D0431919

DAYTON MEMORIAL LIBRARY
REGIS UNIVERSITY
3333 REGIS BLVD.,
DENVER, CO 80221

CURRIC
BUS
SEC
GLE
2002
Grs. 9-12

Marketing Essentials

Third Edition

Lois Schneider Farese
Marketing Education Teacher-Coordinator
Northern Highlands Regional High School
Allendale, New Jersey

Grady Kimbrell
Educational Consultant
Santa Barbara, California

Carl A. Woloszyk
Professor
Consumer Resources and Technology
Western Michigan University
Kalamazoo, Michigan

Glencoe
McGraw-Hill

New York, New York   Columbus, Ohio   Woodland Hills, California   Peoria, Illinois

Marketing Essentials Program Components

Program Resources
Student Edition
Teacher Wraparound Edition

Reinforcement
Student Activity Workbook
Marketing Math Workbook
School-to-Work Activity Workbook

Enrichment
Marketing Research Project Workbook
Business Week Case Studies

Teacher's Resources
Student Activity Workbook TAE
Marketing Math Workbook TAE
Marketing Research Project Workbook TAE
School-to-Work TM
Impact! Simulation TM
ExamView User's Guide and Testbank
Reproducible Tests
Block Scheduling Implementation Guide
Lesson Plans
Blackline Masters
Internet Resources

Technology-Based Resources
Interactive Lesson Planner (ILP) CD-ROM
ExamView Pro CD-ROM
PowerPoint Presentation Software
Knowledge Matters Virtual Business
Impact! Simulation
Marketing Essentials Web site
   (www.marketing.glencoe.com)

NOTICE: Information on featured companies, organizations, their products and services is included for educational purposes only, and it does not present or imply endorsement of the *Marketing Essentials* program. Permission to use all business logos has been granted by the businesses represented in this text.

Glencoe/McGraw-Hill

A Division of The McGraw-Hill Companies

Copyright © 2002 by the Glencoe/McGraw Hill Division of McGraw-Hill School Publishing Company. All rights reserved. Except as permitted under the United States Copyright Act, no part of this publication may be reproduced or distributed in any form or by any means, or stored in a database or retrieval system, without prior written permission of the publisher.
Send all inquiries to:

GLENCOE DIVISION
McGraw-Hill
21600 Oxnard Blvd. Suite 500
Woodland Hills, California 91367-4906

ISBN 0-02-644191-8 (Student Edition)
ISBN 0-07-824951-1 (Teacher's Wraparound Edition)

Printed in the United States of America.

5 6 7 8 9 027 05 04 03 02

About the Authors

Lois Schneider Farese, a nationally recognized secondary marketing educator, has been the marketing teacher and DECA advisor at Northern Highlands Regional High School in Allendale, New Jersey, for more than 30 years. She has been involved in organizing and running New Jersey regional and state DECA conferences and has also participated as series director and event manager at state and national DECA conferences. The State Officer Action Team presented Farese with the Outstanding Service Award for her dedication, professionalism, and commitment to New Jersey DECA in 1993, 1996, and 1999, as well as with the Honorary Life Membership Award in 1990 for setting a new level of professionalism for local advisors. She was inducted into the DECA Hall of Fame in 1996.

As a result of her outstanding teaching methods and involvement in numerous marketing-related activities, Farese was named "Teacher of the Year" in 1981 by the Marketing Education Association of New Jersey. In 1982 she was recognized by the New Jersey Division of the American Vocational Education Association. In 1986 she became the first recipient from her school of the prestigious New Jersey Governor's Teacher Recognition Program. In 1993 and 1999, the University of Richmond recognized Farese for her contributions to the intellectual growth and achievement of students who graduated from her marketing program. In 2000, Farese was the nominee from Northern Highlands Regional High School for the Princeton Prize for Distinguished Secondary School Teaching.

Farese holds a bachelor's degree in business and distributive education and two master's degrees (one in business and one in psychology) from Montclair State University in New Jersey. She has numerous additional credits in education, administration, and supervision.

Grady Kimbrell, a nationally recognized author and consultant on career education, began his career in education teaching high school business in Kansas. After relocating to Southern California, Kimbrell taught business courses and coordinated students' in-class activities with their on-the-job experience. He later directed the work experience program for the high schools of Santa Barbara, California.

A pioneer in the use of computers as a tool for educational research, Kimbrell has assisted school districts with a wide variety of research and evaluation activities. His research into on-the-job work activities led to the development of a new type of career interest inventory used in career guidance. In addition, Kimbrell has served on numerous state instructional program committees and writing teams, designed educational computer programs, and produced educational films.

Kimbrell holds degrees in business administration, educational psychology, and business education.

Carl A. Woloszyk is a university professor with an extensive background in marketing education. He teaches undergraduate and graduate courses in career and technical education (CTE) at Western Michigan University in Kalamazoo. He has served as a state department of education consultant for marketing and cooperative education, DECA and Delta Epsilon Chi state advisor, CTE administrator for a regional education service agency, and a secondary marketing teacher-coordinator. As a secondary marketing teacher-coordinator, he taught beginning and advanced marketing courses, supervised a school store, placed cooperative education students in work-based learning situations, and served as a local DECA chapter advisor. His students have received numerous awards at district, state, and national DECA conferences. Woloszyk has served on the board of directors for National DECA and the Marketing Education Association Foundation, and as a state representative to MarkED, a national marketing research and curriculum development center in Columbus, Ohio. He is a charter and board member of the Michigan Marketing Educators' Association.

Woloszyk received his undergraduate degree in business administration and his doctorate in business and distributive education from Michigan State University. He also holds a master's degree in business education from Eastern Michigan University and an educational specialist degree in occupational education from the University of Michigan.

Reviewers

Anne Cocroft Agyemang
Randolph Vocational
Technical Center
Detroit, MI

Elizabeth Battle
Wake Forest Rolesville High
School
Wake Forest, NC

Miranda Nixon Blocker
Heyward Career and
Technology Center
Columbia, NC

Allen Buntin
Cactus High School
Glendale, AZ

Jennifer Clock
Indian River High School
Chesapeake, VA

Barb Crum
Vidalia High School
Vidalia, LA

Holly DeMarco
Amherst High School
Amherst, NY

Anna Diekman
Clay High School
Oregon, OH

Todd Faar
Palmdale High School
Palmdale, CA

Matt Kuffel
Hartford High School
Hartford, WI

Dennis C. Lane
Parkway North High School
St. Louis, MO

Lucinda Mason
Demopolis High School
Demopolis, AL

Kay Masonbrook
Mt Carmel High School
San Diego, CA

LouGene McKinney
Laramie High School
Laramie, WY

Patrick J. O'Reilly
Woodland Hills High School
Pittsburgh, PA

Laurie Jean Orszulak
Covenant Academy
Town of Tonawanda, NY

Elizabeth S. Pitts
Cass High School
Cartersville, GA

Mark Rael
Cooper City High School
Cooper City, FL

Stephen Rappaport
Beverly Hills High School
Beverly Hills, CA

Kathy Rudinsky
Lake Wales High School
Lake Wales, FL

Michael Stanzione
Beach Channel High School
Rockaway Park, NY

Bradley Tichenor
Amherst High School
Snyder, NY

Contibuting Writer

Priscilla McCalla
Professional and Program
Development Director
DECA
Reston, VA

CONTENTS

v

CONTENTS

CONTENTS

CONTENTS

UNIT 6 LAB

UNIT 7 Distribution — 372

CONTENTS

CONTENTS

CONTENTS

Understanding the Unit

Unit Structure

Marketing Essentials is divided into 12 units, each beginning with a unit opener. The unit opener utilizes exercises and graphics to prepare the student for the information that will be covered in the following chapters.

Portfolio The portfolio feature offers you the opportunity to demonstrate the skills that you master after you read the chapters in the unit. After completing a portfolio project, you can highlight your work in a portfolio that you can take with you when you begin looking for a career. A portfolio contains pieces of successful projects and samples of outstanding work.

Unit Overview The unit overview offers a brief summary of materials covered in the unit. It introduces the concepts that will be explored, acting as a preview for what is to follow.

Foundations and Functions Studied in this Unit This section refers to the marketing wheel and shows which marketing foundations and functions will be the focus of the chapters in each unit.

Marketing Wheel The marketing wheel is a visual representation of the National Marketing Education Standards. The wheel illustrates the foundations and functions of marketing. The foundations of marketing are broad areas that are essential to understanding the concepts of marketing. These include: Business, Management, and Entrepreneurship; Communication and Interpersonal Skills; Economics; and Professional Development. The seven functions of marketing are more specific and relate to how marketing is practically applied in the business world. The seven functions are Distribution, Financing, Marketing-Information Management, Pricing, Product/Service Management, Promotion, and Selling.

Understanding the Chapter and Section

Chapter and Section Structure

The chapter and section openers give you a brief introduction to the new material that will be covered in the chapter. Each chapter is divided into sections. Each section begins with a list of the skills and knowledge you can expect to have mastered once you have completed the section.

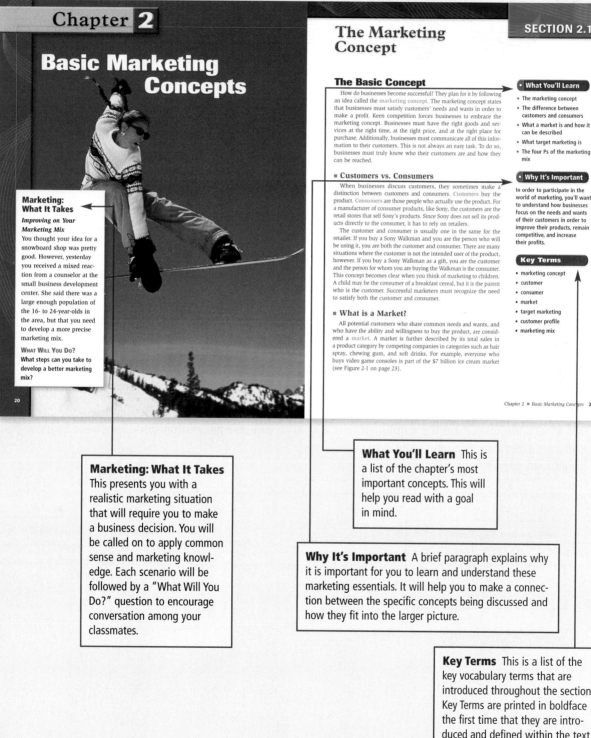

Chapter 2

Basic Marketing Concepts

Marketing: What It Takes

Improving on Your Marketing Mix

You thought your idea for a snowboard shop was pretty good. However, yesterday you received a mixed reaction from a counselor at the small business development center. She said there was a large enough population of the 16- to 24-year-olds in the area, but that you need to develop a more precise marketing mix.

WHAT WILL YOU DO?
What steps can you take to develop a better marketing mix?

20

SECTION 2.1

The Marketing Concept

The Basic Concept

How do businesses become successful? They plan for it by following an idea called the marketing concept. The marketing concept states that businesses must satisfy customers' needs and wants in order to make a profit. Keen competition forces businesses to embrace the marketing concept. Businesses must have the right goods and services at the right time, at the right price, and at the right place for purchase. Additionally, businesses must communicate all of this information to their customers. This is not always an easy task. To do so, businesses must truly know who their customers are and how they can be reached.

■ Customers vs. Consumers

When businesses discuss customers, they sometimes make a distinction between customers and consumers. Customers buy the product. Consumers are those people who actually use the product. For a manufacturer of consumer products, like Sony, the customers are the retail stores that sell Sony's products. Since Sony does not sell its products directly to the consumer, it has to rely on retailers.

The customer and consumer is usually one in the same for the retailer. If you buy a Sony Walkman and you are the person who will be using it, you are both the customer and consumer. There are many situations where the customer is not the intended user of the product, however. If you buy a Sony Walkman as a gift, you are the customer and the person for whom you are buying the Walkman is the consumer. This concept becomes clear when you think of marketing to children. A child may be the consumer of a breakfast cereal, but it is the parent who is the customer. Successful marketers must recognize the need to satisfy both the customer and consumer.

■ What is a Market?

All potential customers who share common needs and wants, and who have the ability and willingness to buy the product, are considered a market. A market is further described by its total sales in a product category by competing companies in categories such as hair spray, chewing gum, and soft drinks. For example, everyone who buys video game consoles is part of the $7 billion ice cream market (see Figure 2-1 on page 23).

● What You'll Learn

- The marketing concept
- The difference between customers and consumers
- What a market is and how it can be described
- What target marketing is
- The four Ps of the marketing mix

● Why It's Important

In order to participate in the world of marketing, you'll want to understand how businesses focus on the needs and wants of their customers in order to improve their products, remain competitive, and increase their profits.

Key Terms

- marketing concept
- customer
- consumer
- market
- target marketing
- customer profile
- marketing mix

Chapter 2 ■ Basic Marketing Concepts 21

Marketing: What It Takes This presents you with a realistic marketing situation that will require you to make a business decision. You will be called on to apply common sense and marketing knowledge. Each scenario will be followed by a "What Will You Do?" question to encourage conversation among your classmates.

What You'll Learn This is a list of the chapter's most important concepts. This will help you read with a goal in mind.

Why It's Important A brief paragraph explains why it is important for you to learn and understand these marketing essentials. It will help you to make a connection between the specific concepts being discussed and how they fit into the larger picture.

Key Terms This is a list of the key vocabulary terms that are introduced throughout the section. Key Terms are printed in boldface the first time that they are introduced and defined within the text.

Understanding Assessment

Assessment Structure

Each section and chapter ends with assessment questions to evaluate your understanding of the chapter. The section assessment is a brief version of the chapter assessment, which goes into more detail and offers you more opportunities to demonstrate your understanding.

> **Thinking Critically** This question offers you the chance to show your application and more in-depth understanding of the concepts in the chapter. You will be asked to interpret, analyze, compare, or make judgments based on ideas from the chapter.

2.2 ASSESSMENT

Reviewing Key Terms and Concepts

1. What do demographics, psychographics, geographics, and product benefits have in common?

2. How can a market be segmented using demographics?

3. What does the study of psychographics involve?

4. Provide one example of how a marketer can segment a market based on product benefits.

5. Of what significance are the combined African-American, Hispanic, and Asian-American populations to marketers?

Thinking Critically

6. How can Procter and Gamble market household products to a male market segment? What problems might P&G encounter in that endeavor?

Integrating Academic Skills

7. **COMMUNICATION** Write an ad campaign theme for Sunsweet Prunes to target baby boomers who are looking for healthy foods. Develop a second campaign theme to target a younger generation with Sunsweet Prunes.

> **Reviewing Key Terms and Concepts** This exercise requires recall of important section material and terms introduced in the text.

> **Integrating Academic Skills** This question will focus on math or communication skills that are related to concepts mastered in the section.

Understanding Assessment

Vocabulary Review This activity will call on your recollection of the vocabulary words introduced throughout the chapter. You may be asked to write sentences, a dialogue, or even play a game that tests your understanding of the application of these words.

Thinking Critically This question offers you the chance to show your application and more in-depth understanding of the concepts in the chapter. You will be asked to interpret, analyze, compare, or make judgments based on ideas from the chapter.

Applying Marketing Concepts This section is intended for students to work on outside of class. All questions incorporate technology with concepts that are studied in the chapter.

The DECA Connection Here is your opportunity to polish your role playing skills for DECA competition. Each of these features is modeled after real DECA events. You will be presented with a situation and perform an activity based on the setting. Each Role Play lists the performance indicators upon which you will be evaluated.

Chapter 2 ASSESSMENT

VOCABULARY REVIEW

Write one paragraph to show your understanding of how the following concepts are related to one another.

- marketing concept
- consumer
- customer
- market
- target marketing
- customer profile
- marketing mix
- market segmentation
- demographics
- psychographics
- geographics

FACT AND IDEA REVIEW

1. What is the marketing concept? (2.1)
2. Provide an example of when a consumer is not the customer of a product purchased in a retail store. (2.1)
3. Define the concept of a market and give an example of one. (2.1)
4. Name the four Ps of the marketing mix and explain how they should be used in target marketing. (2.1)
5. Explain market segmentation and the four main ways a market can be segmented. (2.2)
6. Why do generations make good markets to segment? Name the three recent generations that marketers use to segment the market. (2.2)
7. What is the difference between disposable income and discretionary income? (2.2)

8. How have cosmetic companies targeted African-American women? (2.2)
9. Which ethnic group is the most affluent? (2.2)
10. How might a shampoo manufacturer segment the market according to product benefits? (2.2)

THINKING CRITICALLY

1. The United States is becoming more affluent. Because of this, change a regular food product to create an upscale image for that product—a premium brand.
2. How can a marketer of consumer products use the data from the U.S. Census 2000?
3. How would you position BENGAY to young adults? How would you position the same product to senior citizens? Would you use the same appeal? Why or why not?
4. Using market segmentation based on income, explain Wal-Mart's success.

BUILDING WORKPLACE SKILLS

1. **Human Relations** A shabbily dressed couple enters a luxury automobile showroom, but the sales associates are not eager to approach them. A younger associate finally does and eventually sells them a $50,000 car. The couple puts down $20,000 cash as a down payment. What is the point of this story? What does it say about how lifestyle characteristics can be misleading?
2. **Technology** You have been hired by a stockbroker to research the geographic areas in the country that include high-income households. What technology is available to help you in this endeavor?

APPLYING MARKETING CONCEPTS

1. **Summarizing Key Concepts** Summarize an article that demonstrates any of the key concepts in this chapter. In the summary, identify the specific concepts in parentheses. Use business publications, such as *Brandweek, Adweek, Business Week, Fortune, Forbes, Marketing News,* and *Nation's Business,* to find an applicable article.
2. **Analyzing Marketing Strategies** Using the Internet, find research that describes characteristics of the teenage market. Then visit the Web sites of five companies (manufacturers or retailers) that target teens. Use a word processing program to write a short report analyzing each company's marketing mix strategies and citing your sources of information. Do all four Ps target teenagers effectively? Select one company to provide recommendations on how it could improve its marketing mix strategies when trying to target teens.
3. **Recognizing Target Marketing** Using the Internet, research the holidays of Kwanzaa (African-American celebration of racial pride and unity), Diwali (Hindu festival of lights), and Hanukkah (traditional Jewish celebration). Report how American marketers use knowledge of such holidays.
4. **Researching Psychographic Trends** Research one of the trends noted in the text. Make an oral presentation to the class using presentation software. Be sure to include current examples of how the trend is being used by different companies in their marketing mix strategies. Lastly, evaluate their effectiveness with your classmates.

LINKING SCHOOL TO WORK

Thinking Skills Develop a profile of a local company's customers based on their geographic, demographic, and psychographic characteristics.

THE DECA CONNECTION

Role Play: Toy Company Intern

Situation You are to assume the role of an intern in the marketing department of a consumer product manufacturing company that specializes in toys and electronic games. A new electronic game is being developed and the Research and Development (R&D) Director (judge) has asked for your input. You are to meet with the R&D Director (judge) in fifteen minutes.

Activity You must decide what you will tell the R&D Director (judge) about the strategies to use for product, place, price, and promotion decisions (the four Ps) of the marketing mix. In your presentation include consideration of the product's consumers and customers, as well as concepts such as target marketing and market segmentation.

Evaluation You will be evaluated on how well you meet the following performance indicators:
- Define target marketing
- Explain the difference between consumers and customers
- Explain the role of market segmentation
- Explain marketing mix strategies
- Demonstrate appropriate creativity

inter NET CONNECTION

Head Count
The Census Bureau undertakes a count of the population every 10 years to track changes in population size and demographics.

Connect
- Locate the U.S. Census Web site. Find the current figures and percentages of age and income by ethnic groups (Caucasian, African-American, Hispanic, and Asian-American).

Fact and Idea Review This exercise requires recall of information found in the text. The numbers after each question identify in which section the material is located in the chapter.

Linking School to Work These activities are designed to relate marketing principles to your work experiences or to the specific work experiences of friends, family members, or people in your community. You will be asked to apply practical and analytical skills as you would on the job, or you may interview someone who is employed to gain perspective. Each question is linked to SCANS competencies.

Internet Connection This element consists of a two-part activity, which is designed to enhance your Internet skills. The first part will state a scenario or other fact that is valuable to your learning. The "Connect" heading contains a Web-based activity for you to complete.

Building Workplace Skills This section challenges students to make realistic applications of chapter concepts. The topics may include human relations, technology, writing, language arts, social studies, or science.

Marketing Essentials Features

Each chapter contains six features, which vary in length and focus. They help you understand the practical application of the concepts that you master throughout this book. While they vary in content, they all show a realistic and creative approach to marketing. Each feature ends with a question, or a series of questions, that asks you to expand on what you learned with critical or creative thinking.

BRIGHT IDEAS

Creative Marketing

This feature focuses on how individuals in history or in modern society have applied creative thinking, knowledge, and problem solving skills to achieve success in marketing. These people were either faced with a business problem, or were able to identify a customer need that was not currently being met. This feature ends with a "Thinking Creatively" question, which will allow you to tackle a marketing problem using your own unique creativity.

Thinking Creatively

This Creativity Challenge asks students to solve a problem using creative thinking skills.

Life In The Diverse

MARKETPLACE

Cross-Cultural Communication

As boundaries become less important and nations move toward a global marketplace, it is important to understand the nuances of global cultures and traditions. Every country is unique and has different ways of handling everything from a proper greeting to a business meeting. This feature will increase your awareness of those global differences that are important to know when moving across boundaries.

Thinking Critically

The Thinking Critically question in each feature asks students to analyze, interpret, and apply a concept in the feature.

Electronic Frontiers

Technology Revolution

Electronic Frontiers focuses on the pervasive impact that technology is having on marketing, and gives perspective on the virtual marketing revolution. You'll evaluate the Internet marketing efforts of famous and not-so-famous companies. This feature shows how marketers use the Internet in their marketing strategies, customer relationships, and day-to-day work. It also discusses the legal and ethical issues often involved with e-commerce.

Thinking Critically:

The Thinking Critically question in each feature asks students to analyze, interpret, and apply a concept in the feature.

REAL WORLD MARKETING

The Real World

This feature is filled with fun facts and stories about important developments in marketing. Some features focus on issues such as product and brand development, advertising, and successful entrepreneurs of the past and present. Other features focus on recent developments in marketing and speculate about what the future holds for this exciting and ever-changing field.

Thinking Critically

The Thinking Critically question in each feature asks students to analyze, interpret, and apply a concept in the feature.

Understanding the Features

Careers in Marketing Careers in Marketing places the spotlight on different careers involved in marketing—some of them may seem obvious, but others you may never have considered as a part of marketing. Each feature contains an interview with a successful marketing professional. In addition to sharing some of their keys to success, these professionals also tell you about their likes and dislikes on the job. Practical information is also listed here regarding necessary experience and skills, as well as the career outlook for those ready to enter the job market.

Careers in Marketing

PRODUCT MANAGEMENT

Lori Tauber Marcus
Director of Brand Management
Pepsico Fountain Beverage Division

What does your job entail?
"I supervise the development, production, and sale of Pepsi brands for Pepsi's fountain beverage division, the part of the company that sells beverages to restaurants and theaters. I conduct research to determine the profitability of products being developed, then I oversee the marketing of the product. I also help with advertising and training the sales force. After the product has been marketed, I conduct follow-up research to determine how well it is doing and what changes may need to be made to increase profitability."

What kind of training did you have?
"A few years after earning a bachelor's degree in marketing in college, I went to work for Pepsi, first in the food service marketing division and then as an associate product manager for Pepsi's Mountain Dew brand. I was promoted to customer marketing manager for retail marketing, customizing Pepsi promotions for mass retailers like Target and Kmart. I became area marketing manager for the eastern seaboard, then senior product manager for new cola concepts."

What skills are most important?
"Leadership skills are essential—as a brand manager you lead teams of many people, each performing different functions who are pivotal in bringing your product to market. It is important to have the ability to think creatively and strategically. It is also important to have an aptitude for gathering and analyzing data and making decisions based on the data."

What is your key to success?
"I really love doing what I do. Also, I have been fortunate to have always worked with very smart and highly motivated people from whom I'm constantly learning."

Thinking Critically
What types of experience would you emphasize when applying for a job as a brand manager?

Career Facts

Education and Training: A bachelor's or master's degree in marketing or business and coursework in communication, economics, and math is recommended. College coursework should be accompanied by several years of sales experience.

Aptitudes, Abilities, and Skills: Analytical skills, organizational skills, leadership skills, communication skills, interpersonal skills, and math skills are necessary.

Career Outlook: Many new jobs are opening in the computer and Internet industry, as well as in the electronics industry in general.

Career Path: A typical path to brand manager is through a management trainee job. A staff position in the marketing department can sharpen analytical skills.

Chapter 2 Basic Marketing Concepts **33**

Case Study This feature gives you an in-depth look at the realistic applications of marketing concepts. Each case study offers a real-world story about a marketing decision or situation facing a company. At the conclusion of the case study, there are three questions to help you understand how the chapter's principles apply to the real-life situation. The final question will ask you to evaluate an issue of ethics.

Case Study

Got Milk?

To get the message to teens to drink milk, MilkPEP and Dairy Management Inc. are using popular athletes as their models in "got milk?" ads. Teenagers' zeal for collecting milk mustache ads of their favorite sports stars is what marketers are counting on to get across a serious message.

Milk consumption drops in the teenage years, just when teens may need it most. It appears that seven out of ten teen boys and nine out of ten teen girls do not get their daily calcium requirements.

To target teens, the message for the promotion must be viewed as "cool" and the media must reach teens. Using popular athletes in the "got milk?" print and TV ads helps to get the message across. Print ads in *TV Guide*, which is read by 5.4 million teens, was one effective vehicle used to communicate the message.

Case Study Review

1. Why were "got milk?" ads popular with teens?
2. How can "got milk?" ads target different market segments by age, gender, generation, and ethnic background?

A MATTER OF ETHICS

3. Is it ethical to use popular athletes to persuade teens to take a specific action? Would it change your opinion if the action were other than "drink milk"?

FEATURES CONTENTS

Life In The Diverse MARKETPLACE

REAL WORLD MARKETING

The DECA Connection

What is DECA?

It is likely that DECA will be an integral part of your learning experience as you explore the world of marketing. DECA is a national association for students of marketing. It was formed in 1946 to improve the education of students in business subject areas, in particular marketing, entrepreneurship, and management.

DECA, which stands for the Distributive Education Clubs of America, offers students the opportunity to develop their leadership and professional skills. This is done through on-the-job experience, activities and projects sponsored by individual schools or chapters, and a series of competitive events in specific occupational areas. All activities apply the concepts of marketing to real-life situations.

What is DECA's mission statement?

"The mission of DECA is to enhance the co-curricular education of students with interests in marketing, management and entrepreneurship. DECA helps students develop skills and competence for marketing careers, build self-esteem, experience leadership and practice community service. DECA is committed to advocacy of marketing education and the growth of business and education partnerships."

How can DECA help me?

Even though some activities may take outside of school time, DECA should be considered more of a co-curricular activity instead of an after-school activity. The basis for the projects and events will come from your classroom learning. You will take information from events with you back to the classroom that will enhance not only your learning experience, but that of your classmates as well.

In addition to enhancing these skills, DECA also offers scholarships and other recognition awards to exceptional students. In general, success in DECA events is a positive addition to your résumé or portfolio.

DECA can help you:

- Develop strong leadership abilities
- Understand the importance of making ethical decisions in your personal life and future career
- Focus on enhancing effective public speaking and presentation skills
- Understand the need for diversity in the global marketplace
- Enhance those skills that are necessary for a career in marketing or as an entrepreneur
- Increase your self-confidence, especially when presenting or speaking in public
- Investigate different career opportunities available in the marketing field
- Develop good social and business etiquette

How are DECA activities related to my marketing class?

Marketing Essentials is designed to prepare you for a career or further study of marketing. It is also helpful in preparing for DECA activities. You will notice that the DECA logo and DECA approved activities are prominently featured throughout your *Marketing Essentials* text. The DECA Connection feature is modeled after DECA individual or team projects. It will allow you to practice applying the knowledge that you have gained from your marketing class. DECA activities can also enhance your classroom learning, as they help you develop stronger communication and analytical skills.

DECA sponsors competitive events, for both teams and individuals, in approximately 30 occupational areas. Some of these areas include:

- Advertising and Visual Merchandising Services Series
- Apparel and Accessories Marketing Series
- Finance and Credit Services Series
- Food Marketing Series
- General Marketing Series
- Hospitality and Tourism Marketing Series
- Retail Merchandising Series
- Quick Serve Restaurant Management Series
- Full Service Restaurant Management Series
- Vehicles and Petroleum Marketing Series
- Sports and Entertainment Marketing Management Team Decision Making Pilot Event
- Travel and Tourism Marketing Management Team Decision Making Pilot Event

Portfolio

Design a Marketing Mix

To demonstrate mastery of the content in this unit, you will design a creative marketing mix for a specific target market and product. Be sure to fully describe the demographics, psychographics, and geographics of your target market. To ensure success, tell how you will follow the marketing concept. Prepare a written report complete with visuals to highlight the main points. Be prepared to orally present your ideas to a prospective employer to demonstrate your knowledge of key marketing terms and principles.

The World of Marketing

Unit Overview

Marketing activities are found in every type of business enterprise. In this unit, you will learn key marketing concepts that will be revisited throughout this textbook.

Through your exploration of Chapter 1, you will learn the benefits of marketing to our society and to you personally. You will also see just how many career options are available in this broad field of study. Chapter 2 lays the foundation for further study of marketing principles and practices. You will learn how marketing decisions are made and what factors go into those decisions. You will also learn the various marketing strategies businesses use to identify their customers and other essential topics, such as the marketing concept, the marketing mix, market segmentation, and target marketing.

In this Unit:

Foundations of Marketing

- Professional Development
- Business, Management, Entrepreneurship
- Economics

Functions of Marketing

- Pricing
- Promotion
- Selling

Functions of Marketing: Marketing-Information Management, Financing, Pricing, Promotion, Product/Service Management, Distribution, Selling. Foundations: Professional Development, Economics, Business, Management, Entrepreneurship, Communication, Interpersonal Skills. Concepts • Technology • Academic Concepts

Marketing Is All Around Us

Marketing: What It Takes

Toy Story

Each holiday season, a toy emerges from obscurity to become the holiday item that everybody wants. Poo-chi, Furby, Tickle Me Elmo, Pokemon, Beanie Babies, and Cabbage Patch dolls are just a few examples of this phenomenon. You think you have an idea for a unique toy that could be the next big thing. You know marketing is essential to your toy's success.

WHAT WILL YOU DO?

What does marketing entail? What functions of marketing must you consider to make your toy the next holiday phenomenon?

Defining Marketing

What Is Marketing?

Marketing is the process of developing, promoting, and distributing products to satisfy customers' needs and wants. Products include goods and services, both of which have monetary value and satisfy customers' needs and wants. Goods are the kinds of things you can touch or hold in your hand. Hammers, automobiles, soft drinks, clothing, and computers are goods. Services are the kinds of things you can't physically touch. Services are tasks performed for a customer. Dry cleaners, amusement parks, income tax preparers, and movie theaters provide services.

Marketing helps connect businesses to their customers. After goods are created, they are sent to the marketplace where they are made available to consumers. The marketplace is the commercial environment where exchanges are made. An exchange takes place every time something is sold in the marketplace.

■ Marketing and You

When you carefully consider the definition of marketing, you'll realize that you experience marketing principles and techniques daily. Let's look at an average day to discover all the ways that marketing touches you.

When you wake up in the morning, you go to the kitchen for breakfast. Perhaps you look at cereals, all with different ingredients and packaging. Think ahead to the products you will use this morning—shampoo, soap, toothpaste—they are all created to meet your needs. *Product planning* and *packaging* are part of marketing.

You check the newspaper for last night's sports news. It's filled with national and local retail advertising. One ad in particular might catch your attention, so you ask a few friends to go with you to the mall after school. *Advertising* is part of marketing.

You go to the mall, where all of the retail stores that help to distribute manufacturer's products are part of marketing. At the mall, enticing window displays encourage you to enter certain stores. Some of the stores have sales featuring price reductions of 20 to 50 percent. *Displays* and *promotional techniques* are part of marketing.

You are greeted in the store by a sales associate who is ready to assist you with your purchase decisions. *Personal selling* is part of marketing.

Did you see trucks on your way to the mall? Those trucks were moving goods from producers of products to consumers. Those products were sold to other businesses for resale or use. During the buying-selling process, prices and delivery as well as credit terms were decided. All those *selling* and *distribution* functions are part of marketing.

● What You'll Learn

- The meaning of marketing
- The foundations of marketing
- The functions of marketing

● Why It's Important

To be successful in business requires being marketing oriented. Learning how businesses and people operate from a marketing point of view will help you in all your future endeavors. You will also get a good idea of whether marketing is a potential career for you.

Key Terms

- marketing
- products
- goods
- services
- exchange

As you leave the mall, a young man with a clipboard approaches you and asks if he can ask a few questions about a new product. If you say yes, you are participating in a *marketing research* study. Why does the company doing the research want your viewpoint? You are part of a *target audience* and you might consider buying its product. *Marketing research* is part of marketing.

As you can see, marketing is truly all around us. If you look for it, you will realize that you observe marketing every day.

■ Foundations of Marketing

As you begin to study marketing, you will learn the four basic *foundations* of marketing. You will see how building on these foundations helps you to acquire marketing skills that are relevant to your own career development.

The topics you will study in *Marketing Essentials* are based on these foundations of marketing:

- *Business, Management, Entrepreneurship*—Understanding the basics of business, management, and entrepreneurial concepts that affect business decision making.
- *Communication and Interpersonal Skills*—Understanding concepts, strategies, and systems needed to interact effectively with others.
- *Economics*—Understanding the economic principles and concepts that are basic to marketing.
- *Professional Development*—Understanding concepts and strategies needed for career exploration, development, and growth.

■ **Marketing Functions** Many marketing functions are evident in grocery stores. *What marketing functions are illustrated here?*

■ Functions of Marketing

All of the marketing activities that you encounter daily can be classified into the seven *functions* of marketing. These can be seen on the marketing wheel that is featured in the unit overview of each unit of *Marketing Essentials*. The seven functions are the categories that make up the wheel's outer wedges. They include distribution, financing, marketing information management, pricing, product/service management, promotion, and selling. These functions define marketing as it is applied in business operations. Functions address marketing from the perspective of how it is practiced. Each function is viewed from its relationship to the marketing of a good, service, or idea.

Distribution involves deciding where and to whom products need to be sold in order to reach the final users. The logistics of physically moving and storing goods are also part of distribution planning. Primary methods of transportation are by truck, rail, ship, or air. Some large retail chains store products in central warehouses for later distribution. Distribution also involves the systems that track products so that they can be located at any time.

Financing is getting the money that is necessary to pay for the operation of a business. Business owners often obtain bank loans to start a new business. Some also form corporations and sell shares of the business, or stock. Financing also involves decisions about whether to offer credit to customers. Most retailers offer customers payment options such as MasterCard or Visa, while some other stores offer their own credit services.

Getting the necessary information to make sound business decisions is known as *Marketing Information Management*. Most of this information is obtained through marketing research. Have you ever been asked to complete a questionnaire about the service at a restaurant or other type of business? If so, you have participated in marketing research. Companies conduct marketing research to learn more about their customers' preferences and how to better market products.

Pricing decisions dictate how much to charge for goods and services in order to maximize profits. Most pricing decisions are based on competitive pricing and determining how much customers are willing to pay. Other pricing goals include gaining market share and achieving a certain return on an investment. Pricing concepts and strategies are utilized in determining and adjusting prices to maximize return and meet customers' perceptions of value.

Product/Service Management is obtaining, developing, maintaining, and improving a product or a *product mix* in response to market opportunities. Product/Service Management decisions are most often made on the basis of marketing research, which highlights consumer needs and wants.

Communicating with potential customers to inform, persuade, or remind them about a business's products makes up *promotion*. Television and radio commercials are forms of promotion known as advertising. Promotion is carried out in other media, including print and online. Promotion is used to improve a company's public image—such as showing that the company is socially responsible, perhaps by recycling materials or cleaning up the environment. This is known as public relations. Promotion concepts and strategies are used to communicate information about products, services, images, and/or ideas to achieve a desired outcome.

Selling provides customers with goods and services they want. This includes selling in the retail market to you, the customer, and selling in the business-to-business market to industrial users. Selling concepts and activities are used to determine client needs and wants and respond through planned, personalized communication that influences purchasing decisions and enhances future business opportunities. It also includes selling in the business-to-business (industrial) market where products are purchased for use in business operations.

All seven functions of marketing contribute to the *marketing concept*, which involves satisfying customers' needs and wants in order to make a profit. You will learn more about the marketing concept in Chapter 2.

Life In The Diverse MARKETPLACE

When In Germany

When you see a friend walking down the street, do you wave to say hello? If you were in Germany, that would be considered rude! To get someone's attention in Germany, you should raise your hand, palm facing out, with only the index finger extended. While Germans are very open and friendly with close friends, they frown upon grand shows of affection in public. Only the rude and impolite would shout or wave. This does not mean that Germans are cold or unfriendly, it is just a different manner of greeting.

Thinking Critically
Why might someone stereotype Germans as cold or unfriendly? Would this be a correct judgment?

1.1 ASSESSMENT

Reviewing Key Terms and Concepts

1. What is an exchange?
2. Which of the seven functions of marketing were illustrated in the average day described in this section?
3. Which of the seven functions of marketing were not illustrated in that same discussion?

Thinking Critically

4. How is a presidential political campaign an example of marketing?

Integrating Academic Skills

5. **COMMUNICATION** Write three questions that could be used to survey students' satisfaction with the prices, selection, and quality of food served in your school cafeteria.

Economic Utilities

Economic Benefits of Marketing

Have you ever thought about the benefits of marketing to businesses and to you personally? Marketing bridges the gap between you and the maker or seller of an item. Marketing makes buying easy for customers. It also creates new and improved products at lower prices.

■ Added Value

The functions of marketing add value to a product. That added value in economic terms is called utility. Utilities are the attributes of a product or service that make it capable of satisfying consumers' wants and needs.

There are five economic utilities involved with all products—form, place, time, possession, and information. Form utility is the only one that is not directly related to marketing; the remaining four are marketing utilities.

FORM UTILITY Form utility involves changing raw materials or putting parts together to make them more useful. In other words, it deals with making, or producing, things.

Let's look at a tree to determine its utility. In its original state, a tree has value as an object of beauty. A tree prevents soil erosion, provides homes for animals, and produces oxygen for us to breathe. When the tree is cut down to use in making other products, however, its usefulness changes. Lumber from the tree might be used to make pencils, paper, furniture, and buildings. The raw material (wood) becomes part of finished items that have a different value to us than the raw material itself.

The same would be true if a manufacturer were assembling parts into a product. The parts of a lounge chair—the wood frame, the fabric used for the upholstery, the glue and nails used to hold the parts together, and the reclining mechanism—are less useful by themselves. Putting them together adds form utility.

PLACE UTILITY Place utility involves having a product where customers can buy it. Businesses study consumer shopping habits to determine the most convenient and efficient locations to sell products. Some businesses use a direct approach by selling their products through catalogs, and other businesses rely on retailers to sell their products.

TIME UTILITY Time utility is having a product available at a certain time of year or a convenient time of day. Marketers increase the value of products by having them available when consumers want them. In order to achieve that goal, marketers must plan their operations in advance.

● **What You'll Learn**

- The benefits of marketing
- The meaning of economic utility
- The five economic utilities and how to distinguish the four that are related to marketing

● **Why It's Important**

By understanding the benefits of marketing, you will see how the functions of marketing add value to products. You will also see how marketing activities lead to lower prices and new and improved products.

Key Terms

- utility
- form utility
- place utility
- time utility
- possession utility
- information utility

Consider toy manufacturers and retailers. Toy manufacturers introduce their new products to retailers each February at a toy fair held in New York City. That is when retailers decide which products they will sell during the holiday season nine months later.

Retailers also offer convenient shopping hours to accommodate their customers. Mall stores are generally open 10 a.m. to 9 p.m., and some convenience stores are open 24 hours a day.

POSSESSION UTILITY How do you come into possession of the items you want? Unless they are given to you as a gift, you generally buy them for a price. The exchange of a product for some monetary value is possession utility.

Retailers may accept alternatives to cash, like personal checks or credit cards, in exchange for their merchandise. They may even offer installment or layaway plans (delayed possession in return for gradual payment). Every one of these options adds value to the product being purchased. In fact, without these options, some customers would not be able to buy the items they want.

In business-to-business situations, companies also grant their customers credit. They may give them a certain period (for example, 30 days) to pay a bill. This adds value to the products they sell.

Possession utility is involved every time legal ownership of a product changes hands. Possession utility increases as purchase options increase.

INFORMATION UTILITY Information utility involves communication with the consumer. Salespeople provide information to customers by explaining the features and benefits of products. Displays communicate information, too. Packaging and labeling inform consumers about qualities and uses of a product. The label on a frozen food entree will tell you the ingredients, nutritional information, directions for preparation, and any safety precautions needed. Advertising informs consumers about products, tells where to buy products, and sometimes tells how much products cost. Many manufacturers provide owners' manuals that explain how to use their products.

Businesses must transform materials into products that have value and use in order to experience successful sales. They do this by employing the five economic utilities. Figure 1-1 on page 9 presents an overview of this process using a single product as an example.

■ Lower Prices

Marketing activities add value to products and increase demand. When demand is high,

BRIGHT IDEAS
This Looks Like a Job for...

It's a bird! It's a plane! It's Superman! Created by then-teenagers Jerry Siegel and Joe Shuster, the legend of Superman has endured for over 60 years, although the character of Superman has had many incarnations. The first Superman was a bald villain with mental powers who appeared in a fanzine called "Reign of the Superman." Later that year, he was molded into a rugged world-traveler, but he didn't catch on with readers. In 1934, Siegel and Shuster created the definitive version of Superman. They tried to sell their creation as a syndicated comic strip, but it was rejected by newspaper editors who thought that a man in a bright red and blue outfit looked ridiculous. In 1938, an editor looking for something new featured Superman in *Action Comics #1*. The superhero became an instant success! Superman has gone on to star in radio, television, cartoons, and major motion pictures.

Thinking Creatively

Create a new superhero. Think about Siegel and Shuster's trials and errors. How would you market your new hero?

FIGURE 1-1

ECONOMIC UTILITIES

Economic utilities reflect the value that producers and marketers add to raw materials when they make them into products and offer them for sale to the public. Consider a backpack like the one you use to carry books.

FORM UTILITY

Fabric, leather, thread, zippers, and dye are useless to a student in their raw forms. However, once processed and put together, they have increased value (or utility) as a backpack.

INFORMATION UTILITY

To encourage sales, retailers may feature information about products and special offers and inform potential customers through ads, signs, or displays.

PLACE UTILITY

The manufacturers ship their backpacks to retail businesses—sporting goods stores, drugstores, school bookstores, and mass merchandisers that make them available to consumers.

TIME UTILITY

Retailers selling backpacks stock them regularly but may offer larger supplies in late summer, near the beginning of the school year.

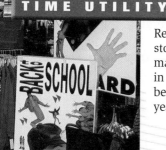

POSSESSION UTILITY

As part of the actual sales transaction, the customer pays for the backpack (with cash, check, credit card, or debit card) and takes possession of it.

manufacturers can make products in larger quantities, which reduces the unit cost of each product. This is because the fixed costs—such as the rent on a building—remain the same whether the company produces 10 units or 10,000 units. When a company produces a larger quantity of a product, it spends less per unit on fixed costs. The company can charge a lower price per unit, sell more units, and make more money.

Here is an example using a fixed cost of $20,000.

Quantity Produced	Fixed Cost Per Unit
10,000	$2.00
200,000	.10

As you can see, the increased quantity significantly reduces the fixed cost per unit.

In addition, when products become popular, more competitors enter the marketplace. To remain competitive, marketers find ways to lower their prices. For example, when they were first introduced, videocassette recorders were priced at more than $600. Now you can purchase a VCR for as little as $100. That's one-sixth of the original price!

■ New and Improved Products

New and improved products are another result of increased competition generated by marketing. As businesses continue to look for opportunities to better satisfy customers' wants and needs, the result is a larger variety of goods and services. For example, personal computers have gotten smaller, more powerful, and less expensive. More people use computers, and this market continues to grow.

A review of detergents demonstrates the change in consumer preference and competition in that market. For years, only powder detergents were available; now, consumers can choose between

Pick a Card—Any Card!

Some people think business is a matter of playing your cards right—and a new generation of business cards is making business a whole lot more interesting. The wallet-size CD-ROM card, which looks like a thick credit card, plays in a CD-ROM tray for either PCs or Macs. It holds enough information for several minutes of text, animation, and graphics. Water Design in New York uses a CD-ROM card in its campus-recruiting program. Maryland-based Ideal-Link uses CD-ROM technology as a calling card for its Networking Mobile Web and IT Reference Library. The Talking Online Business Card combines e-mail technology and sounds files, eliminating the need for a card altogether! CD-ROM technology has upped the ante in business—but who knows how the rules may change in the future.

Thinking Critically

Compare and contrast the advantages and disadvantages of the CD-ROM card to the Talking Online Business Card. Which would work better for a large business? A small business?

powder and liquid detergents. They can also choose other options like detergent with bleach and unscented detergent. Easy-to-use containers with measuring caps demonstrate how marketers have responded to changing consumer trends.

1.2 ASSESSMENT

Reviewing Key Terms and Concepts

1. What is meant by the economic concept of utility?

2. Which economic utility is not classified as a marketing utility? Why?

3. Besides added value, what are two other benefits of marketing?

Thinking Critically

4. Explain the following statement: Marketing is more than just promotion.

Integrating Academic Skills

5. **MATH** Fixed costs for manufacturing widgets are $25,000. Determine the fixed cost per unit when the quantity produced is (a) 5,000 and (b) 75,000.

Careers in Marketing

Why Study Marketing?

By studying marketing, you will have the opportunity to evaluate marketing as a potential career. Even if you don't think marketing is for you, you will learn how important it is for personal success. The skills and knowledge you gain from studying marketing will help you in school and on the job.

Marketing skills are useful in any career because they involve understanding business, as well as relating and communicating effectively with others. These are basic skills that employers expect from all levels of employees.

Through the study of marketing, you will learn how businesses function on a day-to-day basis. In order to apply marketing practices in our free enterprise system, you must understand how businesses operate.

Marketing is communicating. A businessperson's ability to present ideas to employees, customers, and others has a direct impact on a business's success or failure.

Interpersonal skills are another important element of studying marketing. Understanding the techniques and principles of human relations will improve your ability to get along with others. This will help you in your dealings with supervisors, coworkers, customers, and friends.

Is Marketing a Career for You?

Throughout this text, you will have opportunities to investigate marketing careers through the *Careers in Marketing* feature. By the time you have finished studying this text, you will have a good idea of the vast array of marketing careers and some that may be the right career choice for you.

■ An Overview of Marketing Careers

About 33 million Americans earn a living in marketing. Marketing provides a great diversity of opportunities in any career field—from buying merchandise to being the president of a company, from selling clothes to designing ads.

Careers in marketing include all the activities required to plan, develop, promote, and distribute goods and services to consumers. When considered in this broad sense, marketing activities account for about one in every three jobs in the United States.

● What You'll Learn

- The importance of marketing careers to the U.S. economy
- The benefits of working in marketing
- Employment opportunities for people trained in marketing
- Examples of jobs within marketing occupational areas and at different skill levels

● Why It's Important

You'll want to learn about the requirements, opportunities, rewards, and trends of marketing if you are considering a career in this exciting field.

Key Terms

- benefits
- occupational area

Case Study

"Fad to Stay" or "Fade Away"?

B ell bottoms, cargo pants, acid washed jeans, virtual pets—these are just some fads that have passed in and out of popular culture. *Fads* are briefly popular fashions or crazes that benefit producers, wholesalers, and retailers. The challenge is to market these products so that their appeal lasts.

Push scooters from Taiwan illustrate this kind of marketing opportunity. Lightweight, foldable, and fun, these scooters became wildly popular among American kids in 2000. They appeal to the market of bicycle owners, skaters, and skateboard enthusiasts.

Smart marketing, however, is aimed at broadening the consumer base. One company is designing push scooters with larger platforms to accommodate larger feet. Larger wheels on these new models address safety issues. Another company is marketing a scooter with three wheels to increase stability. These changes appeal to adult consumers. Advertising campaigns address adult consumers by stressing the ease of transportation and fewer parking problems when commuting by push scooter. Upscale models with more features are planned to appeal to an even broader market.

Although marketing campaigns stress safety features such as handlebars and low platforms, experts do not seem to agree about scooter safety. Despite that, production companies and thousands of retailers hope that this fad will not fizzle.

Case Study Review

1. How does the evolution of push scooters support the theory that marketing helps to create new and improved products?
2. Two appeals of scooters are that they are inexpensive and maintenance free. Is it wise for manufacturers to add "upscale" features that increase price and maintenance? Why or why not?

A MATTER OF ETHICS

3. If safety experts do not agree that push scooters are safe, is it ethical to promote their safety in ad campaigns? How might advertisers improve safety in the use of these products?

▪ Employment Trends

According to the Bureau of Labor Statistics (BLS), employment in marketing and sales is projected to increase 20.6 percent in the period 1992–2005 (2,671,000 new jobs). During that same time period, employment in service-related industries is expected to increase 33.4 percent (6,462,000 new jobs).

The occupational structure of employment opportunity in marketing is based on the type of employment, regardless of the industry. This measure indicates that there has been an increase in managerial, sales, and service positions in all industries. Department of Labor projections indicate that managerial jobs in marketing-related fields will continue to be plentiful.

Job opportunities in marketing are growing, while those in production are decreasing. This is because production jobs lend themselves to automation and mechanization. In recent years, the number of production workers in many companies has been reduced. Marketing, on the other hand, has not been mechanized as much because it requires personal contact.

As an example, consider the use of computers. A single computer and a series of industrial robots can replace a whole production line of workers. A computer system installed in a marketing department, however, is far more likely to enhance the capabilities of its employees than it is to replace them.

Indeed, changes in the marketplace have created the need for more, rather than fewer, marketing professionals. Factors such as changing gender roles, the rise in the number of single-parent households, changing preferences in recreational activities, and the increase in foreign competition must be monitored through market research and marketing information systems. To track these and other quickly developing trends, companies need to expand their marketing programs and staffs.

■ Benefits of a Marketing Career

Perhaps the most obvious benefit of a career in marketing is the opportunity to make an above-average income. Even in an entry-level job, however, it's nice to know that potential earnings in marketing are excellent.

Besides providing a good salary, a position in marketing may entitle you to some helpful and valuable extras. Benefits are privileges, or monetary payments beyond salary or wages, that go with a job. Examples include the use of a company car, an expense account, and bonuses for outstanding work.

In addition, most jobs in marketing, especially those beyond entry-level positions, are interesting and varied. Many involve a great deal of contact with people.

You will usually have more opportunities to advance in a marketing career than in almost any other area of business. This is because of the high visibility that many marketing positions have.

Consider a few examples. People who work in marketing frequently present and shape their ideas in meetings with company managers and executives. People who work in sales get constant feedback on their efforts in the form of sales figures that are

REAL WORLD MARKETING

Harry Potter's Secret to Promotion

Mystery and magic draw fans to Harry Potter, the fictional British schoolboy/magician. To promote the fourth book in the series and propel sales, the book's publishers, Bloomsbury and Scholastic, tried a little wizardry themselves. They cast a spell of secrecy, distributing no advance copies of the book to critics and reviewers. The plot, cover design, and even the title were all kept secret to increase anticipation and to spark the imaginations of their readers. Author J.K. Rowling had a different reason for the secrecy: Her intention was to not spoil children's enjoyment of the book with advance word about the plot.

Thinking Critically
Can you name an advertising campaign that has used secrecy to launch a product?

regularly reviewed by upper-level management. People who work in advertising may develop ad campaigns that win critical acclaim from professional associations. What all these situations make clear is that people who work in marketing do the kinds of things that command attention, especially from management. They are far more likely to be credited and rewarded for successes. In terms of a job, this means that individuals typically win promotions faster in marketing than they do in other careers.

In fact, because of their high visibility, marketing and sales careers offer the fastest route to middle and top management. A recent survey showed that more chief executive officers (CEOs) reach the top of their organizations through marketing and sales than through any other career area. Figure 1-2 on page 14 lists just a few of the companies whose CEOs fit this description. All of these CEOs earn several hundred thousand dollars per year plus bonuses—some earn millions.

Marketing Occupational Areas

Dividing occupations into areas makes it easier to see the thousands of jobs available in marketing. An occupational area is a category of jobs that involves similar skills and aptitudes. It's much easier to find information about the career area that interests you if you can focus on one or two areas. There are 21 generally accepted areas, or career applications, within the field of marketing. Job titles within the following career applications are featured throughout this text in the *Careers in Marketing* feature. These areas include:

- Advertising
- Customer Service
- E-Commerce
- Entrepreneur
- Fashion Merchandising
- Financial Services
- Food Marketing
- Hospitality Marketing
- Importing/Exporting
- International Marketing
- Marketing Research
- Product Management
- Professional Sales
- Public Relations
- Real Estate
- Restaurant Management
- Retail Management
- Sales Management
- Service Marketing
- Sports Marketing
- Travel/Tourism Marketing

Job Levels in Marketing

Many jobs exist within each of the occupational areas, or career applications, of marketing. In apparel marketing, you could work as a cashier in a small shoe store or as a women's sportswear buyer for a large department store chain. These two jobs would have different educational, skill level, and experience requirements. Jobs in each marketing area can be categorized according to five skill levels: entry level, career sustaining, marketing specialist, marketing supervisor, and manager/owner. Figure 1-3 on page 15 shows possible job titles at each of the skill levels.

FIGURE 1-2

Corporate CEOs with Marketing Backgrounds

Avon	Andrea Jung (1999–)
WalMart.com	Jeanne Jackson (2000–)
Campbell Soup	David W. Johnson (1990–)
Colgate-Palmolive	Reuben Mark (1984–)
E-bay	Meg Whitman (1998–)
General Mills	Stephen W. Sanger (1995–)
Hewlett-Packard	Carly Fiorina (1999–)
IBM	Louis V. Gerstner (1993–)
Kmart	Charles Conaway (2000–)
Kraft Foods	Betsy D. Holden (2000–)
McDonald's	Jack M. Greenberg (1999–)
Nordstrom	John J. Whitacre (1996–)
Ogilvy & Mather	Shelly Lazarus (1997–)
Oxygen Media	Geraldine Laybourne (1998–)
Pearson	Marjorie Scardino (1997–)
J.C. Penney	J.E. Oesterreicher (1998–)
Quaker Oats	Robert S. Morrison (1997–)
Ralston-Purina	W.P. McGinnis (1992–)
Sears Roebuck	Arthur C. Martinez (1995–)
Xerox	Paul A. Allaire (1990–)

■ **Marketing Education** Corporate CEOs are frequently drawn from the ranks of marketing professionals. *Why do you think that marketing professionals make good candidates for CEOs?*

Entry-level jobs usually require no prior experience and involve limited decision-making skills. Entry-level jobs are usually characterized by routine activities, such as working as a cashier at a fast food restaurant or clothing store. These acquired skills increase general employability and job readiness. They also help an individual to develop good business skills and learn appropriate behavior in the workplace.

FIGURE 1-3

Job Titles at the Five Skill Levels in Marketing Occupation Areas

Career Applications	Entry Level	Career Sustaining	Marketing Specialist	Marketing Supervisor	Manager/Owner
Advertising	Proofreader, Assistant display specialist	Copywriter, Display specialist	Ad campaign manager	Account executive	President
Customer Service	Customer service clerk	Sales clerk	Customer service representative	Customer service manager	Sales manager
E-Commerce	Web site tester	Web designer	E-Commerce marketing specialist	E-Commerce marketing manager	Interactive marketing agency owner
Entrepreneur	Business owner's assistant	Small business manager	Small business marketing manager	Marketing supervisor	Sole proprietor of retail or wholesale business
Fashion Merchandising	Buyer's assistant	Salesperson, Model, Display specialist	Buyer, Manufacturer's showroom salesperson	District sales manager	Store manager
Financial Services	Bank teller	Bookkeeper	Loan officer, Accountant	Accounting department manager	Vice president
Food Marketing	Grocery bagger, Stock clerk	Cashier	Food buyer, Food broker	Bakery manager	Store manager
Hospitality Marketing	Maid, Bellhop	Desk clerk	Cruise ship or resort social director	Hotel manager	Chain manager
Importing/Exporting	Shipping/receiving clerk	Warehouse manager	Transportation specialist	Inventory manager	Broker
International Marketing	Marketing assistant	International marketing associate	International trade economist	Agency manager	Agency owner
Marketing Research	Research assistant	Interviewer, Report writer	Statistician, Analyst	Field work director	Director, Consultant
Product Management	Quality control clerk	Sales representative	Finance/research specialist	Associate manager, Brand manager	Category manager
Professional Sales	Cashier	Appliance sales, Auto sales, Insurance sales	Manufacturer's sales representative	Department manager	Owner of retail or wholesale business
Public Relations	Office assistant	Copywriter	Account manager	Public relations representative	Owner of public relations firm
Real Estate	Office staff	Real estate agent	Real estate broker	Sales manager	Owner of real estate office
Restaurant Management	Waiter, Hostess, Cook	Head waiter, Shift manager	Restaurant manager	Chef	Owner, Executive chef
Retail Management	Cashier, Stock clerk	Assistant buyer/manager	Buyer, Department manager	District manager	V.P. of Operations
Sales Management	Telemarketing	Sales representative	Regional sales manager	National sales manager	V.P. of Sales
Service Marketing	Customer relations clerk	Assistant manager of customer relations	Manager of customer relations	V.P. of customer relations	Owner of service marketing company
Sports Marketing	Ticket agent	Airline clerk, Car rental agent	Booking agent	Venue manager	Team owner, Agency owner
Travel/Tourism Marketing	Receptionist, Car rental service attendant	Travel agent	Specialized tour guide	Agency manager	Travel agency owner

■ **Pick a Job** This table shows examples of the types of jobs in each career application, at each of the five skill levels. *What skills are required at the Import/Export Broker level?*

Career sustaining jobs require a higher level of skills and more decision making than entry-level jobs. It is often the second step for someone considering a career in marketing. These jobs allow the employee some control over the work environment as well as more responsibility.

Marketing specialist employees must show leadership ability and make many decisions on a daily basis. Being a marketing specialist is a long-term career goal for many people in marketing. This type of job requires not only strong job-related skills, but also good leadership skills.

Marketing supervisors must have good management skills, the ability to make many decisions on a daily basis, and excellent marketing skills. This is a career level many people aspire to reach. The prestige and income are generally quite high, and there is less risk involved than at the top management level.

Manager/owner is the top level. People at this level are competent to run a small business or a significant part of a large business. They must be highly skilled in a number of areas. They are responsible for the final success of the enterprise. They are also responsible for any failures or problems that occur along the way. People at this level must be ready to accept responsibility for both the successes and failures of the business.

■ **Business Class** Travel to interesting places may be one benefit to a career in marketing. *What are some other possible benefits?*

1.3 ASSESSMENT

Reviewing Key Terms and Concepts

1. What proportion of the U.S. work force is involved in marketing activities?

2. Name one employment trend.

3. List two major benefits of working in marketing.

4. What basic skills are needed for success in a marketing career?

5. According to the Bureau of Labor Statistics, approximately how many new marketing and sales jobs will be created between 1992 and 2005?

Thinking Critically

6. Discuss how the marketing skills you would learn in a fast-food restaurant could be transferred to an industrial sales position.

Integrating Academic Skills

7. **MATH** In your entry-level job as a sales-clerk, you made $15,000 a year. After many years of hard work and a long series of promotions, you became director of marketing at $150,000 a year. This is what percent of your original salary?

Careers in Marketing

HOSPITALITY MARKETING

Mark Bingle
Hotel Manager, Four Seasons Hotels,
The Regent Beverly Wilshire Hotel

What do you like most about your work?

"There are never two days alike in the hotel business. Daily activities are dictated by which guests are arriving and what needs to be done before their arrival. Let's say that the First Lady is arriving today—I am most likely meeting with Secret Service to discuss the arrival plans. Imagine instead that it is the CEO of Coca-Cola checking in—I could be ensuring that any non-Coke products have been removed from the private bar in the room prior to arrival. There is no monotony in my business—it changes every moment."

How did you get into hotel management?

"The hiring philosophy for Four Seasons hotels is that we can train anyone to do anything. The only condition, however, is a friendly disposition and positive attitude. Our industry is service, and we can teach anyone to serve, but the smile has to be there ahead of time. I had no experience when I joined, but I wanted to work in a beautiful environment where quality was a top priority. The hotel took me under its proverbial wing, based on my educational background and commitment to service, and gave me a chance."

What training do you recommend?

"Go to a five-star hotel and watch the interaction of the guests and staff. The enthusiasm has to be there all day long, almost as if one is on stage; if you can keep that up, you've won half the battle. A college education is important for management candidates who want to move up, but not required. Being multilingual is a huge incentive for any employer to hire a candidate, especially in this business."

What is your key to success?

"The key to success in the hotel industry is understanding people's needs and wants. My number one success tool is my education at Georgetown University. Attending an internationally integrated university allowed me to travel and live abroad, which broadened my perspective."

Thinking Critically
What aspect of this job do you find most appealing?

Career Facts

Education and Training: High school classes in marketing, speech, food, accounting, and computer science are helpful, as well as part-time work in hotels or restaurants. Post-secondary training is recommended in business administration, accounting, and food service management.

Aptitudes, Abilities, and Skills: Good people and communication skills (especially in stressful situations), strong problem-solving abilities, good organizational skills, and experience with numerical and clerical data are helpful.

Career Outlook: Positions are expected to grow as fast as the average for all occupations through the year 2006. Manager jobs will not grow as rapidly as the hotel industry in general due to the increase in economy-class accommodations.

Career Path: Many managers are promoted from within the ranks. Geographical mobility is essential for advancement in chain-operated hotels.

Chapter **1** ASSESSMENT

VOCABULARY REVIEW

In a paragraph, define marketing and then explain the relationship of the following terms to it.

- products
- goods
- services
- exchange
- utility
- form utility
- place utility
- time utility
- possession utility
- information utility
- benefits
- occupational area

FACT AND IDEA REVIEW

1. What is marketing? (1.1)

2. Identify the seven functions of marketing. (1.1)

3. Of the four marketing utilities, is one the most important for business success? (1.2)

4. Which of the five economic utilities are related to marketing? (1.2)

5. Using a ballpoint pen as an example, explain the concept of form utility. (1.2)

6. How can marketing help lower prices? (1.2)

7. Explain marketing's role in developing new and improved products. (1.2)

8. Why is the study of marketing helpful in any career? (1.3)

9. What do Department of Labor projections predict for marketing jobs? (1.3)

10. How do the trends in marketing and production compare? What accounts for the differences in the trends? (1.3)

THINKING CRITICALLY

1. It is often said that marketing costs represent approximately 50 percent of the selling price of an item. Select a product of your choice to justify the need for marketing and its related costs in the sale of that product.

2. When handheld calculators were introduced, they sold for $100. As they became popular, more companies introduced better and less expensive ones. Now you can purchase a handheld, solar-powered calculator for as little as $5. Provide examples of other products that were more costly when they were first put on the market than they are now.

3. Explain the meaning of the following statement: Marketing is more than just promotion.

4. Why do you think employers want employees who have an understanding of business as well as good interpersonal and communication skills?

5. You have decided to be a marketing entrepreneur. What kinds of character traits and interpersonal skills will you need?

BUILDING WORKPLACE SKILLS

1. **Human Relations** Assume you are a salesperson in a computer store. A customer is hesitant about buying the mid-priced laptop computer you've been showing her. Her objection is that it will sell for much less in a year. Do you think she's correct? What would you say to her?

2. **Technology** You're interested in marketing as a possible career, but you're not sure about the availability of jobs in marketing. Using career Web sites on the Internet, research the current availability of marketing jobs. Prepare a brief written report on your findings.

APPLYING MARKETING CONCEPTS

1. **Understanding Marketing Functions** With 2–3 classmates, use a word processing program to write a short report about a new fruit beverage that you believe will be popular with teenagers. Assume your team develops this new product and wants to start selling it. Cover all of the seven marketing functions in your report. When you introduce each function, note this in parentheses.

2. **Applying Economic Utilities** Using the short report written in the first project, identify examples of the five economic utilities. What did your group do to create form, time, place, possession, and information utility? What challenges did you face addressing these?

3. **Summarizing Key Concepts** Using a word processing program, summarize an article related to one of the seven functions of marketing or the five economic utilities. Use business publications such as *BrandWeek, Adweek, BusinessWeek, Fortune, Forbes, Nation's Business, Sales & Marketing Management,* or *Marketing News.* Share your article summary with classmates.

4. **Preparing Presentations** Use a computer and a presentation program to prepare a graphic representation of the seven functions of marketing.

LINKING SCHOOL TO WORK

Basic and Information Skills Ask an employer to identify five-to-ten characteristics of an effective employee. Categorize those characteristics as a *business understanding,* an *interpersonal skill,* or a *communication skill.* Were there any characteristics that did not fit into one of those three categories? Which characteristic was regarded as most important to your employer? Why?

THE DECA CONNECTION

Role Play: Store Manager

Situation You are to assume the role of manager of a local supermarket. A disgruntled customer (judge) complains to you about how manufacturers and retailers waste money on marketing. The customer (judge) thinks retail prices could be significantly reduced if manufacturers spent less money on marketing their products.

Activity Take this opportunity to respond to the customer (judge).

Evaluation You will be evaluated on how well you meet the following performance indicators:

- Describe marketing functions and related activities
- Explain the concept of marketing and market identification
- Explain marketing and its importance in a global economy
- Handle customer inquiries
- Determine forms of economic utility created by marketing activities

*inter*NET CONNECTION

Marketing Degrees
You have decided that you would like to learn more about earning a marketing degree.

Connect
- Locate the Web sites of two colleges that offer bachelor's degrees in marketing and two community colleges that offer associate's degrees in marketing.
- Locate information about distance learning and marketing institute programs.
- Contact schools for further information and share the information with your class as part of an information bulletin board.

Basic Marketing Concepts

Marketing: What It Takes

Improving on Your Marketing Mix

You thought your idea for a snowboard shop was pretty good. However, yesterday you received a mixed reaction from a counselor at the small business development center. She said there was a large enough population of the 16- to 24-year-olds in the area, but that you need to develop a more precise marketing mix.

WHAT WILL YOU DO?
What steps can you take to develop a better marketing mix?

The Marketing Concept

The Basic Concept

How do businesses become successful? They plan for it by following an idea called the marketing concept. The marketing concept states that businesses must satisfy customers' needs and wants in order to make a profit. Keen competition forces businesses to embrace the marketing concept. Businesses must have the right goods and services at the right time, at the right price, and at the right place for purchase. Additionally, businesses must communicate all of this information to their customers. This is not always an easy task. To do so, businesses must truly know who their customers are and how they can be reached.

▪ Customers vs. Consumers

When businesses discuss customers, they sometimes make a distinction between customers and consumers. Customers buy the product. Consumers are those people who actually use the product. For a manufacturer of consumer products, like Sony, the customers are the retail stores that sell Sony's products. Since Sony does not sell its products directly to the consumer, it has to rely on retailers.

The customer and consumer is usually one in the same for the retailer. If you buy a Sony Walkman and you are the person who will be using it, you are both the customer and consumer. There are many situations where the customer is not the intended user of the product, however. If you buy a Sony Walkman as a gift, you are the customer and the person for whom you are buying the Walkman is the consumer. This concept becomes clear when you think of marketing to children. A child may be the consumer of a breakfast cereal, but it is the parent who is the customer. Successful marketers must recognize the need to satisfy both the customer and consumer.

▪ What is a Market?

All potential customers who share common needs and wants, and who have the ability and willingness to buy the product, are considered a market. A market is further described by its total sales in a product category by competing companies in categories such as hair spray, chewing gum, and soft drinks. For example, everyone who buys video game consoles is part of the $7 billion game console market (see Figure 2-1 on page 23).

What You'll Learn

- The marketing concept
- The difference between customers and consumers
- What a market is and how it can be described
- What target marketing is
- The four Ps of the marketing mix

Why It's Important

In order to participate in the world of marketing, you'll want to understand how businesses focus on the needs and wants of their customers in order to improve their products, remain competitive, and increase their profits.

Key Terms

- marketing concept
- customers
- consumers
- market
- target marketing
- customer profile
- marketing mix

FIGURE 2-2

MARKETING MIX

The strength of a particular marketing mix depends on two things—how well the target market is defined and how well all marketing decisions are directed toward that market. The target market for Polaroid's I-Zone camera is males and females, 12 to 18 years old. *How does the marketing mix for this product measure up to these two standards?*

1 PRODUCT STRATEGIES

Product strategies include what product to make, how to package it, what brand name to use, and what image to project. Polaroid's choice is a pocket-size instant camera with an indoor flash that produces self-developing miniature photos or photo stickers. Polaroid Pocket Film is designed for use with the I-Zone camera. The cameras come in fashionable colors and carry the Polaroid I-Zone brand name.

2 PLACE STRATEGIES

Place strategies determine how and where a product will be distributed. Polaroid's choice is to reach customers through mass market and specialty stores in the United States.

3 PRICE STRATEGIES

Price strategies should reflect what customers are willing and able to pay. Polaroid's choice of suggested retail price for the I-Zone camera is $24.99, which includes a trial pack of six-exposure sticker film and two AA batteries; Polaroid Pocket Film has a suggested retail price of $5.99 (non-sticker) and $6.99 (sticker) film.

4 PROMOTION STRATEGIES

Promotion strategies deal with how potential customers will be told about the new product, what the message will be, when and where it will be delivered, and with what inducements to buy. Polaroid's choices include television commercials, a public relations effort, and a Web site offering users a variety of interactive activities. The image Polaroid wants to create is "self expression" and "creativity."

Satisfying the needs and wants of all customers in a product category would be difficult without further defining and analyzing the current and potential customers of a given commodity. That is where target marketing comes in. Target marketing is focusing all marketing decisions on a very specific group of people who you want to reach. The more information you have on your target market, the easier it is to make the marketing decisions.

To develop a clear picture of that target market, businesses create a customer profile. A customer profile can include information about the target market with regard to the age, income level, ethnic background, occupation, attitudes, lifestyle, or geographic residence of the targeted customer. Marketers spend a lot of money on research to clearly identify the most important characteristics of the target market's customer profile to help them make intelligent marketing decisions.

■ Marketing Mix

The marketing mix comprises four basic marketing strategies, collectively known as the four Ps—product, place, price, and promotion. These strategies involve the decisions that a business must make. The marketing mix is dependent on how well the target market is defined and how well all strategies are directed toward that target audience. Once a target market is clearly identified, it is easier to make decisions regarding strategies that hit the mark.

The four elements of the marketing mix are interconnected. Actions in one area affect decisions in

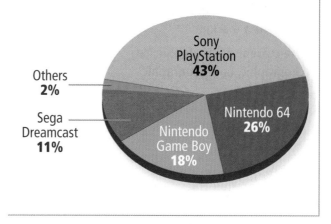

FIGURE 2-1

1999 U.S. Game Console Market

Sales $7 billion

■ **Fun and Games** A market can be described as the people who are potential customers of a product, as well as by the classification of a product in a category. *Would you be considered part of the market for game consoles? Why or why not?*

another. Each part of the marketing mix contains countless alternatives. From all of the alternatives, management must strategize a combination of marketing mix decisions that will satisfy target markets and achieve organizational goals.

Let's use a specific product in the instant camera category, Polaroid's I-Zone camera, as an example. (See Figure 2-2 on page 22.)

(See Figure 2-2 on page 22.)

2.1 ASSESSMENT

Reviewing Key Terms and Concepts

1. What does the marketing concept state?
2. Who are the customers of Sony Electronics and Hershey Chocolates? Who are their consumers?
3. What is a market?
4. What is target marketing?
5. What are the four Ps of the marketing mix?

Thinking Critically

6. Many women's magazines like *Glamour* and *Elle* publish advertisements for men's cologne. Explain the rationale for this practice.

Integrating Academic Skills

7. **MATH** Baking soda toothpastes presently represent 25 percent of the $1.4 billion toothpaste market. What does that percentage represent in dollar sales?

Market Segmentation

What You'll Learn

- What market segmentation is and the four methods used to segment a market
- The current demographic, psychographic, and geographic trends

Why It's Important

Businesses must know who their customers are to achieve success. In other words, they must know their markets. This section will introduce you to the U.S. marketplace and the different ways businesses classify and characterize its segments.

Key Terms

- market segmentation
- demographics
- Baby Boom Generation
- Generation X
- Generation Y
- disposable income
- discretionary income
- psychographics
- geographics

Analyzing Markets

Market segmentation is a way of analyzing a market by specific characteristics in order to create a target market. Once that target market is clearly identified, a business can customize its product offerings and marketing strategies to that specific group of potential customers. To accomplish that goal, businesses may segment a market by demographics, psychographics, geographics, and product benefits. With the vast technological resources now available to marketers, all four methods might be used to identify a very specific group of people—a target market. Let's look at each one separately for now.

■ Demographics

Demographics refers to statistics that describe a population in terms of personal characteristics. These include age, gender, income, ethnic background, education, and occupation. Once marketers know the demographics of a particular market, they can categorize and develop their products to appeal to its members.

AGE Marketers can easily use age to segment the market in product categories such as toys, clothing, and food products. For example, toy manufacturers often identify on the packaging the recommended age group for each toy or game. Jeans manufacturers create jeans for toddlers, children, teens, and adults. Cap'n Crunch cereal is targeted to kids, while Kellogg's All Bran cereal is marketed to adults.

When marketers study age, they classify everyone according to certain generations. The reason for this practice is that each generation tends to have common bonds because of their collectively shared experiences. This makes them good market segments to target. The last three generations were the Baby Boom Generation, Generation X, and Generation Y.

The 76 million babies born in the United States between 1946 and 1964 are called the Baby Boom Generation. Tracking this group's life pays off for marketers because of its large size. Also, as baby boomers get older, their income and spending power increases. In fact, they control $2.6 trillion and have about 51 percent of the wealth in the country. Thus, they are prime targets for all types of luxuries and recreational items. Marketers are watching the baby boomers' age—the oldest baby boomers will turn 65 in 2011 and the number of Americans over 65 will nearly double by 2030. The graying baby boomers will certainly remain a strong market for all kinds of products related to an aging population.

Case Study

Got Milk?

To get the message to teens to drink milk, MilkPEP and Dairy Management Inc. are using popular athletes as their models in "got milk?" ads. Teenagers' zeal for collecting milk mustache ads of their favorite sports stars is what marketers are counting on to get across a serious message.

Milk consumption drops in the teenage years, just when teens may need it most. It appears that seven out of ten teen boys and nine out of ten teen girls do not get their daily calcium requirements.

To target teens, the message for the promotion must be viewed as "cool" and the media must reach teens. Using popular athletes in the "got milk?" print and TV ads helps to get the message across. Print ads in *TV Guide*, which is read by 5.4 million teens, was one effective vehicle used to communicate the message.

9 essential nutrients.

Want game?
Milk is packed with vitamins and minerals that active bodies need.

got milk?

MIA HAMM © 1999 AMERICA'S DAIRY FARMERS AND MILK PROCESSORS

Case Study Review

1. **Why were "got milk?" ads popular with teens?**
2. **How can "got milk?" ads target different market segments by age, gender, generation, and ethnic background?**

A Matter of Ethics

3. **Is it ethical to use popular athletes to persuade teens to take a specific action? Would it change your opinion if the action were other than "drink milk"?**

The more than 40 million Americans born between 1965 and 1976 are called Generation X. Many members of Generation X are products of dual-career households or divorced parents. They have been bombarded with media from an early age, therefore the members of Generation X tend to be savvy and skeptical consumers. Generation Xers are better educated than any previous generation, and they are more financially cautious and conservative. They are prime consumers of cosmetics, fashionable clothing, movies, and electronic items. To reach this group, marketers must use sharp images, music, a sense of humor, and a little irreverence.

The 77 million Americans born between 1977 and 1997 are referred to as Generation Y. This generation is growing up during a computer revolution. They are accustomed to interactivity and used to doing more than one thing at a time. They strive to be different from their parents, and they are very comfortable using computers and "surfing the net." This group has $130 million in spending power and influences $250 billion in purchases. It is easy to see why marketers are interested in Generation Y. They want to build brand loyalty by attracting consumers when they are teens. Marketers have learned that teens buy many of their own personal

Electronic Frontiers

Pixels or Paper?

E-book readers, electronic devices that can store and display the text of books, were introduced with great fanfare in 1998. However, the infant industry faces many obstacles. E-book manufacturers are caught up in a classic chicken-and-egg quandary. To attract readers, they must offer cheap e-book devices and a wide variety of titles, but to persuade publishers to sell titles, they have to show that there is a market and that the technology is secure from piracy. Although not everyone agrees about how and when e-books will take hold, Microsoft has predicted that e-titles will outsell their paper counterparts by 2010.

Thinking Critically:

Do you agree with Microsoft's prediction? Why or why not?

care products, including deodorant, shampoo, and toothpaste. According to Sony, 60 percent of 12– to 17-year-olds have their own CD players. Teens also do the family shopping and influence big-ticket family purchases, like autos and computers. Therefore, smart marketers target teens. MCI Communications Corp has targeted teens with a collect phone call service 1-800-COLLECT.

GENDER Gender helps to create market segments as well. Jockey, a men's underwear company doubled its sales when it entered the women's market with Jockey underwear for women.

Sensor razors for men and new Sensor razors for women, as well as Mennen Speed Stick and Lady Speed Stick demonstrate how companies that traditionally marketed men's products can extend their product lines to enter the women's market. Gender-neutral products may use different advertising media and messages when trying to reach men and women. For example, ads for the Palm Pilot have featured famous professional women when trying to attract the female segment and famous professional men when trying to reach the male market.

■ **The Generation Gap** Generations share common bonds because they experienced their lives during the same era—politically, socially, and economically. Thus, they tend to have the same values and attitudes about life in general. Marketers who want to reach a specific generation must understand that generation's thinking. *Which generation do you think marketers are trying to reach in this advertisement? Why?*

INCOME Marketers want to know how much money is available for spending on different products. For this reason, they look at two types of income measurement: disposable income and discretionary income.

Disposable income is the money left after taking out taxes. Marketers who produce and distribute products that are necessities are interested in changes in consumers' disposable income. Discretionary income is the money left after paying for basic living necessities such as food, shelter, and clothing. Marketers who sell luxury products are interested in changes in consumers' discretionary income.

Marketers also study the different income levels in the United States. In many cases, income levels help to distinguish different socioeconomic groups from one another. The affluent are a small percentage of the population. In 2000, approximately eight million households reported household income of $100,000 or more. Even though these affluent households are small in number, they account for upwards of half of all discretionary spending in the United States.

ETHNIC BACKGROUND The U.S. population is becoming more mulitcultural and ethnically diverse, mainly as a result of increased immigration. The Caucasian population is declining, while other ethnic populations increase. Combined African-American, Hispanic, and Asian-American populations make up 28 percent of the U.S. population. By 2025 these ethnic groups will represent 37.2 percent of all Americans (see Figure 2-3 on page 28). Let's take a look at these growing markets.

African-Americans number approximately 35 million, represent 12.2 percent of the total population, and spend roughly $400 billion annually.

To reach the African-American market, businesses may use ethnically targeted magazines, such as

¡Yo Quiero Taco Bell!

Taco Bell's creative advertising helped it to become the nation's leading Mexican fast-food restaurant. Its sales now exceed $5 billion. In addition to its popular advertising campaign featuring a talking Chihuahua, the company integrated many other promotional activities. They include offering talking Chihuahua dolls as in-store premiums and entering into licensing agreements with major retailers to sell keychains, hats, backpacks, T-shirts, and full-size versions of the Chihuahua. Taco Bell's integrated marketing campaign has proven to be a huge success.

Thinking Critically
Do you think Taco Bell's advertising targets only one ethnic group? Why or why not?

Essence and *Black Enterprise*. Businesses have learned that to effectively reach this market they must back up promotional activities with community support. An example is Maybelline, who formulated the Shades of You line of cosmetics for African-American women. The company also runs Black History Month promotions and has worked with The Coalition of 100 Black Women, a national organization dedicated to improving the lives of women.

Understanding the culture and religion of an ethnic group is important. For example, J.C. Penney utilized the African-American tradition of wearing white to church on the fifth Sunday of a month to promote white suits in African-American women's magazines. That promotion helped to sell out white suits in the chain's urban locations.

Hispanics number approximately 32 million, representing over 11 percent of the U.S. population. Hispanics will surpass African-Americans as the largest U.S. ethnic group by 2010.

Marketers would be wise to understand that the Hispanic culture is diverse and comprises 21 nationalities, including Mexican, Spanish, Puerto Rican, Cuban, Dominican, Caribbean, and others of Central and South American ancestry. Approximately 70 percent of Hispanics are Roman Catholics. Hispanic

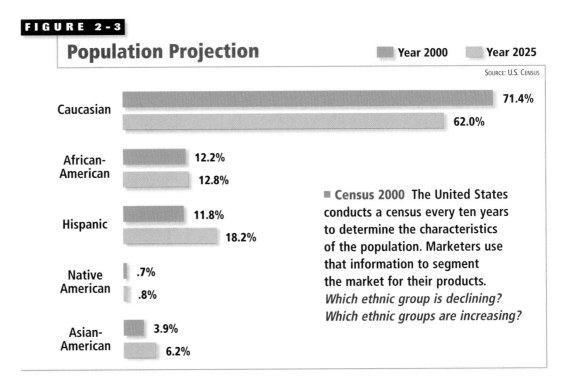

FIGURE 2-3

Population Projection

Year 2000   Year 2025

Source: U.S. Census

Caucasian — 71.4% / 62.0%
African-American — 12.2% / 12.8%
Hispanic — 11.8% / 18.2%
Native American — .7% / .8%
Asian-American — 3.9% / 6.2%

■ **Census 2000** The United States conducts a census every ten years to determine the characteristics of the population. Marketers use that information to segment the market for their products. *Which ethnic group is declining? Which ethnic groups are increasing?*

■ **Who's Watching TV?** Marketers of products for the Hispanic population look for Spanish-speaking media to get their message out. Univision has become America's number one growth network by catering to a Spanish-speaking audience. *Why is television a good medium to use when targeting the U.S. Hispanic population?*

culture centers around the family, and these families tend to be larger than the U.S. average (3.4 people vs. 2.6 for all U.S. families). Food marketers know that when they sell products in Hispanic neighborhoods, the package sizes must be big.

To reach Hispanics, marketers should consider using Spanish-language television. Statistics show Hispanics watch television approximately four hours on weekdays, and most of that time is spent watching Spanish-language programming. Two magazines that can be used to target Hispanics are *People en Espanol* and *Latina*. Radio advertising is also a good medium to reach Hispanics because music is a major part of the Latino culture.

The Asian-American population numbers a little more than 11 million, representing almost 4 percent of the total U.S. population. Americans of Asian descent are the fastest-growing and most affluent population group. Like Hispanics, Asian-Americans are a diverse ethnic group. This group includes

16 different nationalities, including Chinese, Filipino, Japanese, Asian-Indian, Korean, and Vietnamese.

To reach the Asian-American market, it is important to understand its culture and priorities. More Asian-Americans are college graduates than any other ethnic group, and a higher percentage hold professional jobs. Marketers of financial services, computers, telecommunications, and new vehicles may target this segment because Asian-Americans are big consumers of such commodities.

Because there is no national broadcast media for Asian-Americans, marketers can use less costly local media to reach them. Asian-Americans prefer to communicate in their native languages, so it is very important for marketers to understand their languages. When advertising a banking institution, the major theme, such as financial security, can be the same for Chinese and Koreans, but the copy and models must be different to reflect the two groups.

■ Psychographics

Psychographics involves studies of consumers based on social and psychological characteristics. People's attitudes and what they value are of importance to marketers, as are their lifestyles. Consumer lifestyles, which include how people spend their time and money, are closely related to people's attitudes and values. If you made a list of all of your present activities, you would come to realize just how many market segments can be identified by psychographics. It is amazing how similar the attitudes are of people who share common interests. You simply need to begin by looking at people involved in certain sports, such as tennis, golf, skiing, and boating, to see similarities in the participants. Magazine publishers recognize psychographic similarities and publish magazines geared to specific consumer interests. *Golf Digest*, *Photography*, *Ski*, and *Sports Illustrated* are just a few examples.

TRENDS In addition to segmenting people by their leisure time interests and membership in a given generation, marketers observe changes in households, the economy, politics, and the workplace. These factors contribute to changes in personal attitudes about health, time, fun, and living in general.

Health, eating properly, and exercising are trend-setting issues for marketers in the twenty-first century. A promotional campaign for Kellogg's Special K cereal tells women to "Reshape Your Attitude" by eating sensibly and encourages them to establish a healthier lifestyle. A walk through the supermarket will also tell the story, as more and more foods come with claims that they are organically grown, low-fat, fat-free, low-sodium, vitamin-enriched, calcium-fortified, and even cholesterol-lowering.

Work, fun, and indulgence are also key lifestyle issues. A current workplace trend is dressing down. Businesses call it business casual attire. Wisk with Wrinkle Reducer is a product that addresses that trend, as casual clothing generally requires more ironing.

Many Americans are being encouraged to take a break and indulge themselves. Ben & Jerry's tells consumers to "Stop and taste the ice cream." The ice cream company is suggesting "work stoppages,"

What Does Yes Really Mean?

In many Asian societies, it is impolite to say "no," so "yes" has multiple meanings. "Yes" can mean that listeners recognize that they are being spoken to, although they don't understand what is being said, or that the speaker's words are understood, but not agreed with. It can also mean that something is understood, but other people must be told of it before any final decisions are made. "Yes" can also mean that an offer is comprehended, but if the situation were to change, their "yes" would also be subject to change.

Thinking Critically

Why is having a keen cultural ear important in cross-cultural marketing?

so workers can take an indulgence break during the workday. Häagen Dazs ice cream ran a similar promotion called "Passport to Indulge."

Time has become a commodity to market. With the stresses of work, time has become a luxury and vacations have become the number one luxury enjoyed by Americans. Enjoying one's leisure time has become paramount. Proof of this trend can be seen in the increase in spending on entertainment, including concerts, museums, theater, theme parks, sports, toys, and electronics.

Upscaling is another trend that has become apparent due to the strong economy. It seems more and more people (upper and middle classes alike) desire the better things in life. In 1975 only 38 percent of Americans said a lot of money was part of a good life; now 63 percent do. Name brand products and premium versions of everyday products are being sold in discount stores. Architect and designer Michael Graves has designed hundreds of everyday items that are sold at Target stores. The luxury market is definitely a consumer trend, as individuals define themselves through the products and brands they buy.

■ Geographics

The term geographics refers to segmentation of the market based on where people live. To segment a market geographically, you can refer to local, regional, national, or even global markets. Some businesses, by their very nature, segment their market locally. For example, a small independent restaurant generally caters to people who live in its vicinity. There are products that are marketed nationally and internationally, such as Coca Cola and Pepsi. Marketers study where their customers live in order to decide which media to use and where to market their products.

Marketers also study geographics in relation to ethnic concentrations. For example, when selecting advertising media to reach the Hispanic market, businesses look at the four states with the highest Hispanic population: New York, Texas, California, and Florida. When segmenting the market for the Hispanic population, the Ford Motor Company created a Spanish language vehicle catalog in 2000 for dealerships in those states.

Where people live is often studied in relation to age, ethnic background, and income. To assist in such study, the U.S. government created Metropolitan Statistical Areas (MSAs). These are specifically defined geographic areas used by the

■ **Need a Vacation?** Two current psychographic trends involve time and indulgence. With the stresses of work, enjoying one's limited free time has become an important commodity. *How did this candy company utilize that trend in this ad?*

BRIGHT IDEAS

Wear Your Office

Clothing designers are responding to customers' desire for style in the new digital age by creating clothing with functional pockets for the portable electronic gadgets we carry. Savvy consumers are now sporting cleverly designed clothing with extra pockets to keep their beepers, pagers, cell phones, and palmtops in handy reach. The gizmo-oriented pocket is even starting to be offered in clothing appropriate for the office. Brooks Brothers has responded to the new portability craze by adding cell phone pockets in all outerwear and an extra inner pocket to its suit jackets.

Thinking Creatively

With the technology revolution all around us, what other products could be redesigned to capitalize on the psychographic trend of being connected wherever you go?

government in the distribution of federal aid. Marketers use MSAs to target consumers and launch promotional campaigns. *Sales and Marketing Management* magazine reports on where people are moving and how much spending power residents have in the various MSAs.

The propensity to use and buy products in a given region is also an important issue to marketers, especially when introducing a new product. Marketers determine which geographic areas would be most receptive to a new product using sales data coupled with psychographic data. For example, a new energy drink, Torq, was first introduced in California and the Pacific Northwest, where research indicated consumers were more receptive to "energy" drinks with special ingredients, like ginseng. Psychographic data show that trendsetters tend to be located in these regions of the country.

■ Product Benefits

Segmenting a market by product benefits involves studying consumers' behaviors, needs, and wants. Companies market benefits, not simply the physical characteristics of a product. For example, sports shoe manufacturers identify separate market segments for people who jog, walk, play tennis, or do aerobics. Each activity requires a shoe with a particular design. Thus, manufacturers market different shoes for each segment. A shampoo manufacturer may segment the market according to people with different types of hair (oily, dry, or normal), people who have dandruff, or people who wash their hair frequently.

MASS MARKETING When products have universal appeal and few features to differentiate them from competitors, mass marketing is used. Mass marketing involves using a single marketing plan to reach all customers. Since most products (even ones with universal appeal) can be segmented by demographics, pyschographics, geograhics, or product benefits, mass marketing is not as poplular as it once was. Even products that use one slogan in their advertising, such as "Got Milk" ads, will use different models or themes to reach different segments of the market. The advantage of market segmentation is that products can be targeted more effectively. The disadvantage is that marketers must be more creative and spend more money getting the message across in different media to reach each segment. The advantage of mass marketing is that the costs involved in the original ad campain are less since only one theme is used. The disadvantage is that the theme must be very general or it may not be understood by all potential customers.

2.2 ASSESSMENT

Reviewing Key Terms and Concepts

1. What do demographics, psychographics, geographics, and product benefits have in common?

2. How can a market be segmented using demographics?

3. What does the study of psychographics involve?

4. Provide one example of how a marketer can segment a market based on product benefits.

5. Of what significance are the combined African-American, Hispanic, and Asian-American populations to marketers?

Thinking Critically

6. How can Procter and Gamble market household products to a male market segment? What problems might P&G encounter in that endeavor?

Integrating Academic Skills

7. **COMMUNICATION** Write an ad campaign theme for Sunsweet Prunes to target baby boomers who are looking for healthy foods. Develop a second campaign theme to target a younger generation with Sunsweet Prunes.

Careers in Marketing

PRODUCT MANAGEMENT

Lori Tauber Marcus
Director of Brand Management
Pepsico Fountain Beverage Division

What does your job entail?

"I supervise the development, production, and sale of Pepsi brands for Pepsi's fountain beverage division, the part of the company that sells beverages to restaurants and theaters. I conduct research to determine the profitability of products being developed, then I oversee the marketing of the product. I also help with advertising and training the sales force. After the product has been marketed, I conduct follow-up research to determine how well it is doing and what changes may need to be made to increase profitability."

What kind of training did you have?

"A few years after earning a bachelor's degree in marketing in college, I went to work for Pepsi, first in the food service marketing division and then as an associate product manager for Pepsi's Mountain Dew brand. I was promoted to customer marketing manager for retail marketing, customizing Pepsi promotions for mass retailers like Target and Kmart. I became area marketing manager for the eastern seaboard, then senior product manager for new cola concepts."

What skills are most important?

"Leadership skills are essential—as a brand manager you lead teams of many people, each performing different functions who are pivotal in bringing your product to market. It is important to have the ability to think creatively and strategically. It is also important to have an aptitude for gathering and analyzing data and making decisions based on the data."

What is your key to success?

"I really love doing what I do. Also, I have been fortunate to have always worked with very smart and highly motivated people from whom I'm constantly learning."

Thinking Critically
What types of experience would you emphasize when applying for a job as a brand manager?

Career Facts

Education and Training: A bachelor's or master's degree in marketing or business and coursework in communication, economics, and math is recommended. College coursework should be accompanied by several years of sales experience.

Aptitudes, Abilities, and Skills: Analytical skills, organizational skills, leadership skills, communication skills, interpersonal skills, and math skills are necessary.

Career Outlook: Many new jobs are opening in the computer and Internet industry, as well as in the electronics industry in general.

Career Path: A typical path to brand manager is through a management trainee job. A staff position in the marketing department can sharpen analytical skills.

Chapter 2 ASSESSMENT

VOCABULARY REVIEW

Write one paragraph to show your understanding of how the following concepts are related to one another.

- marketing concept
- customers
- consumers
- market
- target marketing
- customer profile
- marketing mix
- market segmentation
- demographics
- psychographics
- geographics

FACT AND IDEA REVIEW

1. What is the marketing concept? (2.1)
2. Provide an example of when a consumer is not the customer of a product purchased in a retail store. (2.1)
3. Define the concept of a market and give an example of one. (2.1)
4. Name the four Ps of the marketing mix and explain how they should be used in target marketing. (2.1)
5. Explain market segmentation and the four main ways a market can be segmented. (2.2)
6. Why do generations make good markets to segment? Name the three recent generations that marketers use to segment the market. (2.2)
7. What is the difference between disposable income and discretionary income? (2.2)
8. How have cosmetic companies targeted African-American women? (2.2)
9. Which ethnic group is the most affluent? (2.2)
10. How might a shampoo manufacturer segment the market according to product benefits? (2.2)

THINKING CRITICALLY

1. The United States is becoming more affluent. Because of this, make a plan to change a regular food product to create an upscale image for that product—a premium brand.
2. How can a marketer of consumer products use the data from the U.S. Census 2000?
3. How would you position BENGAY to young adults? How would you position the same product to senior citizens? Would you use the same appeal? Why or why not?
4. Using market segmentation based on income, explain Wal-Mart's success.

BUILDING WORKPLACE SKILLS

1. **Human Relations** A shabbily dressed couple enters a luxury automobile showroom, but the sales associates are not eager to approach them. A younger associate finally does and eventually sells them a $50,000 car. The couple puts down $20,000 cash as a down payment. What is the point of this story? What does it say about how lifestyle characteristics can be misleading?
2. **Technology** You have been hired by a stockbroker to research the geographic areas in the country that include high-income households. What technology is available to help you in this endeavor?

APPLYING MARKETING CONCEPTS

1. **Summarizing Key Concepts** Summarize an article that demonstrates any of the key concepts in this chapter. In the summary, identify the specific concepts in parentheses. Use business publications, such as *BrandWeek, Adweek, BusinessWeek, Fortune, Forbes, Marketing News,* and *Nation's Business,* to find an applicable article.

2. **Analyzing Marketing Strategies** Using the Internet, find research that describes characteristics of the teenage market. Then visit the Web sites of five companies (manufacturers or retailers) that target teens. Use a word processing program to write a short report analyzing each company's marketing mix strategies and citing your sources of information. Do all four Ps target teenagers effectively? Select one company to provide recommendations on how it could improve its marketing mix strategies when trying to target teens.

3. **Recognizing Target Marketing** Using the Internet, research the holidays of Kwanzaa (African-American celebration of racial pride and unity), Diwali (Hindu festival of lights), and Hanukkah (traditional Jewish celebration). Report how American marketers use knowledge of such holidays.

4. **Researching Psychographic Trends** Research one of the trends noted in the text. Make an oral presentation to the class using presentation software. Be sure to include current examples of how the trend is being used by different companies in their marketing mix strategies. Lastly, evaluate their effectiveness with your classmates.

LINKING SCHOOL TO WORK

Thinking Skills Develop a profile of a local company's customers based on their geographic, demographic, and psychographic characteristics.

THE DECA CONNECTION

Role Play: Toy Company Intern

Situation You are to assume the role of an intern in the marketing department of a consumer product manufacturing company that specializes in toys and electronic games. A new electronic game is being developed and the Research and Development (R&D) Director (judge) has asked for your input. You are to meet with the R&D Director (judge) in fifteen minutes.

Activity You must decide what you will tell the R&D Director (judge) about the strategies to use for product, place, price, and promotion decisions (the four Ps) of the marketing mix. In your presentation include consideration of the product's consumers and customers, as well as concepts such as target marketing and market segmentation.

Evaluation You will be evaluated on how well you meet the following performance indicators:
- Define target marketing
- Explain the difference between consumers and customers
- Explain the role of market segmentation
- Explain marketing mix strategies
- Demonstrate appropriate creativity

inter NET CONNECTION

Head Count

The Census Bureau undertakes a count of the population every 10 years to track changes in population size and demographics.

Connect

- Locate the U.S. Census Web site. Find the current figures and percentages of age and income by ethnic groups (Caucasian, African-American, Hispanic, and Asian-American).

The Zazz Lab...

A Sports and Entertainment Marketing Simulation

WELCOME

Welcome to Zazz Sports and Entertainment Marketing Company. Zazz is devoted to serving the needs of its clients who include college, university, and professional sports teams, professional athletes, sporting events, and sports arenas plus major consumer product corporations, as well as television networks and movie studios. As an intern, you will have the opportunity to work on different clients' projects. All of your work will be assigned and reviewed by your department supervisor.

MARKET A SPORTS DRINK

SITUATION

Your client is RJF Beverage Company, the creator of a new sports drink. The company is entering the "active thirst" market—beverages consumed by people when they're hot and sweaty. The market has been dominated by Gatorade, the sports drink made by Quaker Oats. Other competing brands are Powerade (Coca-Cola) and AllSport (Pepsi). Your client thinks it has a formula for a new sports drink that's even better than Gatorade's. Your client believes that affiliation with a popular sport would help get this new product off the ground.

ASSIGNMENT

Your supervisor wants you to conduct an analysis of the current sports drink market for the new client. You have also been asked to generate creative ideas with regard to the marketing mix for the new product. *Product* ideas should include designing the container and naming the product. *Place* suggestions involve deciding how to get the product into the hands of the consumer. *Price* recommendations should be based on the competitor's pricing strategies. *Promotion* ideas should be creative. Consider sponsorship of a sports team or an endorsement by a professional athlete as part of the promotional mix.

Tools and Resources

To complete this assignment, you will need to conduct research at a library or on the Internet. You will also need a word processing program, a spreadsheet program, and presentation software. Trade publications that may be helpful include *BrandWeek, Advertising Age, Sports Business Journal,* and *Sports Business Daily.*

Research

Research the sports drink market and the major competitors. Find out how much is sold and who buys it. For your customer profile, research geographics, demographics, and psychographics. Determine the market share (percentage of total market) each competitor enjoys. Study each major competitor's product, pricing, promotion, and place decisions. Find out which sports drinks are being endorsed by sports personalities, teams, or leagues, and whether they have special agreements. See if any of the main competitors have Web sites; if they do, find out what is included. Secure samples of competitors' advertising and promotions if possible. You want to see what the RJF company needs to do to break into the sports drink market.

Presentation and Evaluation

In addition to your written report, your supervisor wants you to present your ideas orally and show him your presentation. The presentation will later be shown to the client. You will be evaluated on your oral presentation skills, including:

- Knowledge of the sports drink market and marketing mix strategies
- Continuity of presentation
- Voice quality
- Eye contact

Portfolio

Print out a copy of your completed report and presentation for your Portfolio.

Report

Prepare both a written report and a computer presentation for the client. Use a word processing program to prepare a double-spaced report. Use a spreadsheet program to create a pie chart to illustrate the current market share of the major competitors in the sports drink market. Include the pie chart in your written report. Also include samples of competitors' advertising. Arrange your written report around the following headings:

- Background on the sports drink market
  - The market
  - Market trends
  - Customer analysis (demographics, geographics, psychographics)
- Analysis of major competitors
  - Product, place, price, and promotion decisions
- Proposed target market for RJF
- Marketing mix decisions for RJF
  - Product (name, container), place, price, and promotion (main theme, slogan, publicity, special promotions, advertising) decisions

Using computer presentation software, prepare a presentation of your ideas for the client that includes:

- Key topics covered in your written report
- Graphic illustrations that are relevant to each slide's topic
- Very little text
- Minimum of 10 slides

THE DECA CONNECTION

DECA Food Marketing Event
Making decisions concerning how to sell the product to the consumer through supermarkets and other food retailers is a possible scenario for a role play in this event.

DECA Business Service Marketing Series
Generating marketing ideas for a client for a fee could be a potential role play for this event.

DECA Marketing Management Series
Strategizing marketing mix decisions is part of this career area.

DECA Food Marketing Research Event
Developing a customer profile and ideas for marketing a food product could be a topic for this event.

DECA Sports and Entertainment Marketing Management Team Decision-Making Event
Working on this project with a partner will make the experience similar to what is expected in a DECA Team Decision-Making Event.

Portfolio

Controlling Interest Rates

Once you have completed this unit, you will research the economy of the United States or another country of your choice for the past year. Assume you are the government agency that controls the interest rates in that country. Analyze the economic indicators and decide what to do to improve the economy. You can decide to keep interest rates where they are, increase them, or decrease them based on your analysis of the economy and what you see as trends in the economy. Using computer software, prepare a written report and a presentation. Begin your report with a review of the recent history of the economy and indicate the trends you see. Then provide your recommendations for interest rates and your rationale for your decision. Prepare charts and graphs of the key economic indicators in your report. Print copies of your report and presentation for your Portfolio.

Economics

Unit Overview

Before you can study marketing, it is essential that you understand the economic principles that govern the way marketing functions in different economic systems. Chapter 3 covers the free enterprise system, characterized by private ownership, competition, profit, and risk. Chapter 4 addresses other types of economic systems found around the world and the operating philosophies that govern them. The second section of Chapter 4 provides the information on how an economy is measured and different stages that an economy can experience.

All these economic concepts will give you a better understanding of how governments, businesses, and consumers function during various economic phases and under different economic philosophies. As future marketers, those economic foundations become essential to knowing where, when, and how to market goods.

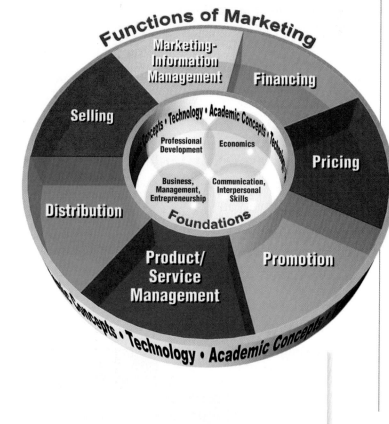

In this Unit:

Foundations of Marketing

⬤ Economics

The Free Enterprise System

Marketing: What It Takes

Exploring the Free Enterprise System

Imagine that you just inherited $25,000 with a restriction that you must invest it to prove you understand the United States free enterprise system. You cannot spend it on yourself.

WHAT WILL YOU DO?

How will you go about investigating possibilities for investment?

trademark for its real estate trading card game equipment. ©1990, 1995 Hasbro, Inc. All Rights Reserved.

Capitalism

Basic Principles

In the United States, we have the freedom to make decisions about where we work and how we spend our money. We also have the freedom to elect the people who represent us in our government. Our nation's founders believed that individuals should have freedom of choice and created the philosophy of the free enterprise system.

In theory, a free enterprise system encourages individuals to start and operate their own businesses without government involvement. The free enterprise system we have today is modified because the government does intervene on a limited basis. It does this to protect citizens and still support the basic principles of free enterprise. Let's look at the basic principles upon which free enterprise is established.

■ Freedom of Ownership

Individuals in our free enterprise system are free to own personal property, such as cars, computers, and homes, as well as natural resources such as oil and land. You can buy anything you want as long as it is not prohibited by law. You can also do what you want with your property in a free enterprise system. You can give it away, lease it, sell it, or use it yourself.

The free enterprise system encourages individuals to own businesses. There are, however, some restrictions on how and where those businesses may operate. Businesses that make things may be forced to comply with certain environmental measures. They may also be restricted in where they can locate. Most kinds of businesses are zoned out of areas intended for private housing.

Intellectual property rights are included in this freedom. Let's say that you get a patent on an invention—you alone own the property rights to that item or idea. To ensure that protection, you would apply for a patent in the U.S. Patent and Trademark Office. Anyone who wanted to manufacture your product would have to pay you for its use through a licensing agreement.

When a company wants to use another's name, symbol, or product, it must get permission to do so and pay a fee for the use. A licensing agreement protects the originator's name and products. A T-shirt manufacturer might be granted a licensing agreement with the National Football League (NFL) so that it can produce T-shirts with NFL logos on them. The company will have to pay NFL Properties a fee for this privilege. It will also have to agree to certain standards of operation imposed to protect the NFL's reputation.

● What You'll Learn

- Basic principles of a free enterprise system
- The role of competition
- The importance of risk and profit

● Why It's Important

In this chapter, you will develop an understanding of how our economic system operates. You will learn how prices are determined, as well as what roles the government and consumers play in that system.

Key Terms

- free enterprise system
- competition
- price competition
- nonprice competition
- monopoly
- risk
- profit

■ **Protecting Tiger** Government regulation protects businesses and individuals from unauthorized use of their personal property. *What evidence of this practice do you see here?*

Even professional athletes make use of licensing agreements to protect their names and images. The professional golfer Tiger Woods has several licensing agreements with a variety of businesses. Some of those businesses include Nike, American Express, Rolex, Titleist, and Wheaties. All of those businesses pay Tiger Woods a fee for the use of his name in their advertising and promotion.

■ Competition

Businesses that operate in a free enterprise system try to attract new customers and keep old ones. Other businesses try to take those same customers away. This struggle between companies for customers is called competition.

Competition is an essential part of a free enterprise system. It is one of the means by which the free enterprise system functions to benefit consumers. Competition forces businesses to produce better-quality goods and services at reasonable prices.

Businesses constantly look for ways to develop new products and improve old ones to attract new customers. Competition results in a wider selection of products from which to choose. The results of these efforts increase the nation's output of goods and services, as well as its standard of living.

Marketing strategies determine how businesses will compete with one another. Marketing helps by determining what customers want and the best way to make those products available. There are two basic ways businesses compete—through price competition and nonprice competition.

PRICE AND NONPRICE COMPETITION Price competition focuses on the sale price of a product. The assumption is that, all other things being equal, consumers will buy the products that are lowest in price.

The marketing strategies used by the Wiz, a discount electronics store, and Ross, the national discount store chain, are examples of price competition. The first insists, "Nobody beats the Wiz,"

bloomingdale's

pinktank
i.n.c. international concepts

Available for both Misses and
Petites. 110.00, melon v-neck
tank dress, also red polyester/
rayon/elastine, misses and
petites 2-14, in Sutton/Studio,
and Shop for Petites in selected
stores. To order, please call
1-800-555-SHOP, #M028.

■ **Price vs. Nonprice Competition** Keen competition
is the key to success for most businesses, especially
in retail. *Which advertisement demonstrates price
competition? Nonprice competition? Why?*

Ask yourself,

"do I need it?

or

do I want it?"

Then look at the price tag

and think,

"does it really matter?"

Walk into Marshalls any day of the week and find brand names and designer fashions for 20%-60% less than department and specialty stores. If you haven't
seen us lately perhaps it's time you did. Over 500 stores nationwide. For the store nearest you, call 1-800-MARSHALLS or visit www.MarshallsOnline.com
Product shown is representative of the merchandise in our stores. Styles and items not vary by store. ©2000 MARSHALLS

Marshalls
Brand names for less. Every day.®

while the second promises to help you "Dress for
Less." Both stress price as the primary focus of their
competitive advantage.

In nonprice competition, businesses choose to
compete on the basis of factors that are not related
to price. These factors include the quality of the
products, service and financing, business location,
and reputation. Some nonprice competitors also
stress the qualifications or expertise of their
personnel. Businesses that use nonprice competition may charge more for products than their
competitors do.

Nordstrom is a fine clothing specialty retailer that
prides itself on providing complete customer satisfaction. Nordstrom's personnel do whatever it takes
to please their customers. The store provides a
unique shopping environment in addition to the
high-quality goods and customer service. One way
the store does this is by providing live piano music
that echoes through the store.

The examples for price and nonprice competition
seem to suggest that businesses adopt one strategy
or the other. It is not uncommon, however, in our
value-oriented society for businesses to try to do
both. As competition increases, you may see more
price-oriented competitors offering services they
never offered in the past. Wal-Mart, the national
discount chain store, offers customers the chance to
meet friends, eat at the food service area, shop,
and listen to Garth Brooks concerts broadcast
throughout the store. Add their huge product selection, and you can see why Wal-Mart is the essence
of one-stop shopping and customer convenience.
Wal-Mart's Web site also offers customers the
ability to check out what's happening in each local
community and store.

Case Study

How's Your Game?

One in every four American homes has a game console, according to Sony, the manufacturer of PlayStation. This is not a surprise as Sony has sold approximately 75 million first-generation PlayStations. Sony is just one of the players in the game console market, which reached $20 billion in 2000, according to *Time* magazine.

This market is so hot that *Newsweek* devoted its front cover and a feature article to the fall release of Sony's PlayStation2 in March 2000. Hype surrounding the release of the new Sony product culminated in Web-based auction sites selling the game console at over 10 times the retail price. PlayStation2 has excellent resolution graphics and sound, generating remarkably lifelike images that can be mistaken for a film of the real thing. Games such as *Madden NFL 2001* and *SSX*, which is an extreme snowboarding game, are already getting attention. A great cost-saving feature is that the PlayStation2 is compatible with all 800 games from the original PlayStation. It features Internet access for online games, Web browsing, e-mail, and capacity for downloading software, music, and video. It also functions as a DVD player as well as a CD player, serving as a home theater and stereo system. Sony is referring to its latest creation as more of a "computer entertainment system" than just a console.

As with any successful product category, there is competition. Nintendo is releasing its next-generation game console, and Microsoft will enter the market with its X-Box game console. Sega's Dreamcast also introduced its online multiplayer game called "ChuChu Rocket" before the other competitors. Sega's Dreamcast also comes Internet-ready.

Sony took risks in developing PlayStation2 with over $2 billion invested in product development. The revenue to cover these costs and expenses will hopefully be covered by selling software, which is the real money maker in the game console business. In the past, seven to eight games have been purchased for every game console sold.

Case Study Review
1. How do consumers benefit from the competition in this game console market?
2. Why is Sony willing to lose money on PlayStation2?

A MATTER OF ETHICS
3. Is it ethical for a company to sell a product at a low price, knowing that it will make more money on the necessary accessories or supplies (i.e. video games and printer cartridges)?

MONOPOLIES When there is no competition and one firm controls the market for a given product, a monopoly exists. A monopoly is exclusive control over a product or the means of producing it.

Monopolies are not permitted under a free enterprise system because they prevent competition. A company can charge whatever it wants without competition. It can also control the quality of a product and who gets it. Without competition, there is nothing stopping a company from acting without regard to customer wants and needs.

One of the most publicized monopoly cases in recent history involved Microsoft, the computer software company. A federal judge declared Microsoft a monopoly. Its technology dominance was said to have "stifled innovation" and "hurt consumers."

The U.S. government has allowed a few monopolies to exist, mainly in industries where it would be wasteful to have more than one firm. These regulated monopolies, however, are on the decline. Telephone service was a government-regulated monopoly until the breakup of American Telephone and Telegraph (AT&T) in 1982. The government decided that deregulating long-distance telephone service would increase competition and benefit consumers. Now many different communication companies, like MCI and Sprint, compete for long-distance telephone business.

Currently, utility companies are being deregulated. This will allow customers to choose their own electric and gas suppliers. In order for the deregulation to work, the government will still control gas and electric companies by imposing price restrictions, forcing the former regulated monopolies to not exceed certain prices. The restrictions will provide an opportunity for unregulated suppliers to compete with the existing utility companies.

■ Risk

Along with the benefits that come from private ownership of property and competition, businesses also face risk. Risk is the potential for loss or failure in relation to the potential for improved earnings. As the potential for earnings gets greater, so does the risk. Putting money in the bank with guaranteed interest rates is less risky than investing in the stock market.

Businesses take risks all the time. Simply starting up is a risk. If you wanted to open your own business, you would probably put your savings into the enterprise. You make money if the business is successful; if the business fails, you lose all your savings and more.

One out of every three businesses in the United States fails after one year of operation. This risk

BRIGHT IDEAS
Stuck on Magnets

"It all started five years ago as a tool I made for myself to help my songwriting," says Dave Kappell, the 36-year-old founder of Magnetic Poetry, Inc. "I suffered from writer's block. At first, I'd photocopy my journal entries or a letter from a girlfriend. I'd cut out the words and move them around until it looked more interesting. It worked great until I sneezed." Kappell later applied the words to magnets and used his refrigerator as a composition board. When friends expressed interest, Kapell interviewed local retailers and gathered sales and marketing information. These retailers sold his first Magnetic Poetry Kits successfully, and Kapell hired sales representatives to sell the kits. Magnetic Poetry, Inc. now offers 50 different products in five languages and has annual sales near $6.5 million.

Thinking Creatively
Give an example of how you could turn your hobby into a business opportunity.

■ **Closing Shop** Going out of business usually means that a business wasn't successful. One in three U.S. businesses fail after one year of operation. *What component of the free enterprise system does this photo demonstrate?*

continues even if a business survives the first few years. When an industry develops and profits are great, more people enter that industry. This increases competition and the risk of failure for individual firms.

Risk is also involved in the development of new products. Product introductions are costly and risky; up to 85 percent of new products fail in the first year. Procter and Gamble (P&G), manufacturer of consumer products such as Tide detergent, Crest toothpaste, and Cover Girl cosmetics, is constantly developing new products. Noxzema Skin Fitness was one product that did not experience much success. Wal-Mart and other dissatisfied retailers discontinued the line of skin care products after only seven months.

■ Profit

Profit is the money earned from conducting business after all costs and expenses have been paid. Profit is often misunderstood. Some people think the money a business earns from sales is its profit. That is not true. The range of profit for most businesses is 1–5 percent of sales; the remaining 95–99 percent goes to pay costs, expenses, and business taxes.

Profit is the motivation for taking the risk of starting a business. It is the reward for taking that risk. It is also the reward for satisfying the needs and wants of customers and consumers.

Profits are good for our economy in many ways. The concept of profit is the driving force in our free enterprise system. It encourages people to develop new products and services in the hope of making a profit. Without profit, few new products would be introduced.

Profit remains high when sales are high, and costs are kept low. This encourages companies to work in an efficient way that helps to conserve precious natural resources. Profits provide money for a company to keep its facilities and machinery up to date. Then the business can produce goods more efficiently.

ECONOMIC COST OF UNPROFITABLE FIRMS An unprofitable business faces many problems. One of the first things businesses do when their profits decline is to lay off employees. When businesses are not profitable, they can lose money. Investors in public companies can lose money if the stock value falls below what they paid for it. As more investors sell their stock in the poorly performing company, the company has fewer resources with which to conduct business. It is forced to cut back on research and development for new products, as well as on the purchase of goods and services needed for operation. This, in turn, affects the profitability of the suppliers and transportation companies that depend on those business transactions.

Government also suffers when business profits decline. Poorly performing businesses pay less money to the government in taxes. When businesses lay off workers, there is a rise in unemployment. This causes an increase in the cost of social services and puts more stress on such agencies. Everyone loses when businesses are not profitable.

ECONOMIC BENEFITS OF SUCCESSFUL FIRMS

Profitable businesses hire more people and pay them well. Employees generally not only have higher incomes, but also have better benefits and higher morale. Investors earn money from their investments, which they spend or reinvest. Vendors and suppliers make more money, too. As employment and profits climb, the government makes more money from taxation of individuals and businesses. Companies and individuals are also more likely to donate to charities when they are doing well.

Remember that profitable companies attract competition, which is beneficial to the consumer. Businesses compete with one another to sell their products to you and other consumers. To satisfy consumer wants and needs, they try to offer new products, the lowest prices, the highest quality, and the best service. For consumers, competition means choice. Companies learn to operate more efficiently in order to lower prices.

As people earn higher incomes they have more money to spend freely. There is an increase in a need not only for expensive products such as cars and homes, but also for services such as vacations.

Ever heard the sound a stoplight makes?

■ **A Greener Car** The Toyota Prius is a "hybrid" electric/gas car that doesn't need to be plugged in. *How does this ad suggest that consumers and the economy can benefit from profitable companies, like Toyota?*

3.1 ASSESSMENT

Reviewing Key Terms and Concepts

1. Provide an example of how freedom of ownership may be limited by government.

2. Provide an example of a business that uses price competition and one that uses nonprice competition.

3. What principle of free enterprise provides the incentive for people to risk their money on business ventures?

4. What is risk, and why is it relevant to a free enterprise system?

5. How do profitable businesses benefit the economy?

Thinking Critically

6. Applications for patents for new technology-related business processes are increasing. Patents for a one-click system for online orders are pending. What are some consequences of such patents being granted?

Integrating Academic Skills

7. **COMMUNICATION** Assume a friend has a great idea for a new computer software product. Write a letter to your friend to give advice about how to make money with that idea in our free enterprise system.

Government and Consumer Functions

• What You'll Learn

- The roles government plays in our free enterprise system
- The supply and demand theory

• Why It's Important

As a consumer, you need to know your power to affect the prices you pay for products. As a voter, you have a responsibility to understand how decisions made by the government affect you, your investments, and your life in general.

Key Terms

- supply
- demand
- surpluses
- shortages
- equilibrium

The Role of Government

Government plays four roles in our free enterprise system. It provides general services, supports businesses, regulates industry, and acts as a competitor in a few instances.

This government involvement in the economy classifies the United States as a modified free enterprise system. To understand what that means, we have to take a closer look at the government's various roles.

■ Provider of Services

To ensure the safety and general welfare of people in the United States, our government provides military, police, and fire protection, as well as free public education. Government expands its educational role to provide retraining for some people who have lost their jobs as a result of changes in the marketplace and/or foreign competition. The Joint Training Partnership Act (JTPA) is one example of this sort of activity.

To improve transportation in the United States, our government supports the building of roads and bridges. Public libraries are paid for with government funds, as is our social welfare system. Medicare and Medicaid are two programs that are part of that system. Both provide medical care—Medicare for the elderly and Medicaid for the poor.

■ Supporter of Business

Our government also serves businesses. Throughout the years, floods and earthquakes have devastated communities nationwide. Government provided disaster assistance to help both businesses and home owners rebuild in the affected areas.

To support and encourage our free enterprise system, our government runs the Small Business Administration (SBA). The SBA provides counseling and educational materials to prospective business owners to help ensure their success. Additional support comes in the form of loan guarantees for some business owners who cannot get conventional loans.

The government is the single largest consumer of goods and services in the United States. All government projects require purchases of goods and services produced by U.S. companies. Those products range from uniforms for military personnel to defense equipment and systems.

Finally, to encourage more global business activity, our government establishes trade alliances and agreements with other countries. Those agreements often make it easier for U.S. companies to do business in foreign markets.

■ Regulator

Making laws is one of the principal functions of government. In the United States, most laws are designed to protect the safety, health, and welfare of individuals and the freedom of businesses to operate in our free enterprise economic system.

CONSUMER AND WORKER PROTECTION At the federal level, laws are carried out by regulatory agencies. Several of these agencies have been set up specifically to protect workers and consumers. They include the Food and Drug Administration (FDA), the Equal Employment Opportunity Commission (EEOC), the Occupational Safety and Health Administration (OSHA), and the Consumer Product Safety Commission (CPSC).

At the state and local levels, government agencies require licensing of people who perform certain services, such as hairstylists and manicurists. Health departments inspect restaurants and other food-handling businesses to protect consumers. Finally,

to ensure that workers can maintain a certain standard of living, both state and federal governments mandate a minimum wage.

The government seeks not only to protect both employees and workers, but also beyond that to control how our natural resources are used. To protect our environment, the Environmental Protection Agency (EPA) was established in 1970. Local zoning ordinances help to maintain the value of residential real estate and provide for uses that are consistent with the public good.

The Securities and Exchange Commission (SEC) regulates the sale of securities (stocks and bonds). It is responsible for licensing brokerage firms and financial advisers. It also investigates any dealings among corporations, such as mergers, that affect the value of stocks. This type of regulation helps protect investors from deceptive practices. The SEC also protects corporations, whose stock is traded, by requiring that all information about the corporation that is given to investors be truthful.

BUSINESS PROTECTION To protect our private property rights, government provides laws and regulations regarding patents, copyrights, and trademarks. These laws protect businesses for a period of time from having others copy their creative ideas and identifying symbols.

■ **Paid for by the U.S. Government** Local, state, and federal governments spend so much money that they are considered the largest single consumer in the United States. *How does that spending benefit business?*

Businesses must try to protect their products from theft by foreign and domestic companies in this new wave of global competition. It is becoming more common to find companies stealing ideas and patents from other companies.

The government regulates trade with other countries. U.S. companies are not permitted to sell certain products abroad if such sales might jeopardize the national defense. To protect domestic industries, the U.S. government sometimes imposes trade restrictions on foreign-made products.

The government also passes laws to regulate how businesses operate (see Figure 3-1 on page 51). One of these laws that prevents monopolies is the Sherman Antitrust Act (1890). It outlawed all contracts and agreements that would limit trade or competition in interstate commerce. It also prevents one company from under-charging for an item or service in order to put the competition out of business. This practice is known as *predatory pricing*.

A second law, called the Clayton Antitrust Act, was passed in 1914 to reduce loopholes in the Sherman Antitrust Act. In that same year, the Federal Trade Commission (FTC) was established to enforce both acts. The FTC's powers have since been expanded to include investigations of deceptive and misleading business practices, like false advertising.

To ensure economic stability for businesses, the government monitors our economy and controls our monetary supply through the Federal Reserve System. This is our nation's banking system. When the Federal Reserve Board of Governors thinks that the economy is moving too fast or too slowly, it reacts to correct the problem. When prices are going up too fast, the board may increase interest rates to slow economic activity. Higher interest rates generally make it more difficult to borrow money and therefore discourage expansion by businesses.

■ Competitor

There are three business operations that our government runs. They are the Tennessee Valley Authority (TVA), the U.S. Postal Service, and Amtrak. The TVA provides electricity to parts of the rural South. It was established during the Great Depression when private companies were unwilling to invest in dams and power plants for the area. The U.S. Postal Service provides mail delivery nationwide. There are several specialized delivery

■ **Fly Like an Eagle** The U.S. Postal Service is a competitor in the free enterprise system. *What competition does it face?*

companies that now compete with the Postal Service—DHL, United Parcel Service (UPS), and Federal Express. Amtrak is a passenger rail service that was established under the Rail Passenger Act of 1970. The act was necessary because rail line owners no longer wanted to offer passenger service.

The U.S. government also runs national parks and campgrounds. These tourist attractions are sometimes in competition with privately owned tourist attractions.

The Role of the Consumer

Most of the goods and services produced in the United States are bought by consumers for personal use. Therefore, the role of the consumer must be part of any discussion of our free enterprise system.

Consumers do two major things in the marketplace. First, they pick the winners—the products and businesses that will be in the marketplace tomorrow. They also determine the demand for any given product, and therefore help determine prices.

FIGURE 3-1

Summary of Legislation that Involves Marketing

Competition Regulating Legislation

LEGISLATION	PURPOSE
Sherman Antitrust Act (1890)	Prohibits monopolies
Clayton Antitrust Act (1914)	Prohibits price discrimination
Federal Trade Commission (FTC) Act (1914)	Establishes FTC and prohibits unfair competition
Robinson-Patman Act (1936)	Strengthens Clayton Antitrust Act; regulates price discounts and allowances
Wheeler-Lea Act (1938)	Extends FTC Act to include unfair competition
Consumer Goods Pricing Act (1975)	Eliminates federal and state laws permitting manufacturers to set retail prices

Deregulation Legislation

Airline Deregulation Act (1978)	To allow competition among airlines
Telecom Act (1996)	To allow for competition in local phone service

Consumer Protection Legislation

Pure Food and Drug Act (1906)	Regulated food & drug labeling and safety
Food, Drug, and Cosmetic Act (1938)	Amended Pure Food and Drug Act of 1906
Automobile Information Disclosure Act (1958)	Post suggested retail price on new vehicles
Fair Packaging and Labeling Act (1966)	Regulates packaging and labeling
Cigarette Labeling and Advertising Acts (1966 & 1969)	Label cigarettes as "hazardous to your health" and prohibits TV advertising of cigarettes
Consumer Product Safety Act (1972)	Established Consumer Product Safety Commission; rules on products that are unsafe
Children's Television Act (1990)	Limits advertising time on children's programs

Worker Protection Legislation

Occupational Safety and Health Act (1970)	Established Occupational Safety and Health Administration for workplace safety and health

■ **Marketing Legislation** The U.S. is considered a modified free enterprise system partially due to the legislation featured in this table. *Why are these laws needed?*

Deciding Which Businesses Survive

The United States is known as a consumer-oriented society. Consumers have the power to decide which products will be produced and which companies will stay in business. They do this by shopping. Every time they make a purchase, they are "voting" with their dollars. The more votes (or sales) a product gets, the more likely that product and the company that produces it will succeed.

Determining Prices

In a market economy, supply and demand determine the prices and quantities of goods and services produced. Consumers play a major role in supply and demand theory. In this role, consumers are responsible for setting the prices for their goods and services. Figure 3-2 on page 53 illustrates how this theory works.

To understand how prices are determined, you have to look at both demand and supply—the willingness and ability of producers to provide goods and services at different prices in the marketplace.

Supply is the amount of goods producers are willing to make and sell. The law of supply is an

Pleased to Meet You!

A handshake is a handshake. Correct? Not in the global marketplace. A handshake is the traditional greeting in North America and Europe, but not in other regions. The Japanese greet each other with a bow, while in Southeast Asia, people press together their palms (as if praying) to welcome another person. Those people who do opt for the handshake should be careful though, as the firm grip characteristic of Americans is looked upon as aggressive by others around the world.

Thinking Critically

You are entertaining Japanese clients for business. What is the appropriate way to greet each other when you meet?

economic rule that price and quantity supplied move in the same direction. This means that as prices rise for a good, the quantity supplied generally rises, and as the price falls, the quantity supplied by sellers also falls. Thus, suppliers want to supply a larger quantity of goods at higher prices so their businesses can be more profitable.

Demand refers to consumer willingness and ability to buy products. The law of demand is an economic theory that states that as the price of a good increases, the quantity of the good demanded falls.

When supply and demand interact in the marketplace, conditions of surplus, shortage, or equilibrium are created. These conditions often determine whether prices will go down, up, or stay the same.

Surpluses of goods occur when supply exceeds demand. If prices are too high or seem unreasonable to the customers their decision will affect the market. When this happens, businesses respond by lowering their prices in order to encourage people to buy more of the product. There may be a promotion or a sale to encourage people to purchase the product.

One of the best examples of surpluses can be found in the produce section of a supermarket. A large supply of peaches, apples, broccoli, or other produce

Trade Across Boundaries

Producing a trade show takes a lot of planning. Organizing travel, meeting space, seminars, and exhibits can be overwhelming; but imagine doing this all in a country under a U.S. trade embargo. Trade show organizer Peter Nathan did this when he produced a medical equipment and pharmaceutical industry trade show in Cuba. He pursued the idea because of the important humanitarian aspect. It took three years to get Washington's approval; however, Havana approved it in just 10 days.

Thinking Critically

Does the government have a right to determine whether a company can organize a trade show in other countries?

FIGURE 3-2

SUPPLY AND DEMAND THEORY

Supply and demand interact to determine the price customers are willing to pay for the number of products producers are willing to make.

DEMAND

Demand refers to consumer willingness and ability to buy products. According to the law of demand, if the price is low enough, demand for a product usually increases. This is reflected in the demand schedule. It provides the points to plot a demand curve.

SUPPLY

Supply is the amount of goods producers are willing to make and sell. The law of supply states that at a higher price, producers will offer a larger quantity of products for sale. At a lower price, they will offer fewer products. This is reflected in the supply schedule. It provides the points to plot a supply curve.

Demand Schedule for Athletic Shoes Sold at Retail	
Price per Shoe	Number Demanded
$155	600
140	800
125	1,100
110	1,500
95	2,000
80	3,000
65	3,400
50	4,600
35	6,200

Supply Schedule for Athletic Shoes Sold at Retail	
Price per Shoe	Number Supplied
$155	6,000
140	5,800
125	5,600
110	5,400
95	5,000
80	4,400
65	3,400
50	2,000
35	1,000

EQUILIBRIUM

Equilibrium exists when the amount of product supplied is equal to the amount of product demanded. On the graph, this is the point where the supply and demand curves meet. It is also the point where both producer and consumer are satisfied with the price. The equilibrium price, therefore, is the price at which customers are willing to buy and producers are willing to sell.

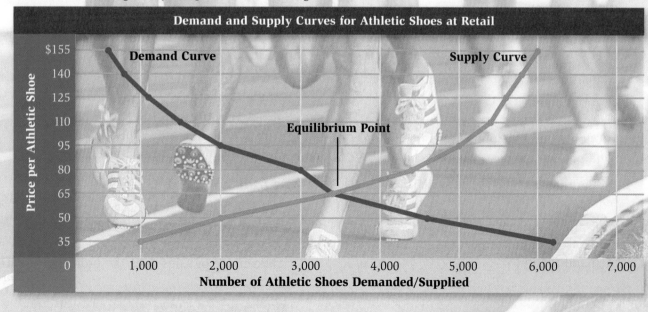

Demand and Supply Curves for Athletic Shoes at Retail

may be priced very low one week due to supply. When there is an excess of a given crop when it is in season, farmers lower their prices to sell large quantities. Supermarkets that buy large quantities of the crop at the low price do the same. The surplus affects the price all the way down the line. Think again of the example of the produce section of a grocery store. You can see how a produce shortage affects produce prices. When there is a poor season for oranges, you will find that the price of oranges is higher. When the product in question is a necessity, customers will pay the price determined by the market.

When demand exceeds supply, shortages of products occur. When shortages occur, businesses can raise prices and still sell their merchandise. An oil shortage increases the price of gasoline, so consumers who want to drive their vehicles pay the higher price.

When the amount of a product being supplied is equal to the amount being demanded, equilibrium exists. When supply and demand are balanced, everyone wins. Customers are able to purchase goods and services at a fair price, and retailers experience a steady flow of business. Customers buy the entire stock of the product that is available. Retailers clear their shelves of merchandise. Everyone's needs and wants are satisfied in the most efficient manner possible.

Electronic Frontiers

Tale or Trail: Cookies

Small text files—called cookies—can be stored and read on a user's computer hard drive. Cookies allow Web sites and advertising companies to see where customers travel on the Internet and which advertisements they view; this information is used by companies to improve their target marketing. To many users, cookies are perceived as an invasion of privacy. Congress is looking into the legality of this issue, sometimes referred to as "data spillage." Data spillage is the distribution of data collected from Web sites that is automatically sent to outside parties, mostly Internet advertising agencies, which track the information.

Thinking Critically

Many advertising agencies claim to use only basic geographic information taken from a user's Internet address to target its ads. Are these practices fair, or an invasion of privacy?

3.2 ASSESSMENT

Reviewing Key Terms and Concepts

1. Name four ways government is involved in our free enterprise system.

2. Why is the United States said to have a modified free enterprise system?

3. What is the FTC, and what does it do?

4. In the U.S. free enterprise system, who decides which businesses will survive and what prices will be charged for the goods sold?

5. What is the equilibrium point in supply and demand theory?

Thinking Critically

6. A new airline starts up with low fares and many new routes. At the same time, established airlines drop their fares and add new flights to match the routes of the new airline. Is this against the law? Explain your position.

Integrating Academic Skills

7. **MATH** Determine the profit a company makes with sales of $2,456,700, costs of $1,246,100, and expenses of $1,112,332. What percentage of sales does the profit represent?

Careers in Marketing

E-COMMERCE

Amber Nevens
Prefer Network
Internet Marketing Specialist

What does an Internet Marketing Specialist do?

"Internet marketing specialists serve as consultants to clients who want to develop or enhance online business Web sites. They develop Internet marketing strategies that include promotional plans and campaigns for product launches. Internet marketing specialists work with technical departments, sales teams, advertising departments, and financial analysts of the companies they represent."

What skills are most important to you?

"Research skills are vital to learn about industry trends. It is important to know what shoppers value in their online experience and what motivates their purchases. This information helps me present my product in a way that drives new customers, ensures a positive shopping experience, and builds a lasting relationship."

What do you like most about your work?

"The small number of employees makes it vital for everyone to work together. This environment is conducive to learning, and being surrounded by bright individuals is inspiring."

How does your workload vary?

"I am constantly juggling many projects at a time. It is important to be aware that things can change unexpectedly—budgets can be cut or technological difficulties can affect your ability to carry out promotions as planned. It is necessary to be able to adapt to these changes quickly."

What is your key to success?

"My key to success is being well informed on breaking industry developments. The Internet industry is always ripe for new ideas; therefore, learning about other's successes and misses is vital to marketing your product or service. I sign up for every relevant newsletter (ClickZ Network and Ebiz) and read industry publications (*The Industry Standard* and *IMarketing News*)."

Thinking Critically
Why is it so important to keep up with changes in the industry of e-commerce?

Career Facts

Education and Training: Most firms require an MBA for management positions, or a bachelor's degree in marketing, journalism, or communications. Candidates should have experience with Web site development.

Aptitudes, Abilities, and Skills: Ability to work independently and with a team, above average communication skills, ability to manage numerous projects at once, and creativity are necessary.

Career Outlook: Opportunities for Internet marketing managers are expected to grow faster than other management-level marketing opportunities as e-commerce expands.

Career Path: Experience in both marketing and Web site design may lead to careers in Internet marketing management. Product management and online advertising production also provide entry into this career.

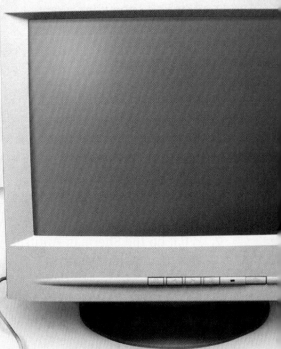

Chapter 3 ASSESSMENT

VOCABULARY REVIEW

Use presentation software on the computer to design a presentation based on this chapter's content. Write captions and select graphics to illustrate ten of the following terms:

- free enterprise system
- competition
- price competition
- nonprice competition
- monopoly
- risk
- profit
- supply
- demand
- surpluses
- shortages
- equilibrium

FACT AND IDEA REVIEW

1. What are the four basic principles of a free enterprise system? (3.1)

2. Why is competition essential to the free enterprise system? (3.1)

3. What role does profit play in our free enterprise system? (3.1)

4. What happens when businesses are not profitable? (3.1)

5. How does the Small Business Administration support and encourage our free enterprise system? (3.2)

6. Name three government regulatory agencies that protect consumers and workers. (3.2)

7. What do the Sherman Antitrust Act of 1890 and the Clayton Antitrust Act of 1914 have in common? (3.2)

8. What might the Federal Reserve do if prices are going up too fast? (3.2)

9. What three major businesses make our government a competitor in the marketplace? (3.2)

10. How do supply and demand interact to determine price in our free enterprise system? (3.2)

THINKING CRITICALLY

1. What, if anything, should the government do to help "mom-and-pop" retailers compete with retail giants like Wal-Mart, Home Depot, and Staples?

2. Are new businesses guaranteed success in our free enterprise system? Explain your answer, and give examples to support your viewpoint.

3. Why are patents and copyrights allowed in a free enterprise system? Aren't they in direct conflict with the concept of competition? Explain.

4. If three of the large automobile manufacturers wanted to merge into one large corporation, do you think the U.S. government would allow them to do so? Why or why not?

5. Provide examples from your own experience of supply and demand theory at work. Then, try to think of one example each to illustrate surplus, shortage, and equilibrium.

BUILDING WORKPLACE SKILLS

1. **Human Relations** A customer questions why your video store's rental fees are 50 cents higher than those of the video store in the next town. You know the competing store does not carry the selection you do, and its late charges are double yours. Given these facts, prepare a response for the customer.

2. **Writing** Write a story about a country that did away with competition as part of its economic system. Tell what life would be like there.

1. **Summarizing Key Concepts** Using current business publications like *Fortune, Forbes, BusinessWeek, Inc., Nation's Business,* or the business section of your local newspaper, find an article related to the content of this chapter. Use a word processing program to summarize the article and explain how it illustrates, reinforces, or extends one or more of the chapter's concepts.

2. **Understanding Regulatory Agencies** Research three federal regulatory agencies on the Internet. Use a computer database program to create a database of your findings. It should include basic information, including headquarter office locations, when the agency was established, its responsibilities, and a current issue that is facing the agency.

3. **Evaluating Licensing** Use the Internet to research professional athletes who have licensed their names on specific products. What are the potential problems for manufacturers that use those celebrities to promote their products? Use presentation software to prepare an oral presentation that you will give to your class.

4. **Understanding Government Regulation** Interview a local business owner about governmental policies that have cost the business owner any money or caused any problems. Using a word processor, write a letter to the governmental or federal regulatory agency addressing the problems that are addressed in your interview.

LINKING SCHOOL TO WORK

Thinking and Information Skills Ask your employer to share the OSHA and EEOC rules that must be followed where you work or in a local business. Share your findings with the class.

THE DECA CONNECTION

Role Play: Salesclerk

Situation You are to assume the role of salesclerk at the Lakeview Drugstore. This local establishment has been serving the residents of your town (which has a population of 30,000) for more than 25 years. In one month, however, a new discount drugstore is scheduled to open just two miles away. The owner of the Lakeview Drugstore (judge) has asked her employees for help.

Activity What would you suggest the owner (judge) do to meet the new competition?

Evaluation You will be evaluated on how well you meet the following performance indicators:

- Explain the concept of competition
- Determine factors affecting business risk
- Identify factors affecting a business's profit
- Make oral presentations

inter NET CONNECTION

My Aching Back!
Your employees work on a computer for long hours. What safety precautions and responsibilities do you have as an employer?

Connect
- Use the Internet to research ergonomics.
- Research ergonomic rules established by OSHA with regard to preventing on-the-job injuries to the neck, back, and wrist.

Global Economies

Marketing: What It Takes

Judging an Economy
Your marketing professor suggests that you study abroad for a semester. You need to select a country that differs from the United States politically and economically. The deadline is approaching for submitting your country request, and you're still not sure where you want to go.

WHAT WILL YOU DO?
What factors will you research in selecting the country?

What Is an Economy?

What Is an Economy?

An economy, or economic system, is the way a nation makes economic choices. The choices that must be made involve how the nation will use its resources to produce and distribute goods and services. Let's take a closer look at the resources common to all nations.

■ Resources

Resources are all the things used in producing goods and services. The technical term economists use for resources is factors of production. Economists also attach special meanings to the four categories that comprise the factors of production: land, labor, capital, and entrepreneurship.

Land refers to everything on the earth that is in its natural state, or the Earth's natural resources. This includes everything contained in the earth or found in the seas. Coal and crude oil are natural resources, and so is a lake and all of the living things in the lake.

Labor refers to all the people who work in the economy. Labor includes full- and part-time workers in both the private and public sectors.

Capital includes money needed to start and operate a business. It also includes the goods used in the production process. Factories, office buildings, computers, and tools are all considered capital resources. Raw materials that have been processed into a more useful form (such as lumber or steel) are also considered capital.

Entrepreneurship refers to the skills of people who are willing to risk their time and money to run a business. Entrepreneurs organize the other factors of production to create the goods and services desired in an economy.

Each of the four factors of production presents its own set of problems and opportunities within an economy. The easiest way to appreciate this is to consider the plight of developing nations. Such nations may want to attract certain kinds of industries; however, they may be limited by the educational level of their workers. The value that an economic system places on education can profoundly impact one of its most important economic resources—its labor pool.

Capital is often an equally difficult problem for developing nations. Capital includes infrastructure, or the physical development of a country, including its roads, ports, sanitation facilities, and utilities, especially telecommunications. These things are necessary for production and distribution of goods and services in an economy. Imagine trying to operate a modern factory without electricity. Think of the challenges of trying to run an international business without dependable phone service.

● What You'll Learn

- What is meant by the term *economy*
- The factors of production
- The three basic economic questions
- The difference between a market economy, command economy, and mixed economy
- Different types of economic philosophies

● Why It's Important

Before you can study international trade, you need to understand how a country's economy is related to its resources and political system. This will help you understand how a country is viewed in terms of its ability to function in our global marketplace.

Key Terms

- economy
- resources
- factors of production
- land
- labor
- capital
- entrepreneurship
- infrastructure
- scarcity
- market economy
- command economy
- capitalism
- socialist
- communist
- privatization

Scarcity

All economies have different proportions of resources. The United States has an educated labor force, a great deal of capital, an abundance of entrepreneurs, and many natural resources. Most underdeveloped nations are not that fortunate. They have natural resources to spare but not the capital or skilled labor to develop them.

Even the United States, with a plethora of resources, cannot meet the needs and wants of all its citizens. It has homeless and other people living below the poverty level. Businesses go bankrupt on a regular basis. It is apparent that nations have unlimited wants and needs for growth and development but limited resources to meet them. This difference between wants and needs and available resources is called scarcity. Scarcity forces nations to make economic choices.

How Does an Economy Work?

Nations must answer three basic questions when deciding how to use their limited resources. The way nations answer these questions defines their economic system.

1. *What goods and services should be produced?*
2. *How should the goods and services be produced?*
3. *For whom should the goods and services be produced?*

Economists have studied the way nations answer the three basic economic questions and have classified their economic systems into two broad categories. They are market (or capitalist) systems and command (or planned) systems.

No economy can be called purely market or purely command. Elements of both systems are found in all economies, making all economies mixed. To establish this, let's consider the two basic types of economic systems in their purest form. Then we can demonstrate how all economies are mixed.

Market Economies

The United States is a market economy, so you already know much about how a market economy operates. In a pure market economy, there is no government involvement in economic decisions. The government lets the market answer the three basic economic questions.

■ **Shop 'til You Drop!** Consumers play an active role in a market system. *What two basic economic questions are being addressed in this scene?*

1. *What?* Consumers decide what should be produced in a market economy through the purchases that they make in the marketplace. Those items that satisfy consumers' needs and wants are purchased, and those are the ones that succeed. Products that do not satisfy consumers' needs are not purchased and therefore will not achieve success.

2. *How?* How products will be produced is left up to businesses in a market economy. Businesses must be competitive in such an economy and produce quality products at lower prices than their competitors. It is necessary for them to find the most efficient way to produce their goods and services and the best way to encourage customers to buy these products.

3. *For whom?* In a market economy, the people who have more money are able to buy more goods and services. To obtain money, people are motivated to work and invest the money they make.

Command Economies

A command economy is a system in which the government controls the factors of production and makes all decisions about their use. In a command economy, the government is responsible for answering the three basic economic questions.

1. *What?* One person (a dictator) or a group of government officials (a central planning committee) decides what products are needed based on what they believe is important. The former Soviet Union, for example, was more interested in creating products for military use than in producing consumer goods for its people. As a result, they had frequent shortages of consumer goods.

2. *How?* Since the government owns all means of production in a command economy, the government runs all businesses. It decides how goods and services will be produced. It employs all workers and controls all employment opportunities and workers' benefits. In the most extreme command economy, the government tells people where they will work and how much they will get paid.

3. *For whom?* The government decides who will receive what is produced in a command economy. Wealth is shared equally among all people, in principle, to ensure that everyone's basic needs are met. The idea is that all people are equal and are offered the same opportunity. The government provides subsidies for housing and food for everyone, as well as medical care, education, and jobs for everyone who wants to work. There is much security for people in such a system—but at the cost of individual freedom and choice.

Mixed Economies

As you learned in Chapter 3, our free enterprise system is not a pure market system. There is some government involvement in the economy through mandatory laws and regulations that businesses follow. These include labor laws that limit how much people can work, at what age they can start working, and the minimum wage they can be paid. Our government provides social programs for those who need help, such as welfare and Medicaid for the poor and Medicare for the elderly. Based on these mixed influences, the U.S. economy is technically a mixed economy.

All economies in the world today are mixed. The most meaningful economic classification is based on how much government interferes with the free market. Looking at the difference between the two economic philosophies on a continuum, it is easier to see the degree of economic freedom permitted. Figure 4-1 shows a continuum of economic systems. Left of center would be more closely related to a command economy, and right of center would indicate a market-driven economy. Economic freedom to the right of center encourages competition and lets the market decide where the resources should flow.

Where a country fits on that continuum is most often determined by its philosophy of government. The philosophy of a government reflects not only the laws and rules, but how individuals are treated. The three political philosophies that have shaped world economies are capitalism, socialism, and communism.

FIGURE 4-1

Continuum of Economic Systems

| Command Economy | Socialism | Market Economy |
| Communism on far left | left of center but right of Communism | Capitalism on far right |

■ **Continuum of Economic Systems** When studying different economic systems, it is best to view them on a continuum, as depicted here. *Where on the continuum would you place the United States? Canada? North Korea?*

CAPITALISM Capitalism is an economic system characterized by private ownership of businesses and marketplace competition. It is the same as free enterprise. Government in a capitalist society is also concerned about its people and cares for those who cannot care for themselves. The number of social services, however, does not match that of a socialist country.

The political system most frequently associated with capitalism is democracy. Nations that practice democracy believe that political power should be in the hands of the people. There is usually more than one political party from which to choose representatives to run the government in a democratic country. People in a democracy are free to elect those candidates who agree with their philosophy on how the government and the economy should be run. The United States and Japan are two examples of countries that are classified as capitalistic and have a democratic form of government.

SOCIALISM In a socialist political system, there is increased government involvement in people's lives and the economy. The main goal is to keep prices low for all people and to provide employment for many. The government runs key industries and makes economic decisions. Those state-controlled, noncompetitive companies are generally found in industries such as telecommunications, mining, transportation, and banking.

Socialist countries tend to have more social services to ensure a certain standard of living for everyone. Medical care is free or low cost in most socialist countries, as is education from elementary school through college. These countries have systems for pensions and elderly care. Businesses and individuals pay much higher taxes than in capitalist countries to pay for all these "free" government services.

Today most countries that are characterized as socialistic also have democratic political institutions. The difference from capitalist nations is the increased amount of government involvement in people's lives and the economy. Canada, Germany, Great Britain, Sweden, and Australia are countries that are generally characterized as socialist.

COMMUNISM Communist countries have a totalitarian form of government, which means that the government runs everything. One political party—the Communist party—runs the government. This is done to ensure that all people share common economic and political goals.

In a communist country all people who are able to work are assigned jobs. Theoretically, there is no unemployment. Employees who don't go to work continue to get paid under this system. The government decides the type of schooling people will receive and also tells them where to live. Housing accommodations are assigned according to need. Food and housing subsidies keep prices low, so everyone has a place to live and food to eat. Medical care is free. As you can see, there is a little or no economic freedom associated with communism.

■ **Work for Food** In a command economy with a communistic philosophy, many people do not work and their standard of living is poor. *Why are these two conditions so prevalent in a command economy?*

Case Study

The Chaebol Economy

In 1961, Park Chung Hee, the autocratic leader of South Korea, passed the Law for Dealing with Illicit Wealth Accumulation. He then arrested leading businessmen and gave them a choice—go to prison or invest in a government-identified industry. The government funneled funds from foreign loans to these companies under the guise of "special capitalistic projects," in addition to loans from domestic banks. The government and business leaders worked together to build up specific industries, starting with textiles and light manufacturing, later moving on to steel and chemicals, and finally electronics and automobiles. This gave the government a degree of control in each of these industries. This created a concentration of capital and profits in the hands of a few key companies called chaebol. What was Park Chung Hee's motive? The South Korean economy needed a strong boost to rise above its poor agrarian state to compete with industrializing nations. Much of South Korea's economic growth has been due to the export-led growth of chaebol, the politically connected, family-owned conglomerates that include such companies as Hyundai, Samsung, LG, and Daewoo.

Chaebol are business conglomerates with a holding company that acts as the controlling arm of the firm. Today, chaebol are no longer dependent on the now democratic government for credit or assistance. In the late 1990s, the chaebol were blamed for plunging South Korea into financial crisis by recklessly and rapidly expanding into a variety of unrelated businesses on borrowed money. This prompted the government to force chaebol to restructure by merging overlapping subsidiaries. This restructuring led to mass layoffs and labor unrest.

Chaebol are also suffering with the Internet explosion as key employees leave to start their own companies. Samsung, one of Korea's top four chaebol, lost 6,000 employees to start-up firms in one year. It now allows employees to set up their own businesses during company time. Samsung lets these in-house ventures spin off if they are successful, taking half of the shares in the new company. Both employer and employee benefit from this arrangement. If the venture does not work, the employees still have a job with Samsung.

Case Study Review

1. Why is it difficult to classify South Korea's economic philosophy in the 1960s when Park Chung Hee first established the "chaebol"?
2. How would you classify today's South Korean economic philosophy, taking chaebol into consideration?

A MATTER OF ETHICS

3. Is it ethical for a company to take half of the shares of a new enterprise that was created by a company employee?

There are very few totally communist countries left in the world today. The economies of such countries have tended to collapse in recent years. In such a system there is no incentive for people to increase their productivity.

The few countries that can still be classified as communist include Cuba and North Korea. Even China, which is politically still dominated by a communist party, is liberalizing its economic practices.

ECONOMIES IN TRANSITION The breakup of the former Soviet Union probably provides the best examples of societies making the difficult change from command to market economies. Most Eastern European countries that were once communist satellites have embraced capitalism. They have also moved to more democratic forms of government.

The state-owned industries have been privatized in many of these nations. Privatization refers to the process of selling government-owned businesses to private individuals. This process generates much-needed revenue for the governments involved. It also demonstrates a high level of commitment to making the transition to a market system.

Today even socialist countries are selling some of their state-run businesses to help balance their budgets as the costs for national health care, unemployment, and retirement programs soar. Great Britain has sold its national phone company, national steel company, and national sugar company, as well

Life In The Diverse

MARKETPLACE

Too Close for Comfort

Arm's length—or 30 inches—is the average amount of personal space that a North American expects while in conversation. Upon leaving the United States, however, one might notice a shift in this space. Asians usually stand farther apart, while Middle Easterners and South Americans might get a little too close for the North American's comfort. It is important not only to respect personal space, but also to respect the person who might seem a little too close. Backing away or shifting uncomfortably may give off an unfriendly vibe!

Thinking Critically
Based on this information, what do you think about the cultural differences regarding touching during a conversation?

as Heathrow Airport, a hotel business, water suppliers, and an automobile company it owned. These sales generated approximately $63 billion for Great Britain.

4.1 ASSESSMENT

Reviewing Key Terms and Concepts

1. What is an economy?

2. Name the factors of production necessary to create goods and services in an economy.

3. Explain how command and market economies answer the three basic economic questions.

4. Why are all economies mixed?

5. How do capitalist, socialist, and communist economies differ from each other?

Thinking Critically

6. How can developing countries improve their economies with regard to the factors of production?

Integrating Academic Skills

7. **COMMUNICATION** Assume your pen pal from a communist or socialist country has asked how people in the United States afford vacations, medical care, and retirement. In your letter of response, compare the U.S. mixed economy with the economic system under which your pen pal lives.

Understanding the Economy

When Is an Economy Successful?

Soon you will be voting on issues and candidates who will represent your interests in government. You may also decide to invest in the stock market. All of these decisions can have an impact on your financial well being. Therefore, you must be able to recognize the signs of a healthy economy. This may affect your choices as you cast your ballot and invest your money. It is the goal of all economies to increase productivity, decrease unemployment, and maintain stable prices. All nations analyze their economies to see how well they are doing. Their analysis helps them determine which phase of the business cycle their economies are in. This determination, in turn, allows businesses, consumers, and governments to make appropriate economic decisions.

■ Economic Measurements

Accurate information about an economy is essential to the whole process. Let's look at key economic measurements that nations routinely use to determine their economic strength. These measurements include employee productivity, Gross Domestic Product (GDP), inflation, and unemployment.

EMPLOYEE PRODUCTIVITY Productivity is output per worker hour that is measured over a defined period of time, such as a week, month, or year. Productivity is a crucial factor in a country's standard of living (see Figure 4-2 on page 66).

Businesses can increase their productivity in a number of ways. They can invest in new equipment or facilities that allow their employees to work more efficiently. Providing additional training or financial incentives can also increase staff productivity. Finally, businesses can reduce their workforces and increase the responsibilities of the workers who remain. This makes an organization more financially efficient and more effective, as well.

Moves such as these have in recent years helped to increase the productivity of American workers. Suppose a steel manufacturer with an aging plant could produce 1.25 million tons of steel a year with a work force of 550. That manufacturer retooled to double its output and reduced its work force by 150. What would the result be? The calculations would look something like this:

$$
\begin{aligned}
\text{Productivity} &= \text{output per year (in tons)} \\
\text{workers} \times \text{hours} \times \text{weeks} &= 2{,}500{,}000 \text{ tons} \\
400 \times 40 \times 52 &= 2{,}500{,}000 \text{ tons} \\
832{,}000 \text{ worker hours} &= 3 \text{ tons of steel per worker hour}
\end{aligned}
$$

The resulting figure is nearly triple the old productivity rate (1.09 tons per worker hour).

● What You'll Learn

- The goals of an economy
- The various measurements used to analyze an economy
- The four phases of the business cycle

● Why It's Important

It is essential that you understand how an economy is measured and what factors contribute to a strong or weak economy. It is important to know how you, businesses, and the government influence the economy.

Key Terms

- productivity
- Gross Domestic Product (GDP)
- inflation
- Consumer Price Index (CPI)
- Producer Price Index (PPI)
- business cycle
- prosperity (expansion)
- recession
- depression
- recovery

FIGURE 4-2

Productivity

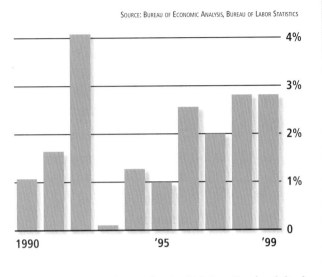

SOURCE: BUREAU OF ECONOMIC ANALYSIS, BUREAU OF LABOR STATISTICS

■ **Productivity and Standard of Living** Productivity is a crucial factor in a country's standard of living. *What can you surmise about the United States' standard of living from 1995 to 1999 based on this chart showing U.S. productivity growth from 1990 to 1999?*

FIGURE 4-3

Gross Domestic Product

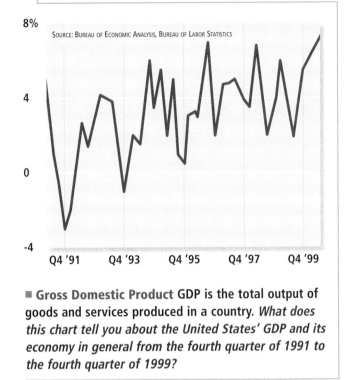

SOURCE: BUREAU OF ECONOMIC ANALYSIS, BUREAU OF LABOR STATISTICS

■ **Gross Domestic Product** GDP is the total output of goods and services produced in a country. *What does this chart tell you about the United States' GDP and its economy in general from the fourth quarter of 1991 to the fourth quarter of 1999?*

GROSS DOMESTIC PRODUCT (GDP) Most governments study productivity by keeping track of an entire nation's production output. Today the principal way of measuring that output in the United States is gross domestic product, or GDP. Gross Domestic Product is a measure of the goods and services produced using labor and property located in this country (see Figure 4-3).

INFLATION RATE Inflation refers to rising prices. A low inflation rate (1–5 percent) is good because it shows that an economy is stable. Double-digit inflation (10 percent or higher), on the other hand, devastates an economy. When inflation gets that high, money does not have the same value as it did with lower inflation. The period from the mid-1960s to the early 1980s was a highly inflationary period. Prices went up threefold in the United States during that time. People who live on a fixed income are especially hurt by high inflation.

Controlling inflation is one of a government's major goals. When inflation starts to go up, many governments raise interest rates to reduce everyone's ability to borrow money. The result is a slowdown in economic growth, which helps to bring inflation down.

Two measures of inflation used in the United States are the Consumer Price Index (CPI) and the Producer Price Index (PPI). The CPI measures the change in price over a time of some 400 specific retail goods and services used by the average urban household. It is also called the cost-of-living index. Food, housing, utilities, transportation, and medical care are a few of its components. The core CPI excludes food and energy prices, which tend to be unpredictable. The PPI measures wholesale price levels in the economy. It is often a trendsetter, as producer prices generally get passed along to the consumer. When there is a drop in the PPI, it is generally followed by a drop in the CPI (see Figure 4-4 on page 67).

UNEMPLOYMENT RATE All nations chart unemployment, or jobless, rates (see Figure 4-5 on page 67). The higher the unemployment rate, the greater the chances of an economic slowdown. The lower the unemployment rate, the greater the chances of an economic expansion. This is true because when more people work, there are more people spending money and paying taxes. Businesses and government both take in more money, and the government doesn't have to provide as many social services.

■ Other Indicators

The Conference Board provides additional indicators to help economists evaluate the performance of the U.S. economy. The Conference Board is a private business research organization that is made up of businesses and individuals who work together to assess the state of the economy. Three Conference Board indicators are the Consumer Confidence index, the Consumer Expectations index, and the "Jobs Plentiful" index, which measures consumers' perceptions regarding the number of jobs available. (see Figure 4-6 on page 68). Consumers are polled to see how they feel about personal finance, economic conditions, and buying conditions. The survey reviews not only how customers feel about the current economic environment, but also how they feel about the future. Retail sales are studied to see if Consumer Confidence polls match consumer actions in the marketplace. Along those same lines, the rate of housing starts are reviewed, as are sales of trucks and autos. These are big expenditures that tend to be affected by the economy and interest rates.

Wages and new payroll jobs provide additional information about the strength of the economy at any given point in time. When everyone is employed, supply and demand theory would suggest that wages would increase due to the shortage of workers. Economists study these factors, as they may effect inflation and other economic indicators.

FIGURE 4-4

Inflation Barometers

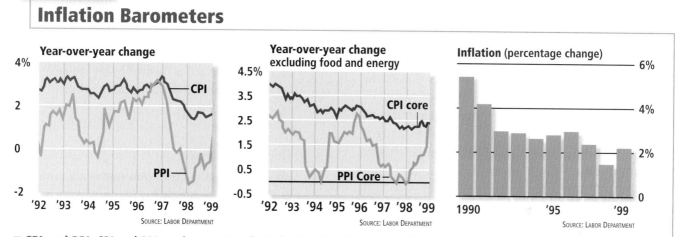

■ **CPI and PPI** CPI and PPI are barometers for inflation. The CPI Core and PPI Core take out the volatile food and energy prices from the indexes. *Based on these three charts, how would you describe inflation in the United States for the latter part of the 1990s?*

FIGURE 4-5

Jobless Rate

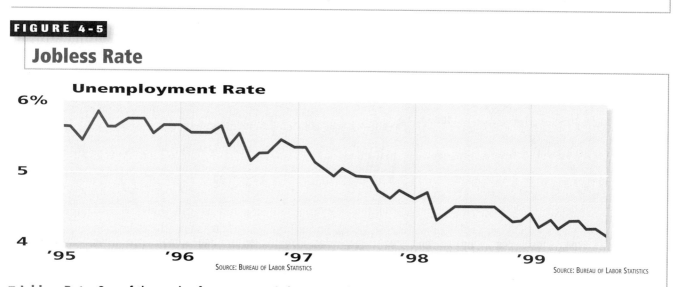

■ **Jobless Rate** One of the goals of an economy is low unemployment. *After viewing this chart on the jobless rate, what can be said about the United States' attempt to reach that goal?*

■ The Business Cycle

Governments keep statistics in order to determine the stage their economies are in at any given time. History shows that sometimes an economy grows, and at other times it slows down. These recurring changes are called the business cycle (see Figure 4-7 on page 69).

The four main phases of a business cycle are prosperity, recession, depression, and recovery. Prosperity, which is also known as expansion, is the time when the economy is flourishing. This is a good time for new businesses to start up.

As business activity slows down, there is always the danger that the economy will move into a recession. A recession is a period of economic slowdown that lasts for two quarters, or six months. Companies reduce their workforces and consumers have less money to spend.

A depression is a period of prolonged recession. During a depression, it becomes nearly impossible to find a job and many businesses are forced to shut down.

The time comes when the economy cannot reach lower depths, often referred to as the *trough*. Eventually, the GDP will slowly begin to increase. This shift in the economic cycle leads to a period of recovery. Recovery is the increase in the overall economic activity. During this stage business picks up, people find jobs, and the demand for goods increases.

Eliminating Bugs

Buggy software is a global headache, so engineers around the world are coordinating their efforts to find a solution. Some of these results show promise. An international movement called "Open Source" draws programmers from around the globe to constantly debug major programs. The Internet provides a platform for discussion and instant feedback. With thousands of programmers pooling their skills to build and test software programs, bugs can be discovered early, saving time and money. Programmers like Linus Torvalds, the creator of Linux, has addressed this problem by including the source code written in comprehensible computer language in his commercial software. This simple code can be read and understood by any computer programmer; therefore problems can be solved easily. Now the industry waits for others to follow Torvalds's lead.

Thinking Critically

Why is the Open Source movement a benefit to the global economy?

FIGURE 4-6

Consumer Confidence

■ **Consumer Confidence** Consumer confidence is an economic indicator that provides a view of how consumers feel about their economic prospects (employment, spending). The green bar represents the 1991 recession. *What conclusions can be drawn from a review of these three charts? What trend is apparent?*

FIGURE 4-7

THE BUSINESS CYCLE

Economists have identified four phases that comprise the business cycle. The phases are prosperity, recession, depression, and recovery.

PROSPERITY

Prosperity is a period of economic growth and expansion. Nationwide there is low unemployment, an increase in the output of goods and services, and high consumer spending. Sometimes this period is called peak prosperity.

RECESSION

Recession is a period of economic slowdown. Unemployment begins to rise, fewer goods and services are produced, and consumer spending decreases. Recessions can end relatively quickly or last for a long period of time.

DEPRESSION

Depression is a period of prolonged and deep recession. During a depression, consumer spending is very low, unemployment is very high, and production of goods and services is down significantly. Poverty results because so many people are out of work and cannot afford to buy food, clothing, or shelter. The Great Depression of the early 1930s best illustrates this phase of the business cycle.

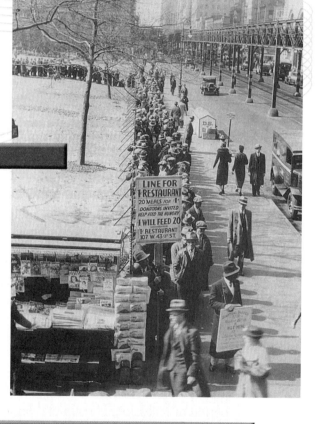

RECOVERY

Recovery is a period of renewed economic growth following a recession or depression. Recovery is characterized by reduced unemployment, increased consumer spending, and moderate expansion by businesses. Periods of recovery differ in length and strength.

FIGURE 4-8

Managing the Economy

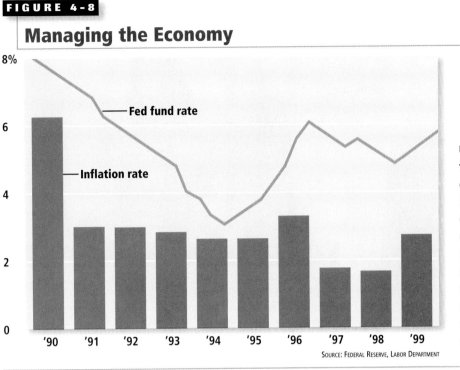

SOURCE: FEDERAL RESERVE, LABOR DEPARTMENT

■ **Manipulating Rates** The federal funds rate (rate banks charge each other for overnight loans) and the discount rate (rate the U.S. Federal Reserve charges banks that borrow money from it) are used to speed up or slow down an economy. *From this chart, what do you think the motivation of the Federal Reserve Board was in 1991? In 1999?*

FACTORS THAT AFFECT BUSINESS CYCLES

Business cycles are affected by the actions of businesses, consumers, and the government. In turn, businesses, consumers, and the government are affected by business cycles.

Businesses tend to react to business cycles by expanding their operations during periods of recovery or prosperity and curtailing their operations during periods of recession. Expansion may involve investments in new properties, equipment, and inventories, as well as hiring more employees. When the economy moves into a recession, one of the first things a business does is lay off workers. Businesses also cut back on inventories to match lowered demand for goods and services in a recession or depression. This has a ripple effect in the economy as business suppliers feel the effects of lost revenues.

During a period of recession, consumers' biggest fear is losing their jobs; the other big fear is a decrease in wages. These fears result in a loss of consumer confidence in the economy, which reduces consumer spending. Reduced consumer spending causes businesses to reduce their operations in response to lower demand. The opposite is true during periods of prosperity and recovery.

During those periods, consumers are more optimistic. They spend more money on material goods and luxury items. Businesses will also respond by producing more goods. This cycle shows how important consumers are to an economy—consumer spending makes up two-thirds of the U.S. GDP.

A government influences business cycles through its policies and programs. Taxation has a strong bearing on what happens in an economy. As the government requires more money to run programs, higher taxes are needed. When taxes are raised, businesses and consumers have less money with which to fuel the economy. When the economy needs a boost, the government may reduce interest rates, cut taxes, or institute federally funded programs to spark a depressed economy. Figure 4-8 illustrates ways the Federal Reserve can control the economy. One example of an action a government can take to spur economic growth involves Japan's decision to hand out free shopping coupons to its citizens. In 1999, Japan slashed income tax rates and distributed nearly $6 billion in shopping coupons to encourage people to spend. The government took the dramatic actions to spur consumption and revive an economy in its worst recession in 50 years.

THE GLOBAL ECONOMY Early in the 1990s there was a *global recession*. This means that many countries all around the world were in recession at the same time. Some countries rebounded more quickly and soundly than others.

The recovery phase for the United States began in March 1991, but this recovery was different from others. Job growth did not increase as quickly. Instead of hiring new employees as conditions improved, businesses asked existing employees to work longer hours. U.S. manufacturing workers who escaped layoff during the recession were working an average of 41 hours a week in 1993. This increased worker productivity.

Increased investment in equipment, which displaced workers but increased output, also contributed to the recovery trend. U.S. workers were rated the most productive in the world by 1994. The U.S. economy continued to grow and expand into the new millennium. The jobless rate fell to the lowest point in 30 years, inflation was low, and economic output continued to increase.

The same was not true for Southeast Asia. Southeast Asian economies appeared to be improving as businesses and governments began big projects for expansion. Most of those projects were supported by large amounts of international capital, much of which was short-term loans in foreign currency. When it was time to pay back those loans, businesses and governments did not have the money. Bank debts reached $1 trillion in the region. The financial fragility caused by these outstanding debts forced devaluation of several countries' currency and led to an increase in interest rates, causing further economic turmoil. Thailand is generally regarded as the domino that set off the devastating Asian economic crisis with the devaluation of its currency—the Baht—in July 1997. The economies in Thailand, Indonesia, the Philippines, Malaysia, Singapore, Hong Kong, and South Korea collapsed in late 1997. Their over ambitious plans were compounded by scandal-ridden banking systems and government interference in the private sector. There was a rippling effect on the stock market, causing stock markets to decline throughout Asia and around the world. On October 27, 1997, the U.S. stock market plunged 554 points in one day after the news about Asia's troubled stock markets. Stock prices also plummeted in Latin American countries, such as Brazil, Mexico, Venezuela, and Argentina.

The economic recession that occurred following this financial crisis created higher import prices and lower wages for workers, which caused a decline in domestic demand. In a global economy, this discouraged foreign investors from investing in a country

BRIGHT IDEAS
Sticking with It

It saves us from tying our shoes, zipping our jackets, and strapping on our watches. What would we do without the miracle of VELCRO? VELCRO—created by Swiss mountaineer George de Mestral—was invented by accident. De Mestral returned from walking his dog to find that both he and his dog were covered with burrs. Intrigued by the small plant seed sac's ability to cling to fur, de Mestral examined a burr under a microscope. The stiff hooks on the seed inspired de Mestral to develop a fastener based on the design of the burr. Initially the idea was met with laughter; after some trial and error in design, de Mestral finally patented the VELCRO product in 1955. Today VELCRO is a multimillion dollar industry.

Thinking Creatively

Inventing requires imagination. Suppose that you were de Mestral and you were stung by a bee while walking that day. What product might you have invented instead?

where they would have a difficult time selling their goods due to low consumer demand. Asian businesses that wanted to succeed had to cut prices in order to boost sales at home and more importantly through exports to pay back their foreign debts. Those lower prices from Asian countries contributed to lower inflation, having a positive influence on European countries and the United States.

There were other reasons why the United States remained stable after the stock market scare of October 1997. Most companies in the United States were financially strong and had lower interest rates on their loans, making the loans easy to repay. Corporate earnings were up, as was productivity. Due to downsizing, which is the reduction of staff to cut costs and increase efficiency, and investment in technology, the U.S. economy continued to grow despite the Asian economic crisis.

Asian countries, like South Korea, rebounded in the new millennium. Many of them were able to "export" their way out of trouble by increasing sales to foreign customers, especially the United States. The economic boom in the United States helped to fuel Asia's recovery by maintaining huge demand for Asian exports like computers, electronics, machinery, toys, and textiles. The International Monetary Fund was also a big influence as it helped countries regulate their currencies by loaning them money and forcing them to restructure their financial sectors. Many countries confronted government corruption to reassure foreign investors of their stability and desirability as a business partner.

REAL WORLD MARKETING

Hold the Anchovies, but Add Two Videos, Please!

TelePizza is Spain's leading fast food company, operating 767 outlets. In 2000, TelePizza had to come up with creative solutions in an effort to expand its business and remain a leader. Rather than offer different menu items, TelePizza joined with Terra, the leading Internet Service Provider in Spanish- and Portuguese-speaking countries. The e-commerce network offers TelePizza customers a wide range of products including videos, compact discs, books, and other entertainment goods along with their pizza orders.

Thinking Critically

What is the benefit for each company of this joint venture?

4.2 ASSESSMENT

Reviewing Key Terms and Concepts

1. What are the goals of any economy?

2. Name four measurements used to gauge the success of an economy.

3. Describe in the briefest terms what each of the following stands for: GDP, CPI, PPI, and Core CPI.

4. Describe the four phases of the business cycle.

5. What stage of the business cycle was the United States in during the year 2000?

Thinking Critically

6. Assume the economy was growing rapidly and there were increases in the CPI, PPI, as well as in employee wages and spending. What might the government do to reduce the risk of inflation?

Integrating Academic Skills

7. **MATH** If inflation is up 2.5 percent from last year and last year the price of a loaf of bread was $1.59, how much would it be selling for now?

72 Unit 2 ■ *Economics*

Careers in Marketing

IMPORTING / EXPORTING

Kara Schick
Epicurean Enterprises
Importer/Exporter

What does your job entail?

"I work in both importing and exporting. I arrange for the purchase and transportation of foreign food delicacies to sell domestically, as well as the purchase and transportation of domestic goods in foreign countries. Dealing with domestic and foreign shipping companies is part of the job. I oversee the staff who handle the necessary documentation for importing and exporting. I am responsible for keeping abreast of shipping and receiving regulations, and training staff in tariff laws as well as import and export quotas."

What do you like most about your job?

"My favorite aspect of my job is the extensive travel. I spend a good deal of time in European cities developing relationships with clients and arranging for the most effective and efficient shipping methods for the products that I buy and sell."

What kind of training do you recommend for students?

"Fluency in a foreign language and knowledge of other cultures are excellent preparation for students interested in the import/export business. This can be attained through travel or study abroad. It is also helpful to take business courses in high school and college."

What is your key to success?

"My key to success lies in my commitment to stay well-informed of changes or trends in the industry. It is important to be aware of any changes in tariff laws or trade embargoes that may affect my business."

Thinking Critically

How could work as a customs entry clerk be effective training for a career in importing/exporting?

Career Facts

Education and Training: Travel abroad is important. Courses in English, business, economics, marketing, accounting, consumer education, and data processing are recommended. Familiarity with currency exchange rate is necessary.

Aptitudes, Abilities, and Skills: An interest in locating and coordinating resources is important in this field. An eye for quality and value is also required. Importers/exporters should have good clerical and numerical skills. They should enjoy meeting people and must have strong communication skills.

Career Outlook: Opportunities will vary with the economy. The impact of e-commerce on the import/export business is unknown.

Career Path: Work as an import/export clerk or a customs-entry clerk provides good background. Experience working as an import/export agent in an import/export agency may also lead to management or buying positions. Experience in shipping and receiving for a retail store, or as a shipping agent for a transportation company is also valuable.

Chapter 4 ASSESSMENT

VOCABULARY REVIEW

Work in groups to develop a story about a new country that incorporates fifteen of the terms below. Assume the country is trying to answer the three basic questions about its economy.

- economy
- resources
- capital
- land
- labor
- entrepreneurship
- factors of production
- infrastructure
- scarcity
- command economy
- market economy
- capitalism
- socialist
- communist
- privatization
- productivity
- Gross Domestic Product (GDP)
- inflation
- Consumer Price Index (CPI)
- business cycle
- prosperity
- recession
- depression
- recovery

FACT AND IDEA REVIEW

1. Explain how the infrastructure of a country is related to the factors of production. (4.1)

2. Into what two broad categories have economists classified all economic systems? (4.1)

3. In which economic system does the government let the market answer the three basic economic questions? (4.1)

4. Why were there always shortages of consumer goods in the former Soviet Union? (4.1)

5. How can businesses increase productivity? (4.2)

6. What economic measurement does the U.S. government use to report the nation's production output? (4.2)

7. Why is double-digit inflation bad for an economy? (4.2)

8. Why is low unemployment good for a nation? (4.2)

9. What three factors affect business cycles? (4.2)

THINKING CRITICALLY

1. Why are most world economies moving to a market system?

2. Would you enjoy living in a country where the government guaranteed employment, housing, food, and medical care for all people? Why or why not?

3. Until the 1990 global recession, Japanese companies offered workers lifetime employment. Do you think U.S. companies should consider offering their workers such an arrangement? Why or why not?

BUILDING WORKPLACE SKILLS

1. **Technology** Look up information on the Asian economic crisis of the late 1990s on the Internet. Prepare an outline of your findings and cite your sources.

2. **Human Relations** Your company hired an efficiency expert to streamline the operations of the business during an economic recession. He would like you to prepare a memo that will warn employees that they may lose their jobs within the next six months due to downsizing.

APPLYING MARKETING CONCEPTS

1. **Summarizing Key Concepts** Summarize an article that demonstrates any of the key concepts in this chapter. In the summary, identify the specific concepts in parenthesis. Use publications, such as *BusinessWeek, Fortune, Forbes,* and *Nation's Business*, to find an applicable article.

2. **Analyzing Economic Phases** Using the government Internet sites and other sources, research the current U.S. GDP and inflation, interest, and unemployment rates. Use the figures you gather to determine the business cycle phase of the U.S. economy at the present time. Using presentation software, create an oral report based on your findings.

3. **Studying Economic Theory** Research the cost-push different theory of inflation and the wage-price spiral associated with that theory. Study how the presidential administration of Richard Nixon handled problems with inflation in the 1970s. Using design software, prepare a report that highlights your findings and utilizes graphics and charts.

4. **Researching Economic Expansion** Using the Internet and other sources, study the economic expansion of the 1990s into the new millennium. Research the factors that contributed to that prosperous period in U.S. history. Write your conclusions in a two-page report using a word processing program.

LINKING SCHOOL TO WORK

Thinking and Information Skills Interview an employer about the cost of government taxes and employee benefits for the employer's company. Ask the employer what can be done to cut down on labor costs. Share your findings with the class.

THE DECA CONNECTION

Role Play: Public Relations Intern

Situation You are to assume the role of intern in a public relations firm. A client has requested that your firm prepare a learning packet on the business cycle to teach children (ages 10–12) about the economy. This project is part of your client's school-business partnership with an elementary school.

Activity Since you are the youngest person in the PR firm, your supervisor (judge) asked you to develop a rough draft of what you think should be included in the learning packet. You have only 15 minutes to organize your ideas.

Evaluation You will be evaluated on how well you meet the following performance indicators:

- Determine the impact of business cycles on business activities
- Explain measures used to analyze economic conditions
- Prepare simple written reports
- Demonstrate appropriate creativity
- Follow directions

interNET CONNECTION

Ups and Downs
Since everyone is talking about the ups and downs of the stock market, you decide to see what it is all about. Conduct research on the Internet to find more information.

Connect
- Find recent (within the past month) articles that reported current economic measurements.
- Find reports on the stock market on the day of and the day after these announcements.
- Write two paragraphs explaining how the announcements of economic measurements affected the stock market.

The Zazz Lab

A Sports and Entertainment Marketing Simulation

WELCOME

Welcome to Zazz Sports and Entertainment Marketing Company. Zazz is devoted to serving the needs of its clients who include college, university, and professional sports teams, professional athletes, sporting events, and sports arenas plus major consumer product corporations, as well as television networks and movie studios. As an intern, you will have the opportunity to work on different clients' projects. All of your work will be assigned and reviewed by your department supervisor.

LICENSE A SPORTS-THEME VIDEO GAME

SITUATION

Prima Sports Videos Company, a designer of sports-related video games, is looking to license sports teams or sports celebrities through Zazz. Prima has developed new video game technology that allows users to "play" alongside professionals. For example, a user could play a simulated golf tournament against Tiger Woods. The games will be available for all game console platforms. Prima Sports Videos expects to pay for the licensing rights of one or more of Zazz's properties. There is also some debate about when to market the product because a majority of video games are launched and sold in the fourth quarter of the year for holiday shoppers. Prima Sports Videos wants Zazz's help to determine if it is best to go with sports that are in season at that time or the most popular sports year-round.

ASSIGNMENT

Your supervisor wants you to select and provide rationale for a sports organization or a specific sports celebrity to license for Zazz's new client. You may assume that Zazz represents or will negotiate a deal with the professional athlete or sports organization of your choice. You must convince Zazz's management that the sports organization or celebrity you have

chosen is a perfect match for Prima Sports Videos. Prepare a brief description of your suggested video game, as well as ideas on how and when the video may be merchandised and promoted.

Tools and Resources

To complete this assignment, you will need to conduct research at a library or on the Internet. You will also need a sample Product Licensing Proposal to use as a guide, and presentation software. *BusinessWeek* and *BrandWeek* may provide you with the business perspective for this assignment, while *Sports Trend* and *NFL Retail Buzz* provide sports related information. Other helpful trade publications include *The Licensing Book, TLB—Team Licensing Business, Street & Smiths Sports Business,* and *Playthings,* a monthly list of best-selling toys and videos.

Research

Research the demographics of sports-theme video game players. Research sports organizations and sports celebrities. Study the demographics of the fans to see which would best fit the sports-theme video game market. Choose three sports organizations or sports celebrities and research current licensing agreements. Determine the popularity and current sales of those licensed products, as well as how they are being merchandised, marketed, and distributed. Research your client's competition. Research the distribution outlets in which these sports video games are sold.

Report

Prepare a written report and a computer presentation. Use a word processing program to prepare a double-spaced report. Include a table showing the correlation between the demographics of video game players and the fans for the sports organization or sports celebrity you selected to license the video game. Be sure to provide a heading for the table and introduce it in the text prior to its inclusion on that page. Arrange your report around the following headings:

- Review of licensed sports-theme video games
  - Popularity of licensed sports-theme video games
  - Video games currently licensing sports teams or figures
  - Method of distribution (sales outlets)
- Review of sports organizations and sports celebrities
  - Criteria used for review
  - Selection of top three
- Correlation of demographic profiles
  - Sports video game players
  - Fans for top three selections
- Current product license agreements for top three selections
  - Products
  - Popularity of products
  - Methods of merchandising, marketing, and distribution
  - Potential conflicts
- Sports organization or sports celebrity selected
  - Rationale
  - Suggested video content
  - Suggested method(s) of merchandising and marketing
  - Suggested distribution method(s)

Presentation and Evaluation

Present your ideas in a written report and an oral presentation. You will be evaluated on your oral presentation skills, including:

- Knowledge of sports-theme video game market
- Knowledge of sports licensing agreements
- Selection of a viable sports organization or celebrity for the new client
- Rationale for licensee (why that Zazz property) and rationale for the licensor (why a video game)
- Ability to persuade others
- Continuity of presentation
- Voice quality
- Eye contact

Portfolio

Print out a copy of your completed report and presentation for your Portfolio.

THE **DECA** *An Association of Marketing Students*
CONNECTION

DECA Business Services Marketing Series
Negotiating product licensing agreements for a client could be a role play in this event.

DECA Marketing Management Series
Developing a plan to market a new sports-theme licensed product could be the basis of a role play in this event.

DECA Retail Merchandising Series, Management Level
A possible role play might involve evaluating the purchase of licensed sports video games, given current marketplace trends.

DECA Sports and Entertainment Marketing Management Team Decision-Making Event
Working in teams on this project ties together all aspects of team decision making, as well as the fields of sports and entertainment marketing.

UNIT·3

Develop a Marketing Plan

To demonstrate mastery of the content in this unit, you will develop a marketing plan for a business that wants to get involved in international trade. You are free to select a country and a product to market in that country. You may change the product to successfully gear it toward the target market in the selected country. Research several countries' economic, political, and social characteristics until you find one that is suitable for your product. Research the company to see if it has any international operations in that country. Prepare an outline with the following topics: rationale for the country selected, rationale for the product selected, target market and rationale, and proposed marketing plan (product, place, price, promotion). Provide a description and rationale for each of the four Ps, including samples when appropriate. Use presentation software to prepare your maketing plan for an oral presentation to the company's marketing team.

Business and International Marketing

Unit Overview

In this unit you will have the opportunity to see what business is all about, in the United States and abroad. Chapter 5 discusses different types of business, as well as social responsibility in the marketplace and workplace. Chapter 6 introduces you to the global marketplace as you review international trade. You will learn why international trade is important, as well as how businesses operate in foreign countries.

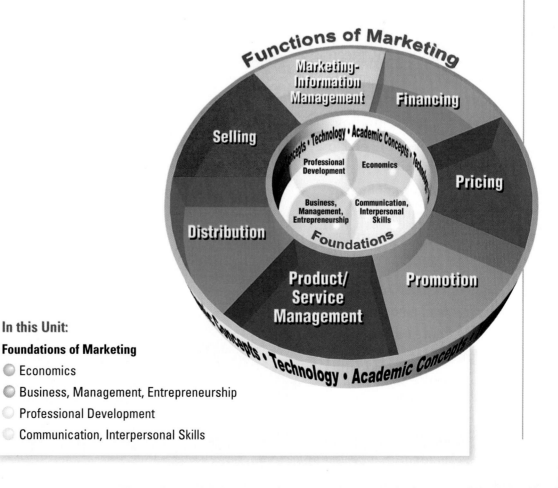

In this Unit:

Foundations of Marketing

● Economics

● Business, Management, Entrepreneurship

○ Professional Development

◐ Communication, Interpersonal Skills

Business and Social Responsibility

ADOPT A HIGHWA
LITTER CONTRO
NEXT 2 MILE:

ASHLAND CHEMICAL, I

Marketing: What It Takes

Responsible Recycling

You are the sales manager at a new company that produces stationery, greeting cards, and journals made from recycled paper products. You are finding that the sales figures for the first three months are not as strong as anticipated. You are currently marketing the products in drug stores and mall card stores.

WHAT WILL YOU DO?

What are some nontraditional avenues that you could explore to market the cards to an audience that values recycled products?

Defining Business

What Is Business?

Business is all of the activities involved in producing and marketing goods and services. Organizations involved in such activities are called companies, or businesses. Every business seeks to satisfy economic needs by planning, organizing, and controlling resources in order to produce and market goods or services.

■ The Functions of Business

Business has two primary functions—the production and the marketing of goods and services. These primary functions depend on the important support activity of management. Management is used to plan, organize, and control all available resources to reach company goals.

PRODUCTION The process of creating, growing, manufacturing, or improving on goods and services is called production. A songwriter *creates* a song. A farmer *grows* wheat. Ford Motor Company *manufactures* cars. Van conversion companies *improve* newly manufactured vans to make them more suitable for camping and travel.

Now consider an extended example. Weyerhauser Lumber Company produces lumber by cutting down tall trees and slicing them up into pieces of wood. The raw goods—freshly cut trees—are processed to make usable lumber and shipped all over the world. Mobile home manufacturing companies buy the processed lumber, which serves as one of the main materials in their product. Harvesting the trees, cutting them into lumber, and making the lumber into buildings are all production activities.

MARKETING When goods or services are created, grown, or manufactured, they must be sold in the marketplace. The marketplace exists wherever a product is sold to a customer. It may be in a store, an outdoor market, or simply wherever two or more people agree to buy and sell a product.

Recall that the selling of something in the marketplace is the essence of the exchange process. The exchange process occurs when customers *exchange* their money (or their promise to pay) for the goods and services offered. The lumber processed by Weyerhauser in the example above earns no profit for the company and cannot be used for building anything until the exchange process has taken place. The exchange process is the focus of the broad range of activities that we call marketing.

● What You'll Learn

- What a business is
- The basic functions of a business
- How to distinguish businesses from each other based on general characteristics
- The importance of e-commerce
- The concept of derived demand
- The major types of businesses that comprise the industrial market

● Why It's Important

Marketing is part of doing business. In order to understand the world of marketing, you will want to understand what's involved in doing business and some of the different types of businesses.

Key Terms

- business
- management
- production
- marketplace
- finance
- nonprofit organizations
- public sector
- private sector
- industrial market
- derived demand
- wholesalers
- retailers
- e-commerce

MANAGEMENT Businesses use natural resources, labor, and capital to produce and market goods or services. These resources must be brought together through good management. Management is the process of achieving company goals by effective use of resources through planning, organizing, and controlling. You will learn more about management in Chapter 11.

The word finance has several meanings in business. It can mean money or anything that can be sold very quickly to get money. It can also mean borrowing money. You may have heard someone talk about financing a car. This means borrowing money to buy the car. As a supporting function for management, finance means money management. You will learn more about finance in Unit 11.

■ Types of Businesses

Businesses come in a variety of shapes and sizes and are classified using various terms. In order to understand their differences, it is important to understand the terminology associated with business classifications. Keep in mind that a business may be classified in more than one category. Businesses can be categorized in the following ways:

- *By size* Is the business large or small?
- *By profit orientation* Is the business a profit or nonprofit concern?
- *By market served* Does the business serve the consumer or industrial market?
- *By kind of product provided* Does the business provide goods, services, or something else?

LARGE VS. SMALL Businesses can be categorized by their size. A small business is one that is operated by only one or a few individuals, and generally has less than 100 employees. A larger business is generally considered one that employs over 1000 people. These organizations are usually national or global and contain many different departments.

Nationwide, there are thousands of small businesses, or "mom-and-pop" operations. They include neighborhood grocery stores, florists, gift shops, photocopy and print shops, and secretarial services. This category also contains many Internet start-up companies and "dot com" businesses that often start off with small budgets and staffs. About 95 percent of all U.S. businesses are classified as small businesses. They employ over half of the private-sector (nongovernment) work force.

DOMESTIC VS. GLOBAL A domestic market comprises buyers in a single country. The global market is the exchange of goods and services among nations.

The advent of the Internet, along with faster transportation and financial flows, makes it easier to do business globally. Products produced in one country are now finding greater acceptance around the world. The trend is moving from domestic markets to a larger global market.

Established companies that have achieved domestic success for many years are now facing international competitors in their own back yards. A company that does not establish a foothold in the global market will forgo profits internationally— and also risk losing business at home.

■ Different Marketplaces These two marketplaces look considerably different. *What makes them similar?*

The free enterprise system of the United States has nourished some of the world's most successful global businesses. One of the most dramatic success stories in modern American business is that of McDonald's Corporation—the fast-food giant.

Founder Ray Kroc, who sold restaurant equipment for a living, borrowed money to start the company. The first McDonald's opened in 1955, and by 1962, the company had domestic sales of $76 million. By 2000, McDonald's was a global leader, with 25,000 restaurants in 119 countries and annual sales of $17 billion in the United States, $10 billion in Europe, $8 billion in Asia/Pacific, and another $2 billion in Latin America. McDonald's is now the largest and best-known food service retailer in the world.

PROFIT VS. NONPROFIT Businesspeople in a free market economy, like that of the United States, may earn a profit for satisfying the needs and wants of consumers. People who want to work for themselves and make a profit establish thousands of businesses each year in the United States. Many of these businesses achieve great success.

Microsoft, the computer software company, was started by Bill Gates in 1975 when he was 18 years old. The company earned more than $12 billion in 2000 and was the worldwide leader in software for personal computers.

While profit is the motivating factor in starting most businesses, this is not always the case. Service organizations, called nonprofit organizations, are not operated for the purpose of making a profit.

Examples include the Boys/Girls Clubs of America, and the YMCA and YWCA.

Like any business, nonprofit organizations must hire employees and pay the costs and expenses of running the organization. All the income remaining after expenses are paid goes for the charitable cause outlined in the organization's charter. That means it does not earn a profit.

PUBLIC VS. PRIVATE In addition to charitable institutions, there are other organizations that operate as businesses do but are not intended to earn a profit. Most local, state, and federal government agencies and services, such as public schools and public libraries, fall into this category. These organizations are said to be part of the public sector.

Public sector organizations purchase one-third of all goods and services sold in the United States each year. Government agencies are usually required to buy the least expensive product that meets written minimum specifications. To be considered by the government, a business usually must submit a bid quoting its prices. Businesses not associated with government agencies are part of the private sector.

GOODS OR SERVICES Another way to classify businesses is by looking at the type of products they provide. Some businesses provide goods, like the bread sold in the supermarket or the flour used to make it. Other businesses provide services, like dry cleaning for your clothes or security for the mall where you work.

■ **Not for Profit** Although most large universities are nonprofit, they are still managed much like a for-profit business. *What do you think they do with their excess income?*

Risky Business

How do you keep readers coming back? Online magazines—especially ones focusing on computer hardware and software—face this challenge. In 2000, the Macintosh News Network (MNN) got in trouble for soliciting and posting a "sneak peak" story with inside information about a new version of the popular software program Adobe Photoshop. Adobe claimed that the unauthorized "exclusive inside look" provided trade secrets to competitors. The online news publisher said the information came from a public Web site and claimed it didn't know that the original source was confidential. Although the story was removed from the site, the damage to Adobe could equal tens of millions of dollars in lost sales.

Thinking Critically

Should "anything go"on the Internet? Is it ethical for MNN to post "sneak peaks"?

There are finer distinctions among types of services. *Business* services include financial planning, insurance, real estate, transportation, shipping, communications, utilities, data processing, and advertising. The services of doctors, dentists, lawyers, and other professionals are called *professional* services. Newspapers and magazines provide *information* services. There are also categories for businesses that promote people, like political candidates, or places, such as tourism destinations.

Beginning in the 1990s, a whole new area of services arose with the rise of the Internet. Such services include Internet service providers, Web page designers, and an explosion of telecommunications providers.

American business will continue to grow during the early years of the 21st century. The direction, though, will be different. More of the growth will be concentrated in service industries than in manufacturing, and the Internet will continue to expand and shape business.

■ Consumer vs. Industrial

The type of market served is another way of classifying businesses. When we think of goods and services, most of us think of the consumer products that satisfy our own needs and wants. There is another side of marketing that is even larger than the consumer market—the industrial or business-to-business market. Business-to-business marketing involves all the customers who make purchases for business purposes.

The industrial market is based on, or derived from, the demand for consumer goods and services. For this reason, the demand for industrial goods is called derived demand.

Marketers of industrial goods need to be aware of how their markets will change as a result of changes in the consumer market. When consumers decide to buy more automobiles, the derived demand for auto components (tires, radios, batteries, electronic parts, etc.) increases. Businesses that are involved in the industrial market are extractors, construction and manufacturing businesses, and wholesalers and retailers.

Extractors are businesses that take something from the earth or sea. They include agriculture, forestry, fishing, and mining. The products are primarily sold to other businesses.

Construction companies build structures like houses, office buildings, and manufacturing plants. *Manufacturing* involves producing goods to sell to other manufacturers or to wholesalers and retailers, which is often referred to as business-to-business marketing.

Wholesalers obtain goods from manufacturers and resell them to industrial users, other wholesalers, and retailers. Wholesalers are also called distributors. Retailers buy goods from wholesalers or directly from manufacturers and resell them to the consumer. For the most part, retailers cater to the consumer market.

E-COMMERCE E-commerce has become a whole new category of business. Short for electronic commerce, e-commerce is the buying and selling of goods through the use of electronic networks, usually the Internet. Electronic commerce can also be classified as any activity that uses electronic communication in the exchange of goods and services.

Electronic commerce has really existed for many years before the World Wide Web came to be in 1996.

■ **Going Online!** It seems like most businesses are entering the world of e-tailing; traditional brick and mortar companies like Sears began marketing washers and dryers online in 2000. *What are some of the benefits of selling products online?*

Consider the familiar task of shopping for groceries. When the supermarket cashier scans your grocery items, data is transmitted through a computer network to the store's suppliers, who track and replenish the store's stock. When you pay for your purchase using an ATM terminal, funds are electronically transferred from your bank account to the store's bank account. This transaction was made possible through the use of electronic networks.

After only the first five years of the World Wide Web, e-commerce rivaled the size of century-old business sectors, such as automotive, energy, and telecommunications. Sector growth that took a

hundred or more years to build during the Industrial Age is being matched by e-commerce at a rate about 20 times faster in the "new economy" of the 21st century.

The market research firm, Socratic Technologies, Inc., found that over half of the businesses it surveyed said the Internet is central to their daily business activities. All types of businesses use the Internet. Even traditional retailers are adapting their marketing to e-commerce—producing the term *e-tailing.*

Use of the Internet for e-commerce will be discussed in greater depth in Chapter 9.

5.1 ASSESSMENT

Reviewing Key Terms and Concepts

1. What is a business?
2. What are the two primary functions of business?
3. List four ways that businesses can be categorized.
4. Discuss the significance of e-commerce.

Thinking Critically

5. Why would someone want to start a small business? Describe the success of a small business with which you are familiar.

Integrating Academic Skills

6. **COMMUNICATION** Conduct a telephone interview with a representative of your local chamber of commerce. Ask what new businesses have joined the organization in the past year. Also, find an evaluation of the economic, political, and other conditions facing businesses in your community. Write about your findings in a one-page report.

Ethics and Social Responsibility

• What You'll Learn

- The areas in which businesses are thought to have social responsibilities
- The ways that business activities have impacted our environment
- The definition of ethics and how marketers can make ethical choices
- The meaning of consumerism and a brief history of the movement
- The current trends and concerns in the workplace for employees

• Why It's Important

You know the importance of being considerate of others in your daily life. As you move toward a career in adult life, you will want to understand the importance of ethics and social responsibility in business.

Key Terms

- green marketing
- ethics
- consumerism

Marketing and Social Responsibility

Anyone can choose to go into business in a free enterprise system, but everyone must abide by state and federal laws that apply to businesses. Some of those laws encourage fair business practices, while others protect consumers, workers, investors, and the environment.

Apart from following the law, should businesses have any further social responsibility? Some businesses feel they should. Society's expectations of businesses in regard to social and environmental responsibility have changed dramatically in recent years. Most consumers feel that businesses should act in a socially responsible manner. Because so many consumers have taken an interest in the issue, organizations have been increasingly encouraged to consider the social and environmental consequences of their actions. Social responsibility means that businesses are part of a larger society and should be held accountable to that society for their actions. Companies that have instituted socially responsible programs and policies include Ben & Jerry's Homemade, Inc., and McDonald's.

Ben & Jerry's, the ice cream manufacturer, donates 7.5 percent of its pretax earnings to the disadvantaged and the needy. The company also contributes to groups that strive for social change and environmental protection.

McDonald's Corporation funds Ronald McDonald Houses near children's hospitals. The parents of young cancer patients stay at these residences while their children are receiving medical treatment. There are more than 150 Ronald McDonald Houses across the United States. McDonald's founder, Ray Kroc, also endowed a charitable foundation that has funded millions of dollars in medical research and programs to combat alcoholism.

Let's look at some of the issues that concern socially responsible companies like these. Those issues include protection of the environment, ethical conduct in the marketplace, and the treatment of both consumers and employees.

■ Environmental Issues

Laws govern many environmental issues that affect us. They prohibit improper disposal of medical, chemical, and other hazardous wastes. Socially responsible businesses follow the laws and understand their roles in helping to preserve our natural resources.

AIR AND WATER POLLUTION The federal government established the Environmental Protection Agency (EPA) to protect the environment from pollution. The EPA is probably best known for the Clean Air Act, which was revised in 1990 to intensify actions to protect our environment. All automobile manufacturers have had to modify their engines to meet EPA emission standards. It is also mandatory that cars use unleaded gasoline to protect people and nature from the harmful effects of lead. Manufacturers are still working to perfect EVs, or Electronic Vehicles, that run on battery energy as opposed to gasoline and oil.

Chlorofluorocarbons (CFCs) were once used as propellants in spray products such as hairspray, insecticide, and paint cans until research proved that they contributed to the depletion of the ozone layer. Less ozone is a health hazard and increases exposure to the Sun's harmful rays. An international agreement was reached to phase out the use of CFCs before 2000, but they are still being used in some countries. Socially responsible companies have substituted different propellants or switched to pump sprays.

One popular CFC, freon, was widely used in automobile and building air-conditioning systems. Federal law now requires manufacturers to use safer chemicals. As of 1996, no freon is produced in the United States. Garages and repair shops are required to recycle freon products under a law passed in 1997.

Although agricultural pesticides and chemical fertilizers are frequently used to grow bigger crops and more attractive fruits and vegetables, the EPA tightened laws regarding food exposure to pesticides with the Food Quality Act of 1996.

Many pesticides have had harmful effects on animals and people. The EPA is constantly checking pesticides to determine possible harmful effects. Some have already polluted our land, streams, lakes, and underground water supplies. This is true for household products that are used as pest control, too. The EPA required S.C. Johnson & Son, Inc. to remove AllerCare Dust Mite Powder and Allergen Spray from store shelves in January 2000 when it was found to cause some customers to have asthma attacks, breathing problems, and skin rashes.

Chlorine gas is the most heavily used pesticide in the United States, acting as a disinfectant for swimming pools, drinking water, and sewage systems. The EPA issued the Chlorine Gas Reregistration Eligibility Decision (RED) to limit the use of chlorine only to trained professionals who understand the hazards of handling this potentially dangerous substance. Chlorine products were to be re-labeled for "restricted use only" beginning in 2000.

■ **Reaching Out** McDonald's is one of many organizations that promotes charitable programs and practices social responsibility. *Why would an organization become involved in activities such as these?*

■ **Recycle, Please** 3M's Scotch-Brite Never Rust Wool Soap Pads appeal to customers because they are made of recycled soda bottles. This makes them more expensive than competing brands. *Do you think that this will affect the environmentally-conscious customer's decision to buy?*

Industrial waste poses another problem for the environment. Industrial waste often finds its way through porous soil into the underground water supplies used by cities. The EPA found that in 1996, 208 million tons of municipal solid waste were generated by the United States. The EPA has increased its efforts to enforce proper waste disposal to protect our water and resources. The executives of some manufacturing companies have even been sentenced to prison for violation of safe disposal standards.

CONSERVATION AND RECYCLING Oil consumption became a concern during the oil crisis of the 1970s, and it still is today. According to the *International Energy Outlook 2000*, worldwide oil demand will reach 113 million barrels a day by 2020. The price and availability of oil is greatly affected by political and economic disruptions; therefore it can often be unpredictable. In 2000, Arab nations restricted oil output, and gas prices rose abruptly. Exploration of other fuels has become necessary. Car manufacturers have responded by producing smaller, more fuel-efficient automobiles.

BRIGHT IDEAS

Be Kind—Rewind and Recycle

A handful of entrepreneurs are making money by erasing, cleaning, and repackaging videotapes. Once recycled, they are sold to a variety of users looking to work within tight budgets. The lower price of a recycled tape versus a new tape appeals to young film students, independent movie studios, and public broadcasting networks. This $30 million dollar industry has continued to grow in the past 30 years as these modern day recyclers find treasure in the unwanted discards from TV networks, corporations, and security-camera outfits. Recyclers also earn revenue by reconditioning used tapes and returning them to the original owners for use. Other customers pay to have their videotapes destroyed, in order to keep their video footage from reappearing elsewhere.

Thinking Creatively
On what other products could these specialized recycling businesses concentrate?

Alternatives to the traditional transportation fuels of gasoline and diesel fuel are currently being developed. Some vehicle fuels, because of physical or chemical properties, create less pollution than do today's gasolines. These are called "clean fuels." These include certain types of alcohol, electricity, natural gas, and propane. Researchers say that a "fuel cell" vehicle will be available to the public before too long.

Gasoline is toxic and emits complex mixtures of compounds that lead to the formation of ground-level ozone. While steps have been taken to reduce the risk of pollution, many large cities still have not seen a reduction of their ozone problem. The use of clean fuel slows the atmospheric buildup of the "greenhouse gas," carbon dioxide, which contributes to the potential for global warming. While combustion of any carbon-based fuel produces carbon dioxide, fuels produced from biomass (crops, trees, etc.) and from natural gas result in less carbon dioxide accumulation than fuels made from petroleum or coal.

While electric or battery-powered vehicles give off virtually no pollution, the driving range of today's electric cars is limited by the amount of power the battery can provide. Currently, the cost of electric vehicles is high and batteries take hours to recharge. Recent developments in electric vehicle technology show much promise for the future—and offer one of the best options for reducing motor vehicle pollution.

Conservation of our natural resources depends heavily on cooperation of business, government, and consumers. Most local governments require mandatory recycling of glass, plastic, and aluminum through local trash collection, and many companies are making similar efforts.

GREEN MARKETING Consumer concern over the environment is increasing, and marketers are paying attention. The growing importance of ecological issues has brought about green marketing. In green marketing, companies make an effort to produce and promote environmentally safe products. Such products are often labeled as ozone-safe, recyclable, environmentally friendly, or biodegradable. Green marketing strategies have become an increasingly important way for companies to build consumer loyalty. A significant number of consumers are willing to pay more for products that are environmentally friendly and ecologically sound.

Life In The Diverse MARKETPLACE

Finding a Balance

Sustainable development is a strategy by which communities seek economic development approaches that also benefit the local environment and quality of life. It provides a framework for communities to use resources efficiently, create efficient infrastructures, protect and enhance quality of life, and create new businesses to strengthen their economies. Efforts to achieve sustainable development have been difficult for developing countries dealing with concerns such as poverty. Organizations work together to develop sustainable development strategies that can help rich and poor countries alike.

Thinking Critically

Why are sustainable development issues important to all nations, not just developing countries?

■ Business Ethics

Ethics are guidelines for good behavior. Ethical behavior is based on knowing the difference between right and wrong—and doing what is right. Ethical behavior is truthful and fair and takes into account the well-being of everyone.

Laws are made to address ethical concerns involving products or marketing. Unethical practices such as bait-and-switch advertising, price fixing, and selling unsafe products are prohibited. Ethical questions that involve debate between our guaranteed freedom of speech and our guaranteed freedom to compete are not as easily answered, however. The ethics of marketing products such as tobacco and liquor as glamorous or romantic is often questioned. To make the right ethical choices, marketers must answer these three basic questions:

1. Is the practice right, fair, and honest?

2. What would happen if the product were marketed differently?

3. What practice will result in the greatest good for the greatest number of people?

Case Study

The Wired Hotel

Hotels depend on business travelers for large profits and therefore compete for their business by offering innovative services. Many chains offer lower room rates for business customers, and some make agreements with airlines to credit customers' accounts with mileage redeemable for airline tickets.

Most big brand hotels have started offering comprehensive business services. Many chains offer high-speed Internet connections, conference rooms, and work areas with speakerphones, fax machines, and printers. Even less expensive hotel chains are getting in the act to meet customers' needs.

The Starwood Hotel company has tapped into this lucrative market with its W hotel chain, which concentrates exclusively on the business travel market. Every W hotel room is a fully wired virtual office with a high-speed Internet connection, Web browser television, fax port, two-line cordless telephone, and multimedia support. The high-speed Internet access connects at speeds up to 50 times faster than conventional dial-up access. W offers meeting spaces called "creative think tanks" that are designed to inspire creative thought. W's guest rooms are luxuriously stocked with Aveda bath products and goose down comforters. Guests even have the option of arriving to a prestocked refrigerator, with their advance order delivered via WebGrocer. At the end of the day, guests can unwind at the spa or state-of-the-art gym, complete with personal trainers.

Examining the needs of business travelers and providing the services that make it easier for them to conduct their business on the road is smart marketing. If business customers have a positive experience, it is likely that they will pass their recommendations on to their business associates.

Case Study Review

1. How are hotels catering to businesspeople who travel as part of their jobs?
2. What are some risks involved in making changes in a hotel to better serve business travelers?

A MATTER OF ETHICS

3. What ethical concerns can you see when a hotel offers lower room rates to a specific type of customer—such as a business traveler?

PRODUCT RECALLS Businesses sometimes look at the legal issues involved in addition to their perceived social responsibility when making choices involving ethics. To reduce losses that could arise from future lawsuits, a socially responsible business will recall an unsafe product before the government forces it to do so. Irresponsible businesses that do not recall a product on their own may be forced to do so by a government agency like the Consumer Product Safety Commission.

Businesses may recall products even if they are not responsible for design flaws or other problems. A historically important example is when McNeil Consumer Products pulled Tylenol products off store shelves nationwide in 1982 after someone was fatally poisoned by a capsule that had been tampered with. The company immediately alerted all Tylenol users to return their capsules to the stores where they had purchased them. The manufacture of Tylenol capsules was temporarily discontinued while McNeil worked with other drug companies to develop tamper-resistant packaging. Thanks to their efforts, today most over-the-counter drugs are packaged with a seal around the bottle top or around the entire package.

CODE OF ETHICS The American Marketing Association has developed a code of ethics for marketers. The code includes detailed provisions about the truthfulness and fairness of marketing activities such as advertising, selling, pricing, marketing research, and product development and use.

■ Consumerism

Social responsibility involves the relationship of marketing with all of society. Consumerism, however, involves the relationship of marketing only with those who buy a company's goods or services. Consumerism is the societal effort to protect consumer rights by putting legal, moral, and economic pressure on business. Individual consumers, consumer groups, government, and socially responsible business leaders share this effort.

Consumerism had its beginning in the early 1900s, when it focused on product purity, product shortages, antitrust concerns, postal rates, and banking. From the 1930s to the 1950s, consumerism concentrated on product safety, labeling, misrepresentation, deceptive advertising, consumer refunds, and bank failures.

CONSUMER RIGHTS The greatest growth in consumerism took place from the early 1960s until about 1980. It involved all areas of marketing. President John F. Kennedy's Consumer Bill of Rights dominated the beginning of this consumer period. It stated that consumers have four basic rights:

- To be informed and protected against fraud, deceit, and misleading statements, and to be educated in the wise use of financial resources
- To be protected from unsafe products
- To have a choice of goods and services
- To have a voice in product and marketing decisions made by government and business

Several widely read books gave impetus to consumerism during the 1960s and 1970s. Ralph Nader's *Unsafe at Any Speed* focused public attention on what the automobile industry could do to make cars safer. Rachel Carson's *Silent Spring* detailed how marketing contributed to a decaying environment. Vance Packard's *Hidden Persuaders* revealed marketing's influence on society.

Consumers were increasingly dissatisfied with poor-quality products, deceptive business practices, and the lack of concern for consumer complaints. They got angry and demanded action. The Federal Trade Commission responded by expanding its role in consumer issues.

Companies are more responsive to customer complaints and environmental concerns than they have been in the past. Many companies now consider consumer concerns when developing their marketing plans. Product containers that can be recycled, for example, are a direct response to consumers' environmental concerns. For example, McDonald's changed their packaging from a difficult-to-recycle polystyrene plastic to a more environmentally friendly kind of packaging in response to pressure from customers.

■ Workplace Trends and Concerns

As interest in traditional social responsibility concerns has receded, other concerns have replaced them. Employee issues have been in the center of public interest since the 1990s.

Figure 5-1 on pages 92 and 93 presents an overview of other trends and concerns in the workplace, including telecommuting, flextime, family leave, on-site child care, help for the physically challenged, and health care reform.

FIGURE 5-1

WORKPLACE TRENDS AND ISSUES

Today's socially responsible businesses are offering their employees a more user-friendly workplace and even redefining the term workplace.

TELECOMMUTING

Telecommuting involves working at home, usually on a computer. Completed jobs are transmitted either by mail-in disk or manuscript form, or by phone, using a fax machine or a modem.

FLEXTIME

Flextime allows workers to choose their work hours. Possible arrangements include early start/early finish (7 A.M.–3 P.M.), late start/late finish (10 A.M.–6 P.M.), and even four-day workweeks (four 9- or 10-hour days followed by three-day weekends).

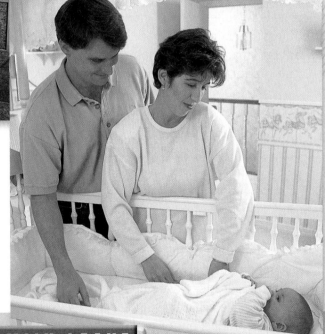

FAMILY LEAVE

Family leave is now legally required by federal law for large employers. Workers are entitled to up to 12 weeks of nonpaid family leave every two years. This allows people to cope with births, deaths, and family illnesses without fear of job loss.

HELP FOR THE PHYSICALLY CHALLENGED

Help for the physically challenged is mandated by the Americans with Disabilities Act (1990). Employers must provide physically challenged people with the same job opportunities and work site access that others have. To make this possible, employers may have to alter their workplaces physically, change the way a job is done, or provide individual assistance.

HEALTH CARE REFORM

Health care reform at the national level is an employee issue because so many Americans receive health insurance benefits through their jobs. Of the 37 million Americans who do work, many are employed by small businesses or hold minimum-wage jobs. How to cover these people and how to hold the line on costs for those who have coverage are key issues in the national health care debate.

ON-SITE CHILD CARE

On-site child care is a benefit that has grown in popularity with the increase in two-income families. Some employers have expanded it to include on-site schools and on-site clinics for children who are ill. Where the benefit is provided in any form, it tends to reduce employee turnover.

Other workplace concerns include sexual harassment, computer privacy and security, and employee computer use. The increase in the number of lawsuits alleging sexual harassment has become one of the most challenging issues businesses face today. The Equal Employment Opportunity Commission (EEOC) defines sexual harassment as unwelcome sexual attention or the creation of "an intimidating, hostile, or offensive working environment." As a response to sexual harassment concerns, many companies have policies defining harassment and procedures for handling complaints.

Computer privacy and security are also emerging as important workplace issues. As more and more companies' computer networks are connected to the Internet, the need for computer security has become increasingly important. To achieve a level of security, computer engineers have developed firewalls. Firewalls are hardware or software that restrict access from a business's internal network to the Internet and vice versa. Think of a firewall as a checkpoint at which all data, incoming and outgoing, is stopped to make sure that it is acceptable.

Many companies also track employee computer use to ensure that computers are being used appropriately and for work-related business only. Employee monitoring is more widespread than ever today, as managers need to ensure appropriate business behavior and high performance levels.

REAL WORLD MARKETING

Pepsi: Back to School

In England's Thames Valley, Pepsi has gained exclusive rights to sell its products in high school vending machines. People who felt schools were becoming overly commercialized opposed the deal. Nutritional concerns were also an issue. In an effort to help fund school activities, the school board decided to accept Pepsi's proposal. The schools will receive 60 percent of the revenue from bottled drinks and 40 percent from cans. Pepsi would probably not have been allowed to sell on school grounds without this marketing idea to raise funds from the proceeds of soda sales.

Thinking Critically

What is Pepsi's motivation in targeting this market?

5.2 ASSESSMENT

Reviewing Key Terms and Concepts

1. What are some areas in which businesses are thought to have social responsibility?

2. In what ways have business activities impacted our environment?

3. Define the term ethics and explain how marketers can make ethical choices.

4. Define consumerism and give a brief history of the movement.

5. What current trends are likely to improve the workplace for employees?

Thinking Critically

6. How are business ethics related to personal ethics?

Integrating Academic Skills

7. **MATH** If the local recycling plant pays $.06 per pound for aluminum cans, how many pounds of cans would it take to get $10?

Careers in Marketing

TRAVEL AND TOURISM MARKETING

Natasha Lawe
Travel Consultant
Liberty Travel

What does your job entail?

"The main focus of my job is making people happy—I sell dream vacations. Travel consultants make travel arrangements for clients, planning travel routes and schedules, determining fares, and reserving seating. They also book accommodations, arrange tours, and reserve rental cars. Travel is a required part of the job—you need to know a destination in order to sell it."

What training do you recommend for students?

"Students should study geography and be familiar with travel destinations. *Travel Weekly* is one magazine that keeps you updated on all of the popular destinations and selling tools."

What skills are most important?

"Patience—it takes time and patience when dealing with customers. It is important to know documentation criteria for international travel. Some customers may never have left their towns, and they count on you for thorough and accurate information. You also need excellent communication skills and computer skills."

How does your workload vary?

"The busy season is normally from October to April, when people are planning their summer vacations; this makes work slower in the summer. On an average day, I confirm about 10–15 reservations and receive approximately 20–30 phone inquiries on sales promotions."

What is your key to success?

"My key to success is knowing my priorities and what I want out of life. To be successful, travel consultants need to know their products and develop personal relationships with their customers. People have to trust you 100% to make their vacations pleasurable."

Thinking Critically

Why would vacationers choose to use a professional travel consultant instead of using a travel Web site to make their plans?

Career Facts

Education and Training: A high school diploma is required. Courses in travel consulting can be taken at vocational schools, community colleges, and some four-year colleges. Recommended courses include business classes, geography, world history, foreign languages, and word processing.

Aptitudes, Abilities, and Skills: Patience, people skills, organizational skills, ability to work under stress and keep up with industry changes are necessary.

Career Outlook: Money spent on travel is expected to increase through 2010 so employment should grow faster than average.

Career Path: Experience as a tour guide, hotel reservation clerk, or receptionist in a travel agency may provide entry into this career. Travel agents may advance to other managerial positions.

Chapter 5 ASSESSMENT

VOCABULARY REVIEW

Use each of the following words in a sentence that demonstrates you know its meaning:

- business
- production
- marketplace
- management
- finance
- nonprofit organizations
- public sector
- private sector
- industrial market
- derived demand
- wholesalers
- retailers
- e-commerce
- green marketing
- ethics
- consumerism

FACT AND IDEA REVIEW

1. Name the two primary functions of business. (5.1)

2. What are the three major functions of management in business? (5.1)

3. What percentage of U.S. businesses are small businesses? (5.1)

4. Explain how the operation of a nonprofit organization differs from a profit-making enterprise. (5.1)

5. Provide an example of both a private-sector and a public-sector organization. (5.1)

6. In what areas are businesses thought to have some degree of social responsibility? (5.2)

7. What are the questions that marketers must ask themselves to make ethical business choices? (5.2)

8. How has consumerism affected the way that businesses conduct themselves? (5.2)

9. What rights do consumers have according to the Consumer Bill of Rights? (5.2)

10. How does flextime differ from telecommuting? (5.2)

THINKING CRITICALLY

1. How should local, state, or federal governments handle industries that pollute the environment?

2. What unexpected benefits might a company receive if it believes in and practices social responsibility?

3. Do consumers have a duty to be socially responsible in their purchasing? What might be some examples of this sort of conduct?

4. Employee benefits, such as on-site childcare, tend to stabilize a company's workforce. Given this fact, why do you think more companies don't offer such benefits?

BUILDING WORKPLACE SKILLS

1. **Writing** Write a letter to a local government official describing the importance and benefits of recycling.

2. **Human Relations** You work for a company that produces textiles, and you have just discovered that the company has been disposing of its wastes in a manner that is unsafe for the environment. What will you do?

APPLYING MARKETING CONCEPTS

1. **Summarizing Key Concepts** Summarize an article that demonstrates any of the key concepts in this chapter. In the summary, identify the specific key concepts in parenthesis. Use business publications, such as *BusinessWeek, Fortune, Forbes,* and *Nation's Business,* to find an applicable article.

2. **Recycling in Your Community** With a group of other students, research the recycling centers in your community. Use a presentation software program to make a presentation with charts, graphs, and other information about the centers. Include their locations, their hours of operation, the materials they accept, and the rates they pay for those materials.

3. **Understanding Small Businesses** Find a local mom-and-pop business and interview the owners. Ask them to give you a brief history of the business. Find out what they like and dislike about having their own business. Use a word processing program to write a two-page report summarizing the interview.

4. **Conserving Resources** Think of a project that would help your school conserve resources and protect the environment. Then use a word processing program to write an editorial for the school newspaper. In the editorial, explain your idea and try to persuade other students to participate in your project.

LINKING SCHOOL TO WORK

Thinking and Personal Skills Ask an employer whether he or she believes business has social responsibilities, and why or why not. Report back to the class and discuss the answers you and your classmates received. Some good interview questions might be:

- In what ways does your business show awareness of social responsibility?
- How do you think it might improve?

THE DECA CONNECTION

Role Play: Plant Employee

Situation You are to assume the role of employee at a plant experiencing a serious problem with productivity. Much of the problem can be traced to days lost by employees with young children. When their day-care arrangements don't work out or when their children get sick, these employees must leave early or take time off. As a result, production and quality drop. The workers have a solution and they've chosen you as their spokesperson.

Activity Make the case to your employer (judge) for an on-site child-care facility. What will you say in your presentation?

Evaluation You will be evaluated on how well you meet the following performance indicators:

- Explain the concept of productivity
- Explain the role of business in society
- Foster positive working relationships
- Convince others
- Make oral presentations

interNET CONNECTION

New Century Social Responsibilities

You are a management trainee in a large corporation that has a poor record for social responsibility. The new management is interested in working toward a more socially responsible image and has asked for your input on what is expected in the 21st century.

Connect

- Use the Internet to research what specific social responsibilities are expected of businesses in the 21st century.
- In your search, use key words and phrases, such as "business responsibility," "environment," "ozone layer," and "pollution."
- Use a word processing program to write a two-page summary of your findings.

International Trade

Marketing: What It Takes

Doing Business Abroad
You have a great idea for a product that you believe could be marketed in China. A potential investor likes your product idea but is not convinced it will sell in China.

WHAT WILL YOU DO?
What information about the country, trade agreements, and trade practices will help you improve your business proposal?

The Global Marketplace

Defining International Trade

International trade involves the exchange of goods and services between nations. Imports are goods and services purchased from other countries. Conversely, exports are goods and services sold to other countries. These exchanges occur between businesses but are controlled by the governments of the countries involved.

■ Interdependence of Nations

Most countries need to get some of their goods and services from other nations. This is called economic interdependence, and it happens because different countries possess unique resources and capabilities.

Resources may include a country's weather, raw materials, labor force, capital sources, and location. Some countries, such as the United States and Canada, have good climates for agriculture. The Middle East, Africa, and Mexico have crude oil, while Russia has coal. Countries such as those in Eastern Europe and Asia, have inexpensive labor forces. Others, like the United States and Japan, have the capital and technology necessary for manufacturing.

Since nations need different things, they find it helpful to trade with each other. There are two types of advantages in international trade—absolute and comparative.

Absolute advantage occurs when a country has special natural resources or talents that allow it to produce an item at the lowest cost possible. China produces close to 80 percent of all the silk in the world, which gives them absolute advantage.

Trade is still valuable even when absolute advantage does not exist. This is because of comparative advantage. Comparative advantage is the value that a nation gains by selling the goods that it produces most efficiently. When countries specialize in products well suited to their capabilities, they may gain a comparative advantage in international trade.

U.S. businesses are well suited to producing high-tech goods and services in the 21st century. Their specialties include products such as airplanes, computers, high-tech machinery, entertainment, and telecommunications. These products give the United States a comparative advantage over less developed nations.

Some emerging nations have large, unskilled labor forces available at low costs. Labor-intensive industries, which rely on labor as opposed to machinery, do well in such an environment. Emerging nations can produce labor-intensive toys, clothing, and shoes at a lower

● What You'll Learn

- The interdependence of nations
- The benefits of international trade
- How government is involved in international trade
- What balance of trade is
- What trade barriers are
- The signifigance of trade agreements and alliances

● Why It's Important

The global marketplace makes all people and businesses in the world potential customers, as well as potential employees or employers. In this chapter you will explore the key concepts that govern international trade and help create the global marketplace.

● Key Terms

- international trade
- imports
- exports
- absolute advantage
- comparative advantage
- balance of trade
- tariff
- quota
- embargo
- World Trade Organization (WTO)
- North American Free Trade Agreement (NAFTA)
- European Union (EU)

cost than most industrialized nations. They have a comparative advantage when making these goods. It is more cost-effective for high-wage countries, like the United States, to buy those items from emerging nations rather than to make them themselves.

■ Benefits of International Trade

Consumers, producers, workers, and nations benefit from international trade in different ways. Consumers benefit from the competition that the foreign companies offer. This competition encourages the production of high-quality goods with lower prices. The variety of goods increases as more producers market their goods in other countries.

Producers can expand their business by conducting operations in other countries. Much of business for many producers now takes place abroad. Almost one-third of the profits of U.S. businesses comes from international trade and foreign investment.

Workers are another group that benefits from trade. Increased trade leads to higher employment rates both at home and abroad. Exports sustained about six percent of U.S. jobs in the year 2000.

■ **The Flower Market** Holland is known for its beautiful flowers, in part due to its research in flower cultivation, packaging, and shipping know-how. Approximately 59 percent of the world's cut flowers come from Holland. *Would you consider that an absolute advantage?*

You can see how nations as a whole benefit from international trade. Increased foreign investment in a country often improves the standard of living for that country's people. Individuals have more options to choose from when making purchasing decisions. These economic alliances often turn into political alliances. Think of the results of ending relations with a country that is a large market for U.S. exports or one that has many business investments here.

Government Involvement in International Trade

All nations control and monitor their trade with foreign businesses. The U.S. government monitors imports through the customs division of the U.S. Treasury Department. All people and goods that enter the United States from a foreign country are subject to search and review by U.S. customs officials. Other countries also check incoming goods. All U.S. citizens and firms must meet the customs requirements of foreign countries when visiting or exporting goods.

■ **Sold in the U.S.A.** Many foreign-made products are sold in the United States. *What are some consumer benefits of international trade?*

Balance of Trade

Nations must keep track of their trade to be aware of their economic status. The difference in value between exports and imports of a nation is called its balance of trade. A positive balance of trade, or trade surplus, occurs when a nation exports more than it imports. A negative balance of trade, or trade deficit, occurs when a nation imports more than it exports.

Figure 6-1 illustrates the large trade deficit in the United States. This trade gap may seem surprising because the United States is the world's largest exporter. Some analysts believe this situation exists because Americans purchase more goods and services than do people of other nations. Others believe that the United States has started to focus more on providing services than on manufacturing and farming, making it more economical to import goods that were once domestically manufactured.

An unfavorable balance reduces a nation's revenue. When more money leaves a country than comes in, that country becomes a debtor nation. Another effect of a negative balance of trade can be increased unemployment. People may lose their jobs as foreign competitors take business away from domestic firms. Domestic businesses must become competitive or they will fail.

Trade Barriers

A nation's government may impose trade barriers or restrictions when it wants to limit trade. These controls restrict the flow of goods and services among nations. The three main types of trade barriers are tariffs, quotas, and embargoes.

TARIFFS A tariff (sometimes called a duty) is a tax on imports. Tariffs may be used to produce revenue for a country. Revenue-producing tariffs were used in the United States as a primary source of income before income taxes were established in 1913. These tariffs exist today, but they are as low as 25 cents or less per item or pound.

Another type of tariff is protective. A protective tariff is generally high. Its purpose is to increase the price of imported goods so that domestic products can compete with them. This kind of tariff can prevent foreign businesses from trading with the United States. This would protect new domestic industries from foreign competition and domestic jobs.

QUOTAS An import quota limits either the quantity or the monetary value of a product that may be imported. The U.S. government might place a quota on foreign automobiles, limiting the number that may be imported. This controls the amount of a good that enters the economy.

FIGURE 6-1

Trade Deficit

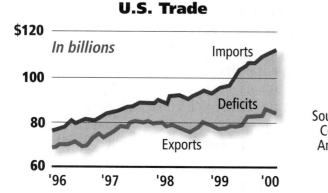

■ **U.S. Trade Deficit** The largest contributors to that trade deficit were countries from the Pacific Rim region. The U.S. trade gap in August 2000 was $29 billion. One effect of a trade deficit is a weaker dollar. *Should that help or hurt U.S. exporters? Why?*

Sometimes one trading partner might voluntarily put quotas on exports to improve relations. Japan placed quotas on its auto exports to the United States to improve trade relations between the two countries.

EMBARGOES An embargo is a total ban on specific goods coming into and leaving a country. A government can impose an embargo for health reasons. The U.S. government embargoed Chilean grapes in 1989 as a precaution after inspectors found poisoned fruit in a shipment. That embargo was lifted within a week.

Embargoes are more often used for political reasons. The United Nations imposed an embargo on Iraq during the Persian Gulf War. The goal of this sanction was to end the war through economic, rather than military, means. The United States still observed that embargo in the early 21st century.

Embargoes based on political differences can continue for a very long time. The United States lifted its 20-year embargo on Vietnam in 1994 so that trade relations could be cultivated between the two nations. The U.S. embargo against Cuba—imposed in 1960 when Fidel Castro created a communist state—still remains in effect. Certain aspects of this embargo were under consideration in 2000; however, there are no plans to completely repeal the embargo.

■ Trade Agreements and Alliances

Governments make agreements with each other to establish guidelines for international trade and to set up trade alliances. Some milestones in the progress toward worldwide free trade are the World Trade Organization, the North American Free Trade Agreement, and the European Union.

THE WORLD TRADE ORGANIZATION The World Trade Organization (WTO) is a global coalition of 135 governments that makes the rules governing international trade. The creation of those rules requires a unanimous vote. This means that agreeing on new rules may take years of negotiating.

The WTO was formed in 1995 as the successor to the General Agreement on Tariffs and Trade (GATT). GATT was an international trade agreement designed to open markets and promote global free trade among agreeing nations. It reduced tariffs and created a common set of trading rules. GATT had no enforcement power, so it created the WTO to police the agreement and resolve disputes among nations.

Understanding Foreign Cultures

If you are considering a career in international marketing, you'll want to learn as much as you can about the cultural norms of other societies. This means understanding other societies' histories, values, lifestyles, and ways of communicating. Learning as much as you can about your target market will help you make the best possible marketing decisions.

Thinking Critically

What are some other ways you can develop a deeper understanding of foreign cultures?

The WTO also manages world trade by studying important trade issues and evaluating the health of the world economy. It addresses the activities that GATT was not able to, including intellectual property rights, investment, and services.

Supporters of the WTO and free trade stress that globalization and the expansion of trade have created enormous wealth in both rich and previously poor countries. Free trade supporters believe global prosperity can be maintained and expanded only through a borderless economy. This requires a set of rules that are universally accepted. Advocates argue that such a system is the only way to ensure fairness and avoid damaging trade wars.

Critics of the WTO raise concerns about democracy, labor rights, and the environment. They charge that the WTO makes decisions affecting all of society on a commercial basis. They do not like the idea of having a non-elected body that has the power to overrule the government on issues of environmental protection and labor rights. Some of the more radical critics want the organization disbanded. Others want to transform it to include social and environmental concerns.

Case Study

The European Union

The European Union (EU) may be the most important regional trade agreement in the world today. Originally called the European Economic Community (EEC), the EU was formed in 1957 in an effort to speed western Europe's economic recovery after World War II. It has grown from six countries in 1957 to 15 countries in 2000, and many more nations have requested membership.

The primary goal of the EU was to create a free trade zone in Europe. The EU's other goal, to have a single currency for Europe, became reality on January 1, 1999, when 11 member nations began using the European Currency Unit (ECU), which is used in setting exchange rates among member nations. In order to participate in the EU's Economic and Monetary Union (EMU), member nations had to satisfy strict economic criteria. Nations with weak economic systems have been excluded from the EMU. In 2002, the Euro hard currency will make its debut, replacing the national currencies of EMU member nations.

Eventually, the EU will have a common currency for over 350 million European consumers. It will rival the United States in market size.

Case Study Review

1. Why was the EU created?
2. What is the Economic and Monetary Union?

A MATTER OF ETHICS

3. Is it ethical for the EU to exclude some member nations from its Economic and Monetary Union?

NORTH AMERICAN FREE TRADE AGREEMENT (NAFTA) The North American Free Trade Agreement (NAFTA) is an international trade agreement among the United States, Canada, and Mexico. It went into effect on January 1, 1994. The principal benefit of NAFTA was increased trade with Mexico.

The goal of NAFTA was to get rid of all trade barriers and investment restrictions among the three countries by 2009. Tariffs were eliminated immediately on more than half of the 9,000 goods traded between Mexico and the United States.

EUROPEAN UNION (EU) The European Union (EU) is the term for Europe's trading bloc. The goal of the EU is to encourage economic integration as a single market. Established by the Maastricht Treaty, the intent of the EU was for free trade among the member nations, as well as for a single European currency and a central bank. Other treaty provisions related to fair competitive practices, environmental and safety standards, and security matters.

Figure 6-2 on page 104 points out those countries that are involved in the EU and NAFTA.

FIGURE 6-2

NAFTA and EU

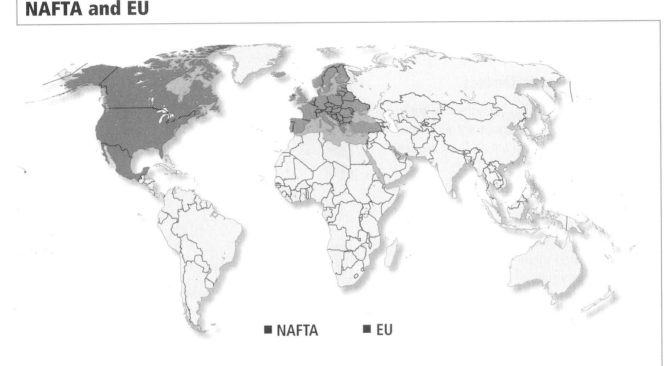

■ NAFTA　　■ EU

■ **International Trade Agreements & Alliances** Depicted on this map are two major trading blocks or markets—NAFTA and the EU. *How do these trade alliances foster free trade?*

6.1 ASSESSMENT

Reviewing Key Terms and Concepts

1. Explain the concept of economic interdependence of nations.

2. Provide an example of comparative advantage and absolute advantage for two different countries.

3. What benefits do consumers and nations derive from international trade?

4. Name three types of trade barriers.

5. What is the common goal or purpose of WTO, NAFTA, and the EU trade agreements?

Thinking Critically

6. What problems occur when trade between nations is not equal? What measures could the United States take in order to reduce its trade deficit with Japan?

Integrating Academic Skills

7. **COMMUNICATION** Translate a magazine ad into a foreign language for international use. Make any changes necessary to promote the product. Present your new ad in class, and report any problems.

International Business

Business Involvement in International Trade

While governments make trade agreements, it is businesses that actually trade with one another. It is important to understand how those businesses operate across international boundaries. There are three basic means of getting involved in international trade—importing, exporting, and setting up shop abroad.

■ Importing

Imports to the United States are subject to more than just the requirements of the U.S. Customs tariff. They must also meet the same standards as domestic products, such as those imposed by the Food and Drug Administration. If these standards are met, most products can be imported without prior government approval. Only special items, such as alcoholic beverages and prescription drugs, require such approval. A quota can also limit entry of certain goods into the country.

Certain imported products may be subject to reduced duties under international trade agreements. Knowing the details of importing is difficult. U.S. businesses usually hire customs brokers, specialists who are licensed by the U.S. Treasury Department. Customs brokers know the different laws, procedures, and tariffs. Customs brokers handle over 90 percent of all imports because of the necessary complex procedures.

■ Exporting

Other nations have similar means of controlling and documenting imports that U.S. businesses must follow when exporting their goods. Most businesses hire international freight forwarders licensed by the U.S. Maritime Commission to handle export details.

You can imagine the risks involved in transporting goods from one country to another. The costs of transportation and insurance needed for these shipments vary greatly. Shipping mink coats would require different handling than shipping steel. It is wise for businesses to purchase special insurance when dealing with international shipments.

■ Setting Up Shop in a Foreign Country

Multinationals are large corporations that have operations in several countries. According to *International Business*, about one-third of the world's private-sector assets are controlled by some 37,000 transnational corporations with over 170,000 foreign affiliates (see Figure 6-3 on page 106).

• What You'll Learn

- How businesses can get involved in international trade
- The standard business practices involved in importing and exporting
- The cultural, economic, and political factors that should be considered when deciding whether to do business abroad

• Why It's Important

Doing business in a foreign country can be very different than doing business in the United States. Besides language barriers, there are many other factors that must be considered in international business. Costly problems may arise without this understanding.

Key Terms

- customs brokers
- freight forwarders
- multinationals
- mini-nationals
- joint ventures
- customization
- globalization
- nationalize

FIGURE 6-3

World's Top 25 Companies, as of April 2000

Company	Country	Sector
General Electric	US	Electrical Equipment
Cisco Systems	US	Telecommunications Equipment
Intel	US	Semiconductors
Microsoft	US	Software
NTT Docomo	Japan	Wireless Telecommunication Services
Vodafone Airtouch	UK	Telecommunication Services
Exxon Mobil	US	Oil
Wal-Mart Stores	US	Discount Stores
Nokia	Finland	Telecommunications Equipment
Citigroup	US	Banks
NTT	Japan	Fixed-line Telecommunications Services
Oracle	US	Software
Deutsche Telekom	Germany	Fixed-line Telecommunications Services
Toyota Motor	Japan	Automobiles
Royal Dutch/Shell	Netherlands/UK	Oil
Lucent Technologies	US	Telecommunications Equipment
BP Amoco	UK	Oil
Intl Business Machines	US	Computer Hardware
AIG Group	US	Insurance
Pfizer	US	Pharmaceuticals
Merck	US	Pharmaceuticals
Ericsson	Sweden	Telecommunications Equipment
France Telecom	France	Fixed-line Telecommunications Services
AT & T	US	Fixed-line Telecommunications Services
Sun Microsystems	US	Computer Hardware

■ **International Business** All the companies listed in this table have subsidiaries or operations in many countries. *How many of these companies do you recognize?*

Mini-nationals are midsize and smaller companies that have operations in foreign countries. The key characteristic that sets multinationals and mini-nationals apart from domestic businesses is foreign investments in factories, offices, and other facilities abroad that are used for operations. These investments are referred to as foreign direct investments (FDI). Some countries attract more FDI than others.

Direct investment is only possible if you have a domestic partner in some countries. Foreign investors are not permitted to own 100 percent of a business in these countries. Such partnerships, called joint ventures, allow companies to participate in a country's economy with a partner. This is often a good idea even when not mandated by law. Domestic business partners know the market and procedures for conducting business in their own country. This is how many U.S. fast-food chains have granted franchises to companies in foreign countries.

Often joint ventures are formed on a country-by-country basis. Royal Crown Cola is one example of a company that forms many relationships with companies in different countries. In one year, they entered the markets in Mexico, Argentina, Syria, Portugal, Australia, and Indonesia.

Globetrotters: UPS

United Parcel Service, the U.S. parcel delivery company with the trademark brown uniforms and trucks, now covers the globe. It already has 17,000 trucks in Europe and lands 300 intercontinental flights daily. UPS has purchased a French postal operation and is thinking about buying a partner in Asia to continue its expansion plans. Despite overseas growth at double-digit rates, UPS still has some cultural obstacles to overcome. Driving a truck was once considered a demeaning job in Germany; and in France, UPS acquired a tombstone delivery company.

Thinking Critically
Why do you think UPS is concentrating on overseas advancement?

Special Considerations in International Business

When doing business internationally, companies must be aware of many special considerations, such as differences in language and customs as well as political and legal considerations (see Figure 6-4 on page 108).

▪ Cultural Factors

Differences in language and culture make international trade more challenging than doing business at home. When General Motors tried to sell its Chevrolet Nova in South America sales did not meet expectations. The reason? The words *no va* in Spanish mean "No go!"

Social and business etiquette is important when doing business abroad. A common practice in one country may take on a different meaning elsewhere. You would not want to cross your legs in Japan because showing the bottom of your feet is considered rude. Gift giving is another area of concern. A gift may be considered part of business etiquette in the Far East; however, it might seem to be an illegal bribe in the United States or Canada.

Building a relationship before doing business is important in Japan and other Asian countries. It is best to plan a night of dinner and entertainment without any mention of business when conducting business in those countries. Once a personal relationship has been established, then business may be discussed. It is important for you to be aware of these cultural differences before a big business meeting.

▪ Economic Factors

You should consider the key factors of economic cost when considering starting up a business in another country. These include infrastructure, cost of labor, taxes, and currency exchange rates. You should also consider the population's standard of living if you want to sell goods in another country.

Infrastructure can be a deciding factor. Things like undependable telephone service or inadequate roads would rule out a location for some businesses. These same factors would be an opportunity for other companies involved in building roads, energy plants, and telecommunications systems.

The quality and cost of the labor force also should be reviewed. You would want to know the educational and skill levels of the workers, as well as the customary wages and employment laws. Employers are responsible for paying a fair amount for mandated employee benefits above and beyond wages in some countries.

Other costs include taxes. Taxes on property and profits are common. Countries that want to attract foreign investment may offer reduced taxes for a period of time as an incentive.

Standard of living can be a consideration if a business is eyeing a country as a market rather than a manufacturing site. When Honda entered China's consumer market, it recognized that most Chinese people could not afford cars. The company targeted the motorcycle market instead and was very successful.

BRIGHT IDEAS

SOS Spells International Rescue

Imagine being in China on business and suddenly facing a medical emergency, or being caught in Rome during a terrorist attack. What would you do? International SOS to the rescue! International SOS began in 1974 as a provider of emergency services to business travelers. The company now operates offices in more than 30 cities around the globe. The need for emergency assistance is greater than ever with the increasing amount of necessary business travel; many companies pay International SOS a fee to have emergency assistance available worldwide. SOS will go into an emergency situation and provide immediate medical care and assistance including transportation and exit clearances if needed.

Thinking Creatively

How might handling international emergencies differ from handling emergencies in the United States?

FIGURE 6-4

CUSTOMIZATION VS. GLOBALIZATION

When marketing products in foreign countries, companies must make product and promotion decisions. Some companies create completely new products for specific countries (customization), while others do not change anything about their product or their promotions (globalization). Between the two are companies that keep their products' brand names while varying their products and/or promotions enough to meet local tastes. Here are some examples of each.

Fuerza Ford para tu vida.

Con sus convenientes cuatro puertas estándar, toda la familia está invitada a pasear.

Ford
Espíritu de Superación
www.fordespiritu.com

PROMOTION ADAPTATION

Many companies do not change their products, only their promotions to better meet the foreign customers' way of thinking. Ford adapted its advertising message because the one it used in the United States would not be interpreted the same way by Spanish speakers.

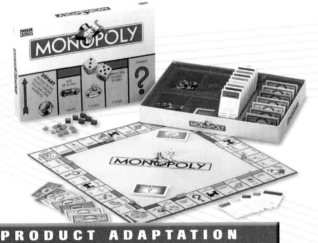

PRODUCT ADAPTATION

Changing a product in some way to make it more appropriate for a country's preferences is a product adaptation strategy. Monopoly is the world's favorite board game. It is available in 25 languages.

CUSTOMIZATION

Customization is inventing a totally new product for a different country's market. Swanson creates soups for different palates around the world. Watercress and Duck Gizzard Soup is a favorite in China.

GLOBALIZATION

Globalization is keeping the product and advertising message the same around the world. Its benefit is global brand recognition. Coca-Cola does not change its products or its ad message for the global market.

The number of middle income workers is increasing in poorer nations in the 21st century. This increases the demand for all types of ordinary consumer goods. U.S. consumer products like soaps, detergents, breakfast cereals, snack foods, and soft drinks are gaining popularity among consumers in emerging nations.

Finally, the exchange rate for a nation's currency based on the U.S. dollar is an important factor to consider. Changes in a nation's currency exchange affect businesses that sell abroad. If a product has a high price in U.S. dollars and is converted into an even higher price on the international market, it may be difficult to attract customers.

■ Political and Legal Factors

A government's stability is an important factor when considering international business operations. There is always the possibility that new rulers might nationalize private property in countries where military takeovers or popular revolutions are common. When a country nationalizes property, the government takes ownership, and the owners generally get nothing in return. Bolivia, for example, nationalized all of its businesses in the early 1950s. You can imagine how costly this would be today

when businesses routinely invest millions of dollars in buildings and equipment.

An unstable government can create problems for a business's employees as well. Business executives may be used as political pawns in countries where political corruption is common. There may be unspoken rules or practices that must be learned. Payoffs to government officials are the only means of getting necessary licenses or approval to conduct business in some countries. The political climate of a county may change very quickly. This can be difficult for businesses to keep up with. There are companies that monitor political situations on a country-by-country basis. Such companies maintain databases that contain information about each country including new laws, the political climate, and potential risk.

Countries that want to be part of the global marketplace, however, may encourage foreign investment. These governments offer stability and support to businesses. They may be moving toward a market economy by privatizing state-run industries. They may reduce tariffs, develop laws to protect intellectual property, and increase the percentage of business ownership allowed by foreign investors (see Figure 6-5).

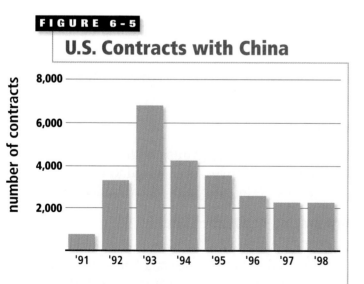

FIGURE 6-5

U.S. Contracts with China

■ **U.S. Investments in China** This graph shows that U.S. companies have been cutting down on their investments in China. *With China being one of the largest potential markets in the world, why do you think companies are reluctant to invest?*

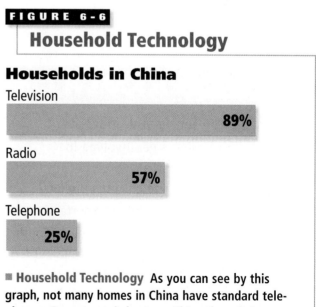

FIGURE 6-6

Household Technology

Households in China

Television — 89%
Radio — 57%
Telephone — 25%

■ **Household Technology** As you can see by this graph, not many homes in China have standard telephones. One reason is because China doesn't have adequate infrastructure, which makes the cost of telephone service very high. *What type of phone is selling like hotcakes in China because of this?*

■ Technological Factors

Technology is changing the ways that businesses can get involved in international trade. When studying a country's technology, you need to look at the use of computers, faxes, voice mail, cellular phones, and the Internet. Some countries, like Finland and the United States, are already well connected, while emerging countries are just beginning to adapt to technological advances (see Figure 6-6 on page 109).

Underlying any economic environment is its technological base—the technical equipment and technical skills and knowledge of the people. The technological base of a country has a great affect on the availability of opportunities.

In general, complex and sophisticated industries are found in countries with advanced levels of technology, while more basic industries are found in countries with lower levels of technology. People in technologically advanced nations have higher incomes than people in less technologically developed markets.

When researching the level of technology in a country, even the most basic technologies should be taken into consideration. Factors such as measurement systems and electric voltage standards can be important. A business cannot assume that the same technology that is available in its home country is available or used in other countries.

Electronic Frontiers

Business to Business: Cutting Costs through Online Ordering

While many of us think of consumer sites like Amazon and CDNOW when it comes to the Internet, business-to-business Internet purchases are 10 or more times larger than consumer purchases. Businesses have found that conducting business on the Internet can streamline operations and cut costs. Consider the example of BOC Company in New Jersey. It places its product orders online and within seconds, its Japanese supplier receives the million-dollar orders. No phone calls or faxes are required, nor are any invoices or shipping orders necessary. Key personnel can access order status instantly, which trims correspondence, processing time, and the chance for human error.

Thinking Critically

What are the advantages to conducting business over the Internet?

6.2 ASSESSMENT

Reviewing Key Terms and Concepts

1. How can a business get involved in international trade?

2. Why do importers use customs brokers?

3. What type of business helps exporters?

4. What difficulty did Chevrolet have in South America with its Nova model automobile?

5. How can a country's poor infrastructure create opportunities for foreign businesses?

Thinking Critically

6. Do you see anything wrong with countries that offer incentives, such as reduced taxes, to foreign investors but not to local businesses?

Integrating Academic Skills

7. **MATH** Assume the currency exchange rate between the United States and Canada is 1.25, which means one U.S. dollar is equal to $1.25 in Canadian currency. How much would a $20 T-shirt cost a U.S. citizen shopping in Montreal?

Careers in Marketing

INTERNATIONAL MARKETING

Sigrid Ann Davison
International Sales
Marketing Director

Career Facts

Education and Training: A degree in international business, or an MBA, and marketing experience is good preparation.

Aptitudes, Abilities, and Skills: Excellent communication skills and an appreciation of other cultures, as well as an ability to travel, flexibility, good decision-making skills, organizational skills, and leadership skills are required.

Career Outlook: Opportunities are expected to increase faster than average with the increased use of Internet technology.

Career Path: Product management, team management, marketing positions, and extensive travel can lead to a career in international marketing. International marketing specialists can advance to VP of international sales.

What does your job entail?

"I am responsible for the sales, marketing, and distribution of motion pictures and television products in the international marketplace. This involves licensing all individual media rights in foreign countries. Most transactions occur at international film markets, including the American Film Market in Los Angeles, the Cannes Film Festival in France, the London Premiere Screening in England, and MIFED in Milan, Italy. Once media rights have been licensed and sold to distributors, the filmmaking begins. I then put together the marketing strategy, including advertising (posters, artwork, trailers, and TV spots), publicity, and promotion, on a territory-by-territory basis. When the film is completed, I oversee the release in each country."

What training do you recommend for students?

"I recommend a bachelor's degree, or preferably a master's degree specializing in international marketing. A knowledge of foreign languages is helpful. Try to start out in a company that handles the type of product or service in which you want to specialize."

What do you like most about your job?

"My favorite aspect of my job is the international travel, which enables me to have business dealings with people all over the world. Not all cultures conduct business in the same manner as the United States, and it is fascinating to figure out the best way to achieve a positive outcome in both sales and marketing."

What is your key to success?

"My key to success—hard work, hard work, and hard work! A willingness to roll up my sleeves and tackle everything that needs to be done, from mundane tasks to challenging international marketing problems, is necessary. I try to learn as much as I can about all aspects of the entertainment industry. Finally, I make a conscious effort to treat everyone I work with and for with respect—in a way that I would want to be treated."

Thinking Critically
How might a strong sense of humor be useful in any job?

Chapter 6 ASSESSMENT

VOCABULARY REVIEW

For each group of terms, write a paragraph explaining the relation of each term to the heading.

- **International Trade:** balance of trade, imports, exports, absolute advantage, comparative advantage, multinationals, mini-nationals, customization, globalization
- **Trade Concerns:** tariff, quota, embargo, joint ventures, customs, brokers, freight forwarders, nationalize
- **Trade Alliances:** World Trade Organization (WTO), North American Free Trade Agreement (NAFTA), European Union (EU)

FACT AND IDEA REVIEW

1. Why do nations trade globally? (6.1)

2. How do producers and workers benefit from international trade? (6.1)

3. Why is it surprising that the United States has a negative balance of trade? (6.1)

4. What are trade barriers? (6.1)

5. What organization was established to police the GATT treaty? (6.1)

6. Compare multinationals to mini-nationals. (6.2)

7. How do the marketing strategies of customization and globalization differ? (6.2)

8. Cite three examples of cultural factors that can make doing business abroad more difficult. (6.2)

9. Cite an economic factor and a political factor that could discourage a business from engaging in international trade. (6.2)

10. What impact can technology have on doing business abroad? (6.2)

THINKING CRITICALLY

1. How have you personally benefited from international trade?

2. Assume a South Korean company sold hair dryers in the United States below market prices. To retaliate, the United States increased tariffs on South Korean automobiles. How would that hurt U.S. consumers and U.S. auto franchisees who carry South Korean autos?

3. When a Japanese investor bought New York City's Rockefeller Center in the 1980s, it brought out xenophobia in many U.S. citizens. Xenophobia is a distrust of foreigners. Since foreign investment is supposed to be good for a country, why do you think these people reacted this way?

4. What measures could a business take to avoid cultural blunders if it wants to get involved in international trade?

5. What are the advantages and disadvantages of international trade?

BUILDING WORKPLACE SKILLS

1. **Human Relations** A customer in your store wants to buy a silk blouse that matches her outfit perfectly. However, the blouse is made in China and she has told you that she only buys American-made products. What would you do?

2. **Public Speaking** You have been asked to make a presentation to the foreign language club on the need for bilingual employees in business. In your presentation, discuss the need to understand different cultures when marketing products in foreign countries.

APPLYING MARKETING CONCEPTS

1. **Summarizing Marketing Concepts** Using a word processing program, summarize an article related to one topic in this chapter. Review publications such as *International Business*, *The Economist*, *BusinessWeek*, *Forbes*, and *Fortune*.

2. **Understanding NAFTA** The NAFTA agreement had many supporters, but there were many people who debated the effects that it would have on Americans. Using the Internet and business magazines, research both sides of this debate. Write a report using a word processing program discussing the viewpoints of those who supported NAFTA and those who were against it. Then give your own opinion based on your research.

3. **Researching Exporting Patterns** International trade provides people access to goods from all over the world. Research the top exports for the following countries: Japan, China, Mexico, India, the United States, France, and Switzerland. Using presentation software, prepare an oral report of your findings. Present your report to your class.

4. **Analyzing Foreign Trade Alliances** Using a word processing program, write a report that explains the trend among multinationals to forge strategic alliances with foreign companies. What are the reasons for these alliances, and what have been the outcomes?

LINKING SCHOOL TO WORK

Thinking and Information Skills Ask an employer if his or her company is involved in international trade. Find out the particulars of its involvement. You can ask companies that are not involved with foreign trade if there are any products manufactured by foreign companies sold by the business. Write a short report of your findings, and share it with your classmates.

THE DECA CONNECTION

Role Play: Marketing Intern

Situation You are to assume the role of an intern in a marketing firm that specializes in international trade. You have been asked to be part of an extensive training program for firm employees doing business in Japan.

Activity Your task is to instruct your fellow employees in the proper way to exchange business cards. Your supervisor (judge) wants to see your presentation before you begin this training program with others.

Evaluation You will be evaluated on how well you meet the following performance indicators:

- Identify the impact of cultural and social environments on world trade
- Develop cultural sensitivity
- Make oral presentations
- Give directions for completing job tasks
- Foster positive working relationships

inter NET CONNECTION

The Emerald Isle

You are a travel agent and your client wants to go on a vacation to Ireland.

Connect

- Use the Internet to plan a written itinerary for your client, who wants information on major cities, castles, the Blarney Stone, and golf.

the Zazz Lab

A Sports and Entertainment Marketing Simulation

WELCOME

Welcome to Zazz Sports and Entertainment Marketing Company. Zazz is devoted to serving the needs of its clients who include college, university, and professional sports teams, professional athletes, sporting events, and sports arenas plus major consumer product corporations, as well as television networks and movie studios. As an intern, you will have the opportunity to work on different clients' projects. All of your work will be assigned and reviewed by your department supervisor.

PLAN A ROCK GROUP WORLD TOUR

SITUATION

Zazz would like to arrange a world tour for a popular rock group to make money and support a worthy cause. Zazz is willing to guarantee $25 million to the rock group if they play 25 shows outside the United States with at least two shows performed in developing countries. The net proceeds from ticket sales will have the following breakdown: 80 percent to the rock group, 10 percent to Zazz, and 10 percent to the chosen cause. The breakdown for merchandising (sale of programs, T-shirts, etc.) will be 80 percent for the rock group and 20 percent for Zazz.

ASSIGNMENT

Your supervisor wants you to suggest the rock group that will have the highest potential for success, as well as the best cause to benefit from the tour. Careful selection of the countries to tour is crucial to ensure that the $25 million guarantee is covered and that Zazz makes a profit.

Tools and Resources

To complete this assignment, you will need to conduct research at a library or on the Internet. You will also need a word processing program, a map of the world, and presentation software. Magazines that report on rock groups and their tours, such as *Rolling Stone* or *Spin*, may be helpful.

Research

Research popular rock groups and worthy causes that have universal appeal, such as AIDS or cancer research, or hunger. Review past record and concert sales as well as new album releases. Review the itinerary and ticket prices of current rock group tours to see how they are organized and what venues are used (stadiums, open fields, arenas). To select the best cities and to determine appropriate ticket prices, you must research economic factors such as the unemployment rate, inflation rate, productivity level, and currency exchange rate. Review the demographics of each tour city, including population by age and average household income. To determine the itinerary, research travel distances between cities and the proximity of countries you want to include in the tour. Research normal weather patterns, which will impact venue selection and travel considerations.

Report

Prepare a written report and a computer presentation. Use a word-processing program to prepare a double-spaced report. Prepare a table with a heading and introduction in the text, showing the current rock group tours you researched. Prepare a map that identifies the tour destinations and dates of your proposed itinerary. Arrange your report around the following headings:

- Current rock group tours
  - Name and description of three current tours
    - Popularity of group
    - Targeted audience
    - Album being promoted (if any)
    - Cities, countries, venues, and ticket prices
- Proposed rock group
  - Popularity of group
  - Targeted audience
  - Album being promoted (if any)
- Proposed cause or charity to benefit from tour
  - Description of cause or charity
  - Rationale for selection
  - Relationship or fit with suggested rock group
- Proposed tour itinerary
  - Countries selected
    - Industrialized nations
    - Developing countries (two)
    - Map showing the location of all concert sites
- Rationale for cities and countries selected
  - Economic factors
  - Demographic factors
  - Proximity to other countries in tour
  - Weather patterns
  - Conflict with other rock group tours
  - Cultural and religious considerations
- Itinerary—(table)
  - Dates
  - Cities, countries, venues, and ticket prices
  - Travel distance between cities (time and mileage)
- Conclusion
  - Potential ease in marketing this tour
    - Tour theme
    - Media selection (i.e. television, radio, magazine, Web site)
    - Tour promotion
  - Potential revenue generated from the tour

Using computer presentation software, prepare a presentation of your ideas for your supervisor that includes:

- Key topics covered in your written report
- Graphic illustrations that are relevant to each slide's topic
- Very little text
- A minimum of 10 slides

Presentation and Evaluation

Your supervisor wants you to present your ideas in a written report and an oral presentation. Your oral evaluation will be based on the following:

- Knowledge of rock group tours
- Selection of a worthy cause/charity
- Knowledge of other countries' economics, demographics, and cultural differences
- Realistic planning of the itinerary
- Ability to persuade others
- Continuity of presentation
- Voice quality
- Eye contact

Portfolio
. . . .
Print out a copy of your completed report and presentation for your Portfolio.

THE DECA CONNECTION

DECA Business Services Marketing Series
Recommending prices and marketing ideas for a rock concert tour could be a role play in this event.

DECA Marketing Management Series
Developing business proposals is part of this career area.

DECA Business and Financial Marketing Research Event
Conducting research for a proposed rock concert tour could be a topic for this written research event.

DECA Sports and Entertainment Marketing Management Team Decision-Making Event
Planning a rock concert tour could be a potential topic for this event.

Portfolio

Handle Customer Complaints

To demonstrate mastery of the content in this unit, you will consider customer service and human relations skills from both angles. You will use a word processing program to compose two letters, following the guidelines for a business letter. The first letter is a letter of complaint to a manufacturer regarding a defective product or to a restaurant regarding recent poor service. Switch letters with a classmate and compose a response to his or her complaint showing the appropriate way to handle an angry or unhappy customer.

Academic Concepts and Skills

Unit Overview

The first three units introduced you to economics, business, and marketing. In this unit, you will learn some of the real world skills that you will need to succeed in a career in marketing.

In Chapter 7, you will review basic skills in math that you may not have used for a while, but will be needed in a marketing career. In Chapter 8, you will see that there is much more to listening than just hearing, and you will learn how to listen to understand the message. In Chapter 9, you will learn new things about computer technology—the fastest-growing field the world has ever known. Chapter 10 will help you in your interpersonal relationships on the job, and Chapter 11 will provide a background in management skills.

In this Unit:

Foundations of Marketing

- Communication, Interpersonal Skills
- Professional Development
- Business, Management, Entrepreneurship

Chapter 7

Basic Math Skills

Marketing: What It Takes

Room for One More?

You are considering opening your own bookkeeping and accounting business. You have a good understanding of basic math and you like working with numbers. You enjoyed your high school bookkeeping class so much that you've taken some accounting courses at the local city college. You feel confident that you could do a good job for your clients, but you're wondering if there is a large enough market for your new business. You are also concerned about the competition you would have to face.

WHAT WILL YOU DO?

How can you determine whether there is a market for your new business venture? How and what can you learn about your competition?

Math Fundamentals

Writing Whole Numbers

The numbering system we use is composed of ten basic symbols: 0, 1, 2, 3, 4, 5, 6, 7, 8, and 9. These symbols are called **digits**. Each digit represents a number and can be combined to represent larger numbers, such as 14; 215; 7,901; and 36,852.

The numbers above are all whole numbers because they can be written without fractions or decimals. Each digit in a whole number represents *how many* of something. The digit on the right represents the number of *ones*. The next digit represents the number of *tens*. So, in the number 25, there are five *ones* and two *tens*.

Knowing the placement name for each digit and for groups of digits is necessary for reading numbers and writing them in words. You use this skill, for example, when you write a check. The check format requires that amounts be written in both figures and words. Follow these five steps when you read whole numbers or write them in words.

1. Separate the number into groups of three digits: units, thousands, and millions. Very large numbers may include groups of digits for billions, trillions, and so on.

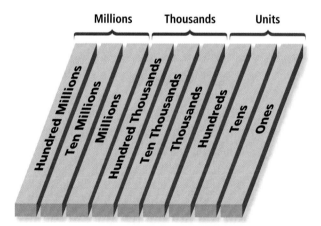

2. Separate the groups with commas.

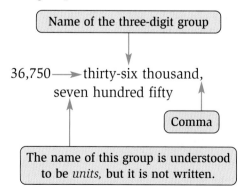

What You'll Learn

- **How to write numbers in words using commas and hyphens correctly**
- **How to understand and know the meaning of fractional amounts**
- **How to perform basic math operations with decimal numbers**
- **How to round answers, especially amounts of money**
- **How to convert fractions to decimal equivalents**

Why It's Important

Virtually every job in marketing and business requires a good understanding of math fundamentals. Many young people have skipped over some of the basic skills. Others need a review to provide a good foundation in math. In this section, you will have an opportunity to sharpen your math skills.

Key Terms

- digits
- fractions
- numerator
- denominator
- mixed number
- decimal number

3. When writing whole numbers, never use the word *and*.

360 ⟶ three hundred sixty

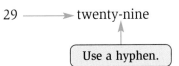

No *and*

4. Use hyphens in numbers less than 100 that are written as two words.

29 ⟶ twenty-nine

Use a hyphen.

5. When a three-digit group is made up of only zeros, do not write the name of the group.

3,000,375 ⟶ three million, three hundred seventy-five

No words are written for the thousands group.

■ **Everyday Math** Despite the rising popularity of ATM and debit card machines as a form of payment, there are still times when you will write out a check the old-fashioned way. This is an example of when everyday math skills are necessary. *Can you think of other daily activities that require an understanding of mathematical foundations?*

Fractions

You learned about fractions when you were in grade school, but you may not have had much practice using them. Many jobs in business, especially in marketing, require a good understanding of fractions.

Fractions are numbers used to describe a part of some standard amount. The top number, the numerator, represents the number of parts being considered. The bottom number, the denominator, represents how many parts in a whole or how many *total* parts are being considered. For example, the shaded area in the rectangle below is $\frac{3}{5}$ (three-fifths) of the total rectangle.

Numerator, the number of parts being considered

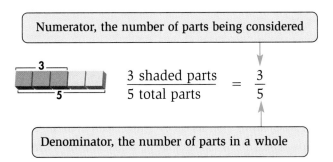

$$\frac{3 \text{ shaded parts}}{5 \text{ total parts}} = \frac{3}{5}$$

Denominator, the number of parts in a whole

In the example below, the number of circles is $\frac{2}{7}$ (two-sevenths) of the total number of shapes.

$$\frac{2 \text{ circles}}{7 \text{ shapes}} = \frac{2}{7}$$

Here are more examples illustrating the same principle. The answers represent the number of *shaded* parts.

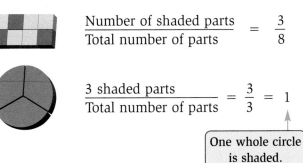

$$\frac{\text{Number of shaded parts}}{\text{Total number of parts}} = \frac{3}{8}$$

$$\frac{3 \text{ shaded parts}}{\text{Total number of parts}} = \frac{3}{3} = 1$$

One whole circle is shaded.

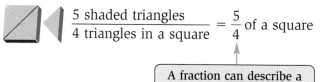

$$\frac{5 \text{ shaded triangles}}{4 \text{ triangles in a square}} = \frac{5}{4} \text{ of a square}$$

> A fraction can describe a number greater than 1.

When the numerator is greater than the denominator, the fraction describes a number greater than 1. It can be written as a **mixed number**, a whole number and fraction together.

$$\frac{6}{5} = 1\frac{1}{5}$$

← Mixed number

Numerator is greater than denominator.

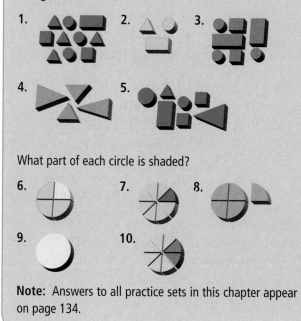

PRACTICE 1

What fraction of the total number of shapes are triangles?

1. 2. 3.

4. 5.

What part of each circle is shaded?

6. 7. 8.

9. 10.

Note: Answers to all practice sets in this chapter appear on page 134.

Decimal Numbers

A **decimal number** is a fraction or mixed number whose denominator is a multiple of 10. The decimal number 5.3 means $5 + 0.3$ or $5 + \frac{3}{10}$ or $5\frac{3}{10}$. The decimal number 935.47 can be broken down as $900 + 30 + 5 + \frac{4}{10} + \frac{7}{100}$.

Knowing placement names is necessary for reading decimals and writing them in words. Decimal placement names apply to digits to the right of the decimal point.

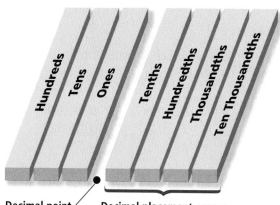

Decimal point / Decimal placement names

To read a decimal number or write it in words, follow the steps below. Use 15.083 as an example.

1. Begin with the whole number to the left of the decimal point *(fifteen)*.

2. Read or write *and* for the decimal point.

3. Read or write the number to the right of the decimal point as a whole number *(eighty-three)*.

4. Use the name of the decimal place of the final digit *(thousandths)*.

The result is *fifteen and eighty-three thousandths*.

There is another way to read numbers with decimal points. You may also hear decimal numbers read using the whole number and only the names of the digits in the decimal places, with *point* for the decimal point. For example, 9.7 could also be read as *nine point seven*; 15.083 might be read as *fifteen point zero eight three*.

Why is it important for you not only to know how to write decimals and fractions, but to understand the relationship between the two as well? Understanding the relationship between decimal numbers and fractions is important when you are writing a check. After writing the amount in decimal form, you must write it again, using words for the dollars and a fraction for the cents.

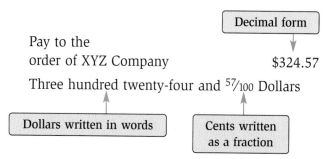

Decimal form

Pay to the
order of XYZ Company $324.57

Three hundred twenty-four and $\frac{57}{100}$ Dollars

Dollars written in words   Cents written as a fraction

Write the decimal numbers in words. Write the amounts of money (as indicated by $) as you would on a check.

1. 5.6
2. 0.7
3. 14.5
4. 0.09
5. 3.12
6. 9.05
7. 10.33
8. 25.48
9. $155.87
10. $545.67

■ Adding and Subtracting Decimal Numbers

To add or subtract decimal numbers, first list the numbers vertically, keeping the decimal points in line with each other. Then add or subtract as you would with whole numbers. Sometimes you may need to write zeros to fill a column.

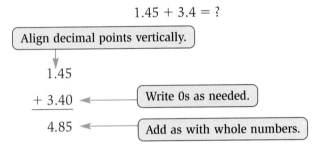

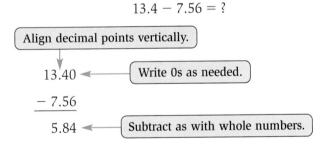

■ Multiplying Decimal Numbers

To multiply decimal numbers, use the following two-step process.

1. Multiply the two numbers as if they were whole numbers. Pay no attention to the decimal points yet.

2. Add the number of decimal places in the two numbers being multiplied. Then, *working from the right,* count off the same number of decimal places in the product and insert the decimal point. *Note:* When counting off places from the right, you may have to add a zero in order to place the decimal point.

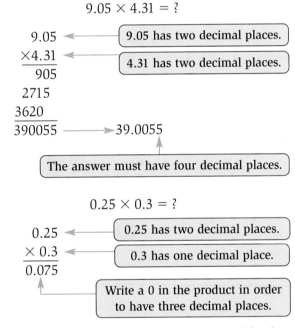

Multiply amounts of money as you would other decimal numbers. Remember to include the dollar sign in your answer.

$$\begin{array}{r} \$4.98 \\ \times\ \ \ \ 2 \\ \hline \$9.96 \end{array}$$

Write the dollar sign.

Complete the following addition and subtraction problems with decimal numbers.

1. 5.4 + 8.6 =
2. 7.5 + 9.6 =
3. 9.8 + 7.5 =
4. 18 + 7.7 =
5. 17.5 + 4.75 =
6. 7.04 + 71.5 =
7. 6.7 + 0.6 + 2.67 + 7 =
8. 4.6 − 3.3 =
9. 45.9 − 7.76 =
10. $8 − $3.76 =
11. 5.7 − 1.11 + 14.078 =
12. 23.6 − 8.431 =

13. Bob's Bicycle Shop paid the following bills in September: $86.45 for gas, $114.86 for electricity, $187.58 for telephone, $98.36 for insurance, and $875 for rent. What is the total?

14. From a 40-yard bolt of fabric, Carol sold the following pieces: 3.33 yards, 4.5 yards, 2.25 yards, 2.125 yards, and 3.875 yards. How many yards are left?

■ Rounding Decimal Numbers

Sometimes you may have to round a decimal number. This is especially common when multiplying with amounts of money, as when figuring tax amounts, discounts, and so on.

Use the following steps to round decimal amounts. Round 16.842, 16.852, and 16.892 to the nearest tenth.

1. Find the decimal place you are rounding to.

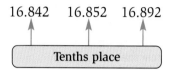

16.842   16.852   16.892

Tenths place

2. Look at the digit to the right of that place.

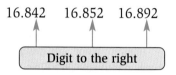

16.842   16.852   16.892

Digit to the right

3. If the digit to the right is less than 5, leave the first digit as is. If the digit is 5 or greater, round up.

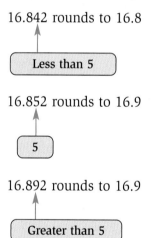

16.842 rounds to 16.8

Less than 5

16.852 rounds to 16.9

5

16.892 rounds to 16.9

Greater than 5

When you are working with amounts of money, use the same steps to round your answer to the nearest cent (the nearest hundredth).

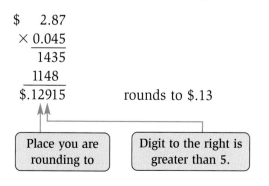

$\begin{array}{r} \$\quad 2.87 \\ \times\ 0.045 \\ \hline 1435 \\ 1148 \\ \hline \$.12915 \end{array}$ rounds to \$.13

Place you are rounding to   Digit to the right is greater than 5.

PRACTICE 4

Complete the following multiplication problems with decimal numbers. Round any amounts of money to the nearest cent.

1. 5.2
    × 7

2. 6.1
    ×4.6

3. 31.4
    × 7.8

4. 31.6
    × 6.3

5. 5.08
    × 0.68

6. 7.75
    × 3.2

7. 0.687
    × 8.02

8. $8.5 \times 7.2 =$

9. $0.83 \times 0.04 =$

10. If you earn \$8.75 an hour, how much pay should you receive for 39.5 hours of work?

11. At Big Al's Pizza, the cost of delivering orders is \$.41 per mile. If the delivery van averaged 458.7 miles per day last week, what is the average daily cost of making deliveries?

■ Dividing Decimal Numbers

Division of decimal numbers is similar to division of whole numbers. Follow the steps below to divide decimal numbers.

1. Set up the division problem as you would with whole numbers.

69.7 divided by 1.7 = $1.7\overline{)69.7}$

69.7 divided by 1.724 = $1.724\overline{)69.7}$

2. Shift the decimal point in the divisor so that the divisor becomes a whole number. Then shift the decimal point in the dividend the same number of decimal places. Write zeros in the dividend, if necessary, in order to place the decimal point.

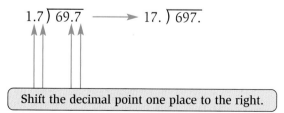

$1.7\overline{)69.7}$ ⟶ $17.\overline{)697.}$

Shift the decimal point one place to the right.

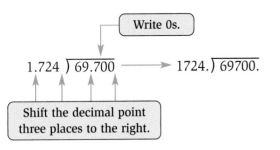

Write 0s.

$1.724\overline{)69.700}$ → $1724.\overline{)69700.}$

Shift the decimal point three places to the right.

3. Place a decimal point in the answer space directly above its new position in the dividend. Then divide as with whole numbers.

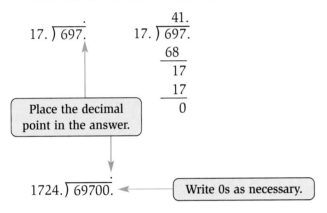

$17.\overline{)697.}$

$$\begin{array}{r} 41. \\ 17.\overline{)697.} \\ \underline{68} \\ 17 \\ \underline{17} \\ 0 \end{array}$$

Place the decimal point in the answer.

$1724.\overline{)69700.}$ ← Write 0s as necessary.

Sometimes you may need to write extra zeros after the decimal point in order to have a remainder of zero.

$$16.38 \div 6.5 = ?$$

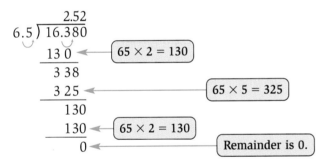

$$\begin{array}{r} 2.52 \\ 6.5\overline{)16.380} \\ \underline{13\ 0} \\ 3\ 38 \\ \underline{3\ 25} \\ 130 \\ \underline{130} \\ 0 \end{array}$$

$65 \times 2 = 130$

$65 \times 5 = 325$

$65 \times 2 = 130$

Remainder is 0.

Electronic Frontiers

Divide and Conquer

The way a computer looks at and sorts data takes more than just a speedy processor. A set of instructions is required to solve complex problems, so an algorithm is created to make sense of the masses of data. An algorithm is a new way of looking at an old problem. Online marketing departments collect huge amounts of data from their customers by tracking information such as customer purchases from frequently visited Web pages. Companies use this information to personalize their Web sites or adjust their pricing. An analyst would not be able to look at every bit of information accurately; instead, algorithms are created to regroup, divide, and merge information into more easily classifiable units. This method of dividing tasks and then regrouping them saves time for individuals and the company as a whole. Algorithms to the rescue!

Thinking Critically
What use do algorithms have in marketing?

Some decimal answers will continue infinitely as you write zeros to the right of the decimal point. *Repeating decimals* will repeat a number or pattern of numbers.

These digits repeat.

$$\begin{array}{r} 2.0333 \\ 3\overline{)6.1000} \\ \underline{6} \\ 10 \\ \underline{9} \\ 10 \\ \underline{9} \\ 10 \\ \underline{9} \\ 1 \end{array} \qquad \begin{array}{r} 0.2727 \\ 11\overline{)3.0000} \\ \underline{2\ 2} \\ 80 \\ \underline{77} \\ 30 \\ \underline{22} \\ 80 \\ \underline{7} \\ 3 \end{array}$$

There is never a remainder of 0.

PRACTICE 5

Do the following division problems. Round answers to the nearest hundredth.

1. $0.75 \div 1.8 =$ **4.** $8.4 \div 0.015 =$

2. $4.76 \div 3.8 =$ **5.** $0.063 \div 2.1 =$

3. $1.758 \div 4.64 =$ **6.** $6.002 \div 0.3 =$

7. Software Corporation paid $2,366.05 for computer paper. If the paper costs $29.95 per box, how many boxes did the corporation buy?

8. Edward averages 80 questions per hour when typing test questions into a computer testbank. How long will it take him to enter 1,800 questions?

■ Converting Fractions to Decimals

As you read in the section on fractions, decimal equivalents of fractions are important in many jobs in marketing. To convert any fraction to a decimal, simply divide the numerator by the denominator.

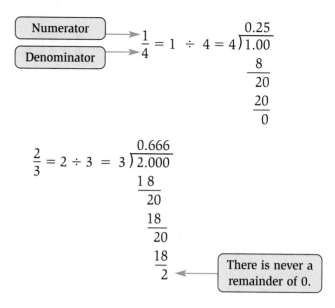

In its decimal form, $\frac{2}{3}$ is a repeating decimal. When working with repeating decimals, you may round to the nearest hundredth for most applications.

Thus, $\frac{2}{3} = 0.67$.

7.1 ASSESSMENT

Reviewing Key Terms and Concepts

1. Write the whole number 2,000,265 in words, using commas and hyphens correctly.

2. Explain the meaning of $\frac{3}{5}$.

3. Multiply: 4.99×5.

4. Round the answer from question 3 to the nearest dollar.

5. Convert the fraction $\frac{3}{4}$ to its decimal equivalent.

Thinking Critically

6. Sometimes rounding decimal numbers to whole numbers makes a complicated math problem easy to do "in your head." Name at least one example when rounding is helpful.

Integrating Academic Skills

7. **COMMUNICATION** Each of the following numbers can be expressed in three ways. Fill in the blanks.

Fraction		Decimal	Percentage
$\frac{3}{5}$	=	_____	_____
$\frac{2}{70}$	=	_____	_____
$\frac{1}{1,000}$	=	_____	_____

Interpreting Numbers

What You'll Learn

- How to use a calculator to solve math problems
- The procedure used to convert percentages to decimals and decimals to percentages
- The ways to read different types of graphs used to present mathematical data

Why It's Important

Most jobs in marketing require the use of a calculator. Many require using a computer to generate graphic presentations. You will improve your skill level on the calculator as you study this section. You will also gain a greater understanding of graphs and charts.

Key Terms

- percent
- bar graph
- line graph
- circle graph
- pie chart

Using a Calculator

Calculators simplify the math that is common in both the business world and in people's personal lives. Many people find calculators vital when paying bills, creating a budget, and balancing their checkbook. Nearly everyone in marketing and business uses calculators. There are two basic types. The most widely used type employs the *algebraic entry system*. This is the type of calculator used in the problems that follow. The other type uses the *reverse-entry system*.

The basic difference is that with the reverse-entry system, you enter the first amount, then the second amount, and then the operation (added to, subtracted from, multiplied by, or divided into the first amount). If you have a calculator that uses the reverse-entry system, read the instruction book that accompanies your calculator very carefully. You will get a very different answer if you enter numbers as if using an algebraic entry system when working with a reverse-entry calculator.

If you expect to be hired in sales or any other marketing job, you will almost certainly use a calculator. Besides simply knowing which buttons to press, you will be expected to work with accuracy, know how to work with fractions and amounts of money, and have an understanding of how the calculator computes with multiple operations.

■ Estimate, then Operate

When using a calculator, many people follow the *guess-and-check method*. They estimate first, then enter the problem in the calculator. Finally, they check the displayed answer against the estimate.

$$388 + 995 = ?$$

Estimate: 400 + 1,000 = 1,400
Enter the problem:

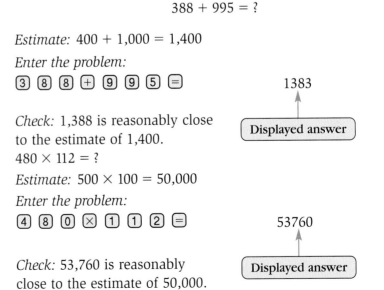

1383

Displayed answer

Check: 1,388 is reasonably close to the estimate of 1,400.

$$480 \times 112 = ?$$

Estimate: 500 × 100 = 50,000
Enter the problem:

53760

Displayed answer

Check: 53,760 is reasonably close to the estimate of 50,000.

You may wonder why it is important to estimate your answers when you use a calculator. Surely the calculator is more accurate than your estimate. Sometimes, though, you may make errors when entering numbers or even press the wrong operation key. It's important to have an estimate of the answer in mind. For example, if you're expecting an answer of about 300, you'll know something is wrong if the displayed answer on your calculator is 3,300.

Another way to ensure accuracy when using a calculator is to check the display after you enter each number and before you press the operation key. If you have made an error, press the Clear Entry key ⒸⒺ to remove the last entry. Suppose you want to multiply 5.8 × 7.2, but you enter ⑤ Ⓘ ⑧ ⓧ ⑦ ②. Press ⒸⒺ to delete the last two keystrokes. Then you can reenter the second number correctly. The first number will remain in the calculator. Press the Equals key ⊜, and the answer will be displayed: 41.76.

■ How to Make Entries

Keep in mind as you enter digits that you can disregard leading zeros to the left of the decimal point (as in 0.6 or 0.375) and final zeros after the decimal point (as in 9.250 or 41.500). You don't need to enter these zeros. The calculator will display all the digits needed.

Number	Keystrokes Entered	Display
0.785	Ⓘ ⑦ ⑧ ⑤	0.785
5.10	⑤ Ⓘ ①	5.1

When dealing with mixed numbers or fractions, you must first convert the fractions to decimal form. Do this by dividing the numerator by the denominator. For example, to enter 5¼, first enter ① ÷ ④. Then add the whole number by entering ➕ ⑤.

When solving problems dealing with money, remember to write the dollar sign in the answer. You may also have to round the displayed answer to the nearest cent.

Display	Answer Written as Money Amount
5.25	$5.25
25.368216	$25.37 (Round to nearest cent.)
46.0194	$46.02 (Round to nearest cent.)
76514.1	$76,514.10 (No commas shown in large numbers on most calculators.)

A calculator can operate on only two numbers at a time. However, you can perform a string of involved calculations on more than two numbers if you are very careful. When only addition and subtraction are involved, the calculator will perform these operations as they are entered.

⑧ Ⓘ ⑥ ➕ Ⓘ ② ⑤ ➕ ① ① Ⓘ ⑨ ⊖ ③ Ⓘ ⑥ ② ⊜ 17.13

When only multiplication and division are involved, the calculator will also perform these operations as they are entered.

⑦ ⑦ ⑤ ⓧ Ⓘ ⑨ ⑥ ÷ ⑤ ⓧ ① Ⓘ ⑨ ⑥ ⊜ 291.648

However, when a calculation involves a combination of addition or subtraction with multiplication or division, not all calculators work the same way. You will need to check how your calculator performs the operations in this type of problem. Most calculators will do the operations as they are entered.

6 + 4 × 6 will be calculated as

6 + 4 × 6 =

10 × 6 = 60.

6 × 4 + 6 will be calculated as

6 × 4 + 6 =

24 + 6 = 30.

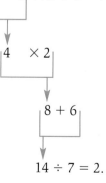

9 − 5 × 2 + 6 ÷ 7 = will be calculated as

9 − 5 × 2 + 6 ÷ 7 =

4 × 2

8 + 6

14 ÷ 7 = 2.

Percentages

Percent means parts per hundred. Thus, a number expressed as a percent represents the number of parts per hundred.

To write a whole number or a decimal number as a percent, multiply it by 100. A simple way to do this is to move the decimal point two places *to the right*.

$0.70 = 0.7 \times 100 = 70\%$ or $0.70 = 70\%$

$0.05 = 0.05 \times 100 = 5\%$ or $0.05 = 5\%$

$2.5 = 2.5 \times 100 = 250\%$ or $2.50 = 250\%$

> Move the decimal point two places to the right.

> Write 0s as needed.

You can use a calculator to do this operation.

$[.][7][\times][1][0][0][=]$ $70 = 70\%$

$[2][.][5][\times][1][0][0][=]$ $250 = 250\%$

■ Converting Fractions to Percentages

To write a fraction or mixed number as a percent, first convert the fraction to decimal form. Do this by dividing the numerator by the denominator. If there is a whole number, add it to the converted fraction. Then multiply by 100. You can use a calculator to do this operation.

$\frac{1}{2} = [1][\div][2][\times][1][0][0][=]$ $50 = 50\%$

$\frac{3}{8} = [3][\div][8][\times][1][0][0][=]$ $37.5 = 37.5\%$

$4\frac{2}{5} = [2][\div][5][+][4][\times][1][0][0][=]$ $440 = 440\%$

■ Converting Percentages to Decimals

Sometimes it may be easier to complete a math problem by changing a percentage to a decimal. There is a simple method that can be followed when you are asked to do this. You can change a percent to a decimal number by dividing by 100. A simple way to do this is to move the decimal point two places *to the left*.

> Move the decimal point two places to the left.

$24.8\% = 24.8 \div 100 = .248$ or $24.8\% = 0.248$

$0.5\% = 0.5 \div 100 = 0.005$ or $0.5\% = 0.005$

> Write 0s as needed.

You can use a calculator to do this operation.

$12.6\% = [1][2][.][6][\div][1][0][0][=]$ 0.126

$1.4\% = [1][.][4][\div][1][0][0][=]$ 0.014

You can also convert a percent with a fraction or mixed number to a decimal by using a calculator.

$7\frac{1}{4}\% = [1][\div][4][+][7][\div][1][0][0][=]$ 0.0725

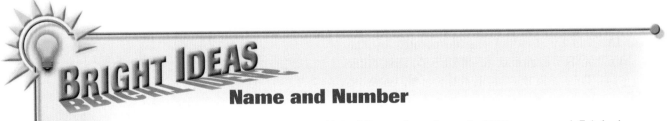

BRIGHT IDEAS

Name and Number

The first Datsun sports car that arrived in the United States from Japan in 1970 was named *Fair Lady*— a tribute to the popular play. The car was never marketed because the executives in the United States feared that the name would turn people off. This name would work in Japan, where cars are named for things like flowers; however, Americans favor cars with huge engines and tough images. There was little time to brainstorm for a new name, so they went with the company's internal designation for the car. The car made its debut in the United States as the 240Z. The name stuck, and the company (now Nissan) still names their sports car with numbers.

Thinking Creatively

What are some other products that are well-suited to number names? What are some products for which a number might not be a suitable name?

Inches or Centimeters?

The rest of the world is hooked on the metric system; however, Americans still favor the standard English system of measurements. NASA learned this lesson in September 1999 when the Mars Orbiter went off track. Why? One team of engineers was working with English units and the other with the metric system. Some countries in the European Union have demanded that they will only import U.S. goods that are metrically labeled. Whether it is inches or centimeters or miles or kilometers, the global marketplace calls for a common unit of measurement.

Thinking Critically
What challenges does the United States face in switching to the metric system?

■ **Calculating Price** It is helpful to understand how to properly use a calculator both in business and when dealing with personal finances. *Why would it be important to have a calculator at your disposal when making an investment like financing or leasing a car?*

■ Percent Problems

Percent problems are often encountered on a job. For example, you may be asked to figure a discount amount or the amount of sales tax. You may have to figure the total selling price, including the tax. Maybe you will be asked to figure the percent commission on your total sales.

Most percent problems will involve finding a percent of a number. To do that, multiply the decimal equivalent of the percent by the number.

Decimal equivalent of $5\frac{1}{2}\%$

$$5\frac{1}{2}\% \text{ of } \$35 = 0.055 \times \$35$$

Of tells you to multiply.

Use these steps to help you solve percent problems.

1. Estimate the answer.
2. Translate the problem into a math statement.
3. Do the calculations.

4. If necessary, round money amounts to the nearest cent.
5. Check your answer.

Many calculators have a Percent key ⊞ that can simplify percent calculations. Read the instructions for your calculator to find out how to use this key.

Two types of percent problems are explained below. The problems can be solved with a calculator without the use of a Percent key.

1. Suppose you have sold a set of skis listed at $395.99 to someone eligible for a 15 percent discount. How much in dollars and cents will you allow as a discount on the skis?

- *First: Estimate the answer.* Round the list price to $400. Figure that 10 percent of $400 is $40. Since 15 percent is $1\frac{1}{2}$ times 10 percent, estimate the discount at about $60 ($1\frac{1}{2}$ times $40).

- *Second: Translate the problem into a math statement.*

$$15\% \text{ of } \$395.99 = 0.15 \times 395.99$$

Creative in Numbers

As calculators grow more sophisticated, so do the opportunities for marketing them to today's students. Graphing calculators, which run graph equation programs, are being credited for changing the way students think about solving math problems. Unfortunately, they are also turning into the next generation of classroom distractions. Programs can now be downloaded to morph the devices into TV and VCR remote controls and even Game Boys.

Thinking Critically
What might marketers of graphing calculators do to resolve the negative criticism they receive?

• *Third: Do the calculations.*

$$0.15 \times \$395.99 = \$59.3985$$

• *Fourth: Round the answer to the nearest cent, if necessary.*

$$\$59.3985 \text{ rounds to } \$59.40$$

• *Finally: Check the answer against your estimate.* The amount $59.40 is reasonably close to the estimate of $60. The discount is $59.40.

2. If sales tax is $6^{1}/_{2}$ percent, how much tax should you collect on the sale of the skis? Before you can figure the tax, you have to find out the net selling price.

List price − discount = net price
$395.99 − $59.40 = $336.59

Now you can proceed, following the guidelines given above.

• *Estimate:* Round $6^{1}/_{2}$ percent to 7 percent and $336.59 to $300. A 7 percent sales tax means that $7 tax is collected on every $100 in sales. So, you can estimate the tax to be $21 $(3 \times \$7)$.

• *Translate:*
$6^{1}/_{2}$ percent of $336.59 = $0.065 \times \$336.59$

• *Calculate:*
$$0.065 \times \$336.59 = \$21.8784$$

• *Round:*
$$\$21.8784 \text{ rounds to } \$21.88$$

• *Check:* $21.88 is reasonably close to the estimate of $21. The sales tax to be collected is $21.88.

Reading Charts and Graphs

Often in marketing, people need to use numbers to describe market trends, growth of sales, and other data. Graphs are a way of presenting such information in a way that is easier to understand than a long series of numbers. Because graphs are drawings, they make it possible for people to *see* information and grasp it more readily. It's easier to tell that one bar is longer than another, or that a line is going up or down, than it is to try to understand data by reading. Usually a graph shows the relationship between two kinds of data, or statistical information.

■ Bar Graphs

A bar graph is a drawing made up of parallel bars whose lengths are proportional to the qualities being measured. The bar graph in Figure 7-1 on page 131 was used by Morning Glory Music in its market research. It shows the relationship between the number of compact disks people bought and the age of the buyers. The bottom of the graph lists the age groups that purchased compact disks. Each group is represented by a bar of a certain height. There is a vertical line along the left side of the graph indicating the number of disks sold.

To discover how many disks 19- to 24-year-olds bought, simply draw an imaginary line across the top of the bar that represents that age group. Then note where that line intersects the left side of the graph. As you can see, 19- to 24-year-olds bought 800 disks that month, more than any other group.

Look at the bar representing 25- to 34-year-olds. The top of this bar is halfway between the 600 and 700 sales level. You can estimate that this group bought 650 CDs that month. You can also easily see that the younger group bought about 150 more CDs than the 25- to 34-year-olds and about 600 more than people over 60. The relative heights of the bars give the store an instant picture of the number of CDs purchased by various age groups.

■ Line Graphs

Another kind of graph you have probably seen often in magazines and newspapers is a line graph. A line graph uses a line that joins points representing changes in a variable quantity, usually over a specific period of time. It is very useful for charting sales, prices, profits, output—things that people expect to change over time. The information is

useful in predicting future trends so that businesses can make plans to prepare for them.

The line graph shown in Figure 7–2 charts the ups and downs in compact disk sales at Morning Glory Music over a 12-month period. Along the bottom of the graph are the months of the year. Along the left side are the number of units sold. As you can see by following the line, by far the most sales (10,000) occurred in December. There was also a big jump in sales at the beginning of the summer and smaller increases in April and September. These were all followed by declines. This kind of information can help the store decide how much merchandise to order the following year.

FIGURE 7-1

Morning Glory Music—Compact Disk Sales by Age Group

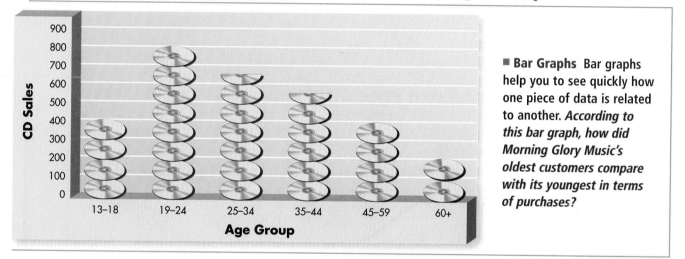

■ **Bar Graphs** Bar graphs help you to see quickly how one piece of data is related to another. *According to this bar graph, how did Morning Glory Music's oldest customers compare with its youngest in terms of purchases?*

FIGURE 7-2

Morning Glory Music Compact Disk Sales

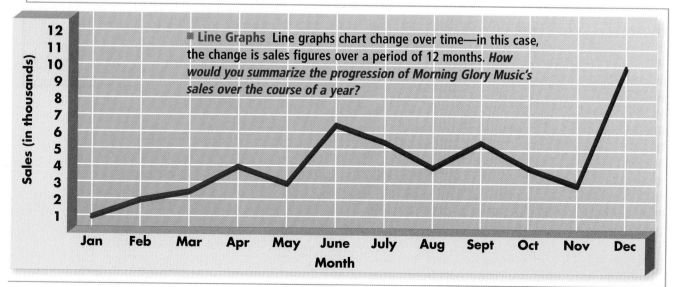

■ **Line Graphs** Line graphs chart change over time—in this case, the change is sales figures over a period of 12 months. *How would you summarize the progression of Morning Glory Music's sales over the course of a year?*

Circle Graphs

A circle graph is a geometric representation of the relative sizes of the parts of a whole. Businesses often choose such a graph to compare things like the costs of different aspects of manufacturing the expenditures of one specific department, or the ways income from sales is used by a company.

Circle graphs offer a visual that is easy to understand when considering how a large figure is broken down into several parts. A circle graph is better known as a pie chart, because it looks like a pie cut into slices of different sizes. The proportions of the different "slices" are sometimes expressed as percentages of the whole circle and sometimes as dollar amounts.

The pie chart in Figure 7-3 shows a percentage breakdown of where the money from the retail sale of a compact disk went. Even without reading the numbers, you can easily see who received the largest portion of the money and who received the least amount. You can see from the chart that twice as much of the sale price went to retail profit as to the artists who made the recording. The biggest portion of the "pie" went to the record company. Look at the area representing manufacturing costs. You can see that it accounted for the smallest portion of the retail price.

This kind of chart enables companies to see at a glance which costs take the largest bite out of their revenues. The companies can then determine whether this breakdown accurately reflects their priorities. If not, they can institute cost-cutting measures as they see fit to restructure the breakdown of the pie.

FIGURE 7-3

Morning Glory Music Retail Price Distribution—Compact Disks

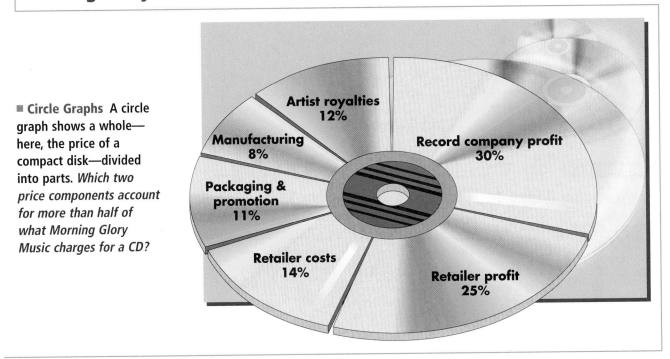

■ Circle Graphs A circle graph shows a whole—here, the price of a compact disk—divided into parts. *Which two price components account for more than half of what Morning Glory Music charges for a CD?*

Artist royalties 12%

Manufacturing 8%

Packaging & promotion 11%

Retailer costs 14%

Record company profit 30%

Retailer profit 25%

Case Study

The Best Deal

More customers are beginning to shop at discount chain stores, attracted by the lower prices and convenience. Discount chains have gained popularity over small local stores as more people shop at them. Does this mean that they offer the best deal? Many customers seem to think so. On the surface, the price is what draws customers in. A lower price, however, does not always guarantee the same quality offered at a specialized store.

Consider the example of a seemingly similar bike sold at two stores—a discount chain store, "Mega-Mart," and a more expensive local bicycle shop. The discount chain store Mega-Mart sells a children's bike for $70. A bike with the same features costs $120 at the small bike shop. The bike from Mega-Mart seems like a better deal; however, research shows that the two bikes are not the same.

The more expensive bike is built from stronger materials and has replaceable parts. It is adjustable for different sized riders. When the rider outgrows the bike after two years, it can probably be resold for $60. This price is a reasonable estimation based on the "wear and tear" that the bike will receive in the two years.

The cheaper bike is not adjustable to account for growth and has a life span of one year. The cheaper materials are more likely to dent, rust, and chip, which makes reselling the bike difficult.

The lesson for the consumer is that the bike that costs more was truly a better buy. There are many factors that must be considered when making such a purchase—and price should not always be the deciding factor.

Case Study Review

1. How much does it cost per year to ride the more expensive bike? The cheaper bike?
2. Express the ratio of the cost of riding the more expensive bike to the cost of riding the Mega-Mart bike as a percentage.

A Matter of Ethics

3. The manufacturer and seller of the Mega-Mart bike make $37 profit on the sale, while the profit on the sale of the expensive bike is $32. Is it ethical to make more profit on a less costly product than an expensive product? Why or why not?

Answers to Practice Sets

Practice 1 (page 121)

1. $^4/_{10}$ (or $^2/_5$)
2. $^1/_3$
3. 0
4. $^4/_4$ (or 1)
5. $^2/_7$
6. $^3/_4$
7. $^1/_8$
8. $^5/_4$ (or $1^1/_4$)
9. No parts shaded.
10. $^2/_8$ (or $^1/_4$)

Practice 2 (page 122)

1. Five and six-tenths
2. Seven-tenths
3. Fourteen and five-tenths
4. Nine-hundredths
5. Three and twelve-hundredths
6. Nine and five-hundredths
7. Ten and thirty-three hundredths
8. Twenty-five and forty-eight hundredths
9. One hundred fifty-five and $^{87}/_{100}$
10. Five hundred forty-five and $^{67}/_{100}$

Practice 3 (page 122)

1. 14
2. 17.1
3. 17.3
4. 25.7
5. 22.25
6. 78.54
7. 16.97
8. 1.3
9. 38.14
10. $4.24
11. 18.668
12. 15.169
13. $1,362.25
14. 23.92 yards

Practice 4 (page 123)

1. 36.4
2. 28.06
3. 244.92
4. 199.08
5. 3.4544
6. 24.8
7. 5.50974
8. 61.2
9. 0.0332
10. $345.63
11. $188.07

Practice 5 (page 125)

1. 0.42
2. 1.25
3. 0.38
4. 560
5. 0.03
6. 20.01
7. 79 boxes
8. 22.5 hours

7.2 ASSESSMENT

Reviewing Key Terms and Concepts

1. Use a calculator to find the decimal equivalent of $^1/_7$.
2. What is the decimal equivalent of 60 percent?
3. What are three forms of graphic representation?

Thinking Critically

4. A market researcher plans to present data about purchases of colas by age group. She can't decide whether to use a bar graph or to list her groups on a chalkboard in order of size. What should she do, and why?

Integrating Academic Skills

5. **MATH** Use a calculator to solve the following problem: You want to start a word processing business. The equipment you want to purchase costs $9,000. How many hours of work will it take to pay for the equipment if you charge your customers an average $25 per hour?

Careers in Marketing

RESTAURANT MANAGEMENT

Bill Duffy
Restaurant Manager
Spike & Charlie's

What does your job entail?

"The main function of my job is to coordinate staff and control the operation of the restaurant. I organize the work of approximately 120 individuals to prepare and serve meals. Some restaurant managers plan the menu and order food and supplies; however, I try to delegate much of that work to the kitchen staff. Restaurant managers are routinely responsible for hiring, training, maintaining schedules, and overall troubleshooting at the restaurant."

What skills are most important to you?

"A restaurant manager must have very good organizational skills. Efficiency is necessary when coordinating activities, resources, and staff. I also believe that it is necessary to have excellent communication skills that enable you to let servers know what is expected of them. This must be communicated clearly and quickly because of the fast-paced environment."

What do you like most about your work?

"The best part about my job is the social experience of meeting many different people who come in to dine. Going out to dinner is like a mini-vacation and I get to be a part of that. I generally get to deal with people on very good terms in a nice environment."

How does your workload vary?

"My duties include keeping track of inventory, maintaining budgets, developing promotional marketing programs or events, coordinating staff, scheduling, and general maintenance of the restaurant."

What is your key to success?

"My motto is 'think big, concentrate small.' If you focus on your objectives (establishing menu prices, planning restaurant decor, etc.) you can work efficiently and effectively."

Thinking Critically

What are the four Ps of marketing in restaurant management?

Career Facts

Education and Training: Many community colleges and four-year colleges offer certificates and degrees in restaurant management and food service management. Employers are increasingly hiring candidates with four-year degrees who have strong backgrounds in business administration, marketing, sales, or hotel management. Experience as a food service worker provides valuable training.

Aptitudes, Abilities, and Skills: The ability to work under stress, good organization skills, good communication skills, good management skills, basic clerical skills, and the desire to serve people are necessary.

Career Outlook: Faster than average growth is expected to occur in restaurant management positions through the year 2006.

Career Path: Restaurant managers are often promoted from within a company. Large restaurant chains offer management-training programs allowing employees to advance to assistant management and then manager positions.

VOCABULARY REVIEW

Build a crossword puzzle using the terms below. Use graph paper to arrange your entries. Then write short definitions for them.

- digits
- fractions
- numerator
- denominator
- mixed number
- decimal number
- percent
- bar graph
- line graph
- circle graph
- pie chart

FACT AND IDEA REVIEW

1. You should separate whole numbers into groups when you write them in words. What are these groups? (7.1)

2. What is a fraction? (7.1)

3. How do you decide whether to round a decimal number up or down? (7.1)

4. Describe how you would convert $5/9$ to a decimal number. Give your answer rounded to the nearest hundredth. (7.1)

5. What can you do to increase accuracy when using a calculator? (7.2)

6. Describe how you would convert a fraction to a percentage. (7.2)

7. What are the five steps in solving a percent problem? (7.2)

8. How is a bar graph different from a line graph? (7.2)

THINKING CRITICALLY

1. Estimating an answer before doing the math on a calculator is a good idea. What are some reasons for estimating before doing the same problem on paper?

2. Should students be allowed to use calculators when taking math exams? Defend your answer.

3. If the price of the compact disks in Figure 7-2 is $15, how would you find out how much money each point on the line represents?

4. You are purchasing computer parts for assembly in your company's plant in California. Locate current world currency exchange rates on the Internet or in a newspaper. Then compute the cost in U.S. dollars for the following orders:

   Order #1 from Japan: 131,087.5 yen

   Order #2 from Great Britain: 850.5 pounds

   Order #3 from Hong Kong: 11,310 Hong Kong dollars

   Order #4 from France: 10,540 francs

BUILDING WORKPLACE SKILLS

1. **Human Relations** You are the supervisor of a telemarketing team. Your records show that the success rate of your workers varies from 10 percent to 70 percent. Do you think it would be helpful to display these percentages in a chart for everyone to see? Why or why not?

2. **Math** Use a calculator to solve the following problem: You want to start a lawn mowing business. The equipment you will need will cost you $6,700. If you charge your customers $22 per hour, how many hours of work will it take to pay for the equipment?

APPLYING MARKETING CONCEPTS

1. **Analyzing Sales Patterns** Imagine that you sell computer parts. In January, you had $15,000 in sales. In February, your sales increased by 15 percent. From March through June, your sales continued to increase 15 percent a month. Use a spreadsheet program to prepare a line graph to show your sales by month.

2. **Researching the Computer** Research the history of the computer at the library or on the Internet. Find out when and where the first computers were built. Compare the uses, memory capacity, and cost of computers in the 1960s with those of today. Use a word processing program to write a 300-word report on your findings.

3. **Comparing Graphing Calculators** Research graphing calculators at the library or on the Internet. Why are they important, and what are some situations in which they are helpful? Use presentation software to prepare an oral report on your research, answering those questions and showcasing the best models you found.

4. **Using Circle Graphs** Keep track of how much money you spend in one week. Include money that you spend on food, transportation, and entertainment (buying CDs, clothing, going to the movies). Using a computer program, create a circle graph based on these amounts. You can divide your graph into as many parts as you would like. Then turn this graph into a bar graph. Which do you find easier to interpret?

LINKING SCHOOL TO WORK

Technology Skills Prepare a demonstration illustrating the way calculators are used at a local business. Include electronic cash registers if you work with one on the job.

THE DECA CONNECTION

Role Play: Motorcycle Dealership Employee

Situation You are to assume the role of employee at a local motorcycle dealership. You will be required to explain the company's two compensation plans to new employees. Employees can choose to work for a salary of $250 a week plus a commission of 8% of the price of the motorcycles they sell. Under that plan, if they don't sell any motorcycles, they get the salary but no commissions. The other choice is to work for commissions only. Under this plan employees will receive a 15% commission on the price of the motorcycles they sell, and no other salary. Prospective employees have average weekly living expenses of $475, so the base salary of $250 is tempting.

Activity You must demonstrate to the dealership manager (judge) that you are capable of presenting these options to new employees.

Evaluation You will be evaluated on how well you meet the following performance indicators:

- Explain the compensation plans
- Calculate financial ratios
- Make oral presentations
- Orient new employees

inter NET CONNECTION

Tax Break
You are figuring out your income taxes and know that the tax rate increases as your income goes up.

Connect
- Locate the Internal Revenue Service Web site and find the tax tables you need.
- Determine where the income break points are for the different tax rates.
- Calculate the tax on a taxable income of $49,700.

Communication Skills

Marketing: What It Takes

Copy House Communications

Imagine yourself as the owner of a copy center. Your services include providing copy machines, fax transmittals, and computers with e-mail and Internet connections. You pride your business on friendly, personal, and quick service. Your marketing advisor suggests you explore training employees on communication skills to enhance your venture.

WHAT WILL YOU DO?

What techniques can you employ to enhance effective communication between your employees and customers?

Defining Communication

The Communication Process

Communication is the process of exchanging information, ideas, and feelings. Good communication is an essential factor when developing interpersonal relations. They are also an important element of conducting successful business activities.

■ Senders and Receivers

The simple act of sending a message is just one facet of communicating—every message must be sent, received, and understood. Both verbal and nonverbal means are used to send and receive messages. Speaking and writing are verbal means. Nonverbal means include facial expressions and *body language*, your gestures, movements, and mannerisms that communicate your thoughts, which will be discussed more in Chapter 10.

You are often a sender and a receiver at the same time in face-to-face conversations. Suppose that you have asked your employer, Mr. Sanchez, how he wants you to arrange a window display. He sends a message by speaking as he explains the arrangement. You receive the message by listening. As you listen, though, you may be sending a message at the same time—even if you don't say a word. The expression on your face may be saying, "I don't understand." Mr. Sanchez may receive this message and start over, or he may rephrase the message.

■ Messages

The substance of any form of communication is the message—the information, ideas, or feelings the sender wants to share. All communication is made up of verbal and nonverbal symbols. Messages are represented by symbols, which can be anything that stands for something else.

Every word is a verbal symbol with a meaning that can be understood by others who know the same language. Avoiding nonstandard language, such as slang expressions and highly technical terms, will increase the chances that your message will be understood.

■ Channels

Channels are the avenues by which the message is delivered. In face-to-face conversations, the channels are sound and sight. The participants listen to and look at one another. The channel in telephone conversations is the sound that is transmitted and received over telephone lines. The participants speak to and listen to one another.

What You'll Learn

- The six primary elements of communication
- How to arrange the setting for a business meeting
- How to use listening skills to improve your understanding of messages
- Three blocks to listening with understanding
- Three skills that will help you read with understanding

Why It's Important

Studies have shown that 70 percent of our waking hours are spent communicating. Most jobs in business, especially in marketing, require good communication skills. You need to understand the communication process to become a more effective communicator.

Key Terms

- communication
- channels
- feedback
- blocks
- setting
- distractions
- emotional blocks
- jargon

Another channel of communication is the written word. On the job, many messages are delivered in the form of e-mail, letters, memoranda, and reports. The participants write messages and read each other's messages.

■ Feedback

Feedback is the receiver's response to the message. When your employer explains your part in a new advertising program, you will probably ask some questions. This is feedback. You may restate some of your employer's words to assure that you understand the message. Feedback is important in communication because it allows participants to clarify the message and know that both (or all) parties gave the same meaning to the message.

When reading reports, you have little opportunity for feedback. You can respond to a letter or memorandum, but it takes more time than it would to give feedback in a conversation. E-mail is fast, but it doesn't allow for reading body language. The greatest opportunity for feedback is in a face-to-face conversation with another person.

■ Blocks

Blocks interfere with understanding the message. The three primary blocks to understanding are *distractions, emotional blocks,* and *planning a response.* These will be discussed later in the chapter.

■ Setting

The setting is where communication takes place. Outdoor settings are varied and often hard to control. Indoor settings in a job situation may vary from a large hall to a small office. You may have control over choosing the room and arranging the furniture.

When you choose the setting for a group meeting, make sure that it is large enough to accommodate everyone who will attend. Arrange the chairs so that everyone can see the main speaker. Check to make sure there is adequate lighting. Make sure that you have the appropriate equipment, an electrical outlet, and an extension cord if you are giving a visual presentation. You may want to bring in coffee, water, and snacks.

When you are discussing something with one other person in a face-to-face conversation, a small room is more comfortable than a large one. You will also be more comfortable in your own workplace

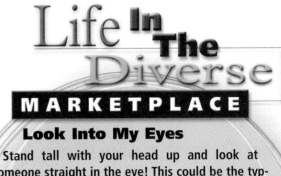

Life In The Diverse MARKETPLACE

Look Into My Eyes

Stand tall with your head up and look at someone straight in the eye! This could be the typical advice given to a young person in North America before the first day of school or a job interview. Eye contact is expected—and respected—in the United States, where it is a sign of confidence and ease. In countries like Japan and Korea, however, young people are trained to avert their eyes during a conversation. It is believed that direct eye contact is intimidating and overbearing.

Thinking Critically

What are some other communication norms in the United States that could be misinterpreted by people from another culture?

than in someone else's. If you want to make a person feel comfortable in a conversation, go to his or her workplace.

Listening

You have learned that about 70 percent of your waking hours are spent communicating. Studies show that approximately 45 percent of that time is spent listening. Unfortunately, some people never learn the difference between hearing and listening. Hearing is primarily a physical process that takes place in the ears. Listening is a mental process that requires using the brain to assimilate information gathered.

■ Listening Skills

Learning to use listening skills is a vital part of being an effective communicator. Listening skills help you understand the messages you receive. These skills involve knowing what to listen for and what to think about as you listen. These same skills can be applied to understanding written messages.

IDENTIFYING THE PURPOSE You should always know the purpose of a meeting that has been scheduled to discuss a particular topic before the speaker begins to talk. When meeting with customers, you may not have advance notice of the purpose of the message. Then you have to identify the purpose from the content of the message. The sooner you can do this, the easier it will be for you to understand the whole message.

LOOKING FOR A PLAN When you listen to a structured speech, try to identify a plan of presentation. This makes it easier to see the different parts of the message fit together to convey the whole message. Sometimes a speaker makes generalizations and then supports them with specific evidence. The speaker may use contrasts and comparisons or show cause-and-effect relationships. When you know the plan, you can often anticipate what the speaker will say next. You will also be able to sort out the relevant and irrelevant information.

Face-to-face conversations between two (or even several) people are usually not as well planned as a formal speech. In these informal conversations, as long as you know the purpose of the message, it is not important to know the plan.

GIVING FEEDBACK If you are conversing with another person or even in a small group, give feedback to show whether you understand the message. Without interrupting, you can nod your head, raise an eyebrow, or frown. You may have an opportunity to ask questions when the speaker pauses. When the speaker has completed the message, summarize your understanding of it in your mind. Ask the speaker for clarification if you think that it is possible that your understanding of the message is different from that intended by the sender.

SEARCHING FOR AN INTEREST On the job, many of the messages you receive from your employer or from co-workers will relate to your job performance. Since you want to succeed at your job, show an interest in anything that will improve your performance.

You may attend meetings or conferences where the messages seem uninteresting and you want to tune them out. This can become a habit that will cause you to miss important information. Remember, you can learn valuable information from even the most uninteresting message. Listen carefully to find something that applies to you or interests you.

■ **All Ears!** Good salespeople are good listeners. *How can this salesman show that he understands what the customer is telling him?*

EVALUATING THE MESSAGE There are times for listening with empathy and times for listening and making judgments. You must be able to distinguish which type of listening is appropriate in every situation.

A friend may express the need to share his or her innermost feelings with you; this is a time to listen with empathy and understanding. Making judgments would be inappropriate.

In most other conversations and when listening to messages, making judgments can help you listen with understanding. Your mind becomes more actively involved in the listening process when you make logical judgments. You will not understand messages you do not like if you let your emotions get in the way. Always keep an open mind.

As you listen, evaluate the validity of the message. Try to distinguish between fact and opinion and evaluate whether the information presented is relevant to the purpose of the message.

LISTENING FOR MORE THAN VERBAL CONTENT There is usually more to the speaker's message than the meaning of the words. The manner in which the speech is delivered affects the meaning of the message. The rate of speech, pitch, volume, and

REAL WORLD MARKETING

Hello Kitty!

Hello Kitty, the tiny Japanese ambassador of friendship, is only one of the popular Sanrio characters that draws huge annual sales. Sanrio has been developing a social communication business since 1960 that ranges from novelty items and greeting cards to apparel and accessories. "In order to get along with one another, we need to respect and love," said Shintaro Tsuji, Sanrio's President and CEO. "Whether one is sad, down, happy or whatever . . . We want people to share these important feelings with one another," adds Tsuji. Mr. Tsuji shouldn't be feeling sad or down based on his company's record annual revenue of over $1 billion!

Thinking Critically
What businesses might be a logical extension of Sanrio's social communication business?

voice quality can add and change meaning. Some experts estimate that 40 percent of the meaning of oral communication is due to vocal cues—not the actual words spoken but the way they are said.

LISTENING FOR A CONCLUSION Listen for the speaker's conclusion. You may want or need to take action based on it. You can summarize the main points and then draw your own conclusion if you don't let your emotions get in the way. Don't jump to a conclusion before the speaker has presented the facts or opinions to support it.

TAKING NOTES Always take notes on the main points presented in a business meeting. Employers appreciate employees who care enough to write down what is being discussed. It may be necessary to refer back to these notes at a later time.

FOLLOWING DIRECTIONS It is important to listen carefully when someone gives you directions. Be sure you understand each step if there is more than one. Give frequent feedback to the person instructing you so that he or she knows you have understood each step.

■ Blocks to Listening with Understanding

Some things interfere with or *block* effective listening. Avoid these blocks, and you will be able to concentrate on the message.

Distractions are blocks to effective listening that include noises, environmental factors, interruptions by other people, and competing thoughts that creep into your mind. To avoid a distraction, you may decide to move to a different area or even postpone a meeting. Most messages that you receive on the job will be important. Exercise the discipline necessary to keep your mind on the message despite distractions.

Emotional blocks are biases against the opinions expressed by the sender that prevent you from understanding. It is especially important to listen and understand, even when you don't agree with the sender's ideas. Otherwise, you will not be able to give a meaningful response.

Planning a response blocks understanding because you can't concentrate on the message and your response at the same time. When the speaker says something that you want to respond to, it's tempting to think about your response and tune out the speaker. You may miss some key points in the message if you do this and respond inappropriately. Listen to the entire message before you plan your response.

Reading

Reading, like listening, is a process of trying to understand a message. Reading with understanding is a necessity in every career. Even when applying for a job you have to read Help-Wanted ads, whether online or in print.

■ Knowing the Purpose of Your Reading

You will be a more efficient reader if you know why you are reading before you begin. When you read a novel or magazine, you are reading for pleasure. You can read as fast or as slowly as you want. When you read a job application form or a company memo, you have to read every word for complete understanding.

■ Reading for Meaning

One of the many things required to succeed on the job is reading and understanding written messages. These three skills can help you: focusing your mind, forming pictures, and improving your vocabulary.

No one's mind focuses on a subject automatically. Your mind will *focus* only through constant concentration. When you don't concentrate, the message will be unclear. Monitor your thoughts when you read, and if your mind wanders, refocus on the subject.

It can be difficult sometimes to comprehend the written word without other visual aids. A message may be easier to understand when you see elements of the message in your mind. Try to *form pictures* of the people, places, things, and situations described when you read.

You may come across words that are unfamiliar when reading. Skipping over these unfamiliar words may cause you to miss key points in the message. Try to figure out the meaning by the way the word is used in the sentence or paragraph and then look up the word in a dictionary. This will *improve your vocabulary* and broaden your understanding of written communication.

You will come across some technical terms called jargon in your job-related reading. Jargon is technical or specialized vocabulary used by members of a particular profession or industry. Many of these words aren't even listed in most dictionaries. Most marketing jobs have their own jargon, which you will learn as you study this book.

■ **A Novel Experience** Good reading skills are necessary in almost all careers. *How is this young man developing good job skills?*

8.1 ASSESSMENT

Reviewing Key Terms and Concepts

1. What are the six primary elements of communication?

2. How would you arrange the setting for a business meeting?

3. What listening skills can help you better understand messages you receive?

4. What are three blocks to listening with understanding?

5. What are three skills you need to read better?

Thinking Critically

6. Describe an appropriate setting for an in-home cosmetics presentation and for a stockbroker's meeting. How and why should the two settings be different?

Integrating Academic Skills

7. **COMMUNICATION** Watch the television or a video with the sound turned off. Make a list of the nonverbal messages you observe. What can you interpret from them?

Elements of Speech and Writing

Why It's Important

You will use spoken and written communication on every job throughout your life. In large part, the success you attain in your career will depend on how well you speak and write.

Key Terms

- parliamentary procedure
- quorum

Speaking

Many jobs in marketing require above-average speaking skills. Whatever your job, you will need to express yourself clearly so your employer, customers, and co-workers can understand the messages you want to send.

■ Knowing the Purpose

Before you decide what you will say, know the purpose of the message you want to send. In most cases, you will speak to inform, persuade, or entertain.

In most casual conversations and business meetings, the main purpose of speaking is to *inform*. Participants exchange information, frequently changing roles from sender to receiver and back again. When speaking to inform, get to the point clearly and concisely.

In any job, there will be times when you will need to *persuade* others to see or do things a certain way. Perhaps the most important skill in persuading others is determining the listeners' needs and showing how you can satisfy at least some of those needs. This is a salesperson's most important skill. You will look at this more closely in Unit 5.

Sometimes the purpose of speaking is to *entertain* others. Salespeople frequently need to entertain clients. It is not necessary to be a comedian to enjoy joking and telling stories. This kind of informal speaking helps create a friendly and comfortable atmosphere.

■ Using Your Voice

You will need to use your voice effectively to be a good communicator. With practice, you can develop a pleasant voice that is neither too high nor too low. Your voice will sound relaxed if you speak in a medium, even tone.

Speak loudly enough to be heard without blasting your listeners. Vary your inflections by stressing certain words and syllables. Variations of speed and loudness will help you communicate your message in an interesting way.

■ Speaking Formally

Many jobs in marketing will require you to inform or persuade others with structured messages, or *oral presentations*. The use of good body language (gestures, movements, and mannerisms) and eye contact with your listeners are necessary skills for an effective presentation.

A formal speech begins with an opening statement and concludes with a closing statement. In between, there are four basic patterns you may use to organize a structured message.

■ Key Words in the Sale
Enumerating the features of a package ski vacation to these customers gives them many reasons to want to buy. *What signal words can the travel agent use to make clear the number of reasons to buy a vacation?*

ENUMERATION *Enumeration* is listing several items in order. When instructing a new worker on how to perform a certain task, you may begin by saying, "There are four steps in performing this task." The new worker will listen for four separate but related things to do. The steps will be easier to understand because the listener is expecting them. Use *signal words*, such as *first, second, third,* or *next,* to help the listener. These signal words show the relationship between what you have already said and what you will say next.

GENERALIZATION WITH EXAMPLE Many speakers use *generalizations*—statements that are accepted as true by most people—to make a point. They support the generalizations with examples and evidence to show that the statement is true. When you make a general statement such as, "Everybody agrees that high definition television has the best picture quality and will soon take over the market," you should back it up with "A Sony survey reported 80 percent of owners say the picture clarity is worth the higher price." Using evidence to support your generalization clarifies your message and helps your listeners remember the main points. Signal words, such as *for instance* and *for example,* can help get your point across.

CAUSE AND EFFECT When you discuss an issue in terms of cause and effect, you lead the listener from the cause of something to the effect. This is an effective way to explain many topics. You can reverse this method by first presenting the effect and then considering possible causes. Use signal words, such as *therefore, consequently,* and *as a result.*

COMPARE AND CONTRAST It may be most efficient to explain something using the compare and contrast method. You can explain new concepts by showing how they are similar to or unlike those your listeners already know. Use signal words, such as *similarly, however, nevertheless,* and *on the other hand.*

■ Training

Training involves a specialized form of speaking and is usually combined with showing one or more other people how to perform a particular task.

When you are responsible for training others, you will find that the following four-step training plan is effective in almost all training situations. First, explain the task that is to be performed. Second, demonstrate how to perform the task—by actually doing it yourself. Third, let the other person or persons try doing the task. Finally, provide a critique that explains what was done correctly and discusses the strong points so the trainee will feel accomplished. After this encouragement, discuss the changes that should be made to perform the task properly and completely. Make the trainee feel as though it is a cooperative effort. This will motivate him or her to improve and minimize any feelings of inadequacy.

■ Parliamentary Procedure

If you have ever been a member of a student organization like the student council, you are probably familiar with parliamentary procedure. Parliamentary procedure is a structure for holding group meetings and making decisions. It is meant to make meetings democratic and decision-making orderly. Parliamentary procedure favors the opinion of the majority of a group. However, this does not mean that the viewpoint of the minority is overlooked. Every issue that comes up is discussed freely and thoroughly before a final decision is reached. Parliamentary procedure is used in government, business, and social clubs. The rules that govern it vary depending on the contexts. Certain elements, however, are almost always present. Learning about them will help prepare you for formal business meetings.

A QUORUM In order for business to be conducted at a meeting, there must be a quorum. A quorum is a proportion of the membership needed to conduct official business. The organization's constitution usually covers what a quorum must be. It may be a set number, like 20, or a percentage of members, like 51 percent.

ORDER OF BUSINESS The meeting follows a standard *order of business*, which is called an agenda. The standard format for a meeting is as follows:

1. *Call to order* The president or chairperson opens the meeting by saying, for example "I now call this meeting to order." This statement alerts all members that the meeting is beginning and that they should be quiet. The chairperson's job is to make sure the meeting runs according to the rules.

2. *Minutes of the meeting* The secretary reads the minutes, which are a written record that outlines the decisions made at the last meeting. The minutes also cover such information as the date and time of the previous meeting and the members who were in attendance. The president or chairperson asks all members if there are any additions or corrections to the minutes. The minutes are accepted as a permanent record of the organization if there are no corrections.

3. *Treasurer's report* The treasurer reports the money that the organization received since the last meeting and the money it spent, as well as the current balance.

4. *Committee reports* Committees are set up in organizations to do research or plan events. Each committee presents a report at a meeting to let the entire membership know what they have done and what they plan to do. Committees that exist year after year are called *standing committees*. Other committees may be established as the need arises. Some standing committees for a local DECA chapter may oversee fund raising or civic-minded projects.

BRIGHT IDEAS

Mouse Potatoes

You've all heard the term couch potatoes, but have you ever heard of a "mouse potato"? Well La-Z-Boy recliner chair manufacturers certainly have. Their latest product—the La-Z-Boy Explorer "e-cliner"—was created with the mouse potato in mind. This comfy recliner lets customers kick back their legs to relax with their computer at their fingertips on the special keyboard tray. The chair also includes a power outlet, a storage tray in the right arm, as well as a WebTV hookup with a two-month free subscription. Mouse potatoes can kick back as they surf the Web, check their stocks, and watch television all from the comfort of their recliner.

Thinking Creatively

The Internet has already made life more convenient for many people. What are other ways that using the Internet can be simplified even more?

■ **Parliamentary Procedure** Parliamentary procedure allows formal meetings to run smoothly, making sure there is a time for all that needs to be discussed. *Why would it be important to read the minutes of the last meeting before moving on to important topics?*

5. *Old business* Any issues that were discussed at the previous meeting but were not decided on become old business. Old business is reported at this point in the meeting.

6. *New business* New ideas that members would like to have considered are brought up at the end of the meeting. It is important to discuss only one new issue at a time.

7. *Adjournment* The president or chairperson entertains a motion to adjourn the meeting. If accepted, this is the official end of the meeting. The secretary records the time of adjournment in the minutes.

THE MOTION After being recognized, or allowed to speak by the chairperson, one member makes a *motion,* or a proposal. Then, another member must *second* the motion. A period of discussion follows when a motion has been made and seconded. If no one seconds the motion, it is not discussed. The procedure of making and accepting motions is one

that can be formal or informal. The formal method calls for much discussion and must repeat the motion, call for a discussion, establish the voting time, and announce the result. In other cases, when a move motion is used, the chair may adopt the policy of *general consent*. In this case, the chair will introduce an issue and propose the logical action that could be taken. He or she would then ask if there were any objections; if not, this would be the decision of the group. This is most often used when discussing issues that are not controversial or sensitive. Once a member is recognized by the chairperson, he or she has the right to speak for a certain length of time without being interrupted. Only one member is permitted to speak at a time to assure that each person is heard. When the time for discussion is up, the chairperson asks for a vote. This is known as *calling the question*. A majority vote is usually enough to *win adoption*, otherwise known as *carrying the motion*.

A Prescription for Success

Is there a doctor in the house? If you have Internet access the answer is "yes." An increasing number of doctors today are making house calls: E-mail house calls, that is. Patients can log onto Web sites like AmericasDoctor.com and ask questions and chat with physicians. With long lines in doctors' offices, restrictive HMO plans, and overbooked doctors, the patient/doctor relationship has suffered. The Internet has helped to bridge the communication gap between patients and doctors. Physicians with their own Web sites believe that this new mode of communication helps inform and educate patients and improves upon the health-care experience.

Thinking Critically

Why are reading and writing skills crucial to Internet physician communication?

Telephone Skills

If you take a job in marketing, you will probably speak to many people on the telephone. A pleasant voice is even more important on the telephone than in face-to-face conversations. Your listener can't see you, so you can't rely on facial expressions and body language to help get your message across.

Answer the telephone with a cheerful but formal greeting. Your greeting should also confirm with the caller that he or she has reached the right number. Working in customer relations, you might say, "Customer relations, this is Maria, how may I help you?"

Use a pleasant tone, enunciate clearly, and speak directly into the mouthpiece. Speak loudly enough for the other person to hear, but don't shout. Listen as well on the telephone as you do in a face-to-face conversation. Develop the habit of being courteous and never interrupt when the other person is speaking.

Be prepared to take a message. Have a pencil and paper ready to write down the time of the call, the

caller's name and message, and the return phone number. Repeat the telephone number to the caller to make sure it is correct. Some businesses have phone logs in which to record every incoming call.

Writing

Writing a message takes more time and thought than simply having a conversation, but there are times when it is more appropriate. Writing a message helps you organize your thoughts.

Many people forget most of the message in a conversation within 24 hours, but a written message is a permanent record. It's hard to ignore a written message. The person receiving it is more likely to take appropriate action than if the same message were delivered in a conversation.

■ Basic Considerations in Writing

In every type of writing, it is important to know the precise reason for which you are writing a message. Three basic considerations when writing are to know your reader, know your purpose, and know your subject.

Before you begin writing even your first draft, think about how well you *know your reader*. Who are the people who will receive your message? Why will they read your message? What do they know about the subject? These answers will help you to write a more meaningful message.

The second consideration before you begin writing your message is that you *know your purpose*. Most of your writing will be done to inform, request, confirm, persuade, inquire, or complain. Some messages, of course, combine two or more of these purposes.

You will need to *know your subject* well to write a clear message about it. You may be well-educated on particular subjects for your job, but sometimes further research will be necessary.

■ Developing a Writing Style

The executives of a company generally establish the writing style. You can read company letters, e-mail, memos, and reports before writing any yourself to help you determine your company's style.

The trend in business writing is toward a direct, conversational style. Remember, you are writing to

Case Study

"Soft Skills" Work!

When the U. S. and global economies are doing well, there is considerable competition for good employees. Companies must develop strategies to hold on to them. Making sure managers and employees are proficient at "soft skills" gives a real boost.

The term "soft skills" refers to interpersonal skills that managers use when problem solving and supervising employees. Employees are more loyal when their managers have good interpersonal skills. Effective communication and teamwork skills are also essential in today's team-based organizations. Schools or private training companies that provide training in these soft skills are enjoying a boom in the 21st century.

Many companies are training their lower-level employees in soft skills as well. Companies have discovered that teams that are low in technical skills but work well together are more productive than teams with good technical skills but poor teamwork.

Companies still save money despite training expenses. One study showed that training current employees saved $12,000 per worker over hiring new employees. Training managers to be more sensitive to employees' needs gives companies an edge in holding on to their best employees—those who could find work anywhere.

Case Study Review

1. How are personal skills important in raising productivity?
2. Is it more important for workers or managers to take soft skills training? Defend your position.

A MATTER OF ETHICS

3. If someone has great technical skills and works harder than his co-workers but has a terrible temper and can't get along with anyone, do you think it is ethical to fire him? Why or why not?

communicate a message to one or more receivers. Use a crisp, clear style that is easy to read. Don't use extensive vocabulary to impress others. Use a word processing program with spelling and grammar checkers to eliminate common errors. You should always review the letter one final time to ensure that no mistakes were overlooked.

Personalize your message by using the name of the person who will receive it. The receiver will have a warmer feeling toward you if you do.

You may need to use some jargon in your messages to people in your career field. However, avoid jargon when you can or explain any jargon you must use when writing to those outside your field.

FIGURE 8-1

BUSINESS LETTERS

M ost business letters include eight standard parts.

1

The return address is the address of the letter writer. Most companies have their addresses printed on stationery called letterhead. When you type a business letter on blank paper, type the return address at the top of the page.

3

The inside address is the name and address of the person who will receive the letter. The same address is typed on the envelope.

Southland Office Supply

11061 West Olympic Boulevard Los Angeles, California 90064

2

The date line shows the reader when the letter was written. In business, it is important to document when you write a letter.

4

The salutation is the greeting. The most commonly used salutation is, "Dear (Mr., Mrs., Miss, Ms.)." If you usually call the person by his or her first name, you can use it in the salutation: "Dear Adam." If you are not sending the letter to a specific person, make the salutation to the department to which you are sending the letter: "Dear Customer Service Department." A colon always follows the salutation in a business letter.

August 30, 2002

Mr. Dan Provost
Super Sports Magazine
3119 South Barrington Avenue
Suite G
Los Angeles, CA 90066

Dear Mr. Provost:

Today we received your written request for four (4) reams of Pale Yellow 24-pound writing bond. We are ordering it for you from our supplier, who promises to have it to us in five (5) days. I will call you as soon as it comes in.

Thank you for thinking of Southland for your office supply needs. We look forward to filling this order and to doing business with you in the future.

Sincerely yours,

Jessica H. Johnston, Manager

jhj/ktb

5

The body is the message of the letter.

6

The closing is a respectful goodbye. Formal closings for business letters are, "Yours very truly" and "Yours truly." Less formal, more friendly closings are, "Sincerely" and "Cordially." A comma should follow the closing.

7

The signature block includes the handwritten and typed name of the writer. Sign your name in ink above your typed name. Write both your first and last name, unless you are on a first-name basis with the reader.

8

The reference initials are the initials of the writer and sometimes the initials of the typist. They are typed two spaces below your typed signature, beginning at the left margin. The writer's initials are always typed first.

Letters, E-mail, Memos, and Reports

There are many types of written communications. In business, most written messages are in the form of letters, e-mail, memos, or reports.

The main form of written communication with people outside your own company will be business letters. Business letters are always typed or word processed and printed on a laser printer (see Figure 8-1 on page 150).

In recent years, e-mail has become the method of choice for fast communication with both those inside and outside of your own company. In many companies, it has almost replaced memos for in-house communication (see Figure 8-2).

E-mail has advantages over other means of written communication because messages are sent immediately. This ensures that urgent messages will be received in a timely manner. It is also cost-effective and environmentally friendly, as no paper is used.

An interoffice e-mail typically contains:

- An informative subject title
- A traditional (not personal) greeting
- A concise, clearly stated body of text
- A statement regarding the type of response needed
- A formal closing and signature (for the signature, type your name, company, address, phone and fax number, and e-mail address)

Although e-mail has a reputation for speed and informality, it is important to compose your e-mail messages carefully. E-mails should have a style appropriate to the situation and conventional business language. Any information that pertains to issues other than those stated in the subject field should be sent in different e-mails.

One of the greatest dangers of business e-mail is that it is often treated informally. E-mail should not be considered private. In fact, it should be considered more permanent than traditional letters, memos, and reports because it will continue to exist in digital form long after it has been deleted or erased from a hard drive. This is because companies store many backups of every computer's hard drive in many places.

When the U.S. Justice Department pursued antitrust charges against Microsoft in 1998 and 1999, the evidence against Microsoft was in the form of millions of pages of internal e-mails. Because of this, more and more companies are developing strict e-mail policies. The following are some general rules found in most e-mail policies:

- Only save essential e-mail
- Don't forward e-mail without the sender's express permission
- Use extreme care when forwarding privileged e-mails
- Delete any copyrighted materials that you don't have permission to use

---

FIGURE 8-2

Business E-mail

From: Jessica H. Johnston <j.h.johnston@southlandoffice.net>
To: Dan Provost <danprovost@supersportsmagazine.org>
Date: Wednesday, August 30, 2002, 4:26 PM
Subject: Your request

— — — — —

Dear Mr. Provost,

Today we received your written request for four (4) reams of Pale Yellow 24-pound writing bond. We are ordering it for you from our supplier, who promises to have it in five (5) days. I will call you as soon as it comes in.

Thank you for thinking of Southland for your office supply needs. We look forward to filling this order and to doing business with you in the future.

Jessica H. Johnston

— —

Jessica H. Johnston
Senior Manager
j.h.johnston@southlandoffice.net
Phone: (800) 867-5309
Fax: (888) 867-5309

■ **Business E-mail** E-mail is commonly used for communication within an office or company. Although e-mail has a reputation for speed and informality, it is important to compose your e-mail messages carefully. *Why do you think this is so?*

A memo, the abbreviation for memorandum, is a written message to someone in your company. It is usually brief and covers only one subject. Most memos are written in a simple format that has a standard set of headings. The standard headings include the sender's and receiver's names, the date, the subject, and then write your message in paragraph form. Look at the sample memo in Figure 8-3.

Business reports cover such topics as yearly sales, survey results, or problems that need attention. Some are called *in-house reports* because they are to be read only by company employees. Others, such as reports to stockholders, are written for a wider audience. An in-house report can be written by a company department to let management know the results of a project, or a report might move from one department to another. The sales department may produce a report to tell the design department how customers like a product. Several people may give input to produce the report, but one person is usually responsible for the final writing.

■ Company Publications

Many marketing companies produce internal publications for their employees. These might include employee handbooks that outline policies and procedures or newsletters. Companies also produce external publications, such as promotional brochures about the company or individual products. Internal publications are usually written by the corporate communications department, while external publications are often written by the marketing department.

FIGURE 8-3

Memorandum

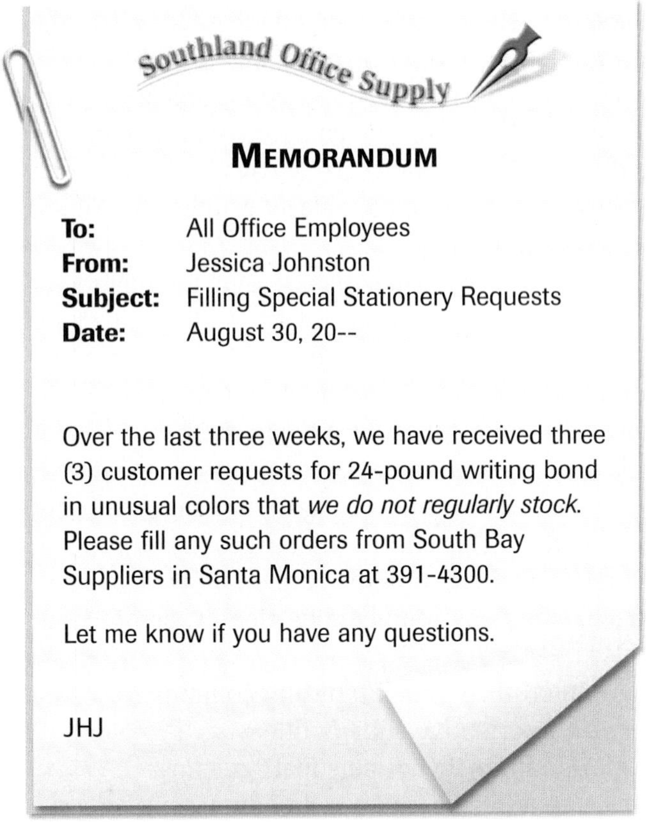

Southland Office Supply

MEMORANDUM

To: All Office Employees
From: Jessica Johnston
Subject: Filling Special Stationery Requests
Date: August 30, 20--

Over the last three weeks, we have received three (3) customer requests for 24-pound writing bond in unusual colors that *we do not regularly stock.* Please fill any such orders from South Bay Suppliers in Santa Monica at 391-4300.

Let me know if you have any questions.

JHJ

■ **Memorandum** Memos are used for communication within an office or company. Their format is more informal than a business letter. *Why do you think this is so?*

8.2 ASSESSMENT

Reviewing Key Terms and Concepts

1. What are the three most common purposes for speaking?

2. What are the four basic patterns used to organize a spoken message?

3. What is parliamentary procedure? Why is it used?

4. What types of information should you write down when taking a telephone message?

5. What are the three basic things you should consider when writing?

Thinking Critically

6. Your co-worker has asked you to review a letter he has written to a customer. What elements will you look for in his business letter?

Integrating Academic Skills

7. **MATH** To send a fax anywhere in the United States, a local business charges $4 for the first page and $1 for subsequent pages. If a fax machine costs $600 to purchase, how many single-page documents could you send commercially for the same price?

Careers in Marketing

William Cusick
Vice President/Real Estate Broker
Birmingham Real Estate Inc.

What does your job entail?

"Real estate brokers are independent real estate agents who sell residential and business property owned by others. Some brokers manage properties for a fee. My primary responsibility is asking people what they need and searching the marketplace to find a match. Brokers may be involved in arranging for title searches, financing, and closing details. Real estate brokers spend time listing properties for sale, as well as hiring and supervising real estate agents, advertising properties, and handling the business matters of their office."

What skills are most important to you?

"Interpersonal skills—especially listening—are important in my field. Real estate brokers and agents must be honest, customer oriented, work well with the public, and have good memories for names and details. Networking with other professionals in the communities where they work and cultivating personal contacts are also important."

What kind of training did you have?

"For most people, real estate is learned from experience. I would recommend that students take Real Estate courses in college in addition to classes dealing with finance, marketing, business, business law, and economics."

What do you like most about your work?

"My job offers a lot of variety. The workload varies tremendously, especially since I work on a client's schedule. A broker could turn down an assignment because he or she is too busy, but one never knows what the "pipeline" of work will be in two weeks once current assignments are completed. I enjoy the sense of being my own boss, and the satisfaction of completing a project where the customer finds what he or she wants and is happy with it."

What is your key to success?

"Timing—I was in the right place at the right time!"

Thinking Critically

How can a real estate broker get feedback to improve his or her marketing skills?

Career Facts

Education and Training: A state license is necessary in order to practice as a broker. Experience as a real estate agent is needed as well as a bachelor's degree, in some cases.

Aptitudes, Abilities, and Skills: Honesty, good decision-making skills, customer oriented, good memory for details and names, and strong knowledge of business conditions and property values are essential.

Career Outlook: Employment of real estate brokers and real estate agents is expected to continue to grow through 2008. The ability of customers to conduct their own property searches through Web sites, however, may decrease the need for brokers and agents.

Career Path: Experienced real estate agents can advance to sales managers or may obtain their broker's license. Experienced agents may also become real estate appraisers. Brokers may move on to the fields of mortgage financing, real estate investment counseling, or property management.

Chapter 8 ASSESSMENT

VOCABULARY REVIEW

Use each of the following in a 250-word paper on communication.

- communication
- channels
- feedback
- blocks
- setting
- distractions
- emotional blocks
- jargon
- parliamentary procedure
- quorum

FACT AND IDEA REVIEW

1. What is communication? (8.1)
2. Describe how the communication of a message is a two-way process. (8.1)
3. Why is it important to give feedback when someone is giving you directions? (8.1)
4. Why is a small room a good setting for a meeting with one other person? (8.1)
5. Discuss when and how making judgments as a listener can be helpful. (8.1)
6. Discuss why taking notes is part of being an effective listener. (8.1)
7. Name the four steps used in training. (8.2)
8. Name the seven parts of a meeting agenda. (8.2)
9. How should you answer a business call? (8.2)
10. What are some of the advantages of a written rather than a verbal message? (8.2)

THINKING CRITICALLY

1. Why is it important to be a good listener? Which listening skills could help you most in school? How?
2. Describe a situation in which it would be appropriate and helpful to make judgments as a listener. Describe another situation in which it would not be helpful.
3. Choose a career that interests you. Describe how being a good reader could help you in that job.
4. Which of the four patterns in this chapter would you discuss when instructing a fellow employee on how to complete a task? Explain.
5. In parliamentary procedure, when is a formal procedure of motions used? When would an informal procedure be appropriate? Why?

BUILDING WORKPLACE SKILLS

1. **Writing** Using a word processing program, write a business letter to the principal of your school, describing a plan to raise funds for new football uniforms. Include all the standard parts of a business letter, and use the spelling and grammar check feature of your program.
2. **Human Relations** You are a manager of a home electronics store. You observe a new salesperson who is trying to impress a customer with his technical expertise and terminology. You can see that his overuse of jargon is offensive to the customer. What should you do?

APPLYING MARKETING CONCEPTS

1. **Defining E-mail Policies** You are the manager at a telecommunications software company that relies on e-mail for internal and external communication. Lately it seems that employees are spending more time using their computers for personal e-mail. Prepare an oral report using presentation software that outlines appropriate e-mail standards and behavior to be discussed at a future meeting.

2. **Preparing a Business Letter** Use a word processing program to write a formal business letter from your company, Jack's Construction, to Acme Hardware. The hardware store has delivered faulty pipe to you, and you are writing to correct the situation.

3. **Researching Marketing Fields** Choose a marketing field you are interested in. Use a word processing program to write a business letter to an executive of a company in this marketing field. (Your librarian can help you find the correct address.) Request information about preparing for the career that interests you.

4. **Creating Marketing Materials** You have just started a new job as the marketing director at a nonprofit organization that provides professional clothing and uniforms to economically-challenged men and women who are looking for employment. The organization's brochures are outdated, and your first duty is to create an up-to-date one. Using design software, create a brochure including information on your organization and how people can help support it.

LINKING SCHOOL TO WORK

Information Skills Interview an employer to find out how often written communication is necessary at the workplace. How often does he or she need to write a business letter, report, or memo? What other types of writing does he or she need to do? Share your findings with the class.

THE DECA CONNECTION

Role Play: Clerk Trainer

Situation Assume the role of a newly promoted assistant manager of the parts department at a local auto dealership. You will be responsible for training new parts clerks.

Activity Before you begin training others, the manager (judge) has asked that you demonstrate to him that you can complete the following tasks: orient new employees; reinforce service orientation through communication; use proper grammar and vocabulary; handle customer/client complaints; and give directions for completing job tasks.

Evaluation You will be evaluated on how well you meet the following performance indicators:

- Explain the four-step plan for training employees
- Understand essential topics that should be covered with new employees
- Use formal speech
- Display effective listening skills

interNET CONNECTION

Meeting Notes

You have been asked to prepare the minutes from the student government meeting, and you don't know what format to use.

Connect

- Find the Web sites of local government agencies, such as the water board and planning commission, and look for links to their meeting records.
- Compare the meeting minutes of two or three different agencies.
- Develop your own format for student government minutes based on your research.

Chapter 9

Computer Applications and Skills

Marketing: What It Takes

Rewarding Regular Customers

You are the assistant manager of a large retail computer store. Because you have more background and experience in advertising than the manager, you are responsible for planning and carrying out the advertising program. Your manager likes the advertisements you have written for the local newspaper, but wonders how you might get more repeat business from those who make purchases at your store.

WHAT WILL YOU DO?
How will you plan to entice more repeat business from current customers?

Computers in Marketing

Computers

Businesses use computers to generate correspondence, maintain lists of customers or clients, and control inventory. They also use computers to create advertising materials, calculate and produce financial reports, and communicate electronically with other computer users. Most businesses today could not compete successfully in the world market without the use of computer technology.

Computers make it possible for businesses to process a large quantity of information with enhanced speed, ease, and accuracy—and at a reduced cost! They also allow businesses to reduce the number of staff members they require, improve their profit margins, enhance inventory control, and effectively track customer sales patterns. Most businesses find that their investment in computer technology is money well spent.

Computers and related technology have been credited for the immense increase in productivity seen in the late 1990s and into the 2000s. The tiny microprocessor—the silicon chip—has expanded the use of computer technology and moved the world into the Age of Technology. Throughout the 1990s and early 2000s, U.S. industry spent more money on computers and communications equipment than on all other types of capital equipment combined. This included all machinery needed for manufacturing, mining, agriculture, construction, and all other fields of production.

It is usually a matter of time before the technological strides that advance one industry are adopted by other industries. This is illustrated by the example of robotics, or the technology of computer controlled machines. In the 1940s, the first simple robots handled dangerous radioactive materials. In the 1950s, scientists at MIT learned how to control robots using computer technology. In the early 1960s, the company Unimation built and promoted the first robots used for manufacturing.

Aided by computer technology, scientists are able to manipulate a robot's "hands" closely. This advancement moved robotics into medicine. Surgeons are beginning to use robots to perform delicate open-heart surgery. The surgeon sits at a computer screen and uses a device similar to a video game's joystick to control the robot. The robot's "hands" are tiny and much steadier than any human hand, making it possible to perform surgery with smaller incisions and less injury to the body.

This technology that was invented for the military was adapted for use in both business and health fields. Shared technology such as this will continue to improve efficiency of work and quality of life.

• What You'll Learn

- The major ways computers are used to save businesses money
- The characteristics of different types of computers
- The functions of basic pieces of computer hardware

• Why It's Important

Computers have changed our personal lives in many ways, including the way that we engage in marketing. Success in the business world increasingly depends on an understanding of and proficiency in the use of computer technology.

Key Terms

- supercomputer
- mainframe
- minicomputer
- microcomputer
- laptop
- PDAs
- hardware
- disk drive
- CD-ROM
- DVD
- scanner
- software

As computer technology revolutionizes the work place, computers are replacing people. Statistics show that effective organizations are decreasing in size. Increased efficiency through computer technology has allowed many businesses to reduce their clerical and managerial staff. People can connect to a server from their home computer and complete the same work previously done in an office. The types of jobs are changing, too. There is an overall shift away from manufacturing toward services. In 2000, white collar jobs had increased to 60 percent of the workforce.

Types of Computers

Computers range widely in size, cost, speed, and power. The largest and most powerful type of computer is called a supercomputer. Supercomputers are used for the most sophisticated work, such as directing space missions or tracking hurricanes.

Mainframe computers are large, sometimes filling a whole room. Mainframe computers are used where many people in a large organization need frequent access to the same information. Large corporations, universities, and government organizations generally use mainframe computers.

Minicomputers are next in size and power, and are used by many businesses. The capabilities of a minicomputer lie somewhere between those of mainframes and those of personal computers. Minicomputers are ideal for organizations and companies that cannot afford or do not need a mainframe system. They enable smaller organizations to deal with large amounts of information and complex processes, and give access to multiple users.

Most medium and smaller businesses use the microcomputer, which is also referred to as the personal computer, or PC. It is the computer most people use at home. Since its introduction in the early 1980s, this machine has thrived as a business tool. Many businesses connect a powerful microcomputer as a *server* to a number of work stations. The server provides computing power and large amounts of storage.

A laptop is a smaller, portable personal computer. Laptops are fully functional microcomputers. Also called notebooks, they can operate on plug-in current or with special batteries. Laptops are rapidly acquiring all capabilities of the nonportable PC.

Celtic Tiger

Green fields, sheep farmers, and Riverdance— these images may be what people associate with Ireland. This is changing as technological and economic growth in Ireland is on the upswing. Ireland surpassed the GDP and standard of living of Great Britain in 1997, overcoming their stereotypes. This showed the world that the "Celtic Tiger" was a force to watch. In addition to the plants operated by Dell and Intel, many Internet start-up companies are being established in Ireland. This makes it clear that the Irish plan to stay a contender.

Thinking Critically
Why would developing countries that are lagging in the technological race look to Ireland for inspiration?

Laptops, in recent years, have become not only smaller and lighter but also more affordable to travelers and students alike.

Personal digit assistants (PDAs) are the smallest of portable computers. Often, they are no larger than the palm of your hand. PDAs, also called palmtops, are much less powerful than notebook or desktop computers. Many PDAs can be connected to larger computers. You can use a palm-size computer for a variety of functions, including sending and receiving e-mail and communicating via the Internet. PDAs are often used as personal organizers, incorporating an address book, memo pad, date book, and calculator. Advanced models have high resolution graphics and can function as entertainment devices capable of playing movie trailers, digital photography, and arcade games!

The wireless cell phone, too, is utilizing more computer technology. Cell phones can now be used to send and receive e-mail messages. Despite their increasingly sophisticated components, cell phones are often affected by factors as simple as the location where they are used.

Computer System Components

The components of a computer system are hardware and software. Hardware and software work together to enable a computer to function. Let's take a closer look at these components.

■ Hardware

Hardware is the equipment—the physical components that make up a computer system. Hardware comprises all of the interconnected electronic devices that you can use to control the computer's operation, input, and output.

The system unit is the main part of the computer, with the central processing unit (CPU) at the heart. Most system units contain one or more disk drives—the device that holds a disk. A disk drive is used to read data from and write data to a disk. Some disks are built into the drive and are not meant to be removed. Other kinds of disk drives enable you to remove and replace disks. The storage capacity of disks varies, but rapid developments in technology continually make it possible to buy more storage capacity for less money.

Other types of data storage devices include CD-ROM and digital versatile disk (DVD) drives. Compact disks (CDs) are used in CD-ROM drives and are a type of optical storage device identical to audio music CDs. A DVD disk is a high-density optical storage device capable of storing a full-length movie on a single disk the size of a CD.

The keyboard is used to type information and commands into the computer and to control its action. It looks like the keys on a typewriter with a numeric keypad and function keys added. People often use a mouse as an input device. You can give a computer commands by moving a mouse on a flat surface and pushing its buttons.

A monitor displays computer output, such as a business letter or computer graphics. A monitor is either a cathode ray tube (CRT) similar to a TV set or liquid crystal display (LCD) similar to digital display clocks or watches. Most monitors today display your work in millions of colors.

A printer reproduces an image from the computer onto paper. Laser and ink jet printers are very popular and have excellent print quality. Color ink jet printers produce outstanding photographic prints and other graphic images.

Computer hardware may also include other options. Scanners have become very popular. A scanner reads and transforms images into digital data. Scanners are also used to convert photographs into digital files for editing and manipulation in a photo editing program (See Figure 9-1 on page 160).

■ **Updated Version** Application software for personal computers is continually being improved. *What types of upgrades do you envision for the next generation of software?*

FIGURE 9-1

COMPUTER PERIPHERALS

Computer Peripherals connect to your computer and make it more versatile and powerful. *Which of these devices have you used? What other peripherals have you used?*

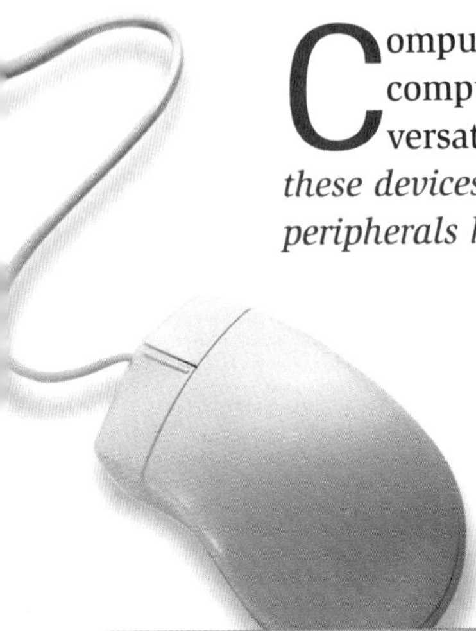

CD-ROM OR DVD DRIVE

A CD-ROM drive is a specialized type of disk drive that enables a computer to read data from a compact disk. DVDs provide high-resolution graphics, animation, video, and digital sound. DVDs can store large amounts of information, including text, pictures, and sound.

MOUSE, TRACKBALL, OR TRACKPAD

A mouse, trackball, or trackpad is a small hand-operated device with a button, ball, or just a pad that is sensitive to movement. These are used to move a cursor or arrow to different locations on the screen, and then "clicked" to perform functions.

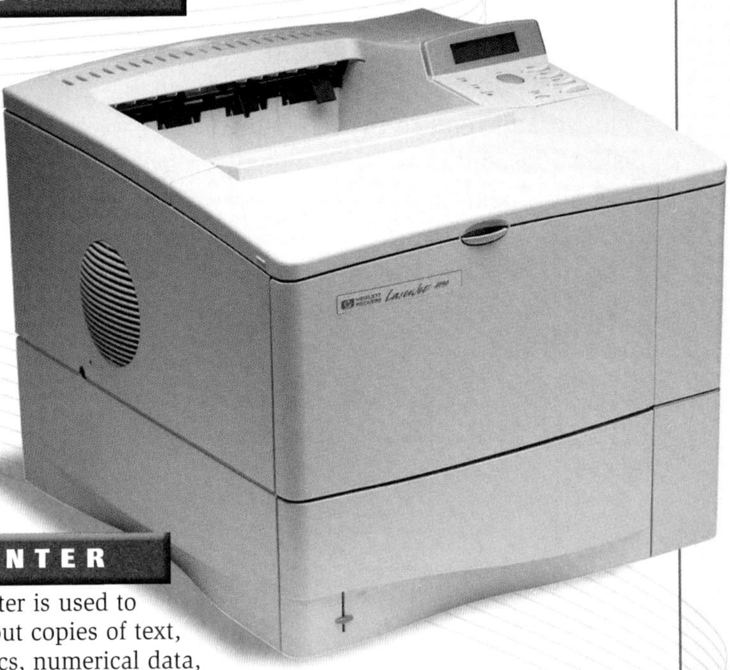

MODEM

A modem connects your computer to the phone, cable, DSL, or ISDN connection lines. It allows your computer to connect with others in a local network, and to connect to the Internet. Most computers have built-in modems.

PRINTER

A printer is used to print out copies of text, graphics, numerical data, or whatever you have created on your computer.

SCANNER

A scanner allows you to input text or a graphic image into your computer. The scanner translates the visual image into digital data. The scanner software then displays the text or graphic image on your computer screen.

■ Software

Software is a set of electronic instructions that directs the CPU to carry out a specific task. These sets of instructions are also known as programs or applications and each one has a specific purpose.

Most software falls into two major categories: system software and application software. One major type of system software, called *operating software*, tells the computer how to use its own components. The operating system basically determines what programs you can run on your computer. Applications must be compatible with the operating system of the computer platform you use. Two widely used platforms are the IBM-compatible—called PC—and the Apple Macintosh. Most Apples use the Macintosh operating system, while most PCs use the Windows operating system.

Application software is used for many different functions, such as word processing or production of graphics. These functions will be described in Section 9.2.

Some companies create specific software to meet their needs. Most common applications, though, are available commercially. Software publishing has become America's fastest growing industry. Major software publishing companies, such as Microsoft, Novell, Borland, and Oracle, continually compete to produce the newest, most technologically advanced products in this booming market.

Linking Technologies

Microsoft has something new up its sleeve with its plans to link all technological devices together. Imagine visiting a zoo to collect information for a report through your handheld computer/phone, then sending digital photos to friends. Your friends could view the images on their televisions and immediately transfer them to a digital picture frame. How about using a mobile phone to find a doctor in a new city, choose which insurance company policy to use for billing, schedule an appointment, and send medical records to the new doctor. While this software is basically developed, Microsoft is waiting for computer hardware to develop accordingly before releasing this technology on the market.

Thinking Critically

What other ideas may become realities utilizing linked technologies?

9.1 ASSESSMENT

Reviewing Key Terms and Concepts

1. What are three ways that computers can save businesses money?

2. What are the functions of four basic pieces of computer hardware?

3. What is the function of a scanner?

4. What is operating system software?

Thinking Critically

5. What are some advantages and disadvantages of the use of robots in the medical field?

Integrating Academic Skills

6. **COMMUNICATION** Your employer wants to upgrade the computer hardware in your marketing firm. The supervisor of information management is an expert on computers. She has been asked to explain the capabilities of the latest equipment and to assess employees' needs. However, she speaks in *computerese* (using technical computer terms). What could you say to this supervisor to help solve the problem?

Computer Applications

What You'll Learn

- Eight types of popular computer application programs
- How these programs are used in business

Why It's Important

Computer technology is the driving force behind the most productive economy the world has ever known. It is likely that you will use computer hardware and software on the job; in fact, your career success may be measured by your understanding and skillful use of these applications.

Key Terms

- word processing programs
- database programs
- spreadsheet programs
- desktop publishing programs
- graphics and design programs
- presentation software
- home page
- Web page editors
- Web page
- hypertext markup language (HTML)
- communications programs
- e-mail

Software

Software application programs have been developed to help us manage just about every facet of our lives. People use software applications to manage their time and money. Medical practices use programs to schedule patients and manage billing. Hotels use software applications to manage room assignments and generate bills. Universities use application software to keep track of thousands of students and their class schedules. Farmers use software to manage their livestock and crops. Architects use computer aided design (CAD) programs to design buildings. There is even software available to help programmers write more software!

There are endless types of software available to meet our needs. In this section, we will discuss eight popular types of software applications commonly used in marketing. These types include word processing, database management, spreadsheets, desktop publishing, graphics and design, presentation, Web page editors, and communications programs.

■ Word Processing Programs

Word processing programs are software applications used to create documents that are primarily text but may also contain some graphics.

Many businesses use word processing programs to
- Write letters and memos
- Produce research papers and reports
- Write business plans
- Create contracts
- Record meeting minutes
- Create announcements

It is likely that you've used a word processing program for writing a letter or preparing a research paper for school; if so, you are aware of how these programs simplify your work. Word processing allows you to make changes in your documents while viewing the changes on screen. Word processing programs help you to produce sophisticated, polished documents in a fraction of the time it would take on a typewriter.

Most word processing programs contain a thesaurus, dictionary, spelling checker, and grammar checker. These features help users produce more accurate documents.

Many word processing programs are available in the commercial market. Among the more popular word processing programs are Microsoft Word and WordPerfect.

Database Programs

Database programs are software applications used to collect related data, which can be sorted, searched through, and printed as needed. Much like a warehouse, a database is a storage area for collections of related data. Database software enables businesses to track products, orders, shipments, customers, and more. Once your information is entered in the computer, the database program allows you to organize and analyze the information quickly and easily.

Database programs can be used to complete many business functions. Businesses use database programs to

- Maintain customer lists for automated mass mailings
- Keep information about guests and vendors for parties and events
- Catalog furniture and assets for insurance records
- Manage time and track billable hours
- Catalog personnel records

Suppose you have entered into the computer your company's mailing list, which contains the names and addresses of 3,000 of your customers. You could alphabetize all the names or group the addresses by zip code or display only those customers who live in a certain location with just one keystroke. Including your customers' birthdays in the database would make it possible to pull up all the customers with birthdays and send them birthday cards each month. Customer purchase history in your database would allow you to quickly pull up all those customers who made purchases during a certain month or who purchased a certain dollar amount of merchandise. Consider the following example of how one business uses database software.

Tim Hilton, owner of Top Dog, a small business that breeds pedigreed Labrador dogs, uses a database to keep information about each of his dogs. The database information includes size of litter, gender, name of the mother and father, the color, weight, date born, and feeding record. It also includes the selling price and information about the owner who purchased the dog. Hilton can use his database to quickly analyze his sales records and use the data for future planning.

There are numerous types of database application programs. Some popular commercial database programs are Filemaker Pro, Lotus Approach, and Microsoft Access.

Spreadsheet Programs

Spreadsheet programs are software applications used to organize, calculate, and analyze numerical data. Spreadsheets enable you to perform financial and scientific calculations, organize numeric information, illustrate data with charts and graphs, and create professional-looking reports. Spreadsheets are used in business to

- Develop a budget
- Analyze financial performance
- Track loans or mortgages
- Track stock and bond performance
- Schedule projects
- Manage business assets
- Produce profit-and-loss statements
- Calculate and produce a payroll

■ **A Penny Saved** Programs that automate bookkeeping tasks save money for small businesses. *How could you use bookkeeping software?*

REAL WORLD MARKETING

Pen Man Ships Pens

The Fountain Pen Hospital may only have 12 employees, but $5 million in annual revenues in the sales and service of new and antique fountain pens is nothing to shake your pen at. The Fountain Pen Hospital has managed to succeed by tracking individual customer preferences and matching them to inventory. To do this, the company hired a computer programmer to design a customer database and inventory management system that can display each customer's contact information, as well as prior sales by date, pen type, and amount spent.

Thinking Critically

How do customer databases assist businesses?

Data are entered into squares, or cells, on a grid. A spreadsheet program calculates the data mathematically with amazing speed and accuracy not possible by hand or with a calculator. Working with a grid like this, you can easily change any one number and all related numbers will be adjusted automatically.

One common use of a spreadsheet is to produce a financial statement. Many businesses and organizations use spreadsheet programs to analyze their annual income and spending. The data can be used to produce a graphic picture, such as a line graph or a pie chart. The chart might depict what percent of the total outlay went toward salaries, building maintenance, research and development, or even phone bills. This pie chart illustration might be included in the annual report or in a presentation to potential investors.

Spreadsheet programs are available to suit a variety of different needs. Some popular commercial spreadsheet programs are Lotus 1-2-3 and Microsoft Excel.

■ Desktop Publishing Programs

Desktop publishing programs are software applications used to design and produce professional printed materials. These programs allow you to combine word processing and graphics. Businesses may use desktop publishing to

- Create layouts for newsletters, books, brochures, advertisements
- Create professional-looking forms, such as invoices and project planning sheets

Many businesses have learned to save large amounts of money by using desktop publishing programs. In the past, they paid a graphic design or printing firm to work for them. Now they can produce the work themselves. Take the following business for example.

Mass Potential is a business that promotes and produces training seminars nationwide. It offers one-day seminars, such as "How to Deal with Difficult Employees," "Time Management," and "Stress Reduction." Using desktop publishing software, it produces elaborate course catalogs that are distributed in mass mailings. At the seminars, each participant receives a nametag and an area map. Both items are produced with desktop publishing. During the seminars, instructors often use overlays on an overhead projector and distribute handouts. Both, of course, are produced with desktop publishing software!

Desktop publishing has become a valuable tool for professionals in all fields. It helps a company put its best foot forward and make a good impression. Desktop publishing software can produce documents that are creative, eye-catching, attractive, professional, and easy to read. Some popular commercial desktop publishing programs are Adobe Pagemaker, Corel-Ventura, and QuarkXPress.

■ Graphics and Design Programs

Graphics and design programs are software applications used to produce drawings and designs. Graphics programs can be used by businesses to

- Create professional-looking illustrations
- Design a logo or letterhead
- Illustrate floor plans and furniture arrangements
- Make flowcharts or seating and organizational charts

■ **Desktop Publishing** Computer technology has revolutionized the publishing world. *What kinds of printed materials can you create with desktop publishing software?*

Graphics and design programs can be used to produce simple drawings or elaborate designs. They can be used to create a simple flowchart of the structure of an organization. They can also be used to create stunning artwork, 3D images, technical drawings, engineering graphics, and elaborate diagramming. Sound and animation can be added for multimedia presentations.

Most graphics and design programs come with professionally created art—called *clip art*. The images are usually grouped together in categories like business, food, sports, people, places, animals, cartoons, or holidays. Some popular graphics and design programs include Adobe Illustrator, and CorelDRAW.

■ Presentation Software

Presentation software is used to create slide shows or multimedia presentations all in one program. It is helpful with organizing, illustrating, and presenting ideas during a meeting or on the Internet. Presentation software can be used by businesses to

- Prepare verbal and visual copy for meetings
- Present ideas interactively with clients that are located in other cities or countries via the Internet
- Create slide shows using pictures or Web pages

Presentation software is used to produce a series of slides. Slides are single screen images that usually contain a combination of text and graphics, such as pictures or charts. Colorful graphics and concise text can be used in sales presentations to persuade clients and close sales.

Presentation software handles both graphics and text with equal ease to create well-crafted presentations. It is possible to add voice narration so that it seems as if you are truly at a conference, though you may be thousands of miles away.

Gone are the days of presentation boards propped up on stands in the front of a conference room. Now large screens can showcase presentations that are put in action with the click of a mouse. Programs like this are useful for large companies like Coca-Cola or McDonald's, who have shareholders and manufacturers located all over the world. The head of a department can create a presentation using text, bulleted lists, graphs, photos, and even screen shots from the company Web page. This can be broadcast to conference rooms in numerous different countries. As global interaction in the business world increases, programs like this simplify communication and cut down on travel time. Some examples of presentation software programs are Microsoft PowerPoint and Metacreations Office Advantage.

■ Web Page Editors

Most businesses either have a Web site or are preparing one. Businesses use their Web sites to promote their company and its products. Most also revise and improve their Web sites regularly. Many Web sites contain a top level home page that has links to other pages throughout the site.

Web page editors are applications used to create Web pages. A Web page usually contains text, photos, graphics, and hyperlinks. Also called HTML editors, Web editing software makes the work of coding a Web page with HTML easier. Web pages are written

Case Study

Buying Online at the Mall

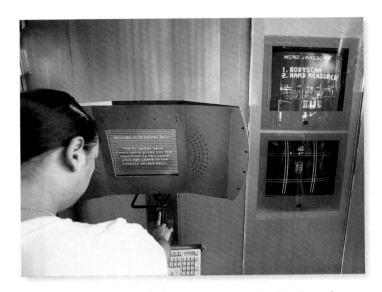

You might think online marketing is limited to people surfing the Web from home. Retail stores are installing Web kiosks so customers can shop online right inside the store.

Executives at Gap, the clothing retailer, don't believe that online shopping causes in-store sales to decrease; rather, they complement each other. Web kiosks bring in online shoppers who browse the store racks. Shoppers who don't find a certain style, size, or color on the shelves can go to the kiosk and order online. They can also find information about Gap products that may influence them to buy in the store.

Some online marketers are opening stores so shoppers can see and test their products before buying. One marketing analyst says that marketers need a physical outlet, in addition to a Web site, to attract a mass market.

Some retailers offer interactive kiosks that don't connect to the Internet but to an in-store intranet. These provide information about products or related activities. A camping equipment store may offer information about camping, fishing, hiking, and canoeing.

Web and information kiosks are creative ways to combine computer and online technology with in-store shopping. Future marketers will use this development to come up with even more ways to market their goods and services.

Case Study Review
1. Why would a store choose to have in-store network kiosks rather than connect to the Internet?
2. How could it help a camping store to provide information to customers about local campgrounds?

A Matter of Ethics
3. What ethical issues are involved when an e-tailer sells your address to another marketer?

in a language called hypertext markup language (HTML). Before a Web page can be viewed in a Web browser, it must be formatted in HTML. The HTML coding tells the browser how to display the text, whether as a heading, a table, or a link. The coding also tells the browser when and how to display images and when to link to another page. Viewing the code "behind" an HTML page reveals a complicated jumble of words and numbers. Basic HTML is relatively simple, and more and more HTML editing

programs are automating coding so that Web page authoring can be as simple as using a standard word processor.

To understand and troubleshoot Web pages that are not working properly, it is important to have a basic understanding of HTML. Fortunately, there are many excellent resources available on the Web that would-be Webmasters can refer to. Among the more popular Web page design programs are Microsoft FrontPage and Adobe PageMill.

■ **Visual Communication** This woman is in her office in New York, yet she is able to see and speak to clients in Hong Kong using technology. *What is this process of meeting with someone using the computer called?*

■ Communications Programs

Communications programs are software applications used to establish communication between your computer and other computers. Many communications programs require a modem to allow the computer to send information—usually through a telephone line or cable. Wireless communication technology allows you to communicate via radio waves. One of the most far-reaching applications of data communications is electronic mail (e-mail). E-mail is a system of exchanging written messages as well as voice and video messages and electronic files through a computer network. Many communications programs allow you to attach data files—such as spreadsheet files or word processed documents—to your e-mail message. This means that people can share files even when they don't have access to the same storage devices. A few of the popular commercial communications programs are Lotus Notes, Microsoft Outlook, and Netscape Messenger.

In addition to e-mail, communications software can also facilitate teleconferencing and videoconferencing. A teleconference is a virtual meeting in which people in different locations conduct discussions by typing messages to each other. Each message can be seen by all of the other people in the teleconference. Users can actually see and speak to each other as they conduct their meeting if they have the necessary hardware and software. This process is known as videoconferencing.

Videoconferencing has many practical advantages. Perhaps the greatest professional advantage to videoconferencing is that it can lessen a business's travel expenses. Travel expenses can be dramatically reduced by holding meetings by videoconference rather than in person.

9.2 ASSESSMENT

Reviewing Key Terms and Concepts

1. What are eight types of software applications commonly used by businesses?
2. What are three tasks that a database program simplifies for businesses?
3. What did businesses have to do to create marketing materials before the creation of desktop publishing programs?
4. What is presentation software used for? What are some examples of presentation software?
5. What is the process of videoconferencing?

Thinking Critically

6. What type of software would you use to track the financial performance of your company?

Integrating Academic Skills

7. **MATH** At your computer shop, orders are placed by e-mail messages. Each e-mail message costs four cents. If the cost of a telephone order was 72 cents, and the shop places eight orders a day, what are the savings per business week?

Computer Technology

• What You'll Learn

- The types of computer systems that are affecting the world of marketing
- How the Internet increases productivity
- Insight into the future of computer technology

• Why It's Important

As in all other fields, technological advances are changing the scope of marketing every day. With innovations that speed up the transfer of information and development of the Internet, new markets are constantly being introduced. This section will help you understand the value of this specialized technology.

Key Terms

- point-of-sale (POS) system
- Internet
- World Wide Web
- browser
- http
- URL

Specialized Computer Technology for Marketing

The uses for computer technology in marketing appear to be endless. In addition to the software applications discussed in Section 9.2, some computer technology that is helping to shape the way we conduct business today includes point-of-sale systems, interactive touch-screen computers, interactive TV, and the Internet.

■ Point-of-Sale Systems

A common use of computers in retailing is the point-of-sale (POS) system. This system uses light pens, handheld laser guns, stationary lasers, or slot scanners to feed information directly from merchandise tags or product labels into a computer. This information is used to update inventory and monitor purchasing patterns. POS systems will be discussed further in Chapters 16 and 24.

■ Interactive Touch-Screen Computers— The Computerized Salesperson

In retail marketing, there is a strong move toward the greater use of interactive technology. This technology allows consumers to interact with the computer. Interactive computers are frequently placed on shelves in retail stores and in stand-alone kiosks in malls and airports. The customer reads and responds to questions on the touch-sensitive screen. In this way, the "computerized salesperson" directs the customer to the correct product.

Cosmetic companies, such as Clairol and Cover Girl, use on-shelf computers to help consumers choose the right shade of hair color or eye shadow. Office supply stores provide an on-shelf computer to help customers select the correct replacement cartridge for their computer printers. Wedding registries in department stores are often computerized using this type of technology. By typing in either of the couple's names and touching the appropriate boxes on the screen, you can find the perfect wedding gift.

Warner-Lambert's Canadian division, a maker of health care and consumer products, has installed on-shelf computers in the cough-cold sections of more than 600 drugstores. The computers help consumers choose the appropriate product for their symptoms. The computer asks a series of questions about symptoms before recommending one of 26 products, 10 of which are competing brands. It then describes the packaging so consumers can find the product.

■ **Point-of-Sale Systems** Point of Sale computer systems are able to provide management with more information than just the amount of sales. *What other functions do they provide?*

■ Interactive TV

Interactive TV is the marriage of television with Internet-style selectivity and interactivity. It uses a new generation of satellite receiving dishes, DVD players, and television set-top units that have modems, microprocessors, hard drives, operating systems, and software, including browsers.

Though the interactive TV market is still in its infancy, it is garnering a lot of attention because it allows businesses and advertisers to provide various kinds of information and hyperlinks within the same frame as a television program or commercial. These allow the viewer to interact with the programming as it progresses. The marketing possibilities for this technology are endless and include interactive television-facilitated e-commerce, product demonstrations, direct-response targeted advertising, and marketing research.

Today, companies are developing and testing ways in which interactive television can be used for advertising and promotion. Businesses are trying to determine what types of interactive TV work best and what consumers consider to be intrusive. Most agree, however, that this technology will revolutionize the way companies advertise.

■ The Internet

You're probably already a user of the Internet, the world's biggest computer network. Actually, it's not one network but a network of networks, all exchanging information. It began in 1969 as ARPANET, a small U.S. Department of Defense (DOD) network, that linked together the DOD and military research contractors. Soon after ARPANET was established, the scientists who had access to the system were given permission to exchange unofficial information through the system. ARPANET originally connected just three computers in California and one in Utah, but it grew quickly to cover the continent then the world. In the mid-1980s, the National Science Foundation used this technology to create NSFNET, a network connecting educational and research sites. After the establishment of NSFNET, ARPANET and NSFNET "internetworked" by linking their networks. This is where the Internet got its name. In 1990, ARPANET and NSFNET bowed out in favor of commercially run networks that allow transfer of much more information—and it became the Internet.

Internet use in the early 2000s is increasing at a pace similar to that of television fifty years ago. In 2000, about 100 million computers were connected to the Internet, and there were about 300 million users. The number continues to grow about 40 to 50 percent each year. As it exists today, the Internet has become a business tool, an advertising medium, a distribution channel, a source of entertainment, and a "virtual" meeting place for people with similar interests.

You can see that the Internet is equally valuable at home and at work. We'll discuss five common uses of the Internet as used in the workplace. Another common use, locating sources of jobs on the Internet, will be discussed in Chapter 38.

■ **Paint by Numbers** Have you ever wanted to buy paint but couldn't remember the color? Kiosks, like this one, can help you select the right house paint. *Can you think of other reasons stores would install interactive computers?*

THE WORLD WIDE WEB Although the terms World Wide Web (Web) and Internet are often used synonymously, they are actually two different things. The Web resides on the Internet as a collection of interlinked documents. You can view these pages with your browser, the software program that lets you see Web pages. They contain *hyperlinks*, or *links*, which direct you to other sites. When you click on a link, your browser brings up the connected page.

The British researcher Tim Berners-Lee invented the technology that created the Web. In addition to creating HTML, Tim developed the hypertext transport protocol (http) that links documents together. Finally, Tim developed the Uniform Resource Locator (URL)—the code used to identify and locate Web pages on the Internet.

Today there are tens of millions of pages on the Web. Thousands of new Web pages are added every week. Because the World Wide Web does not have a system for locating or categorizing content, an assortment of Web directories and search engines are available. One of the most comprehensive is Yahoo! It is an extensive directory with a menu that lists thousands of Web sites, organized by topic. Yahoo! also offers a search engine that looks for specified words in titles and addresses of the Web sites within the Yahoo! directory.

ELECTRONIC MAIL The single most common use of the Internet is for the exchange of e-mail. E-mail can be sent within a computer network or using the Internet. There are many Web-based e-mail services for which you don't need any special software other than a Web browser.

The greatest advantages of e-mail is that it is very efficient and inexpensive. An appliance store employee can e-mail an order for new merchandise to the shipper. The shipper can acknowledge the order within minutes, and the merchandise can be prepared for shipment almost immediately. E-mail users also find it convenient, economical, and ecological—no envelopes, stamps, or long-distance phone calls are needed!

INFORMATION RETRIEVAL If you are involved in business or do any type of research, the Internet has already changed your world view. Useful information can be accessed on computers at any time. If you are considering starting up a new business, you can research the competition on the Internet. You are also able to locate people you have lost track of in directories that search phone books and other sources throughout the entire United States. You can plan vacations and business trips, and make airline, hotel, and car rental reservations all on a single Web site. You can buy and sell stocks on the New York Stock Exchange. The possibilities truly are endless!

INTRANETS AND EXTRANETS Many businesses use e-mail and Web technologies within their companies on their own internal networks, called *intranets*. An intranet is a private, secure network usually within a company or organization, that contains proprietary company data and restricts access to designated personnel. They work like a private World Wide Web, but only internal users are allowed to access information or resources on an intranet system. Some businesses have developed networks for their customers, employees, partners, and suppliers. These networks, called *extranets*, enable external users to access a portion of an organization's internal network. By setting up an extranet, a company can enable customers to access data stored on an internal server. The security of such sensitive information is maintained through a firewall. A firewall is hardware and software checkpoint at which all data, incoming and outgoing, are stopped to make sure that the data are acceptable.

ELECTRONIC COMMERCE Electronic commerce, usually called e-commerce, means the process of conducting business transactions on the Internet. The Internet makes possible new ways of doing business that are simpler, faster, and cheaper. E-commerce is redefining the relationship between the seller and the buyer. Web markets differ from traditional markets in that they are open for business 24 hours a day, seven days a week. They are also unencumbered by costly middlemen and distribution channels.

Retail businesses that sell directly to the consumer through the Web are known as *e-tailers*. Another common term for e-tailing is *B2C*, shorthand for business to consumer. You may have purchased products on the Internet, perhaps from a company like Amazon, the book and music superstore. Major companies are adapting to this trend as they promote and sell their products through Web pages.

Many companies request personal information, like your e-mail address and credit card number, when you make online purchases. E-tailers often store at least some of the personal information you provide, along with your preferences regarding their products. Later, they will use this information to promote their products on their Web sites and even in messages sent directly to your e-mail address.

E-commerce is much more than companies selling directly to consumers via the Internet. Business-to-business (*B2B*) sales are expected to be ten times as big as B2C by 2002. B2B allows manufacturing companies using the Internet to be in quick and constant communication with suppliers of parts and materials needed for production. Business analysts agree that B2B transactions will total more than $1 trillion a year before 2005.

The Future of Computer Technology

As more powerful and smaller technology is developed, one can't help but wonder what the future holds. One example that shows how quickly technology is changing the face of the market is the automobile industry. Jaguar used voice-activated technology in its 2000 models that enables the driver to control features such as temperature and the radio. Jaguar's "Global Positioning System" uses satellites to monitor position on the road and then offers the driver voice and visual guidance to reach the desired location. This technology, which seemed advanced at its introduction, will be further developed with sensors placed on cars and highways that

BRIGHT IDEAS

Radical Marketing of Storage Devices

Radical marketers focus on listening to their customers and making these concerns a top priority. This style of marketing is usually employed to counteract hefty advertising budgets of large competitors. EMC, a mainframe data storage company, employed this technique when going up against IBM. EMC convinced customers that their systems were a technological weapon and customers listened. As a result, EMC owns 32 percent of the market for large external storage systems, compared to IBM's 22 percent. L.L. Bean discovered that they could process transactions so fast that they added a full day to their holiday shopping season and still promised on-time delivery of goods. It is radical tactics such as these that keep customers coming back for more.

Thinking Creatively

How could you use radical marketing when starting a new online company that sells art posters and prints?

can judge a car's location, maintain a safe speed, and control traffic. The ability to verbally tell your car to change the radio station is just the beginning.

Technology is reducing everything from books to the human voice to small bits that can be read, translated, and manipulated by computers. In addition, the plug is becoming less necessary as the wireless technology that produced remote controls and cellular phones expands. Wireless Internet access will become the standard, as messages and news updates will be obtained on watch-size devices that can be worn on the wrist.

In the future, bits of electronic data will primarily be read by machines instead of people. In time, machines will communicate between each other and cut out the need for the human middleman. The days of grocery shopping lists and spoiled milk will end as your appliances will keep track of this information for you. Your refrigerator will keep track of its food inventory, using wireless scanners to read bar codes on your food packages.

This technology explosion will not be limited to the Western world. In the early 2000s, use of the Web all over the world will skyrocket. Most of these new Web users will be from other countries, especially China. This change may lead to a marked decrease in the U.S. dominance of the Internet. The changing face of Internet use will open the global market to more countries and may level the playing field between technology-rich countries and the developing world.

■ **Global Positioning** The computer in this car is constantly calculating the car's location. It communicates with a global positioning satellite in space. In case of an accident, the computer can notify emergency personnel exactly where the car is. *What other functions can computers have in automobiles?*

9.3 ASSESSMENT

Reviewing Key Terms and Concepts

1. What are five types of computer systems?
2. What are two advantages that the Internet provides businesses?
3. What is the difference between the Internet and the Web?
4. What is a URL?
5. What is one change in computer technology that is expected in the future?

Thinking Critically

6. What are some ways in which using the Internet will increase your productivity, both in your personal life and on the job?

Integrating Academic Skills

7. **MATH** If there are 500 million users of the Internet now, and the number of users is expected to rise 40 percent each year over the next five years, how many Internet users will there be in five years?

Careers in Marketing

Dan Linfield
Web Designer
Discovery.com

What does a job in Web design entail?

"Web designers design, develop, and maintain home pages for use on the Internet, working closely with advertisers, staff, and customers. Web designers are responsible for overseeing Web site usage and security policies. When working with online shoppers, Web designers provide technical assistance, validate credit card information, and supply information."

What kind of training did you have?

"I have a BS degree in Visual Communications and I worked in print design for seven years before getting into Web design. I learned most of the software that I use on the job."

What training do you recommend for students?

"I would suggest finding a college program that starts out with a solid foundation in design principles, such as color theory and typography. They should have software training in Adobe Photoshop, Adobe Illustrator, and Macromedia Flash, which is getting bigger on the Web. Basic knowledge of html and javascript is helpful."

What skills are most important to you?

"Good design skills are a must no matter what the medium. There are a lot of people doing Web design who know the software very well, but do not have strong skills in color, typography, and layout."

What is your key to success?

"The key to success in the Web world is keeping up with technology and your competition. The capabilities of the Web expand every day, and you need to keep up with these changes to stay successful. The easiest way to do this is to look at the Web every day and look for new innovations."

Thinking Critically

Why is flexibility so important in the field of Web design?

Career Facts

Education and Training: High school students should take college preparatory classes in computer science, science, mathematics, and accounting. A bachelor's degree in computer science with course work in operating systems and database language is recommended.

Aptitudes, Abilities, and Skills: Design skills, creativity, ability to learn new technologies quickly, good logic skills, and attention to detail are all helpful.

Career Outlook: The rapid expansion of the Internet should increase the demand for Web designers through 2006.

Career Path: A typical path to Web designer is employment as a computer programmer or experience with database languages and the Internet.

VOCABULARY REVIEW

Choose at least eight of the words below and write a 250-word paragraph explaining how you would use a computer in business.

- supercomputer
- mainframe
- minicomputer
- microcomputer
- laptop
- PDA
- hardware
- disk drive
- scanner
- software
- word processing programs
- database programs
- spreadsheet programs
- desktop publishing programs
- graphics and design programs
- presentation software
- Web page editors
- Web page
- hypertext markup language (HTML)
- communications programs
- point-of-sale (POS) system
- e-mail
- browser

FACT AND IDEA REVIEW

1. What is the difference between a mainframe and a microcomputer? (9.1)

2. What does a modem do? (9.1)

3. Why is computer software necessary? (9.1)

4. Why would you use a word processing program rather than a typewriter when producing a business document? (9.2)

5. What is a database program? (9.2)

6. When would you use desktop publishing? (9.2)

7. What is a graphic and design program used for? (9.2)

8. How is a point-of-sale system used? (9.3)

9. What advantages does e-mail have over traditional mail? (9.3)

THINKING CRITICALLY

1. Some people have discussed the possibility of everyone in the country being in one database with credit and income information and personal histories included. What kinds of concerns might this kind of database raise?

2. What do you think has been the effect of desktop publishing software on the book and magazine publishing industry?

3. Explain the possible effects of the widespread use of e-mail.

BUILDING WORKPLACE SKILLS

1. **Human Relations** You are the manager at an exclusive make up and beauty supply chain store. Your district manager has decided to install an interactive touch-screen computer in each store to assist shoppers in making choices. Prepare a brief presentation to explain the benefits of the new computer and to explain that the role of the salesperson will be in conjunction with the computer device.

2. **Technology** Your company's computer system provides access to the Internet, and you've noticed several employees writing e-mail messages and doing personal research not related to their work assignments. What can you do to prevent or minimize employees' personal use of company computers?

APPLYING MARKETING CONCEPTS

1. **Analyzing Computer Use in Marketing Careers** Choose a possible marketing career and use the Internet to research how computers are used in it. Speculate on what new uses computers might have in the future in that career. Use a word processing program to write a two-page report and present your report orally to the class.

2. **Interacting With Your Television** Research interactive television programs and participate in the program of your choice. Using a word processing program, write a summary of your experience.

3. **Understanding Publishing Software** Visit a local book publisher or newspaper publisher with your class or on your own to learn how these businesses use desktop publishing software. Ask for a demonstration, and then use graphics design software to produce a newsletter about class activities.

4. **Using Everyday Computer Skills** You are searching for the book of your choice for summer reading. Using the Internet, check the price of the book (with shipping and handling) at three e-tailers. Then, check the price of the book at three local retailers. Create a spreadsheet comparing the prices. Which offers the best value?

LINKING SCHOOL TO WORK

Technology Skills Find out from an employer how many different computer applications are in use at the workplace. List their names and what they are used for. Share your findings with the class. Tally which seem to be most popular.

THE DECA CONNECTION

Role Play: Software Salesperson

Situation You are to assume the role of a salesperson selling computer software to a record store owner (judge). As a salesperson, you will be expected to help the record store owner choose the software needed to keep track of the store's expanding customer base.

Activity Give a general explanation of the benefits of each part of the computer system.

Evaluation You will be evaluated on how well you meet the following performance indicators:

- Demonstrate basic database skills
- Explain the use of databases in organizing marketing data
- Design a database for retrieval of information
- Use database information analysis

interNET CONNECTION

The Choice Is Yours
You are interested in doing graphic design as a career, and you want to choose the best computer platform and software for the job.

Connect
- Find the Web sites of graphics software manufacturers.
- Read about the various features of different graphics software programs and how they run on different platforms.
- Choose software and hardware that most suit your needs.
- Write a one-page report explaining and providing rationale for your choice.

Chapter 10

Interpersonal Skills

Marketing: What It Takes

The Importance of Being Flexible

You are a salesperson in a sporting goods store. Most of your time is spent helping customers select items to purchase and answering their questions. Sometimes you help set up displays of new merchandise. Recently, your supervisor asked you to help with the repackaging of products to be returned to manufacturers. You were not told that this was one of your job responsibilities when you were hired, and you don't like doing it. Yesterday, you nearly snapped at your supervisor, telling her that repackaging is not part of your job.

WHAT WILL YOU DO?

Should you point out to your supervisor what duties were discussed when you were hired? Should you try looking differently at your job and the duties you are asked to do?

Human Relations

Understanding Others

The first step in getting along with others is getting to know them. Finding out others' interests helps you understand them better. Interests often reflect values, and an understanding of a person's values is helpful in a relationship.

Trying to understand the reasons for others' behavior also facilitates good relationships both on and off the job. You can learn to be sensitive to certain aspects of everyone's behavior. Observe the way a person deals with others. Does the person relate differently to different people in the same situations? Can you figure out why? Which of the person's personality traits might affect your relationship with him or her?

Observing body language is another key way to learn about a person. Body language is the gestures, posture, mannerisms, and eye contact through which a person communicates thoughts with others. A person who leans slightly forward and nods in agreement with you is obviously paying attention. A person with an expressionless stare is looking but not listening.

Facial expressions are often good indicators of emotions and feelings. A pleasant, smiling expression, for instance, usually indicates a positive outlook. Your eyes tell a lot about you, too. When you are happy, for example, your pupils get larger; when you are unhappy, your pupils constrict. Suppose you are interviewing a candidate to help you with an advertising campaign. As you explain the job responsibilities, look into the person's eyes for an indication of his or her feelings.

One study of body language found that people sometimes say one thing verbally and another through body language. Body language is often the more accurate indicator of the person's thoughts and feelings. By observing people in many different situations, you can learn to read body language with considerable accuracy.

Personal Traits

Understanding others is only the first step in getting along with them. The way you interact with others will determine how successful and satisfied you are in the marketing world. The traits described here will help improve your interpersonal relations, on the job and with your friends and family.

■ Friendliness, Courtesy, and Tact

Getting along well with others is a lot easier when you display a friendly, outgoing personality. It's not always easy to do, especially if you're naturally quiet or shy. Show sincerity and you will be treated the same way.

• What You'll Learn

- The importance of understanding others
- The personal traits that can help you be more effective in relations with other people
- The personal skills you should master for successful interpersonal relations
- How interpersonal skills may be used in marketing

• Why It's Important

You use interpersonal skills in your personal life every day. Getting along well with others will serve you well on any job. In fact, studies show that between 80 and 85 percent of a person's success in the world of work is due to good interpersonal skills.

Key Terms

- body language
- initiative
- empathize
- assertive

■ **Body Talk** A person's body language sometimes speaks louder than words. *What message is the listener in this conversation conveying?*

Baby's First Cell Phone

Interested in a flip phone that features a picture of Queen Amidala of *Star Wars: Episode One* legacy? You might not be, but you might know an eight-year-old who would love one. Tiger Electronics is now empowering kids with the same electronic tools that adults have. Along the lines of cellular phones, Tiger's Power Talk sends and receives short voice messages up to 90 feet. The toy runs about $25 and replaces the toy push-button phone of the past. Another Tiger device, Lightning Mail, is capable of wireless sending and receiving of text messages at up to 50 feet. When the same device is plugged into a standard telephone jack, it can communicate via e-mail to anywhere in the world.

Thinking Critically

What other toys might you create that imitate an adult tool or product?

Courtesy is closely related to friendliness. Good manners and a polite demeanor should come naturally, even in awkward situations. It is not always easy to be courteous and pleasant, but tactfulness is always necessary. When you act with tact, you show respect in handling a situation and all the people involved. There is always a way to provide constructive criticism without offending or hurting someone unnecessarily.

■ Personal Ethics

Demonstrating personal ethics is essential in every aspect of life, especially on the job. Ethical behavior includes honesty, integrity, and a sense of fair play—things that all people desire and deserve. When you behave ethically, people trust you. This is particularly important on the job. You may be giving people information to help them decide whether to buy something. Being untruthful or withholding negative information leads to customer dissatisfaction.

It's also important to demonstrate good personal ethics toward your employer and coworkers. Honesty is a job requirement that cannot be overlooked.

■ Creativity, Initiative, and Responsibility

Creativity is the act of using your imagination to be inventive. It allows you not only to come up with new products but also to find new ways of doing your job. Incorporating creative thinking into daily tasks at work will make your job even more enjoyable.

Creativity is a form of self-expression that lets personality traits, which often go unnoticed at work, shine through. Creativity also helps you analyze situations and problems from a new and fresh perspective.

Initiative means doing what needs to be done without being urged. Once you have used your creativity to come up with a new idea, it will go nowhere unless you use your initiative to act on it.

Responsibility is being accountable for your actions and doing your duty. After taking the initiative to begin a job, you must accept responsibility for completing it. Employers value responsible employees because they can be counted on to work without much supervision.

■ Attitude

Your attitude refers to the mental outlook you have toward people and situations. Try to see the good in the people you deal with. People with a positive attitude welcome a difficult assignment as a challenge. People with a negative attitude complain.

Specific traits that foster a positive outlook are interest and enthusiasm. You can develop interest in a particular subject by learning more about it. Finding out why inventory is necessary makes the process more interesting. It will help you do the job with more enthusiasm.

■ Self-Control and Orderliness

People who exercise self-control are tactful and slow to anger. They don't indulge their impulses, but behave in a disciplined way. This is important in marketing where you will be in contact with the public. Self-control and orderly behavior inspire confidence in customers and in coworkers. People who can't control themselves and do things in a sloppy, inattentive way are not likely to be given much responsibility.

■ Self-Awareness and Willingness to Change

Knowing yourself is the first step in making personal changes. You can begin by making a list of all your personal strengths and weaknesses. Then decide which weaknesses you would like to work on improving. Practice the traits that will help you improve your weaknesses.

■ **Service with a Smile** Good customer service is one key to success. Cashiers at Safeway grocery stores show courtesy by thanking all customers by name (which they learn from the ATM card or by asking). *What are other ways that employees in retail can be courteous?*

It's also important to be willing to listen to the feedback of others and act on it. Sometimes we aren't aware of the effect we are having on other people. We can move ahead in our own personal growth if we are willing to change attitudes and

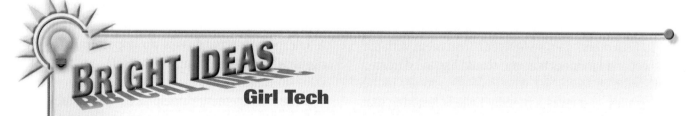

BRIGHT IDEAS
Girl Tech

Dr. Janese Swanson, a founder of Girl Tech, does more than come up with bright ideas—she brings them to market. Dr. Swanson has created a line of affordable electronic gadgets for girls. One item, the Password Journal, is a book-size voice-activated plastic box that holds a diary. Using voice recognition technology, this diary is accessible only when its owner speaks the password. Girl Tech's Door Pass sets off an alarm when someone tries to sneak into the owner's bedroom. Dr. Swanson's inspiration comes from her ten-year-old daughter, who is always searching for "cool" toys for girls. Girl Tech most certainly fills this niche with its very cool gadgets.

Thinking Creatively

Think of a cool toy that you would have loved when you were ten years old. Invent this product now with the help of modern technology.

REAL WORLD MARKETING

For Women Only

It was a 175-mile bike ride that inspired Gary Erickson to create an energy bar that was not only healthy, but tasty, too. Gary Erickson and Lisa Thomas entered the power bar industry in 1992. The Clif Bar, and the company bearing the same name, was born. The next challenge that these entrepreneurs undertook was to enter a territory in food marketing where few companies tread—food for women only. The LUNA Bar, packaged in a blue wrapper featuring a woman leaping under the moon, is geared toward active women. Its flavorful approach includes vitamins, soy, calcium, and something to satisfy a sweet tooth.

Thinking Critically
What approaches might Clif Bar Inc. take if it was marketing a new energy bar to men only?

behaviors that are negative. Being willing to change also means being willing to adapt to changes around you. Flexibility is essential.

Self-Esteem

Self-esteem is your perceived worth or value. Good self-esteem helps you see yourself as being able to do your job. It helps you get along with others.

To help others gain self-esteem, treat them with the respect and kindness that you would like to be treated with yourself. A cashier who looks a customer in the eye, smiles, and gives a friendly hello is fostering that person's self-esteem.

Empathy

You can earn a person's trust and respect faster by empathizing. To empathize means to understand a person's situation or frame of mind. Learn to respect the other person's point of view, even when you don't agree with it. This technique is especially important in dealing with customers who are upset or angry. There may be other factors contributing to their moods.

Personal Skills

There are some personal skills that can help you get along with people on the job, in addition to the personal traits discussed earlier. Using the following skills can help you succeed in your career.

Assertiveness

Being assertive means standing up for your rights, beliefs, and ideas. People will respect you if you can be assertive without being pushy or aggressive. Show confidence and speak with authority. This does not mean you should sound like a know-it-all, but you do have to know what you are talking about.

Assertiveness is a skill that takes a while to learn. You will gain confidence as you gain more experience. This will put you in a better position to influence others.

Solving Someone's Problem

People are far more willing to listen to a new idea when they can see how it will benefit them. Look for ways your idea will solve a problem for others. It may save them time or make it unnecessary for them to perform some unpleasant tasks. Always keep those benefits foremost in your mind—and in their minds—when presenting your idea. Phrase your idea in terms of their needs.

Time Management

Learning to budget your time and to record important deadlines or appointments are part of time management. It's not possible to be effective in your work unless you are able to use time wisely. A salesperson who misses an appointment with a client is not likely to make the sale—or any other sale—to that client.

Time management principles involve establishing goals, setting deadlines, allocating enough time for each task, tackling the most difficult task first, and being realistic.

Goal Setting

Setting goals for your career and personal development is essential. How can you get anywhere if you don't know where you are headed? Procedures for setting goals are outlined in Chapter 37.

Case Study

Schmoozing

The word "schmooze" has a bad reputation! For many, it implies being nice to others just to get something from them—a job contact or a sales opportunity. To some, schmoozing involves using someone or unfairly taking advantage of a situation. There is more to schmoozing than that. It's a way of using your interpersonal skills to turn strangers into friends and friends into customers. Learning the elements of schmoozing can also help you get along with people in your workplace.

Schmoozing is about being generous with sincere compliments. It requires people to move out of their comfort zones and strike up conversations with people they don't know. To perfect the art of schmoozing, it is important to get over any fears of being rejected. Be confident, be yourself, and be prepared by "knowing your audience." To know your audience you must understand what the people you want to schmooze with will want to talk about. It is also important to find ways to help people. If you've just met a person who has a need you can solve, be sure to give the person your business card and assure him or her that you will follow up. A handy way to remember such promises is to get the person's business card and write what you promised on the back of the card. This will help you remember to write down the task on your to-do list. Be sure to end the conversation by thanking the person and reiterating your promise to follow up on anything you may have offered. If they've talked to you about something that they're involved in and you're interested in, ask them to keep you informed on their progress.

The key to schmoozing is sincerity. If you have an ulterior motive, people will not feel comfortable with you. Good schmoozers are able to find interests and attitudes they share with others. They ask questions and are sincerely interested in the responses. They are good listeners. They smile when they meet people and maintain eye contact. Most importantly, they truly enjoy people. They value what they can offer to a person just as much as they value any potential benefits from the relationship.

Many people at the top of their fields are great schmoozers. They've learned that making others feel valued and appreciated is great for business. It's time to downplay the negative connotations of the word schmooze and develop your own schmoozing skills!

Case Study Review

1. What interpersonal skills do good schmoozers show?
2. How do you think learning to be a good schmoozer could help you in working in a team environment?

A Matter of Ethics

3. Do you see a connection between schmoozing's bad reputation and ethical concerns? What are those concerns?

Interpersonal Skills in Marketing

Certain interpersonal skills are needed to deal with the special relationship between marketing employees and their customers. The following is a list of some basic procedures you may be asked to handle that will require the use of your interpersonal skills.

1. *Handle customer requests and questions.* You will need to learn the proper procedures for handling customer requests and questions. You will also need to know what you should say to customers if you cannot answer their questions yourself.

2. *Provide customers with directions to your store location.* You will need to be able to give clear and concise directions.

3. *Understand management's role in customer relations.* You will need to know under what circumstances a manager should be called to talk to a customer. Policies differ from business to business.

4. *Understand procedures for handling difficult customers.* Having clear procedures helps to prevent you from becoming upset when dealing with customers who may be angry.

5. *Explain business policies to customers.* This includes return or exchange policies and whether the business accepts checks or credit cards.

6. *Handle customer complaints.* You will be better able to provide a customer with an acceptable response, whether positive or negative, if you have a specific procedure to follow.

■ **Customer Assistance** Having good interpersonal skills can help you avoid problems in working with customers. *What skills can this employee use to try to ensure the customer's satisfaction?*

10.1 ASSESSMENT

Reviewing Key Terms and Concepts

1. Why is it important to understand others?

2. What are the personal traits that can help you be more effective with other people?

3. What are four personal skills that you should master for successful interpersonal relations in the marketing world?

4. How can interpersonal skills be used in marketing?

Thinking Critically

5. Describe the body language you would expect to see in a shy person, a defensive person, and a self-confident person.

Integrating Academic Skills

6. **COMMUNICATION** As an insurance agent, you have just met with a prospective buyer and discussed a particular health insurance plan. Write a brief, effective follow-up note.

Working Together

Teamwork

Have you ever been on a team? While you were growing up, did you play baseball, basketball, or other sports on the playground? Have you ever participated in a school or club car wash or decorated the gym for a dance? All of these activities were performed by teams. A team is a group of people who work together to achieve a goal. Teamwork is the skill they use to achieve that goal.

Teamwork is important in the business world. You will learn in Chapter 11 about new models of management where entire companies are organized into teams. A manager at Sun Life Insurance Company said, "People rise and fall according to how they work with their peers."

■ Training

To be an effective team member, you must have training for all the tasks you will perform. You have probably heard of cross-training in sports. That's a way of staying in shape that includes doing many different activities—swimming, running, and weight training, for example. Each one of the sports uses a different set of muscles and leads to a different kind of strength.

On the job, people are cross-trained for many tasks on a team. This gives the team flexibility and several strengths. Work becomes more enjoyable when you know you will not be doing the same thing every day.

At Hallmark Cards, teams of editors, writers, artists, and production specialists oversee the entire process of making greeting cards. Twenty percent of the team's time during the first year is spent in training.

■ Team Planning

Imagine that you and your friends have decided to throw a surprise birthday party. If each friend goes ahead and does what he or she thinks should be done, the result may be chaos. If, however, you plan who will send invitations, set up decorations, be in charge of music, and buy the food, the result will probably be a great party. The same goes for running a successful team project at work. Before you start, make a plan. Since you will be working as a team, plan as a team. Team planning involves setting goals, assigning roles, making agreements, sharing responsibility, and communicating regularly.

● What You'll Learn

- The importance of teamwork in the business world
- Six aspects of successful teamwork

● Why It's Important

Teamwork in business is like teamwork in the sports arena. You may not wear a uniform in the work world, but you will be a member of a team dedicated to achieving a specific goal. Develop the habit of being a good team member by always fulfilling your responsibilities, and you won't let your team down on your job.

Key Terms

- consensus
- agreement

■ **Working Together** Effective teamwork requires respect for each other. *What other qualities help you get along with others in the workplace?*

■ Team Goals

Before a team can begin to act, the team has to have clearly defined goals. Team members must feel involved in defining a goal in order to feel committed to it. At Subway sandwich shops, for example, production teams set goals for the time required to make each sandwich and for the quality of the product. Companies that involve employees in setting goals show that they respect and value employee opinions. This results in greater company loyalty and stronger team spirit.

Team members set specific goals for their teams, in addition to setting company goals. Usually, members must reach a consensus about goals. A consensus is a decision that each member agrees to. In order for this to happen, it is important that all team members be allowed to state their opinions. Other members must respect this right and not interrupt. Respectful discussion continues until the group reaches an agreement. The final agreement may require team members to make a compromise. This means that some members may need to adjust their original positions. It is important that all members be comfortable with the final decision of a compromise. This prevents employees from saying later that their opinions were not acknowledged.

■ Assigning Roles

Remember the party you planned? You could have chosen one friend to oversee the process. Then the tasks might have been done more efficiently. Likewise, team projects often work more smoothly if the team appoints a team leader. This is especially true for self-directed teams. The facilitator coordinates the tasks so that the team works efficiently. It is also important to assign roles to each member of the team.

Each person on the team needs to know which part of the process he or she is responsible for each day. Members are usually assigned tasks based on their skills and experience. Sometimes a less experienced member will be paired up with someone more skilled, so he or she can receive training while completing the task.

■ Agreements

An agreement is a specific commitment that each member makes with the group. It is similar to a contract or a promise to perform a certain task within a certain period of time. When team members make agreements, the team becomes more cohesive and stronger. A team's agreements must be consistent with its goals.

At some franchises of Pizza Hut, the agreement is that dine-in customers receive their pizza in 20 minutes or the pizza is free. Each affected team member must complete his or her part of the process. Sometimes this can be accomplished by cutting out unnecessary steps, or it may be that people have to work at top speed. In another situation, all employees at a retail store might agree to greet customers with the same greeting.

Each person is motivated to keep his or her agreement when everyone has agreed on the goal. The whole team's performance suffers if one person doesn't keep his or her agreement. It is important that each team member feels connected to company goals as well as the team as a whole. Team loyalty and positive peer pressure help to encourage people to keep their agreements.

■ Shared Responsibility and Shared Leadership

Each member must feel responsible for the whole team's efforts in order for a team to work. That is shared responsibility. If a team is to function effectively and efficiently, then a standard must be set by the whole team. It's not enough to do your own job well and then complain if others don't seem to be doing theirs. That's where shared leadership comes in.

Team members take action to bring the whole team's performance up to the standards the team has agreed on in shared leadership. Teams do this by having meetings at which they give feedback about individual performance and about specific parts of the team's work. Feedback about someone's performance must be given with respect. If it is done in a way that is overly critical or harsh, it will not serve its purpose and it will alienate the team member in question.

If the feedback is about some aspect of the team process, it needs to be specific so team members can provide specific responses. For example, rather than saying, "We seem to be wasting a lot of time walking around," more specific feedback would be, "It takes two minutes to walk from my work station to the pizza oven." A team member might then suggest, "Could we move the work station closer to the oven to save time?"

Shared leadership allows all team members to perform some management functions. As employees get a glimpse of other roles and responsibilities in an organization, it gives them a greater appreciation for management. It makes employees feel more powerful because it actually gives them more power. Shared responsibility and shared leadership are essential elements of teamwork.

In your marketing career, you will certainly be a member of many teams. Any group that works together to achieve something—reach a sales goal, perform an inventory—is a team. A department can act as a team. You may serve on different teams for various projects that you work on or clients that you represent. You may also serve on interdepartmental or cross-functional teams. Teamwork skills will always be valuable interpersonal skills.

■ **Team Players** Teamwork can improve productivity, creativity, and customer satisfaction. *How does working in teams prevent the process from being dominated by one person?*

■ Being a Valuable Team Member

A team can only be as successful as its members. For a team to be successful, it is important that each member is willing and able to work to achieve the team's goals.

What makes a person a good team member? The following list describes valuable attitudes and actions. As you read the list, consider how following these conventions can help teams overcome obstacles.

- Make the team's goals your top priority
- In meetings, listen actively and offer suggestions
- Build positive group dynamics with team members
- Continue to communicate with team members outside meetings
- Follow up on what you've been assigned to do
- Work to resolve conflicts among team members
- Respect the other members of your team
- Try to inspire other employees to get involved

Life In The Diverse
MARKETPLACE

There's No "I" in Team

People in the United States put an emphasis on individual excellence and winning, which in turn encourages competition and entrepreneurship. In Japan, the emphasis is placed on teamwork and consideration of others. Taxi drivers wear white gloves, and sick individuals wear surgical masks to prevent infecting others. High school baseball teams bow to each other at the beginning of each game. The point is to enjoy harmony, or common experience, in all aspects of life. Perhaps this emphasis is a result of population size and square footage—125 million Japanese live in an area the size of California.

Thinking Critically

Can Japan succeed as an economic superpower with its view toward harmony in the workplace?

10.2 ASSESSMENT

Reviewing Key Terms and Concepts

1. What is teamwork? Why is it important in the business world?
2. List six aspects of successful teamwork.
3. What is a consensus?
4. What is the idea behind shared leadership?

Thinking Critically

5. Why would employees be more motivated to perform well on a team than in an individual effort?

Integrating Academic Skills

6. **MATH** You have calculated that your idea to use plastic instead of metal when manufacturing your company's paper towel holders would save $.13 per item. If your company can produce 600 paper towel holders per day, and there are 250 production days in the year, how much will your idea save the company in a year?

Careers in Marketing

HOSPITALITY MARKETING

Krista Brennecke White
Flight Attendant
USAirways

Career Facts

What does your job entail?

"My job as a flight attendant is ultimately to ensure the safety and comfort of the passengers on board the aircraft. I serve as the main link between USAirways and its customers, which draws on the public relations and customer service aspects of my job. Flight attendants not only serve the customers during the flight, but are also responsible for preparing the aircraft and galleys for each trip. This entails ensuring that necessary supplies and food are on board and that all equipment is working. Aside from greeting and assisting passengers, other duties include answering questions, enforcing regulations, and assisting during emergencies."

What kind of training did you have?

"My training consisted of an eight-week rigorous schedule of classes and drills that covered customer service, first aid, federal air regulation safety procedures, and emergency evacuations. We also learned about the history of USAirways and the airline industry as a whole. High school students who are interested in this career should take courses in English, geography, health, and foreign language."

How does your workload vary?

"My workload varies constantly. One flight may be completely full and the next may be very light. Some of the flights are as short as thirty minutes, while others are more than eight hours. Passengers' demands also fluctuate depending on various times of the year and different regions of the country."

What is your key to success?

"I'm always flexible, patient, and open to different personalities."

Education and Training: Most employers require that applicants have a high school diploma or equivalent. Most companies have their own mandatory training programs that prepare you for this career. Knowledge of passport and customs regulations is required. Training as a nurse is helpful, but not required.

Aptitudes, Abilities, and Skills: Good health, keen hearing, corrected eyesight of at least 20/50, stamina to endure long shifts and irregular hours, adequate strength and dexterity to operate safety and emergency equipment, and knowledge of first aid procedures are necessary. You must also have good people skills, good communication (especially verbal) skills, and an outgoing personality.

Career Outlook: The market for flight attendants is expected to grow much faster than the general employment market through the year 2006.

Career Path: Employment as a travel agent in a private company or as a ticket or reservation agent for an airline can lead to a flight attendant position. Flight attendants may advance to positions of in-flight supervisors, flight attendant instructors, or sales representatives.

Thinking Critically

How is the flight attendant a key to the marketing success of an airline company?

VOCABULARY REVIEW

Write a paragraph that includes all the following words. Use them in ways that demonstrate that you know their meanings.

- body language
- initiative
- empathize
- assertive
- consensus
- agreement

FACT AND IDEA REVIEW

1. Why does finding out other people's interests help you understand them better? (10.1)

2. What three personal traits allow you to come up with and follow through on new ideas? (10.1)

3. What attitudes can you cultivate that will foster a positive outlook? (10.1)

4. How can self-awareness help you to change weaknesses to strengths? (10.1)

5. What does it mean to be assertive? (10.1)

6. In a teamwork context, what is cross-training? (10.2)

7. How does a team arrive at a consensus? Why is consensus important? (10.2)

8. What must a team do before it can act? (10.2)

9. Why does shared responsibility and shared leadership help a team to work well? (10.2)

10. Name three conventions that can help teams overcome obstacles. (10.2)

THINKING CRITICALLY

1. Why is it necessary for people in the marketing world to behave ethically?

2. How do the personal traits of initiative and responsibility aid in building teamwork?

3. Describe some ways in which you can increase other people's self-esteem.

4. In teamwork, team members make agreements with the group. Describe some agreements you have made in your own life.

5. Would you prefer to work on a team where you do different tasks requiring different skills from day to day or to work alone on the same sort of work each day? Explain your choice.

BUILDING WORKPLACE SKILLS

1. **Human Relations** Go to a store and ask a salesclerk for assistance in finding a type of product. Do not smile at the salesclerk. Go to another store. This time, make eye contact with the clerk and smile. Describe the two experiences.

2. **Public Speaking** You have just been hired as the manager at a sandwich shop. Some employees don't respect your authority. They come in late and avoid eye contact with you. You think that they are trying to see how far they can push the limits with a new boss. You need to set team standards; however, you do not want to come off only as a stern disciplinarian. Prepare a speech to present at the next staff meeting to discuss these issues and to tactfully establish yourself as the boss. What kind of body language will you use when speaking?

APPLYING MARKETING CONCEPTS

1. **Understanding Empathy** Imagine that you work for a company that is suffering financially and needs to terminate jobs. Put yourself in the position of both the manager who needs to carry out the job terminations and the assistant who will lose his or her job. Describe your feelings, concerns, and needs. Write your descriptions using your word processing program.

2. **Using Time Management Principles** Use time managment principles to create a schedule for planning a marketing career fair to be held six weeks from today. Present the schedule to your class using presentation software.

3. **Researching Training Opportunities** Use the Internet to research training in assertiveness or self-esteem. Find out what kinds of classes are available and how they relate to success in business. Pick one and use design software to create a flyer advertising it.

4. **Analyzing Teamwork Skills** Use a word processing program to write a report comparing and contrasting the teamwork skills involved in playing a team sport with the teamwork skills used on the job. Describe how each type of team uses the six aspects of teamwork discussed in the chapter.

LINKING SCHOOL TO WORK

Interpersonal Skills Are the employees at your workplace organized into teams? If they are, report to the class on how the teams work. If they aren't, write a 250-word description of how you would organize your coworkers into a team.

THE DECA CONNECTION

Role Play: Fast Food Manager

Situation You are to assume the role of new day assistant manager at a local fast-food restaurant. You believe production would improve if the restaurant used a team approach to cooking and serving the food.

Activity It's your job to convince the restaurant manager (judge) that the team approach is worth a try.

Evaluation You will be evaluated on how well you meet the following performance indicators:
- Participate as a team member
- Foster positive working relationships
- Treat others fairly at work
- Explain the nature of staff communication
- Persuade others

inter NET CONNECTION

Skills Training
Your company wants to hire a career-training company to train employees in how to deal effectively with customer complaints.

Connect
- Find Web sites of career-training companies.
- Narrow your search to training related to customer relations.
- Compare offerings of different companies and choose the one that you feel addresses the complaint issue best.
- Write a one-page report explaining and providing rationale for your choice.

Management Skills

Marketing: What It Takes

Promoting Initiative

Imagine that you are a management trainee for a full-service restaurant with about 20 employees. You notice that many of the employees don't do any work until told directly by the manager exactly what to do.

WHAT WILL YOU DO?

Suppose that you are made the manager of this location. What changes would you consider making?

Management Structures

Types of Management Structure

Management is the process of reaching goals through the use of human resources, technology, and material resources. To facilitate effective management, businesses are organized in two ways—vertically and horizontally.

■ Vertical Organization

Managers look up to higher levels of management or down to employees within a single department in large, traditional companies. The managers' goal is to perform a particular department function well. The up-and-down structure of this kind of organization is called vertical organization.

There are three basic levels of management in the traditionally organized company: top management, middle management, and supervisory-level management. Figure 11-1 on page 192 distinguishes these three levels.

■ Horizontal Organization

Today, purely vertical organization is being displaced by new ways of structuring management. While vertical management will continue to exist in many companies, it will no longer be the only option. Many corporations downsized in the late 1980s and early 1990s to increase their efficiency and productivity. The thought was that if fewer workers could produce the same amount or an increased amount of a product, profits would rise. Unfortunately, this was not the result for more than half of the companies that downsized. Employee morale suffered, customer dissatisfaction rose, and profits fell as a result.

Clearly, more than staff cuts were needed to make companies more efficient. The answer was a new kind of management structure—horizontal organization. Horizontal organization involves self-managing teams that set their own goals and make their own decisions. It is organized by process instead of function and is customer-oriented.

The movement toward horizontal organization in business is definitely a trend. For some companies, it has been extremely successful. Ford, for example, reduced the time it takes to develop and produce a new model from five years to three. That's a 40-percent reduction!

Not all companies, however, have been quick to restructure their workforces. Shifting from the familiar vertical model, with its levels of management, requires reorganization that can take years. For many companies, there will probably always be a mix of the two types.

● What You'll Learn

- How horizontally organized companies differ from traditionally organized companies
- The three levels of management
- How a self-managing team functions

● Why It's Important

You will probably have an opportunity to work in management at some point in your career. Management involves the communication and interpersonal skills discussed in the last two chapters. A job in management is a challenge for anyone, and a basic understanding of management structure and functions, presented in this section, will give you an advantage.

Key Terms

- vertical organization
- top management
- middle management
- supervisory-level management
- horizontal organization
- empowerment

FIGURE 11-1

LEVELS OF MANAGEMENT

All managers perform the same basic functions, but their responsibilities differ according to their management level.

TOP MANAGEMENT

Those who make the planning decisions that affect the whole company are top management. CEO (Chief Executive Officer), President, COO (Chief Operating Officer), and Vice President are some top management titles. Their decisions have the broadest effect on the company.

MIDDLE MANAGEMENT

It's the job of middle management to implement the decisions of top management. They plan ways that departments under them can work to reach top management's goals. They communicate with and support supervisory level managers.

SUPERVISORY-LEVEL MANAGEMENT

These front-line managers supervise the activities of employees who carry out the tasks determined by the plans of middle and top management. They assign duties and evaluate the work of production or service employees.

SELF-MANAGING TEAMS At the heart of horizontal organization is a restructuring of the traditional management hierarchy. Levels of management have been eliminated and the number of supervisors reduced. This is known as "flattening" the organization. Instead of reporting up a chain of command, employees are organized into teams that manage themselves.

Here's the way it works. Each team has someone called an "owner." This person is the nearest to an overall manager. He or she has ultimate responsibility for making sure the team meets its goals. The owner doesn't do this by issuing orders, however. He or she acts more like a coach than a boss. The owner works together with the whole team to define all the individual steps necessary to meet its goals.

This is based on the idea that the people actually doing the work are the best source of information about how the work should be done. The team manages itself by sharing opinions and brainstorming. It also shares responsibility for the consequences of its decisions.

Encouraging team members to contribute to and take responsibility for the management process is known as empowerment. Empowerment reinforces team spirit and contributes to company loyalty. It ultimately increases profits and productivity.

ORGANIZATION BY PROCESS A second characteristic of horizontal companies is organization by process. Self-managing teams are organized around particular processes, such as developing new products or providing customer support. Teams made up of people with different specializations replace functional divisions, like the finance department or engineering department. The product development team, for example, might include people from marketing research, design, engineering, and finance. These team members share opinions, decisions, and responsibility for the success or failure of the products they develop. One challenge of organization by process is that it may require many levels of organization. A company that produces sophisticated technical equipment, for example, will require more levels of management than a company that produces golf balls.

CUSTOMER ORIENTATION The third characteristic of horizontal organization has to do with where teams get their direction. The source of direction is management in vertical organizations; in horizontal companies, it's the customer. This type of organization supports the principle of customer satisfaction. Customer orientation can be based on a type of industry or the channel of distribution used. A firm may have one department that deals specifically with wholesalers and another that deals with retailers. By focusing on customers instead of product or process, managers have direct access to customer feedback. The ideal results of customer satisfaction for a company are large profits, high productivity, and satisfied investors.

11.1 ASSESSMENT

Reviewing Key Terms and Concepts

1. What is the principal difference between the structure of a vertical company and the structure of a horizontal company?

2. What are the three levels of management?

3. Why did many companies choose to downsize in the 1980s and 1990s?

4. What is the role of the "owner" in a self-managing team?

Thinking Critically

5. Would you feel more comfortable in a traditional company, where you answer to only one supervisor, or in a horizontal company, where you have many people giving you feedback about your efforts? Compare the advantages of each organizational model, as you see them.

Integrating Academic Skills

6. **COMMUNICATION** Imagine that you are the manager of a large bookstore. One of your salesclerks makes a suggestion about rearranging the children's section to include a few small tables and chairs. You like the idea and intend to carry it out. Write a note to the salesclerk praising the suggested improvement.

Management Functions

• What You'll Learn

- The three functions of management
- The management techniques used by effective managers
- How to motivate employees through a system of rewards

• Why It's Important

The concept of management is changing. It is allowing more employees to fulfill management functions, whatever their job titles. Understanding the functions of management will help you to excel in any career you choose.

Key Terms

- planning
- organizing
- controlling
- mission statement

What Managers Do

All managers perform certain basic functions of planning, organizing, and controlling during their career. The decisions that a manager makes in these areas affect all employees. This means that communicating and motivating people are especially important management skills.

■ Basic Management Functions

All managers must plan when they set goals and determine how to reach them. They organize when they decide who will do what and how each task will be done. They control when they set standards and evaluate performance.

All three of these management functions involve making decisions. Some decisions will be fairly simple or routine, while others may be difficult and complicated. Following the formal, six-step procedure shown in Figure 11-2 (page 195) can be helpful when making complicated decisions.

PLANNING The first step in the management process is planning. Planning involves deciding what will be done and how it will be accomplished. A CEO who sets a sales goal to increase profits by 10 percent by expanding the company's product line is engaged in planning.

Good management planning at any level is realistic, comprehensive, and flexible. It includes plans for the short- and long-range uses of people, technology, and material resources.

To be an effective management tool, a management plan should be reduced to written form. When writing their plans, managers or management teams should not try to anticipate every possibility. An overly long and detailed document offers too many opportunities for misinterpretation.

Once the written plan is complete, it should be distributed to and discussed with everyone who is involved. Managers should keep their plans flexible so that they can be easily revised in response to comment or change. Plans should be reviewed and revised often to reflect changes in the organization.

ORGANIZING Organizing is a coordinated effort to reach a company's planning goals. It involves assigning responsibility, establishing working relationships, staffing, and directing the work of employees.

Assigning responsibility and establishing working relationships (see Figure 11-3 on page 195) are functions usually carried out by top and middle management, even in horizontal companies. Staffing, which includes selecting and training new employees, is often shared by middle management and supervisors. Because supervisors usually direct an employee's work, it is important that they be part of the hiring process.

The organizing function in large companies is complex. There may be hundreds of middle-level managers, thousands of supervisors, and tens of thousands of employees. Since the work is divided among so many people, middle managers and supervisors in traditional companies are usually given a narrow range of responsibilities.

In horizontal companies, middle management responsibilities are much wider. Because employees are empowered to do much of the organizing themselves, managers are able to advise and troubleshoot rather than give orders. Managers in smaller vertically organized companies usually have a wide range of organizing responsibilities as well.

CONTROLLING Controlling is the process of comparing what you planned with actual performance. It involves three basic activities—setting standards, evaluating performance according to those standards, and solving any problems revealed by the evaluation. A manager must analyze the financial records for the year to monitor progress toward financial goals. Controlling helps identify problems and ways to avoid or solve them.

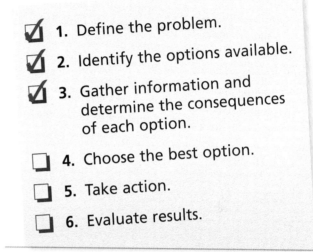

FIGURE 11-2

Decision-Making Process

■ **Investigate All Options** In order to reach a wise decision on complex questions, it's important to consider all the options. A process like this can help assure that decision-makers do not leave out important considerations. *What could happen if the problem is not well defined at first?*

☑ 1. Define the problem.

☑ 2. Identify the options available.

☑ 3. Gather information and determine the consequences of each option.

☐ 4. Choose the best option.

☐ 5. Take action.

☐ 6. Evaluate results.

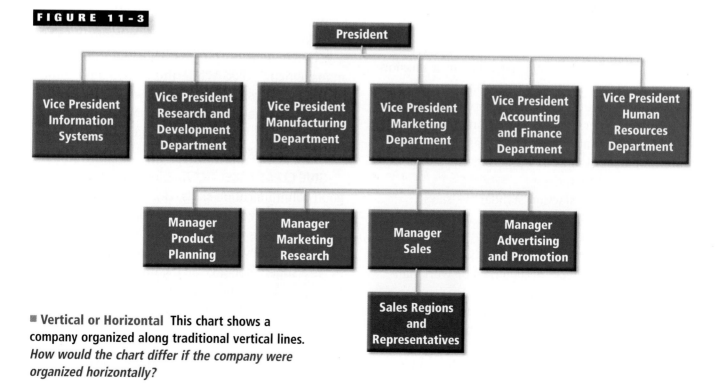

FIGURE 11-3

President

Vice President Information Systems

Vice President Research and Development Department

Vice President Manufacturing Department

Vice President Marketing Department

Vice President Accounting and Finance Department

Vice President Human Resources Department

Manager Product Planning

Manager Marketing Research

Manager Sales

Manager Advertising and Promotion

Sales Regions and Representatives

■ **Vertical or Horizontal** This chart shows a company organized along traditional vertical lines. *How would the chart differ if the company were organized horizontally?*

Chapter 11 ■ *Management Skills* **195**

FIGURE 11-4

Federal Express Mission Statement

MISSION STATEMENT

Federal Express is committed to our PEOPLE-SERVICE-PROFIT PHILOSOPHY. We will produce outstanding financial returns by providing totally reliable, competitively superior global air-ground transportation of high-priority goods and documents that require rapid, time-certain delivery. Equally important, positive control of each package will be maintained utilizing real-time electronic tracking and tracing systems. A complete record of each shipment and delivery will be presented without request for payment. We will be helpful, courteous, and professional to each other and the public. We will strive to have a satisfied customer at the end of each transaction.

David Bronczek,
Chairman and CEO

■ **United with the Company** A mission statement is designed to outline the goals and values of a company. *What are some ways that employees at Federal Express can uphold their mission statement?*

Before setting standards, many companies compose a mission statement. A mission statement describes the ultimate goals of a company in a brief paragraph or two. A mission statement summarizes why a company exists. It identifies products or services offered and the target market. While mission statements may vary in length and detail, the goal is the same for all—to support the company's mission. An example of a longer mission statement, for Federal Express, is shown in Figure 11-4.

Once a company establishes goals in a mission statement, it will adopt standards that are consistent with them. These standards will apply to all aspects of the firm's operation. Here are some possibilities:

- Financial standards—profit, cash flow, sales
- Employee standards—productivity, professional conduct, dress
- Customer satisfaction standards—sales returns, customer complaints, repeat business, referrals
- Quality control standards—production line checks for defects in materials or workmanship, repair requests, recalls

Once standards have been established, managers can then use them to evaluate both company and individual performance. When performance does not meet established standards, managers must identify and solve the problem. The defect rate in company products may be up sharply because of malfunctioning equipment. A solution to this case might involve replacement of the equipment.

■ Effective Management Techniques

Whether you find yourself a supervisor in a traditionally organized company or a member of a self-managing team, you will need to develop management skills. While this may sound intimidating, the most effective management techniques are usually a matter of common sense. You can judge for yourself as you read the suggestions below for effective management.

GIVE CLEAR DIRECTIONS Directing others requires good communication skills. Good communication is necessary at every level of management. Even the best employees will not be productive if they don't know what they are expected to do.

As a supervisor, give all the direction required for each job. Remember that you may need to repeat some of your directions, perhaps using a different approach. Encourage employees to ask questions about your directions. Communication will improve dramatically when they feel comfortable doing this.

TRAIN NEW EMPLOYEES WELL All new employees need some on-the-job training and orientation. As a supervisor, you may train new employees yourself or delegate this task. You may choose to delegate the task of training to someone else. Choose a person who knows the job well and is a good teacher, and supervise the training. Make sure that all job duties are explained and that the new employees understand how to complete them.

Orienting new employees includes more than simply training them for their positions. New employees may be frightened at the prospect of a new workplace, new coworkers, and new skills to learn. It is important to make new employees feel valued and welcome and to familiarize them with the working environment. Studies have shown that properly oriented employees are more satisfied with their work, more productive, and more likely to stay in the job.

Orientation may take as little as a couple of hours or as long as a few days. It commonly includes the following:

- Tour of the company and introduction to coworkers
- Discussion of the company's history, mission and values
- Description of what the company does
- Training on equipment, such as cash registers and computers
- Information on where key facilities are located
- Information about payroll, benefits, and company policies

REAL WORLD MARKETING

Downsizing

As a result of corporate downsizing and the Internet boom in the 90s, many companies have removed layers of management between top executives and people in the field to create a flatter organization structure. A recent study conducted by the University of Southern California found that 78 percent of companies had removed at least one layer of management in the last decade. This flatter structure allows companies to react quickly to changing market conditions, consumers' needs, and technology. With fewer people to communicate with, companies are able to speed up processes and transfer information more efficiently. Advocates of the flatter structure include successful companies such as Cisco and Wal-Mart.

Thinking Critically

How might a flatter structure help management work more efficiently?

■ **Management Roles** Managers are planners, organizers, and controllers. *Which function of management is the standing woman performing?*

BE CONSISTENT If you have decided that a job must be done in a certain way, make sure that all employees follow this standard. Don't make exceptions unless there is a good reason to do so.

Always follow through on what you say. If you announce that you intend to deduct part of an employee's salary for being late to work, do it. It will be hard to gain employee respect if you don't follow through on your decisions.

TREAT EMPLOYEES FAIRLY Whenever possible, do what is best for your employees. You do not need to say yes to every employee request; however, you should always consider the employees' point of view when making decisions. Listen to suggestions from your employees and consider acting on them. Take time to explain your reasoning if you believe an employee is wrong.

Take any necessary actions that can help them without sacrificing the amount or quality of work that is done. Talk with your immediate supervisor about changes that will benefit your employees. Employees will be more productive when treated fairly. Set reasonable standards of performance and apply those standards to everyone. Don't give special privileges to a few favorites.

BE FIRM WHEN NECESSARY Sometimes supervising others requires a firm hand. This can be done without losing your temper.

Each situation requiring disciplinary action is different. A friendly suggestion may be all that is necessary to get most employees on the right track. Others may not respond to the friendly approach, and you may have to be direct and firm. Give whatever directions are appropriate, and be certain the employee understands what you expect.

Employee problems that are caused by the inappropriate behavior of one employee toward another may be difficult to handle. A discussion may be the only way to clear up anger and solve the problem. Listen to what both parties have to say, and be reasonable but firm.

SET A GOOD EXAMPLE Set a good example in everything you do on the job. Doing this one simple thing will make your supervisory job much easier.

Let's consider the example of Frank, a department manager in a large retail store. He wrote computer programs at night to earn extra money and seldom went to sleep before 2 a.m. He found it very difficult to arrive at the store on time. Other employees in his department noticed that Frank was usually a half hour late. They decided they could sleep 20 minutes longer and still arrive at the store ahead of him. By following Frank's example, the whole department began arriving late for work. After several weeks of this, Frank was replaced.

Maria, the new department manager, always arrived at the store a few minutes early. When the other employees realized this, they reset their alarm clocks and began arriving early, too. Maria didn't have to say a word to anyone. She simply set a good example.

■ **Delegation** Managers who fail to delegate suffer the consequences—stress and lack of time for family and other interests. Sometimes it's necessary to bring work home, but if it happens too often, it could be a sign you have too much responsibility. *How could doing less of the work yourself be good for the company?*

Case Study

Long Distance Management

Many managers offer the option of telecommuting to attract top prospects to their companies. Some perks for the telecommuter are the ability to work from home, set your own hours, and avoid a commute to the office.

Managing telecommuters requires new approaches because managers are used to dealing with people they can see throughout the day. Managers must clearly state what they expect from telecommuting employees. E-mail and online chats can help keep communication clear.

How do managers know the employee is working on the job and not on his or her vegetable garden? In reality, they can't know. They need to focus on results and meeting schedules.

Managers find that it is important to have face-to-face contact—once or twice a week if possible, and less often if travel time is long. This helps telecommuters stay connected with the rest of the team and keeps relations fresh and friendly. It is important that full-time telecommuters understand that telecommuting is a privilege, not an entitlement. Clear lines of communication and contact with coworkers is crucial in maintaining a productive work environment. Coworkers who work on-site must feel comfortable calling telecommuters at home. There are also internal benefits for employers who allow employees to telecommute. This invests a certain amount of trust in the individual, who, in turn, should want to prove to his or her employer that this was not a poor decision. Another benefit of employee telecommuting is cost-avoidance. Employees who work from home may use their own computer, which will defray the costs of an employer providing them with one. Recruiting costs and training replacements can be expensive, costing upwards of $12,000 for some employees. It is more cost-efficient to make allowances for employees who have already proven responsible and reliable.

As information technology continues to grow, there will be more people who spend their workdays at home rather than in office cubicles. Learning how to manage these workers benefits both the company and the employee.

Case Study Review

1. **What can managers do to encourage team spirit in people working away from the office?**
2. **Which management structure, horizontal or traditional, do you think is more compatible with using telecommuters? Defend your position.**

A Matter of Ethics

3. **Some workers are allowed to telecommute, while others must come to the office each day. Do you think that is unfair? Why or why not?**

DELEGATE RESPONSIBILITY Some supervisors and many middle managers simply do too much work themselves. Some take work home almost every night. This may be necessary at times, but it usually means resources are not being managed well. Those who take work home are probably not delegating many tasks and responsibilities to others. Yet they often have capable employees with lighter workloads who would be willing to do more.

As a supervisor, don't try to do everything yourself. Organize your work responsibilities, and then decide which ones you can delegate to others. Decide which employee can best handle each task. Take time to teach some employees how to do new tasks. Follow up by monitoring and evaluating the tasks that have been delegated. This will allow you more time to concentrate on the most important tasks.

Empowering employees is company policy in horizontal organizations. You will be expected to delegate. That way, you will do a better job with your remaining responsibilities. Your employees, in turn, will appreciate the chance to show that they can handle more responsibility. They will become more productive.

FOSTER TEAMWORK As mentioned earlier in the chapter, teamwork is especially important in horizontally organized companies. As a manager or group "owner," you can foster teamwork in a number of ways. Encourage team members to step outside their areas of specialization and learn about other aspects of the process for which they are responsible. Try to promote honest and frank discussion before decisions are made. Listen respectfully to the comments and opinions of other team members, and encourage others in the group to do likewise. Respond to the comments and concerns of team members to develop a feeling of trust. You must ensure that all team members feel they are treated equally and fairly. A team will not succeed if members believe that some individuals are treated differently.

■ Employee Motivation

The more people feel that they are appreciated, the harder they will work. Keep this in mind when you become a manager. Provide frequent feedback to employees and formally evaluate them each year. Identify goals to be achieved over a period of years. Then reward employees who contribute to these goals.

It is important to reward smart work, not busy work. A person who looks busy may not necessarily be getting the work done; if you reward results, however, you will get results in return.

It is also important to reward those individuals who simplify work as opposed to creating more complexities on the job. Ordering a $2.79 pen from the supplies department at Intel Corporation, for example, used to take 95 steps and 12 pieces of

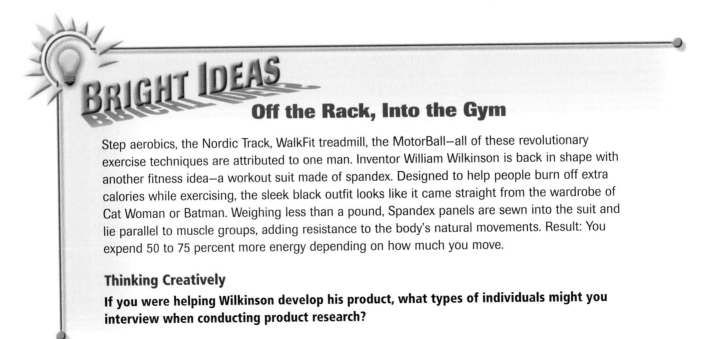

BRIGHT IDEAS

Off the Rack, Into the Gym

Step aerobics, the Nordic Track, WalkFit treadmill, the MotorBall—all of these revolutionary exercise techniques are attributed to one man. Inventor William Wilkinson is back in shape with another fitness idea—a workout suit made of spandex. Designed to help people burn off extra calories while exercising, the sleek black outfit looks like it came straight from the wardrobe of Cat Woman or Batman. Weighing less than a pound, Spandex panels are sewn into the suit and lie parallel to muscle groups, adding resistance to the body's natural movements. Result: You expend 50 to 75 percent more energy depending on how much you move.

Thinking Creatively

If you were helping Wilkinson develop his product, what types of individuals might you interview when conducting product research?

paper. Intel recognized the problem and simplified the procedure. Now it takes 8 steps and 1 piece of paper.

Doing the job right the first time lowers costs and increases productivity and worker pride. Identify those workers who value quality, not speed. Ask them to suggest ways to improve job performance. Seek out those employees who quietly do a good job. Take a sincere interest in them, and they will perform even better.

A reasonable amount of conformity is necessary in every company, but do not let conformity stifle creativity. Encourage employees to be creative and remind them that they won't be penalized for mistakes. Sometimes it is necessary to take risks when avoiding conformity, but these risks may produce positive results and should be rewarded.

A young engineer named Steve Wozniak was bored with his job working on computer chips. He asked on three occasions if he could work on designing a personal computer. His manager said no each time. So he built the first Apple computer in his garage and became one of the most successful entrepreneurs in history.

Enthusiastic long-term employees are the key to success in most companies. Reward loyalty by investing in continuing education for employees and promoting from within.

Life In The Diverse MARKETPLACE

Trading Cards

The exchange of business cards cannot be taken merely at face value—in many countries it is more of an art. While in the United States it may be quite casual to give someone your card, in other parts of the world there is more ritual. Japanese people always offer their *meishi*, or business cards, with two hands. The person who is receiving the card must accept it with two hands, study the card, and bow slightly to it. The card is then placed in a special case and placed in a jacket or shirt pocket, never in the pants pocket or the wallet.

Thinking Critically

Why do you think that giving someone your card has the potential to become a ritual?

■ **Employee Rewards** Companies often give gifts or awards to employees who excel. Continental Airlines gives employees a monetary bonus every month that the airline is in the top five of on-time flight arrivals. *Why is it important to reward effective work?*

Leadership in the 21st Century

The business world should expect to face many changes in the 21st century. As corporations dominated by controlling executives become obsolete, global competition increases. The expanding vision of international business and technology will affect organizations, people, production, and the fundamentals of management.

In light of these changes, many product life cycles may be counted in months, not decades. There will be fewer projects led by one executive. Management is turning to teams of cooperative leaders to create a vision and rally the organization around that vision to achieve exceptional results. This prevents one single person from being responsible for a product failure.

A recent study shows that marketing and sales is the fast track to top management. Considering the global economy, international experience follows marketing as the quickest way to advance in business.

Effective managers are making increased use of new technology, and customer satisfaction is a top priority as competition heats up. New leaders are diverse, even in jobs at the very top level. There are more women in positions such as CEO or Senior Vice President for large corporations. Global competition is creating companies and managers who are united by common goals and ideals.

Electronic Frontiers

Big Brother

Nearly three-fourths of major U.S. companies monitor their employees at the workplace. Common practices consist of reviewing e-mail, monitoring Internet usage or computer files, or listening in on telephone conversations. Special software, which costs companies between $25,000 to $65,000, is available to analyze online communication patterns without the knowledge of those being monitored. These software programs help companies cut down on this problem of "cyberslacking." Reasons cited for the extra eye included legal protection, productivity measures, and performance reviews.

Thinking Critically

If you were a manager in a large corporation, would you employ the practice of monitoring employees in the workplace? Explain your reasoning.

11.2 ASSESSMENT

Reviewing Key Terms and Concepts

1. What are the basic functions of management?
2. What is the value of employee orientation?
3. What does it mean to delegate responsibility?
4. What are two ways to reward employee loyalty?

Thinking Critically

5. How could a manager's openness to suggestions from employees influence employee loyalty to a company?

Integrating Academic Skills

6. **MATH** The vice president of a company makes an annual salary of $65,000 and works an average of 40 hours per week. The president of the company makes an annual salary of $100,000 and works an average of 60 hours per week. Assume both work 50 weeks a year. What does each person earn per hour? On a per-hour basis, who earns more money?

Careers in Marketing

FASHION MERCHANDISING

Carole Friedman
Fashion Merchandiser
Basically Kids

What does your job entail?

"It is my job to develop products, which sometimes requires working with the design department and/or sales department. In design, you have to determine what designs are fashionable and what sells, while in sales, you have to work with how to sell your designs to satisfy customer needs. It is nice to be involved with everything from product planning to product placement, and it keeps you traveling frequently. It is often necessary to visit retailers and buyers and find out what they need—and how best to help them move product."

What skills are most important?

"Typically, one needs to be good with numbers and math—especially when working on the sales end. You also really need to know your product. This is a two-sided occupation, and you need to have solid skills in design and sales while keeping your ear on the pulse of the industry."

What training would you recommend to students?

"Students should develop a strong marketing background. Most fashion merchandisers come up through either the sales or design departments. Getting training at a reputable fashion school, like the Fashion Institute of Technology or the Parsons School of Design, is important because the school will train you in the knowledge of fashion. Combining knowledge of design and fabric textures with creativity will take you far in this business."

What is your key to success?

"The secret to success in this field is to be able to go into the market and have a feeling for the trends. The buyers won't know what they want, so you have to look at what is selling and make judgments from there. It's like going shopping: you need to know what you want before you can buy it."

Thinking Critically
Think of another career that requires knowledge of both sales and design. Why are those skills important to the career you chose?

Career Facts

Education and Training: High school courses in marketing, business administration, consumer education, foreign language (especially French), and economics are valuable preparation for this career, as well as college preparatory courses. A college degree is not essential, but many universities and trade schools offer programs in merchandising and retailing.

Aptitudes, Abilities, and Skills: A highly developed sense of personal fashion and knowledge of trends is essential, in addition to communication skills, a strong ability to coordinate data and resources, and a good sense of color, design, and textiles.

Career Outlook: Competition is very keen; however, other management positions in the fashion industry may be more plentiful and may lead to fashion merchandising positions.

Career Path: Assistant to fashion coordinator positions or department management positions prepare employees for this position. Advancement often means moving to a larger company.

VOCABULARY REVIEW

Write a paragraph that includes all the following words. Use them in ways that demonstate that you know their meanings.

- vertical organization
- horizontal organization
- top management
- middle management
- supervisory-level management
- planning
- organizing
- mission statement
- controlling
- empowerment

FACT AND IDEA REVIEW

1. Describe traditional management structure. (11.1)

2. A vice president in a vertically organized company would be part of which management level? (11.1)

3. What does a supervisor do? (11.1)

4. What does it mean to "flatten" an organization? (11.1)

5. What is the main difference between a department and a self-managing team? (11.1)

6. What are the characteristics of a good management plan? (11.2)

7. What is usually involved in the organizing function of management? (11.2)

8. Why is it important to ask for feedback after giving directions to an employee? (11.2)

9. How can the owner of a management team foster teamwork in the group? (11.2)

THINKING CRITICALLY

1. Compare top-level management in a large company to what you think it would be in a small company.

2. Discuss why being fair is an effective and important management skill. Describe experiences you have had or heard about in which managers were not fair. What were the results of the unfair treatment?

3. Why do you think rewards get better results than punishments?

4. Do you think a company's mission statement should include a commitment to doing business ethically? Should ethics be as important as profits? Defend your answer.

BUILDING WORKPLACE SKILLS

1. **Technology** Use the Internet to find information about management opportunities in marketing. Then use a word processing program to write a summary of your findings.

2. **Human Relations** Ramesh works as a travel agent. The manager of the travel agency has just hired a new agent who happens to be a close personal friend. The manager is showing her friend obvious favoritism. Ramesh likes his job, but he feels increasingly uncomfortable with the manager's unfair behavior. What should he do?

3. **Science** Calculate the square feet of space required to reorganize an office to accommodate six employees. Each cubicle requires a minimum of 8 feet by 8 feet and 3 feet of walking space between three of the cubicles.

APPLYING MARKETING CONCEPTS

1. **Planning an Event** Use your word processing program to describe what would go into the planning, organizing, and controlling of a school club car wash.

2. **Building a Cohesive Team** You are the manager of a bookstore that recently merged with a neighboring coffee shop. While all employees will remain under their former manager, it is necessary to create a united group of workers. Brainstorm ideas for team-building activities. Pick your favorite activity and, using design software, make a flyer describing your event.

3. **Creating a Mission Statement** Use the Internet to research a company's mission statement of your choice. Then imagine that you are starting a similar company in the same field. Using the mission statement as a model, write your own mission statement. Use presentation software to prepare a presentation of your mission statement and of how you created it.

4. **Developing a Training Program** You are a manager at a phone card telemarketing company. You have just hired three new employees who need training. You have received feedback in the past that the training process is ineffective and could be more intensive. Using a computer program, develop a schedule for a two-day orientation.

LINKING SCHOOL TO WORK

Resource and Systems Skills Ask a supervisor or employer what he or she thinks about the newer management structures that emphasize teamwork and organization by process. Report your findings to the class. After everyone has shared the various responses he or she obtained, discuss any trends that are apparent and speculate about the reasons for them.

THE DECA CONNECTION

Role Play: Management Trainee

Situation You are to assume the role of management trainee at a local outlet of a traditionally organized national sporting goods company.

Activity As part of your training, you have been asked by the store manager (judge) to draw up a chart showing the different management levels in your local branch of the company. Once you have completed the chart, you must explain it to the store manager (judge).

Evaluation You will be evaluated on how well you meet the following performance indicators:

- Explain the concept of management
- Demonstrate orderly and systematic behavior
- Follow directions
- Prepare simple written reports

inter NET CONNECTION

Which Is Better?

Your company is considering changing from a traditional to a horizontal organization. You are concerned and decide to find out which is more effective.

Connect

- Use the Web to research and compare the corporate culture and financial performance of several traditional and horizontal companies.
- Write a report making comparisons between the two types of organization.

the Zazz Lab...

A Sports and Entertainment Marketing Simulation

WELCOME

Welcome to Zazz Sports and Entertainment Marketing Company. Zazz is devoted to serving the needs of its clients who include college, university, and professional sports teams, professional athletes, sporting events, and sports arenas plus major consumer product corporations, as well as television networks and movie studios. As an intern, you will have the opportunity to work on different clients' projects. All of your work will be assigned and reviewed by your department supervisor.

ESTABLISH A CHILDREN'S SOCCER CAMP FRANCHISE

SITUATION

One of Zazz's long-standing properties—a professional soccer player—is preparing to retire. To stay involved in soccer and to generate retirement income, he wants to run children's soccer camps around the United States. The camps would cater to three age groups—6–9, 10–13, and 14 and older. He has asked Zazz to establish the format and prospectus so his name and concept for the camps can be franchised. The new camps will be in competition with established camps that have been catering to soccer players for many years.

ASSIGNMENT

You must determine the four *P*s of the marketing mix, as well as guidelines for consistent management of the camps. *Place* strategies should discuss minimum requirements for location sites. *Product* suggestions involve camp format and a sample daily schedule for each age group. Besides soccer drills, include team-building activities and social skills for the first two age groups and game strategies for the older age group. Also include leisure activities. *Promotion* efforts include a letter and brochure. Determine a realistic pricing structure for the camps. Write a mission statement discussing the philosophy and goals of the camps. Compile an employee handbook discussing the client's philosophy, job responsibilities, behavior guidelines, and management's expectations. Provide two human relations scenarios for employees to analyze and respond to—one situation involving coworkers and the other involving children. These can be used for employee training.

Tools and Resources

To complete this assignment you will need to conduct research at a library or on the Internet. You will need a word processing program and computer presentation software. Required reading would include *Soccer America*, a national soccer magazine.

Research

Research soccer to get an appreciation for the sport and its popularity. Research soccer camps for children, including where and when they are held, average length, who runs them, cost, typical activities, and promotional activities. Research team-building activities and human relations skill development for inclusion in the camp's schedule and employee handbook. Study management strategies for training employees and keeping them motivated.

Report

Prepare a written report and a computer presentation for the client. Use a word processing program to prepare a double-spaced report. Within the report, prepare a table that shows a comparison of four existing camps. Also create a table for the daily schedule for each age group, listing the times and activities in an easy-to-follow format. Be sure each table has a title and is introduced in the text prior to its inclusion on the page. Arrange your written report around the following headings:

- Background on soccer
  - Worldwide and United States
  - Current trends
- Analysis of existing soccer camps—(table)
  - Formats, locations, pricing structure, and promotion
- Proposed soccer camps
  - Mission statement
  - Location requirements (place)
  - Suggested format (product)
    - Duration (weekly, overnight)
    - Classifications (age, gender)
    - Activities
      - Sample daily schedule (table)
      - Sample team-building activity
      - Sample social skills activity
  - Promotion of camps
    - Sample letter and brochure
- Pricing structure
- Employee handbook
  - Role plays
  - Camp philosophy
  - Job responsibilities
  - Guidelines for behavior

Using computer presentation software, prepare a presentation of your ideas for the client that includes:

- Key topics covered in your written report
- Graphic illustrations that are relevant to each slide's topic
- Very little text
- A minimum of 10 slides

Presentation and Evaluation

Your supervisor wants you to present your ideas in a written report and an oral presentation. The oral presentation will later be shown to the client. You will be evaluated on your oral presentation skills, which include:

- Knowledge of soccer and soccer camps
- Proposed ideas for soccer camp franchise
- Comprehensiveness of report
- Continuity of presentation
- Enthusiasm
- Voice quality
- Eye contact

Portfolio
Print out a copy of your completed report and presentation for your Portfolio.

THE DECA CONNECTION

DECA Business Service Marketing Series
Creating the format and promotional ideas for a business franchise could be a potential role play for this event.

DECA Marketing Management Series
Preparing an employee handbook and training plan is part of this career area.

DECA Hospitality and Recreation Marketing Research Event
Conducting research and planning a soccer camp for children is a possible topic for this written event.

DECA Entrepreneurship Participating Event
Developing a business proposal for a soccer camp for children is a possible topic for this event, as long as financial information is included.

DECA Sports and Entertainment Marketing Management Team Decision-Making Event
Working on this project with a partner will make the experience similar to what is expected in a DECA Team Decision-Making Event.

Portfolio

The Sales Presentation

Upon completion of this unit, you will be expected to conduct an actual sales presentation, demonstrating mastery of each step of the sales process. Have your teacher select a classmate to play the role of your customer, and if possible, videotape the presentation. To prepare for this activity, you will need to research a product of your choice, prepare a written feature-benefit chart for it, and decide on your sales situation (retail or business-to-business). Prepare an evaluation sheet for your teacher and classmates to use in judging your sales demonstration. Include spaces to rate all the steps of the sale (approach, determining needs, product presentation, handling objections, closing the sale, and suggestion selling), as well as relationship marketing and ability to communicate. Under each step of the sale, indicate items to be evaluated and points assigned to each. The evaluation sheet should total 100 points.

Selling

Unit Overview

This unit is designed to prepare you for employment in a sales position. The practical aspect of this unit will be beneficial to you even if you don't pursue a specific career in sales—selling an idea, being elected to a political position, and even getting hired for a job often requires these skills.

Chapter 12 helps you prepare for the sale by performing product and customer research. Chapter 13 introduces you to the steps of a sale in retail and business-to-business sales, focusing on approaching customers, determining their needs, and offering excellent customer service. Chapter 14 discusses product presentation and how to handle any customer questions or objections. Chapter 15 explains how to close the sale, conduct suggestion selling, and begin a long-standing relationship with your customers. The final chapter in this unit addresses the mathematical aspect of selling, including operating a sales register and filling out necessary forms.

Functions of Marketing

Marketing-Information Management

Financing

Selling

Professional Development · Economics

Technology · Academic Concepts

Pricing

Business, Management, Entrepreneurship · Communication, Interpersonal Skills

Distribution

Foundations

Product/Service Management

Promotion

Technology · Academic Concepts

In this Unit:

Foundations of Marketing

○ Communication, Interpersonal Skills

Functions of Marketing

◗ Selling

◗ Financing

◗ Distribution

◗ Pricing

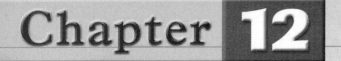

Preparing for the Sale

Marketing: What It Takes

Fashion, Fabrics, and Styles

You have just been accepted as an intern for a clothing manufacturer. You will be working in the manufacturer's showroom in New York City as a sales consultant for the summer. Prior to starting your internship, you decide that it would be a good idea to learn about the company's products and customers.

WHAT WILL YOU DO?

What information will you need? How will you find it?

Knowing Your Product and Your Customer

Selling

The act of personal selling occurs in a retail setting, a business-to-business setting, or even over the telephone. Personal selling is any form of direct contact occurring between a salesperson and a customer. The key factor that sets it apart from other forms of promotion is that there is two-way communication between the seller and the buyer.

Retail selling is unique because customers come to the store. Non-personal selling techniques, such as advertising and displays, help to create store traffic. The salesperson's job in the store is to offer customer service. The salesperson is available to answer any questions about the product or its features.

Business-to-business selling may take place in a manufacturer's or wholesaler's showroom (inside sales) or a customer's place of business (outside sales). In the latter case, it is up to the salesperson to make contact with the customer. Sales representatives, in most cases, will call to make an appointment prior to their visit. In other cases, a sales representative may make a "cold call," which means he or she will appear without an appointment.

The last type of personal selling situation is telemarketing, which is the process of selling over the telephone. Consumer products and services that are commonly sold over the telephone include magazine or newspaper subscriptions; service contracts for newly purchased appliances, televisions, and computers; and long distance telephone services. Products that may be telemarketed to businesses are items that are purchased on a regular basis, such as stationery, cleaning supplies, or office supplies like computer paper.

The goals of selling are the same regardless of the sales situations. They are to help customers make satisfying buying decisions, which create ongoing, profitable relationships between buyer and seller. Repeat business is crucial to the success of any company. It is easier and less expensive to keep current customers happy than it is to generate new customers. If a business is successful at keeping customers happy, it is likely that the customers will pass along positive recommendations to friends and family.

Salespeople accomplish those goals by offering customer service, which involves solving customers' problems and by understanding their needs and wants. A customer may say that she is having a problem with her feet because she stands all day in her new job. An alert salesperson will suggest shoes designed for people who stay on their feet all day. This analysis of the customer's needs combined with product knowledge should please the customer and make the sale.

What You'll Learn

- The definition and goals of selling
- The various sales situations encountered in the business world
- The definition of feature-benefit selling
- How customers make decisions and the difference between rational and emotional buying decisions

Why It's Important

Learning how to research products and customers is helpful when selling any type of product or idea. Learning how to find customers is also essential. In this chapter you will learn key selling concepts that link products to customers.

Key Terms

- personal selling
- business-to-business selling
- telemarketing
- feature-benefit selling
- product features
- customer benefits
- rational motive
- emotional motive
- extensive decision making
- limited decision making
- routine decision making

■ Feature-Benefit Selling

Matching the characteristics of a product to a customer's needs and wants is a concept called feature-benefit selling. Many people believe that customers do not buy products; rather, they buy what the products will do for them. Leather shoes are purchased for their appearance, easy care, comfort, and longevity. A computer is purchased for increased productivity. Insurance is purchased for emotional and financial security.

PRODUCT FEATURES A salesperson needs to learn how a product's features will benefit the customer. Product features may be basic, physical, or extended attributes of the product or purchase. The most basic feature of a product is its intended use. A person buys an automobile for transportation or a watch to tell time.

Consumers look for certain physical qualities in products that differentiate competing brands and models. In a vehicle a consumer might consider price, color, automatic transmission, car stereo system, tires, air bag, and antilock brakes.

Additional features add more value to a product and provide the reasons for price differences among product models. An iron that turns itself off after sitting unused will cost more than the basic model. Then there are extended product features. Extended features for a vehicle might include the warranty, service policy, and available financing. Customers might even consider the reputation of a company to be an extended feature because there is reduced risk doing business with a secure, well-established company. Customers are faithful to a reputable company that stands behind its products.

CUSTOMER BENEFITS When the features of a product are developed into customer benefits, they become selling points. Customer benefits are the advantages or personal satisfaction a customer will get from a good or service. It is a salesperson's job to analyze the product features from the customer's point of view to determine the benefits.

You, as a salesperson, will need to answer two questions about each product feature:

1. *How does the feature help the product's performance?* The answer to this question represents the first step in developing a customer benefit. For example, air pockets in the heel of a running shoe cushion the impact on pavement.

2. *How does the performance information give the customer a personal reason to buy the product?* What value is the product to the customer? In the case of the running shoe, the air pockets give the wearer more comfort when running or walking and help to protect the foot from injury.

After identifying the features of a product and their benefits, you should put together a feature-benefit chart. This is a chart in which each product feature is listed with its corresponding customer benefits. In preparing such a chart, remember that the more useful a feature, the more valuable the product is to the customer. Figure 12-1 on page 213 shows a feature-benefit chart for a digital video camera.

■ **A Phone Call Away** Telemarketing may be used to sell all types of goods and services for personal and business use. In some cases, businesses are using computer-generated voices to conduct telemarketing instead of human beings. *Why do you think some businesses use computer-generated voices for sales?*

FIGURE 12-1

Feature-Benefit Chart for Sharp VL-SD20U Digital Video Camera

FEATURE	BENEFIT
3″ High Resolution Color LCD View Screen (fingerprint reduced) and Low Reflectivity	Viewing area is 4.27 square inches with 89,856 pixels, which means you will be able to see a very clear image of what you are recording. It allows you to make adjustments while you are recording, so you don't waste any footage. Screen is coated with a special resin that reduces fingerprints (cleaning is simple with a clean, soft cloth). The low reflectivity (one percent) feature absorbs 99 percent of all reflective light, making it easy to perform well in all lighting conditions, indoors and outside.
100x Digital Zoom	The 100x digital zoom is in addition to the 10x optical zoom (regular analog recording). It kicks in as soon as you zoom in past 10x and allows you to magnify that image 100 times. Great for those times when you cannot get close to the subject you want to record, like in a zoo or during a sporting event, where you are restricted in distance from the subject.
Digital Gamma Brightness Correction	This feature has a new backlight compensation which adjusts only the dark spots of a shot to optimal brightness levels and leaves the bright sections untouched, so they don't become glaringly washed out. No more worry about the degree of lightness in the area in which you are recording—you are guaranteed clear recordings all the time.
i.LINK™ Digital Interface In/Out (IEEE 1394)	the iLINK cable capability allows for incredibly high-speed (up to 400 Mbps) transfer of full motion video from digital camcorders to computers or other i.LINK capable camcorders. Since there is no need to convert digital data into analog, there is no loss of image quality. It is the ideal vehicle for transmitting digital camcorder data. (iLINK is a trademark of Sony Electronics, Inc.)
Digital Image Stabilization (D.I.S.)	The D.I.S. circuit senses movement of the user holding the camera and helps to reduce image shake and jitter, delivering a more stable picture.
270 degree Variable Angle Recording	You can hold the Viewcam in a variety of angles to record over people and objects or close to the ground. You can even record yourself by rotating the view screen 180 degrees.
Dimensions (W × H × D Inches) 16.2 × 3.8 × 2.9 and Approximate Weight: 1.2 lbs. (without tape or battery)	Compact and lightweight Viewcam makes it easy to handle and transport.
Suggested retail price is $999.99, which includes the following accessories: AC Adaptor/Charger (for the house), Battery Pack, Two Lithium Ion Batteries, DC Cable (for the car), Shoulder Strap, A/V Cable (for television), and Lens Cap	Good value for all the features and benefits of this new technology, as well as all the included accessories.
Sharp Electronics	A reputable electronics company that stands behind its products.
90-day limited warranty	The warranty is reassurance of the good quality of the product. Worry-free because anything that goes wrong with the Viewcam will be fixed during the warranty period free of charge.

SOURCE: SHARP ELECTRONICS WEB SITE.

■ **Feature-Benefit Chart** Combining a product or extended feature with its corresponding customer benefit creates selling points. *In this feature-benefit chart, which features are product features and which ones are extended features?*

■ Customer Buying Motives

To understand relevant consumer benefits for certain product features, salespeople must develop knowledge of customers. They must know what motivates customers to buy and what decisions customers make before the final purchase.

Customers may have rational or emotional motives for making purchases. A rational motive is a conscious, logical reason for a purchase. Rational motives include product dependability, time or monetary savings, health or safety considerations, service, and quality. An emotional motive is a feeling experienced by a customer through association with a product. Emotional motives are feelings such as social approval, recognition, power, love, or prestige. Many buying decisions involve a combination of both buying motives.

Successful salespeople determine customers' rational and emotional motives in a potential buying situation. Then they suggest the features and benefits of the product that best matches those motives. People buy automobile tires for safety reasons (rational motive) because they care about loved ones that will share the vehicle with them (emotional motive).

■ Customer Decision Making

Some customers need no help from salespeople, and others require significant time and effort. This difference has its roots in three distinct types of decision making—extensive, limited, and routine. How a person makes a decision is affected by the following factors:

- Previous experience with the product and company
- How often the product is purchased
- The amount of information necessary to make a wise buying decision
- The importance of the purchase to the customer
- The perceived risk involved in the purchase (fear that the product will cause financial loss or will not function properly)
- The time available to make the decision

EXTENSIVE DECISION MAKING Extensive decision making is used when there has been little or no previous experience with an item. This category includes those goods and services that have a high degree of perceived risk, are very expensive, or have high value to the customer. Products in this category include expensive manufacturing machinery, land for a new building site, or an individual's first home.

LIMITED DECISION MAKING Limited decision making is used when a person buys goods and services that he or she has purchased before but not regularly. There is a moderate degree of perceived risk involved, and the person often needs some information before buying the product.

Consumer goods and services in this category might include a second car, certain types of clothing, furniture, a vacation, and household appliances. Goods and services that a firm might buy using limited decision making include accounting services, ad agency services, computer programs, office equipment, and certain products used in manufacturing.

■ **Making the Sale** There are three degrees of decision making for most sales situations. They are routine, limited, and extensive. *Which decision-making process do you think this customer is using?*

ROUTINE DECISION MAKING Routine decision making is used when a person needs little information about a product that he or she is buying. This is generally attributed to a high degree of prior experience with it or a low perceived risk. The perceived risk may be low because the item is inexpensive, the product is bought frequently, or satisfaction with the product is high. Some consumer goods and services in this category are grocery items, newspapers, dry-cleaning services, hairdressing services, and certain brand name clothing and cosmetics. Customers who have developed brand loyalty for a product will use routine decision making. Expensive items, such as automobiles, may be purchased routinely if the customer has strong brand loyalty to one car manufacturer. This is the same for electronic or computer products. A customer may be more likely to routinely purchase, for example, Sony electronics because of Sony's good reputation and overall popularity.

Businesses that simply reorder goods and services without much thought are using routine decision making. Products that businesses often buy routinely include raw materials, office supplies, maintenance services, and other staple goods. Many offices may have a standing order with an office supply company for computer paper, pens, and stationary. They know how much they use each month and assume that those quantities will remain constant. These items will continue to be routine purchases until there is a problem with the product or with the supplier. When this happens, limited decision making would be required to change suppliers or products.

Electronic Frontiers

Viral Marketing: It's Spreading

Getting your customers to become a part of your salesforce is a great way to conduct business. Instead of relying on banner advertisements or expensive marketing campaigns, companies look to their customers as a source of publicity. Many companies include "e-mail this information to a friend" buttons on their Web sites. On the Internet, word of mouth via e-mail can propel product recognition into purchases, especially if your happy customer is able to recommend a great experience to others. A customer who discussed the benefits of a particular make-up brush in an online discussion group provided a link to a beauty retailer. Over the next five days, that beauty retailer sold 3,000 brush sets. Companies hope that once the message is e-mailed, it spreads from person to person.

Thinking Critically

Customers are becoming aware that their endorsement is valuable to a company. Would it make sense for a company to reward them? If so, how?

12.1 ASSESSMENT

Reviewing Key Terms and Concepts

1. What is personal selling?
2. Name three settings where personal selling may occur.
3. What are the goals of selling?
4. Explain the concept of feature-benefit selling.
5. What are the three levels of decision making that customers may use when purchasing goods or services?

Thinking Critically

6. Explain this statement: Customers do not buy products, they buy what the products will do for them.

Integrating Academic Skills

7. **COMMUNICATION** Write a classified advertisement for a sales position in a school store. Include job responsibilities and required skills.

Preparation

What You'll Learn

- Sources for developing product information
- Prospecting sources and methods
- How leads are developed
- Preparation for the sale in business-to-business selling and retail selling

Why It's Important

As a salesperson, you will need to prepare for the sale by learning about the industry and the products you will be selling. In specific sales situations, you may also need to find customers. The tools and techniques for accomplishing these tasks are covered in this section.

Key Terms

- preapproach
- prospect
- referrals
- endless chain method
- cold canvassing

The Preapproach

There are some steps that a salesperson follows when preparing to assist customers. The preapproach is getting ready for the face-to-face encounter in a selling situation.

Salespeople prepare for the sale by studying their products, keeping abreast of industry trends, researching potential customers, and developing familiarity with their company's policies and procedures.

■ Product Information

Product knowledge is essential for success in selling. Knowing how to use and care for a product is essential when educating consumers and demonstrating a product.

Developing product knowledge is easy—if you know where to look for the information. Salespeople can generally find all the product information they need through four main sources—direct experience, written publications, other people, and formal training.

Using a product is probably the best source of direct experience. Some businesses offer discounts to their salespeople to encourage employees to buy and use the company's merchandise. You can also get direct experience with a product by studying display models or visiting the manufacturing facility to see how the product is made.

Printed materials can offer facts and background necessary to develop familiarity with a product. These include user manuals, manufacturer warranties and guarantees, catalogs, and promotional materials. Labels provide important information for clothing items or prepackaged goods. Manufacturers, retailers, and wholesalers often have Web sites where products may be explained and purchased.

A personal opinion is valuable because it offers a human touch when sharing a product with a customer. Friends, relatives, and customers can tell you what they liked about the product as well as how they used it. Coworkers, supervisors, and manufacturers' representatives who have extensive product knowledge can also share their expertise.

Formal training may be the best way to educate salespeople on certain products. Most industrial sales representatives receive much of their product knowledge through formal training sessions. Some sales representatives spend several months attending classes and observing experienced sales representatives before going out on their own. In retail settings, training is likely to be less structured. Information might be funneled informally to the sales staff as new merchandise is received or selected for promotion.

■ Industry Trends

Sales representatives read periodicals related to their trade to gain insight into the industry. As a sales representative for an apparel manufacturer, you might read *Women's Wear Daily*. At the retail level of selling, a sales representative may read consumer fashion magazines, such as *Vogue*, to stay current with up-to-date colors and trends. All industries have trade publications related to their industry.

Standard & Poor's is another publication that is a must for researching industry trends. This publication offers a trade report by industry. It is available in most college libraries, in some public libraries, and online.

■ Sources and Methods of Prospecting

Looking for new customers is called prospecting. A **prospect**, or a lead, is a potential customer. Many types of businesses require salespeople to find prospects, while others do not. Most retail selling situations are not involved with prospecting because salespeople do not need to go out and find customers—customers come to the store.

Prospecting is especially important in business-to-business selling situations. Salespeople are evaluated on how many new accounts they open through prospecting efforts. A rich supply of prospect sources is available to enterprising salespeople, including various kinds of directories, periodicals, lists, and suggested leads.

■ **Customer Catalogs** A manufacturer's catalog provides details of products as well as important information regarding their purchase by other businesses. *How could the information on this catalog page be helpful to a sales representative for RefrigiWear?*

■ **Getting the Word Out There** Standard & Poor's provides data on industry trends, as do trade journals. *How could all these trade journals be useful to a company like RefrigiWear, an insulated clothing manufacturer?*

EMPLOYER LEADS Some firms employ entire telemarketing teams to generate leads for their sales staffs. Telemarketers in such firms often perform preliminary research on these leads so that salespeople have information about the prospects before meeting them. Other firms rely entirely on their salespeople to find new customers.

Most businesses probably fall somewhere between those two extremes. Many employers do what they can to help locate potential customers for their salespeople. Figure 12-2 on page 219 provides some insight into how leads are created and pursued.

TELEPHONE DIRECTORIES The White Pages telephone directory provides names, addresses, and telephone numbers of potential customers in given geographic areas. The Yellow Pages lists businesses that may be potential customers for certain industrial goods and services.

TRADE AND PROFESSIONAL DIRECTORIES Business-to-business sales representatives can use trade and professional directories to locate potential customers by type of business. One well-known directory frequently used by sales representatives is *Thomas' Register of American Manufacturers*.

NEWSPAPERS Newspapers provide good leads for some salespeople. Birth announcements are good leads for insurance salespeople. Engagement announcements provide bridal shops, caterers, florists, and printers with prospects. Reports of business mergers and announcements of new personnel in business firms provide leads for business-to-business salespeople.

COMMERCIAL LISTS Salespeople may buy lists of potential customers from companies that specialize in categorizing people by such criteria as education, age, income, credit card purchases, and location. Lists of businesses categorized according to net sales, profits, products, and geographic locations are also available.

E-mail lists of people interested in the same subject or employed in the same industry are also available. Most e-mail list services are free, making them an economical way to identify potential customers.

Life In The Diverse MARKETPLACE

Small Talk in Sales

In today's fast-paced society, American salespeople have been trained to make the sale with as little small talk as possible. This is not the case in Europe, where sales presentations take a different pace. Small talk and conversation about current events, sports, art, and other unrelated topics are part of the sales process. This practice of "friendly" selling is so common, in fact, that most Europeans are suspicious of a hard sale, where there is little talk and complete focus on making the deal.

Thinking Critically

Why are many Americans turned off by overly chatty salespeople and sales presentations that involve more talking than selling?

CUSTOMER REFERRALS Satisfied customers often give salespeople referrals—the names of other people who might buy the product. Referrals open the market to those potential customers you might not have reached without a recommendation. When salespeople ask previous customers for names of potential customers, they are said to be using the endless chain method. Some companies offer discounts or gifts to customers who give referrals.

COLD CANVASSING In cold canvassing, a salesperson tries to locate as many potential customers as possible without checking out leads beforehand. In cold canvassing, potential customers are selected at random, such as by going door-to-door or selecting names from a telephone directory. This is also sometimes called blind prospecting. One example is a real estate agent going door-to-door in a neighborhood, asking people if they would like to sell their homes. Another example of cold canvassing is a stockbroker selecting names from a telephone book at random and calling them.

FIGURE 12-2

HOW EMPLOYER LEADS ARE DEVELOPED

Many firms generate leads for their sales staff. They help locate potential customers for their salespeople.

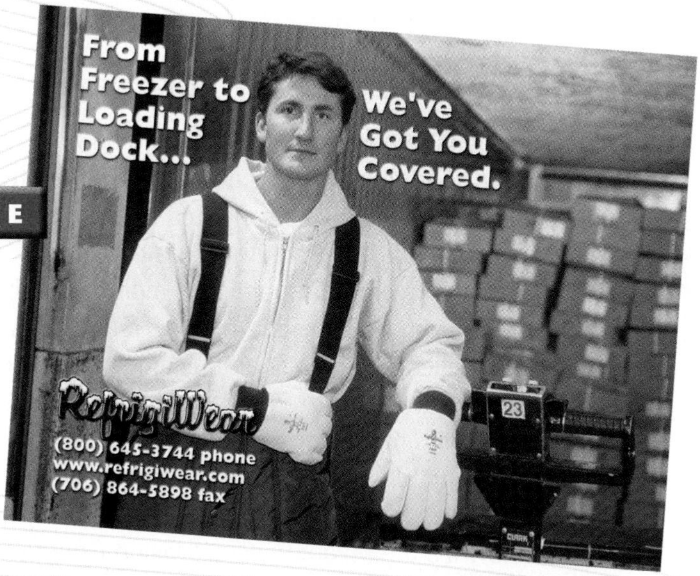
From Freezer to Loading Dock...
We've Got You Covered.
RefrigiWear
(800) 645-3744 phone
www.refrigiwear.com
(706) 864-5898 fax

1 BUSINESSES ADVERTISE

Employers often get leads from their involvement in trade shows and from advertising in trade journals and consumer magazines. Some firms send direct mail, while others subscribe to computer database services to get names, addresses, and telephone numbers of prospective customers.

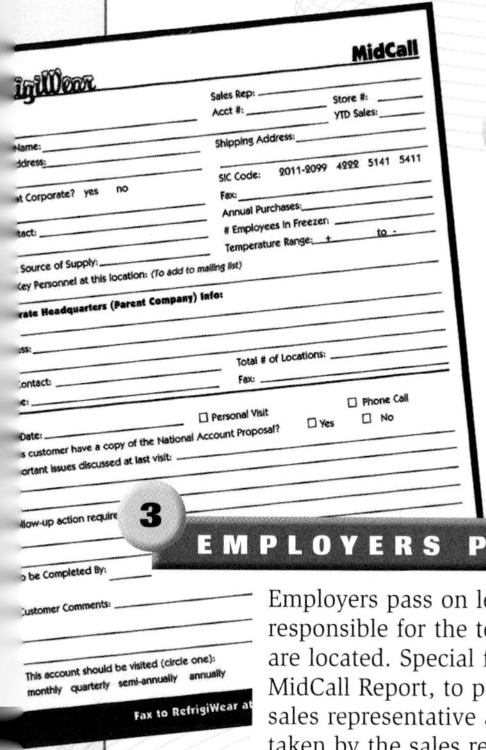

MidCall
Sales Rep: Store #:
Acct #: YTD Sales:
Name: Shipping Address:
ddress:
SIC Code: 2011-2099 4222 5141 5411
at Corporate? yes no
Fax:
Annual Purchases:
tact: # Employees in Freezer:
Temperature Range: + to -
Source of Supply:
Key Personnel at this location: (To add to mailing list)
rate Headquarters (Parent Company) Info:
ss:
Total # of Locations:
ontact: Fax:
e:
Date: ☐ Personal Visit ☐ Phone Call
s customer have a copy of the National Account Proposal? ☐ Yes ☐ No
ortant issues discussed at last visit:
llow-up action require
o be Completed By:
Customer Comments:
This account should be visited (circle one):
monthly quarterly semi-annually annually
Fax to RefrigiWear at

2 PROSPECTIVE CUSTOMERS RESPOND

Prospective customers respond to this promotion by requesting further information.

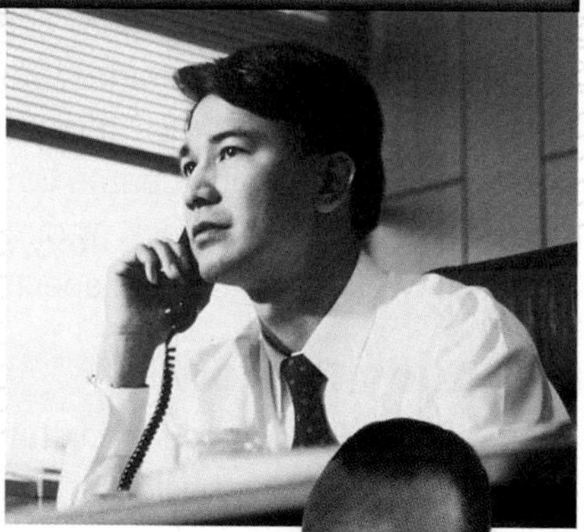

3 EMPLOYERS PASS ON LEADS

Employers pass on leads to the sales representatives responsible for the territories in which the prospects are located. Special forms are often used, like this MidCall Report, to pass along the information to the sales representative and to keep track of the action taken by the sales representative.

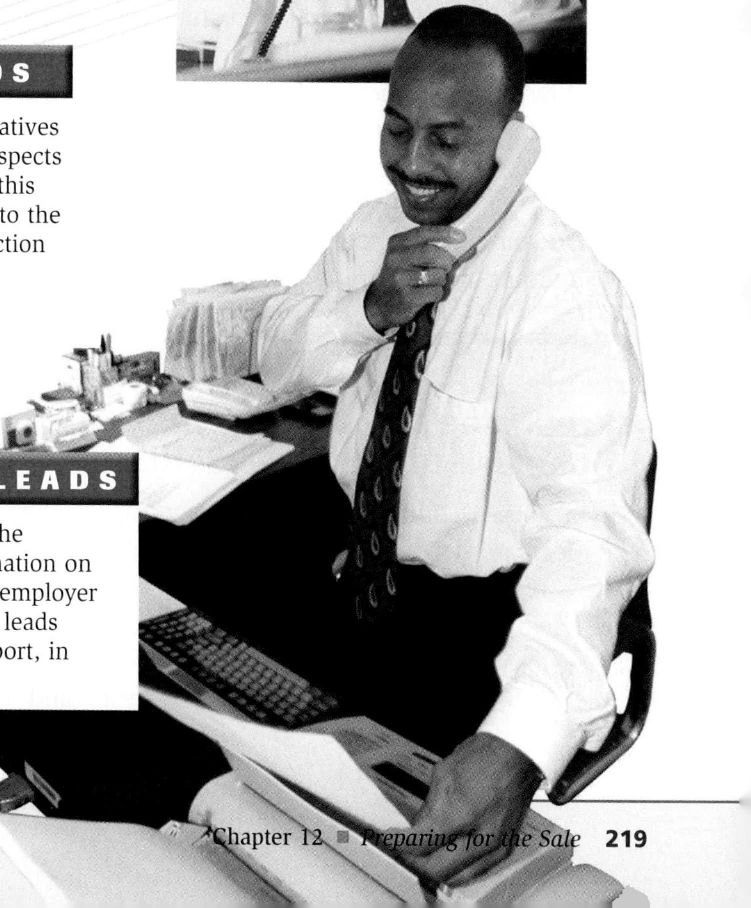

4 SALESPEOPLE ACT ON LEADS

Salespeople act on leads by calling to qualify the prospects. Salespeople report back with information on the disposition of the prospects. That way the employer knows the salesperson has followed up on the leads sent to him or her. The completed MidCall Report, in this case, would be faxed back to RefrigiWear.

Customer Management Software

Customer management software is changing how companies keep track of their customers. The software company Siebel Systems Inc. has created a program that helps sales representatives track their customers and analyze markets. The program publishes monthly analyses that detail customer problems and needs. Honeywell, a company that makes jet engines and avionics, uses Siebel's software. In Honeywell's first report, they found that airlines were frustrated with managing parts inventories. Honeywell executives responded with new services that will spare airlines that headache. "Our focus used to be from the inside out. Now it's the reverse," says division General Manager Lynn Brubaker.

Clarify, another software company, has a program that combines multiple databases into one huge database so companies can view all customer information in one place. H&R Block, for example, uses Clarify software to combine and coordinate the customer records at its tax offices, discount brokerage, Web site, and customer-service center. With easy access to this central warehouse of information, salespeople in the company's stock trading division can look at detailed descriptions of tax customers and size up who would be good prospects.

Case Study Review

1. How did Honeywell's use of customer management software provide the company with an opportunity to increase its business with the airline companies?
2. How did H&R Block's salespeople in the stock trading business benefit from the company's adoption of Clarify's software?

A Matter of Ethics

3. Do you think it is ethical for H&R Block to use its database from one operation to sell products in another division of the company? Why or why not?

■ Preparing for the Sale in Business-to-Business Selling

In business-to-business (B-to-B) sales, preapproach activities vary depending on whether the sales call is with a previous customer or a new prospect. When dealing with previous customers, salespeople analyze past sales records and review their notes about the buyer's personality, family, interests, and hobbies.

When dealing with a new customer, the salesperson must do some homework before jumping into the selling process. Questions that the salesperson should research include the following:

- Does the prospect need this product or service?
- Does the prospect have the financial resources to pay?
- Does the prospect have the authority to buy?

To find answers to these questions, you may make inquiries by calling other sales representatives who sell noncompeting lines. You may read the company's annual reports. A visit to the retail store or the manufacturing facility can answer some questions. To determine if the prospect has the appropriate financial resources, you may subscribe to a company like Dun & Bradstreet, which offers credit services.

Some of the above concerns can be addressed during your telephone conversation with the prospect. By asking tactful questions such as what competing products the prospect carries, you can determine satisfaction with the present supplier. You may find that your product could better satisfy your prospect's needs. Other questions might help to determine how your product could help improve the prospect's business.

All of this research brings you to the final step—the appointment to see the prospect. This is necessary in most business-to-business selling situations whether or not the client is a regular customer or a new prospect. Your research will have saved you time and money, especially if a prospect is not a likely customer for your product. If the prospect is a good lead, your research can be the basis of a strong sales presentation when you finally meet face-to-face.

REAL WORLD MARKETING

Zing It to Me

Tired of lugging around folders of photos and computer software to every presentation? Making a long distance presentation can be easier and more colorful, thanks to online photo sharing and storage Web sites. The online photo sharing company Zing allows you to store and organize your photos or PowerPoint slides for free and update presentations when necessary. You create a ZingAlbum with a personalized title that is available to clients or coworkers from any location. Companies such as Adobe, Intel, and Kodak are catching on and offering similar services.

Thinking Critically
Why would online companies offer free services such as photo sharing?

BRIGHT IDEAS

From Thousands of Users to Millions—Yahoo!

Yet Another Hierarchical Officious Oracle. Sound familiar? Those are the words that are abbreviated in the acronym Yahoo!, the online Web directory guide. In 1994, David Filo and Jerry Yang, Ph.D. candidates in Electrical Engineering at Stanford University, started keeping track of their personal interests on the Internet. They soon found their lists to be too cumbersome, and they converted their hobby into Yahoo!. "What we did took 20 hours a day, but we were one of the first to [try and organize the Web], and we did it better than anyone," says Yang. Today, Yahoo's income is mainly generated from advertisers. Yahoo! generates over 95 million daily page views and now serves more than 30 million users monthly.

Thinking Creatively
What are some challenges in having a business like Yahoo! grow from thousands to millions of users in just a few years?

■ Preparing for the Sale in Retail Selling

Since the customer comes to you in retail selling situations, the preparation centers around the merchandise and work area. It involves stockkeeping and housekeeping activities. Those activities include:

- Straightening, rearranging, and replenishing the stock
- Adjusting price tickets before and after special sales
- Learning where stock is located and how much is available
- Taking inventory
- Arranging displays
- Vacuuming the floor, dusting the shelves, and keeping the selling area neat and clean

The above activities are important because they give you an opportunity to learn about the merchandise. You can learn what goods go well together, as well as the prices of the merchandise. Keeping all the merchandise in an orderly fashion is beneficial—especially when you have to look for a specific item requested by a customer.

■ **House-Keeping** Much of the preapproach in retail selling involves stockkeeping and housekeeping. *How does folding and arranging stock in a retail store help a salesperson prepare for the actual face-to-face sales situation?*

12.2 ASSESSMENT

Reviewing Key Terms and Concepts

1. What are four categories for sources of product information?
2. Why don't all businesses require salespeople to find prospects?
3. Name five sources of prospecting.
4. What is the difference between the endless chain method and cold canvassing as methods for prospecting?
5. What is the focus of the preapproach in retail sales?

Thinking Critically

6. You have been asked to research a new prospect for your boss. Your research of this lead found that the company's owner is a 90-year-old sole proprietor. The company is financially sound and pays its bills on time. The only concern is that there is no heir-apparent (someone to take over if the owner is no longer capable of running the business). Would you qualify this prospect as a worthy customer? Why or why not?

Integrating Academic Skills

7. **MATH** In preparing a sales presentation for your company's all-purpose cleaner, you gather the following data on your products and a competitor's products:

Cleaner	Fluid Ounces	Price
A	22	$3.79
B	28	$4.29
C	40	$6.99
Yours	44	$7.19

Calculate the price per ounce for each cleaner. Then identify which, if any, competing product beats your own.

Careers in Marketing

SALES MANAGEMENT

Michael Dougherty
Vice President of Sales
Unilever

What does your job entail?

"It involves working with teams and knowing how to motivate people. Unilever is a British-Dutch consumer products company. Its brands include Lipton, Ragu, Skippy, Slim-Fast, and Dove and Ponds skin care products. I manage a concept and a team of professionals who have the responsibility of acting as entrepreneurs within our company. It is my responsibility to select people for the team from areas within our organization who represent marketing, sales, distribution, and finance. This is far different from the way we operated ten years ago, when each department acted on its own. Today, every new product has a team behind it. The team brainstorms the idea for the new product and develops a business plan for it. After input from all the areas (marketing, sales, distribution, and finance), the team decides if the product is worth a go or not. It is my job to see that these teams are functioning well. "

What skills are most important?

"Flexibility and working well with people are the two most important skills I need for my job. With the emphasis on teamwork, it is important to leave your ego at the door. That means you need to be able to win through a group instead of being a solo player. That is why flexibility and getting along with others are so important. Integrity, honesty, and being goal oriented are essential, in addition to being a good listener. "

What is your key to success?

"Never giving up. Believing in your idea and staying with it is essential to success. You can't let yourself get frustrated when you encounter obstacles. Although you must base your decisions on facts, you still must go with "gut" instincts in the decision-making process. The last guiding principle is "follow the consumer." You want to make products the consumer will need in the future; so you never want to forget that the consumer is your end game. "

Thinking Critically

What skills do you have that would make you a good Vice President of Sales?

Career Facts

Education and Training: An MBA, or at least minimum courses in marketing, accounting, finance, economics, international business, and data processing systems. As many as ten years sales and supervisory experience may be necessary for promotion to such a top-level job.

Aptitudes, Abilities, and Skills: Excellent problem-solving and decision-making skills, sound business judgment, outstanding verbal and written communication skills, and diplomacy in working with customers and employees are needed for this job. Leadership and administrative skills that foster organizational growth are also required for top-level executives.

Career Path: Participation in management development programs is a typical point of entry for aspiring executives.

Career Outlook: Average growth is predicted for executive positions through the year 2008.

Chapter 12 ASSESSMENT

VOCABULARY REVIEW

Work in groups to create an outline for a sales training session that defines and organizes the following topics:

- feature-benefit selling
- product features and customer benefits
- rational and emotional motives
- extensive, limited, and routine decision making
- retail and business-to-business sales preparation
- preapproach
- prospect
- referral
- endless chain method
- cold canvassing

FACT AND IDEA REVIEW

1. Why is it important for customers to be pleased with their purchases? (12.1)

2. What is a basic, a physical, and an extended product feature for a camera? (12.1)

3. When do product features become selling points? (12.1)

4. What two aspects of a product feature help a salesperson determine a customer benefit? (12.1)

5. Explain the difference between a rational motive and an emotional motive. (12.1)

6. In all selling situations, what can salespeople do to prepare for the sale? (12.2)

7. What is prospecting? (12.2)

8. What is cold canvassing? (12.2)

9. What is the final step of the preapproach in a business-to-business selling situation? (12.2)

THINKING CRITICALLY

1. Determine a customer benefit for each of the following product features: remote access on a telephone message machine; automatic focus on a camera; and ten-CD capacity on a CD player.

2. You are the manufacturer of a unique jacket designed so that parts of it can be added or removed for various weather conditions. What would you do to train your sales force? What would you do to help retailers train their salespeople to sell the jacket?

3. Assume you are selling a diamond engagement ring. What rational and emotional motives might the customer have in this situation?

4. Explain your reasons for agreeing or disagreeing with the following statement: Customers love to buy but hate to be sold.

BUILDING WORKPLACE SKILLS

1. **Writing** To prepare for a sales demonstration with a product of your choice, write a letter to the product's manufacturer. Introduce yourself and tell the reason for writing the letter. Explain why you selected that company's product for your research. Identify the specific information you are requesting. Request the information in a way that makes it easy for the reader to comply.

2. **Human Relations** Assume you work for a local ski shop and receive a 20-percent employee discount, which can only be used by you and your immediate family members. Your friend is in the market for a new pair of skis and asks you to buy them for him so he can benefit from your discount. What would you do? Why?

APPLYING MARKETING CONCEPTS

1. **Categorizing Sales Jobs** Using a spreadsheet program, prepare a table on the various requirements for sales positions found in newspaper or Internet "Help Wanted" ads. Organize the table in these categories: retail, business-to-business, and telemarketing; previous experience required; educational requirements; and salary.

2. **Preparing Feature-Benefit Charts** Select a product and prepare a feature-benefit chart for it, using a spreadsheet program. The product should be one that would require limited decision making. You will use this project to develop a sales training manual in later chapters.

3. **Researching Potential Customers** Your publishing company is launching a new extreme sports magazine. Your first step is to research potential customers. Using a word processing program, list three ways that you could pinpoint your target audience. Write a script to be used by your staff of telemarketers to encourage subscriptions.

4. **Understanding Consumer Motives** Your company has launched a marketing campaign for a new children's car seat. Research your competition on the Internet. Using presentation software, create a presentation to appeal to the rational and emotional motive of the typical car seat buyer.

LINKING SCHOOL TO WORK

Thinking Skills and Information Prepare a background report on a company, including its history and how it sells its products. Discuss what types of salespeople are employed and what company policies related to sales are important for a new salesperson to know.

THE DECA CONNECTION

Role Play: Sales Associate

Situation You are to assume the role of an employee at a clothing store. Every day when you arrive, your assistant manager (judge) tells you to check the incoming stock, return clothes left in the dressing rooms, and rearrange stock. You were hired as a sales associate, but you have not yet met your weekly sales quotas.

Activity At this point you are discouraged and decide you must discuss the situation with your manager (judge).

Evaluation You will be evaluated on how well you meet the following performance indicators:
- Prepare for the sales presentation
- Acquire product information for use in selling
- Facilitate customer buying decisions
- Use appropriate assertiveness

*inter*NET CONNECTION

Features, Features, Features!
It is important to learn all you can about the product featured in this chapter, as it will be revisited in other chapters.

Connect
- Use the Internet to obtain all the features of the digital video camera featured in Figure 12-1 (page 213).
- Add those features to the feature-benefit chart provided in Figure 12-1.

Chapter 13

Initiating the Sale

Marketing: What It Takes

One-on-One

You have completed your research on fabrics and industry trends during training for your new position as a sales associate at a retail furniture store. You feel you are ready to meet with customers, but your sales instructor is not so sure. She wants to know exactly what you will say and do when you are face-to-face with your first retail customers and your first business-to-business customers.

WHAT WILL YOU DO?

How will your sales approach and method of determining needs be different in the two selling situations?

The Sales Process

Steps of a Sale

Professional salespeople go through seven steps when helping a customer make a purchase (see Figure 13-1 on page 228).

1. *Approaching the customer*—greeting the customer face-to-face

2. *Determining needs*—learning what the customer is looking for in a good or service in order to decide what products to show and which product features to present first in the next step of the sale

3. *Presenting the product*—educating the customer about the product's features and benefits

4. *Overcoming objections*—learning why the customer is reluctant to buy, providing information to remove that uncertainty, and helping the customer to make a satisfying buying decision

5. *Closing the sale*—getting the customer's positive agreement to buy

6. *Suggestion selling*—suggesting additional merchandise or services that will save your customer money or help your customer better enjoy the original purchase

7. *Relationship building*—creating a means of maintaining contact with the customer after the sale is completed

In this chapter, we will concentrate on the first two steps—the approach and determining needs. The other five steps will be examined in later chapters.

Approaching the Customer

The approach is the first face-to-face contact with the customer. Although different selling situations require the use of different methods in the approach, the importance and general purposes of the approach are the same in all selling situations.

Salespeople can make or break a sale during their first few minutes with a customer; therefore, the initial approach is critical. Customers who are turned off by the approach will be difficult to win over later on.

The approach sets the mood or atmosphere for the other steps of the sale. It has three purposes: to begin conversation, to establish a relationship with the customer, and to focus on the merchandise. Let's look at how these purposes are accomplished.

To begin conversation, you need to be alert to customers' interests. This may be easier in business-to-business selling because you can conduct research prior to the initial meeting. In retail selling, you must observe the customer from the moment he or she enters the store.

• What You'll Learn

- The seven steps of a sale
- The importance and purposes of the approach in the sales process
- How business-to-business sales representatives conduct the initial approach
- The three initial approach methods used by retail salespeople

• Why It's Important

Knowing the seven steps of a sale gives you an overview of how a sale is conducted from beginning to end. Learning the various methods of approaching a customer is the first step in that process.

Key Terms

- service approach method
- greeting approach method
- merchandise approach method

FIGURE 13-1

Steps of a Sale

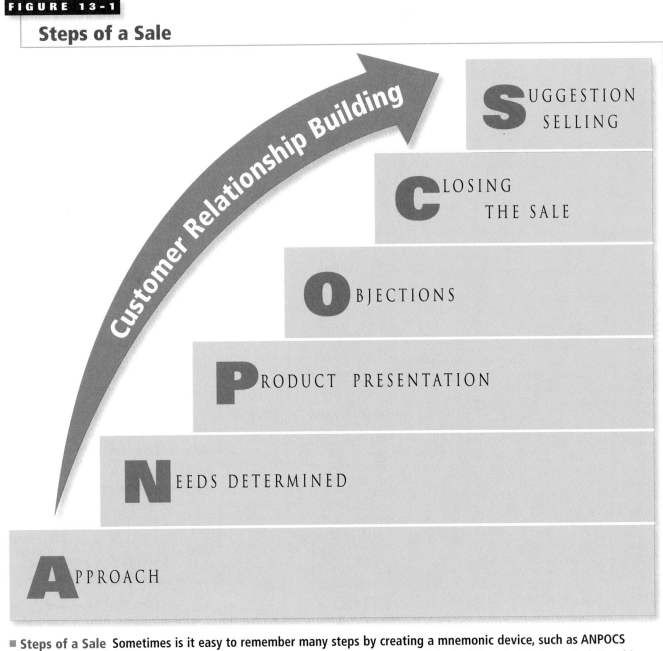

Customer Relationship Building

SUGGESTION SELLING

CLOSING THE SALE

OBJECTIONS

PRODUCT PRESENTATION

NEEDS DETERMINED

APPROACH

■ **Steps of a Sale** Sometimes is it easy to remember many steps by creating a mnemonic device, such as ANPOCS for the steps of a sale. *What is the significance of each letter in this mnemonic device? How is "Customer Relationship Building" part of the sales process?*

To establish a relationship, treat the customer as an individual. There should be no stereotyping of a person because of age, sex, race, religion, or appearance or any other reason.

You must be perceptive about the customer's buying style. Some customers like to do business quickly. Others prefer a more methodical, slower pace. In any case, a customer likes to feel important.

To put a customer at ease and establish a positive atmosphere you should be enthusiastic, courteous, and respectful. Show sincere interest by maintaining good eye contact and showing genuine friendliness. It may be useful to learn the customer's name to personalize the sale. Time the approach appropriately in a retail situation; this could mean giving the customer time to browse before initiating communication. Always ask business-to-business customers if it is a good time to see them. This courtesy is appreciated by busy business people.

The Approach in Business-to-Business Selling

In business-to-business selling, the salesperson will set up an appointment in the preapproach stage of the sale. Then the salesperson calls on the customer at his or her place of business. Arriving early for the appointment will show your customer that you are interested, and give you time to organize your thoughts. Introduce yourself and your company with a firm handshake and a smile. Use the customer's name. Some salespeople may give the customer a business card. It is sometimes appropriate to give your customer a gift. See Figure 13-2 for some hints for approaching customers in a cross-cultural business-to-business selling situation.

The initial approach depends on your prior dealings with the customer or the work you did in the preapproach. When meeting with customers you visit frequently, you can be more personal. Comments on recent happenings in the customer's industry or personal recollections about the customer's family, interests, or hobbies can create a smooth initial meeting. When used correctly, this technique puts the customer at ease and helps open lines of communication. Learning what is appropriate to say regarding personal matters is critical. When personal conversation is not appropriate, you can still engage in small talk to establish a relationship with the customer.

When meeting a new customer, choose your words carefully. Some good opening statements in business-to-business settings discuss how your company can help the customer reduce costs, increase productivity, improve profits, and generate more business. Prior research on the prospect conducted in the preapproach will suggest other possible opening comments.

The Approach in Retail Selling

Good technique must be learned when approaching customers in a retail setting. When customers are in an obvious hurry, you should approach them quickly. When customers seem undecided, it is best to let them look around before making the approach. Encourage customers who are comparison-shopping to look around and ask questions.

■ **Equal Attention** Salespeople often take turns greeting and waiting on customers based on a rotating system. *In this photo, assume that both customers arrived at the same time when only one salesperson is available. How could the salesperson tactfully handle this situation?*

FIGURE 13-2

DOs AND DON'Ts OF THE SALES APPROACH IN FOREIGN COUNTRIES

Saying and doing the appropriate thing is important when selling your products in a foreign country. Simply scheduling the right time for an appointment can be a challenge if you don't know the appropriate time for meetings! Knowing what to do and say when you first meet your prospective customer is equally challenging. Let's look at the some of the basics of that first face-to-face encounter when dealing with customers from other countries.

GIFT GIVING

Do not give a French person wine as a gift, but do give a gift of French origin. The Japanese prefer a gift from the United States, especially one with a well-known brand name. Also, take the time to wrap the gift nicely, even elaborately if the person receiving it has a high position in the company. Do not send red or yellow flowers as a gift in Mexico because those colors represent evil and death. In Belgium it is not a good idea to send white chrysanthemums, because they are used in funerals.

THE GREETING AND HANDSHAKE

In Arab and South American countries, the handshake is light and lasts for a long time. In the United States, Poland, and Hungary the handshake is firm and short in duration. In Japan, one firm handshake coupled with a slight bow is appropriate. In Singapore your greeting (salaam) involves sliding palms together and bowing.

APPOINTMENTS

In France, do not schedule a sales appointment before 10:00 A.M. Do not schedule a sales meeting during siesta time in Spain. In Germany, do not schedule a breakfast meeting and always be on time. Punctuality is very important not only in Germany, but in Japan as well. Power breakfasts are appropriate in the United States, but not in very many other countries.

REAL WORLD MARKETING

Ad Campaign Brews Results

In an effort to raise coffee drinkers' understanding of the importance of freshness in quality coffee, Peet's coffee created Coffee Freshness Week. Freshness is actually determined by how long ago the beans were roasted. Peet's contracted an interactive advertising company to custom-blend their advertising approach. An online sweepstakes giveaway of 25,000 one-pound gift packs attracted Peet's online visitors to the coffee maker's promotional Web page. Banner advertising generated 78 percent of the traffic while targeted e-mail campaigns pulled more than 14 percent of the online visitors. Results: Peet's online sales increased 16 percent during the promotional period.

Thinking Critically
In what ways do you think online advertising helped Peet's to initiate sales?

Many customers prefer to shop around before buying and appreciate salespeople who show interest while giving them the space to make their own decisions.

There are three methods you can use in the initial approach to retail customers—the service approach, the greeting approach, and the merchandise approach. You must evaluate the selling situation and the type of customer to determine which method is best.

SERVICE APPROACH METHOD In the service approach method, the salesperson asks the customer if he or she needs assistance. This is often best stated as "How may I help you?" Open-ended questions such as this one offer the customer a greater opportunity to respond with more than "yes" or "no." This method is acceptable when the customer is obviously in a hurry or if you are an order-taker for routine purchases. In most other sales situations, this method is ineffective because it usually elicits a negative response, such as "No,

■ **Service Approach Method** Counter salespeople generally fill the role of an order-taker. *In this selling situation, is it okay to use the service approach method? Why or why not?*

■ **Merchandise Approach** The merchandise approach is the most effective when a customer fixates on a specific item. *What might you say to this customer to demonstrate the merchandise approach?*

I'm just looking." In this case, you lose control of the sales situation. In addition, the customer may feel awkward asking for help later after initially rejecting it. If such a situation occurs, take a moment to remind the customer to ask any questions that he or she may have later on. You might say, "Please feel free to ask any questions after you have had some time to look around. My name is Janice and I'll be on the floor if you need anything."

GREETING APPROACH METHOD In the greeting approach method, the salesperson simply welcomes the customer to the store. This lets the customer know that the salesperson is available for any questions or assistance. The greeting can be formal, such as "Good morning." When you know the customer, an informal greeting is appropriate with a personal comment specifically related to the customer. When using the greeting approach, it is important to use a rising tone in your voice. A falling tone sounds unfriendly and would start the sale off on the wrong note. Regardless of whether the customer responds in a friendly or unfriendly manner, it is extremely important that the sales person smiles and continues to act friendly.

After greeting the customer, pause for a few seconds. Out of courtesy, most customers will respond. If they need help, they will tell you how you can assist them. If they are just looking, they will let you know. While this approach method does not highlight the merchandise, it does establish a positive atmosphere and opens the lines of communication.

MERCHANDISE APPROACH METHOD In the merchandise approach method, the salesperson makes a comment or asks questions about a product in which the customer shows interest. This method can only be used if a customer stops to look at a specific item. You may open with a statement about the product's features and benefits.

In the merchandise approach, the salesperson walks up to the customer and starts talking about the merchandise without asking the customer whether he or she wants to be waited on. The opening comment that is used in the merchandise approach should be the most appropriate to the situation. Ideally, it should give the customer some information that is not immediately apparent to the eye.

Notice what interests the customer and make that the focus of your conversation. If a customer is looking at a label, you might say, "That shirt is made of a cotton and polyester blend, so it's machine washable." If a customer is simply looking at an item and you have no indication of the exact interest, you can talk about the item's popularity, its unusual features, or its special values. You can also ask a question about the item, such as "Is that the size you need?" or "Are you interested in a specific color?"

The merchandise approach method is usually the most effective initial approach in retail sales because it immediately focuses attention on the merchandise. It also gives you an opportunity to tell the customer something about the features and benefits of the merchandise. This helps arouse customer interest and could encourage a purchase.

It is possible that customers might not see their desired style, size, or color on the selling floor. The merchandise approach can easily clear up this confusion and opens lines of communication.

Customer Service Online

Have you ever browsed through a virtual mall, then made your purchase at a brick-and-mortar shop because you have unanswered questions? Liveperson.com is here to serve you. Liveperson.com makes it possible for Web sites to have customers consult with customer service representatives in real time. It is one of a growing number of businesses that provides e-commerce companies with a solution to customer service issues. One satisfied client is iQVC.com, a virtual shopping mall, which has live salespeople available 24 hours a day. Customers can ask questions about sizes and colors, or get advice on the best products available to meet their needs. This approach works—many new customers are returning for the quality products and the quality service. This is proof that personalized service increases sales.

Thinking Critically
Why is personalized service important to consumers?

13.1 ASSESSMENT

Reviewing Key Terms and Concepts

1. List the seven steps of a sale.
2. What are the purposes of the approach in selling?
3. What three general things would a business-to-business sales representative say and do during the initial approach?
4. Name the three approach methods retail salespeople use, and suggest when it is appropriate to use each method.
5. Of the approach methods used in retail sales, which is generally the most effective? Why?

Thinking Critically

6. You are given the opportunity to train new retail sales associates in the art of approaching customers. What three key concepts would you make sure you covered first? Why?

Building Workplace Skills

7. **COMMUNICATION** You are approaching a new customer for the first time in a business-to-business selling situation. Introduce yourself and your company to a classmate. Be sure to use the prospect's name and offer an opening statement that will get your customer's attention. Was this easy or difficult for you? Why?

Determining Needs in Sales

• What You'll Learn

- Why determining needs is an essential step in the sales process
- Three methods used for determining needs

• Why It's Important

A thorough analysis of customers' needs and wants is necessary when planning and executing effective sales presentations. Customers vary greatly in their perceptions and requirements, so salespeople must learn how to uncover those differences. This section will help you to accomplish that goal.

Key Terms

- nonverbal communication
- open-ended questions

Determining Needs

Customer needs are directly related to buying motives. As you may recall from Chapter 12, these motives can be rational, emotional, or a combination of both. These buying motives will greatly affect the outcome of the sales process.

In this step of the sale, your job is to uncover the customer's reasons for wanting to buy. In some instances, these motives or needs may be quite obvious, but that is not always the case.

Whether the customer's needs are obvious or not, taking a sincere interest in the customer is essential. Everyone benefits when the customer's needs are satisfied. Not only does the business profit, but the satisfied customer may become a repeat customer as well. When customer needs are met, the salesperson experiences a feeling of success.

■ When to Determine Needs

The salesperson's focus should be to determine the customer's needs as early in the sales process as possible. Here is an example of what can happen when a salesperson does not determine needs early on.

Salesperson: "This is one of our most popular tennis racquets. It's perfect for you—the grip is the correct size and the large sweet spot can improve your game."

Customer: "That's very interesting, however I'm not buying the racquet for myself. It's actually a gift for my nine-year-old daughter."

In this example, the salesperson went right into the product presentation before determining the customer's needs. After the initial approach, the salesperson could have asked, "Are you interested in a racquet for yourself?"

The answer to that simple question could have guided the salesperson into additional questions about the person for whom the racquet was being purchased. It also could have helped the salesperson decide which racquet to show the customer and which features to emphasize. In the situation above, the racquet recommended for a child would be quite different than the one the salesperson chose to introduce.

In retail selling, the salesperson should begin to determine needs immediately after the approach. In business-to-business selling, needs can be determined in the preapproach. In both situations, the salesperson should continue determining needs throughout the sales process.

■ **Reading Body Language** Body language is often very telling with regard to a customer's feeling about a product. *In this photo, what does this customer's body language tell you?*

■ How to Determine Needs

There are three methods that will help you determine customer needs. They are observing, listening, and questioning.

OBSERVING When you observe a customer, you look for buying motives that are communicated nonverbally. Nonverbal communication is expressing yourself through body language. Facial expressions, hand motions, eye movement, and other forms of nonverbal communication can give you clues about a customer's mood and interest in a product and mood.

There are other details you can observe in retail and business-to-business selling situations that may provide more clues about customers. Observing how long a customer in a retail store looks at a product can give you an initial idea about the level of interest. How long the customer holds the product during a sales presentation (if he or she holds it at all) can indicate the level of feelings for it.

In a business-to-business selling situation, you can generally get ideas about a buyer's interests by looking around his or her office. For example, you

may observe trophies from company-sponsored tennis tournaments, paintings of horses, or educational certificates and diplomas. All of these are likely to indicate personal interests.

When calling on a retail buyer, walk through the store first. This will give you information about the types of customers the retailer serves, the price levels of lines carried, complementary and competing products offered, and opportunities for additional sales.

The key to observing is the proper selection of facts. You want only those that are important to the sales process. Avoid stereotyping people or drawing conclusions from your observations before getting additional facts.

LISTENING Listening helps you pick up clues to the customer's needs. You can use this information for the product presentation. Here's an example.

Customer: "I want a copier for my home business that is simple to use and reliable. My last copier broke down often, which was a problem. I usually make one or two copies at a time. However, I occasionally may make up to 50 copies at once."

■ **Analyzing Free Time** Knowing what interests the customer sometimes creates a common bond if the salesperson shares those interests. *In this photo, what can you tell about the prospective customer's interest? How could that knowledge be helpful in the sales process?*

From these statements, you've learned that the customer is not looking for a top-of-the-line copier. Since the copier is for a home business, size is a factor.

In Chapter 8 we explored listening skills as well as the potential blocks to listening with understanding. To develop good listening skills, you must learn how to listen to and understand others. Remember these five important listening skills when you are talking to your customers:

- Maintain good eye contact
- Provide verbal and nonverbal feedback
- Give customers your undivided attention
- Listen with empathy and an open mind
- Do not interrupt

QUESTIONING In order to listen to customers, you must get them talking. One way of engaging a customer in conversation is to ask questions. Not all customers can clearly express their needs and motives when making a purchase. In such a situation, well-chosen questions can help you uncover needs and buying motives while putting the customer at ease.

When you begin determining needs, first ask general questions about intended use of the product and any previous experience with it. Build your questions around words like who, what, when, where, how, and why. You might ask the following questions of someone who wants to purchase a copier:

BRIGHT IDEAS

Freebord–On a Roll

Freebord Manufacturing has brought snowboarding to suburbia. Half snowboard, half skateboard—this six-wheeled contraption can spin 360 degrees and is sure to impress anyone in the concrete jungle. The goal is to imitate the slippery slide of a downhill ski slope on city streets. Now you can work on your boarding technique in your board shorts before hitting the slopes in winter. Freebord Manufacturing co-owner Steen Strand developed the product at Stanford University to merge his two loves—skateboarding and snowboarding. Strand designed two dozen models before he hit on just the right product. In business and in debt since 1997, the company recently sold 4,000 boards through 225 independent retail outlets. In a time when board sports are hot, Strand is finally looking to turn a profit.

Thinking Creatively

What type of sales approach would you suggest Freebord take to initiate future sales with independent retail outlets?

Case Study

The Personal Touch

Approximately 25 to 30 percent of all customers are not satisfied with the service they receive from online businesses. Online retailers are striving to provide better service by adding a human touch.

HomeTownStores.com and Cameraworld.com have human beings personally greet each visitor with a typed offer of help. Other businesses have humans available to answer typed questions, while still others provide Internet-telephone capability for customers to talk with sales reps at the same time they view their computer screen.

Software needed for this extra service may cost upwards of $500,000, and that does not include installation, maintenance, or people expense.

Is it worth the expense? Some online retailers think it is. At HomeTownStores.com, sales rose 30 percent within a month after a new personal-greeter service was started. Cameraworld.com reported that after it added the human sales reps via Internet phone calls, 25 percent of the customers bought something, as compared with 3 percent for all visitors to the site.

Case Study Review

1. Why did the e-tailers noted in this article add live support to their Web sites?
2. Of what significance are the first two steps of a sale (approach and determining needs) to online selling?

A MATTER OF ETHICS

3. Is it ethical for online retailers to use the "personal touch" in the electronic age because most people can manage their purchases without such help (especially since the cost of doing so will most likely be passed on to consumers in the form of higher prices)?

- *Who* will be using the digital copier?
- *What* type of copier is the person presently using?
- *How* much experience has the person had with copiers?
- *How* many copies will the person be making every week or month?

Once you have an idea of the customer's general needs, then you can ask more specific questions relating to the product. These might include inquiries about size, color, and any special features desired.

In the case of the copier, questions could be asked about the need to enlarge or reduce the size of copy, as well as the need to collate and staple copies.

Questioning is an important skill that must be done carefully. Always bear in mind that some customers will be protective of their privacy; they may resent even general, nonpersonal questions. When selling skis it is often necessary to determine the customer's weight. In such a situation, you might have the various weight classes listed on a sheet of paper that you hand the customer. Then you can simply ask which category the customer falls into. In this way, you avoid asking the person, "How much do you weigh?"

Here are some other dos and don'ts guidelines for questioning.

1. *Do ask open-ended questions that encourage customers to do the talking.* Open-ended questions require more than a yes or no answer, such as "What do you dislike about the copier you're presently using?" The answer to such a question will provide valuable information about a customer's needs.

2. *Do ask clarifying questions to make sure you understand customers' needs.* To do this, use opening lines such as "Let me see if I understand you" or "Am I correct in assuming you're looking for a product that can...?"

3. *Don't ask too many questions in a row.* This will make customers feel as if they are being cross-examined.

4. *Don't ask questions that might embarrass customers or put them on the defensive.* Never ask, "How much do you want to spend?" Instead, ask about intended use of the product and any past experience. That should give you enough information to determine the correct price range on your own.

Life In The Diverse

MARKETPLACE

Beware 13!

Have you ever suffered a bout of triskaideka-phobia? You might have and not realized it as triskaidekaphobia is the fear of the number 13. Many people in the United States are so superstitious about the number 13 that most hotels have banished this floor number from their buildings. In many Mexican cultures, however, the number 13 has more positive connotations of the sun and positive energy. Is it silly to market based on superstitions like these? Apparently Tiffany & Company doesn't think so. They sell their glassware only in sets of five in Japan, where the number four, "shi," also means death.

Thinking Critically

Do you think that it is important for companies to know the traditions and superstitions of other cultures?

13.2 ASSESSMENT

Reviewing Key Terms and Concepts

1. Why is determining needs an essential step in the sales process?

2. When should you begin determining needs in the sales process?

3. At what point in the sales process do you stop determining the customer's needs?

4. Name three methods used to determine customers' needs.

5. Without asking a direct question, how could you find out how much a customer weighs in order to properly outfit him or her with the proper size skis?

Thinking Critically

6. You are a salesperson in a rug store that carries inexpensive area rugs, medium-priced area rugs, and very expensive handmade rugs. How would you determine your customer's price range so you know which category of rugs to show?

Integrating Academic Skills

7. **MATH** Your customer is located 100 miles from your office. You can travel an average of 45 miles in one hour. If you have a 10:30 a.m. appointment and you want to arrive 15 minutes early, what time do you have to leave your office?

Careers in Marketing

PROFESSIONAL SALES

Al Watson
Vice President of Pharmaceutical Sales
Pfizer, Inc.

What does your job entail?

"My job is to oversee the sales of our product. Our clients include physicians, hospital personnel, pharmacists, nursing home personnel, and other health care organizations. We sell through one-on-one sales contacts, as well as in group situations to multiple physicians. My staff conducts educational programs on Pfizer products to educate physicians on guidelines and recommendations for product use. It is important to sell the benefits of products—it must be clear to the client how the product will help them. The most important aspect of my job is to continually strive to increase my technical knowledge."

What skills are necessary?

"The most essential skill is technical knowledge—pharmaceutical detailers must be able to answer all questions on their products. All Pfizer representatives need to have a good understanding of the diseases that our products treat, and a thorough knowledge of the competition. In all careers it is necessary to be self-motivated, responsible, determined, and persistent, but these traits are particularly important in sales. Once the sale is made, consistency and follow-up with customers help ensure repeat business."

What kind of training do you recommend?

"Pfizer offers three types of ongoing training—technical, comprehensive sales, and professional development. The technical training focuses on disease facts and product awareness; if you are selling antibiotics, you need to know what diseases these medicines would be used for. Comprehensive sales training focuses on how to sell in one-on-one situations and large group settings. Professional development courses increase professional and personal development."

What is your key to success?

"I find that the key to my success has been a strong work ethic. A solid academic background is necessary. A strong liberal arts background exposes students to many different ideas."

Thinking Critically

Why must salespeople learn to make their points in a short period of time?

Career Facts

Education and Training: Students interested in a career in pharmaceutical sales should take high school and college courses in biology, chemistry, marketing, business, accounting, speech, and data processing.

Aptitudes, Abilities, and Skills: Ability to read and understand technical material, good record keeping skills, self-motivation, good telephone skills, and a willingness to travel and work long hours are necessary.

Career Outlook: Average growth is expected through the year 2008.

Career Path: Previous work for a physician or pharmacy can lead to a pharmaceutical detailer position. Sales representatives can advance to sales management positions.

VOCABULARY REVIEW

Work in groups to develop a story about two salespeople using the following terms:

- service approach method
- greeting approach method
- merchandise approach method
- nonverbal communication
- open-ended questions

FACT AND IDEA REVIEW

1. Why is the approach a critical part of the sales process? (13.1)

2. What is wrong with saying, "May I help you?" as a retail approach? (13.1)

3. What should a salesperson do after using the greeting approach method with a retail customer? (13.1)

4. Which retail approach is most effective? (13.1)

5. When should you begin determining needs in retail selling and in business-to-business selling? (13.2)

6. What can you look for when you observe customers in retail situations? In business-to-business selling situations? (13.2)

7. What questions should be asked first when determining customer needs? (13.2)

8. What is the best way to encourage customers to do the talking? (13.2)

9. What two things should you avoid doing when questioning a customer? (13.2)

THINKING CRITICALLY

1. Do you think all seven steps of a sale are followed in every sale? Why or why not?

2. With the rise in e-tailing, hypothesize about the need for retail salespeople in ten years and in fifty years.

3. You are stuck in traffic and are going to be late for your first meeting with a potential customer. What should you do? How could you prevent this situation from happening again?

4. You are responsible for training new retail sales associates in the art of approaching customers. What three concepts would you make sure you covered first?

5. How can retail salespeople know the needs and wants of their customers prior to these customers entering the store? Explain.

BUILDING WORKPLACE SKILLS

1. **Human Relations** Role-play the determining needs steps of a sale with a classmate by using a personal product, such as a jacket, calculator, or purse. Make a list of guidelines for listening, observing, and asking questions. At the conclusion of the role play, provide the salesperson with constructive criticism. Change the product and switch roles with your partner to repeat the assignment.

2. **Writing** Write merchandise approaches that can be used in a retail selling situation for a cellular phone, a pair of jeans, and a pair of work boots.

APPLYING MARKETING CONCEPTS

1. **Training Sales Associates** Create a sales training manual using the product for which you prepared a feature-benefit chart in Chapter 12. Write the approach section, using a word processing program. Explain how to approach a customer properly and provide a few suggested sample approaches in dialogue form.

2. **Determining Needs** Using presentation software, prepare a presentation about determining needs. Begin with a brief description of the importance of determining needs. Present ten questions that could be used to determine a customer's needs. Begin with general questions regarding intended use and previous experience. End with specific questions about the particular features of the product. Base your questions on the product for which you prepared a feature-benefit chart. Print out your presentation and include it in your sales training manual.

3. **Comparing Retail Approach Methods** Pretending to be a customer, conduct your own informal survey of the professionalism of three retail salespeople. After your encounter with each, note what he or she did (or failed to do) to put you at ease and establish a positive atmosphere in the initial approach. Identify which retail approach method each salesperson used. Using a word processing program, write a two-paragraph summary of your findings.

LINKING SCHOOL TO WORK

Thinking and Interpersonal Skills, Personal Qualities Interview two sales representatives of a firm to determine how well prepared they are to approach customers and determine customers' needs.

THE DECA CONNECTION

Role Play: Sales Trainer

Situation You are to assume the role of assistant manager of a shoe store. You are responsible for training and evaluating the sales staff. Omar (judge), a new employee, is having difficulty making sales. Each time you observe him with a customer, you see several pairs of shoes in front of the customer. The sad part is that nine times out of ten, Omar's (judge's) customers don't make a purchase.

Activity You must have a talk with Omar (judge) and help him with his sales technique.

Evaluation You will be evaluated on how well you meet the following performance indicators:
- Determine customer/client needs
- Address the needs of individual personalities
- Identify customers' buying motives
- Assess customer/client needs
- Give directions for completing job tasks

interNET CONNECTION

Online Sales
As a wholesaler of electronics, you want to try selling your products online. You will need to create questions to help a customer decide on a purchase.

Connect
- Investigate the Web site of a computer e-tailer.
- See how customers' needs are determined through questions.
- Adapt those questions to your company's needs by writing five questions that may be used when selling a digital camera for business or personal use.

Presenting the Product

Chapter 14

Marketing: What It Takes

What's Next

Your customers—parents of an active high school athlete—are in the market for a new camera. Currently, they scan photos of their child's activities into their computer and e-mail them to friends and grandparents. The only problem is that they have to get the photos developed first. You think a digital camera is the best option for this couple.

WHAT WILL YOU DO?

How will you effectively present the digital camera's selling points? What objections or obstacles do you anticipate?

Presenting the Product

Product Presentation

During the product presentation phase of a sale, you show the product and tell about it. As you determine the customer's buying motives, you should display products that match the needs you have discovered. The goal of the product presentation is to match the customer's needs with appropriate product features and benefits. You can achieve this goal by following certain guidelines that can make your product presentation smooth.

■ Show and Tell

Your first decision in the product presentation step of the sale is what product or products to show your customer. Then you must think about what you are going to say and how you are going to say it. This is the step of the sale where you have the opportunity to share your expertise with the customer. The preparation that you have put into learning about the product or products you sell and how to communicate their selling points will assist you now.

WHICH PRODUCTS TO SHOW After you have learned the intended use of the product, you should be able to select a few items that match those needs. You may select a technically advanced camera for a customer who wants a camera for professional use. Novice customers might want to select a fully automatic camera.

WHAT PRICE RANGE TO OFFER When you don't know the customer's price range and your knowledge of the intended use is insufficient to determine a price range, begin by showing a medium-priced product. You can move up or down in price once you begin to get the customer's feedback.

HOW MANY PRODUCTS TO SHOW To avoid overwhelming your customer, show no more than three products at a time. It is difficult for most people to remember all the features of more than three items during a presentation. When a customer wants to see more than three, put away the displayed products in which the customer shows no interest.

WHAT TO SAY In this step of the sales process, talk about the product's features and benefits. This is a good time to use your feature-benefit chart. Tell your customer the product features that match his or her buying motives and needs.

Use highly descriptive adjectives and active verbs when describing product features. Avoid unclear words, such as nice, pretty, and fine.

● What You'll Learn

- The goal of the product presentation
- How products are selected for the presentation
- What to say during the product presentation
- Four techniques that will make a lively and effective product presentation

● Why It's Important

Selling is, in many ways, like putting together a jigsaw puzzle. When you do a puzzle, you analyze the various parts by shape and size. You select the straight-edged pieces to use for the frame. When you sell, you analyze your customer's needs and buying motives. Then you use that information to begin framing your product presentation.

Key Terms

- layman's terms

■ **Displaying the Product** How you display the product has a bearing on the customer's image of it. *Do you think this product is properly displayed? Why or why not?*

Demo or Doom

In the world of computer software and hardware manufacturing, the marketplace leaders are those who are able to stand before a crowd and demonstrate how products work in real time. Successful demonstrations strike the imagination and hearts of customers. Hand Technologies uses a team of sales consultants to demonstrate computer products in homes and at local seminars to win customers. Every sale begins with a handshake and continues with hand-holding to get a customer started and supported down the line. Hand's product line includes well-respected brands, and its prices are comparable to those of electronic superstores.

Thinking Critically
Have you ever seen any product demonstrations? Explain.

You might say, "This full-cut sleeve allows complete rotation of the arm, making it extremely comfortable for skiing."

Choose your words carefully. Avoid slang and double meanings. For example, when selling an expensive suit to an executive, you would not say, "You look cool in that suit."

When selling industrial products, use the appropriate jargon to communicate with industrial buyers at their level of expertise. As mentioned in Chapter 8, *jargon* is technical or specialized vocabulary used by members of a particular profession or industry. When selling products to retail customers, use layman's terms. Layman's terms are words the average customer can understand.

■ Make the Presentation Come Alive

Planning is necessary for an effective product presentation. Consider how you will display and handle the merchandise. What will you do to demonstrate the product's selling points? What sales aids will add to your presentation? Finally, how will you involve the customer?

DISPLAYING AND HANDLING THE PRODUCT Creatively displaying the product is the first step in an eye-catching presentation. Some products, of course, lend themselves more naturally to visual display. Others will challenge your creativity. Diamond rings, for example, look best on a black velvet display pad. An attractive display of vacuum cleaners, on the other hand, takes more creative planning.

The way you physically handle a product presents an image of its quality. Handle it with respect and use hand gestures to show the significance of certain features. Expensive crystal goblets, for instance, should be held up to the light to show the quality of the glass.

DEMONSTRATING Demonstrating the product in use helps to build customer confidence. This is especially true if you are showing an item that requires manipulation or operation, such as a television, camera, CD player, food processor, or computer. To demonstrate the features of a copier, you may show how it can enlarge or reduce a document, as well as collate and staple multiple copies.

To prove selling points or claims made by the manufacturer, you may need to demonstrate a

Case Study

Sales Techniques Using E-Commerce

Customer involvement is important in the product presentation step of a sale. To make use of that concept when selling online, businesses customize their Web sites and make them interactive. Fannie May Candies online sales tripled when they let customers select their favorite candies and bypass the ones they did not like to create their box of candy.

Getting customers involved helps increase "stickiness," which means a site is so attractive that customers "stick" to it for a long time. Fannie May customers stay at the site for an average of 19 minutes, which is longer than most of the popular sites. Ebay.com is among the most "sticky" sites with visitors staying for 15 minutes. For Fannie May, not only do customers stay longer, they buy more, too.

Stickiness can also be helped by virtual tours. Customers use a computer mouse to navigate up, down and around and to zoom in within photos. This on-screen mobility may be used to show off aircraft, automobiles, or building interiors. Gulf Stream, the jet manufacturer, sold a used jet online for $22.9 million. Other businesses that use virtual tours include real estate, automotive, travel, and hospitality companies, such as Century 21 Real Estate, Princess Cruises, and Hilton Hotels.

Case Study Review

1. How did Fannie May utilize the concept of customer involvement in its online sales process?
2. What types of companies are making use of virtual tours to sell their products on the Internet?

A MATTER OF ETHICS

3. Is it ethical for a business to replace its salespeople by selling its products over the Internet?

---

product in a more dramatic way. To prove that a fabric is water resistant, you can pour water on the garment to show how the fabric repels water. At Saturn car dealerships, salespeople jump up and down on a car door that has been removed to show high durability and dent-proof construction.

USING SALES AIDS When it is impractical to demonstrate the actual product or when you want to emphasize certain selling points, you can use sales aids in your presentations. Sales aids include samples, reprints of magazine and newspaper articles, audiovisual aids, models, photographs, drawings, graphs, charts, specification sheets, customer testimonials, and warranty information.

Computers play an increasingly important role in product presentations as many business-to-business sales representatives make use of computer presentation software.

Be creative when determining which sales aids will help you in your particular product presentation. A manufacturer of industrial machinery might show a videotape of how quickly a machine performs. An insurance salesperson might use graphs and charts to show how dividends will accumulate or to compare the benefits of one policy to another. He or she might even use a computer to personalize the presentation of that information for each customer and show different policy plans for that person.

INVOLVING THE CUSTOMER It is best to get the customer physically involved with the product as soon as possible in the sales presentation. You could have your customers hold and swing golf clubs, try on and walk around in a pair of shoes, use a computer keyboard or mouse, test-drive an automobile, or taste and smell food products.

You can also involve your customer verbally during the sales presentation by confirming selling points. You might say, "This camera is extremely versatile with its power zoom and panorama feature. Did you ever feel torn between wanting a camera that could take great close-ups of the kids and one that could take wide-angle shots of a gorgeous view?" (Pause for customer's answer.) "Now you can have both of those cameras in one." Getting the customer's agreement on several selling points helps to ensure that you are on the right track with the selected product.

When you involve a customer in the sale, you help the person make intelligent buying decisions. You also help yourself because a customer is generally more attentive when doing more than just listening to what you say.

When you are losing your customer's attention, ask a simple question. You might say, "Now that you've seen the features of this camera, what do you think about it?" Regaining your customer's attention is essential if you are to continue with the sales presentation. The key is keeping the customer involved.

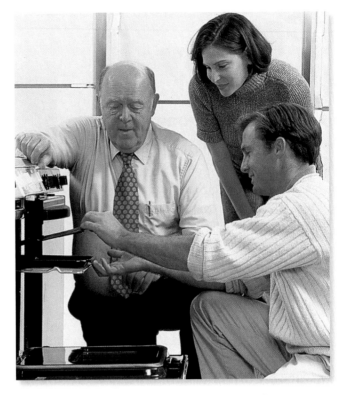

■ **Free Demonstrations** This salesperson is demonstrating how easy it is to take apart the oven for cleaning purposes. *What other sales aids might be appropriate to use in this sales situation?*

14.1 ASSESSMENT

Reviewing Key Terms and Concepts

1. What is the goal of the product presentation?
2. Which products and how many of them should be selected for the presentation?
3. Give some guidelines for what to say during the product presentation.
4. Describe four techniques that will make the product presentation lively and effective.

Thinking Critically

5. Tell what is wrong with these selling statements: "You look great in that suit," and "This fabric is made of 420/420 denier nylon."

Integrating Academic Skills

6. **COMMUNICATION** Select an item you have in your backpack or purse to sell to a classmate. Assume you have already approached your customer (classmate) and determined his or her needs. Demonstrate your ability to effectively present the item's features and benefits. Role-play with your partner and then switch roles. When you play the role of the customer, evaluate your partner's knowledge of the product presentation step of the sale and his or her sales ability.

Objections and Rejections

Understanding Objections

Objections are concerns, hesitations, doubts, or other honest reasons a customer has for not making a purchase. Objections should be viewed as positive because they give you an opportunity to present more information to the customer.

Objections can be presented as either questions or statements. An example of a question would be: "Do you carry any other brands?" and a statement would be: "These shoes don't fit right."

Excuses are insincere reasons for not buying or not seeing the salesperson. Customers often use excuses when they are not in the mood to buy or when concealing real objections. Here are some general excuses:

"I'm too busy to see you today."

"We don't need any more . . . ."

"I'm just shopping around."

"I didn't plan to buy anything today."

It is often hard to distinguish between objections and excuses. A statement or question that seems to be an objection may really just be an excuse. When you are faced with this in a retail selling situation, be polite and courteous. Encourage the customer to look around and ask you any questions he or she may have.

In a business-to-business selling situation, the procedure is different. Leave a business card if a potential customer refuses to see you when you make a call, and ask if it is possible to see the person at a more convenient time.

There are cases when excuses are actually attempts to hide real objections. "I didn't plan to buy today" may really mean, "I don't like the styles you have available." When you suspect that may be the case, ask additional questions to get to the real reason for the disinterest in your product or products.

■ Welcome and Plan for Objections

Objections can occur at any time during the sales process and should be answered promptly. A customer who must wait to hear responses to questions or concerns tends to become preoccupied with the objection. When that happens, you may lose the customer's attention and confidence.

Objections can guide you in the sales process by helping you redefine the customer's needs and determine when the customer wants more information. A customer may say, "This item is very expensive." What the person may really mean is "Tell me why this product costs

What You'll Learn

- The difference between objections and excuses
- The five buying decisions upon which common objections are based
- The general four-step method for handling customer objections
- The six specific methods of handling objections and when each should be used

Why It's Important

Anticipating and planning potential answers to objections will help you feel more confident in your responses to customers. Selecting the most appropriate method for handling those objections will make you a superior salesperson.

Key Terms

- objections
- excuses
- objection analysis sheet
- paraphrase
- boomerang method
- superior point method
- third party method

so much." This objection not only lets you know why the customer is reluctant to buy but also gives you an opportunity to bring out additional selling points.

You should therefore welcome objections—they are not necessarily the sign of a lost sales process. Research shows that there is a positive relationship between customer objections and a successful sales outcome.

You can prepare yourself for most objections that might occur in a sales situation by completing an objection analysis sheet, which lists common objections and possible responses to them. Although the actual objections may be slightly different from those you anticipated, thinking of the responses gives you an idea of how to handle other objections.

You can incorporate anticipated objections into your product presentation so they do not become objections. You must be cautious about this, however. You don't want to include so many objections in your product presentation that you introduce doubt —especially if none existed before. Saying "I guess you're worried about the safety of this snowmobile," may introduce a fear that was not a previous concern.

A better way to handle the same situation would be to emphasize the safety features of the vehicle. You might say, "The suspension on this snowmobile is specially designed to keep it stable. It's very safe to operate."

■ Common Objections

When you list general customer objections, you will see that they fall into certain categories. Most objections are based on key decisions the customer must make before buying—decisions about need, product, source, price, and time. This is true for both retail and business-to-business sales situations. The actual objections will vary due to the difference in purchase motivation. Retail customers generally are making a purchase for personal use, while business-to-business customers are buying for a company's operation.

The following are examples of customer objections in a retail situation. Both provide a starting point for the creation of an objection analysis sheet.

NEED Objections related to need usually occur when the customer does not have an immediate need for the item or wants the item but does not truly need it. A comment such as "I really like this sweater, but it doesn't match anything I have," is an objection based on a conflict between a need and a want.

PRODUCT Objections based on the product itself are more common. They include concerns about such things as construction, ease of use, quality, color, size, or style. "I don't like the way this jacket fits me," is such an objection.

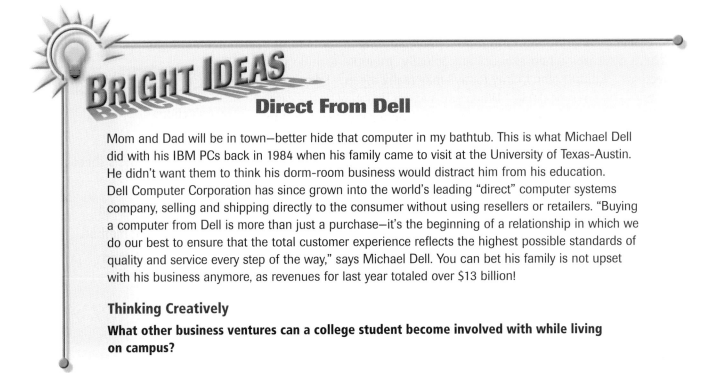

BRIGHT IDEAS

Direct From Dell

Mom and Dad will be in town—better hide that computer in my bathtub. This is what Michael Dell did with his IBM PCs back in 1984 when his family came to visit at the University of Texas-Austin. He didn't want them to think his dorm-room business would distract him from his education. Dell Computer Corporation has since grown into the world's leading "direct" computer systems company, selling and shipping directly to the consumer without using resellers or retailers. "Buying a computer from Dell is more than just a purchase—it's the beginning of a relationship in which we do our best to ensure that the total customer experience reflects the highest possible standards of quality and service every step of the way," says Michael Dell. You can bet his family is not upset with his business anymore, as revenues for last year totaled over $13 billion!

Thinking Creatively

What other business ventures can a college student become involved with while living on campus?

Shopping for Knowledge

Imagine replacing your traditional classroom experience with an online teacher and interactive classroom. It's already happening. You can read course materials on your monitor and submit homework by e-mail. Now, a group of Internet entrepreneurs is trying to capitalize on this new trend by offering online students a variety of products while they study. Students enrolled in photography courses may be offered cameras and film. Someone learning French may be offered a travel guide or airline tickets. Some educators, however, view the combination of sales and classrooms as purely advertising and not instructional.

Thinking Critically

Do you think that marketing to students interferes with learning?

SOURCE Objections based on source often occur because of negative past experiences with the firm or brand. A retail customer might say, "The last time I put an outfit on layaway, you couldn't find it for a week. I'm not so sure I want to take that chance again."

PRICE Objections based on price are more common with high-quality, expensive merchandise. You might hear statements like "That's more than I wanted to spend."

TIME Objections based on time reveal a hesitation to buy immediately. These objections are sometimes excuses. Customers usually have a real reason for not wanting to make a purchase on the spot. A customer might say, "I think I'll wait until July when you have your summer sale to buy those sandals."

You will probably hear many different kinds of objections once you begin selling. You should note them for future reference.

■ Four-Step Process for Handling Objections

Successful salespeople have learned to use a very basic strategy when answering all objections. It consists of four basic steps for handling objections—listen, acknowledge, restate, and answer.

LISTEN CAREFULLY To demonstrate sincere concern for your customer's objections, follow the key rules you learned in Chapter 8. Remember to be attentive, maintain eye contact, and let the customer talk.

ACKNOWLEDGE THE CUSTOMER'S OBJECTIONS Acknowledging objections demonstrates that you understand and care about the customer's concerns. Some common statements used to acknowledge objections are "I can see your point" or "Other customers have asked us the same question."

These acknowledgments make a customer feel that his or her objections are understandable, valid, and worthy of further discussion. It does not mean that you agree with the customer, but it acknowledges the objection. Disagreeing with the customer, or saying "You're wrong," will put the customer on the defensive, and you might lose the sale. Always try to acknowledge a customer's objections in a positive way.

RESTATE THE OBJECTIONS To be sure you understand the customer, you can restate his or her objections in a number of ways:

"I can understand your concerns. You feel that . . . . Am I correct?"

"In other words, you feel that . . . ."

"Let me see if I understand. You want to know more about . . . ."

Don't repeat the customer's concerns word for word. Instead, paraphrase the objections, or restate them in a different way. A customer might say, "The style is nice, but I don't like the color." You could paraphrase the objection by asking, "Would you be interested in the jacket if we could find your size in another color?"

When paraphrasing, don't change the meaning or content of what your customer says. Accurate paraphrasing shows the customer you are listening and understand the objections. It also helps you open the lines of effective communication when a customer has difficulty expressing concerns.

ANSWER THE OBJECTIONS Answer each objection tactfully. Never answer with an air of superiority or suggest that the person's concern is unimportant.

Think of yourself as a consultant, using the objections to further define or redefine the customer's needs. When price is the objection, go back to determining the customer's needs. Offer a higher-priced item to a customer if it is warranted. Explain the features and benefits of the more expensive model and why that item is better suited to the customer.

■ Specialized Methods of Handling Objections

There are six specialized methods for handling objections: boomerang, question, superior point, denial, demonstration, and third party. Some of these techniques are effective only in specific situations, while others are used more commonly. Any one of these methods may be used as the last step in the four-step process for handling objections.

BOOMERANG An objection can be returned to the customer in the same way that a boomerang returns to the thrower. The boomerang method brings the objection back to the customer as a selling point. Here is an example:

Customer: "This ski jacket is so lightweight. It can't possibly keep me warm."

Salesperson: "The jacket is so light because of an insulation material called Thinsulate. The manufacturer guarantees that Thinsulate will keep you warmer than fiberfill insulation, without the bulk and extra weight."

When using the boomerang method, you must be careful not to sound as if you are trying to outwit the customer. Use a friendly, helpful tone to explain how the objection is really a selling point.

QUESTION The question method is a technique in which you question the customer to learn more about the objections. Your questions may reveal hidden objections and may help you learn more about the customer's needs and wants. While answering your inquiries, the shopper may even come to realize that an objection may not be valid. Here is an example:

Customer: "I don't see the point of having two sinks in our master bathroom, as featured in your suggested layout."

Salesperson: "Do you and your husband ever need to get ready to go out at the same time?"

Customer: "Yes."

Salesperson: "Do either one of you have to wait for the other to finish using the sink on those occasions?"

Customer: "Yes. I see your point."

Never ask questions in an abrupt manner—this may seem rude and create a defensive atmosphere. Suppose a customer comments, "I don't think my sister will like this purse." Never respond with a simple "Why not?" Show courtesy and respect instead by asking a more complete question, such as "Why don't you think she'll like it?"

■ **A Perfect Fit** Successful salespeople use a four-step method to answer objections. *If the customer does not like the color or fit of a garment, how would you use the four-step method to handle this objection?*

SUPERIOR POINT The superior point method is a technique that permits the salesperson to acknowledge objections as valid yet still offset them with other features and benefits. The superior point method allows you to admit disadvantages in certain products but then present superior points to offset or compensate for them. This technique puts the customer in a position to decide between the different features and thus see additional reasons for buying. Here is an example:

Customer: "Your prices are higher than the prices of your competitors."

Salesperson: "That's true. Our prices are slightly higher, but with good reason. We use better quality nylon in our garments that will last five to ten years longer than our competitors'. Plus, we guarantee the quality for life. You can return the product if you ever have a problem with it and we'll repair it free of charge."

DENIAL The denial method is when the customer's objection is based on misinformation. It is best to provide proof and accurate information in answer to objections. This method is also used when the objection is in the form of a question. When using the denial method, you must back up the negative reply with proof and accurate facts. Consider an example:

Customer: "Will this shirt shrink?"

Salesperson: "No, it won't shrink because the fabric is made of 50 percent cotton and 50 percent polyester. The polyester will prevent shrinkage."

DEMONSTRATION The demonstration exemplifies the adage "Seeing is believing." Here is an example:

Customer: "I can't believe that food won't stick to the bottom of the pan if you don't use oil or butter."

Life In The Diverse

MARKETPLACE

Thumbs Up!

In America, the upturned thumb signals a job well done or another positive message. However, giving a "thumbs up" to someone in a country such as Australia, Poland, Nigeria, or Russia just might get you in some trouble. In these countries the thumbs up sign is offensive. AT&T learned this the hard way and they had to change their ads showing upturned thumbs to make sure that the back of the hand, not the palm, was shown for ads in Eastern Europe.

Thinking Critically

What are some other basic hand symbols used in the United States that may be misinterpreted by visitors from another country?

■ **Counteracting Objections** Columbia Sportswear brand jackets have unique features that set them apart from the competition. *Which specialized method would you use to handle an objection based on price for Columbia Sportswear jackets? Why?*

Salesperson: "I'm glad you brought that up. Let me demonstrate how the Teflon coating lets you cook without fats of any kind."

The demonstration method can be quite convincing and should be used when appropriate. Only conduct demonstrations you have tested, and make sure they work before using them on a customer in a sales situation.

THIRD PARTY The third party method involves using a previous customer or another neutral person who can give a testimonial about the product. Some salespeople keep letters from satisfied customers to use as testimonials when handling objections. Others get permission from previous customers to allow prospective customers to call and verify the salesperson's claims. Here's how the method works:

Customer: "I can't see how this machine can save me $1,000 in operating costs the first year."

Salesperson: "Frank Smith, one of my customers, questioned the same point when he bought his machine a year ago. He now praises its efficiency and says that his costs have gone down by $1,200. Here's a letter I recently received from him."

In any given sales situation, it is unlikely that you will use all six methods of handling objections. You will create effective combinations over time that work best for you.

■ **On Recommendation** Customers may sometimes have concerns about the quality or capabilities of a product or the need and cost of repairs. *Which specialized method for handling objections might be best to use in those cases? Why?*

14.2 ASSESSMENT

Reviewing Key Terms and Concepts

1. Distinguish between objections and excuses.
2. Why should you welcome objections in the sales process?
3. Name the five buying decisions upon which common objections are based.
4. List the four steps involved in the process for handling customer objections.
5. Name six specific methods of handling objections.

Thinking Critically

6. Why is restating the objective often a successful method in turning around objections?

Integrating Academic Skills

7. **MATH** Your customer wants to buy 6¾ yards of fabric and the price per yard is $12.50. How much would you charge?

Careers in Marketing

SALES MANAGEMENT

Ken Montgomery
District Sales Manager
L'Oreal

What does your job entail?

"I manage four regional managers and one national account manager who are responsible for the eastern United States. We sell and merchandise our products to drug chain stores, mass merchandisers, and food chain stores. My job is to attain my quarterly and yearly sales quota and to keep within budget. I work with the marketing and sales planning departments to develop strategies for selling new items and supporting existing brands. I set goals with key regional and account managers. My goal is to keep people focused on our marketing plans."

How does your workload vary?

"When I am not in internal planning meetings or making account calls, I work with the regional or district managers visiting stores to check on the display conditions and to measure stock. I travel weekly and am away from home one to three nights a week and two to three weekends per year."

What skills are most important?

"Superior verbal and written communication is important. The demands of time and speed have made communication skills even more important—people want answers quickly so that they can move on to the next issue. Other helpful skills are computer literacy, organization, and good time management."

What is your key to success?

"You have to be flexible and open as your career progresses. Companies expect you to adapt and be willing to do many different jobs while developing your career. Finding a mentor is also important, as that person can support your efforts and help you move up in a company. Treat everyone with respect—remember names and say good morning. It is good to have a friendly working relationship with people across all levels in an organization."

Thinking Critically

Why is it especially important to develop good relationships with all employees as a district sales manager?

Career Facts

Education and Training: In addition to having sales experience, a college degree and a background in business administration are helpful, with courses in marketing, accounting, economics, psychology, and communications.

Aptitudes, Abilities, and Skills: Understanding of the industry, excellent supervisory experience, strong people skills, and good decision-making skills are needed for this job.

Career Outlook: Opportunities for sales management positions should remain stable through 2008.

Career Path: Promotion from within a company is the most common entry into district sales management. Successful managers may advance into regional, national, or international sales management positions.

Chapter 14 ■ *Presenting the Product* **253**

Chapter 14 ASSESSMENT

VOCABULARY REVIEW

Write a paragraph incorporating the following terms:

- layman's terms
- objections
- excuses
- objection analysis sheet
- paraphrase
- boomerang method
- superior point method
- third party method

FACT AND IDEA REVIEW

1. When you cannot determine a customer's intended price range, what priced product should you show? Why? (14.1)

2. When is it appropriate to use jargon? When should you use layman's terms? (14.1)

3. Name five sales aids you can use in the product presentation. (14.1)

4. How could you involve a customer in the product presentation physically and verbally? (14.1)

5. When can objections occur? (14.2)

6. Why should objections be answered promptly? (14.2)

7. How can you prepare for objections? (14.2)

8. What happens to a customer's objection when you use the boomerang method? (14.2)

9. Which specialized method of handling objections allows you to offset an objection with other features and benefits? (14.2)

THINKING CRITICALLY

1. How would you effectively display a set of china during a sales presentation?

2. What would you do to involve your customer if you were selling a copying machine for a business? A universal gym for home use?

3. Identify the best method for handling these objections:

   a. "This is the smallest TV I've ever seen. How can it have a clear picture?"

   b. "I didn't think automatic focus cameras cost so much."

   c. "I'm not sure I need a copier that enlarges and reduces, especially at $300 more than the basic model."

   d. "Will this nylon and polyester fiberfill vest need to be dry-cleaned?"

   e. "These running shoes are so lightweight. Are they definitely for avid runners?"

4. Why should you welcome objections in the sales process?

BUILDING WORKPLACE SKILLS

1. **Human Relations** A woman looking at the size 8 dresses says, "I used to wear size 8, but I've gained a few pounds." In reality, the customer is probably a size 12. How would you direct her to the correct size?

2. **Technology** Choose one product to sell (investment services, an automobile, or makeup and hair coloring) and identify the hardware, software, and audiovisual capabilities that can help you effectively present that product to a prospective customer.

APPLYING MARKETING CONCEPTS

1. **Communicating Product Features** Using the product for which you prepared a feature-benefit chart in Chapter 12, prepare a detailed plan for the product presentation step in the sales training manual. For each product feature, include what you will say, how you will demonstrate that feature, what sales aids you will use, how you will use them, and how you will involve your customer with each feature. When appropriate, incorporate sample dialogue. Prepare this report using a word processing program.

2. **Handling Objections** Use a word processing program to write the section of your sales training manual that deals with handling objections. Include an objection analysis sheet for the product for which you prepared a feature-benefit chart. Present one objection for each of the specialized methods you learned in this chapter (total of six).

3. **Analyzing Objection Approaches** Interview a salesperson in retail and one in business-to-business sales. Ask both salespeople what the most common objection is that they hear and how they handle it. Ask what the most unusual objection is that a customer ever raised, and how they responded. Finally, ask how they prepare for objections that occur during a sales presentation. What similarities did you find in their responses? What differences? Use a word processing program to report your findings.

LINKING SCHOOL TO WORK

Basic Skills and Information Ask an employer how the company's computer system provides the sales force with information needed to make effective product presentations.

THE DECA CONNECTION

Role Play: Product Presentation Trainer

Situation You are to assume the role of sales associate for a home electronics store. Because you have one of your store's best sales records, your supervisor (judge) has asked you to take part in a company training program. The portion of the program for which you will be responsible is titled, "Making Product Presentations Come Alive."

Activity You must make a presentation for your company training program in which you share your secrets for success.

Evaluation You will be evaluated on how well you meet the following performance indicators:
- Recommend specific products
- Demonstrate products
- Explain the nature of sales training
- Make oral presentations
- Demonstrate interest and enthusiasm

interNET CONNECTION

Internet "Show & Tell"
You are creating a new Web site for your company and must decide on the design for product presentation and overcoming objections.

Connect
- Find Web sites of three manufacturers and three retailers that sell products to the consumer.
- Evaluate their Web site design for effectiveness of product display and addressing questions.

Chapter 15

Closing the Sale

Marketing: What It Takes

Making Customers Happy

This growing family has just bought their first new car from you. You explained and demonstrated the features and benefits of this car, and you just made the sale.

WHAT WILL YOU DO?

How will you make sure these customers are satisfied with their buying decision? How can you keep them as customers?

Customer Buying Signals

Closing the Sale

Closing the sale is obtaining positive agreement from the customer to buy. All your efforts up to this step of the sale (preapproach, approach, product presentation, and handling objections) have involved helping your customer make buying decisions. Closing the sale should be a natural part of the sales process; sometimes, it is so natural that your customer closes the sale for you by saying, "I'll take it." In many sales situations, however, the customer waits for you to initiate the close. That is why it is important for you to learn when and how to close a sale.

■ Timing the Close

Close the sale when your customer is ready to buy. Some customers are ready to buy sooner than others; therefore, you must be flexible. You may show a customer a product and almost immediately detect an opportunity to close the sale. Other times, you may spend an hour with a customer and still find that he or she is having difficulty making a decision.

You should never feel obligated to complete an entire sales presentation just because you have planned it that way. Remember, the key to closing the sale is customer readiness.

BUYING SIGNALS When trying to close a sale, look for buying signals, the things customers do or say to indicate a readiness to buy. Buying signals include facial expressions, body language actions, and comments. A customer who is holding merchandise and smiling is usually sending you buying signals. A customer who has removed a jacket from its hanger and draped the garment over his or her arm is also sending buying signals. Comments that imply ownership are buying signals. You know a customer is ready to buy when he or she says "This is exactly what I was looking for."

TRIAL CLOSE You may attempt a trial close to test the readiness of a customer and your interpretation of a positive buying signal. A trial close is an initial effort to close a sale.

Trial closes are beneficial for two reasons. First, even if the close does not work, you will learn from the attempt. The customer will most likely tell you why he or she is not ready to buy. Second, if the trial close does work, you will reach your goal of closing the sale. You have control of the sale in both situations and are in an excellent position to continue with the sales process.

• What You'll Learn

- The buying signals that a customer sends
- The rules for closing a sale
- The specialized methods of closing a sale

• Why It's Important

At a certain point in the sales process, your customer will be ready to make a purchase. Sometimes the decision to buy is quick and easy. At other times, it's more difficult. In this section, you will learn how to recognize customer buying signals and how to close a sale.

Key Terms

- closing the sale
- buying signals
- trial close
- which close
- standing-room-only close
- direct close
- service close

■ **Judging Buying Signals** Buying signals may be verbal or nonverbal. *How would you interpret this customer's body language—ready to buy or not?*

■ General Rules for Closing the Sale

Professional salespeople start closing the sale the first moment they begin talking to the customer. They rely on proven and tested techniques, and they often have the following behavioral traits in common:

- They radiate enthusiasm throughout the sales process
- They are sincere and confident
- They truly want to help solve their customers' problems
- They enjoy their profession
- They watch for early buying signals and close as soon as possible
- They constantly practice sale-closing techniques

You will find it easier to attempt trial closes and to close more sales if you follow a few simple guidelines. Professional salespeople use guidelines, including recognizing opportunities, helping customers make a decision, and creating an ownership mentality for the customer. There are also a few things that you want to avoid saying or doing when closing a sale.

RECOGNIZE CLOSING OPPORTUNITIES You should always use major objections that have been resolved to close the sale. The effect of having a major obstacle removed usually makes a customer receptive to buying the product or service. You can also use effective product presentations to close the sale. Dramatic product presentations often prove important selling points and get a customer excited about owning the product. Take advantage of high customer interest at these times and attempt to close.

HELP CUSTOMERS MAKE A DECISION When a customer is having difficulty making a buying decision, stop showing additional merchandise. You should also narrow the selection of items by removing those things that are no longer of interest to the customer. You can do this by asking, "Which of these items do you like the least?" Once you get the selection down to two, you can help a customer decide by summarizing the major features and benefits of a product. You can also explain any advantages or disadvantages of the item being considered. Both methods help you to focus the decision making on important considerations.

CREATE AN OWNERSHIP MENTALITY Use words that indicate ownership, such as *you* and *your*. When presenting selling points, say things such as, "You'll enjoy using this camera on your vacation." Look for minor agreements from the customer on selling points that lead up to the close. Ask questions such as, "Those walking shoes are comfortable, aren't they?" In general, if you get positive reactions from your customer throughout the sales process, that same positive frame of mind will help create a natural closing.

DON'T TALK TOO MUCH AND DON'T RUSH A CUSTOMER If you think the customer is ready to make a buying decision, stop talking about the product. Continuing to sell to a ready customer may have a negative effect or even cause you to lose the sale.

Don't rush a customer into making a buying decision. Be patient, courteous, polite, and helpful, and always remember that your primary interest is customer satisfaction.

■ Specialized Methods for Closing the Sale

Attempt to close the sale as soon as you recognize a buying signal. How you go about this depends on the selling situation. Certain selling situations warrant the use of specialized methods, such as the *which, standing-room-only, direct,* and *service closes.*

WHICH CLOSE The which close encourages a customer to make a decision between two items. If you follow the general rules for closing a sale, you will remove unwanted items to bring the selection down to two. Review the benefits of each item and then ask the customer, "Which one do you prefer?" This method makes it easy for a customer because only one simple decision must be made.

STANDING-ROOM-ONLY CLOSE The standing-room-only close is used when a product is in short supply or when the price will be going up in the near future. This close should be used only when the situation honestly calls for it because it may be perceived as a high-pressure tactic. In many situations, a salesperson can honestly say, "I'm sorry, but I can't promise that I'll be able to make you this same offer later." This approach is often used in selling high-demand real estate. Customers must often be prompted to act on a hot property that will be off the market quickly.

Life In The Diverse MARKETPLACE

The Universal Sign

The smile, a universal sign, generally needs no translation across boundaries. A smile in the wrong place, however, might cause some confusion. In Thailand, Singapore, and the Philippines, a smile or nervous laughter is often used to cover up embarrassment or an awkward situation. Japanese people smile not only when they are happy or amused but also when they are confused or angry. How can you interpret a smile? Look at the eyes. A genuine smile will cause other changes in the facial expression, such as the crinkled skin in the corner of the eyes.

Thinking Critically

How might a misinterpreted smile cause a problem?

■ **Asking the Right Questions**
In business-to-business sales situations, closing the sale often requires signing a contract. *What preliminary questions or statements could the salesperson have used in this situation to access the customer's readiness to sign on the dotted line?*

REAL WORLD MARKETING

Ladies and Gentlemen, Start Your Computer Engines

One-third of all car buyers use the Internet for auto product and pricing information. General Motors just made this process easier with their Web site, Gmbuypower.com. Consumers can choose the vehicle options they want, find a dealer in their area that has the make and model in stock, and even schedule a test drive. Dealers get hot leads at a lower cost than through traditional television, print, and radio advertising. Customers can shop from the comfort of their homes and then purchase from 500,000 cars at 6,000 dealers without ever having to leave their living rooms.

Thinking Critically

What are some challenges of shopping for a car online?

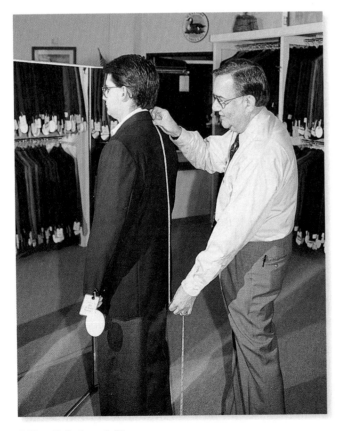

DIRECT CLOSE The direct close is a method in which you ask for the sale. You would use the direct close method when the buying signal is very strong. Here are a few direct close approaches:

- "Based on what I've shown you, how do you feel about this product?"
- "Can I assume that we're ready to talk about the details of your order?"

Positive statements by the customer to direct close approaches lets you know that the customer is ready to buy. You can continue the closing by addressing the specifics of the order. In a retail situation, you might simply ask a question regarding payment, such as "How would you like to pay for this purchase—cash, check, or credit card?"

SERVICE CLOSE Sometimes you may run into obstacles or instances that require special services in order to close the sale. The service close explains services that overcome obstacles or problems. Such services include gift-wrapping, a return policy, special sales arrangements, warranties and guarantees, and bonuses or premiums. You might want to explain the store's return policy when a customer hesitates but seems to be willing to make the purchase anyway. This is an especially good idea when the item is being purchased as a gift for someone else.

Special sales arrangements are used to close the sale when the customer needs help in paying for the item or order. In an industrial selling situation, the sales representative would talk about the terms of the sale, discussing such points as when payment is expected. For example, payment could be due 30 or 60 days after the date of the invoice. A customer may also need information about credit terms to help him or her decide to buy. In a retail selling situation, the use of credit and checks, as well as special buying plans such as layaway, can be suggested. When a customer questions the quality of the merchandise, perhaps you can explain that a warranty, or guarantee, is offered on the product. When your business offers the same quality merchandise at the same price as your competitors, your service may be the only factor that affects the buying decision.

■ **Special Circumstances** In some sales situations, the salespeople need to solve customers' problems by providing special services. *In this case, what do you think helped to close this sale?*

■ Failure to Close the Sale

Don't despair if your initial attempts to close a sale are unsuccessful. It should not be inferred that every sales presentation should result in a sale. Even the best salespeople can sell only a fraction of the prospects called upon. You will have many more opportunities for success, particularly if you treat your customers with courtesy and respect. Research suggests that perseverance is the way to succeed.

In a retail setting, invite the customer to shop in your store again. In business-to-business selling, the sale is rarely closed on the first call. Business-to-business salespeople may negotiate with large accounts for over a year before closing the sale.

Experienced salespeople are able to capitalize on defeat and come away from an unsuccessful selling experience with something to show for it. It is important to keep in mind that even a customer who does not make a purchase is still a prospect for future business. Be alert to what purchases today's nonbuyer might make in the future.

In a business-to-business selling situation, ask if you may call again. Remember that every sales contact has the potential to become a successful sale in the future. In some business-to-business selling situations, the buyer has some feelings of guilt for rejecting your sales proposition in favor of a competitor's. This is especially true when you and the buyer have established a good relationship. In such a case, the buyer may respond to an appeal for consideration on the next order.

If you have established excellent rapport with the buyer, you may be able to ask him or her what factors led to the decision to buy from another source. An appeal for constructive criticism may work for you if you have earned the buyer's respect.

The attitude of the salesperson who has not made the sale should be no different than that of the successful salesperson. It is very important for the salesperson to smile and act friendly after trying in vain to make a sale. In business-to-business selling situations, it is not uncommon for a buyer to be convinced by a sales presentation, but not yet ready to buy. In such a situation, it is extremely important that the salesperson leave an opening for a return sales call. If you clearly sense an impending turndown, it is better to make a graceful exit, leaving the door open for a future sales call. You should carefully consider the situation before bowing out, as it will greatly increase selling costs.

One popular misconception about selling is that salespeople are born, not made. Success at selling, like success at any career, is the result of training, apprenticeship, and experience.

15.1 ASSESSMENT

Reviewing Key Terms and Concepts

1. What are customer buying signals?

2. When is the right time to close a sale?

3. Provide an example of each of the following closing methods: which close, standing-room-only close, direct close, and service close.

4. Why is the failure to close not a true failure?

Thinking Critically

5. A customer seems to be frustrated because she likes three of the items you have shown her. How can you make her buying decision easier?

Integrating Academic Skills

6. **COMMUNICATION** As a salesperson, how do you close the sale when a customer says, "Your presentation was terrific, and I like those skis. But I think I'll wait until they go on sale."

Effective Selling

What You'll Learn

- Why suggestion selling is important
- The rules for effective suggestion selling
- Specialized suggestion selling methods
- The concept of relationship marketing and how it is related to the sales process

Why It's Important

The goal of selling is to help customers make satisfying buying decisions so they buy from you again. In this section you will learn how to create a relationship with your customers so they will continue to do business with you in the future.

Key Terms

- suggestion selling
- relationship marketing

Suggestion Selling

Suggestion selling is selling additional goods or services to the customer. It does not mean loading customers with unneeded or unwanted goods and services. Instead, it involves selling customers other items that will ultimately save time and money or make the original purchase more enjoyable.

Consider the customer who buys a camera, takes it home, and only then realizes that he or she has no film for it. That means another trip to the store before the camera can be used. The salesperson would have had a sure sale by suggesting that the customer buy film.

■ Benefits of Suggestion Selling

Suggestion selling benefits the salesperson, the customer, and the company. You benefit because customers will want to do business with you again. Your customer benefits because he or she is more pleased with the original purchase. The firm benefits because the time and cost involved in suggestion selling is less than the cost of making the original sale.

Selling is a process of persuasion, and the principles of persuasion apply to it. When a counter clerk at McDonald's asks you whether you would like a drink, French fries, or a hot apple pie with your meal, the clerk is using a suggestion selling approach.

Consider the two purchases below. The second includes an extra item, a suggestion from the salesperson.

Purchase		Purchase	
pants	$75	pants	$ 75
		shirt	35
Total	$75	Total	$110
Cost of goods	−37	Cost of goods	−55
Gross Profit	$38	Gross Profit	$ 55
Expenses	−12	Expenses	−15
Net profit	$26	Net profit	$ 40

Note that the extra time spent on suggestion selling significantly increased the firm's net profits. Expenses rose—but not in proportion to the sales volume. There are two reasons for this. First, less time and effort are needed for suggestion selling compared to the initial sale. Second, certain business expenses (such as utilities and rent) remain the same despite the extra sales activity.

■ **A Perfect Match** Evaluate this salesperson's suggestion selling technique. *What is the salesperson doing right?*

■ Rules for Suggestion Selling

There are five basic rules for suggestion selling.

- *Do suggestion selling after the customer has made a commitment to buy, but before payment is made or the order written.* Introducing additional merchandise before the sale has been closed can create pressure on the customer. The only exception to this rule involves products whose accessories are a major benefit, like film for a camera or clothes for a doll. Salespeople who sell such products often introduce the additional items during the sales process to help close the sale.

- *Make your recommendation from the customer's point of view and give at least one reason for your suggestion.* You might say, "If you want to use your camera immediately, you might want to buy film for it." A customer is usually willing to listen to your suggestion when it seems that you seem to have his or her best interests at heart.

- *Make the suggestion definite.* Don't ask, "Will that be all?" Instead say, "This oil is recommended by the manufacturer for this engine." In most cases, general questions invite a negative response.

- *Show the item you are suggesting.* Merely talking about it is not enough. In many cases, the item will sell itself if you let the customer see and handle it. You may put a matching purse next to the shoes a customer just decided to buy, particularly with some commentary. You might say, "This purse matches your shoes perfectly, doesn't it?"

- *Make the suggestion positive.* You could say, "This scarf will complement your coat beautifully. Look how perfectly it matches the color and how fashionable it looks." You certainly would never say, "You wouldn't want to look at scarves for your new coat, would you?" Such a negative statement shows a lack of enthusiasm or a lack of confidence on the part of the salesperson.

How to Pamper Customers? Get to Know Them!

Knowing your customers gives you an edge. With today's computer technology, Marriott tracks customers' needs and preferences from their previous stays at the hotel chain. Personal planners from the chain's resorts are able to access the central Marriott database so they can anticipate the amenities repeat customers want. The spa at Marriott's Camelback Inn in Scottsdale, Arizona, is so popular that guests must book their spa services well in advance of their stay there. Personal planners, who know that a guest had spa services in the past, are in a good position to suggest those services again. They even take care of making the required reservations.

Marriott's personal planners also are prepared to plan an entire itinerary for a guest. This may include restaurant reservations, golf tee times, shopping sprees, and sightseeing tours. These personal planners can also arrange for child care and activities while parents enjoy an evening at the theater. Flowers for a spouse upon arrival also can be arranged. Personal planners may suggest fee-generating activities, such as hot-air balloon rides. All these services make guests' vacations hassle-free, which makes them want to repeat their positive experience in the future.

Case Study Review

1. How is the Marriott hotel chain following the concept of relationship marketing?
2. How are Marriott's personal planners making use of suggestion selling?

A MATTER OF ETHICS

3. Is it ethical for the Marriott to keep such detailed records of guests? How could such a practice cause problems with regard to privacy issues?

■ Suggestion Selling Methods

There are three methods used in suggestion selling. They are offering related merchandise, recommending larger quantities, and calling attention to special sales opportunities (see Figure 15-1 on page 265).

OFFERING RELATED MERCHANDISE Related merchandise can be a good or service that would increase the use or enjoyment of the customer's original purchase. Introducing related merchandise is probably the easiest and most effective suggestion selling method. There are usually accessory items that can be sold with the original purchase—a tie to match a new suit or a special service contract for a new appliance.

RECOMMENDING LARGER QUANTITIES Suggesting a larger quantity usually works in retail settings when selling inexpensive items or when savings in money or time and convenience are involved. You may tell a customer who wants to buy one pair of pantyhose, "One pair costs $4, but you can buy three pairs for $10. Buying three pairs will save you a trip to the store next time you need a pair and will also save you $2."

FIGURE 15-1

SUGGESTION SELLING METHODS

After customers have made a commitment to buy, it is a good practice to suggest something specific that will help them better enjoy their original purchase. There are three methods of accomplishing that goal. Let's examine how they may be used in a business-to-business sales situation that involves the sale of cameras to an electronics retailer.

LARGER QUANTITIES

In business-to-business sales situations, a sales representative may suggest larger quantities of goods to make a customer eligible for special discounts, payment terms, or delivery charges. Sometimes qualifying retailers may be given free merchandise when they buy a larger quantity of goods.

RELATED MERCHANDISE

The sales representative should suggest these related items of merchandise to the retail store buyer. The rationale for the suggestion would be that these accessories may be needed or wanted by the retailer's customers.

SPECIAL SALES OPPORTUNITIES

When a company runs a special promotion on products unrelated to the original purchase, or wants to introduce a new product, it is up to the sales representative to share that information with the customer. That information is often disseminated after the commitment to buy the original item has been made.

In business-to-business sales situations, the salesperson may suggest a larger quantity so the customer can take advantage of lower prices or special considerations. Some manufacturers also include special services in addition to a better price per item. Buying a certain quantity, for instance, may allow a retailer to take advantage of an opportunity for free freight or free advertising.

CALLING ATTENTION TO SPECIAL SALES OPPORTUNITIES Salespeople are obligated to communicate special sales opportunities to their customers. This is true even if those opportunities are not related to the original purchase. Often they involve new merchandise, special sales, and holiday items.

In retail sales, routinely inform your customer of the arrival of new merchandise. Regular customers appreciate this special service because they like having the opportunity to see new merchandise before others do.

Most shoppers appreciate the opportunity to take advantage of a bargain. Salespeople are obligated to both the store and the customer to pass along such information. You could comment on a special sale by explaining, "We're having a one-day sale on all items in this department. You might want to look around before I write up your purchase."

Special occasions and holidays present an opportunity to sell more merchandise. You can suggest gift items to customers around occasions such as Christmas, Kwanzaa, Hanukkah, Valentine's Day, Father's Day, and Mother's Day. Here's an example of what you can say: "If you haven't finished your holiday shopping for the men in your life, you may want to look at the special display of gift ideas we have in the men's department. You'll be amazed at the variety and creativity of some of the items. If you would like to follow me, I'll show you what I mean."

In business-to-business sales situations, sales representatives often show new items to their customers after they have completed the sale of merchandise requested. Thus, the salesperson has an opportunity to establish a rapport with the customer before introducing new merchandise.

Relationship Marketing

A popular trend among companies today is relationship marketing. Relationship marketing involves the strategies businesses use to stay close to their customers. In today's competitive marketplace, customer service is an important part of this trend. After-sale activities are used to develop and nurture customer relationships.

The value of a good relationship is not a new idea. Marketers have long recognized that identifying the needs of customers and satisfying them can be profitable. However, it is only recently that firms have made a dedicated effort to use relationship marketing. By examining successful partnerships in

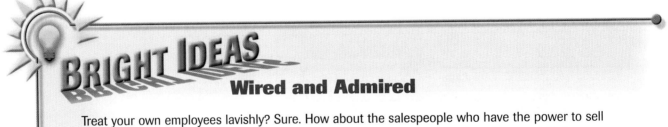

BRIGHT IDEAS
Wired and Admired

Treat your own employees lavishly? Sure. How about the salespeople who have the power to sell your product? Noel Lee of Monster Cable says why not treat salespeople well, especially because he depends on suggestion selling to make a profit. When selling a new home entertainment system, salespeople may promote Monster's gold-tipped electromagnetically shielded cable. The high cost ($3 to $125 per foot) encourages salespeople to have a good sales push, because the average cable is 25 cents per foot. To spur sales, Monster Cable's Noel Lee flies top producers from electronics stores to all-expenses-paid weekends in Napa Valley, Hawaii, and Germany. He also lets them drive one of his sports cars. Sometimes, salespeople need motivation to move the product.

Thinking Creatively

What other incentives could be offered to motivate a salesforce?

business and elsewhere, marketers have discovered that enduring relationships are built on trust and commitment and require a lot of time and effort to maintain.

Relationship marketing is alive and well in both traditional and e-commerce marketing. Consider the example set by Harley Davidson, the motorcycle manufacturer. The company established a club for its members, and it markets services such as motorcycle insurance and travel assistance to those members. An e-commerce example of relationship marketing is Amazon.com's practice of collecting information about customers' book purchases and then e-mailing personalized information about promotions and merchandise within the customer's established range of interest.

Customer loyalty cannot be taken for granted, especially with the high levels of competition in today's market. A company can stay close to its customers and keep them happy by having the sale be the first step in developing a relationship, not the final one. Think of after-sale activities as part of an ongoing dialog with customers in preparation for future sales. This is simplified with the use of e-mail, which can be used to keep customers informed about sales, new products, and important company news.

■ Taking Payment/Taking the Order

Take payment or the order with courtesy. Work quickly to complete the paperwork. Avoid saying or doing anything to irritate your customer at this stage of the sale. You have probably heard an annoyed customer say, "Forget the order. I don't want it anymore." If you are courteous and efficient, you can usually avoid this type of negative response from an unhappy or disappointed customer.

■ Departure

Before the customer departs, or before you leave your client's office, reassure the person of his or her wise buying choices. If an item needs special care or specific instructions, take the time to educate your customer about it. You may want to remind the

E-mail as a Sales Tool

Make millions fast...Special Customers Online Clearance—these are just two examples of subject lines for possible e-mail advertisements. E-mail is a potent Web technology when it comes to customer service. It provides businesses with an inexpensive form of communication that can easily focus on specific customers and address their particular interests and needs. For customers, receiving e-mail from companies about order status, sales, special discounts, and even a personalized newsletter can make them feel as if they are part of a family. It's important, however, to ask customers whether they want company e-mail. Giving consumers control over the volume of information they receive means they won't feel that they are being "spammed," or loaded with unwanted e-mail. Unsolicited messages or too many e-mail messages can turn off customers.

Thinking Critically
How could you use e-mail to encourage sales?

customer, for example, that to get the best results from a Teflon-coated frying pan, it is best to preheat the pan. If you are selling a customer a new automobile, this would be a good time to remind him or her when the oil should be changed and when tune-ups are necessary. Helpful comments like this will make your customer feel you are interested and concerned. They also help ensure customer satisfaction.

Always thank your customers. Even when a customer does not buy, express your gratitude for the time and attention given to you. Invite him or her back to the store, or ask for permission to call again in the near future.

■ Follow-Up

The follow-up includes making arrangements to follow through on all promises made during the sales process. It also includes checking on your customer's satisfaction with his or her purchase. Some follow up ideas:

- Call the shipping department to confirm a special delivery date.
- Check to make sure that delivery occurs as promised.
- Call the customer and explain any delay.
- Phone the customer a week or two after the purchase to see if he or she is happy with his or her selection.
- Send a thank-you note with your business card attached.

You can use the time immediately after the sale to plan for your next encounter with the customer. Take notes on your conversation with the customer. Keep this in a file for future reference. In retail sales, note a customer's preference in color, style, and size, as well as the person's address and telephone number. In business-to-business selling, record personal information on the buyer's marital status, children, and hobbies to assist with future sales visits. Record changes in buying patterns that may lead to future sales. You also want to note any future service dates for appliances or cars so that you can send a reminder when the time comes.

■ Evaluation

Some businesses send questionnaires or call customers to check on how well they were treated by the sales and service staff. The results of such surveys are passed on to salespeople so they can improve their technique.

Even if your company has a formal method of reviewing your efforts, you should conduct your own evaluation. In your evaluation, consider the following:

- What were the strong points of your sales presentation?
- What did you do wrong?
- How could you have improved your performance?
- What would you do differently next time?
- What can you do now to solidify your relationship with your customer if you made the sale?

Objective self-evaluation is a helpful tool in any career. Asking yourself these questions can help you improve your selling skills as well as your business skills in general. They will enable you to look forward to your next sales opportunity. That kind of attitude will help you become more effective with each sales contact. It will also help you become more successful in building a strong relationship with your customers.

15.2 ASSESSMENT

Reviewing Key Terms and Concepts

1. What is suggestion selling, and why is it important?
2. Suggest two rules for suggestion selling.
3. Identify three methods used for suggestion selling.
4. What is relationship marketing and how is it related to the sales process?
5. Why are after-sale activities (such as departure, follow-up, and evaluation) important?

Thinking Critically

6. Assume you work for a bank and are in charge of selling commercial loans. You just sold a real estate developer a $3.5 million loan for a new shopping center. What could you do now to solidify your relationship with this customer?

Integrating Academic Skills

7. **MATH** What is the total amount due from a customer who purchases three shirts at $25 each, two pairs of pants at $40 each, and four ties at $14 each? The sales tax on the clothing is 5 percent.

Careers in Marketing

SALES MANAGEMENT

Martin Swinehart
Sales Promotion Manager
Revolution Marketing

Career Facts

Education and Training: A bachelor's degree in marketing is the ideal preparation. Experience in negotiating complex contracts and facilitating market research is necessary.

Aptitudes, Abilities, and Skills: The ability to coordinate information, make decisions based on numerical and statistical information, and promote the cooperative work of various groups of employees. Analytical skills and above average communication and presentation skills are helpful.

Career Outlook: Average growth in opportunities is projected through the year 2006. Growth in e-commerce sales promotion is likely to be stronger.

Career Path: Sales promotion directors must have several years of increasingly responsible sales and marketing experience. They may advance from regional to national sales promotion directors, and finally to global sales promotion directors.

What does your job entail?

"I am in the business of sampling and promotion. My job is to assist clients with selling their product or service. When you are at an event and are given a free can of soda or box of cereal, that is sampling and promotion. My company does direct hand-to-hand promotions, as opposed to mail order; this allows consumer interaction, which creates greater logo recognition. Direct promotion offers higher quality sampling and a better sampling of the demographic. It saves money over mailing, costing only 15 to 20 cents per impression, while a mailing can cost more than 33 cents per impression."

What skills are most important?

"Communication on all levels is the most important skill to have in this business. You need to keep a straight head and be able to transition from the high-pressure business meetings to a casual climate in a second. "

How does your job vary?

"It changes every day—there is a huge amount of variety in my job. I am the captain of my own fate because I pick my own clients and run my business my own way. I have quite a bit of variety and freedom, which really allows for a lot of creativity."

What kind of training would you suggest for students?

"It's important to get out into the real world. You have to understand trends, demographics, how people work, how they think, and how they communicate. You need to gain insight about how people really are, as opposed to reading about something in a book. For this job, you need to be out in the field."

What is your key to success?

"Innovative thinking and presenting solutions to clients. I am in the business of problem solving, and must base my actions on that."

Thinking Critically

Why is it important to understand human behavior in the sales promotion field?

VOCABULARY REVIEW

Write a story, using the terms below, about a sales situation in which you are asked to close the sale for a colleague.

- closing the sale
- buying signals
- trial close
- which close
- standing-room-only close
- direct close
- service close
- suggestion selling
- relationship marketing

FACT AND IDEA REVIEW

1. Why are trial closes important? (15.1)

2. Why should a salesperson stop talking about a product once strong buying signals are detected from a customer? (15.1)

3. What are the three steps of the which close method? (15.1)

4. When should the standing-room-only close be used? (15.1)

5. What should you do if you did not close the sale in a retail situation? In a business-to-business situation? (15.1)

6. How does suggestion selling benefit the salesperson, the customer, and the company? (15.2)

7. When should you try suggestion selling? (15.2)

8. How can a salesperson use the time immediately after the sale to plan for his or her next encounter with that customer? (15.2)

9. Why should you evaluate yourself when the sales process is over? (15.2)

THINKING CRITICALLY

1. Select the most appropriate closing method and provide your rationale.

   a. "I like this TV, but I don't have the money with me to buy it today."

   b. "You've shown me so many pairs of gloves I like that I can't make up my mind."

   c. "My parents are fussy. What if I buy them this clock and they don't like it?"

   d. "I had a bad experience with my last computer and am concerned about this one's reliability."

2. List three related items that could be used for suggestion selling after a customer's decision to buy a suit, a camera, and a bicycle.

3. What are five criteria that you think should be used when evaluating a salesperson's technique?

BUILDING WORKPLACE SKILLS

1. **Writing** Prepare a memo explaining the importance of suggesting related merchandise to customers to all new sales employees. Include examples, recommendations, and guidelines to encourage suggestion selling.

2. **Human Relations** A customer wants to return a clock radio because he was not able to set the time or the alarm. The customer is probably not aware of a memory key that must be depressed while such settings are being made. How would you handle the return? How could the whole situation have been avoided?

APPLYING MARKETING CONCEPTS

1. **Developing Sales Strategies** Write about closing the sale and suggestion selling for your continuing sales training manual project. Explain each step's importance and timing, then write four different dialogues to demonstrate each of the different closing methods. List all the related merchandise that can be sold with your product. Select one related item and write a dialogue of exactly what you would say to demonstrate the rules of suggestion selling. Use a word processing program to prepare this report.

2. **Recognizing Relationship Marketing** Use a word processing program to write the conclusion for your sales training manual. Stress the concept of relationship marketing.

3. **Developing Customer Relationships** Using presentation software, show ways a computer business and a car dealership can ensure customer satisfaction and develop ongoing relationships with their customers.

4. **Reaching Out to Customers** You manage a funky clothing store that caters to Generation Xers. You are inviting valued customers to a special preseason sale. Using design software, create a flyer to be mailed to your regular customers encouraging them to come back to your store.

LINKING SCHOOL TO WORK

Thinking, Interpersonal, and Information Skills Interview a salesperson from a company to find out what closing techniques he or she uses, as well as what is done to develop an ongoing relationship with customers. Prepare a written report on your findings.

THE DECA CONNECTION

Role Play: Sales Associate

Situation You are to assume the role of sales associate in a sporting goods store. A new store manager (judge) has asked all employees to share with him or her the sales practices they have found most successful.

Activity Develop a master plan that can be used storewide to ensure customer satisfaction through effective closing techniques, suggestion selling, and relationship marketing.

Evaluation You will be evaluated on how well you fulfill the following performance indicators:
- Demonstrate sale-closing techniques
- Demonstrate suggestion selling
- Explain the selling process
- Plan follow-up strategies for use in selling
- Explain the nature of effective verbal communications

interNET CONNECTION

Who Closes the Sale?
You have been asked to design a Web site for a sporting goods business. Before beginning, research the sales-closing strategies and relationship marketing techniques of other e-tailers.

Connect
- Report on how various e-tailers close the sale.
- Report on how these businesses develop a relationship with customers.
- Create a flowchart from the home page for the sporting goods dealer, including closing the sale and relationship marketing links.

Chapter 16

Using Math In Sales

Marketing: What It Takes

Ski Lodge Inn— A Mountain High or a High-Risk Idea?
You and three friends are giving serious thought to opening a restaurant in a ski resort area. The four of you have been meeting regularly to study the feasibility of opening the restaurant. Your discussions have included the potential market, start-up costs, sources of financing, food and equipment suppliers, and many other issues. Now it's time to begin your research. Your first responsibility is to learn about the advantages and disadvantages of accepting various credit cards for payment.

WHAT WILL YOU DO?
How will you research the advantages and disadvantages of accepting credit cards for payment?

Cash Registers

Cash Register Operations

The sales transaction is the process of recording a sale and presenting the customer with proof of payment. Most retailers today use cash registers to record sales and provide customers with receipts. Cash registers fill three important functions of sales transactions:

- *Recording sales* Cash registers provide a convenient way to enter information about a sale. This usually includes the department, the type of transaction, the salesperson, and the amount of the sale. The salesperson also enters the amount of money given by the customer. The register responds with the amount of change due.
- *Storing cash and sales documents* Cash registers provide a convenient, organized way to keep cash, personal checks, credit sales checks, and refund slips. Coupons and other sales-related documents may also be kept in the cash register drawer.
- *Providing receipts* Cash registers automatically provide a receipt for the customer. This is the customer's record of the sale and proof of payment.

Most salespeople operate a cash register. In some retail stores, including many department stores and all supermarkets, cash register operations are the responsibility of a cashier or checkout clerk. Before you assume the responsibility of using a cash register and handling money, you will need to become familiar with all aspects of cash register operations.

■ Electronic Cash Registers

Electronic cash registers automatically perform many functions of a sales transaction, including totaling quantity purchases, figuring sales tax, subtracting refunds and returns, and calculating the change due to a customer.

Information on sales transactions can be entered into an electronic cash register in a number of ways:

- *Manual key entry* Even with electronic cash registers, some businesses have their salespeople enter sales transactions manually, using the register keys. All registers provide a numeric keyboard for entry in case other input devices don't function properly.
- *Electronic wand entry* More and more retailers (especially department and clothing stores) are using electronic wands to enter sales transactions. The salesperson moves the point of the wand across the data printed on a tag attached to the article sold.

• What You'll Learn

- The three general functions of all cash registers
- The arrangement of currency and coins in a cash register drawer
- The two methods of making change
- The two most important rules for safeguarding money at the cash register
- The general content of sales checks and the basic ways of generating them

• Why It's Important

Your customer's decision to buy does not conclude the sales process. You must record the transaction and present the customer with proof of payment —or secure a promise to pay in the future. In this section, you will explore cash register operations. You will learn the basics of operating both manual and electronic registers.

Key Terms

- sales transaction
- Universal Product Code (UPC)
- Universal Vendor Marketing (UVM)
- till
- opening cash fund

■ **UPC** There are two types of product codes. *Which is shown in this photo? Why might it be more effective?*

- *Optical scanning* Supermarkets have improved their efficiency in recording sales transactions by installing optical scanners at checkout counters. Salesclerks drag items across the scanner so it can read the bar codes on the product packaging. If the scanner cannot read the code, the salesclerk keys the information manually.

Two types of codes are widely used for electronic entry. The Universal Product Code (UPC) is the bar code referred to in the photograph above. Bar codes are composed of a series of vertical parallel black and white lines and a row of numbers. Each item has its own distinctive UPC. The Universal Vendor Marketing (UVM) code is another code that appears as a series of numbers across the top of a price tag. A UVM code is designed to be read by an electronic wand.

Once read and entered into a register, coded information can be transferred to a mainframe computer for further processing. Many electronic cash registers are linked to such computers as part of a POS system (see Figure 16-1 on page 275). Using the data, the computer can update inventory records with each sale and automatically reorder items in short supply. It can also store customer information and make it available for marketing or credit-check purposes. It can also print out financial statements, sales trends, and sales personnel productivity reports.

■ The Cash Drawer

Checks and currency collected in sales transactions are generally deposited in the till. The till is the cash drawer of a cash register.

CASH DRAWER ARRANGEMENT The till normally has ten compartments—five in the back and five in the front. Although some companies vary the arrangement, bills are usually kept in the back of the drawer and coins in the front.

In the section for bills, the first compartment on the left often remains empty. It is reserved for checks or other special items. The second compartment contains $20 bills, the third $10 bills, and the fourth $5 bills. The last compartment on the right is used for $1 bills. When a customer tenders a $2 bill, it is placed under the $1 bills.

In the section for coins, the first compartment on the left is used for silver dollars and half-dollars. The next compartment is for quarters, the following one for dimes, and the one after that for nickels. The last compartment on the right is for pennies.

This arrangement facilitates making change because the bill and coin compartments are related and in descending order of value. Each pair has at least one digit in common. The $20 bills are behind the quarters ($.25). The $10 bills are behind the dimes ($.10). The $5 bills are behind the nickels ($.05), and the $1 bills are behind the pennies ($.01).

OPENING CASH FUND The manager or other designated person will provide a limited amount of money for the cash register at the beginning of each business day. This opening cash fund consists of the coins and currency designated for the register for a given day's business. To verify the fund, the assigned person first counts the coins and places them, one denomination at a time, in the correct compartment; then he or she does the same with the currency.

As the coins and currency are counted, the amount is written down to make sure the total matches the amount planned for the register. The change fund is even when it matches exactly. When there is more than planned, the fund is over; if there is less than planned, the fund is short. An opening cash fund that is short or over should be reported immediately to the person who supplied the money.

FIGURE 16-1

POS TERMINAL FUNCTIONS

Point of sale (POS) computer terminals are connected to an in-store network that keeps track of sales, inventory, and often the ordering of new merchandise.

```
TAX DUE          .24     Today is
EFT TOTAL      39.59     Friday  09/29/00
SC 7088 JM LT ST/BAN            .17-F
SC 7088 JM LT PEACH            .17-F
SC 7088 JM LT.LMN.CF          .17-F
SC 7290 RP LAFAYETTE         1.00-F
              TAX DUE          .24
MC     SCANNED COUPON         .75-
SC     DOUBLE COUPON          .75-F
              TAX DUE          .24
00.00 lb   Balance    $39.59
SSC I    (III) n max=2999
CAPACITY/CAPACITE : 29.99x.01 lb / 15 x .005 kg
```

SCANNING PRODUCTS

The checker passes each item over the scanner so that it can read the code printed on the package. The checker will key in the sale amount if the code label is torn or missing.

TRANSFERRING INFORMATION

The price and name of each item are displayed on the screen. The terminal also shows the total amount of the sale after it computes any special discounts. Customers can pay by cash, check, or credit or debit card. This terminal also sends the information to the central store computer, where store inventory is updated and new merchandise can be ordered if stocks are low.

RECORDING SALES

The terminal calculates the amount of change that the customer is due and prints a tape receipt listing each item sold along with prices, the date and time of sale. If the sale was by credit or debit card, usually the customer's name and some account information are also printed on the tape. The checker gives the customer any change due and the receipt. This completes the sale.

■ **Cash Flow** The money in a cash drawer is laid out in order of value from right to left. *Why do you think this arrangement is always the same?*

MAKING CHANGE A salesperson who handles a large number of cash transactions during a business day may run short of certain denominations at some time. Check your cash drawer during any slack time you have to see if you need any bills or coins, and request the change then. This procedure can prevent delays when customers are waiting for service.

A customer who has made a decision to buy usually wants to pay quickly and move on. That is why accuracy and speed are of primary concern in recording sales. You should take special care with cash transactions. Be thorough and accurate when making change, and follow these five steps:

1. Once the transaction has been entered in the cash register, announce to the customer the total amount of the sale. You might say, "That will be $17.65."

2. Announce the amount tendered when the customer offers payment in cash, saying, for example, "Out of $20."

3. Place the money on the cash drawer ledge and leave it there until you have given change to the customer. This eliminates most disputes over amount tendered.

4. Count silently while removing change from the cash drawer. The most common method is to count up from the purchase price, taking out smaller denominations of coins and currency first. Use as few coins as possible in making change.

5. Count aloud when handing the change to the customer. Say, "That's $17.65 out of $20—$17.75 (giving the customer a dime), $18 (giving a quarter), $19, and $20," (giving two $1 bills, one at a time).

Many customers try to avoid accumulating small change by tendering an odd amount of change to pay for their purchases. A customer might give you $20.39 for a sales total of $18.39. You would use the 39 cents to cancel the "odd cents" of the sale and give change for the $20 bill. The same customer might also tender $20.50, in which case you would count the odd cents first, starting at $18.39.

Most newer cash registers calculate and display the amount of change. You may find it easier to begin with the largest denomination when using this type of machine. When the register displays $2.35 due the customer for a $17.65 purchase, you may select the change from the cash drawer by taking out two $1 bills, a quarter, and a dime. The customer knows from the display what change is due; therefore, you can count it out the same way.

PRACTICE 1

How would you make or arrange for change in the following situations using the smallest number of bills and coins possible?

1. A customer gives you a $50 bill to pay for a $22.61 purchase. What change would you give her?

2. A customer is buying two audio cassettes that total $15.09, including tax. The smallest bill he has is $20, and he doesn't want too much change back. What is your response?

3. A customer gives you $40.15 for a $27.15 purchase. How would you count back the change?

4. You are a cashier at Long's Drugstore, and a customer gives you $20.75 to pay for a purchase of $13.63. Count the customer's change back to him. Why did he give you the change along with the $20 bill?

Note: Answers to all practice sets in this chapter appear on page 287.

SALES TALLY Salespeople and cashiers who use a cash register must account for the day's sales and money at closing. This process goes by a number of names, including balancing the cash or balancing the till.

FIGURE 16-2

Sales Check—Single Purchase

masons

15154 RYLAND AVENUE
ABINGTON, PA 19001

LUGGAGE & FINE LEATHER GOODS

Date ___5-11___ 20 _--_

Sold to ___CASH___

Address ___—___

Emp. # ___11335___

Dept	Qty	Article	Price	Amount	
511	1	WALLET	24.99	24	99
		Mdse Subtotal		24	99
		Sales Tax		1	50
		Total		26	49

■ **Single Purchase Sales Check** A sales check like this provides more information than a simple cash register receipt. *Why would a customer prefer to have a record like this one?*

Most cash registers automatically keep a sales tally, or summary of the day's sales. This makes the job of balancing the cash much simpler. The person responsible for each register counts the money and fills out a brief closing balance report. Then he or she removes the tape from the cash register and sends the money, report, and tape to management.

Some older cash registers do not keep an automatic sales tally. Sales checks may be written for each sale and the information recorded on a tally sheet after each transaction. At the end of the day, sales must be reviewed to balance the cash.

SAFEGUARDS AGAINST THEFT Every employee who uses a cash register should be familiar with some safeguards against the theft of money. The first rule is always to close the cash drawer between transactions. While you are counting change to a customer, you should partially close the drawer.

Remove the money tendered by the customer from the register ledge after giving change. You should always lock the register if you leave it.

You may occasionally encounter a customer who interrupts you while you are counting change. It is best to ignore the interruption while you are making change. Don't allow yourself to get distracted, because this could cause you to make incorrect change. You can respond politely once the transaction has been completed.

Counterfeit bills show up in almost every city at some time. Every company has, or should have, printed information on how to identify counterfeit money. Recently, changes were made to the design of U.S. currency to thwart counterfeiters. To make the currency more secure from reproduction techniques, the U.S. Department of the Treasury redesigned most denominations with new security features. The redesigned bills include a polymer thread embedded vertically in the bill, concentric fine-line printing, a watermark, color-shifting ink, and an enlarged, off-center portrait.

The best way to guard against counterfeit money is to become very familiar with U.S. currency. Examine suspect notes and look for difference in the quality of printing and paper characteristics.

Genuine currency has tiny red and blue fibers embedded throughout. The portrait on a genuine bill appears lifelike and stands out distinctly from the background. Counterfeit portraits are usually lifeless and flat, with details merged into the background. Also, the fine-line printing on the border of a genuine bill is clear and unbroken. On a counterfeit, the lines on the border scrollwork may be blurred and indistinct.

■ Sales Checks

Since small firms account for such a large percentage of U.S. businesses, you may find yourself working for a company that does not use automated cash registers. That means you will have to prepare a handwritten sales check like the one shown in Figure 16-2 for every sale. Take the time to familiarize yourself with its basic entries.

A sales check is a written record of a sales transaction. That includes such information as the date of the transaction, the items purchased, and the purchase price. It is valuable to a customer as an itemized receipt in this form. In its most complete form, a sales check can contain customer information (name, address, and phone number) and details such as the time of the sale and the identity of the salesperson. This is additional information that a business would find valuable.

Most businesses use electronic cash registers and POS systems, which result in fewer handwritten sales checks. The electronic registers provide customers with a portion of the cash register tape as a receipt. The POS systems provide computer-generated sales checks. (Sales and customer information are input by keyboard. The computer then prints out a sales check for the customer and a duplicate for the store.)

With technological advances like these, why would you concern yourself with written sales checks? Many small businesses do not have access to electronic registers and POS systems. Their salespeople record transactions by hand in sales check books that contain two or three copies of each form. They also use sales check registers, metal or plastic devices that contain a supply of continuous sales checks in duplicate or triplicate form. (When a slip is completed, you simply pull a handle and eject one or two copies. A second or third copy is kept inside the sales register, and a new sales check moves into place for the next transaction.) In these instances, the written sales checks provide both customer and company with the details that the cash register tape does not.

Life In The Diverse MARKETPLACE

Thumbs Up?

Standing at a crowded fast food restaurant, you may hold up your index finger to say "just one soda." This seems simple enough; however, it is not if you are abroad. In Germany, the upright thumb represents the number one and the forefinger shows the number two. While most Westerners begin counting with the thumb, the Japanese start with the index finger. This means that number five is reached at the thumb, not the pinky finger. Holding up your thumb may result in five sodas! Count on the wrong finger and you just might find yourself with one, two, or five hamburgers, depending on how your signal is interpreted!

Thinking Critically

Why is it helpful to know the differences in hand gestures for counting when travelling abroad?

16.1 ASSESSMENT

Reviewing Key Terms and Concepts

1. What are three functions that all cash registers perform?

2. From left to right, how are the coins arranged in a typical cash register drawer? The bills?

3. A customer gives you a $50 bill for a purchase of $37.73. How will you count the change back to her?

4. What can you do to help prevent theft from a cash register?

5. What sort of information does a sales check use to detail a sales transaction?

Thinking Critically

6. What advantages do you think using an electronic wand would have over manually entering prices?

Integrating Academic Skills

7. **COMMUNICATION** Write a memo to all cashiers at Francisco's grocery explaining the reasons you are switching from manual to electronic cash registers.

Sales Transactions

Retail Sales

As a salesperson or cashier, you will handle several types of sales transactions. Most will be cash and debit or credit card sales, in addition to layaway (or will-call) sales, on-approval sales, and cash on delivery (COD) sales. You will also be dealing with returns, exchanges, allowances, sales tax, and shipping charges.

■ Cash Sales

A cash sale is a transaction in which the customer pays for the purchase with cash or a check. The simplest sale occurs when the customer pays in cash. The cashier records the transaction on the register, gives the customer change and a receipt, and wraps the purchase.

Each business has rules about accepting checks, and you will have to learn the policy of your company or store. When a customer writes a check, you may need to verify his or her identity by requesting a driver's license and another form of identification.

Some math is necessary when preparing handwritten sales checks. The five steps of this process are shown in Figure 16-3 on page 280. Occasionally, you will not be given a unit price, and it is necessary to calculate it on your own. This occurs when items are sold in multiple quantities, such as three pairs of stockings for $12. To find the selling price of one item in an instance like this, you divide the price instead of multiplying it. One pair of stockings in this example would be $4 ($12 ÷ 3).

When the division is uneven, any fractional amount is charged to the customer. The price of one pair of stockings when three pairs are $10.99 is calculated as follows: $10.99 ÷ 3 = $3.663 or $3.67.

• What You'll Learn

- The various types of sales transactions
- The math calculations necessary to fill out sales checks

• Why It's Important

Although cash is used for payment in many transactions, an ever-greater proportion of sales involves the use of a debit card or a credit card. Understanding how to handle such sales will be necessary on many sales jobs, and this section explains how it is done.

Key Terms

- cash sale
- debit card
- floor limit
- layaway
- on-approval sale
- cash on delivery (COD) sale
- return
- exchange
- allowance
- sales tax
- parcel post

PRACTICE 2

Do the sales calculations indicated below.

1. Calculate the amount for each item by multiplying the unit price times the quantity purchased.

Dept.	Quantity	Item	Unit Price
12	10	Vests	$85.00
16	5	Footballs	$15.95
18	11	Clocks	$26.50
21	20	Irons	$39.95

2. If all of the above items were part of a single purchase, what would be the merchandise total?
3. Determine the price for one can of soda when a six-pack sells for $2.17.
4. Determine the price for two rolls of film when three rolls sell for $12.25.

FIGURE 16-3

Sales Check—Multiple Purchases

Step 1—Multiply unit price times quantity for each item and extend the amounts to the last column. Remember that the last two digits on the right are cents. Place a decimal point to their left, or enter them to the right of the vertical line dividing the last column into two unequal parts.

Step 2—Add item amounts to arrive at a merchandise subtotal. Enter this figure on the appropriate line.

Step 3—Calculate sales tax or look it up in a tax table. Sales tax must be paid by the buyer on all retail sales. It is calculated as a percentage of the merchandise subtotal. In most states, food and prescription medicine are exempt from sales tax, as are shipping charges.

Step 4—Calculate shipping charges. You need to decide if you will use Parcel Post or a specific express mail carrier.

Step 5—Add subtotal, tax, and shipping to get the purchase total. This is the amount the customer will pay.

ODEL'S CAMERA, INC.
1329 Walnut Street • Santa Barbara, CA 93101

NEW CUSTOMER ☐ YES ☐ NO DATE 6/17/--

NAME CASH

COMPANY

ADDRESS

CITY & STATE

PHONE (RESIDENCE) PHONE (OTHER)

SOLD BY TYPE OF SALE

	CASH	CHECK	C.O.D.	CARD TYPE	ACCOUNT	PURCHASE ORDER NO.
		✓				

CODE	QTY	DESCRIPTION	PRICE	AMOUNT	
511	1	MET2 45 CT-4 Flash	325.00	325	00
X	6	Konica 220 Color Film	6.19	37	14
X	12	Kodak 120 B&W Film	2.49	29	88

SPECIAL INSTRUCTIONS

HANDLING	—	—
SUB TOTAL	392	02
TAX	31	36
SHIPPING	15	00
TOTAL AMOUNT	438	38
PAID	438	38
BALANCE	0	00

SHIP VIA:

PAID ON # _____ TC # _____
CC # _____

7932

■ **Multiple Purchase Sales Check** Customers often buy more than one item and more than one unit of each item, which creates a more complicated sales check. *What can you do to ensure that the sales check is correct in the end?*

■ Debit Card Sales

Many businesses offer customers the option of using their automatic teller machine (ATM) cards to purchase products. When a customer uses an ATM card to make a purchase at a store, the card becomes a debit card. This means that the amount of the purchase is debited (or subtracted) from the customer's bank account.

A customer slides his or her ATM card through a device that reads the information from the magnetic strip on the card. After the sale is totaled on the cash register, the cardholder enters his or her *personal identification number (PIN)* into a keypad to authorize the debit. If there is money in the customer's bank account to cover the purchase, the sale is approved electronically. The customer then receives a receipt.

Debit cards provide advantages for both customers and businesses. The business has access to money much sooner than with a check. Customers benefit from not having to carry large amounts of cash or checkbooks. It is also harder for thieves to use a debit card because they can't make a purchase without knowing the cardholder's PIN number.

■ **Debit or Credit** Card readers such as this make it easier and easier to use a credit card to complete retail sales. *Why would retailers want to make it easier for people to use credit cards?*

REAL WORLD MARKETING

Plastic Fantastic

Have you ever polished off a huge meal only to realize that you are just short of money for the bill? That happened to Frank McNamara while dining in Manhattan in 1950. Based on this experience, McNamara created the Diners' Club—the first American credit card. The idea caught on and was followed with more cards, such as American Express, marketed as a benefit to traveling salespeople for use on the road. As credit card mania increased in the 1970s, Congress had to ban such common practices as the mass-mail distribution of active credit cards to individuals who did not request them.

Thinking Critically
Why would Congress want to stop the mass mailing of active credit cards?

■ Credit Sales

Most businesses today accept one or more of the major credit cards, such as Visa, MasterCard, and American Express. Many large oil companies and department stores issue their own cards in addition to accepting the major ones. The goal is to make it easier for the general public to shop. This, of course, increases sales.

In many businesses now, the amount of each credit card sale is electronically deposited to the business's bank account as the sale is made. A combination credit card sales check and receipt is issued by the cash register. With this procedure, the credit card company is able to deduct its service charge from the store's bank account immediately. The store normally has access to its funds the next day. This is much faster than if credit card sales checks had to be delivered to a bank.

GETTING CREDIT AUTHORIZATIONS Credit cards have become an efficient, popular alternative to more traditional forms of payment. Some people, however, abuse the privilege of using a credit card by charging more than they can pay. Thus, many

businesses (especially retail stores) have a set limit on credit card charges. The floor limit is the maximum amount a salesperson may allow a customer to charge without getting special authorization. Usually, the manager or someone in the credit department must approve charges that exceed the floor limit.

To confirm that a customer has been approved to charge the amount of a sale, most businesses use electronic credit authorizers. Many POS systems, in fact, include an integrated credit authorizer. Other electronic credit authorizers are separate pieces of equipment. These devices, smaller than a telephone, read data encoded on credit cards. The sales clerk inputs the amount of the sale into the device. The data is transmitted to a computer, which offers approval or disapproval in less than a minute.

Companies that do not use electronic credit authorizers obtain approval of charges in other ways. With a major credit card, for example, you may wait while a salesperson calls a central authorization telephone number for approval of charges. The salesperson may also look for your credit card number on a list of delinquent account numbers.

Get Smart!

Everyone is familiar with ATM and credit cards, but are you familiar with smart cards? By the year 2010, smart cards are likely to be as familiar as paper money—and maybe even more common. While they have been popular in Europe and Asia since their invention in France 25 years ago, smart cards are gaining momentum the United States.

Although smart cards look like credit or debit cards, there is a big difference. Credit and debit cards have a magnetic strip with identifying information, while smart cards have computer chips embedded in the plastic. What this means is that a smart card is much more closely related to your personal computer than to your regular VISA card. The tiny microchips embedded in the plastic of a smart card are electronics capable of memory and processing.

The simplest cards have a dollar value attached to them, and the chip records the amount spent and the balance after every purchase. With a more powerful chip, a smart card can be used to download money from a customer's bank account directly into the card's memory. Instead of getting cash from a machine, you "fill up" your card by inserting it into a card reader on a computer or specially equipped phone. Then it can be used like cash to shop in stores or to pay bills over the telephone. The card stores the account information, which you can download into your computer later. Smart cards can also be used for payment of telephone calls, payment of parking and tolls, storage of identification and medical records, and access to satellite television. The use of smart cards addresses many security issues that people have regarding using their credit cards or debit cards when shopping online. Because the smart card stores account information on a computer chip rather than through an account number embossed on a card, it is much more secure from theft.

In 2000, Visa U.S.A. introduced the first smart credit card, which combines the purchasing power of traditional payment cards with smart chip technology. With the growth in e-commerce, technologically enhanced payment products such as the smart credit card will meet the evolving needs of consumers for greater convenience and control over their account information.

Case Study Review

1. Why would online marketers be interested in increasing customer security?
2. How would it benefit banks to have people use smart cards rather than write checks or use cash?

A MATTER OF ETHICS

3. Some smart cards allow marketers to collect data about the customer's spending habits. What ethical concerns does this bring up?

Credit card sales slip (General Credit Forms, St. Louis 63045):

DEBORAH MURCHAK
4322 WENONA RD.
EVERETT, WA 98208
3770-494965-01001

QTY.	CLASS	DESCRIPTION	PRICE	AMOUNT
1	G	Shawl	69.00	69 00
2	B	Gloves	23.99	47 98
2	D	Stocking caps	12.98	25 96

DATE 11/8/-- AUTHORIZATION K-111023 SUB TOTAL 142 94
REFERENCE NO. REG./DEPT. 2 TAX 9 29
FOLIO/CHECK NO. SERVER/CLERK 12A TIP / MISC. — —
MasterCard OR VISA 5827410 TOTAL 152 23

CUSTOMER SIGNATURE X Deborah Murchak

The issuer of the card identified on this item is authorized to pay the amount shown as TOTAL upon proper presentation. I promise to pay such TOTAL (together with any other charges due thereon) subject to and in accordance with the agreement governing the use of such card.

DO NOT CIRCLE EXPIRATION DATE — USE BOX BELOW — THESE AMOUNTS MUST AGREE

EXPIRATION [X] DATE CHECKED

DO NOT WRITE ABOVE THIS LINE

MERCHANT COPY   SPLIT CARBONS HELP PREVENT FRAUD

SNAP HERE DISCARD CARBONS   SPLIT CARBONS PREVENT FRAUD   SNAP

■ **Credit Card Slip** A credit card slip provides information not usually seen on a cash sales check or receipt. *What is that information?*

RECORDING SALES As a salesperson in retail business, you will probably sell merchandise to customers who want to charge their purchases on a credit card. In this case, you will have to know how to complete credit card sales checks. This is not very difficult, since the math calculations are identical to those for a cash transaction.

There are usually at least three copies of each sales check—one for the customer, one for the seller, and one for the bank or credit card agency. You might use a mechanical imprinter to transfer the customer's name and account number to the sales slip, or you might write the information on the sales check by hand.

Some businesses do not use credit card sales checks at all, but instead record all necessary information electronically. Electronic recording of credit card sales is becoming more common.

OBTAINING PAYMENT Credit card sales checks for charges to bank cards (VISA, MasterCard, etc.) may be deposited when you deposit checks in your company account. A special deposit slip must be prepared for the bank so that your accounts are credited quickly.

Copies of sales checks for travel and entertainment cards and oil company credit cards are sent for payment to the company that originated them. It takes longer to turn these charges into cash.

If your company accepts credit cards, it pays a fee to the bank or agency that handles the billing and record keeping. This fee is a percent of credit sales based on a sliding scale. Suppose your store had VISA sales of $100,000 during the same period that another store had VISA sales of only $2,000. Your company would pay a smaller percentage for handling. The handling fee for travel and entertainment cards is usually slightly higher than for bank cards.

PRACTICE 3

Calculate the impact credit card fees would have on the business described below.

1. At Rachel's Gifts, VISA sales are usually between $13,000 and $15,000 per month. The VISA handling charge for $10,000–$14,999 is 3 percent of sales; for $15,000–$19,999, 2.5 percent; and for $20,000–$29,999, 2 percent.

   a. Rachel had $15,500 in VISA sales one month. How much more would she net than if sales were $14,300?

   b. How much would Rachel net in that month if her shop did $21,000 in VISA sales?

2. Rachel has decided to accept the Diner's Club card in her shop. The handling charges are 1 percent higher than for VISA at each sales level. If Rachel had $21,000 in Diner's Club sales, how much more would she pay in handling fees than she does for VISA sales?

3. Rachel had $13,600 in cash sales, $14,800 in Diner's Club sales, and $15,200 in VISA sales one month. What were her net sales after handling charges?

Layaway Sales

Merchandise is removed from stock and kept in a separate storage area until the customer pays for it with layaway, or will-call. Layaway appeals to many shoppers and increases sales. The customer will make a deposit on the merchandise and agree to pay for the purchase within a certain time period. The customer may have the merchandise when it is fully paid for; if it is not paid for within the agreed-upon time, the goods are returned to stock. Any money paid need not be returned to the customer.

On-Approval Sales

Some department and specialty stores extend a special privilege to their regular customers —on-approval sale. This agreement permits a customer to take merchandise (usually clothing) home for further consideration. If the goods are not returned within an agreed-upon time, the sale is final. The customer must then send a check or return to the store to pay for the merchandise. Credit card information may be taken from the customer so that the sale can be processed if the customer keeps the item. This practice is a safe way for retailers to handle on-approval sales because there is much less risk involved.

COD Sales

A cash on delivery (COD) sale is a transaction that occurs when a customer pays for merchandise at the time of delivery. Because the customer must be on hand when the merchandise is delivered, however, COD sales are not as efficient as other types of sales transactions.

Returns, Exchanges, and Allowances

A return is merchandise brought back for a cash refund or credit. Gifts that do not suit the recipient's taste are one of the most common categories of returns.

An exchange is merchandise brought back to be replaced by other merchandise. Items of clothing that are the wrong size or color are commonly exchanged.

An allowance is a partial return of the sale price for merchandise that the customer has kept. These are usually given when there is a defect in the merchandise, such as a missing button.

Each of these situations will require you to do a different type of sales transaction. Some businesses adopt a policy of no returns; however, most feel that accepting returns is an important part of good customer relations. Some businesses accept returns

FIGURE 16-4

Refund Slip

Nicky's Dress Shop

REFUND SLIP

STORE NO.	DATE	ITEM RETURNED	AMOUNT	
	10/20/--	DRESS	89	90

NAME	Deborah Murchak		
ADDRESS	4322 Wenona Rd.		
CITY & STATE	Everett, WA 98208		
TELEPHONE NO.	206-882-0252	TAX	5	84
CUSTOMER'S SIGNATURE	Deborah Murchak	TOTAL AMOUNT	95	74
EMPLOYEE NO. 12A	AUTHORIZED BY K. Allen	REASON FOR RETURN Too small	

No refunds after 30 days; No refunds without receipt.

■ **Refund Slip** Most businesses give customer refunds or exchanges under certain circumstances. *Why would the store insist the customer have a sales receipt before giving a refund?*

Electronic Frontiers

Fly with the Web

In the "new economy," the nation's airlines are facing more and more competition as Web-based airline ticket brokers, such as Travelocity.com, Expedia.com, and Priceline.com, sell discounted airline tickets online. Airlines have realized that they need to hit the Web to stay competitive. Loyalty marketing programs offering incentives to frequent flyers have become widespread. Many airlines regularly send out e-mails about special fares and sales to frequent fliers and loyal customers. Many airlines now also offer last minute deals, or e-savers, which are fights that customers can book online at discounted prices only days before flying!

Thinking Critically

How can airlines benefit from offering discounts or mileage to customers who book online?

but issue credit slips that can be used to pay for other merchandise purchased from the same business instead of a cash refund.

Most businesses are happy to make exchanges because they want their customers to be satisfied. Transactions that involve returning an item for a replacement that is priced the same is an even exchange; if not, it is an uneven exchange.

Suppose Nigel decides he needs a calculator for his personal use but wants a less expensive one than he was given for his birthday. The original calculator was priced at $90 (excluding sales tax), and Nigel wants to exchange it for one priced at $60. You would refund the difference, $30, plus the sales tax on $30. The procedure would be reversed for a customer who wants to exchange an item for one that is more expensive. The customer would pay the extra cost of the exchanged item and the extra sales tax on that amount.

Consider how a sales check is prepared. Each item is not taxed individually in multiple purchases; instead the subtotal is used to calculate the sales tax. When looking at the sales check, simply find the item being returned, calculate the difference between that item and the item the customer is taking in exchange for the item returned, and tax the difference between the two amounts. The customer already paid tax on the original item. The tax due is on the difference between the two items and is paid by the customer if the customer wants a more expensive item or by the store if the customer wants a less expensive item.

When you refund cash to a customer on a return or an exchange, you will probably have to fill out a refund slip. One of these is shown in Figure 16-4 on page 284.

■ Sales Tax

A sales tax is a fee placed on the sale of goods and services. These rates differ from state to state and combine local and state charges. Local sales and use taxes in addition to the state tax cannot exceed 2 percent. The state tax rate in Texas is 6.25 percent, making the highest possible tax rate 8.25 percent in Texas.

Sales tax is only paid once by the final user; in other words, it does not apply to goods bought for resale. Customers handle the costs of sales taxes. Problems arise with this because the sales tax is *regressive*, meaning that there is a flat rate to be paid by all income levels. It is more of a challenge for a lower-income individual to pay this fee than for someone who makes a higher salary. Sometimes certain items, such as food, clothing, or drugs, may be exempt from sales tax for this reason.

New challenges have developed with the sales tax with the rise in e-commerce. The Federal Commission on Electronic Commerce was created by the Internet Tax Freedom Act of 1998. This limits new laws taxing Internet access and sets standards for taxes for online purchases.

PRACTICE 4

1. Assuming a sales tax rate of 6 percent, find the tax and total amount due for each purchase listed below. Round the tax to the nearest cent.

Item	Price
Tires	$315
Ski Boots	$185
Clock	$105
Books	$110
Washer	$429

■ Shipping Charges

Most retailers use the United Parcel Service (UPS), Federal Express, or the U.S. Postal Service to deliver merchandise. Because delivery charges are generally exempt from sales tax, they are added after the sales tax has been calculated.

PARCEL POST The cost of shipping merchandise depends on the service used, the weight of the shipment, and the distance it is being sent. Parcel post is one type of standard surface package delivery that is offered by the U.S. Postal Service. Parcel post is a good option if you take your packages to the post office and your customer is willing to wait for delivery.

When you ship COD, the postal carrier will collect the amount due and forward it to your company. Your company must prepay the shipping charges; however, the amount due to the customer may include both the totals for merchandise and shipping costs. The customer must pay a fee for the COD service, which varies depending on the amount collected. Up to $500 may be collected on delivery by a postal carrier.

Many businesses prefer using United Parcel Service for COD shipments. This is because UPS does not limit the amount that can be collected at delivery to $500 and the shipping charges do not have to be prepaid.

EXPRESS MAIL When you need to ship something fast, you may use the express mail service provided by the U.S. Postal Service. This faster delivery service, of course, costs more. A number of private parcel carriers also provide such service. They include Federal Express, UPS, Airborne Express, DHL Worldwide Express, and Emery Worldwide Courier.

All of these private package delivery companies compete vigorously with each other and with the U.S. Postal Service for the overnight delivery market. This market is extremely competitive, and the various package delivery firms try to outdo each other in regard to price, pickup and delivery time and speed, tracking technology, and customer service.

> ### PRACTICE 5
>
> How much will be returned to or paid by the customer in each of the following cases? Assume a sales tax rate of 7 percent.
>
> 1. Mrs. Smith returned a $150 dress that was too large and selected a smaller size in another style priced at $115. How much will you return to her?
>
> 2. Mr. Jordan returned a $45 radio because it was apparently defective. He selected another model priced at $75. How much more will you charge him?

BRIGHT IDEAS
The Incorruptible Cashier

Cash registers are commonplace in most businesses, from large retail stores and neighborhood ice cream shops; but, it wasn't always this way. James Ritty invented the first mechanical cashier in 1884, receiving a patent under his company name of National Manufacturing. That same year, John H. Patterson recognized that Ritty's invention provided security and saved time. He bought out Ritty and the patent rights, then launched the National Cash Register Company (NCR) to manufacture and sell cash registers. The invention—nicknamed the "Incorruptible Cashier"— came complete with the familiar bell ringing referred to in advertising as "The Bell Heard Round the World". Patterson improved upon the patent by attaching a paper roll that kept track of transactions. In 1906, an electronic motor was added to the cash register to increase efficiency.

Thinking Creatively
The "Incorruptible Cashier" was revered for time saving and security. How might employers screen applicants to be able to meet their security needs?

Answers to Practice Sets

PRACTICE 1 (PAGE 276)

1. Four pennies, a dime, a quarter, two $1 bills (or a $2 bill), a $5 bill, and a $20 bill. Note: If customer has the penny (for the $.61), then a nickel could substitute for the four pennies.

2. Ask if customer has $.09 in change or at least a dime.

3. By disregarding the exact change provided, the cashier is less likely to get confused. Disregard the $.15 and simply say "That's $27 out of $40; $28, $29, $30 (giving back three $1 bills, one at a time); and $40 (giving back $10).

4. "That's $13.63 out of $20.75; $.64, $.65 (handing off two pennies), $.75 (handing a dime)"; then say, "That leaves $13 out of $20; $14, $15 (handing off two $1 bills), and $20 (handing off a $5 bill)." By tendering the $.75, the customer reduces the amount of small change to be returned to him.

PRACTICE 2 (PAGE 279)

1. Vests $850; footballs $79.75; clocks $291.50; irons $799

2. $2,020.25

3. $.37

4. $8.17

PRACTICE 3 (PAGE 283)

1. a. $1,241.50

   b. $20,580

2. $210

3. $42,628

PRACTICE 4 (PAGE 285)

1. Tires $333.90; boots $196.10; clock $111.30; books $116.60; washer $454.74

PRACTICE 5 (PAGE 286)

1. $37.45

2. $32.10

16.2 ASSESSMENT

Reviewing Key Terms and Concepts

1. How is a credit card sale different from a debit card sale? A will-call sale? An on-approval sale?

2. What is the difference between a return and exchange?

3. Kim is considering the purchase of a new guitar for $950, plus $24 shipping. The state sales tax is 8 percent. How would Kim go about figuring the total purchase amount?

Thinking Critically

4. People have suggested that as more buyers use debit cards, checks will become obsolete. Do you think this is likely? Why or why not?

Integrating Academic Skills

5. **MATH** A department store offers a 20 percent discount to senior citizens. If your grandmother purchased items at $17.99, $15.95, and $3.59, what would be her total bill, assuming the sales tax rate is five percent?

Purchase Orders and Invoices

Business-to-Business Sales

• What You'll Learn

- To calculate and verify extensions on purchase orders and invoices
- To use appropriate tables to determine shipping charges

• Why It's Important

In this section, you will learn some math applications that are regularly used by buyers and vendors. In many marketing jobs, including sales, you will need to understand the costs and methods of shipping.

Key Terms

- purchase order
- extension
- invoice

Much of the math that a buyer does in business-to-business sales is for purchase orders; for vendors, the comparable form is the invoice. The calculations for both forms are very similar to those performed by retail salespeople on sales checks.

■ Purchase Orders

To place an order, most companies prepare a purchase order (PO), a legal contract between the buyer and the supplier. The PO lists the quantity, price, and description of the products ordered, along with the terms of payment and delivery. In Figure 16-5 on page 289, notice the information routinely included in a purchase order:

- *Item number*—the vendor's catalog designation that identifies the merchandise being ordered
- *Quantity*—the number of units ordered
- *Description*—what is being ordered
- *Unit*—how the item is packaged and priced (individually, by the dozen, by the ream, etc.)
- *Unit cost*—the price per unit
- *Total*—the extension, or result of multiplying the number of units by the cost per unit

Note that if you order several items on the same purchase order, the total of all extensions is entered at the bottom of the Total column. This amount is used to compute any sales tax.

■ Invoices

When filling an order based on a PO, a vendor will include an invoice with the delivered merchandise. The invoice in Figure 16-6 on page 290 uses check marks to indicate that the information has been checked for accuracy. The invoice numbers and amounts are correct when they match the PO and other documents, as are the extensions.

Notice the entries at the bottom of the invoice. In addition to the merchandise total (or subtotal), there are also places for sales tax, shipping charges, and the amount to be paid by the customer.

In Figure 16-6, Mountain-Air pays the tax because its purchases are clearly intended for business purposes; if it purchased ten bikes for resale, however, there would be no sales tax entry. The sales tax would be paid by the customers.

Regardless of the nature of its purchases, Mountain-Air is entitled to take advantage of the specified payment terms (2/10, N30). Note, however, that discounts apply only to merchandise—shipping charges are not discounted.

FIGURE 16-5

Purchase Order

Mountain-Air Bicycle Shop

			PURCHASE ORDER NUMBER: 1004			

Invoice and ship to:
Mountain-Air Bicycle Shop
123 State Street
Van Nuys, CA 91423

DATE: Oct. 15, 20 - -

Vendor:
Channel Paper Distributors
436 Ocean Avenue
Mission Hills, CA 91345

ITEM NO.	QUANTITY	DESCRIPTION	UNIT	UNIT COST	TOTAL
K2007	10	Photocopy paper	500	$ 5.16	$ 51.60
K94	2	Calculators	ea.	19.95	39.90
J411	15	Binders	ea.	11.75	176.25

TOTAL AMOUNT:	$ 267.75
TAX	22.09
TOTAL DUE:	$ 289.84

■ **Purchase Order** A purchase order is a legal contract between buyer and seller. *How would you determine the extension cost of an item from its unit cost?*

■ Dating Terms

Dating terms state when a bill must be paid and the discount permitted for paying early. Ordinary dating occurs when the dating terms are based on the invoice date. Consider, for example, ordinary dating of 2/10, net 30. It specifies the percent of discount permitted for paying early (2 percent), the number of days the buyer has to take advantage of the discount (10 days), and the number of days within which the invoice must be paid (30 days).

■ Shipping

Part of the selling arrangement negotiated between the buyer and seller involves delivery—specifically who will pay and when change of title (ownership) will take place. Both of those issues are part of the agreement between the buyer and seller in business-to-business sales.

The terms for delivery are all variations of F.O.B. (free on board). There are four options:

- *F.O.B. destination*—The title or ownership of the goods remains with the seller until the goods reach their destination. The seller pays transportation charges and is responsible for the condition of the goods until they arrive to the buyer.
- *F.O.B. shipping point*—The buyer pays the shipping costs and is responsible for losses for damages that occur in transit.
- *F.O.B. factory freight prepaid*—The goods become the buyer's property. However, the seller pays for shipping.
- *F.O.B. destination charges reversed*—The merchandise becomes the buyer's when goods are received. The buyer pays for transportation, but if the goods are lost or damaged in transit, the buyer's investment is protected.

FIGURE 16-6

Invoice

CHANNEL PAPER DISTRIBUTORS

SOLD TO: Mountain-Air Bicycle Shop
123 State Street
Van Nuys, CA 91423

INVOICE NO: K5005
DATE: Oct. 24, 20 - -

YOUR ORDER NO.	DATE SHIPPED	SHIPPED VIA	FOB	TERMS
1004	10/24/- -	UPS	M. HILLS	2/10, N30

ITEM NO.	QUANTITY	DESCRIPTION	UNIT	UNIT COST	TOTAL
K2007 ✓	10 ✓	Photocopy paper ✓	500	$ 5.16 ✓	$ 51.60 ✓
K94 ✓	2 ✓	Calculators ✓	ea.	19.95 ✓	39.90 ✓
J411 ✓	15 ✓	Binders ✓	ea.	11.75 ✓	176.25 ✓

TOTAL AMOUNT:	$ 267.75 ✓
TAX	22.09 ✓
UPS	14.22 ✓
TOTAL:	$ 304.06 ✓

■ **Invoices** The vendor (seller) prepares an invoice based on the buyer's purchase order. *What categories of information does an invoice include that are missing from a purchase order?*

16.3 ASSESSMENT

Reviewing Key Terms and Concepts

1. Who prepares a purchase order?
2. A customer orders six triple packs of adhesive tape at $1.79 each—6 × $1.79 on your invoice. What term describes this calculation?
3. What is the meaning of the letters F.O.B. in terms of delivery?

Thinking Critically

4. How could using a computer to generate invoices save time?

Integrating Academic Skills

5. **COMMUNICATION** You are the buyer for a men's retail clothing store. There have been repeated requests for a certain brand of trousers, but your manager doesn't like doing business with the company that makes them. Use your word processing program to write a memo to your manager describing the increased sales that would result if you were allowed to buy these trousers.

Careers in Marketing

FOOD MARKETING

Danielle Ellis
Cashier
Fresh Fields

What does your job entail?

"I handle money—ringing up groceries, making change, and processing credit and debit cards. I must always greet customers with a smile and ensure customer satisfaction. In the year that I have worked here, I have mastered the register, which is especially important during the 'crunch times.' Saturdays, Sundays, and Mondays are our busiest days, and with the number of people that we have coming through the lines, things can get crazy. It is necessary to keep your focus. I also have to be comfortable handling the customer service desk and bagging groceries when we are short-staffed."

What kind of training did you have?

"I started working here bagging groceries for customers. I volunteered often, which helped me learn the skills required for working as a cashier. I also showed enthusiasm and learned all of the codes for the register on my spare time. When it came my time to train as a cashier, my supervisors found that I didn't need much training at all."

What skills are most important?

"Two of the most important skills to my job are math and problem solving. When things are hectic, you must concentrate on the numbers and make sure you give out the right change. There are also times when a customer might disagree with a price on a certain item and you have to make sure that they don't think that you don't know how to do your job."

What is your key to success?

"The secret to my success is 'the customer is always right, even when they are wrong.' You have to be strong and handle rude comments when they come your way. You encounter many different customers every day, which can be draining. Despite that, working here is a wonderful experience because while you occasionally encounter mean people, you also work with some truly wonderful people."

Thinking Critically
How might technology affect those who work as cashiers?

Career Facts

Education and Training: Employers prefer high school graduates with experience in cash handling and clerical skills. Recommended courses include marketing, business math, accounting, data processing and communication. Training on the job is usually informal, but some employers may have established programs; vocational schools also provide formal training.

Aptitudes, Abilities, and Skills: Good arithmetic skills, ability to work well with the public, a friendly personality, and appropriate hand-eye coordination skills are a must. Cashiering involves standing for long hours in a confined area and performing repetitive tasks.

Career Outlook: The outlook is expected to be average through the year 2006. Jobs will be affected by technological changes, including online shopping and self check-out equipment.

Career Path: Many cashiers begin working at lower-level jobs, stocking shelves or carrying groceries, or working part-time while attending school. Cashiers may be promoted to supervisory positions, or with further education, to management positions.

VOCABULARY REVIEW

Study each pair of terms and then, in your own words, tell how they are related to each other.

- UPC—UVM code
- till—opening cash fund
- layaway—will-call
- sales transaction—exchange
- cash sale—personal check
- debit card—PIN
- credit sale—floor limit
- return—allowance
- on-approval sale—COD sale
- purchase order—invoice

FACT AND IDEA REVIEW

1. What information does a cash register provide about a sale? (16.1)

2. List the three methods of entering information into electronic cash registers. (16.1)

3. What is a UPC? (16.1)

4. What two factors are important to the customer about the way you make change? (16.1)

5. When a customer pays for a purchase by check, what else is he or she usually asked to supply? (16.2)

6. How is an ATM card used as a debit card? (16.2)

7. What is an electronic credit authorizer? (16.2)

8. What items are usually exempt from sales tax? (16.2)

9. What information is usually listed on a purchase order? (16.3)

10. What are dating terms? (16.3)

THINKING CRITICALLY

1. Why would a store want a list of all its customers' names and addresses?

2. How could having a POS system make taking inventory easier?

3. How do you think a no-return policy would affect sales in a store?

4. A gas station allows customers to pay for gas using debit or credit cards. Customers pump their own gas and use an electronic pay point near the pump to pay. They never directly interact with a station employee. What advantages and disadvantages might there be to allowing customers to complete sales without help?

5. Some businesses use combination purchase order/invoice forms. What advantages would there be to this?

BUILDING WORKPLACE SKILLS

1. **Human Relations** You work as a cashier, and today has been exceptionally busy. You give change to a woman for a $10 bill. She claims she gave you a $20 bill. Unfortunately, you neglected to leave the bill out while making change. How would you handle this situation?

2. **Technology** You work as a cashier in a children's clothing store where an old-fashioned cash register requires entering the amount of each sale by hand. The owner of the store has asked you to research what POS systems would be appropriate for the store and how much these systems cost. Use the Internet to do this research. Then use your word processing program to prepare a report.

APPLYING MARKETING CONCEPTS

1. **Researching Optical Scanners** Use the Internet to research information on grocery store conversion to optical scanners. Use a word processor to write a report that describes how the increased speed and accuracy of these systems affect a grocery store's profits.

2. **Understanding UPC Codes** Use the World Wide Web to research what the bars and numbers in a UPC represent. Prepare an oral report using presentation software to present your findings to the class.

3. **Preventing Profit Loss** Discuss the ways that a store manager might train employees to prevent loss through credit card fraud, bad checks, and counterfeit currency. Use presentation software to prepare an oral report on this topic.

4. **Comparing Purchase Order and Invoice Forms** Ask several local businesses for copies of their purchase orders and invoice forms. Use a spreadsheet program to compare the formats based on ease of use.

5. **Comparing Sales Tax Rates** Choose five different states and research the sales tax rates that are applied there. See if you can find any states that don't have any sales tax. Create a chart using a spreadsheet program comparing these rates.

LINKING SCHOOL TO WORK

Basic and Thinking Skills Inquire about the payment methods customers prefer at local businesses. Specifically, try to determine what percentage of customers use cash, debit cards, personal checks, and credit cards. Compare your findings with other class members, and discuss why you think different payment methods are used depending on the type of business.

THE **DECA** CONNECTION

Role Play: Cashier

Situation You are to assume the role of newly hired cashier at a music and video store. Your job will include completing sales using cash, checks, and credit and debit cards.

Activity You must demonstrate to the store manager (judge) that you are competent at accurately completing transactions. Assume a customer purchased a DVD movie for $29.95 and there is a 6% sales tax on that item.

Evaluation You will be evaluated on how well you meet the following performance indicators:
- Calculate charges
- Process sales documentation
- Prepare simple written reports

inter NET CONNECTION

Selling Online
You are in charge of setting up the retail sales end of your company's Web site.

Connect
- Research the ease of buying and customer privacy protection at a variety of popular e-tailers.
- Select the company with the most customer-friendly procedure.
- Write a report detailing your findings, focusing on the strategies you thought were the most successful.

The Zazz Lab

A Sports and Entertainment Marketing Simulation

WELCOME

Welcome to Zazz Sports and Entertainment Marketing Company. Zazz is devoted to serving the needs of its clients who include college, university, and professional sports teams, professional athletes, sporting events, and sports arenas plus major consumer product corporations, as well as television networks and movie studios. As an intern, you will have the opportunity to work on different clients' projects. All of your work will be assigned and reviewed by your department supervisor.

SPONSOR A NASCAR DRIVER

SITUATION

Jose Ramirez, a professional race car driver involved with NASCAR, is one of Zazz's newest clients. Your job is to secure a primary sponsor or several companies that will sponsor the Jose Ramirez Car. NASCAR hopes to attract new spectators and Hispanic fans with this outgoing, charismatic, bilingual race car driver.

ASSIGNMENT

Your challenge is to raise a minimum of $1 million for the new client, the cost for him to race in this year's racing series. Jose will be driving a Ford Taurus as a member of the Tony Pessolano Race Team. You can sell space on any part of the driver's suit, pit crew's uniforms, or auto (hood, dashboard, spoiler, doors, front fender, rear quarter panels). You can also sell sponsored merchandise and arrange personal service contracts, including retail point-of-purchase material, TV commercials, or public appearances. Sponsors must be category exclusive (you cannot sell McDonald's and Burger King sponsorships on the same car) and must represent different categories of goods and services.

Your supervisor wants you to develop a sales training manual with a Ramirez-specific feature-benefit table and script for telephone solicitation of potential

sponsors. Additionally, you have been asked to generate a list of potential sponsorship leads, taking into consideration the demographics of Jose's and NASCAR's fan base. To demonstrate your selling skills, your supervisor expects you to role play your complete sales presentation. Use your sales training manual as the basis of the role play and incorporate a computer presentation.

Tools and Resources

To complete this assignment you will need to conduct research at a library or on the Internet. You will also need a word processing program, a spreadsheet program, and presentation software. Helpful trade publications include *Brandweek, Advertising Age, Sports Business Journal, Sports Business Daily, Team Marketing Report, Motorsports Sponsor FactBook,* and *National Speed Sport News.*

Research

Research NASCAR drivers, sponsorships, and fans. To generate a list of potential sponsors, research consumer products and companies that target the same market, as well as identify untapped markets. Research sponsorship agreements for other race car drivers so you can develop selling points that you can use to create a feature-benefit chart.

Report

Prepare a written sales training manual, a computer presentation for the sales presentation, and a telephone script to qualify prospects. Use a word processing program to prepare the double-spaced documents. The feature-benefit chart in the sales training manual should be in table format. Arrange your written report around the following headings:

- Plan to generate $1 million
  - Strategy (one sponsor vs. many sponsors)
  - What's for sale?
- Prospecting
  - Rationale for selection of prospects
  - List of suggested leads (minimum of 20)
  - Telephone script for use in qualifying prospects
- Sales training manual
  - Introduction
  - Feature-benefit chart for Jose Ramirez
  - Sample approach dialogue
  - Determining needs
    - Observations that should be made
    - Sample dialogue to demonstrate good listening skills and effective questioning techniques
  - Product presentation
    - Two sample selling sentences
    - Suggested sales aids
    - Demonstration of selling points
    - Involvement of customer in presentation
  - Handling objections
    - Two potential objections
    - Suggested answers to potential objections
  - Closing the sale
    - Suggested closing methods (minimum of two)
    - Sample dialogue to demonstrate closing methods
  - Suggestion selling
    - Suggested products or services
    - Sample dialogue to suggest additional product or service
  - Relationship marketing
    - Suggested follow-up strategies

Using computer presentation software, prepare a presentation of your ideas for the client that includes:
- Key selling points
- Graphic illustrations and/or figures
- Very little text
- A minimum of 10 slides

Presentation and Evaluation

Present your ideas in a written report and an oral presentation. In your oral presentation, conduct a role play that demonstrates how to utilize the telephone script to qualify prospects and a role play for a salesperson calling on a prospective sponsor. You will be evaluated on your selling and oral presentation skills, including:
- Knowledge of motorsports, especially NASCAR
- Demonstration of effective selling techniques
- Ability to communicate with prospects
- Ability to handle questions and objections
- Continuity of presentation
- Voice quality
- Body language and eye contact

Portfolio

Print a copy of your completed report and presentation for your Portfolio.

THE DECA CONNECTION

DECA Business Services Marketing Series
Selling sponsorships for a professional race car driver could be a potential role play in this event.

DECA Marketing Management Series
Developing a sales training plan for the sale of sponsorships could be a role play in this event.

DECA Hospitality and Recreation Marketing Research Event
Researching potential sponsors and developing an effective sales presentation for the sale of sponsorships could be a topic for this event.

DECA Sports and Entertainment Marketing Management Team Decision-Making Event
Working on this project with a partner will make the experience similar to what is expected in a DECA Team Decision-Making Event.

U N I T · 6

Portfolio

The Promotional Plan

Once you have completed this unit, you will select a particular product to promote. Design a promotional plan for the product. Be sure to describe your target audience, product features, and sales appeal as well as your planned promotional and media strategies. Prepare a written report, complete with visuals, to highlight your promotional plan.

Promotion

Unit Overview

Businesses spend large amounts of money annually on promotional activities. In this unit you will learn about promotion and promotional strategies.

Through your exploration of Chapter 17, you will learn the importance of promotional strategies when selling goods and services or developing an image. Chapter 18 explains the importance of visual merchandising and display. Chapter 19 details the different types of advertising media used for product and institutional promotion. Chapter 20 highlights the essential parts of print advertisements and explains how to create effective advertising layouts.

In this Unit:

Foundations of Marketing

○ Professional Development

Functions of Marketing

◤ Promotion

Promotional Concepts and Strategies

Marketing: What It Takes

Attracting Young Professionals

You thought your promotional plan for a new line of baseball hats was exciting, organized, and complete. The manager of the advertising department, however, was not as enthusiastic. He questioned your promotional mix of advertising, sales promotions, and public relations activities to reach young professionals in the city.

WHAT WILL YOU DO?

How will you evaluate this difference of opinions to determine the most effective promotional plan?

The Promotional Mix

The Concept of Promotional Mix

Promotion is any form of communication a business or organization uses to inform, persuade, or remind people about its products. Promotion is also used to improve the public image of an organization.

To achieve promotional goals, it is important to decide on the right promotional mix. Promotional mix is a combination of the different types of promotion. A business decides on the promotional mix that will be most effective in persuading potential customers (wholesalers, retailers, and consumers) to purchase and support its products. The communication process used in promotional activities follows a pattern of first attracting attention, then building interest and desire, and finally asking for action. This communication process is often referred to by the acronym AIDA.

The purpose of any promotion may be directly related to the product or to the image of the business. A business uses product promotion to convince potential customers to buy products instead of buying from a competitor. The business also explains the major features and benefits of its products, identifies where those products are sold, advertises product sales, answers customer questions, and introduces new products.

Institutional promotion is used by a business to create a favorable image for itself, as opposed to promoting a product or service. Businesses may maintain Web sites to provide news, product information, and answers to questions as part of institutional promotion. While institutional promotion does not directly sell a certain product, creating a favorable image may result in increased sales for a company.

■ Types of Promotion

There are four basic types of promotion: personal selling, advertising, sales promotion, and public relations. Each plays a vital role in promoting businesses and their products. Figure 17-1 on page 300 illustrates how the Oscar Mayer Division of the Kraft Foods company uses all four types of promotion.

Advertising, public relations, and sales promotion are forms of non-personal selling—communicating with customers in ways other than through direct contact. Personal selling, on the other hand, requires direct personal contact with the customer.

PERSONAL SELLING Personal selling is one of the largest forms of promotion. It requires individuals to make contact with potential buyers, making it the most expensive form of promotion. Personal selling is designed to complete a sale once a customer is attracted to a business by advertising, sales promotion, or public relations. You learned more about personal selling in Unit 5.

• What You'll Learn

- The role of promotion in marketing
- The concept of promotional mix
- The characteristics of personal selling and advertising
- The nature and scope of publicity

• Why It's Important

Since businesses must continually promote their organizations, products, and policies to gain customer acceptance, you will need to learn successful promotional strategies.

Key Terms

- promotion
- promotional mix
- product promotion
- institutional promotion
- advertising
- sales promotion
- public relations
- publicity
- push policy
- pull policy

FIGURE 17-1
THE CONCEPT OF PROMOTIONAL MIX

Promotion involves a total approach to selling a product. The *Share the Smiles* promotion by Kraft's Oscar Mayer division included advertising, personal selling, sales promotion, and public relations.

Bologna makes me happy up to here!

Cara Owada
our 1998
Talent Search winner!

for the name you trust & the taste they love — Just Whistle!

SALES PROMOTION

Manufacturers frequently provide incentives to both the retailer and the customer to promote sales. Retailers who placed large orders received plush toys to give to customers and to use as gifts in a customer raffle.

PUBLIC RELATIONS

Promotions that benefit the community generate positive publicity toward the company and its products. Customers who donated $1 to Second Harvest National Food Bank received consumer incentives.

ADVERTISING

Oscar Mayer's Weinermobiles advertise Oscar Mayer products in a unique and fun way. Local and national advertising announced the arrival of the Weinermobile and brought large crowds of onlookers.

SELLING

Manufacturer sales representatives convince supermarket owners to support the promotion by purchasing additional quantities of hot dogs, bologna, and bacon products. Shared advertising, consumer promotions, and point-of-purchase displays are designed to boost sales for both the manufacturer and the retailer.

And if you plan to get one, you may want to do it before April 15, 2000. That way, you're sure to get the exact sled you want. You don't want to miss out on the hot new 2001 models. Sleds with unbelievable innovations that you just have to see to believe. Including our all-new Limited Edition sleds with great customized features. Plus you'll find awesome deals on all models you won't want to miss. Just remember to see your dealer and order **ARCTIC CAT** before April 15. Or there may be nothing left to wait for. Call 1-800-3-ARCTIC for a dealer near you or visit www.arctic-cat.com. *What Snowmobiling's All About.*

tread lightly!   See dealer for details. Always wear a helmet and don't drink and ride. ©2000 Arctic Cat Sales Inc., ®™ Trademarks of Arctic Cat Inc., Thief River Falls, MN 56701.
(218) 681-4999. Printed in the U.S.A.

■ **Attention Grabber** Advertising is a form of non-personal presentation and promotion. *How does advertising differ from other forms of promotion?*

REAL WORLD MARKETING

Touchdown!

Football teams aren't the only ones who struggle to score a touchdown during the Superbowl. Advertisers hope to score by spending big money to sell to a huge TV audience. What happened when more than a dozen Internet-based companies spent an average of $2.2 million for 30-second spots during the 1999 Superbowl? Several of the companies ran into financial troubles by fumbling through their cash reserves, and some were forced to close. For example, despite spending $1.6 million on Superbowl advertising in 1999, Epidemic Marketing ran out of capital and left the business market in 2000.

Thinking Critically
How can a business formulate an effective promotional strategy within budget?

ADVERTISING Advertising is any paid form of non-personal presentation and promotion of ideas, goods, or services by an identified sponsor. Advertising can be found everywhere, from magazines and newspapers to television and Web sites. Advertising involves one-way communication, whereas personal selling is communication between seller and buyer. Nationally, businesses spend approximately $200 billion annually on various types of advertising. A more detailed explanation of the various forms and purposes of advertising is given in Chapter 19.

SALES PROMOTION According to the American Marketing Association, sales promotion represents all marketing activities, other than personal selling, advertising, and public relations, that are used to stimulate consumer purchasing and sales effectiveness. The objectives of sales promotions are to increase sales, to inform customers about new products, and to create a positive store or corporate image. Later in this chapter, you will study specific sales promotion activities.

PUBLIC RELATIONS AND PUBLICITY Public relations refers to any activity designed to create a favorable image toward a business, its products, or its policies. Public relations activities and the audiences to which they are targeted will be covered in the last section of this chapter.

Publicity is a specific kind of public relations that involves placing positive and newsworthy information about a business, its products, or its policies in the media. Publicity differs from advertising as a promotional tool because it is free. A one-minute story on the evening news about a company or one of its products costs nothing. Fifteen seconds of advertising time on the same broadcast costs thousands of dollars.

Cost is not the only advantage of publicity. Newspapers, news programs, and news reporters are usually viewed as more objective than advertisers. People are more likely to pay attention to and believe news stories than advertisements. Publicity often appears as a media story, which makes the information appear more credible to many people.

■ **Positive Publicity** Awarding scholarships is one way a company generates good publicity. Here, Best Buy Co., Inc. Divisional Human Resources Manager Daniel Fleischman awards a scholarship to Colin Eide. *Why is this good publicity?*

Click to Win

"You may have already won $100,000,000!" "Just click here to win!" Online promotions represent one of the fastest-growing Internet advertising segments. Nearly ten percent of all Web ads include promotions and sweepstakes. The Gap has offered laptops, and Radio Disney has offered trips to Walt Disney World. One million dollars was offered to loyal customers at Snap.com. Why the increase in Internet advertising? First, it establishes a relationship with the customer. Advertisers know that customers want to return to sites that offer incentives. Second, running a sweepstakes is a method of collecting data. Customers who perceive they may win a grand prize are likely to provide accurate data. In turn, advertisers get a better picture of their customers.

Thinking Critically

What are the benefits of online sweepstakes and promotions?

The disadvantage of publicity is that its content, unlike paid advertising, cannot be controlled by the business. The media selects the content, as well as deciding when and how that content is presented. Negative stories, such as an accident or an unsafe product, are as likely to get publicized as positive stories about company successes or work in the community. Businesses work to generate positive publicity through public relations activities whenever possible.

The principal function of publicity is building an image. Image is the way a business or organization is defined in people's minds. It is an impression based on a combination of factors including physical surroundings, personal experiences, and media exposure. The right kind of publicity can create and maintain a company's positive image. People like to do business with companies that have a respectable and positive image. Some business activities that can be great image-builders include sponsoring cultural events, awarding scholarships, and donating land or equipment for public use.

■ Coordination of Promotional Mix

Most businesses use more than one type of promotion to achieve their promotional goals. The Oscar Mayer division of the Kraft Foods company uses a combination of local and national advertising, personal selling in the form of manufacturer sales representatives, sales promotions, and public relations. This assures them that their product will be widely recognized.

Each type of promotion is designed to complement the other types. Advertising creates awareness of a business's product, while public relations creates a favorable image for the business itself. Sales promotion efforts stimulate sales, reinforce advertising, and support selling efforts. Finally, personal selling builds on all of these previous efforts by helping the individual customer and completing the sale.

All types of promotion must be coordinated. National advertising should be accompanied by local promotional efforts. Many consumer products manufacturers will give or sell retailers decorations

Case Study

Action in the Toy Stores

Bright costumes! Superpowers! X-Treme Sports! When you think of action figures, what comes to mind? Star Wars? X-Men? Pokemon? How about a snowboarding college student? That is exactly what toy makers Hasbro and Mattel want you to think, when you think of action figures!

Even the most popular action figures have short-lived fame. The most successful superheroes of the 1980s—Masters of the Universe, Teenage Mutant Ninja Turtles, and Power Rangers—had great initial popularity but faded quickly.

Research shows that boys age two to five fantasize about Batman-like heroes; by age six, however, they focus on more realistic heroes. In an attempt to capitalize on these results, Mattel, Inc., and Hasbro are shaping new products for development.

Mattel's *Action Man* and Hasbro's *Max Steel* action figures rely on less fantasy and are designed to be more "real." Competing for the same target market, each company hopes to generate sales of $100–$150 million, and success will be primarily based upon promotion.

Mattel's *Action Man* will star in a computer-animated TV show on Fox's Kids Network. In addition, the company is sending CD-ROMs with "game missions" to three million boys whose families own computers and have purchased action figures before.

Hasbro's *Max Steel* action figure will have a Saturday morning TV show produced by Sony Pictures and will also be on Time-Warner's Kids WB Network. Mattel is also planning to sponsor extreme sporting events, like snowboarding, around the country.

Case Study Review

1. What are unique challenges to toy companies marketing to this age group?
2. What other promotional strategies would you suggest to the companies to reach this target market?

A MATTER OF ETHICS

3. Is it ethical to use children in marketing research activities? Does your opinion change depending on the toys that are developed? Why or why not?

or in-store displays that promote a national campaign. At the local retail level, the national and local efforts need to be communicated to the store personnel. Sales personnel should be made aware of coupons, rebates, contests, and any other featured promotional tools so that they can encourage customer participation. Sales are lost and customer dissatisfaction is created when advertised products are not available or the sales staff is uninformed about the promotion.

PROMOTIONAL BUDGET In large companies, the marketing department has many roles. It establishes a promotion budget, allocates resources, coordinates the campaign, and determines the right promotional mix for the company. It is important to consider all aspects of promotional activities when designing the promotional budget. Determining the ideal amount for the promotional budget can be difficult because there is no precise way to measure the exact results of spending promotional dollars. Promotional budgeting methods are discussed in further detail in Chapter 19.

THE PUSH-PULL CONCEPT When deciding on a promotional mix, manufacturers often need to develop a promotional mix for each member of the distribution channel. To promote a product to its larger retailers, a manufacturer might want to use a mix of personal selling, advertising (direct mail and/or trade publications), and buying discounts. This type of promotion—known as the push policy of promotion—is used only with the next partner in the distribution channel. It is helpful when a manufacturer is trying to "push" a product through a channel. The main purpose of the promotion is to convince a retailer to stock the products being promoted. A push strategy relies heavily on personal selling and sales promotion, especially at trade shows. It is a helpful strategy for manufacturers of business products and consumer goods that do not have strong brand identity.

The manufacturer *pushes* the product in to the retailer. The same manufacturer might use a different promotional mix of local and national advertising, in-store displays, sales promotions, and public relations to reach consumers. The pull policy directs promotion towards customers. This pull policy of promotion is designed to create consumer interest. Consumer demand can *pull* or encourage retailers to carry the product being promoted. This strategy relies on heavy advertising geared toward consumers, in addition to premiums, samples, and demonstrations.

17.1 ASSESSMENT

Reviewing Key Terms and Concepts

1. What is promotion?
2. Describe the concept of promotional mix.
3. What is the difference between product and institutional promotion?
4. Why is personal selling the most expensive form of promotion?
5. What is the difference between publicity and advertising?

Thinking Critically

6. Some people think that advertising is a waste of money and needlessly raises the prices of goods and services. What do you think? Is the money spent on advertising justified? Provide an argument to support your position.

Integrating Academic Skills

7. **COMMUNICATION** Find stories about local or national companies in a local newspaper. Identify each company and then categorize the publicity in the newspaper as either positive or negative. Support your conclusions in each case with a paragraph or two explaining what the facts are and how the publicity may help or harm the business.

Sales Promotion

Sales Promotion

Sales promotion is a short-term incentive offered to encourage buying a good or service. The purpose of sales promotions is to increase demand and stimulate sales. Sales promotions can be directed toward manufacturers, wholesalers, retailers, and consumers. Sales promotions can also be directed toward a company's employees, encouraging a sales force to sell products aggressively. Sales promotions are usually supported by advertising activities.

Sales promotions may be either trade (business-to-business) oriented or consumer oriented. Let's take a closer look at the different types of promotions.

■ Trade Promotions

Trade promotions are sales promotion activities designed to gain manufacturers', wholesalers', and retailers' support for a product. More money is actually spent on promoting to businesses than to consumers. Major trade promotions include slotting allowances, buying allowances, trade shows and conventions, and sales incentives.

SLOTTING ALLOWANCES A slotting allowance is a cash premium paid by the manufacturer to a retail chain for the costs involved in placing a new product on its shelves. Slotting allowances can range from a few thousand dollars to more than $100,000 per product. In addition to buying space in the store, slotting allowances also pay for a retailer's discount specials on a product, charges for store shelves, penalties for poor sales, and store advertising and display costs.

BUYING ALLOWANCES A buying allowance is a price discount given by manufacturers to wholesalers and retailers to encourage the purchase of a product. It is sometimes used to encourage buying a larger quantity of a product. The price discount results in more money for wholesalers and retailers for each sold product. They are more likely, therefore, to promote the product to customers.

TRADE SHOWS AND CONVENTIONS Trade shows and conventions are designed to reach wholesalers and retailers. They provide businesses with opportunities to introduce new products, encourage increased sales of existing products, and gain continued company and product support.

SALES INCENTIVES Sales incentives are awards given to managers and employees who successfully meet or exceed a sales quota. Such quotas can apply to a specific period of time, such as a month, one-day sale, or a year, or for a particular product or line of products.

What You'll Learn

- The characteristics of sales promotion
- The concept of trade promotions
- The different kinds of consumer sales promotions

Why It's Important

To be successful, a business must continually promote its products. This section introduces you to the concept of sales promotion and to the techniques used to increase sales and inform customers about a company's products.

Key Terms

- sales promotion
- slotting allowance
- sales incentives
- premiums
- incentives
- promotional tie-ins

Business-to-Business Promotion Trade shows and conventions are forms of business-to-business promotion. *What are other examples of trade promotions?*

Sales contests may also be used to provide incentives for a company's own staff or even for a company's channel partners. In the latter case, a manufacturer's distributor may win points for the sales generated for that manufacturer's products. The points may then be redeemed for prizes. Sales incentive awards vary from business to business but may include prizes such as merchandise, travel, or cash.

A manufacturer of housing units might offer its top dealer (distributor) a group travel award to motivate the dealer's sales force. The prize for selling a certain number of housing units could be an all-expense-paid vacation for the entire sales force. On a smaller scale, a distributor's top salesperson may win a weekend getaway for two.

■ Consumer Sales Promotions

Sales promotion efforts designed to encourage customers to buy a product are called consumer promotions. More than half the households in the United States take advantage of sales promotions each year.

Major consumer sales promotion devices include premiums, sponsorships, incentives, product samples, loyalty marketing programs, promotional tie-ins, product placement, and visual merchandising and displays.

PREMIUMS Premiums are low-cost items given to consumers at a discount or for free. They are designed to increase sales by building product loyalty and attracting new customers. They also can persuade nonusers to switch brands.

The fundamental concept behind premium marketing is that people will be more motivated to buy a product when they are offered an "added value" gift in exchange. While viable, worthy

BRIGHT IDEAS

Make Me Up—Before You Go-Go!

Have you ever been on a plane ride that seemed to last forever? How did you feel when you finally reached you destination? Dirty? Tired? Sweaty? Low humidity and poor air circulation in the cabin dry out the skin, making it look chapped and fatigued. Not only is traveling stressful on your body, it is hard on your skin–and cosmetic companies are honing in on that truth! Guerlain, a French cosmetic company, has developed a skin-care line for travelers. Their line, Blue Voyage, includes a moisturizer to be used in-flight and a recovery cream to be used upon arrival. Their packages are designed to not break or spill in transit. So far, the in-flight beauty therapy seems to be very popular with both male and female business travelers. So now, when you are jetlagged, at least you won't look like you are!

Thinking Creatively
What other types of cosmetics would be good for business travelers?

products may sell themselves, the element of competition increases the need for differentiation. While in many instances price is the determining factor in the consumers' decision to purchase a product, a well planned and targeted premium can override price considerations.

Four types of popular consumer premiums are coupons, factory packs, traffic builders, and coupon plans. Let's take a closer look at each of these four types of consumer premiums.

Coupons are certificates which entitle customers to cash discounts on goods or services. Manufacturers use coupons to introduce new products, to enhance the sales of existing products, and to encourage retailers to stock and display both. Coupons reach potential customers through a variety of routes. They are placed on or inside product packages, sent through regular mail, made available on a business's Web site, and printed in newspapers and magazines. Sometimes they are placed by themselves into newspapers as freestanding inserts. Coupons are probably the most popular type of premium.

Factory packs, or *in-packs*, are free gifts placed in product packages, on product packages, or as a container premium. This form of premium is especially popular with cereal manufacturers, who use it to increase their products' appeal to children. The prize in the box of Cracker Jacks is a classic example of an in-pack premium. A container premium is a product container which, when empty, may be used as a container for other items.

Traffic builders are low-cost premiums, such as pens, key chains, and calendars, which are given away free to consumers for visiting a new store or for attending a special event.

Coupon plans are ongoing programs offering a variety of premiums in exchange for labels, coupons, or other tokens from one or more purchases. A customer might send a manufacturer three specific soup can labels in exchange for a recipe book. Available premiums are often shown in special catalogs. A variation of this program is called the part-cash redemption, whereby a customer returns proof-of-purchase seals from a product plus a cash amount in exchange for a gift.

There are costs involved in using premiums. These costs are ultimately paid by the businesses offering them. Stores accepting manufacturers' coupons send them to their company headquarters or to a clearinghouse to be sorted and passed along to redemption centers. The centers, in turn, reimburse the stores for the face value of each coupon plus a handling charge of about eight cents per coupon. They then bill the manufacturers.

SPONSORSHIP Sponsorship has become an integral part of promotion. Sponsorship involves the promotion of a company in association with a property. A property can be a physical site (such as a stadium, hospital, museum, or performing arts center), an event (such as a concert, film festival, or yacht race), or a group (such as a car racing team). The sponsoring company pays a fee for the right to promote itself and its products or services in association with the property. Sponsors often negotiate the right to use a property's logos and termnology on products for retail sale. When a sponsor is a title sponsor, the sponsor pays to have its name incorporated into the name of the sponsored property, such as the Mattel Children's Hospital at the University of California, Los Angeles.

Because sponsorship is a high-profile promotional medium, sponsorship deals must be able to withstand public and media scrutiny. Potential sponsors should do research in advance to determine the level of public acceptance. Sponsorship is measured by changes in awareness and attitude among patrons of the spoonsored property versus the general population.

INCENTIVES Businesses use incentives to promote many products because they create customer excitement and increase sales. Incentives generally are higher-priced products earned and given through contests, sweepstakes, and rebates. Let's take a closer look at each of these types of consumer incentives.

Contests are games or activities that require the participant to demonstrate a skill. This can include writing a short story or essay about a product, naming a new product, or creating a new advertising slogan. Contest winners are awarded such prizes as scholarships, vacations, and money.

■ **A Small Sampling** Product samples are free trial size products sent through the mail. *Why do manufacturers use product samples?*

Sweepstakes are games of chance. One example is customers at fast-food restaurants receiving a game card with or without a purchase. By law in most states, customers cannot be required to make a purchase in order to enter a contest or sweepstakes. Their game card might earn them a small prize or a chance at a bigger prize.

Rebates are discounts offered by manufacturers to customers who purchase an item during a given time period. Auto and household appliance manufacturers frequently use rebates to encourage customers to buy their products.

PRODUCT SAMPLES Another form of consumer sales promotion is the product sample. A product sample is a free trial size of a product sent through the mail, distributed door-to-door, or given away at retail stores and trade shows. Detergents, toothpastes, shampoos, deodorants, and colognes are frequently promoted this way.

Samples are especially important in promoting new products. Drug manufacturers frequently give samples to doctors and dentists to try with their patients. Teachers sometimes receive sample textbooks to encourage them to buy classroom sets.

PROMOTIONAL TIE-INS Promotional tie-ins involve sales promotional arrangements between one or more retailers or manufacturers. They combine their resources (advertising and sales promotional activities) to do a promotion that creates additional sales for each partner. Promotional tie-ins can be complex and involve several companies. An example is the link between McDonald's *Happy Meal*, Disney studios, and Fisher-Price Toddler Toy promotion of the *Goofy* Movie. Successful tie-ins can also be done on a regional, state, or local basis with only a single partner. Tie-ins are designed to stimulate customer response to a product or products offered and combine the resources of each partner in the arrangement.

PRODUCT PLACEMENT When Apple introduced the iMac in 1999, the new computer popped up in television shows from Ally McBeal to the X-Files. This is known as *product placement*. An organization can develop product recognition by making sure that it is featured in special events, on television, or in the movies. One of the most well-known merges for product placement took place between Warner Brothers movie studios and America Online (AOL) for the film "You've Got Mail." The onscreen exposure in this movie is said to have cost AOL between $3 and $6 million. The benefits: Warner Brothers cut down on production costs and created a realistic aspect of the film, and AOL received international film exposure.

The hope is that the strategic placement of an item will increase or enhance the public's knowledge about a particular product. James Bond is known as much for his Rolex watch and BMW as he is for his espionage and fancy footwork. Product placement in movies, television, or on the sports field may reach a wider audience for a reduced cost.

VISUAL MERCHANDISING AND DISPLAYS *Visual merchandising* refers to the coordination of all physical elements in a place of business so that it projects the right image to its customers. *Displays* refer to the visual and artistic aspects of presenting a product to a target group of customers. Window, floor, counter, and other in-store display techniques are all forms of visual merchandising.

By exposing potential customers firsthand to a company's products, visual merchandising stimulates sales and serves as in-store advertising. A complete discussion of visual merchandising and display can be found in Chapter 18.

LOYALTY MARKETING PROGRAMS Loyalty marketing programs, also called frequent buyer programs, reward customers for making multiple purchases. Loyalty marketing was popularized in the 1980s by the airline industry, which instituted frequent flier programs. These programs reward customers with free air travel after accumulating a set amount of paid travel. The hotel industry has adopted similar programs in which consumers can win free lodging after spending a set amount on paid lodging.

Loyalty exists when a customer, because of past experience, is sufficiently satisfied with a particular brand or retailer that he or she buys that brand or from that retailer when the need arises without considering other alternatives. Loyalty marketing offers consumers incentives not to consider other alternatives.

Other industries have adopted loyalty marketing programs. Sears has a program called Kidvantage in which parents are rewarded with discounts after purchasing a certain amount of children's clothing. Online versions of loyalty marketing programs have also become popular. The Internet search engine Yahoo! awards points to Web surfers who buy from certain retailers or visit certain Web sites. Yahoo! has negotiated with the airline industry to allow consumers to convert their points into frequent flier miles.

■ **Frequent Flier** Loyalty marketing programs reward customers for making multiple purchases. *Why would a business institute a loyalty marketing program?*

17.2 ASSESSMENT

Reviewing Key Terms and Concepts

1. Why do businesses use sales promotions?
2. What unique characteristics do sales promotions have?
3. What are trade promotions?
4. What are consumer promotions?
5. Explain the difference between a sweepstakes and a contest.

Thinking Critically

6. Why don't manufacturers who issue coupons simply lower the price of their products to attract customers? What is the value of coupons to such businesses?

Integrating Academic Skills

7. **MATH** Promotional discounts are given to stores by manufacturers to place products in preferred locations or to pay for ads, displays, or in-store demonstrations. Calculate the store's cost to stock the following items and the percentage of the discount given.

Item	Purchase Amount	Discount Amount	Net Cost to Store	Percent Discount
Snowboards	$5,650	$847.50	_____	_____
CD Players	$535	$42.80	_____	_____

Public Relations

• What You'll Learn

- The nature and scope of public relations
- The different audiences for public relations
- The duties of public relations specialists
- How to prepare a news release

• Why It's Important

Public relations is image-building. A company is concerned with how its employees, customers, and the general public (including its stockholders) view it. This section explains how the public relations department of a company fosters goodwill among the public.

Key Terms

- customer advisory boards
- consumer affairs specialists
- community relations
- news release
- press kit
- press conference

The Nature and Scope of Public Relations

Businesses want to present a positive image to their customers, employees, and the general public. Public relations specialists attempt to create goodwill for their companies by creating public relations events. Here are some examples:

- Grand opening of a new mall
- Interview with a company official about hiring plans
- Launch of a new product or product line
- Announcement of employee promotions or retirements
- Presentation of an award to the company or to one of its employees
- Company-sponsored sports event
- Community activity, such as a scholarship program sponsored by the business
- Charitable activity, such as a walkathon for a local charity, in which the business participates
- Cultural activity, such as support for a new exhibit at a museum

The goodwill generated by such public relations events benefits the business in many ways. Well-planned and organized public relations efforts can increase sales, reinforce a good reputation, and increase the willingness of consumers to respond to advertising efforts for the company's products.

■ Customer Relations

Good communication between employees and customers is vital in promoting a favorable business image. Courtesy, helpfulness, interest, tolerance, and friendliness help make customers come back. This repeat business is what makes a company successful.

Many businesses, however, go further than just friendliness and courtesy. They offer special services and amenities in order to maintain good customer relations. These services and amenities might include on-premise restaurants, child-care facilities, gift wrapping, check-cashing services, fax and copying services, and free delivery.

Other public relations efforts are less obvious. Customer advisory boards are panels of consumers who make suggestions about products and businesses. Manufacturers, wholesalers, and retailers use customer advisory boards to test new products. A supermarket might want to learn about customer preferences regarding store hours and preferred cultural or health food products to stock. It may also want to learn whether customers like in-store promotional devices, such as electronic coupons and videocarts. By consulting with an advisory board, the supermarket can adjust or change policies, products, or promotional efforts to meet customers' needs.

Some larger department stores also hire consultants to assist customers with their purchases. Fashion, cosmetic, travel, bridal, and interior decorating consultants, as well as personal shoppers are examples of employees with specialized training who are hired by some retail firms.

National companies often employ consumer affairs specialists to handle customer complaints and to serve as consumer advocates within the firm. Consumer affairs specialists design programs to reflect customer needs for information on topics such as nutrition, health and wellness, and product safety.

■ Employee Relations

Successful businesses have loyal and well-motivated employees who feel they are important to the company. The public relations staff works with management and employees to design programs that foster positive attitudes. Some examples include providing:

- Tuition reimbursement for college courses
- Newsletters for and about the company and its employees
- Recreational programs
- Employee recognition programs for improvements in performance and efficiency

Positive employee relations are necessary for all companies. They are the building block for developing a good reputation—made up of positive public and community relations.

■ Community Relations

Community relations refers to the activities that a business uses to acquire or maintain the respect of the community. Businesses foster good community relations by participating in and sponsoring activities that benefit the civic, social, and cultural life of a community. Some examples of community relations activities include sponsoring Special Olympics, providing mentors for marketing students, and matching employee donations to local charities.

Companies encourage employees to join and remain active in civic organizations, such as the Optimists, Rotary Club, or the Lions. In addition,

GOOD HANDS.

IN AN ERA THAT'S SHORT ON POSITIVE ROLE MODELS, ALLSTATE AGENT ANTHONY SAMPSON STANDS OUT. HE SPENDS 10-15 HOURS A WEEK WORKING WITH YOUTH GROUPS, AND BELIEVES THAT A THRIVING COMMUNITY BENEFITS EVERYONE WHO'S PART OF IT. **AT WORK.**

AMERICA'S PROMISE
THE ALLIANCE FOR YOUTH

Allstate is proud to support America's Promise.   www.allstate.com

Allstate.
You're in good hands.

■ **Part of the Community** Businesses need to be actively involved in community activities. *How does this ad publicize Allstate's commitment to gain the goodwill and respect of community members?*

involvement with school and community organizations, such as business advisory committees, business and school partnership programs, or the local chamber of commerce, provide recognition for individual employees and present a favorable image for the business. Some companies release employees from normal job responsibilities for limited time periods to chair important charitable fund-raising efforts, such as United Way campaigns.

Effective businesses need to be active participants in their communities. Although the primary aim of community relations work is to promote civic pride and help the local residents, these events also help create goodwill for their business participants. Customers and the general public pay attention to the sponsors of community-wide activities.

The Role of Public Relations Specialists

Companies often hire public relations firms or establish public relations departments. Public relations specialists work with more than just customers, employees, and the media. They also consult with civic and professional groups, legislators, government officials, consumer activists, stockholders, environmentalists, and suppliers.

Public relations specialists work in both the public and the private sector. The public sector includes schools, hospitals, universities, government agencies, charitable organizations, and the military. Like private businesses, public agencies also have a need to project a favorable image.

The principal task of a public relations specialist is to publicize the good news about a company and its products—and to control the damage done by any negative news.

In 1999, two different production problems in Belgium affected the taste, quality, and external odor of some Coca-Cola products. This prompted the Belgium health minister to take precautionary measures. Although no health or safety issues were discovered, the negative publicity affected the overall image and sales of Coke products in Europe. Coca-Cola Belgium removed all old products from the marketplace and destroyed them in an environmentally safe manner. The company also took steps to restart production with all new ingredients, performed more rigorous testing on all production lines, added new equipment, and improved monitoring systems. By acting quickly and responsibly, Coca-Cola was able to overcome the bad publicity.

WRITING NEWS RELEASES The public relations specialist's principal publicity tool is the news release. A news release is a prewritten story about a company that is sent to the various media. It usually contains information about the company's employees, stores, operations, products, corporate philosophy, or participation in an event or program. Publicity projects should be selected for multiple uses. Information gathered for a news release should also be appropriate for use in a new company brochure or ad.

A news release must contain a certain amount of newsworthy information in order to be picked up

Life In The Diverse MARKETPLACE

Naming Names

For Westerners, addressing someone in Malaysia can be complex. Malaysia is a constitutional monarchy with nine royal houses, so it is quite possible that you could meet royalty in Malaysia! When addressing people, use their titles (Teacher, Doctor, Engineer, etc.) and their names. To further complicate matters—each of the three main groups in Malaysia (Chinese, Muslim, and Indian) have different naming conventions. To ask a Malaysian what to call him or her, be direct and polite—he or she may be just as confused about what to call you!

Thinking Critically

What U.S. naming standards might cause confusion to a visitor from abroad?

and carried by the media. There are certain guidelines that public relations personnel must observe in planning and carrying out publicity projects.

A public affairs staff should send only important news releases to the media. A news release telling of a shopping mall expansion that will result in many new jobs created in a community has a good chance of being run by the media. When a media source is overwhelmed with submissions, it will tend to disregard them. By sending significant news releases periodically, a business has a better chance of having its material published. It is also helpful to send news releases to all media, both print and broadcast, at the same time. The chances that one will use the material are greater when all are contacted.

News releases should have a continuity of theme extending over many months or even years. Similar repeat messages will achieve maximum impact on an audience. A consistent message might be that a business is community minded. Such is the case with the Dayton Corporation community involvement program. Since 1946, the company has

FIGURE 17-2

NEWS RELEASES

News releases sent through regular mail to the media should be double-spaced and written on letterhead stationery. Margins should be about $1\frac{1}{2}$ inches to allow the editor to make notes. Always type or word process copy, and be sure it is clean and free of spelling errors. News releases published through electronic means on the World Wide Web are limited by the design of the Web site, but still must identify the company and follow the rules listed below.

1

The first paragraph should answer the Who, What, When, Where, and Why questions.

4

When identifying people in a news release include the full name and title or position of the person, but avoid using Mr., Ms., Mrs., Dr., etc. After you have used the complete name refer only to the last name in the remaining part of the news release.

Adidas' Olympic Mission: More Sports, More Athletes

Colorado Springs, May 16—Why would a company spend a lot of time and resources developing a fencing shoe for the 2000 Olympics in Sydney? For Adidas, the answer is simple: They are committed to more athletes and more sports than any other brand.

Adidas' roots and heritage are linked to the Olympic Games. Adi Dassler, founder of Adidas, was producing track shoes for Olympic athletes as early as the 1928 Games in Amsterdam. Since then, the company has consistently been making advances in technologies specifically designed for Olympic competitors.

Adidas is committed to producing revolutionary products to enhance the performance of all athletes at all levels. Throughout every stage of the development and testing process, Adidas works closely with athletes. The athletes' requirements and preferences, coupled with Adidas' expertise and knowledge, produce the most technologically advanced shoes and apparel available.

For more information, please contact Adidas Public Relations:
Nigel Wright
Phone: (818) 555-2609
Fax: (818) 555-2674
Mobile: (818) 555-4064
E-mail: nigel.wright@yourname.com

# # #

2

The story with important facts should be developed within the next few paragraphs.

3

More information that is slightly less important can follow. This information could be cut by an editor without losing vital information.

5

The news release should always include the name, address, and phone number of the contact person sending out the release. All pages should be numbered except for the first page.

6

The entire news release should be brief—usually one or two pages is enough. If the news release runs more than one page, write "more" at the bottom of each page except the final one. Identify and number each succeeding page at the top. On the last page, put "---30---" or "###" at the bottom to signify the end of the news release.

contributed over $200 million to the communities where it operates stores. The money goes to support local job training and dropout prevention programs, dance, music, theater, and arts groups. As a result, Dayton and its family of stores (Target, Mervyns, Hudson's, Dayton's, and Marshall Field's) are recognized as good corporate citizens and respected in the community.

Remember that the media are interested in news, not publicity. The word publicity should never be used when communicating with media personnel.

A news release should be properly formatted. It also must answer five basic questions: *who, what, where, when,* and *why*. Try to avoid editorial comment and personal opinion; your focus should remain on the facts and details, not personal commentary. When an opinion must be included, attribute it to the originator by using quotes. Use simple and accurate words. Words that are unfamiliar or jargon used in a business might confuse news personnel. Be as brief as possible but be sure to cover important facts about the event. Figure 17-2 on page 313 illustrates the necessary components of an effective news release. It gives all of the necessary information regarding dates and places and offers contact names for further information. It also has an enthusiastic tone.

OTHER PUBLIC RELATIONS DUTIES News releases are the major written documents for which public relations specialists are responsible, but they are not the only ones. Public relations staff members also prepare annual reports for investors and interested customers. They also prepare brochures and responses to customer inquiries. Occasionally, they even write short feature articles for trade magazines. Public relations staff members may help keep a company web site updated with noteworthy and interesting news. They also develop press kits.

A press kit is a folder containing articles, news releases, feature stories, and photographs about a company, product, or person. Press kits are given to the media to assist them in reporting on the intended news item. These save time for public relations specialists because frequently asked questions can be covered in one place.

Public relations personnel frequently meet customers and the public face-to-face. They attend public relations events and organize press conferences. A press conference is a meeting in which a business or organization invites media members to hear an announcement about a newsworthy event. Examples of announcements usually covered in press conferences include corporate officer changes, reorganizations of corporate divisions, or mergers with different corporations. They also include new product developments, expansions, and closings of company plants or offices.

17.3 ASSESSMENT

Reviewing Key Terms and Concepts

1. Name three ways in which the goodwill generated by public relations can benefit a company.

2. What are customer advisory boards?

3. What is meant by community relations?

4. What is the primary task of public relations specialists?

5. What are three reasons why a company may call a press conference?

Thinking Critically

6. What is meant by the statement, "To the customer, the employees are the company"?

Integrating Academic Skills

7. **COMMUNICATION** Write a news release announcing the attendees of a DECA Leadership Development Conference.

Careers in Marketing

Beth Gillespie
Public Relation Specialist
Edelman Public Relations Worldwide

Career Facts

How does your workload vary?

"It's actually a consistent workload and doesn't vary all that much, though the Internet has been cause for adjustment. Our Internet-based clients want things yesterday, so we have had to learn new skills to make us better, smarter, and faster. We work with editorial services to develop the content for the press releases, and must ensure that all outgoing information is 100 percent correct."

What kind of training would you recommend for students?

"Communications and journalism are the most commonly recommended subject areas. I was lucky enough to get into a good PR department in college. Getting into any kind of writing program is very important—the written word is our best form of communication. Don't just stock up on newspaper writing courses—take creative writing classes as well. Strong writers make great PR people!"

What is your favorite part of your job?

"I enjoy the account management elements of my job, but my favorite part is when we get a 'hit', which is when the media picks up a story. Behind every story, there are weeks of hard work trying to convince the media that it is a story worth picking up. In addition, when it 'hits,' it's an amazing feeling to say, 'I was responsible for that!'"

What is your key to success?

"My product is my communication skills—it is my job to determine the needs of my clients and the best way to communicate and articulate the value of their product to the media. I am a press person, and at the end of the day, my client wants to see clips of their product in the news."

Education and Training: Increased competition raises the need for a college degree. Coursework in journalism, English, speech, communications, marketing, media production, and computer applications is recommended. Working on high school and college publications and in clubs provides valuable experience.

Aptitudes, Abilities, and Skills: The ability to relate well to people is the primary required skill. Strong communication abilities, good listening and persuasion skills, assess confidence, quick decision-making skills, and strong management and supervisory skills are necessary.

Career Outlook: Employment is expected to grow faster than average through the year 2006. It is not known how the use of the Internet will affect job growth.

Career Path: Media workers, public relations production workers, and public relations assistants are all entry positions into public relations work. Experienced public relations specialists may advance to administrative positions such as Director of Public relations for government or private organizations.

Thinking Critically
How could a course in Creative Writing improve your skills as a PR Specialist?

Chapter 17 ASSESSMENT

VOCABULARY REVIEW

Write one correct sentence for each of the following terms.

- promotion
- promotional mix
- product promotion
- institutional promotion
- advertising
- sales promotion
- public relations
- publicity
- push policy
- pull policy
- slotting allowance
- sales incentives
- premiums
- incentives
- promotional tie-ins
- customer advisory boards
- consumer affairs specialists
- community relations
- news release
- press kit
- press conference

FACT AND IDEA REVIEW

1. For what specific purposes do businesses typically employ promotion? (17.1)

2. List the four basic types of promotion. (17.1)

3. Explain the differences between trade promotions and consumer sales promotions. (17.2)

4. Explain the difference between contests, sweepstakes, and rebates. (17.2)

5. Distinguish between employee, customer, and community relations. (17.3)

6. List three programs or policies that businesses use to improve their image to employees. (17.3)

7. Give three examples of public relations events. (17.3)

8. What is a news release? (17.3)

THINKING CRITICALLY

1. Saturn has a good promotional mix for their cars. What does this statement mean?

2. Some manufacturers are upset that they are forced to pay slotting allowances. Why do retailers feel that they are justified in charging manufacturers these fees?

3. Besides working with customers and the media, public relations specialists also consult with civic and professional groups, legislators, government officials, consumer activists, stockholders, environmentalists, and suppliers. Explain why public relations specialists should respond to these groups.

4. The Dayton Corporation gives five percent of its taxable profits to communities where it does business. The contributions are made in social service programs and local arts. Analyze the reasons why the company gives to these causes.

5. Why is it important to keep news releases brief and to the point?

BUILDING WORKPLACE SKILLS

1. **Human Relations** Each month a certain amount is automatically deducted from a manager's paycheck at your company and donated to established charities. Your boss has asked you to participate. You are reluctant because you already donate to your own given charities and you prefer to pick where your money goes. How would you explain your position?

2. **Technology** Research and prepare a brief report on the advantages of electronic coupon machines as promotional devices.

APPLYING MARKETING CONCEPTS

1. **Understanding Promotional Devices**
Research the advantages and disadvantages of coupons as promotional devices. Prepare a one-page outline using a word-processing program.

2. **Planning Promotions** Plan a promotion for a product of your choice. Use a word processing program to write a report about your plan. Describe your target market, as well as the public image you would like for your product. Choose a product name and explain why it will appeal to your audience. Describe where you will sell your product (catalog, retail store, discount store, or industry). Discuss any premiums you might offer to promote your product and what kind of premiums would not be suitable.

3. **Analyzing Promotions** Choose a product that is heavily promoted in the marketplace. Prepare an oral analysis of the product using presentation software. Answer the following questions in your analysis: What market is being targeted? What type of image is the company trying to project? What types of promotion are used? Are the promotions effective? Why or why not?

4. **Researching Publicity** Identify an event that brought a business negative publicity. Could the business have avoided the outcome? Could it have limited the damage? Explore your answers in a word-processed one-page report.

LINKING SCHOOL TO WORK

Information Skills Visit a local store or cooperative education training station to review products offered for sale. Photograph or bring examples to class of consumer sales promotions being used to sell products at the store.

THE DECA CONNECTION

Role Play: Promotion Planner

Situation You are to assume the role of assistant manager of a local bookstore. Your manager (judge) has recently asked you to develop a promotional mix to attract people aged 16 to 24 to your business.

Activity You must identify the proper promotional mix for your store by using various promotional devices (advertising, publicity, sales promotions, and personal selling) available in your area and explain your ideas for the promotional mix.

Evaluation You will be evaluated on how well you meet the following performance indicators:

- Identify elements of the promotional mix
- Coordinate activities in the promotional mix
- Develop a sales promotion plan
- Analyze use of specialty promotions
- Explain the nature of a promotional plan

inter NET CONNECTION

About Our Company

As public relations specialist for a national consumer products company, you are required to develop a Web site to assist customers in understanding company events, products, and services.

Connect

- Find three consumer products company sites on the Web.
- Identify at least three elements on each Web site that can be described as public relations tools.

Chapter 18

Visual Merchandising and Display

Marketing: What It Takes

Matching the Season

You work as a sales associate for an apparel and accessories store. You have been asked by the assistant manager to design a visually appealing interior display for a spring promotion. You must suggest a possible plan for the display to match the store's image.

WHAT WILL YOU DO?

What ideas will you use to plan an appropriate seasonal display for your store?

Display Features

What Is Visual Merchandising?

Visual merchandising refers to the coordination of all of the physical elements in a place of business that are used to project the right image to its customers. The "right" image is one that invites interest in the merchandise or services being offered, encourages purchasing, and makes the customer feel good about where he or she is doing business. It creates the whole vision of an organization and draws in the customer.

Successful businesses create distinct, clear, and consistent images for their customers. A good image sets a business apart from the competition. This image is a unique blend of store characteristics, location, products, prices, advertising, public relations, and personal selling. A store's image should highlight what sets it apart from the competition. Its most important component, however, is sales promotion. While this chapter primarily focuses on visual merchandising in retail stores, manufacturers and wholesalers also use visual merchandising to sell their products. Visual merchandising is used extensively at manufacturers' showrooms, trade shows, and conventions.

The term *visual merchandising* is sometimes used interchangeably with the term *display* even though the two are not the same. Display is a much narrower concept and makes up only one part of visual merchandising. Display refers to the visual and artistic aspects of presenting a product to a target group of customers. Visual merchandising, by contrast, involves the visual and artistic aspects of the entire business environment.

Visual merchandising has increased tremendously in importance because of the growth of self-service, superstores, and box stores. There is little personal selling in the warehouse environment of the box store—products must sell themselves. This has spurred box stores to develop giant signs, graphics, and banners to designate areas within the store. Individual displays are set off the main or drive aisles with merchandise presented on fixtures behind each display. Home Depot, an example of a box store, has over 100,000 square feet and specializes in home improvement products. These visual merchandising activities have had a strong influence on the promotional activities of other self-service and full-service retailers.

It is the visual merchandisers that are responsible for the total merchandise or service presentation, the overall business image, and even the building and placement of design elements. They are active members of the decision-making team that promotes a business and its products.

What You'll Learn

- The concepts of visual merchandising and display
- The important display features that contribute to a store's image
- The various types of displays

Why It's Important

Since visual merchandising helps sell products and build store image, you will need to know about the different types of store displays and how to create them.

Key Terms

- visual merchandising
- display
- storefront
- marquee
- store layout
- fixtures

■ The Superstore Phenomenon Superstores are often 20,000- to 100,000-square-foot buildings of concrete, cement, steel and glass with a vast assortment of one specific kind of product. *Why are these types of stores often called category killers?*

Elements of Visual Merchandising

Visual merchandising is used to create a positive shopping experience—and that makes customers want to return. Stores may consider four key elements to achieve this: *storefront, store layout, store interior,* and *interior displays.*

■ Storefront

The total exterior of a business is known as the storefront. The storefront includes the store's sign, marquee, outdoor lighting, banners, planters, awnings, windows, and the building itself (its design and setting). Consider K-Mart superstores, which are typically large buildings with bold graphics, signage, and colorful facades that are conveniently located near a main highway with a large, well-lit parking lot to attract customers.

The importance of an effective storefront cannot be overestimated. It projects the image of the store as discount or expensive or conservative or trendy. It can also attract potential customers by making the business stand out from its competitors.

SIGNS The store sign offers the first impression and therefore should make a statement about the business. It should be original and easily recognizable. The letters, building materials, and colors that are used help create the store's image. An upscale department store might use an elegant script, while a discount merchandiser, such as Wal-Mart, uses bold, block-like capital letters in signage. Signs are designed primarily to attract attention and help to advertise a business.

MARQUEE A marquee is an architectural canopy that extends over a store's entrance. Marquees can be found over most theater entrances, where the times and dates of the latest plays or movies are highlighted. Older stores and some specialty stores also use marquees to display the store's name. A marquee extends out over an entrance and is highly visible. This gives greater prominence than other store signs.

ENTRANCES Entrances are usually designed with customer convenience and store security in mind. Smaller stores normally have only one entrance, while larger stores (such as department stores) have several. The average midsize business probably needs at least two entrances—one leading in from the street for pedestrians and another adjacent to the parking lot for patrons who drive to the business.

There are several types of entrances, including revolving, push-pull, electronic, and climate-controlled entrances. Climate-controlled entrances are most frequently found in enclosed shopping malls. Each of these projects a certain image. Electronically controlled sliding doors, for example, suggest a practical, self-service business. Push-pull doors, which often have fancy metal or wooden push plates or bars, suggest a full-service establishment.

■ **It's One of a Kind** A unique storefront can attract customers by being different from its competitors. *What features make this store stand out from its competitors?*

WINDOW DISPLAYS Display windows, when available on a building's exterior, are especially useful for visual merchandising. Displays placed in these windows can begin the selling process even before the potential customer enters the store.

Window displays are designed to attract the customer by suggesting both the type of merchandise and the type of atmosphere inside the store. Two basic kinds of window displays are promotional displays and institutional displays.

Promotional displays promote the sale of one product, a line of related products, or a variety of products. They do so by presenting items with special lighting, signs, and props. Promotional displays frequently are used to sell a particular product or related product line, such as athletic clothing for golfers. Often promotional displays emphasize a particular theme, such as Mother's Day or Labor Day. Promotional displays are also used to promote storewide events, such as anniversary, pre-season, or end of season sales.

Institutional displays promote store image rather than specific products. Such displays are designed to build customer goodwill and enhance store image by showing that the business is interested in the welfare of the community. Institutional displays focus on public causes, worthy ideas, or community organizations. They might feature the activities of the national groups, such as the American Cancer Society, or local volunteer efforts.

■ Store Layout

Store layout refers to the way store floor space is used to facilitate and promote sales and to best serve the customer. A typical store layout divides a store into four different kinds of space:

- *Selling space* assigned for interior displays, product demonstrations, and sales transactions
- *Merchandising space* allocated to items that are kept in inventory for selling
- *Personnel space* assigned to store employees for lockers, lunch breaks, and restrooms
- *Customer space* assigned for the comfort and convenience of the customer, including a café or food court, dressing rooms, lounges, and recreation areas for children

Once selling space has been allocated, visual merchandising personnel work closely with store layout specialists to decide the best locations for particular kinds of merchandise. In conjunction with management, visual merchandisers have input about where each product category area will be located. They also help to determine which products and services should be located closest to doors, exits, elevators, and parking lots.

Decisions are made about how much selling space to have and the type of interior and window displays to use for various products and related items. Store layout planners and visual merchandisers design traffic patterns to promote extended shopping within the store.

■ Store Interior

Once the general placement of merchandise has been determined, store personnel can develop the visual merchandising approaches for the building's interior. The selection of floor and wall coverings, lighting, colors, and store fixtures can powerfully affect the store image.

Take flooring, for example. Many supermarkets use linoleum or tile floors to project an inexpensive, practical image. Specialty stores often use thick carpeting to send the opposite message to their customers.

Colors and lighting can be used in a similar fashion. Bright colors and light pastels (or plain white) appeal to different types of customers. Stores catering to teens might favor bright colors and lighting. Stores catering to adults often choose pastels and soft, subtle lighting effects. Superstores choose fluorescent or high-intensity discharge lighting, while prestige retailers might install expensive chandeliers.

The principal installations in a store, however, are the fixtures. Fixtures are permanent or movable store furnishings, such as display cases, counters, shelving, racks, and benches.

A business seeking an upscale image might enhance its fixtures by painting them or covering them with textured materials (carpeting, fabric, cork, or reed, for example). A business catering to discount buyers would most likely leave its fixtures plain.

Walls are interior features that can be covered to reinforce store image. Women's specialty stores often use small or subtly patterned paper, while department stores tend to favor soft pastels. Walls are also used to display merchandise. Clothing can be pinned to the surface. This technique has the advantage of both saving space and attracting customers with higher-than-eye-level displays.

The width of a store's aisles may influence behavior more directly than any other element of visual merchandising. Different aisle widths create different images for a store.

Finally, the size, variety, and quality of the merchandise assortment carried by a store affects its clientele. Brand name merchandise conveys a different image from generic goods; each will attract (or put off) a different kind of customer.

■ **Supporting the Arts and Education** Institutional displays promote public causes, institutions, and organizations. *How do stores benefit from institutional displays?*

■ Interior Displays

Interior or in-store displays are technically part of the general store interior. As elements of visual merchandising, however, they are so significant that they are commonly considered in a category of their own. This is because such displays generate one out of every four sales. If interior displays are done exceptionally well, they enable customers to make a selection without personal assistance. Thus, they occupy an important place in today's selling environment, where many stores are self-service.

Five types of interior displays are closed displays, open displays, architectural displays, point-of-purchase displays, and store decorations. Figure 18-1 illustrates the five types of interior displays.

Interior displays use fixtures and props to showcase merchandise. The types of fixtures and props visual merchandisers use will vary depending on the merchandise displayed.

FIGURE 18-1

TYPES OF INTERIOR DISPLAYS

Retailers use interior displays to show merchandise, provide customers with product information, get customers to stop and shop at the store, reinforce advertising, and promote the store's image.

ARCHITECTURAL DISPLAYS

Architectural displays consist of model rooms that allow customers to see how merchandise might look in their homes. Area rugs or the arrangement of the furniture itself can be used to suggest the setting instead of walls or partitions.

STORE DECORATIONS

Store decorations are displays that coincide with specific seasons or holidays. Banners, signs, props, and similar items used to invoke the spirit of Valentine's Day, Halloween, summer, or fall are examples.

OPEN DISPLAYS

Open displays allow customers to handle and examine merchandise without the help of a salesperson. Hanging racks for suits and dresses or countertop and shelf displays for cosmetics are examples.

CLOSED DISPLAYS

Closed displays allow customers to see but not handle merchandise. They are found in catalog showrooms or businesses such as jewelry stores where security or breakage is a concern.

POINT-OF-PURCHASE DISPLAYS

Point-of-purchase displays are displays designed mainly to promote impulse purchases. Point-of-purchase displays are usually more effective at supporting new products than established ones. Point-of-purchase displays are usually supplied by a product manufacturer for use at or near the cash register.

It is important to create a clean and organized visual display regardless of which type of display you choose. It is also helpful to group merchandise by type or with related items to simplify the shopping experience for customers.

As you can see in Figure 18-1, different sales situations call for different types of displays. Items like clothing would be difficult to showcase in a closed display. One typical department store department that often combining many different displays is the cosmetic department. Some items may be part of an open display, such as brushes or accessories; other items could be contained in a closed display to prevent customers from sampling goods other than the tester; finally, a point-of-purchase display may feature a computerized touch screen terminal that can evaluate the best cosmetics for each customer's preferences, coloring, and skin type. These different types of displays all compliment each other and create a positive, interactive buying experience.

Props used with interior displays are generally classified as *decorative* or *functional*. Decorative props include background scenery used to indicate a season or to create an interesting setting. Functional props include functional items for holding merchandise, such as mannequins and shirt forms. Display designers often look for unusual props or unusual ways to use common items as props. Imaginative jewelry display designers, for example, may use open candy boxes to display colored stone.

Electronic Frontiers

One Stop Shop

A loaf of bread, a carton of milk, tickets to the symphony—in Japan, a trip to the convenience store can yield much more than groceries or a newspaper. In a country where physical space is extremely limited, product display and delivery have become a major concern. Enter *Loppi*. *Loppi* is a computer terminal located in convenience stores that increases product offerings. Using a touch-pad screen, shoppers can order concert tickets, make travel reservations, or order meals online to be delivered. Need a book? Order online, then pay and pick it up at your local 7-Eleven the next day. This seems like a perfect fit for Japanese consumers, who are more reluctant than their American counterparts to use their credit cards online.

Thinking Critically

What other products might *Loppi* offer to its customers?

18.1 ASSESSMENT

Reviewing Key Terms and Concepts

1. What is visual merchandising?
2. Why is a display considered part of visual merchandising?
3. How do exterior and interior features help a store's image?
4. List two different types of window displays.
5. Describe the five different types of interior displays used by retailers.

Thinking Critically

6. Is it necessary for staff members who work with visual merchandising to know basic sales promotion techniques? Justify your response.

Integrating Academic Skills

7. **COMMUNICATION** You work as a visual merchandiser for a large department store. You would like to devote one of the main display windows to a public service, rather than using a less visible space within the store as suggested by the manager. Write a formal proposal detailing your views. Be sure to name the public service, describe the display, and indicate how you believe the store will benefit.

Artistic Design

Display Design and Preparation

In the retail environment, a display has about three to eight seconds to attract a customer's attention, create a desire, and sell a product. This limited time frame means that a business must target its displays carefully to appeal to its customers. Failing to do this not only risks losing sales but may ruin a business's image as well. The traditional clothing store that suddenly begins showing abstract displays of trendy merchandise is likely to attract some new style-conscious customers. It also might alienate many of its regular customers.

A business needs to identify its customers, the desired image, and the kind of merchandise concept that it wants to promote before building displays. Display design and selection involves the following five steps.

▪ Step 1: Selecting Merchandise for Display

The first important step when preparing a display is to select the right merchandise. Merchandise selected for display must have sales appeal. New, popular, and best-selling products are often selected for display for this reason. Display merchandise must also be visually appealing and current to attract customers. It must be appropriate for the season and for the store's geographic location. Displays often address the latest fashion, fad, or trend.

▪ Step 2: Selecting the Display

The merchandise selected largely determines the type of display that is used. There are four kinds of displays.

A *one-item display* is used to show a single item. An example would be an Anne Klein shoe displayed on a show box with a promotional logotype. One-item displays are usually constructed for a single product promotion or an advertised special.

A *line-of-goods display* shows one kind of product but features several brands, sizes, or models. An example would be a display unit showing tennis shoes by different manufacturers, such as Reebok and Nike, or a display of styles of shoes put out only by Nike.

A *related-merchandise display* features items that are meant to be used together. In an apparel store, a related-merchandise display might feature casual wear—shirts, pants, sweaters, and shoes. Related-merchandise displays are designed primarily to entice the customers to buy more than one item.

An *assortment display* features a collection of unrelated items. Such displays usually emphasize price and tell customers that a wide variety of merchandise is available for sale. They are typically used by variety stores, discounters, and supermarkets to have a special appeal to bargain hunters.

● What You'll Learn

- The steps used in designing and preparing displays
- The artistic considerations involved in display preparation
- The maintenance considerations for displays

● Why It's Important

Visual merchandisers must know the rules of artistic design for displays that attract customers and keep them coming back.

Key Terms

- complementary colors
- adjacent colors
- proportion
- formal balance
- informal balance

Step 3: Choosing a Setting

Displays can be presented in a number of different types of settings. The setting a business selects will depend largely on the image it wants to project.

A *realistic setting* depicts a room, area, or recognizable locale. The scene could be a restaurant, a park, or a party. Props, such as tables, chairs, plants, risers, books, dishes, and mannequins provide the details.

A *semirealistic setting* suggests a room or locale but leaves the details to the viewer's imagination. A cardboard sun, beach towel, surfing poster, and a sprinkling of sand would be enough to invoke the rest of the scene—an oceanfront beach—in the viewer's mind. Businesses use semirealistic settings when either space or budgets do not permit realistic settings.

An *abstract setting* does not imitate (or even try to imitate) reality. It focuses on form and color rather than reproducing actual objects. Wide bands of torn colored paper used as an accent behind or around merchandise can create an attractive visual image that has little or nothing to do with reality.

Abstract settings are gaining popularity, mainly because they are inexpensive and do not require large amounts of storage space for accumulated props. Display specialists are increasingly accenting products with items such as cardboard, paper, string, yarn, ribbon, and paint instead of more traditional items.

Step 4: Manipulating Artistic Elements

The artistic elements of a display include *line, color, shape, direction, texture, proportion, balance, motion,* and *lighting.* These elements influence your perception of a display in ways that you are probably not aware of.

LINE As you know, people read English from left to right. They also tend to read displays the same way. Lines are created within displays to travel from left to right over featured products.

Various types of lines create different impressions. Straight lines suggest stiffness and control; curving lines suggest freedom and movement; diagonal lines give the impression of action; vertical lines offer height and dignity; and horizontal lines give width and confidence.

■ **Creating a Brand Image** A single item display is designed to promote the sale of a particular product and create a distinct image. *What techniques are used to create a brand image for this product?*

REAL WORLD MARKETING

Targeting Teens

Chasing teen dollars has reinvented the way traditional malls treat some of their most valued customers. Most teens visit a mall 54 times annually—each spending nearly $2,000 on clothes, CDs, and gadgets per year. Competing with the Internet is the mall's biggest challenge; however, malls are making strides for two reasons—many teens don't have credit cards, and they prefer shopping with friends. Capitalizing on these facts, malls like the Glendale Galleria in California are unveiling teen zones, complete with live DJs, big screen TVs, and Internet kiosks. Older patrons aren't enthused; but many retailers are asking to be moved closer to the center of activity.

Thinking Critically
What types of stores would benefit from being nearest to teen zones?

FIGURE 18-2

The Color Wheel

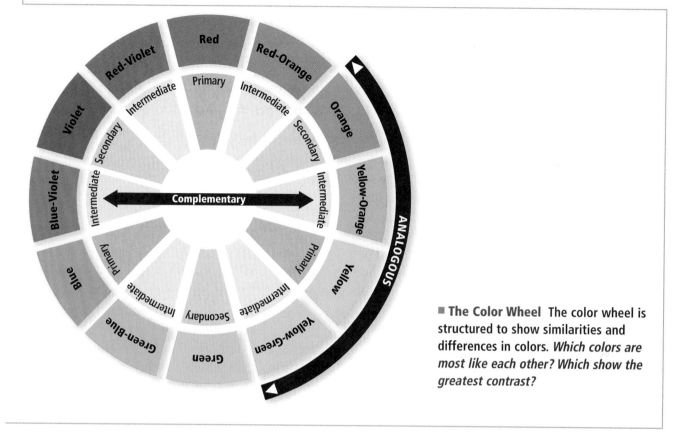

■ **The Color Wheel** The color wheel is structured to show similarities and differences in colors. *Which colors are most like each other? Which show the greatest contrast?*

COLOR can make or break a display. Displays whose colors match their surroundings too closely may not catch the customer's eye. Displays whose colors are too bright or contrasting may overwhelm the merchandise.

The colors selected for a display should contrast with those used on the walls, floors, and fixtures around them. A store decorated in pastels should have displays featuring darker, stronger colors.

Which colors make the most effective contrasts? The answers can be found in the standard color wheel (see Figure 18-2), which illustrates the relationships among colors. Complementary colors are found opposite each other in the color wheel and create the greatest contrasts. Red and green, blue and orange, and violet and yellow are examples of complementary colors.

Adjacent colors, also called analogous colors, are located next to each other in the color wheel and contrast only slightly. Successive adjacent colors (such as blue-green, blue, and blue-violet) form families, or groups of colors that blend well with each other.

Effective displays use color groupings to create visual calm or excitement. Colors from the warm side of the color wheel, such as red and yellow, convey a festive, party mood that works well with lower-priced merchandise. These colors must be used cautiously. Their contrast is so great that it can detract from the merchandise and even irritate customers. This problem can usually be avoided by varying the shades of the colors somewhat to lessen their contrast yet still retain their warmth and friendliness. Colors from the cool side of the color wheel, such as blue and green, represent calm and refinement. They are often associated with higher-priced merchandise.

Customers' expectations about color are also important in planning displays. People have come to expect certain color schemes at certain times of the year, such as earth tones in the fall and bright colors in the spring. Finally, customers' reactions to color also figure into planning displays. Red evokes excitement, so you would not use it in a display designed to convey tranquillity.

SHAPE Shape refers to the physical appearance, or outline, of a display. It is important to consider shape when selecting display units and the merchandise used in a display.

Shape is determined by the props, fixtures, and merchandise used in the display. Squares, cubes, circles, and triangles are some of the shapes that display units may resemble. Displays that have little or no distinct shape—called *mass displays*—are also possible. Mass displays are used to display large quantities and to convey a message of low price.

DIRECTION A good display guides the viewer's eye over all the merchandise, moving smoothly from one part of the display to another. It does not skip around. This smooth visual flow is called *direction*. Good displays create direction by using color, repetition, lighting patterns, and ribbons. This is done by arranging merchandise in a pattern to guide the customer's eye.

Displays should have a focal point. A good method of creating a focal point is to build a display around an imaginary triangle (having more merchandise at the bottom of the display than at the top, for example). This arrangement helps keep the eyes moving up and center.

Displays that lack direction are said to be *unfocused*. Typically, an unfocused display contains too many unrelated items, too many colors, or too many lines that confuse the customer and detract from the merchandise.

TEXTURE The way the surfaces in a display look together is texture. These surfaces can be either smooth or rough. The contrast between them creates visual interest. Products that are smooth, such as flatware, should be placed against backgrounds or props that are rough.

PROPORTION Proportion refers to the relationship between and among objects in a display. The merchandise should always be the primary focus of a display. Props and signs should be in proportion to the merchandise—they should never overshadow it in importance.

BALANCE Placing large items with large items and small items with small items in a display is called formal balance. When a large item is placed on one side of a display, an equally large item should be placed on the other side for balance.

The opposite technique can also be exciting in a display. Balancing a large item with several small ones is called informal balance. An example would be a display in which an adult mannequin is juxtaposed with several shallow baskets of flowers raised to the mannequin's height.

MOTION Motion can be made part of a display through the use of motorized fixtures and props. Animated figures, such as mechanical mannequins, have been used for years in holiday displays. Motion should be used sparingly to accentuate merchandise.

BRIGHT IDEAS

I Smell Sales!

When you walk into the Rainforest Café, you are greeted by tropical noises, simulated rainstorms, and what is that . . . the smell of wildflowers? Just your imagination? Probably not. The latest addition to retail purchasing is "environmental fragrancing." This innovation is now believed by many to be as important as traditional design elements such as lighting, layout, and music. Retailers are looking to enhance their customers' shopping experiences and influence purchasing. The Christmas Store at Walt Disney World pumps in scents of evergreen and spiced apple cider to put shoppers in the right mood year round. The Rainforest Café infuses fresh-flower extracts into its retail section in an effort to open consumers' minds, make them curious, and drive sales. Shoppers at Jordan's Furniture in Massachusetts smell bubble gum in the children's room displays or a hint of pine in the country-style section.

Thinking Creatively
What type of "environmental fragrancing" would be appropriate in other retailing outlets?

Case Study

Redefining Nordstrom

In early 2000, Nordstrom department stores set out to create a fresh new look in the company's stores, fashion lines, and advertising. The venerable Seattle-based national retailer undertook the image makeover to attract a trendier clientele and boost sagging sales. The company redesigned stores to make them brighter, more fun, and easier to navigate. Store displays were made flashier and casual clothes more prominently displayed. Even the piano players relaxed, losing their tuxedoes after customer surveys deemed the look too formal and rigid. The company also undertook a $40 million advertising campaign, the largest in company history.

Nordstrom developed the makeover strategy after an extensive 18-month study, complete with customer interviews and focus groups. However, the redefining of Nordstrom eventually proved to have been more controversial than the company's management estimated. The approach was somewhat lost on the store's traditional audience. Some loyal customers, accustomed to a more genteel and upscale shopping experience, were alienated by the "Reinvent Yourself" campaign and found the new store layouts confusing. Although the company said it was not trying to attract the young market at the expense of its loyal customer base, the Nordstrom family halted the campaign in September 2000.

With the Nordstrom family members as focused as ever on the quality and customer service, the company is likely to prosper even in the face of shifting trends.

Case Study Review

1. Why did Nordstrom undertake a campaign to reinvent its image?
2. Why did the Nordstrom makeover fail?

A MATTER OF ETHICS

3. Is it ethical for an established company to change its image?

LIGHTING Proper lighting makes merchandise appear more attractive in displays. It is recommended that display lighting be two to five times stronger than a store's general lighting. Colored lighting can be used in displays to create dramatic effects.

It is important to consider lighting when displaying delicate, reflective items such as crystal, jewelry, and fine china. The lighting that would be used to create an elegant atmosphere in the fine housewares department would be very different than the lighting that would be used to make a bold statement in the teen clothing department. Although the lighting in the dressing rooms is technically not part of a display, it should be considered as well. Dressing room lighting that is glaring and unflattering will negatively affect a consumer buying decisions.

■ Step 5: Evaluating Completed Displays

Visual merchandisers should evaluate completed displays by checking to see if they enhance the store's image, appeal to customers, and promote the product in the best possible way. Other factors that should be evaluated include whether the display is creatively and appropriately themed, artistically pleasing, and clean and orderly.

Display Maintenance

Once a display has been constructed, it needs to be maintained and eventually dismantled. Individual businesses have different policies regarding the duration of displays. Most businesses check displays daily for damage, displacements, or missing items caused by customer handling. Clothing items that are folded and stacked in a display should be organized and restocked frequently.

Proper display maintenance can keep the merchandise fresh and attractive to customers. Poor maintenance can create a negative image not only of the merchandise but of the store as well. Display units and props should be cleaned and merchandise dusted on a regular basis. Customers are not likely to be enthusiastic about purchasing items that are dusty or displayed on dirty shelves.

Colors of Success

As you have already learned, serious thought must go into planning color schemes. When working in a global marketplace, the importance of colors becomes an even greater priority. A company that chooses to highlight the marketing of its new product with the color white might run into some trouble in Japan and other Asian countries. In contrast to the clean, pure image that white represents in the United States, it is the color of mourning for most Asian countries. Red may be a better choice, as it is considered a lucky color in many of the same countries.

Thinking Critically

Will the color wheel change in different countries?

18.2 ASSESSMENT

Reviewing Key Terms and Concepts

1. What decisions must be made before displays are prepared?

2. Name the five steps involved with display preparation.

3. How does a business select the display setting it desires?

4. Describe five of the artistic elements used in displays.

5. How should displays be evaluated?

Thinking Critically

6. Manufacturers often provide point-of-purchase displays to retailers. If you were a retailer, what criteria would you use in deciding whether or not to accept such a display?

Integrating Academic Skills

7. **MATH** You must recondition a half dozen mannequins (two adult and four youth). If reconditioning a youth mannequin costs $150 and reconditioning an adult mannequin costs 50 percent more, what amount should you budget for the entire job?

Careers in Marketing

RETAIL MANAGEMENT

Robin Kramer
Visual Merchandising Coordinator
KramerHutchison

What does your job entail?

"I communicate the designer's image using plastic, metal, and wood in the arrangement of shelves, mannequins, and other fixtures upon which clothes or items are displayed. The smallest nuances—ranging from where a purse is placed on a shelf to the lighting used in a department—come together to create the atmosphere. Creating a lifestyle and an environment that speaks to the customer gives him or her a reason to choose one store over another. My company works not only with the visual display but also with the architecture, graphics, and packaging for our clients. I've helped create a brand image for companies such as Tommy Hilfiger, Donna Karan, Coach, Narciso Rodriguez, and Barneys New York."

What kind of training did you have?

"I graduated from Syracuse University and the Fashion Institute of Technology before working for Calvin Klein for seven years. As the vice president of store planning and visual display, I learned the art of carrying an image through even the smallest details. In 1996, I went into business with a single client (Isaac Mizrahi) and a single employee (my mother). KramerHutchison now has 60 employees with an ever-growing client list."

What skills are most important?

"It is imperative to have an eye for design and a flair for innovation."

How does your workload vary?

"My workload varies depending on the client's needs—some clients need one freestanding store and some need 1,500 shops in department stores."

What is your key to success?

"The key to success is to maintain a happy, motivated team while developing good relationships with clients. It is important to understand your clients and to be able to interpret their goals and wishes on the design floor."

Thinking Critically

Why are good communication skills particularly important in visual merchandising?

Career Facts

Education and Training: Degrees in design and marketing are excellent preparation for visual merchandising coordinators, as well as classes in graphic arts and architecture.

Aptitudes, Abilities, and Skills: Creativity and an eye for design are important, as well as organizational skills, the ability to work under pressure, and strong communication skills.

Career Outlook: The overall outlook for visual merchandising is good but will likely vary according to the general economy and geographical location.

Career Path: Visual merchandising managers may be promoted to visual merchandising directors, or creative directors, assuming responsibility for several locations.

VOCABULARY REVIEW

Organize the class into two teams for a game of "Marketing Tic-Tac-Toe." Team members will give the definition for the terms and will place an "X" or "O" on the board for each correct definition.

- visual merchandising
- display
- storefront
- marquee
- store layout
- fixtures
- complementary colors
- adjacent colors
- proportion
- formal balance
- informal balance

FACT AND IDEA REVIEW

1. What is visual merchandising? (18.1)

2. What is "store layout"? (18.1)

3. Name the four types of space found in most store layouts. (18.1)

4. Why are interior displays important? (18.1)

5. Which interior display type is most effective for new product introductions? (18.1)

6. Explain the difference between decorative and functional props. (18.1)

7. What three issues must every business address before constructing displays? (18.2)

8. Locate complementary and adjacent colors on the color wheel. How do the colors contrast with each other? (18.2)

9. How is formal and informal balance achieved in a display? (18.2)

THINKING CRITICALLY

1. Assume you are in charge of hiring visual merchandisers for a large department store. What basic skills would you require in any display specialist you hired?

2. Explain why it is important to know your community and your customers when designing store displays.

3. Retailers in some locations are limiting the number of customer entrances due to concern over shoplifting and theft. Discuss what could be done to reduce theft risks around or near store entrances.

4. The trendy colors this season, hot pink, lime green, and iridescent orange, clash with your store's conservative, beige-on-brown decor. How can you creatively display the merchandise without creating jarring or irritating effects?

BUILDING WORKPLACE SKILLS

1. **Human Relations** Your store installed lock racks for all leather merchandise, which are secured with locks, keys, and metal cords that must be removed by store personnel before an item can be tried on. The fixtures have cut theft losses by half but are unpopular with customers. Unfortunately, it is the salespeople who are taking the brunt of the criticism. How would you respond to customers if you were a salesperson?

2. **Science** Using the library or the Internet, conduct research about color. Use a word processing program to write a report detailing the physical properties that determine various colors and the psychological uses of color as an artistic element in visual merchandising.

APPLYING MARKETING CONCEPTS

1. **Designing Store Layouts** Use a computer aided design program (CAD) to draw a floor plan showing the layout of a local business (or one floor of a department store). Code those areas provided for merchandise, selling, customers, and personnel. Then critique the layout in terms of ease of entry, traffic flow, utilization of display space, and availability of customer conveniences.

2. **Planning Holiday Displays** Select a holiday or season, and use a word processing program to describe an effective window display based on that theme for both an apparel and accessories store and an auto parts store. Specify five kinds of merchandise you would feature in each store.

3. **Comparing Display Technique** Visit a department store to observe and rate five different displays. After creating a simple sketch for each display, use a spreadsheet program to create a chart indicating color, the featured merchandise, and apparent theme. Evaluate each display in terms of the artistic elements from this chapter.

4. **Recognizing Display Tactics** Visit a local pharmacy to observe the point-of-purchase displays. Use a camera to photograph at least five different displays. Scan these into your computer and create a slide show using presentation software.

LINKING SCHOOL TO WORK

Thinking Skills Visit a cooperative education training station or a business in your community. Identify at least eight different types of interior displays, and specify the kinds of merchandise featured.

THE DECA CONNECTION

Role Play: Display Designer

Situation You are to assume the role of sales associate in an apparel and accessories department. Your department manager (judge) has asked you to create an interior display for the department. You will be given an assortment of merchandise to be displayed and the following supplies: scissors, fish line, straight pins, safety pins, foam board, a small iron, and white tissue paper.

Activity You must construct an effective display within a specified time period using the materials and merchandise provided.

Evaluation You will be evaluated on how well you meet the following performance indicators:
- Demonstrate appropriate creativity
- Demonstrate product
- Demonstrate initiative
- Demonstrate orderly and systematic behavior
- Persuade others

inter NET CONNECTION

About Our Company
As an assistant display manager, you are required to develop a list of prospective suppliers of store fixtures, mannequins, and props.

Connect
- Use the Internet to find five suppliers of store fixtures.
- Write a summary of the products and services provided by each supplier.
- Research visual merchandising trade shows and conventions for the upcoming year.

Chapter 19

Advertising

Marketing: What It Takes

A Master Media Plan
Imagine that you work as an account executive for an advertising agency. Your supervisor has asked you to design a media plan for a new client. The client, a national chain of sports-themed restaurants, wants to use different types of advertising media to reach different target markets. It is your job to review the different types of advertising media and make recommendations based on your research and the client's needs.

WHAT WILL YOU DO?
How will you determine the best ways to advertise the restaurant chain?

Advertising Media

Advertising and Its Purpose

Advertising is everywhere—television, radio, magazines, newspapers, stores, the World Wide Web, billboards, and even on buses. The average person is exposed to more than 2,000 advertisements a week.

Recall from Chapter 17 that *advertising* is any paid form of non-personal promotion of ideas, goods, or services by an identified sponsor. Advertising is different from other forms of promotion because the time or allotted space is paid for. In advertising, a message is carried by a set format rather than by personal selling. Advertising usually identifies the sponsor of the message.

There are two main types of advertising—promotional and institutional. Advertising designed to increase sales is known as promotional advertising. It introduces new products and businesses, encourages an interest in products, and explains product and service features. Promotional advertising also supports personal selling efforts and creates new markets for a business.

Institutional advertising attempts to create a favorable impression and goodwill for a business or an organization. It does this by providing positive information about a business. Support of community projects and community-endorsed ideas about important public topics such as the environment, public health, and education can create a favorable image.

Advertising allows large numbers of people to see the advertiser's message. The main purpose of advertising is to present a message that encourages the customer to buy the product or accept the ideas. Advertising identifies the good, service, or idea and special features such as price, benefits, location, and business hours. Advertising costs per potential customer (whether that customer is a viewer, reader, or listener) are usually lower than other forms of promotion. Businesses must choose the most appropriate advertising for their target market, for example, billboards, newspapers, radio, or television; a business then prepares the content of an advertisement. This differs from publicity because it can be controlled. Advertisements are subject to repeat viewing, which keeps the advertiser's message in people's minds. Finally, advertising can "presell" products—influencing people's decisions about a product or service before they even go shopping!

■ Advertising Drawbacks

While there are advantages to advertising, it does have its drawbacks. Advertising cannot focus on individual needs because the same message is conveyed to all customers. Some forms of advertising, such

What You'll Learn

- The concept and purpose of advertising
- The different types of advertising media

Why It's Important

Advertising is an important element of promotion. You need to know the different ways a business can use advertising media to promote its image and products.

Key Terms

- promotional advertising
- institutional advertising
- media
- print media
- broadcast media
- online advertising
- banner ad
- specialty media

as television, can be too expensive for many businesses. Advertising can be inefficient—not everyone who reads a magazine ad is a potential customer. Advertising messages are often very short. A page of advertising or a few words on a billboard cannot inform a potential buyer in the same way that other forms of promotion, such as a personal sales presentation, can.

Types of Media

Media are the agencies, means, or instruments used to convey advertising messages to the public. The four general categories of advertising media are print, broadcast, online, and specialty. Figure 19-1 illustrates media expenditures and Figure 19-2 on page 340 illustrates the different types of media.

■ Print Media

Print media is written advertising that may be included in everything from newspapers and magazines to direct mail, signs, and billboards. They are among the oldest and most effective types of advertising.

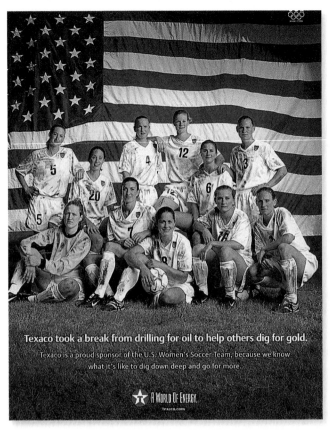

■ **Get the Picture?** Institutional advertising creates good relationships between a business and the public. *How does this advertisement seek to accomplish this?*

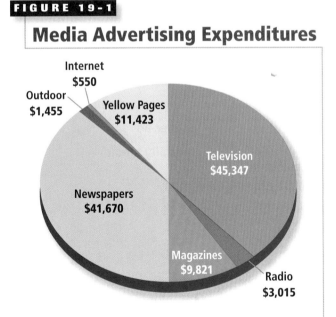

FIGURE 19-1

Media Advertising Expenditures

Internet $550
Outdoor $1,455
Yellow Pages $11,423
Television $45,347
Newspapers $41,670
Magazines $9,821
Radio $3,015

■ **U.S. Advertising Expenditures** Advertising is a multibillion-dollar business. Given the 1999 figures shown in the pie chart, calculate the total spent on advertising among all types of media. *What percentage was spent on television advertising?*

NEWSPAPER ADVERTISING Newspapers are the main form of print media for many businesses. Newspapers can be daily or weekly and may be local, regional, or national in scope.

Local newspapers are sold to community subscribers. National newspapers, such as *USAToday* and *The Wall Street Journal,* are distributed to regional markets and throughout the country.

Daily and weekly newspapers feature local news and advertising about area businesses. One type of community paper is called a *shopper.* Shoppers contain little editorial content, but are delivered free to persons who live in certain areas.

Advantages of newspaper advertising include large readership and a high level of reader involvement. Newspapers carry high interest content that attracts readers. It is estimated that 55 percent of U.S. adults read a newspaper every day. Since newspaper circulation is known, advertisers can target their advertising to people living in certain areas or with certain interests. The cost of newspaper advertising is relatively low because the quality of reproduction (paper and print) is less than that used in magazines and direct mail. Subscribers pay for some of the publishing costs. Newspaper ads are timely and advertisers can easily change ads, often up to 24 hours before the paper goes to print.

Newspaper advertising does have some limitations. Wasted circulation can occur, as when papers are sent to a wider area than the target market. Advertising life is short, because newspapers are thrown away. Finally, the black-and-white format of most newspapers makes ads less appealing than other print media. This can be overcome with the use of freestanding inserts and supplements.

MAGAZINE ADVERTISING Magazines can be classified as local, regional, or national, as well as weeklies, monthlies, and quarterlies. Local and regional magazines are often developed for cities or metropolitan areas to promote businesses in their immediate geographical area. Many national magazines have regional editions and rates. *Field and Stream,* for example, has seven regional editions. Examples of national weeklies include news magazines such as *U.S. News and World Report, Time,* and *Newsweek.*

Magazines can also be classified as consumer or business (trade) magazines. Consumer magazines are read for personal pleasure or interest and include such publications as *Reader's Digest, Vogue,* and *Sports Illustrated.*

Business magazines appeal to people with an interest in general business or a particular business field. Examples of general business publications include *Business Week, Fortune,* and *Forbes.* Some business magazines or trade journals, such as *Supermarket News, Advertising Age,* or *Stores,* are directed at individuals in a certain field of business. Special interest magazines are important to smaller companies selling products to specialized markets because they reach target audiences with little wasted circulation or irrelevant editorial content.

Magazine advertisers, like newspaper advertisers, can target their audiences because they know the circulation and characteristics of regular readers. Magazines have a longer life span and are often read more slowly and thoroughly than newspapers. The information in a magazine ad is more likely to be remembered. The print quality in magazines is generally better than that in newspapers. People tend to keep magazines for a more extended period of time, increasing the chance that they (and the ads in them) may be reread. Magazines offer a variety

MARKETPLACE

Not Just the ABCs

Imagine creating a typewriter with over 3,000 keys! The Japanese language, containing over 3,000 separate characters, or ideographs, creates a challenge for keyboard and typewriter manufacturers. The ancient Chinese symbols—known as *kanji*—are the symbols upon which Japanese is based. And that's not all! The Japanese also use two other alphabets—*katakana* for English and foreign words and *hiragana* for Japanese grammar and pronunciation. Creating more work for advertising typesetters, most billboards in Japan combine both alphabets to communicate with everyone!

Thinking Critically

Why is it important to use both alphabets in Japan?

of presentation formats, including full page ads, two-page spreads, gatefolds (a page folded into itself), return cards, and heavy stock inserts.

Despite these advantages, there are drawbacks to magazine advertising. Compared to newspapers, magazines have less mass appeal within a geographical area and are more expensive. Deadlines for inserting magazine ads are often many months before actual publication, which makes them less timely.

DIRECT-MAIL ADVERTISING Direct-mail advertising, as its name suggests, is sent by businesses directly through the mail to prospective customers. Types of direct-mail advertising include newsletters, catalogs, coupons, samplers, price lists, circulars, invitations to special sales or events, postage-paid reply cards, and letters. Businesses often enclose direct-mail advertising with their monthly bills and statements. Large retailers and manufacturers send direct-mail catalogs and price lists to prospective customers.

Mailing lists are assembled by the advertiser from current customer records. They may also be purchased from a direct mail specialty firm that offers lists of potential customers. Mailing lists must be accurate or using them is a waste of a resources.

■ **Drive-by Advertising** Billboards are outdoor signs that advertise. *Do you think this is a local or national advertisement?*

Direct mail advertisers can be highly selective about who will receive their mailing. They control the timing of the mailing and prevent competitors from seeing the initial mailing. The advertiser has a wide choice of advertisement sizes and formats—such as letters, catalogs, and postcards—limited only by certain postal regulations. Direct mail advertisers can use coupons or other incentives to get customers to try the product. The advertiser can use direct mail, such as product catalogs or magazine or music club subscriptions, to actually make the sale. Customers can order or subscribe directly using an order form or a toll-free number.

There are some disadvantages to direct-mail advertising. There is a low level of response in relation to the number of items sent—usually less than one percent. Many people think of direct-mail advertising as "junk mail" to be discarded without opening or careful reading. This problem is compounded when customer lists become dated and items are sent to the wrong target audience. The cost of direct mail is high, including producing and printing each piece of the mailing, maintaining and buying mailing lists, processing, and postage.

DIRECTORY ADVERTISING Directory advertising is an alphabetical listing of households and businesses. The best known of these listings are telephone *directories*, which are commonly divided into the White Pages (alphabetical listings) and the Yellow Pages (categorical and alphabetical listings).

In the White Pages, businesses receive a free alphabetical listing along with noncommercial telephone customers. In the Yellow Pages, businesses pay for an alphabetical listing and, if desired, a larger display ad. These appear under general headings, such as florists, physicians, recreational vehicles, or travel agencies. The Yellow Pages help consumers find suppliers of goods and services.

Directory advertising has some unique advantages. It is relatively inexpensive and can be used with all demographic groups (telephone directories are found in 98 percent of American households). Directories are usually kept for at least a year until another is provided. One advantage, however, is also a disadvantage—directories are usually printed yearly. Advertisers cannot adjust their prices, advertise sales, or change their message easily.

Service businesses like to use directory advertising, which is illustrated in the local Yellow Pages. You will see ads for such service providers as accountants, electricians, plumbers, and physicians. These are all businesses that you are likely to call only when you have a particular need. These services are used infrequently; therefore, such businesses often combine directory advertising with other forms of advertising to attract customers before there is a service need.

OUTDOOR ADVERTISING Both local and national businesses use outdoor signs, or billboards, for advertising. There are two types of outdoor signs—*nonstandardized* and *standardized*.

Nonstandardized outdoor signs are used by local firms at their places of business or in other locations throughout the community. Businesses usually pay rent to the owners on whose property the signs are displayed for the off-site signs.

Standardized outdoor signs are available to local, regional, or national advertisers. These signs, which are purchased from outdoor advertising companies in standard sizes, are placed near highly traveled roads and freeways where there is high visibility.

■ **E-billboards** E-billboards are digital video screens that display advertising. *Why is a train station a good place to put these screens?*

Three types of standardized outdoor signs are *posters, painted bulletins,* and *spectaculars. Posters* are pre-printed sheets put up like wallpaper on outdoor billboards. They are changed three to four times each year. *Painted bulletins* are painted billboards that are changed about every six months to a year. *Spectaculars* are outdoor advertising signs which use lights or moving parts and are situated in high traffic areas, such as densely populated metropolitan cities.

Outdoor advertising is highly visible and relatively inexpensive. It provides a 24-hour a day message and can be located to reach specific target markets. However, despite its popularity with some advertisers, its use is becoming more restricted. In fact, four states (Alaska, Hawaii, Maine, and Vermont) have completely banned billboards on the premise that the signs mar scenic views and distract drivers. In many urban areas, outdoor billboards have size restrictions and spacing requirements. They also have to be a specified number of feet away from schools, parks, and playgrounds. Outdoor advertising is primarily used along roadways in areas zoned for commercial and industrial uses.

Some limitations for outdoor advertising include limited viewing time, a largely unknown audience of viewers, and increasing government regulations.

TRANSIT ADVERTISING *Transit advertising* uses public transportation facilities to bring advertising messages to people. It includes:

- Printed posters found inside business and commuter trains
- Exterior posters on the outside of taxis and buses
- Station posters located near or in subways and in railroad, bus, and airline terminals

Transit advertising reaches a wide and (in the case of bus and train passengers) captive audience. It is economical and has a defined market, usually an urban area. Unfortunately, transit advertising is often unavailable in smaller towns and cities, is subject to defacement, and is restricted to predetermined travel routes.

A new type of popular advertising in bus stops, train stations, and gas stations are *e-billboards.* These are video screens that advertisers use to promote their products. E-billboards can also be used in stores, lobbies of hotels or buildings, elevators, and even at lines in amusement parks.

■ Broadcast Media

Broadcast media includes radio and television. The average person will spend nearly ten years watching television and almost six years listening to the radio over a lifetime of 70 years. You can see why advertising through broadcast media is popular.

People use television and radio not only for entertainment, but also to get information. In fact, people are more likely to believe the information they get from television than the information they get from print media. Since they can both see and hear the television message, it comes alive for them.

In the United States, there are approximately 10,000 AM and FM radio broadcast stations. Most of the 1,200 commercial television stations are affiliated with one of the major networks—ABC, CBS, NBC, or FOX. In addition, there are about 11,600 cable systems. Over 66 percent of the estimated 98 million TV households are cable television subscribers.

Given the tremendous availability and the popularity of broadcast media, it is no surprise that many businesses use it to sell their products, despite the higher advertising costs involved.

FIGURE 19-2

ADVERTISING MEDIA

A business can use different types of advertising media to promote its image and products in different ways. Media are the agencies, means, or instruments used to convey advertising messages to the public. The four general categories of advertising media are print, broadcast, online, and specialty media. The advertising media should be determined much in the same way as the advertising message, by the appeal and the target audience. *How would you categorize each of these specific advertising mediums?*

MAGAZINES

Magazines generate a high level of reader involvement and the messages can be seen repeatedly. *TV Guide* and *People* have been ranked first and second, respectively, in gross revenues for the past several years among the top 300 magazines with advertising revenues of $1,080,118 in 1998 (dollars in thousands).

NEWSPAPERS

Newspapers are a convenient way for a local advertiser to present a message in selected geographical areas.

TELEVISION ADVERTISING

Television advertising combines audio, visual, and live action effects to present an often-entertaining message.

DIRECT MAIL

Direct mail advertising sends a message right to your home. Direct mail items encourage customers to try new products, since they are convenient and can be used with little effort.

TRANSIT ADVERTISING

Transit advertising uses public transportation facilities and vehicles to bring advertising messages to people.

TELEVISION ADVERTISING Television is the ultimate advertising medium for many businesses because it can communicate a message with sound, action, and color. Prime time for network and cable television is between 8 p.m. and 11 p.m., when millions of viewers are watching.

Most television commercial advertisements are 30- or 60-second spots. An exception is the infomercial, which is a 30-minute advertisement. Infomercials promote products such as cookware, exercise equipment, and appliances using a talk-show type setting. Viewers can order the advertised merchandise by calling a phone number or writing to an address.

Perhaps more than any other medium, television can pull together all the elements necessary to produce a creative advertising message. Television is also great for demonstrating a product's features and benefits. Television advertising is very appealing to large companies with widespread distribution. Think of the catch phrases and jingles you know by heart simply from hearing them on TV commercials.

Television can be directed to an audience with a specific interest—such as news, comedy, history, movies, sports, or science—through cable networks. A televised advertising message can be adapted to take advantage of holidays, seasonal changes, and special-events programming, such as the Super Bowl, the NCAA basketball tournament, or entertainment specials.

There are drawbacks to using television as an advertising medium. Television has the highest production costs of any type of media and a high dollar cost for the time used. Prime-time costs, in particular, are sometimes prohibitive. They keep many smaller companies from using television advertising or force them to buy time in less desirable periods when fewer people are watching. Actual audience size is not assured, and many viewers consider television commercials to be an opportunity to leave the room. As a result, advertising dollars don't always pay off.

RADIO ADVERTISING It is estimated that radio reaches 96 percent of all people age 12 and over in a given week. This ability to reach a wide audience makes radio an extremely effective advertising medium.

The best times for radio advertising are when people are driving to work in the morning and when they are coming home during the afternoon or early evening. These are called prime times or "drive times" for radio advertising because advertisers are guaranteed a concentrated audience.

Radio advertisements are presented in 15-, 30-, or 60-second time periods. The messages are effective in encouraging people to buy because the announcer or actors—along with background music, jingles, slogans, and sound effects—add excitement, drama, or humor.

Radio advertisers can select an audience, such as teenagers, various ethnic groups, and professionals, by advertising on stations targeting that particular market. Radio is more flexible than print advertising because messages can be changed easily. An advertiser can make changes in the script for an advertising message a few days, or even just a few minutes, before the message is recorded. Radio is a mobile medium that can be taken just about anywhere—shopping, jogging, hiking, or driving.

There are also several disadvantages to radio advertising. Radio advertisements have a short life span. When a message is broadcast, it is over—unless the business pays to have it rebroadcast later. In fact, radio advertisers usually buy several time slots instead of just one. In larger markets with many stations, several stations often compete for the same audience. Potential advertisers must decide on which radio station to advertise, or advertise on several.

The lack of visual involvement causes some listeners to become easily distracted and miss some, most, or all of the message. That is why the catchy jingle is so useful.

■ **Would You Like to Have Something to Eat?**
HomeGrocer.com is one company that uses a catchy jingle in its television ads. *What are the benefits of this?*

■ Online Advertising

Online advertising involves placing advertising messages on the Internet. Online advertising is still a small part of overall advertising spending, but it is growing quickly. Estimates call for spending to go up to $10 billion by 2002. Most online advertising appears as banner ads. A banner ad is usually a wide shallow rectangle seen at the top or bottom of Web pages, which takes the user to the advertiser's Web page if clicked with a mouse. Banner advertisements that use technology known as "rich media" include animation, sound, and even video. Similar to banner ads, but smaller in size, are button ads placed in a strategic position on a Web page. Both banner and button ads are designed to attract viewers to click through to the advertiser's Web site. Some advertisers use *interstitial ads,* which are screens that pop up to interrupt Web surfing. A viewer must click on the billboard to get to the Web site or close the ad window to resume surfing.

Unlike other forms of print advertising, online advertisers can easily measure effectiveness by the number of *click-throughs,* or times the ad has been visited. Online advertisers have found that bold colors, top-of-page placement, animation, calls to action, and limited frequency of exposures help increase that number of click-throughs. Even using these techniques, online advertisers report response rates as low as one percent. In other words, for every 100 banner ads, only one in one hundred Web users click the ad. Although online advertising is now part of the advertising media mix, its overall selling effectiveness is still uncertain.

REAL WORLD MARKETING

The Outer Limits of Advertising

These are the voyages of the Starship Radio Shack!?! Radio Shack, in an effort to brand itself as a leader in consumer technology, is joining forces with a space mission. In exchange for an undisclosed dollar amount, LunaCorp will allow Radio Shack to place its logo on the new moon rover, scheduled to land on the moon in 2003. The mission's objective is to explore ice on the moon. The marketing endeavor will allow Radio Shack customers to participate in the mission via the Internet. Radio Shack's marketing department believes the effort will be an effective way to stimulate brand interest.

Thinking Critically
Are there any areas that should be considered safe from advertising? What are the pros and cons?

Some people find online advertisements an annoyance or a distraction from the Web page that they are visiting. Other Internet users may be concerned about the reliability or privacy issues associated with unfamiliar Web sites that may appear in banner ads.

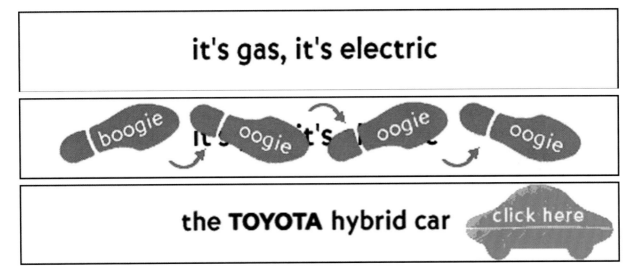

■ **Banners Galore** Online advertising involves placing advertising messages on the Internet. *What characteristics of banner ads cause the viewer to click to the advertiser's Web site?*

Case Study

A Free Ticket on the Internet Express

How would you like free unlimited Internet access? Companies such as AltaVista, Blue Light, Juno, and NetZero offer customers just that. But there is a catch. After signing on, you'll be required to fill out a personal questionnaire. This information helps advertisers target advertising messages to you.

Free Internet services are popular in the United States with teenagers and their parents. They are also immensely popular overseas, like in Great Britain where people have to pay a "per-minute" fee for local phone calls. Other individuals avoid free Internet service providers because they worry about their privacy. They are concerned about how the information they would submit about themselves will be used. All free Internet companies have privacy policies and promise to keep any personal information private. Free Internet access works well for people who don't mind the questionnaires and aren't bothered by the advertisements.

Case Study Review

1. What factors should a potential user consider in evaluating free Internet service providers?
2. Why are free Internet services popular with teenagers and their parents?

A MATTER OF ETHICS

3. Is it possible for Internet providers to uphold a privacy code on the Internet? Why or why not?

■ Specialty Media

Specialty media are relatively inexpensive, useful items with an advertiser's name printed on them. The items are usually given away with no obligation attached to receiving and keeping them.

To be successful as advertising tools, specialty items must be practical, subject to frequent use, and likely to be placed in locations with high visibility. Common items that fit this description include bottle openers, calendars, magnets, pens and pencils, memo pads, and key chains. When designed well, specialty items carry the name and address of the business sponsoring them and an advertising message urging the reader to action. Sometimes, however, the size of the item prevents the use of a message, and there is only room for the name and address of the business.

Specialty advertising has some limitations. The distribution of the items is usually limited. In addition, the items might be given to people who would never consider buying the product or patronizing the business.

■ Other Advertising Media

Businesses are constantly creating innovative means of transmitting their messages to potential customers. Examples include sports arena billboards, ads in movie theaters and home video rentals, ads placed on hot air balloons and blimps, skywriting, and airplanes pulling advertising banners. Increasingly, advertising techniques, such as electronic shelf ads, supermarket cart advertising displays, and instant coupon machines, are being used to advertise products in the store.

Selection of Promotional Media

The choice of an advertising medium ultimately depends on the product to be advertised, the habits and lifestyles of the target audience, and the types of media available in the area.

To determine the type of promotional media to use advertisers need to address three basic questions:

- *Does the medium have the ability to present the product and the appropriate business image?*
- *Does the medium have the ability to target the desired customers?*
- *Does the medium have the ability to obtain the desired response rate?*

The selected advertising medium ideally illustrates the company's product or product line well. It provides the opportunity to present an effective selling message, which stirs excitement for a customer to buy. The advertising medium should portray the desired business image with an appropriate measure of prestige and distinction.

It is important that the medium reaches the targeted audience and covers the appropriate geographical area. Flexibility, in terms of making last-minute changes, can allow the advertiser to take advantage of special promotions and events more easily.

The medium must have the capability to reach the greatest number of potential customers. Hopefully, the selected medium will also generate high response rates for the business at the lowest possible cost per customer.

Electronic Frontiers

The Ad is in the E-mail

In May 2000, CBS officials were worried that their newest show—a departure from their typical target market—wouldn't catch on with audiences. In fact, CBS was so worried about promoting its new show that it e-mailed a miniature television commercial to over 29,000 viewers. It was CBS's hope that even if they didn't tune in, recipients would forward the e-mail to their friends. The show—Survivor—became a critical financial success for CBS. E-commercials have become popular not only because they are cheaper than television commercials but also because (unlike radio and television advertising) marketers can track who watches the commercial and for how long. Who knows . . . your next e-mail message just might be from your favorite television network!

Thinking Critically

How could e-mail ads help a musician sell albums? What would the benefit be?

19.1 ASSESSMENT

Reviewing Key Terms and Concepts

1. What is advertising?
2. What is the main purpose of advertising?
3. List the six different types of print media.
4. What are two forms of broadcast advertising?
5. What is online advertising?

Thinking Critically

6. If response rates are very low with online advertising, why do some advertisers continue to use it?

Integrating Academic Skills

7. **COMMUNICATION** Gather information about one product from three different types of media. Use a word processor to create a one-page summary of how these sources differ from each other in their presentation of the products.

Media Rates

Media Costs

To reach customers, advertising uses a set format that is defined in terms of time (a 30-second television commercial) or space (a half-page newspaper ad). Media costs vary greatly, not just with type of media but with geographical location as well. For example, a quarter-page newspaper ad in a large-city daily newspaper could cost four to eight times more than the same size ad in a small-town weekly. Given such variations, it is virtually impossible to quote exact rates for each type of media advertising. It is possible, however, to generalize about how those rates are set.

When businesses want to access rates for the various media, they can look up the rates in the publications of Standard Rate and Data Service. It publishes rate cards for most major media according to general categories, such as print media or broadcast media.

Another advertising industry service important to both advertisers and print media is the Audit Bureau of Circulation (ABC). Print media publishers subscribe to the ABC to have it verify their circulation figures. This is important in print media because advertising rates are based on circulation. Circulation figures are important selling points for the media to use when trying to attract advertisers to the publication.

■ Newspaper Rates

Newspaper advertising rates are classified into two categories depending on whether the ad is a *classified ad* or a *display ad.* Classified ads can advertise everything from services to houses for sale to job openings. They are called *classified* because they are grouped or classified into specific categories, such as help wanted, real estate, personals, and auto sales. People or businesses that buy classified ads usually pay by the word or line of type.

Display ads involve the creative illustration of the product being advertised. They are a mix of art or photographs, headlines, copy, and a signature or logo of the product or business. Display ads are generally larger than classified ads and their cost is based upon the amount of space used.

Newspapers quote display advertising rates by the column inch. A column inch is an area that is one column wide by one inch deep. If a newspaper quotes a column inch rate, you simply multiply the number of inches by the number of columns to determine the total number of column inches. Then you multiply the total column inches by the rate. An example is if the rate for a column inch is $17, then an ad that measures four inches long by three columns will cost $204.

$$\$17 \times 4 \text{ inches} \times 3 \text{ columns} = \$204$$

• What You'll Learn

- How various media rates are set
- The costs of print media
- The standards for selecting promotional media

• Why It's Important

Since businesses need to reach as many customers as possible within limited budgets, you will need to know how to calculate media costs to best reach your potential audience.

Key Terms

- cost per thousand (CPM)
- network radio advertising
- national spot radio advertising
- local radio advertising
- cooperative advertising

A number of factors can change the regular newspaper rates charged to advertisers. Display ads are usually sold at *run-of-paper* rates. Run-of-paper allows the newspaper to choose where to run an ad in the paper. However, for a higher rate advertisers can run ads in guaranteed or preferred locations, such as the last page of a section.

The use of color also affects the advertising rate. Color ads are sold at a higher rate than those done in black and white. The frequency of advertising lowers the rate charged for display ads. The more a business advertises, the lower the rate charged.

Businesses that advertise in a newspaper generally pay an *open rate*. The open rate, often referred to as the noncontract rate, is the basic charge for a minimum amount of advertising space. The open rate varies depending on when an advertisement will appear in a paper. A newspaper may charge a Monday through Thursday rate of $28 per column inch, a Friday rate of $29, a Saturday rate of $31, and a Sunday rate of $35 per column inch.

Businesses that advertise in the newspaper more frequently may contract with a newspaper to guarantee that they will use a certain amount of space for a specified time period. They are granted *contract rates*, which are discounted from the open rate. Contracts can be written in a number of ways. A yearly frequency contract guarantees that an advertiser will use a minimum number of column inches each week for 52 weeks. A bulk space contract guarantees that a minimum number of inches will be used when the advertiser chooses, within a 12-month period.

Another important rate is the cost per thousand (CPM) rate, which is the media cost of exposing 1,000 readers to an ad. It is useful in comparing the cost of advertising to reach 1,000 readers in one newspaper to the cost of advertising to reach 1,000 readers in another newspaper. The comparison is made by using the following formula:

$$\text{Cost of the ad} \times 1,000/\text{Circulation} = \text{cost per thousand (CPM)}$$

Suppose the cost of an ad in the *Times* is $500 and the paper has a circulation of 500,000. Its cost per thousand rate would be calculated as follows:

$$\$500 \times 1,000/500,000 = \$500,000/500,000 = \$1 \text{ per } 1,000 \text{ readers.}$$

The cost of an ad in the *Tribune*, a competing paper, is $600, and the paper has a circulation of 300,000. Its cost per thousand rate would be calculated as follows:

$$\$600 \times 1,000/300,000 = \$600,000/300,000 = \$2 \text{ per } 1,000 \text{ readers}$$

All other things being equal, an advertiser would probably choose the *Times* over the *Tribune* because it would cost less per 1,000 readers. Of course, all other things might not be equal. The *Tribune's* circulation could include more of the advertiser's target market, or the paper could offer a special ad placement. The point is that the CPM is a convenient measure that allows you to compare costs among newspapers.

■ Magazine Rates

Magazine rates are based on circulation, quality of readership, and production technique. To calculate the actual cost of magazine advertising, you need to become familiar with some terms found on magazine advertising rate cards, including *bleed, black-and-white rates, color rates, premium position, discounts,* and the *cost per thousand rate (CPM)* discussed earlier.

Bleed means that half- or full-page ads are printed to the very edge of the page, leaving no white border. Magazines generally charge between 15 to 20 percent extra for bleeds.

The lowest rate magazines offer for display ads are black-and-white rates for black-and-white advertisements. *Color rates* are offered for color ads. Each time the magazine adds color to the ad, the rates increase. Four-color advertisements, also called *full-color,* are the most expensive magazine ads.

Premium position refers to where ads are placed in the magazine. Ads placed in premium positions, such as on the back cover or the inside first page, are more expensive to run. The back cover is considered the highest premium position because people will see the ad whenever the magazine is placed cover down. The inside front cover and first page are also premium positions because most people begin reading a magazine from the first page.

Frequency discounts are offered to advertisers who run the same ad several times during the year. The magazine may publish an entire schedule of rates for the number of times during the year an advertiser contracts to advertise. The rate per issue decreases as the frequency increases.

FIGURE 19-3

Magazine Rate Card

General Rates

RATE BASE: Rates based on a yearly average of 1,100,000 net paid A B C
A member of the Audit Bureau of Circulation

SPACE UNITS	BLACK & WHITE	BLACK & ONE COLOR	FOUR COLOR
1 page	$16,000	$19,630	$23,300
2 columns	11,620	14,560	18,170
½ page	10,130	13,550	17,200
1 column	5,920	9,530	12,180
½ column	3,020		
Covers			
Second Cover			$25,520
Third Cover			23,300
Fourth Cover			27,020

BLEED CHARGE: 15%
AGENCY COMMISSION: 15%
CASH DISCOUNT: 2% 10 days, net 30 days

Bleed accepted in color, black & white, and on covers, at an additional charge of 15%. No charge for gutter bleed in double-page spread.

Premium Positions: A 10% premium applies to advertising units positioned on pages 1, 2, and 3. A surcharge of 5% applies to bleed units in premium positions.

Rate Change Announcements will be made at least two months in advance of the black & white closing date for the issue affected. Orders for issues thereafter at rates then prevailing.

ISSUANCE AND CLOSING DATES

A. On sale date approximately the 15th of month preceding date of issue.

B. Black & white, black & one color, and four-color closing date, 20th of the 3rd month preceding date of issue. Example: Forms for August issue close May 20th.

C. Orders for cover pages noncancellable. Orders for all inside advertising units are noncancellable 15 days prior to their respective closing dates. Supplied inserts are noncancellable the 1st of the 4th month preceding month of issue. Options on cover positions must be exercised at least 30 days prior to four-color closing date. If order is not received by such date, cover option automatically lapses.

■ **Ad Rates** Ad rates are based on color. *Based on this magazine rate card, what is the cost of a half-page four-colored ad paid in ten days from the issuance of the invoice?*

Another discount is a *commission*—a percentage of sales given by the magazine to the advertising agency for placing the ad for the advertiser. A typical commission is 15 percent.

Finally, a cash discount may be offered for paying the bill earlier than its due date (this may be written 2/10, net 30). This cash discount would permit the advertiser or ad agency to take a two percent discount if the bill is paid within ten days from the date of the invoice. The payment, if the discount is not taken, is due 30 days from the date of the invoice.

Take a look at the rate card in Figure 19-3. You would calculate the cost of a full-page, four-color advertisement with bleed as follows:

$23,300	1 page, four-color rate
× .15	bleed
$ 3,495	extra for bleed
$23,300	1 page, four-color rate
+ 3,495	bleed
$26,795	for 1 page, four color, with bleed

An ad agency placed the ad and it took the commission and the cash discount. The total cost of the above ad to the agency would be:

$ 26,795	1 page, four color, with bleed
× .15	ad agency's commission
$ 4,019.25	
$26,795.00	1 page, four color, with bleed
− 4,019.25	agency's commission
$22,775.75	net cost of ad to agency after commission
× .02	cash discount percentage if paid within 10 days of invoice
$ 455.52	cash discount
$22,775.75	net cost of ad to agency after commission
− 455.52	cash discount
$22,320.23	net cost to advertising agency for one full-page, four-color ad, with bleed after cash discount and agency commission.

As with newspapers, the CPM can be used to compare the cost of advertising in several magazines. A magazine that has a circulation of 2 million and a full-page, black-and-white ad rate of $35,000, would have a CPM rate $17.50.

$$\$35,000 \times 1,000/2,000,000 = \$17.50$$

■ Online Rates

Online advertising rates are based upon the type of format the customer desires. Banner ads, rich-media enhanced banner ads, button/text links, and interstitial ads are some of the options. Online advertising rates are set on a CPM rate of page views. Rates vary based on the volume of monthly page views.

Like newspapers and magazines, online advertisers also look at the CPM rate to determine the medium's effectiveness. A recent study by AdKnowledge of approximately 1200 Web sites found that the average CPM rate was about $40 per thousand or $.04 per banner ad. However, there is a wide range for individual sites. Some very popular sites targeted to high-income professionals averaged over $100/CPM, others were as low as $10/CPM. Discounts are offered to high volume advertisers. Last-minute purchasers of unused advertising space are able to buy banner ads at as low as $1/CPM.

Many online advertisers also engage in barter arrangements, whereby each advertiser agrees to run banner ads for the other. Companies that have the same target market or that sell complimentary products can benefit from such a relationship. Barter arrangements can lead to more traffic for each business and is another method to use unsold advertising capacity.

■ Radio Rates

When purchasing radio time, a business needs to decide what kind of radio advertising to use. There are three options—network radio advertising, national spot radio advertising, and local radio advertising.

Businesses with a national scope usually choose network radio advertising or national spot radio advertising. **Network radio advertising** is a broadcast from a studio to all affiliated radio stations throughout the country. Network radio advertising allows an advertiser to broadcast an ad simultaneously to several markets through sponsorship of a special program, activity, or radio personality.

National spot radio advertising is used by national firms to advertise on a local station-by-station basis. It is used to target select markets in the country. **Local radio advertising** is done by a local business for its target market. It is limited to a specific geographical area.

When selecting advertising, it is important to know the difference between spot radio and spot commercials. Spot radio refers to the geographical area an advertiser wants to reach with its advertising. Spot commercials are advertising messages of one minute or less that can be carried on network or spot radio.

BRIGHT IDEAS
Wouldn't You Like to Be a Pepper, Too!

Have you ever wondered what flavor Dr. Pepper is? Some say it is grape juice, others say cherry juice and still others claim it is prune juice! In truth, Dr. Pepper's flavor is a closely guarded secret created by Charles Alderton, who combined soda flavors to serve customers of Morrison's Old Corner Drug Store in Waco, Texas. One soda combination in particular became very popular. Alderton and store owner Wade Morrison were overwhelmed by demand for the drink and had trouble making enough soda to supply customers. Morrison spoke to the owner of Circle "A" Ginger Ale Company about bottling the drink. Alderton, not wanting to pursue the business of soft drink manufacturing, dropped out while Morrison got help from the Artesian Manufacturing and Bottling Company. In 1904, the company introduced Dr. Pepper to 20 million people at the World's Fair Exposition.

Thinking Creatively
Dr. Pepper has changed its advertising campaign several times. Develop an advertising slogan for the company appropriate for the next decade.

Each radio station determines actual advertising rates by time of day. Rates are higher during peak listening times, also called "drive times" (early mornings and late afternoons). Radio stations also offer less costly, run-of-schedule (ROS) airtimes. ROS airtime allows a radio station to decide when to run the ad spot. Target audiences, audience size, rates, weekly package plans, and discounts vary from station to station; therefore, a business should carefully review and compare the rates of the radio stations on which it might advertise.

■ Television Rates

Advertising rates for television also vary with time of day. It is more expensive, for example, to advertise during the hours of 8 p.m. to 11 p.m. (known as Class AA time) than during other hours. The rates charged for other time slots, such as Class A, Class B, Class C, and Class D, are lower based on diminishing viewership. Businesses try to place their advertisements in time slots during which their potential customers will most likely see them.

A business considering the purchase of television time contacts a television media representative. The representative helps the business determine coverage times available. He or she also arranges package deals that can be developed to give the advertiser more advertising spots, volume, or seasonal discounts.

Cooperative Advertising

Cooperative advertising is a cost-sharing arrangement whereby both a supplier and a local advertiser pay for advertising. Cooperative advertisements feature both the supplier's (typically a manufacturer's) product name and the name of the local advertiser. In a cooperative advertising campaign, a variety of advertising and promotional materials are usually supplied to the local advertiser. These might include print newspaper ads with space for the advertiser's name and address, scripts for television and radio ads with time allotted for the local advertiser's name and location, in-store advertising displays, and posters. An example of a cooperative advertisement might be a newspaper display promoting Calvin Klein products at Lord & Taylor. This ad tells people that Lord & Taylor carries the Calvin Klein line and also encourage shoppers to come to the Lord & Taylor to shop. Both parties benefit from this.

To participate in cooperative advertising campaign, a local advertiser must follow certain guidelines and sign an agreement with the supplier. The guidelines include specific conditions for featuring the supplier's product or service in the media, such as size of a print ad and its placement.

Each time a local advertiser purchases a supplier's goods or services, a certain number of advertising credits are earned—usually three to five percent of the total purchase price. A local advertiser can use these credits to offset advertising that meets with the supplier's approval. Sometimes, the local advertiser pays for all the advertising and then presents the ads to the supplier to receive reimbursement. Up to 50 percent of the total pre-approved advertising expenses are normally reimbursed to the local advertiser.

■ **Cooperative Advertising** Cooperative advertising displays a manufacturer's products along with the name of the local advertiser. *How do cooperative advertisers share in costs and benefits?*

There are advantages and disadvantages to cooperative advertising for the manufacturer and retailer. Advantages to cooperative advertising may include shared advertising expenses (between supplier and local advertiser) and pre-prepared print advertisements, in-store displays, and TV and radio scripts for local use. Retailers specifically benefit from cooperative advertising as they gain access to greater amounts of promotional funding. Manufacturers benefit specifically as they can gain local recognition—people are made aware of where they can purchase their products nearby. Disadvantages may include loss of control over content, placement in various media, and the need for local advertisers to follow guidelines of suppliers.

Promotional Budget

Once a company decides on promotional methods, it must create a budget. The promotional budget considers not only the cost for the advertising, but for the staff necessary to make it all happen as well. This budget must be considered not only in short-term, but also in the long-term benefits that advertising brings about. There are numerous methods that a company might use when deciding on a budget. Four common promotional budgeting methods are *percentage of anticipated sales, all you can afford, following the competition,* and *objective and task*.

In the *percentage of anticipated sales* method the budget is decided based on a percentage of past or anticipated sales. An example of this might be that the budget for advertising this year is five percent of last year sales. An advantage of this is that there is little financial risk. On the other hand, if sales are down, the promotional budget may be decreased. As you know, it is advertising and promotional effects that could boost sales.

The *all you can afford method* turns all monies to promotional activity only after all other company expenses are paid. The objective is to build sales and reputation in the beginning. This method is often used for only a short period of time. It is popular in small businesses, especially Internet start-up companies.

In the *following the competition* method, the competitor's promotional expenditures are matched or spending is planned in proportion to market share. This is generally considered to be a weak promotional budgeting method because it is based on the competition's promotional objectives.

In the *objective and task* method, the company determines goals, considers the necessary steps to meet goals, and determines the cost for these promotional activities. This method considers the current situation that a company is in and where they want to be going. This is the most effective of the three methods as it considers what the company wants and how it will get there. It is an efficient use of company funds.

19.2 ASSESSMENT

Reviewing Key Terms and Concepts

1. Name three factors that affect newspaper rates.
2. What is the difference between an open rate and a contract rate?
3. What is the formula for figuring cost per thousand?
4. What determines the rate television and radio stations charge for advertising?
5. Name three factors that affect the selection of promotional media.

Thinking Critically

6. Will a prime-time television slot always guarantee an advertiser the best results in selling a product? Why or why not?

Integrating Academic Skills

7. **MATH** Calculate the per thousand rate for a magazine that has a circulation of 1.5 million and charges $25,000 for a full-page black-and-white advertisement.

Careers in Marketing

George Karaleks
Advertising Producer

Career Facts

What does your job entail?

"Advertising producers create media commercials. They select scripts and directors, and handle the financial arrangements for the project, which includes drawing up a budget, negotiating with unions, contracting with staff, and securing investors. Part of my job is to give recommendations to companies about how best to spend their money when given an array of statistics, demographics, and channels."

What do you recommend for students who want to go into advertising production?

"No one gets into advertising production fresh out of college. In business, the more specific the job function, the harder it is to get into. You need to build a reputation first. My advice is to become an assistant and take a low-level job that you can move up from."

What skills are most important?

"The ability to organize and prioritize is vital. It's my role to bring everyone together—from the actors to the person bidding on the music. I am the person to whom everyone turns when there is a problem. This requires thinking on your feet and doing what is best for both you and the client."

What kind of training did you have?

"I originally wanted to be an actor, because I knew that I wanted to communicate and convey a message. When I realized that I was not getting far in my acting career, I decided to go behind the camera. I went on to work for Grey Advertising and was made vice-president of the company within three years. I currently work on my own with many different clients, troubleshooting when problems come up in an advertising campaign."

What is the secret to your success?

"In this business, you have to be a jack-of-all-trades and master of all of them."

Thinking Critically

Why is it difficult to immediately get a job as an advertising producer?

Education and Training: Coursework in communication technologies, photographic arts, English, drama, speech, media, business management, and accounting is helpful. A bachelor's degree in dramatic arts also provides a good background.

Aptitudes, Abilities, and Skills: Ability to coordinate people, money, ideas, and resources, and above average communication skills for negotiating good business deals. The ability to multitask, and foresight to visualize the finished project are helpful.

Career Outlook: Faster than average growth is expected through the year 2006 due in part to increased use of Internet advertising.

Career Path: Advertising producers may first gain recognition as advertising copywriters. One can advance from associate producer to line producer to executive producer.

VOCABULARY REVIEW

Use the following vocabulary terms in a 250-word paper on advertising media.

- promotional advertising
- institutional advertising
- media
- print media
- broadcast media
- online advertising
- banner ads
- specialty media
- cost per thousand (CPM)
- network radio advertising
- national spot radio advertising
- local radio advertising
- cooperative advertising

FACT AND IDEA REVIEW

1. Identify advertising media categories. (19.1)

2. What are some advantages and disadvantages of using newspaper advertising? (19.1)

3. In what respect is magazine advertising superior to newspaper advertising? (19.1)

4. What is direct-mail advertising? Give five examples of direct-mail advertising. (19.1)

5. Why is outdoor advertising losing popularity in some areas of the country? (19.1)

6. Why is a knowledge of cost per thousand rates helpful to newspaper, magazine, and online advertisers? (19.2)

7. Why is broadcast media popular for advertising? (19.2)

8. What determines the rates charged for television advertising? (19.2)

9. What is the most effective way to create a promotional budget? (19.2)

THINKING CRITICALLY

1. How might consumer buying habits be different if advertising in all of the forms discussed in this chapter did not exist?

2. Why do companies use institutional advertising? Do you think that this is an effective method of advertising?

3. Assume you are a member of a legislative committee considering a ban on "junk mail" advertising. What information would you like to have from people on both sides of the issue before making your decision?

4. As more television and cable network channels develop, television advertisers are confronted with the problem of "channel surfers." These are people who use their remote control to switch channels to avoid viewing advertising commercials. Come up with one creative way that advertisers can try to limit the amount of channel surfing.

BUILDING WORKPLACE SKILLS

1. **Science** Environmentalists believe that advertising conducted on the Internet and online shopping will have positive effects on the environment. They believe that valuable resources can be saved or recycled. Develop a one-page outline (use broad topic headings such as Energy, Resources, Social Costs, etc.) on possible ways that electronic advertising and online shopping can preserve the environment.

2. **Language Arts** Why do some parents and school administrators believe that advertising should not occur within school buildings? Do you personally believe there should be limits on in-school advertising? Why or why not? Write a one-page paper explaining your position.

1. **Identifying Different Types of Advertising**
Look through newspapers and magazines to find examples of promotional and institutional advertising. Clip four appropriate ads, convert them into electronic form using a scanner, and create a computer presentation to show to the class.

2. **Analyzing Television Viewing** Use a spreadsheet computer program to prepare an advertising log for one hour of your television viewing. List the products advertised, characterize the advertising approach taken, and identify the sponsor as either national or local.

3. **Creating an Advertising Plan** Develop an advertising plan for a product of your choice. Use a word processing program to write a report about your plan that identifies what media you will use, your target audience, and times you want the ad to run. Decide whether you will use institutional or promotional advertising or a combination of both. Research the costs of each advertising medium and your estimated advertising budget per month and per year.

4. **Writing a Direct-Mail Piece** Using a word processing program, write a direct-mail marketing piece to promote either a Caribbean cruise adventure or a charity or special interest group of your choice. As you write your letter, think about your target market. Decide what other pieces should go into the package with the letter, such as reply cards, incentive discounts, or testimonial letters from famous people.

Information and Basic Skills Bring examples of the print advertisements produced by a local business to class. Be prepared to explain how often the print ads are run and in what types of print media they appear.

THE **DECA** CONNECTION
An Association of Marketing Students

Role Play: Direct Advertising Strategist

Situation You are to assume the role of sales associate in a newly opened apparel and accessories store. Since your store is new, procedures need to be established to create a customer mailing list.

Activity Your store manager (judge) has asked you to develop a plan for a direct-mail campaign to target new and current customers.

Evaluation You will be evaluated on how well you meet the following performance indicators:

- Explain the types of advertising media
- Write informative messages
- Write persuasive messages
- Explain the nature of written communications
- Explain the nature of direct advertising strategies

inter **NET** CONNECTION

About Our Company
You work for an advertising firm that develops online advertisements specializing in travel. You are required to review various banner ads developed by companies.

Connect
- Identify three travel-related Web sites that use banner advertisements.
- Write a report summarizing the features of each ad.
- Identify which banner ad you think is the best and explain why.

Chapter 20

Preparing Print Advertisements

Marketing: What It Takes

Advertising 101

As the manager of a new travel agency, you must prepare an ad layout announcing the agency's grand opening. Be sure to include the following: a headline, an illustration, copy that includes any introductory offers and special pricing that will be featured, and a signature plate including the location and hours.

WHAT WILL YOU DO?

What steps can you take to make sure you develop a great print advertisement?

Essential Elements of Advertising

The Advertising Agency

To advertise a product, a company must first determine the target audience it wants to reach and how much money it can spend. The next step is to develop an advertising campaign. An advertising campaign involves the creation and coordination of a series of advertisements (both broadcast and print) around a particular theme to promote a product. The size and the financial resources of a business determines whether an advertising campaign is developed by an "in-house" advertising department, a few designated individuals, or an advertising agency.

Advertising agencies work jointly with business clients to develop advertising campaigns. Depending on the scope and size of the advertising campaign and the needs of the business, agencies can serve as a *full-service agency* or a *limited-service agency*. Full-service agencies perform advertising research, media selection, copy development, and artwork for an advertising campaign. Larger advertising agencies employ specialists, such as copywriters, artists, media experts, marketing researchers, and legal advisers to assist with advertising campaigns.

Limited-service agencies specialize in one aspect of the campaign, such as creative services. *In-house agencies* provide full or limited advertising services based upon the size of the company.

Frequently, larger businesses select an advertising agency to be an *agency of record* to handle all aspects of the advertising campaign. The agency of record does all necessary research, media selection, copy development, and artwork. Increasingly, larger companies are selecting from specialists to develop different aspects of the advertising campaign. In addition, technology and e-commerce opportunities have caused many businesses to employ their own people to perform certain aspects of advertising, such as Web site development and maintenance.

Agency Organization

Advertising agencies are usually organized into four service departments: client, creative, research, and media.

Client service departments work with agency groups and individual businesses to identify opportunities for advertising. Employees—called account executives—look at client needs, create advertising plans, and coordinate advertising with other promotion activities related to the account.

What You'll Learn

- How advertising campaigns are developed
- The creation of advertising headlines
- The preparation of advertising copy
- The selection of advertising illustrations
- The significance of advertising signatures

Why It's Important

In order to understand how successful advertising campaigns help sell products, you need to know how essential advertising elements are used to develop effective advertisements.

Key Terms

- advertising campaign
- advertising agencies
- headline
- copy
- illustration
- clip art
- signature
- slogan

Stamping Out Unwanted E-mail

Everyone loves getting e-mail, right? Wrong! It might be nice to get an e-mail from a family member, coworker, or long lost friend, but what about unwanted junk e-mail? In an effort to limit unwanted e-mail, Congress approved the Unsolicited Electronic E-mail Act in 2000. The bill places restrictions on e-mail marketers. These restrictions include requiring "spam e-mail," or unsolicited e-mail, to include a valid reply-to-address. It also forces people and companies to stop spamming consumers upon request. Internet Service Providers, also referred to as "ISPs," are allowed to establish their own spam policies either accepting, limiting, or charging companies for sending spam. Those ISPs that are compensated for accepting spam must offer their subscribers the ability to opt out of spam e-mail.

Thinking Critically

Why would the government place restrictions on Internet advertising?

Creative service departments develop the advertising messages and produce the ads. Graphic artists, copywriters, commercial designers, and art directors work together in this department to create advertisements.

Research service employees study the target markets, the attitudes of potential customers, and buying behaviors toward a company's products. This department helps determine the type of message that will have the greatest appeal for a particular market segment.

Media service departments advise clients on their media choices. This department suggests an advertising budget for television, radio, newspapers, magazines, and other forms of advertising, such as billboards and direct mail. This department also coordinates the timing, placement, and frequency of various advertisements. The media plans developed by this department for a company's products are based on the region, city, population, gender income, education, and the reading and television viewing habits of people in the target market.

New Models for Advertising Agencies

Advertising experts predict that new models for advertising agencies will be used in the future. These new models will include business formats, such as creative boutiques, project team agencies, and virtual agencies.

A *creative boutique* is a specialized service agency where creative production is sent outside the business, but copy is provided by the business. This results in faster layout and production.

Project team agencies provide copywriting, creative execution, and media placement without larger agency overhead. Teams can come together to do one project, and then move on to the next project when the ad campaign is complete.

Virtual agencies provide services coordinated by an individual who works with a network of experienced freelancers. A *freelancer* is a self-employed person who sells work or services by the hour, day, or job, rather than working on a regular salary basis for one employer.

Developing Print Advertisements

Although they are only one part of an advertising campaign, print advertisements are very important to most campaigns. Print advertisements must contain four key elements, which include *headline, copy, illustrations,* and *signature* (see Figure 20-1 on page 360). Some advertisements also include the company's slogan, which is often presented with or near the signature. Each of the four key elements enhances the overall theme of a product promotion. The four fundamental elements of a print advertisement are applicable for ads in other media. As you read this section, think of ways these concepts would apply to preparing television and radio commercials, as well as online advertising.

Headline

The headline is the saying that gets the readers' attention, arouses their interest by providing a benefit, and leads them to read the rest of the ad. Headlines are responsible for the overall effectiveness of most advertising campaigns, so many experts consider them the most important part of an advertisement.

PURPOSES OF A HEADLINE The purposes of a headline are to attract readers' attention, select an audience, provide a benefit to the reader, and lead to the illustration and copy.

Headlines must be attention-getters, or the advertisement may not be read. More than 80 percent of the people who look at a print advertisement just read the headlines. Headlines that use words such as *new, now,* and *free* universally attract attention.

Effective headlines select an audience. They must have advertising appeal and provide a reason for purchasing a product or service. The motivation for purchase is what will help to identify a targeted group of potential customers. Headlines can appeal to people for a variety of reasons including profit, love, fear, fun, and vanity. Effective headlines can create the image a product wants to project toward a specific type of customer.

A headline provides a benefit to the reader. You want to promise the reader something that matches a need or want. Some benefits include free offers, more miles per gallon, better service, or fewer cavities.

Headlines are used to lead to the copy and illustration. Headlines are often written so that a reader can grasp the entire point of the ad by simply viewing the headline, seeing the illustration, and reading a few words of the copy. Other times, headlines have a subheadline to clarify or expand on the main idea expressed in the headline. Subheadlines are usually found in smaller type close to the headline. Headlines should be powerful enough to draw potential customers into reading the copy.

WRITING EFFECTIVE HEADLINES Most headlines are brief because many people cannot take in more than seven words at one time. One effective and short headline is that for Charmin bath tissue—"Ultra Soft. Ultra Strong." This headline utilizes an illustration to tell the rest of the story.

Charmin's a great combination of softness and strength. Maybe that's why it's the number one bath tissue today.

Everyone wants that Charmin feeling.

■ Effective Headlines A brief, catchy headline is often an effective method of attracting a reader's attention. *Why are most headlines brief?*

Wouldn't it be great if someone thought of the solution before you knew you had a problem?

Someone already has.

Someone with a proven record of solving some of the most difficult and complicated production and engineering problems imaginable.

That someone is Invensys.

The fact is, it's problem anticipation that's now become the name of the game. Except that we don't play games.

At Invensys we combine analytical skills, experience and intelligence with vision. Producing solutions to give one result. Increased performance.

That is no idle boast. Our experience in the highly sophisticated world of automation and controls is acknowledged as unique.

Whatever you require, our people will make it happen. Improving efficiency, raising standards and adding value at every conceivable level. Especially on to your bottom line.

Your next step? Visit us right now at www.invensys.com

invensys™
Technology for an intelligent world.

INTELLIGENT AUTOMATION · DRIVE SYSTEMS · POWER SYSTEMS · CONTROLS
INVENSYS PLC, CARLISLE PLACE, LONDON SW1P 1BX U.K. TEL+44 (0) 171 834 3848

■ **Creative Writing** This ad uses a paradox in the headline. *Why is the headline a paradox?*

It is possible to create longer headlines that are effective if they are provocative. In a recent study, creative directors from major advertising agencies analyzed award-winning print ads to determine what their headlines had in common. They discovered that 32 percent of the headlines used familiar sayings with a twist. About 23 percent of the headlines made use of opposites such as "up/down" and "lie/truth." For example, a headline used by a boot manufacturer made the following statement: "After a Day of Downhill Skiing, Getting a Fine Meal Shouldn't Be an Uphill Battle."

Every headline should have a single focus or main idea. Before writing a headline, try to sum up the main idea in a single sentence. This technique will help you stay focused on the subject and produce a headline with impact.

Here are some other techniques you can use when writing headlines:

- *Alliteration* (repeating initial consonant sounds)—Win with Wireless (Samsung)
- *Paradox* (a seeming contradiction that could be true)—It's an environmental movement all by itself. (Honda Insight)
- *Rhyme*—Bounty. The Quicker Picker-Upper
- *Pun* (a humorous use of a word that suggests two or more of its meanings or the meaning of another word similar in sound)—Beauty and the Beef (Ball Park Franks)
- *Play on Words*—For Soft Babies and Baby Soft Hands

■ Copy

The copy is the selling message in a written advertisement. It directly expands on the information in the headline or the product shown in the illustration. It should also stress the benefits and features of the product advertised to encourage customers to try this product or service.

Good copy, like a good headline, is simple and direct. Copy can vary from a few words to several paragraphs. Copy does not need to be extensive to get a message across. As with all aspects of advertising, a few well-chosen words will intrigue the customer while not bombarding them with information.

Copy might be a conversation, an educational tool, a testimonial to the benefits of using the product, or a description of how an institution can help you. Your copy will be competing with hundreds of other advertisers for the reader's attention; therefore, it must be noticeable or dramatic.

Copy should appeal to the senses. Through the words, the customer should be able to see, hear, touch, taste, or even smell a product. This can be done through using descriptive adjectives.

Give your copy news value by providing specific information. Tell the *who, what, when, why, where,* and *how* of your product. Remember that facts about your product are more powerful than claims. Use case histories, statistics, performance figures, dates, and quotes from experts whenever possible. While it is helpful to include quotes from satisfied customers, facts are most helpful when trying to win new customers.

■ **A Call to Action** The Internal Revenue Service ad shown here is an example of an ad with well written copy. *In what ways does this ad demonstrate effective copy techniques?*

Key words used in copy, such as *compare, introducing, now, price, save, easy,* and *new,* establish immediate contact with the reader. They arouse interest, encourage awareness, and create desire. Customers enjoy knowing that they are on the cutting edge when trying new products, and words such as *improved* and *introducing* offer this impression.

Advertising copy should provide a call to action to shoppers. It should always be written in the active voice. You would write, "This item will help you," rather than "You will be helped by this item."

Including a penalty for not acting now—such as *before it's too late* or *without delay*—help create this sense of action.

Asking for action is especially important in local advertising, which generally seeks immediate action. On the other hand, most national advertising is not looking for immediate action; its purpose is to keep the name of the product in front of the public. It is trying to build brand awareness for new prospects and brand loyalty for current customers. In this case, no action is requested in the print ad.

FIGURE 20-1

PARTS OF A PRINT ADVERTISEMENT

Print advertisements must contain four key elements: *headline, copy, illustrations,* and *signature.* Some advertisements also include the company's *slogan,* which is often presented with or near the signature. Each of the key elements enhances the overall theme of a product promotion.

1

Headlines attract readers, arouse interest and get them to look at the illustration and copy. What is the headline?

3

Illustrations help to expand on the copy by showing how the product works or how it is used. What is the illustration in this ad?

2

Copy represents the selling message in the ad. What does the copy tell about the product in this ad?

TRUCK SEASON NEVER ENDS.

THE TRUCK knows endurance. Just like you, it's always out there in all kinds of weather. That's why we put it through over 150,000 miles of real-world testing under maximum payload conditions. It's also why we offer the most powerful V8 of any 4x4 pickup on the planet. More powerful than Ford. More powerful than Dodge. Throw in the biggest extended cab of any half-ton pickup' and the widest fourth door opening," and you're good to go. And go. And go. Proof positive that Silverado' isn't just any truck. It's The Truck. From Chevy." The most dependable, longest-lasting trucks on the road." 877-THE TRUCK or chevrolet.com/silverado

SILVERADO

LIKE A ROCK

Based on available V8 horsepower; †Based on overall exterior cab dimensions. ''Measurement based on widest distance between open doors. 1981-1998 full-line light duty truck company registrations. Excludes other GM divisions. ©2000 GM Corp. Buckle up, America!

4

The signature, or logotype (logo), is the distinctive identification symbol for a business. What is the signature in this ad?

5

A slogan is a catch phase or small group of words that are combined in a special way to identify a product or company. What is the slogan in this ad?

▪ Illustration

The illustration is the photograph or drawing used in a print advertisement. Its primary function is to attract attention and to encourage a purchase of the advertised product. It should also tie into the headline and copy. The illustration, together with the headline, should lead the potential customer to read at least the first sentence of the copy.

The illustration should transmit a total message that would be hard to communicate just with words. Illustrations should show the product, how the product works, and safety features. Illustrations should also project the appropriate image desired for the product, such as convenience, entertainment, leisure, or status. Sometimes it is necessary for customers to see the product in use, such as models wearing the featured clothing items. Businesses also want to be careful when choosing an image that it will not become outdated quickly. Once a business selects an illustration, it normally does not change for a period of time. To maintain its image, therefore, a business should not only carefully select its illustrations, but also periodically evaluate them for consistency.

Life In The Diverse

MARKETPLACE

The Way of the Words

Attempting to produce print ads for Arabic-speaking Middle Eastern countries can be a disorienting experience for the novice. Where does the challenge lie? The placement of words! Arabic is read from right to left, not left to right as is English. Pictorial sequences must also be shown in that order, therefore, because that is how the mind reads—words on a page or pictures on an ad. One U.S. laundry detergent manufacturer learned this the hard way. An ad for an Arab client showed a step-by-step illustration of doing laundry. When the client "read" the ad, it appeared that clean clothes became dirty after being exposed to the detergent!

Thinking Critically
What are some other goods that could be mistranslated if the ad was read the opposite way?

Think different.

▪ **Advertising Transmittal** The purpose of advertising illustrations is to transmit a message. *What kind of message does the above ad transmit? Do you like it? Why or why not?*

Photographs should be used in advertisements when a sense of reality is necessary. Sometimes it's important for the customer to know exactly what the product looks like or how it's used. Consumer products such as cars, computers, cosmetics, electronic equipment, furniture, and sporting equipment should be illustrated with photographs.

Drawings are often used to show a part of a product that the reader would not normally see. Cutaway drawings and illustrations of constructed or manufactured products and equipment can help show important features not visible in a photograph.

SOURCES FOR ILLUSTRATIONS Businesses often use clip art in their print advertisements. Clip art takes the form of images, stock drawings, and photographs. It is often provided by suppliers, manufacturers, or trade associations for print advertisements. Clip art can also be found in published books, compact disks, and on the Web. Because clip art is ready for reproduction and printing, it is inexpensive, quick, and easy to use. When stock art work is not sufficient, professionals may be hired to photograph situations or products.

How Do You Want to Fly?

Delta Airlines recently unveiled a new $100 million advertising campaign created by the full-service advertising agency Leo Burnett. The old slogan "On Top of the World?" did not produce the results that Delta's management wanted.

Delta's reputation suffered during the 1990s when cost-cutting measures reduced customer service and satisfaction. When Delta realized that it was time to develop a new advertising campaign, they turned to the The Leo Burnett Company, which is responsible for the advertising for seven out of the 25 most valuable global brands, according to Interbrand. The new advertising campaign slogan entitled "How Do You Want to Fly?" is turning things around.

Burnett researchers conducted airport interviews with travelers and found out that most flyers simply want hassle-free travel. Many consumers find that advertising often makes big promises that companies do not honor. The new campaign, which utilizes print, television, and radio media, differs from traditional airline advertising, which often features breathtaking shots of planes with signature background music. The new advertising campaign is designed to meet customers' simple requests.

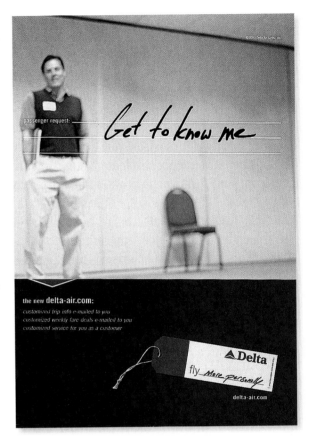

The campaign's print advertisements will feature luggage tags with flyer requests printed on them, such as "Fly with more magazines," "Fly efficiently," and "Fly according to schedule." These ads will be featured in 20 business publications. Television ads will feature real-life experiences of passengers, with no slogan, musical jingle, or big name announcers.

In place of an ending tagline, all new ads will end with a customer travel request on a Delta baggage tag. In conjunction with the new ad campaign, Delta has revamped its Web site to make it more user and customer friendly. Delta Airlines is betting that the new campaign will improve its image for service by placing importance on the airline traveler's time and keeping travel hassles to a minimum.

Case Study Review

1. How can Delta ensure that the new advertising campaign is successful?
2. Why is Delta relying on providing simple service?

A MATTER OF ETHICS

3. Do you think that Delta implies in this advertising theme that all service requests will be honored? If yes, is this ethical for the company to do? Why or why not?

■ Signature

No advertisement is complete without naming its sponsor. The signature, or logotype (logo), is the distinctive identification symbol for a business. A well-designed signature gets instant recognition for a business.

In national ads, the signature is the name of the firm. It may also include the corporate symbol and slogan. The signature in local advertisements usually includes the business's name, address, telephone number, business hours, or slogan. Many advertisers also include their Web addresses in the signature.

SLOGAN To support a firm's signature, many businesses create and use slogans that help customers identify with the firm and its image. A slogan is a catch phase or small group of words that are combined in a special way to identify a product or company.

Slogans create a distinct image for the company, its products, or its corporate mission. Headlines frequently become the slogan for an advertising campaign. An example of an advertising slogan is *Melts in your mouth, not in your hand.*

Figure 20-2 highlights some of the most popular slogans of the twentieth century. Each of these advertising slogans had the power to attract attention and arouse interest. It is important to notice how all of these slogans used fewer than seven words to get their point across.

FIGURE 20-2

Top slogans of the 20th Century

1	Diamonds are forever.	**A**	Maxwell House
2	The pause that refreshes.	**B**	Nike
3	Good to the last drop	**C**	public service
4	Does she . . . or doesn't she?	**D**	Crest
5	Where's the beef?	**E**	Clairol
6	Let your fingers do the walking.	**F**	Wendy's
7	Just do it!	**G**	General Electric
8	We try harder.	**H**	Yellow Pages
9	Breakfast of champions.	**I**	Avis
10	When it rains, it pours.	**J**	Wheaties
11	Look ma, no cavities!	**K**	Morton Salt
12	Loose lips sink ships	**L**	DeBeers
13	We bring good things to life.	**M**	Coca-Cola

■ **Super Slogans** These advertising slogans were judged to be some of the best of the 20th century. *Can you match the slogan to the product?*

1-L; 2-M; 3-A; 4-E; 5-F; 6-H; 7-B; 8-I; 9-J; 10-K; 11-D; 12-C; 13-G

20.1 ASSESSMENT

Reviewing Key Terms and Concepts

1. How are advertising campaigns developed?

2. Why are headlines considered by many to be the most important part of print advertisements?

3. What is the main purpose of advertising copy?

4. What should illustrations show about a product?

5. What is the signature in an advertisement?

Thinking Critically

6. What is a problem with a well-designed ad that does not have a signature?

Integrating Academic Skills

7. **COMMUNICATION** Identify five household or consumer products you are familiar with and develop advertising headlines for each. Assume that the product is being advertised by the manufacturer. Base your headlines on opposite words such as up/down, hot/cold, or inside/outside.

Ad Layouts

• What You'll Learn

- The importance of advertising layouts
- The principles of preparing an ad layout
- The advantages and disadvantages of using color in advertising
- How typefaces and type sizes can be changed to add variety and emphasis to print advertisements
- How to check advertising proofs

• Why It's Important

Since print advertisements have only a few seconds to reach a reader, you'll want to learn how to develop an advertising layout that will attract your target audience.

Key Terms

- ad layout
- advertising proof

Developing Print Advertising Layouts

An ad layout is a rough draft that shows the general arrangement and appearance of a finished ad. It clearly indicates the position of the headline, illustration, copy, and signature. There are different sources of ad layout services, including newspaper salespeople, a magazine representative, or a printer. You submit a rough draft of your idea and the provider will create the ad based on your information.

Ad layouts should be prepared in exactly the same size as the final advertisement. The illustrations should be large enough to show all product features. The ad should make generous use of white or unused space for an uncluttered look. A proper balance of white space and color highlights the image or drawing that you want the consumer to focus on. White space also helps to make copy legible and creates an eye flow for the ad. The image projected in the layout should be appropriate for the target audience. The *typeface*, style of printing type, and size should be easy to read and appropriate for the target audience. A car dealership may use bold block letters to draw customer's attention, while an antique store or Victorian bed and breakfast may utilize a gothic print or fancy script.

When designing advertisements, pay careful attention to where the reader's eyes will be directed. The best ads contain *lines of force* that guide the reader to the copy through illustrations. The models in photos or drawings should be facing or looking at the copy. A model in an illustration that looks out of the ad space moves the reader's eyes away from the copy.

■ Using Color in Print Advertisements

Color makes an advertisement stand out on the printed page. Color ads draw higher response rates than black-and-white ads do because they are more realistic. A color ad is also more visually appealing and commands the reader's attention more than a black and white advertisement does. In fact, research has proven that color newspaper ads can increase the reading of copy by as much as 80 percent over black-and-white ads. Studies have also shown that because of the response rates full-color ads are usually more cost effective than two-color ads (usually black plus a color).

Although color adds excitement and realism, each added color raises the cost of the advertisement. Adding another color can increase costs by as much as 35 percent. Therefore, when businesses use color in advertisements, the added cost must be continually measured against the desired results.

■ **Color Excitement** Color photos often receive better reception than black and white. *How has Xerox used color to illustrate its product and corporate image?*

■ Selecting Typefaces and Type Sizes for Print Advertisements

There are a variety of typefaces and type sizes available for use in print ads. Advertisers make sure that the size of the type and the typefaces they select are distinctive, yet appropriate for the business and target audience. Large, bold type is usually chosen when the words contained in a headline are to be shouted. Smaller, lighter type is usually chosen when the words in a headline are to be whispered. Different typefaces and type sizes can affect the way a reader feels about an advertisement. A typeface that is too small or difficult to read will lower the readership of an ad. A study done by the Newspaper Advertising Bureau found that nearly one-third of readers over 65 had trouble reading newspaper type. This means that some one-third of newspaper readers over 65 may not be reading ads at all unless they have large, simple type and an uncluttered design.

In general, print advertisers should use one typeface for headlines and prices and another typeface for copy. You can add variety and emphasis by using different sizes, italics, and boldface versions of the two basic typefaces selected for the advertisement. A variety of combinations of capital and lowercase typefaces can be used to create different effects. The message may remain the same; however, the effect may be changed by capitalizing different words.

BRIGHT IDEAS

Slinking Its Way to Success

What walks down stairs alone or in pairs and makes a slinkity sound? Everyone knows it's Slinky! How did everyone come to love the Slinky? Richard James invented the Slinky by accident while trying to develop an antivibration device for the Navy. Knocking some experimental springs off a shelf, he was surprised at how they 'slinked' down, as opposed to just falling. In 1945, James first demonstrated the Slinky at the Gimbles department store in Philadelphia. Afraid no one would buy the product because it was so simple, James gave a friend a dollar so that at least one person would buy one. Within 90 minutes of the demonstration, James sold 400 Slinkys! To date, over 250 million Slinkys have been sold!

Thinking Creatively

Can you think of any other products that might have been invented "by accident"?

■ Checking Advertising Proofs

When advertisements are given to a newspaper or magazine staff for preparation, an advertising proof is developed. The advertising proof shows exactly how an ad will appear in print.

The advertising proof is sent to the advertiser for review and approval. The advertiser carefully checks the proof to make sure that the ad was done exactly as planned. It is particularly important to make sure that all prices are accurate and all brand names and company names are correctly spelled. Any errors found in the proof must be marked and returned to the newspaper or magazine publisher for correction.

Before giving final approval to a written advertisement, the advertiser performs an evaluation of each advertisement. The evaluation should be based on the following criteria.

- The ad should be bold enough to stand out on a page, even if it is placed next to other ads.
- The overall layout should look clean and uncluttered and should guide the reader through the copy.
- The typefaces and type sizes should be easy to read and help further develop the image of the company.
- The signature plate should be apparent and distinctive.
- The intended message and image projected must be appropriate for the target audience.

REAL WORLD MARKETING

Fingerhut: Making it Great!

How can you shop from a catalog if there is not one available in your language? Fingerhut Companies, one of the nation's largest retailers, considered this obstacle. The result was a new advertising campaign of 300,000 Spanish-language catalogs. The campaign included a series of newspaper, television, radio, and outdoor advertisements. The response rate more than doubled when Fingerhut used what is called a "push-pull complementary strategy." They pushed catalogs, while at the same time pulling in customers through ads aimed to educate consumers about catalog shopping. Fingerhut's ads also stressed the convenience of mail order and the reliability of delivery from the U.S. Postal Service.

Thinking Critically
Why was it important for Fingerhut to use advertising to promote its catalogs?

20.2 ASSESSMENT

Reviewing Key Terms and Concepts

1. What is an ad layout?
2. Why is color important in print advertisements?
3. How can variety be added to the type selected for print advertising?
4. What is the purpose of an advertising proof?
5. What should an advertiser review before submitting an advertising proof to a newspaper?

Thinking Critically

6. In what ways are online banner ads similar to print advertisments?

Integrating Academic Skills

7. **MATH** Your office supply store has a cooperative arrangement with a computer manufacturer. The store receives a 3.5 percent advertising credit on total yearly computer purchases. What is your advertising credit on purchases totaling $42,000?

Careers in Marketing

ADVERTISING

Deborah Brumfield
Illustrator
Brumfield Studios, Inc.

What do you like the most about your work?

"I am self-employed and enjoy setting my own course. I like the creative aspect of my job—I bring an idea to life on paper. The reason for working is to either bring you fame, fortune or fun. When a job meets all three criteria, it's heavenly!"

How did you get into art?

"I have wanted to be an artist since kindergarten. I went to a college and got a two-year degree in Advertising Art (now called Graphic Design). Competition was rough and I spent time working in unrelated fields while looking for work. I searched the phone book and made appointments with every printer, ad agency, and photographer to show my portfolio. I got my first break as Art Director at a local television station."

What training do you recommend for students?

"I recommend a four-year degree in illustration, fine art, graphic design, photography, or another major that emphasizes creative expression as well as business courses. An internship at an ad agency, magazine, or related business shows how companies work from the inside. Students should seek out a mentor—most artists are happy to take the time to talk to someone who is starting out."

What is your key to success?

"Success takes persistence, confidence, thick skin, flexibility, and creativity. Never take rejection of your art personally—it means that you haven't found the right person or company to appreciate your work yet. Remember that there are record companies that turned down the Beatles, and movie companies that turned down *Titanic*. Be willing to try to new things, learn new skills, and tap new markets. Finally, look at things in your own unique way."

Thinking Critically

Why is it essential to maintain a positive attitude in any job?

Career Facts

Education and Training: An art or design degree, and classes in computer design, communication skills, business, advertising, and marketing are recommended.

Aptitudes, Abilities, and Skills: Illustrators must be creative and artistic, as well as detail-oriented and capable of working with precise tools. Ability to visualize two-dimensional representations is necessary, in addition to flexibility and good people skills to work with clients.

Career Outlook: The need for illustrators is expected to grow rapidly, but competition for the best jobs is likely to be high.

Career Path: Work as a layout artist or paste-up artist may lead to the position of illustrator. Illustrators and designers may advance to art or design directors.

VOCABULARY REVIEW

Construct a crossword puzzle using the following vocabulary terms. Below the puzzle, include appropriate clues for each term.

- advertising campaign
- advertising agencies
- headline
- slogan
- copy
- illustration
- clip art
- signature
- ad layout
- advertising proof

FACT AND IDEA REVIEW

1. Compare a full-service and a limited-service advertising agency. (20.1)

2. What are the four essential elements of a written advertisement? (20.1)

3. What are the purposes of headlines? (20.1)

4. Why should headlines consist of no more than seven words? (20.1)

5. Identify three techniques you can use to develop attention-getting headlines. (20.1)

6. What is the purpose of advertising copy? (20.1)

7. What are the two types of illustrations used in print ads and when should each be used? (20.1)

8. What is included in an ad signature? (20.1)

9. List five principles that should be followed in developing print advertising layouts. (20.2)

10. What should an advertiser do if there is an error on an advertising proof? (20.2)

THINKING CRITICALLY

1. What are some of the predictions for advertising agency models of the future?

2. Why do you think local supermarkets, banks, pharmacies, and department stores frequently use print advertising?

3. Why would a business develop different print ads for the same product if it advertised the same product in both newspapers and magazines?

4. Why are some businesses beginning to employ their own specialists to develop and maintain their Web sites?

5. Advertisers often debate whether the price of the product should be included in an ad. How would you determine when price should or should not be included in print advertisements?

BUILDING WORKPLACE SKILLS

1. **Human Relations** A customer wishes to purchase an item that was advertised improperly in a print advertisement. The item actually costs more than the advertised price. When told about the higher price the customer is upset and angry, but still wants the product. What procedures would you use to calm the customer and still complete the sale?

2. **Technology** Using a graphics design program, select a product to advertise. Develop an advertising layout with computer-generated clip art. The ad should appeal to a customer's need for convenience, vanity, or health. Then write a paragraph describing how your advertising layout creates a particular appeal.

APPLYING MARKETING CONCEPTS

1. **Preparing a Display Advertisement** As an advertising account executive for a newspaper, you have been asked by a potential advertiser (a local flower shop) to prepare a display advertisement. Use a word processing program to prepare the sample ad, including a headline, copy, illustration, and signature.

2. **Addressing Advertising Concepts** Use a word processing program to prepare a one-page summary of special concerns that need to be addressed when advertising to senior citizens.

3. **Developing Headline Writing Techniques** There are five techniques that can help you write memorable headlines. They are alliteration, paradox, rhyme, puns, and plays on words. Develop a headline for each of these techniques.

4. **Summarizing Key Elements of Print Advertisements** Using a presentation software program, prepare a slide presentation with at least 10 slides summarizing the key elements of a print advertisement.

5. **Identifying Popular Slogans** Conduct Internet research on five companies. Write each company's name and slogan on an index card. Read each slogan aloud and have your classmates identify the business using it.

LINKING SCHOOL TO WORK

Speaking and Information Skills Collect a print advertisement from a place of business and evaluate the headline, copy, illustration, and signature for completeness and appropriateness. Be prepared to present your findings orally to the class.

THE DECA CONNECTION

Role Play: Marketing Coordinator

Situation You are to assume the role of assistant marketing coordinator for a restaurant chain. Currently your restaurant is running a print ad that features a pair of absentminded elderly spinsters. The general public apparently finds the ad both amusing and persuasive (purchase of the specials is up by 30 percent). However, members of a local senior citizens group are not amused and have complained about the ad. Your marketing manager (judge) has asked you to create a new ad that targets senior citizens.

Activity You must develop a layout of your ad and present it to the marketing manager explaining the strengths of the ad.

Evaluation You will be evaluated on how well you meet the following performance indicators:
- Explain the components of advertisements
- Write promotional messages
- Address needs of individual personalities
- Evaluate effectiveness of advertising
- Demonstrate appropriate creativity

inter NET CONNECTION

Understanding Advertising Agencies
Advertising agencies assist businesses with product promotions. They frequently perform market research, perform creative work, and coordinate advertising campaigns for their clients.

Connect
- Investigate an advertising agency online and write a one-page report detailing the name of the company and summarizing the types of services it provides to clients.

the Zazz Lab

A Sports and Entertainment Marketing Simulation

WELCOME

Welcome to Zazz Sports and Entertainment Marketing Company. Zazz is devoted to serving the needs of its clients who include college, university, and professional sports teams, professional athletes, sporting events, and sports arenas plus major consumer product corporations, as well as television networks and movie studios. As an intern, you will have the opportunity to work on different clients' projects. All of your work will be assigned and reviewed by your department supervisor.

PLAN A SUPER BOWL PROMOTION

SITUATION

Two major corporations—Crystal Airlines and J.T. Burgers—want to run special promotions to tie in with the Super Bowl. Crystal Airlines, a Midwest airline known for on-time flights and friendly staff, has just started coast-to-coast service. J.T. Burgers is a Southern fast food restaurant that has been quickly expanding its popular franchise across the United States. Both companies are looking for national exposure which Zazz can make happen by affiliating them with the Super Bowl. To capitalize on the popularity of this major event, the promotional plan will be carried out throughout the local level, as well as in the national media.

ASSIGNMENT

You have been asked to prepare a promotional plan for one of the above companies. Your supervisor wants you to prepare a complete promotional package, as well as a budget and calendar of events. Begin with your idea for a unique special promotion, such as a contest or sweepstakes. You will need to explain any contest rules and any prizes (Super Bowl tickets, etc.). You will need to promote through product packaging, in-store displays, various advertising media, and the company's Web site. Create a product package design for food and drinks served in J.T. Burgers restaurants or refreshments served on the airline. Design an in-store

display, which would be placed in the airline terminal or inside the restaurant. Plan the promotion's ads for television, radio, direct mail, magazine and/or newspaper, and the company Web site. Determine the costs for every promotional idea and create a promotional budget. Prepare a promotional calendar of events with deadline dates for insertion and publication. You also want to generate free publicity if possible.

Tools and Resources

To complete this assignment you will need to conduct research at the library or on the Internet. You will also need a word processing program, a spreadsheet program, and presentation software. Trade publications that may be helpful include *Brandweek, Advertising Age, Sports Business Journal,* and *Sports Business Daily.*

Research

Research previous Super Bowl promotions. Investigate promotions run by the client's competitors in the past. What qualities or characteristics of the promotions were successful? Research the cost of television commercials aired during the Super Bowl, as well as all other suggested advertising media. You also will need research regarding how much money is normally spent on a promotional mix of this magnitude.

Report

Prepare a written report and a computer presentation for the client. Use a word processing program to prepare a double-spaced report. Use a spreadsheet program to create a promotional budget. To prepare the promotional calendar, use a table format found in your word processing program or a spreadsheet program. Arrange your written report around the following headings:

- Market analysis
  - Competitors
    - Participation in other Super Bowl promotions
    - Current promotions and their costs
  - Previous Super Bowl promotions
    - Characteristics of successful promotions
    - Cost of television advertising
- Suggested promotional mix
  - Special promotion
    - Type (contest, sweepstakes) and rationale
    - Theme, rules, and prizes
  - Advertising media rationale and design samples
    - Broadcast
    - Print
    - Direct mail
    - Internet
  - Product packaging rationale and design samples
  - In-store displays rationale and design samples
  - Publicity
  - Promotional calendar of events
  - Promotional budget
- Conclusion

Using computer presentation software and other visual aids (sample ads, etc.), prepare a presentation for the client that includes:

- Key topics covered in your written report
- Graphic illustrations that are relevant to each slide's topic
- Very little text
- A minimum of 10 slides
- Samples of all promotional materials suggested

Presentation and Evaluation

Present your ideas in a written report and an oral presentation. The presentation will later be shown to the client. You will be evaluated on your oral presentation skills, including:

- Proposed promotional plan
- Creativity
- Ability to meet the customer's needs
- Continuity of presentation
- Enthusiasm
- Voice quality
- Eye contact

Portfolio

Print a copy of your completed report and presentation for your Portfolio.

THE DECA CONNECTION

DECA Business Services Marketing Series
Planning a promotional campaign for a client is part of this occupational area because it is a business service.

DECA Marketing Management Series
Planning a promotional campaign for any type of business is a possible role play situation in this event.

DECA Quick Serve Restaurant Management Event
Developing a Super Bowl promotional campaign for a quick serve restaurant could be a potential role play for this event.

DECA Advertising Campaign Event
Developing a promotional campaign and presenting it to a client/advertiser is the essence of this DECA competition.

DECA Sports and Entertainment Marketing Management Team Decision-Making Event
Working on this project with a partner will make the experience similar to what is expected in a DECA Team Decision-Making Event.

Portfolio

Choosing a Distribution Plan

To demonstrate mastery of the content in this unit, select a consumer or industrial product to investigate. Using the library, media, Internet, and company resources such as annual reports, press releases, and publications, prepare a detailed research report, using a word processing program, on the manufacturing and distribution process for the selected product. Be prepared to present the information in an oral report to demonstrate what you learned by creating your distribution plan.

Distribution

Unit Overview

In this unit, you will learn about the various aspects of distribution. Chapter 21 discusses the concept of distribution planning and channels of distribution. The effect of the Internet on distribution planning is covered, as well as challenges in foreign market distribution. Chapter 22 explains that physical distribution involves the transportation of the product or its physical movement to various locations. The nature and scope of purchasing is detailed in Chapter 23. An explanation of how purchasing is conducted in both the industrial market and the resale market is included, along with vendor analysis and the effect of business-to-business e-commerce. Chapter 24 concentrates on the process of stock handling, inventory control, and stock management, all of which are essential for efficient control of products in industrial and consumer markets.

In this Unit:

Foundations of Marketing

- Business, Management, Entrepreneurship

Functions of Marketing

- Distribution

Channels of Distribution

Marketing: What It Takes

Changing Channels

The Research and Development department in your toy company just designed a new line of toys for pets. You know that your company's current customers (toy wholesalers and retailers) do not want to carry this new line. Since your company has never produced pet toys before, you have been asked to suggest the most effective channels of distribution for selling the new products.

WHAT WILL YOU DO?
What channels of distribution should be considered for the new line of pet toys?

Distribution

Distribution—How It Works

How do you get somebody to buy your product? By marketing it! Now the question is who do you market to, or who is your target audience? This is the place decision, one of the four Ps of the marketing mix. Shampoo manufacturers, for example, know that customers like to buy personal convenience items in supermarkets, drugstores, or hair salons. A shampoo manufacturer would therefore want its products to be sold to these stores.

To make a place decision, marketers must decide on their channel of distribution. The channel of distribution is the path a product takes from producer or manufacturer to final user. When the product is purchased for use in a business, the final user is classified as an industrial user. When the product is purchased for personal use, the final user is classified as a consumer.

Using the shampoo example, you can see how the same product may be classified as both a consumer and an industrial product. Manufacturers of shampoo sell their product to the customer through retail operations but may sell it as an industrial product for use in a business too. Hair salons buy shampoo in bulk to wash their customers' hair, while hotel chains buy small bottles of shampoo for customers to use during their hotel stay.

■ Channel Members

All the businesses involved in sales transactions that move products from the manufacturer to the final user are called intermediaries or middlemen. Intermediaries provide value to producers because they often have expertise in certain areas that producers do not have. Intermediaries that sell to the final consumer are experts in displaying, merchandising, and providing convenient shopping locations and hours for customers. Intermediaries reduce the number of contacts required to reach the final user of the product. In a case of four customers who wanted to buy a digital camera, a producer would have to make four sales transactions. By using an intermediary (such as Computer City), the number of contacts is reduced to one. This is illustrated in Figure 21-1 on page 376.

Intermediaries are classified on the basis of whether or not they take ownership (or title) to goods and services. Merchant intermediaries take title; agent intermediaries do not. Agent intermediaries, usually called agents, are paid a commission to help buyers and sellers get together. The two major types of merchant intermediaries are wholesalers and retailers.

• What You'll Learn

- The concept of a channel of distribution
- Who channel members are
- The different non-store retailing methods
- How channels of distribution differ for consumer and business-to-business products

• Why It's Important

As you know, the marketing mix includes decisions about product, price, place, and promotion. In this chapter you will explore the place decision—that is, how the product will be distributed and sold in the marketplace. Making the correct place decision has an impact on the entire operation of a business.

Key Terms

- channel of distribution
- intermediaries
- wholesalers
- rack jobbers
- drop shippers
- retailers
- brick and mortar retailers
- e-tailing
- agents
- direct distribution
- indirect distribution

FIGURE 21-1

Intermediaries

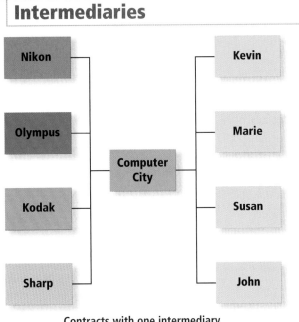

Contracts with one intermediary
4 producers + 4 buyers = 8 contracts

■ **Intermediary Role** Intermediaries reduce the number of transactions required by manufacturers to reach their final customers. *What expenses of doing business are lowered by this reduction in transactions?*

■ **Wholesalers** Some large mass merchandisers have specialized wholesalers manage certain product lines they carry, like health and beauty aids. *What type of specialized wholesaler is the person in this photo?*

WHOLESALERS Generally, wholesalers buy large quantities of goods from manufacturers, store the goods, and then resell them to other businesses. They are called wholesalers and their customers are called retailers. They may be called distributors when their customers are professional or commercial users, manufacturers, governments, institutions, or other wholesalers. In either case, they take title to the goods they buy for resale.

Two specialized wholesalers are rack jobbers and drop shippers. Rack jobbers are wholesalers that manage inventory and merchandising for retailers by counting stock, filling it in when needed, and maintaining store displays. As the name implies, they provide the racks for display of the product in a retail store and manage that product for the retailer. They bill the retailer only for the goods sold, not for all the items on display. Products that are handled by rack jobbers include compact discs, hosiery, health products, and beauty aids.

Drop shippers own the goods they sell but do not physically handle the actual products. They deal in large quantities of items in bulk, such as coal, lumber, and chemicals that require special handling. Drop shippers sell the goods to other businesses and have the producer ship the merchandise directly to the buyers. The products are owned, but never handled by the drop shipper.

RETAILERS Retailers sell goods to the final consumer for personal use. Traditional retailers, called brick and mortar retailers, sell goods to the customer from their own physical stores. These retail stores display, store, and merchandise the products they buy from manufacturers or wholesalers. They serve as the final link between the manufacturer and consumer. They often provide special services, such as offering credit or providing delivery to help solidify customer relationships.

Aside from brick and mortar retailers, there are a number of non-store retailing operations that serve the customer. They include automatic retailing, direct mail and catalog retailing, TV home shopping, and online retailing.

Vending service companies buy manufacturers' products and sell them through machines that dispense goods to consumers. These companies often place their vending machines in stores, office buildings, restaurants, hospitals, schools, and other institutions for free. They make their money from the items sold through the machines, which are regularly stocked. You can purchase a variety of food and snacks—sandwiches, fresh fruit, cookies, candy, soda, and hot drinks—from vending machines.

Direct mail and catalogs also reach the final consumer. Many large brick and mortar retailers produce their own catalogs to reach those consumers who prefer shopping at home. There are catalog houses that buy goods from different manufacturers and display them in a catalog for sale to the customer. Sometimes these catalog businesses have their names put on the products they sell in the catalog. This makes it appear as though they manufactured all the items in the catalog.

Television home shopping networks are TV stations that sell products to consumers. These companies buy the products in set quantities and sell them via television programs. Consumers phone in their orders while watching shows. One example of this is the Home Shopping Network.

Online retailing, or e-tailing, involves retailers selling products over the Internet to the customer. People with computers equipped to access the Internet can buy goods directly from e-tailers' Web sites. Some of the big e-tailing companies are solely found on the Internet, such as Amazon.com or the music seller CD-NOW.

Not to be left out of the technology revolution, many brick and mortar retailers, such as Toys R Us and Barnes & Noble, have created Web sites. Some of the top e-tailing sectors with high sales volume are depicted in Figure 21-2, with air travel, books, and hardware leading the list. This list can change quickly based on new competitors in the market and time of year.

AGENTS Unlike wholesalers and retailers, agents do not own the goods they sell. Agents act as intermediaries by bringing buyers and sellers together. You may be familiar with real estate agents who sell people's homes for them. They are paid a commission for that service, which is a percentage of the sale price of the home. This type of agent is called a *broker*. A broker's principal function is to bring buyers and sellers together in order for a sale to take place. They usually do not have a continued relationship with either party. They negotiate the sale and then look for other customers. Brokers are found in seasonal industries, where they represent producers of items such as fruits and vegetables, as well as in the real estate business.

■ **Brick and Mortar** Brick and mortar retailers sell goods to consumers through their own physical stores. *In what ways do these intermediaries help manufacturers?*

FIGURE 21-2

Shopping on the Web

Buying plane tickets on the Web has taken off. January 2001 shopping revenues:

Top e-tailing sectors	MILLIONS OF DOLLARS
Air Travel	$318
Books	224
Hardware	224
Software	187
Apparel	182
Hotels	164
Toys/games	146
Music	143
Health, beauty	143
Electronics	126

Source: Dow Jones

■ **Shopping on the Web** Note the millions of dollars attributed to online sales by e-tailers in January 2001. *Which three sectors lead the list? How might this list be changed if the month was December?*

FIGURE 21-3

DISTRIBUTION CHANNELS FOR CONSUMER PRODUCTS AND SERVICES

Historically, most consumer goods have not been marketed using direct distribution (channel A) because consumers have become accustomed to shopping in retail stores. Of the indirect channels available, Manufacturer/Producer to Retailer to Consumer (channel B) is the most commonly used in the consumer market.

CHANNEL A

There are five ways in which direct distribution is used for consumer goods.

1. Selling products at the production site. Examples include a farmer's roadside stand or a factory outlet.

2. Having a sales force call on consumers at home. Examples include Avon and Tupperware.

3. Using catalogs or ads to generate sales. One example is an Infomercial, which is a 30- or 60-minute television commercial that explains a product in detail and tells viewers how to order it directly from the manufacturer.

4. Having a sales representative call a consumer on the telephone (telemarketing). Examples include magazine subscriptions and telecommunications services.

5. Using the Internet to make online sales. Examples include manufacturers' Web sites where they sell their products to consumers without help from retailers.

CHANNEL B

This is the most commonly used channel for merchandise that dates quickly or needs servicing. Fashion apparel and automobiles are sold this way. Chain stores also use this channel because they handle the physical distribution of the products they buy. Online retailers will use this method, too; however, they must handle the distribution of products to the final consumer as well.

CHANNEL C

This is the most common distribution method for staple goods, which are items that are always carried in stock and whose styles do not change frequently. The manufacturer sells to the wholesaler, who then handles the sales, warehousing, and distribution of the goods to retailers. Consumer goods sold this way include supermarket items, flowers, candy, and stationery supplies.

CHANNEL D

This is the channel for manufacturers who wish to concentrate on production and leave sales and distribution to others. The agent sells to wholesalers who are involved in storage, sale, and transportation to retailers. The retailer then sells to consumers.

CHANNEL E

This is the channel chosen by manufacturers who do not want to handle their own sales to retailers. The agent simply brings the buyer and seller together. Expensive cookware, meat, cosmetics, and many supermarket items are sold this way.

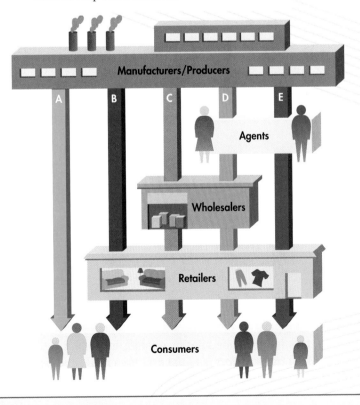

FIGURE 21-4

DISTRIBUTION CHANNELS FOR INDUSTRIAL PRODUCTS AND SERVICES

Because industrial users shop differently and have different needs than consumers, they use different channels of distribution. In fact, the least commonly used channel in the consumer market—direct distribution (channel A)—is the most commonly used in the industrial market.

CHANNEL A

This is the most common method of distribution for major equipment used in manufacturing and other businesses. The manufacturer's sales force calls on the industrial user to sell goods or services. For example, a Xerox sales representative sells copiers directly to manufacturers and commercial businesses. Note: All methods of direct distribution listed for the consumer market are used in the industrial market as well.

CHANNEL B

This channel is used most often for small standardized parts and operational supplies needed to run a business. Industrial wholesalers (distributors) take ownership of the products, stock them, and sell them as needed to industrial users. For example, a restaurant supply wholesaler buys pots, pans, utensils, serving pieces, and paper products from various manufacturers to sell to restaurant owners.

CHANNEL C

Small manufacturers who do not have the time or money to invest in a direct sales force may prefer this channel. The agent sells the goods to the industrial wholesaler who stores, resells, and ships them to the industrial user. The advantage of this arrangement is that both agent and industrial wholesaler are likely to be experts well known in the industry. Their reputation and services may be impossible for a small manufacturer to duplicate on its own.

CHANNEL D

This is another channel used when a manufacturer does not want to hire its own sales force. The agent represents the manufacturer for sale of the goods but does not take possession or title. The merchandise is shipped directly from the manufacturer to the industrial user. Construction equipment, farm products, and dry goods are often marketed this way.

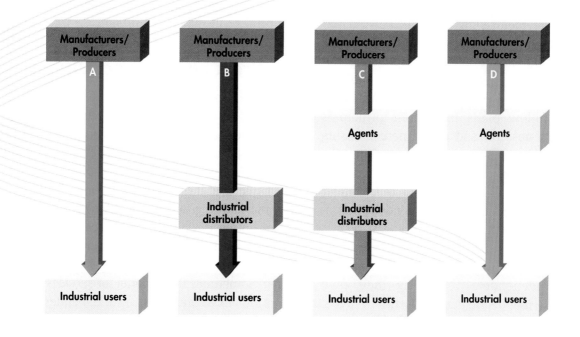

■ **Shop From Home** Retailers can take many different forms. *Why is the Home Shopping Network considered a non-store retailer?*

■ **Retailing Giants** Home Depot is a retailing giant. As such, it has a lot of clout in the channel of distribution. *If you were a manufacturer of lighting fixtures, would you want to sell your products to Home Depot? Why or why not?*

Food brokers, however, are an exception to this rule. Food brokers represent several manufacturers of products sold in supermarkets, convenience stores, and other specialty food stores. Most food brokers sign agreements with their principals (manufacturers they represent) that outline their responsibilities. A food broker may be responsible not only for selling the goods, but for merchandising them as well. Food brokers' employees are often expected to follow plans from their principals regarding shelf position and other merchandising requirements when displaying and stocking the products in supermarkets.

Another type of sales agent is an *independent manufacturer's representative*. Independent manufacturers' representatives represent several related (but noncompeting) manufacturers in a specific industry. They are not on any manufacturer's payroll. They work independently, running their own businesses. An independent manufacturers' agent might carry a line of fishing rods from one manufacturer, lures from another, insulated clothing for

hunters from a different manufacturer, and outdoor shirts from still another manufacturer. This manufacturers' agent would sell the merchandise to sporting goods wholesalers and retailers who specialize in hunting and fishing.

■ Direct and Indirect Channels

Channels of distribution are classified as direct or indirect. Direct distribution occurs when the goods or services are sold from the producer directly to the customer; no intermediaries are involved. Indirect distribution involves one or more intermediaries.

Direct and indirect distribution are both common in marketing goods. The channel of distribution is more often direct when services are performed by the service business itself. Employees in a hair salon actually perform such services as cutting customers' hair. Sometimes the channel for services can be indirect, for example, when an independent insurance agent sells insurance policies from different insurance companies to consumers or businesses.

Channels in the Consumer and Industrial Markets

To get a clearer picture of how channels are structured in the consumer and industrial markets, study Figures 21-3 and 21-4 on pages 378–379. Note that while the individual channels may be different, both markets make use of direct and indirect channels of distribution.

Different channels of distribution are generally used to reach the customer in the consumer and industrial markets. A manufacturer of paper products might sell napkins to both markets by using two different and distinct channels. When selling to the industrial market, the company would sell napkins to industrial distributors who, in turn, would sell the napkins to restaurants. When selling to the consumer market, the company would sell napkins to a wholesaler or use food brokers to sell to retailers. The retailers would then sell the napkins to consumers for personal use at grocery stores or party supply shops.

It is important for any manufacturer, whether industrial or consumer, to weigh all of its options when selecting the best channels of distribution. Not every option works best for every kind of product or company. Despite the potential for success that any product may seem to have, it can fail if the wrong channels of distribution are used.

REAL WORLD MARKETING

Make-up to Go

The main channel of distribution for high-end make-up brands has long been the upscale department store. That is fine for a New Yorker, but what if you live in Lewiston, Idaho, and can't get to a Bloomingdale's? Enter Sephora. Between its flagship stores and online marketplace, Sephora is changing the face of shopping for beauty supplies. Customers have access to make-up without having to wait at counters or peer through the glass. All tubes and containers are within sight and reach, or are just a mouse click away. In addition to marketing its original products, Sephora carries high-end products such as Shiseido, Christian Dior, and Stila.

Thinking Critically
How do expensive make-up companies benefit from Sephora's services?

21.1 ASSESSMENT

Reviewing Key Terms and Concepts

1. What is a channel of distribution?
2. Name two major types of merchant intermediaries.
3. What type of intermediary is a rack jobber? A drop shipper?
4. Distinguish between brick and mortar and online retailers.
5. Which type of distribution channel—direct or indirect—is used more frequently for consumer products? For industrial products?

Thinking Critically

6. Do you think e-tailing will eventually replace brick and mortar retailers? Explain.

Integrating Academic Skills

7. **COMMUNICATION** Prepare and deliver a three-minute speech on the value created by intermediaries for producers in a specific channel of distribution.

Distribution Planning

Understanding Distribution Planning

Distribution planning involves decisions about a product's physical movement and transfer of ownership from producer to consumer. In this chapter, we address only transfer of ownership concerns. You will study physical distribution concerns in Chapter 22.

Distribution decisions affect a firm's marketing program. Some of the major considerations are the use of multiple channels, control versus costs, intensity of distribution desired, and involvement in e-commerce.

■ Multiple Channels

Multiple channels are used when a product fits the needs of both industrial and customer markets. Consider Greenfield's Healthy Foods, a company that produces fat-free cookies and brownies. Presently Greenfield's sells its fat-free snacks to supermarkets and convenience stores, as well as to airlines. It is also looking to expand into other markets, such as schools and hospitals. Each new market poses questions regarding the exact channel of distribution needed to reach it.

Retailers also use multiple channels. A retail stationery store, for example, generally carries stationery supplies, greeting cards, and some convenience items for consumers. Much of its business, though, may involve selling office supplies to businesses in the local area. To cater to this industrial market, the stationery store might offer credit, trade discounts, and delivery services.

■ Control vs. Costs

All manufacturers and producers must weigh the control they want to keep over the distribution of their products against costs and profitability. This means deciding between using an in-house sales force or independent sales agents, in some cases. It can also mean accommodating one's business to the dominant member in a particular channel of distribution.

WHO DOES THE SELLING? A manufacturer must make decisions regarding the amount of control it wants over its sales function. It can decide to use its own sales force or hire agents to do the selling.

A direct sales force is costly. In-house sales representatives are on the company payroll, receive employee benefits, and are reimbursed for expenses. The manufacturer, though, has complete control over them. It can establish sales quotas and easily monitor each sales representative's performance.

● What You'll Learn

- The key considerations in distribution planning
- When to use multiple channels of distribution
- How to compare the costs and control involved in having a direct sales force versus using independent sales agents
- The three levels of distribution intensity
- The effect of the Internet on distribution planning
- The challenges involved in distribution planning for international markets

● Why It's Important

Distribution decisions affect the entire company, so it is important for you to know how these decisions are made. It is also helpful to know how these decisions are carried out in different markets, including international and e-marketplaces.

● Key Terms

- exclusive distribution
- integrated distribution
- selective distribution
- intensive distribution
- e-marketplace

E-business ideas that turn on your brain.

VIGNETTE Platform, services and applications software to help you build a powerful online business.
WWW.VIGNETTE.COM

■ **Getting Started** E-business is so big that there are companies that will help businesses become established on the Internet. *What types of services would you expect a company like Vignette to offer to help you start your own e-business?*

When sales volume is very high and a company is well established in the marketplace, it may be less costly to use an in-house sales force. That is because the selling effort is minimal, and the company can hire sales representatives on a salary basis to service established accounts.

With an agent, a manufacturer loses some of its control over how sales are made. An agent serves primarily as the independent selling arm of producers. There are two different types of agents: manufacturer's agents and selling agents. Manufacturer's agents, or manufacturer's representatives, work for several producers and carry non-competitive, complementary merchandise in an exclusive territory. Selling agents represent a single producer. However, the relative cost of using agents can be lower than hiring an in-house sales staff. No employee benefits or expenses must be paid because agents are independent businesspeople. Another benefit is that agents are paid a set percentage of

sales, assuring that the cost of sales is always the same in relation to the sales generated.

WHO DICTATES THE TERMS? A cost and control consideration that has emerged in recent years is the increasing power of retail giants like Wal-Mart and Home Depot. Manufacturers that want to do business with such retailers must often adhere to strict criteria. These criteria relate to selling direct and offering special services in areas like shipping, pricing, packaging, and merchandising. These added services cost manufacturers money. Despite that, most manufacturers adhere to these wishes because of the large volume of business generated by the retail giants.

There are those manufacturers, however, that cannot or do not get involved with the giants. They distribute their products through smaller retailers instead. They follow such a policy so they don't become totally dependent on one customer as their main source of revenue.

Case Study

Getting Fit & Trim

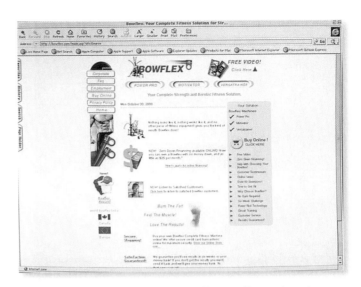

Direct Focus is making strides in the exercise equipment industry. The company manufactures and sells Bow-flex exercise rod-resistance equipment. They do it through direct marketing channels, using 30-minute infomercials and spot cable TV ads that target baby boomers interested in health and fitness. Industry reports note that the average sale is between $1,150 and $1,200. Another direct channel of distribution Direct Focus uses is the Internet. Direct Focus has its own Web site, which generated $5 million in sales in its first three months of operation. The Web site stresses the satisfaction guarantee, which encourages customers to trust Direct Focus. It also offers a free video to customers demonstrating the different machines that are available.

The commercial market for exercise equipment is ten times larger than the home exercise equipment market. To compete in that arena, Direct Focus bought Nautilus International Inc., a brand of commercial (weight resistance) fitness equipment. To sell this new line, Direct Focus plans to use its current direct marketing channels, as well as through indirect channels, including specialty retailers and sporting goods stores. Some of the problems that Direct Focus will face with this indirect method of distribution are meeting shipping demands, pricing pressures, and competing for shelf space.

Case Study Review

1. Explain Direct Focus's channels of distribution for its home exercise equipment and for its Nautilus commercial equipment.
2. Why do you think Direct Focus is using multiple channels of distribution?

A MATTER OF ETHICS

3. How ethical is it for a company to target the same market with two different brands of exercise equipment?

■ Distribution Intensity

Distribution intensity has to do with how widely a product will be distributed. There are three levels of distribution intensity—exclusive, selective, and intensive.

EXCLUSIVE DISTRIBUTION Exclusive distribution involves protected territories for distribution of a product in a given geographic area. Dealers are assured that they are the only ones within a certain geographic radius that have the right to sell the manufacturer's or wholesaler's products. Prestige, image, channel control, and a high profit margin for both the manufacturer and intermediaries are characteristic of this distribution strategy. When there is an exclusive distribution agreement, the retailer is usually tied by contract to the manufacturer. Franchised operations are examples of exclusive distribution planning. This is because only licensed franchises can sell the product.

Wholesalers may also sponsor voluntary groups in which a retailer agrees to buy and maintain a minimum inventory of the wholesaler's products. The wholesaler services the account regularly. This includes checking inventory, telling the retailer what needs to be reordered, and sponsoring special promotions to sell those products to customers. One example of a voluntary group sponsored by a wholesaler is the National Auto Parts Association (NAPA). Retailers affiliated with NAPA buy most of their stock from NAPA and participate in its promotions.

Guidelines given by the manufacturer, franchiser, or the wholesaler cooperative ensure exclusivity of the product line to the retailer. The retailers have limited competition in the sale of the product. The product's image is maintained through the exclusivity of distribution. It is assumed that buyers will seek the outlets that carry these products.

A variation on exclusive distribution is found in manufacturers that own and run their own retail operations. This is called integrated distribution. The manufacturer acts as wholesaler and retailer for its own products. Sherwin-Williams sells its paints in company-owned retail stores.

SELECTIVE DISTRIBUTION Selective distribution means that a limited number of outlets in a given geographic area are used to sell the product. The objective is to select channel members that can maintain the image of the product and are good credit risks, aggressive marketers, and good inventory planners. The manufacturer may exert some pressure on intermediaries to move the product with this type of distribution strategy. Frequent local advertising may be required of the intermediaries, as well as maintenance of a well-stocked and well-balanced inventory.

The intermediaries chosen are selected for their ability to cater to the final users that the manufacturer wants to attract. Ralph Lauren selects only top department and specialty stores to appeal to the affluent target market that will buy its clothing and dry goods. They would not choose to sell their goods in a chain megastore or a variety store for different reasons. The cost of Ralph Lauren goods is in line with those goods carried by fine department stores or specialty shops. This makes it more likely that customers will purchase their goods. The company also chooses top quality stores to ensure that their high quality image is maintained.

Life In The Diverse MARKETPLACE

Going Global

It's not just the big names that head overseas for international expansion. Sure, McDonald's and Pepsi are known worldwide, but many smaller companies have learned the art of business abroad as well. For example, the dry cleaning franchise One-Hour Martinizing opened its first business outside of the United States in Ecuador. Why Ecuador? The heat and sticky humidity require some business people to change shirts three times a day! It looks like One-Hour Martinizing has found its international niche.

Thinking Critically

What are some challenges that smaller companies face with international expansion?

INTENSIVE DISTRIBUTION Intensive distribution involves the use of all suitable outlets to sell a product. The objective is complete market coverage, and the ultimate goal is to sell to as many customers as possible, wherever they choose to shop. Motor oil is marketed in quick-lube shops, farm stores, auto parts retailers, supermarkets, drugstores, hardware stores, warehouse clubs, and other mass merchandisers to reach the maximum number of customers.

Industrial supplies fall into this category. One such product manufactured by 3M is a facial respirator. To reach all possible users of facial respirators, 3M has included welding supply channels, farm supply distributors, and specialty chemical channels in its distribution planning.

With the use of the Internet, businesses are opting for their own Web sites to make their products available to final users in consumer and industrial markets. This creates more intensive product distribution. Individuals who might not have had access to a brick and mortar store in their town can shop online to find any specialized or hard-to-find products.

FIGURE 21-5

Jet Set

Led by airline tickets, online travel sales are expected to reach $29 billion
by 2003, or more than double the total online travel sales in 2000.

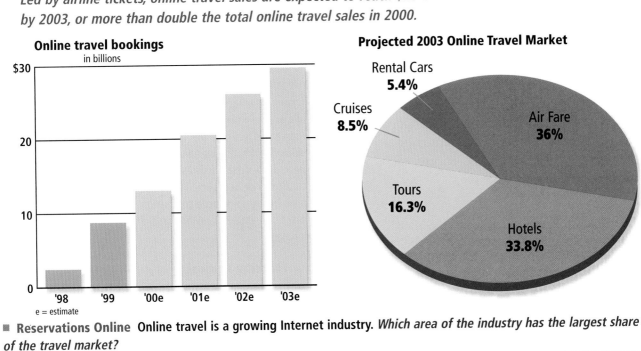

Online travel bookings
in billions

Projected 2003 Online Travel Market

Rental Cars **5.4%**

Cruises **8.5%**

Air Fare **36%**

Tours **16.3%**

Hotels **33.8%**

e = estimate

■ **Reservations Online** Online travel is a growing Internet industry. *Which area of the industry has the largest share of the travel market?*

E-COMMERCE E-commerce is the means by which products are sold to customers and industrial buyers through use of the Internet. You already learned that e-tailing is when retailers sell over the Internet. This online shopping location is called e-marketplace. In 2000 almost half of America's top retailers sold online. To get an idea of how significant the Internet business is for consumer products, consider Ticketmaster.com, which has over $1.5 million in Internet ticket sales daily. Online travel is also becoming increasingly popular, which is illustrated by the interest in Web sites such as Travelocity.com, Priceline.com, and Expedia.com, all of which offer vacation planning services online. The increasing popularity of online travel planning is illustrated in Figure 21-5.

Over 2.2 million small businesses were online in 1999. According to market researcher Forrester Research Inc., business e-commerce sales are expected to reach $2.7 trillion by 2004. The conclusion is that the Internet is here to stay as a channel of distribution for consumer and industrial products.

Panasonic, a consumer electronics maker, provides a business-to-business (B2B) Web site for its retail dealers. The Web site enables them to check on orders, products, pricing, and promotions, in addition to purchasing goods. On Panasonic's business-to-consumer (B2C) Web site, its dealers are able to add their store locations so consumers can find them. Panasonic is not selling directly to the consumer; it is simply using its consumer Web Site for informational purposes.

E-marketplaces for B2B operations provide one-stop shopping and substantial savings for industrial buyers. Online catalogs of products supplied by different companies make it easier for corporate buyers to compare prices and get the best deal. E-marketplaces provide smaller businesses with the exposure that they could not get elsewhere. An e-marketplace company in the chemical industry is ChemConnect. ChemConnect allows companies in the chemical market to sell goods and services and buy supplies over the Web. Even a large company like Dow Chemical, which has its own Web site to sell to its business customers, has signed up with ChemConnect for those customers that want to go to a central site where other products are sold as well. According to Forrester Research, 17 percent of all B2B trade will take place via the Internet by 2004. Figure 21-6 on page 387 illustrates the projected explosion of growth in the sales of goods and services via electronic marketplaces.

Distribution Planning for Foreign Markets

Distribution planning takes on a new dimension when businesses get involved in international trade.

Different environments in foreign markets require that businesses adjust their distribution systems. This situation also gives businesses the opportunity to experiment with different distribution strategies. For example, in the United States, General Motors distributes automobiles through franchised retail car dealerships. However, in Taiwan, GM owns its own retail dealers and sells cars directly to consumers. In that nation, GM is free from franchise dealer constraints and has been able to test systems for selling cars to consumers directly over the Internet.

Cultural considerations should also be weighed when planning distribution in foreign markets. For example, when Reebok owners wanted to sell their athletic shoes in Europe, they studied European culture and found that Europeans visit sporting goods stores far less often than Americans. This led them to decide to distribute Reebok's shoes through hundreds of traditional retail shoe outlets. Within one year of adopting this distribution strategy, Reebok's sales in France doubled.

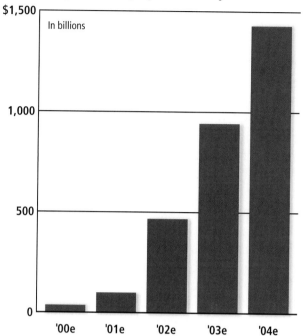

FIGURE 21-6

Going To Market

Sales of goods and services via electronic marketplaces are projected to skyrocket

■ **E-Marketplace or Private Web Site?** E-marketplaces for B2B operations provide one-stop shopping and savings for industrial buyers. *Why would a business opt to be part of an e-marketplace rather than having its own Web site?*

BRIGHT IDEAS

Have Your Pie...And The Tin Too

What to do with the pie tin when the pie is all gone? New England college students in the mid-1900s found that empty pie tins made excellent toys for flinging back and forth across college lawns. Talk about creative recycling! These pie tins came from Frisbie Baking Company of Bridgeport, Connecticut, which sold pies to many New England colleges between 1871 and 1958. In 1948, W. F. Morrison and Warren Franscioni invented a plastic version of the pie tin "Frisbie" that could fly farther with better accuracy. The two men went separate ways before their product had achieved any success. Morrison later marketed the toy as the "Pluto Platter," feeding into America's growing fascination with UFOs. Morrison sold his design rights to Wham-O in 1957 but retained the patent. Wham-O named the product Frisbee and promoted it as a new sport. Sales soared, and Morrison received more than $1 million in royalties for his invention.

Thinking Creatively

What household products might be given new life and reinvented as possible toys?

A look at Japan's system of doing business can serve as an example of challenges companies face when doing business abroad. Japan has a unique distribution system, called *keiretsu* (which means alignment), in which intermediaries have strong social and economic bonds with producers. They are often groups of anywhere from 20 to 45 companies that are all connected to one bank. Keiretsu are groups of closely related companies that do business with one another on a regular basis. Through distribution keiretsu, the manufacturer dominates the marketing channels for its products. Understanding these relationships and becoming a part of them is important for any business wanting to do business successfully in Japan. The Japanese Fair Trade Commission estimated that 90 percent of domestic business takes place between parties in a relationship such as the keiretsu. Warner Lambert needed to utilize a Japanese wholesaler in order to sell its Schick razors and blades in Japan.

Why are wholesalers so important in Japan? One reason is simply tradition and the other is a lack of storage space. As a comparison, it may take five intermediaries to sell soap in Japan and only one or two in the United States. Thus, distributors remain the main links into the marketplace. Foreign business approaching the Japanese market should study the players and their relationships with each other very carefully.

Pick, Pack, and Ship

In addition to marketing and selling their products, most Internet companies ship more than 1,000 packages a day. Amazon.com usually ships 10,000 packages; during the holiday season, however, numbers rise to as high as 60,000 packages. This task is too large for even the dot.com giant Amazon. The cost of hiring employees alone would be a challenge, but building a one-million square-foot warehouse would take two years and cost between $60 million and $80 million. To solve this problem, third-party distribution organizations, also known as pick, pack, and ship fulfillment specialists, help to meet demand, and receive roughly ten percent per order. Outsourcing, or looking outside of your own resources to fill needs, is a practical alternative for time-, space-, or cash-strapped companies.

Thinking Critically

What other services can a company outsource?

21.2 ASSESSMENT

Reviewing Key Terms and Concepts

1. What key factors are considered when developing an effective distribution plan?

2. When are multiple distribution channels used?

3. Give two reasons for using a direct sales force instead of independent sales agents.

4. What are the levels of distribution intensity?

5. Explain the challenges businesses face when getting involved with distribution planning in Japan.

Thinking Critically

6. What problems might be created by a clothing manufacturer that establishes its own Web site to sell to the final consumer, while it also sells the same items to retailers for resale to consumers?

Integrating Academic Skills

7. **MATH** Assuming a manufacturer's sales were $2,000,000 last year and the commission paid to independent sales agents was 8 percent, what was the company's yearly sales expense? What would be the difference in its yearly sales expense if that company hired its own sales force at a cost of $600,000? Assuming the projected expenses for an in-house sales force remained the same, determine the sales volume at which point the manufacturer could switch from independent sales agents to an in-house sales force without being hurt financially.

Careers in Marketing

Sheryl Modesti
Watson and Associates
Food Broker

What does your job entail?

"I assess operators' needs, identifying their concepts and target markets and taking into consideration their food costs. I get to know all people responsible for making decisions in each facility—ranging from the owner or the purchasing director to the kitchen staff and the wait staff. I train food facility staff and distributor sales representatives in my products. I am the link between the manufacturer, the operator, and distributor."

What kind of training did you have?

"I have no formal training in the food industry, only a love of food and cooking. It is very important to your success that you have a passion for what you do. I was a national sales manager, copywriter, and national trainer for a skincare, cosmetic, and nutrition line for 11 years. I traveled 70 percent of the time, hiring, training, selling, and establishing accounts. This gave me a background in sales and marketing and paved the way for my current career. I recommend that students keep focused on their dream."

What do you like most about your work?

"Meeting chefs and absorbing information from them is my favorite part of the job, and it makes me a better consultant. I also enjoy the manufacturer training at our brokerage facility, where we have a test kitchen to experiment with recipes."

What is your key to success?

"Developing good relationships with operators and distributors is the key to my success. Without cultivated relationships, you will not be able to accomplish your end result—closing the sale!"

Thinking Critically
What kinds of research can food brokers do to keep up with the industry?

Career Facts

Education and Training: Many more companies are requiring college degrees in business or marketing. Sales experience and familiarity with brands are also valuable. Many companies have training programs for new sales representatives.

Aptitudes, Abilities, and Skills: Good organizational skills to prepare reports, analyze data, maintain expense accounts, and schedule appointments are required. Food brokers must be goal oriented and able to work independently or on a team, in addition to having a pleasant personality and strong desire to sell.

Career Outlook: Opportunities are expected to grow more slowly than average through 2008.

Career Path: Successful food brokers may be assigned to larger territories or advance to sales supervisors, district managers, or sales trainers.

Chapter 21 ASSESSMENT

VOCABULARY REVIEW

Working in a group, choose a company and tell how it sells products to consumers and industrial buyers. Include the following terms:

- channel of distribution
- intermediaries
- wholesalers
- retailers
- e-tailing
- agents
- direct distribution
- indirect distribution
- exclusive distribution
- selective distribution
- intensive distribution
- integrated distribution
- e-marketplace

FACT AND IDEA REVIEW

1. How are intermediaries classified? (21.1)

2. Do independent sales agents carry competing products from different manufacturers? Why or why not? (21.1)

3. What is the difference between direct and indirect distribution? (21.1)

4. What channel of distribution is generally used for services? (21.1)

5. A manufacturer wants to concentrate solely on production. What channel of distribution would be used in the consumer market? In the industrial market? (21.1)

6. How are giant retailers becoming powerful in the channels of distribution? (21.2)

7. Why would a business opt for intensive distribution of its product(s)? (21.2)

8. Why would retailers want to be part of an exclusive distribution agreement with a manufacturer? (21.2)

9. What is e-commerce and what effect is it having on how businesses sell their products? (21.2)

10. Explain why the *keiretsu* system of distribution makes it difficult for foreign businesses to sell their products in Japan. (21.2)

THINKING CRITICALLY

1. Why do you think that small retailers tend to use the services of wholesalers?

2. How much do you think e-tailing will change the way brick and mortar retailers operate?

3. Under what circumstances would an established business replace its independent sales representative with a direct sales force?

4. Which level of distribution (intensive, selective, or exclusive) would you chose for personal computers, expensive imported sweaters, a new brand of hair spray, and an automobile? Why?

BUILDING WORKPLACE SKILLS

1. **Writing** A new sporting goods equipment company wants to sell its products through infomercials. The vice president of marketing has asked your opinion. As the new marketing manager, you think the Internet would be more effective. Prepare a memo addressing this.

2. **Human Relations** You are a salesperson for Fanny Farmer candies. A customer complains that the selection is small and that she would like to see candy made by other manufacturers sold in the store. What would you say to the customer?

APPLYING MARKETING CONCEPTS

1. **Summarizing Key Concepts** Summarize an article that demonstrates any of the key concepts discussed in this chapter. In the summary, identify the specific concepts in parentheses. Use business publications, such as *BusinessWeek, Fortune, Forbes, Marketing News,* and *Nation's Business,* to find an applicable article.

2. **Defining Channels of Distribution** Using design software, diagram the channel of distribution for two products—one that is meant for the final consumer and one that is sold to industrial buyers. Prepare a written report that depicts and explains each channel of distribution.

3. **Analyzing Sales Costs** Using a spreadsheet program, prepare an analysis of the sales costs associated with hiring independent sales agents to sell your company's products. Assume that the sales of your company are $15,000,000 and that the percentage paid to independent sales agents range from five percent to ten percent in your industry. Show what the effect is at each percentage point from five percent to ten percent.

4. **Understanding E-Commerce** Using presentation software, prepare an oral presentation that addresses e-commerce and its effects on channels of distribution.

LINKING SCHOOL TO WORK

Information, Thinking, and Interpersonal Skills
Ask an employer to tell you from whom it buys selected goods. Trace those goods back to the manufacturer or producer in order to diagram the channels of distribution to the final user. Share your findings with your class in both oral and written reports.

THE DECA CONNECTION

Role Play: DECA Fundraiser

Situation You are to assume the role as chairperson of your DECA chapter's fund-raising efforts this year. You have developed a unique board game based on trivia about your state. You have identified two target markets within your state—consumers age 12 and over and businesses, which might be able to use the game as a premium for customers. A local businessperson, John Ruiz, has given you a quote on manufacturing the game, but you need to present your marketing teacher (judge) with a thorough distribution plan before you can ask people to invest.

Activity Present your distribution plan to your marketing teacher (judge).

Evaluation You will be evaluated on how well you meet the following performance indicators:
- Explain the nature of channels of distribution
- Explain the nature and scope of distribution
- Explain the relationship between customer service and distribution
- Select channels of distribution
- Demonstrate orderly and systematic behavior

inter NET CONNECTION

E-Everything
Brick and mortar businesses are establishing Web sites to sell their products directly to consumers.

Connect
- Find the Web sites for three competing catalog companies.
- Analyze the purpose of each company's Web site and how it fits into the company's channels of distribution.
- Prepare a written report that provides a comparison of the three companies' channels of distribution.

Chapter 22

Physical Distribution

Marketing: What It Takes

A Decision to Make: Common Carriers, Private Carrier, or Both? You have been asked to evaluate the current transportation system for your company. The company is deciding between a common carrier, its own private fleet, or a combination of both to transport its products. Management has asked you to identify the pros and cons of each transportation alternative.

WHAT WILL YOU DO? What advantages and disadvantages will you present for each type of transportation choice?

Transportation Systems and Services

The Nature and Scope of Physical Distribution

After a company decides on its channels of distribution, it must plan for actually moving the products through those channels. Physical distribution comprises all the activities that help to ensure that the right amount of product is delivered to the right place at the right time. Physical distribution is also known as *logistics*. Physical distribution or logistics involves order processing, transporting, storing, stock handling, and inventory control of materials and products. Figure 22-1 on page 394 presents an overview of the functions of physical distribution. Physical distribution is an important link between a business and its customers.

Physical distribution involves moving products quickly with minimal handling to reduce costs and maximize customer satisfaction. Marketing experts believe that between 20–25 percent of the value of a product can be assigned to physical distribution expenses.

Businesses try to make the physical distribution system as efficient and cost effective as possible. At the same time, physical distribution needs to be coordinated with other business functions, such as purchasing, finance, production, packaging, and promotion. Promotional activities are planned in advance, therefore the distribution system must be able to deliver the correct products at the right time and to the right place.

As you can imagine, transporting, storing, and handling products is expensive—physical distribution is the third largest expense for most businesses. It is surpassed only by the costs of material and labor.

Types of Transportation

Once something has been sold, it usually needs to be moved from the seller to the buyer. Transportation is the marketing function of moving products from a seller to a buyer. Transportation costs are a significant part of each sale; therefore, manufacturers, wholesalers, and retailers look for the most efficient and cost-effective delivery methods.

There are five major transportation forms that move products, including motor carriers, railroads, waterways, pipelines, and air carriers. Figure 22-2 on page 395 shows the percentage of freight carried by each transportation mode. Most businesses that transport goods are subject to federal and state regulations of the rates they charge and their operating procedures.

• What You'll Learn

- The nature and scope of physical distribution
- How transportation systems are used to move products
- The different kinds of transportation services

• Why It's Important

To gain a competitive advantage and succeed in today's business environment, you will want to learn how businesses are delivering products to buyers around the country and the world.

Key Terms

- physical distribution
- transportation
- common carriers
- contract carriers
- private carriers
- exempt carriers
- ton-mile
- carload
- freight forwarders

FIGURE 22-1

PHYSICAL DISTRIBUTION

Physical distribution involves the functions of order processing, transportation, storage, stock handling, and inventory control.

ORDER PROCESSING

The purchase of a product initiates the movement of products through a physical distribution system.

TRANSPORTATION

Transportation involves the actual physical movement of products. It is estimated that up to 8 percent of a company's sales are spent on the transportation function.

STORAGE

The storage function facilitates the actual movement of products through the distribution channel as products are sold.

STOCK HANDLING

Receiving, checking, and marking items for sale are an important step in the physical distribution system.

INVENTORY CONTROL

Proper inventory control ensures that products are kept in sufficient quantities and available when requested by customers.

■ Trucking

Trucks (or motor carriers) are the most frequently used form of transportation. They carry higher-valued products that are expensive to carry in inventory. Lightweight shipments transported over moderate distances are generally handled by trucks—nearly 80 percent of those shipments weigh less than 1,000 pounds each. Businesses use trucks for virtually all *intracity* (within a city) shipping and for 26 percent of the *intercity* (between cities) freight traffic in the United States.

State and federal transportation agencies regulate motor carriers used for interstate commerce. State transportation agencies regulate fuel taxes, safety issues, and rates charged for *intrastate* (within a state) trucking. The Interstate Commerce Commission (ICC), a federal agency, regulates transportation of goods between states. The Staggers Rail and Motor Carrier Act of 1980 relaxed many ICC rules, allowing interstate motor carriers and railroads to negotiate competitive rates and services.

TYPES OF CARRIERS Businesses that use trucks to move their products have different options to choose from. They can use *for-hire carriers, private carriers,* or a combination of both. For-hire carriers include common carriers and contract carriers.

Most motor carriers are for-hire or common carriers. **Common carriers** provide transportation services to any business in its operating area for a fee. A common carrier receives a "certificate of convenience and necessity" from the state and federal governments.

A common carrier must publish its freight rates to prevent discrimination against shippers. Carriers can change their rates or geographical areas, as long as they do not charge rates that are different from their published rates or provide different services. More than one-third of all motor freight is handled by common carriers. Common carriers are primarily used for less-than-full truckloads to several long distance locations over infrequently traveled roads or for full-truckload shipments over major highways.

Contract carriers are for-hire carriers that provide equipment and drivers for specific routes, according to agreements between the carrier and the shipper. A contract carrier can provide services on a one-time basis or on a continuing basis.

■ **Delivering the Goods** Common carriers handle different commodities but often specialize in handling a single commodity. *Why are common carriers important to the trucking industry?*

FIGURE 22-2

Transportation Systems

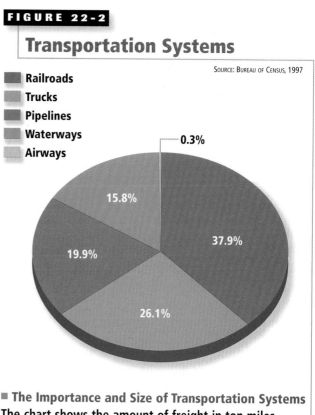

Source: Bureau of Census, 1997

- Railroads
- Trucks
- Pipelines
- Waterways
- Airways

0.3%
15.8%
37.9%
19.9%
26.1%

■ **The Importance and Size of Transportation Systems** The chart shows the amount of freight in ton miles shipped by each form of transportation. *Why is the percentage spent on air transportation small in relation to other types of transportation?*

Chapter 22 ■ *Physical Distribution* **395**

Contract carriers negotiate their fees with each customer, and the fees may differ from agreement to agreement. Contract carriers often transport goods for more than one business, and they can charge different rates to each business. They must file their contracts with the appropriate state or federal regulatory agency.

A business that uses for-hire common or contract carriers does not need to invest in transportation equipment; however, its shipments are subject to the carriers' schedules, routes, and available equipment. For-hire carriers also offer less flexibility for special pick-ups or handling, rush deliveries, and direct shipments.

PRIVATE CARRIERS Private carriers transport goods for an individual business. The transportation equipment can be owned or leased to meet the specific transportation needs of the business. Transportation companies, such as the Ryder System, Inc., make a variety of private carrier options available to a business. These options include full service leasing, finance leasing, and dedicated contract logistics. Significant capital investment is required if a business decides to own and maintain its own private fleet.

Cost is certainly a major factor in selecting transportation. Starting a private carrier operation involves a large investment in equipment and facilities. A business that regularly ships a large amount of merchandise may like the flexibility of owning its own means of transporting its products.

Private carriage lets a business maintain total control over equipment, maintenance, availability, routes, delivery times, and handling procedures. Private carriage also allows a business to rapidly change schedules, routes, and delivery times to meet customers' needs.

Many businesses use a combination of for-hire and private carriers. They may use their own trucks for local deliveries and common or contract carriers for shipments beyond their local service areas.

Exempt carriers, which commonly carry agricultural products, are free from direct regulation of rates and operating procedures. In most cases, they carry agricultural products. Their rates are lower than those charged by common carriers because of their exempt status. Exempt carrier status can also be granted to local transportation firms that make short-distance deliveries within specified trading areas in cities.

At 1500 ... Or 3:00?

Aside from the different time zones that one must be familiar with, different countries also utilize different methods of telling time. What is known in the United States as "military time" is just plain time for our global partners. 8:00 a.m. in U.S. time is 800 hours; 3:00 p.m. is 1500 hours. The trick? Add 12 to the p.m. hours. While in casual conversation all people might not use the 24-hour system. In fact, many Europeans drop the "hours," calling the time just by the number. Don't be surprised if your international travel agent reminds you that your flight leaves at 2200!

Thinking Critically

What are some benefits of the 24-hour time system?

ADVANTAGES AND DISADVANTAGES OF TRUCK TRANSPORTATION Trucks are a convenient form of transportation. They can pick up products from a manufacturer, wholesaler, or retailer and deliver them door-to-door to any geographical location. Trucks help reduce the packaging costs for some products because goods require less protective packaging. Trucks can make rapid deliveries of large amounts of goods and therefore reduce the need to carry large inventories between shipments.

The disadvantages of using motor carriers include susceptibility to delays due to traffic jams, equipment breakdowns, and traffic accidents. Trucks are also subject to size and weight restrictions enforced by states.

■ Rail Transportation

Railroads are a major type of transportation in the United States. Trains transport nearly 38 percent of the total intercity *ton-miles* of freight. A ton-mile is the movement of one ton of freight one mile.

Trains are important for moving heavy and bulky freight, such as coal, steel, lumber, chemicals, grain, farm equipment, and automobiles over long distances. To compete with motor carriers, railroads have aggressively advertised the benefits of shipping by rail.

■ **The Best of Both Worlds** Piggybacking loaded truck trailers on railroad flatcars combines two different forms of transportation. *What are the advantages of piggybacking?*

PRICING AND DELIVERY SERVICES Railroads offer several specialized and innovative pricing and delivery services, including *piggyback service, fishyback service, specialized service, package cars, diversion-in-transit,* and *processing-in-transit.*

PIGGYBACK AND FISHYBACK SERVICE *Piggyback service* gets its name from carrying (piggybacking) loaded truck trailers over land on railroad flatcars. *Fishyback service* is shipping loaded truck trailers over water on ships and barges. Piggyback and fishyback services combine the advantages of truck transportation with the lower costs of rail and water transportation.

Some products need to be hauled in special railroad cars. Refrigerated cars keep perishable products such as milk or fresh vegetables from spoiling over long distances. Other specially designed freight cars haul combustible or hazardous materials, such as chemicals.

Shippers pay lower rail transportation rates if they fill an entire boxcar. A carload is the minimum number of pounds of freight needed to fill a boxcar. Carload weights are established for different classifications of goods. Once a shipment reaches the minimum weight, the shipper pays the lower rate, regardless of the size of the car. A *less than carload* is a shipment that falls short of minimum weight requirements for filling a freight car. Rates charged for less than carload shipments are more expensive because partial carloads have to be unloaded at each destination. Unloading time and the extra effort involved increase the rates charged to shippers.

Package (or pool) arrangements allow several shippers who are sending their items to a common destination to combine their items to fill an entire carload. If sold separately, each shipper would have to pay a higher rate since it would be shipping less than a carload. *Diversion-in-transit* service allows the redirection of carloads already en route. A vegetable grower in the South can send vegetables north and find the best price for them while they are en route. The railroad will divert the shipment to the buyer for a fee—even if the buyer is not at the originally anticipated destination. *Processing-in-transit* permits shippers to have products processed, repackaged, and assembled while in transit to their final destination.

ADVANTAGES AND DISADVANTAGES OF RAIL TRANSPORTATION Railroads can ship at relatively low costs by handling large quantities. Trains are seldom slowed or stopped by bad weather.

The biggest disadvantage of train transportation is the lack of flexibility. Trains can pick up and deliver goods only at stations along designated rail lines, and therefore can not reach as many places as motor carriers are able to.

■ Water Transportation

Shipment over water is one of the oldest methods of transporting merchandise. Ships carry merchandise from one part of the United States to others, as well as around the world. The United States Maritime Commission regulates U.S. water transportation.

INTERNAL AND INTRACOASTAL WATERWAYS

Internal shipping is shipping from one port to another on connecting rivers and lakes. The St. Lawrence Seaway, the Mississippi River, the Ohio River, and the Great Lakes are important internal shipping routes. The St. Lawrence Seaway, which is a combination of rivers, canals, and lakes, and the Mississippi and Ohio Rivers all give ocean-going vessels access to the heartland of America. Agricultural and industrial products of the Midwest are regularly shipped from the Great Lakes to other parts of the world.

Intracoastal shipping is the shipping of goods between ports along the Atlantic or Pacific coasts or from one coast to the other. Shipments can be sent from the New York Port Authority to the San Francisco Port Authority through the Panama Canal.

INTERNATIONAL WATERWAYS

International waterways are the oceans and rivers that connect continents and countries. Transportation by water is particularly important for international product shipments. Almost all overseas freight is transported by ships and barges because of the low cost. Products commonly shipped by international waterways include heavy equipment, steel, ore, forest products, grain, and petroleum. As international trade continues to increase, so will the use of shipping by international waterways.

■ **Waterways** Waterways are a transportation method of choice for many companies. *Why is this true?*

ADVANTAGES AND DISADVANTAGES OF WATER TRANSPORTATION

The biggest advantage of waterway transportation is low cost—ships and barges are the cheapest form of freight transportation. However, they are also the slowest form of transportation. Speed is not a problem when shipping bulky, non-perishable items, such as coal, forest products, and cement. Perishable goods such as dairy products, however, require shippers to use other forms of transportation so they can reach their destination before they perish.

Water transportation has some other disadvantages. Buyers that are located far from the port city must have products off-loaded from ships onto railroad cars or motor carriers to reach their destination. This added cost of distribution reduces the cost advantages of water transportation.

Water transportation is affected by bad weather. Great Lakes shipping, for example, is generally closed for two to three months in the winter.

■ Pipelines

Pipelines are normally owned by the company using them, so they are usually considered private carriers. There are more than 200,000 miles of pipelines in the United States.

Pipelines are most frequently used to transport oil and natural gas. They move crude oil from oil field to refinery, where it is processed. The refined products, such as gasoline, are then trucked to retail outlets such as your local gasoline station.

Pipelines are more important in the physical distribution process than most people know. They carry approximately 20 percent of the ton-miles of freight transported in the United States.

ADVANTAGES AND DISADVANTAGES OF PIPELINE TRANSPORTATION

The construction of pipelines requires a high initial investment, but operational costs are small. The risk of a pipeline leak is small, but when a leak does occur the damage to the environment can be extensive. The National Transportation Safety Board and the U.S. Department of Transportation have determined that pipelines have the best safety record among all major transportation systems. Products carried through pipelines move slowly but continuously, suffer minimal product damage or theft, and are not subjected to delivery delays due to bad weather.

■ **Overnight Delivery** Air transportation is a growing segment of the transportation industry. *What items are generally sent by air?*

■ Air Transportation

Currently, air transportation is less than one percent of the total ton-miles of freight shipped. High-value, low-weight items such as overnight mail are often shipped by air. Certain high-value products, such as emergency parts, instruments, medicines, flowers, and perishable food products are also shipped by air.

Air freight is the most costly form of distribution. However, its speed may create some savings in lower inventory. Because air freight has space constraints, the items usually carried are valuable, light-weight, and time sensitive. Products transported in containers are also well-suited to this form of shipment. There are specialized firms that offer ground support to businesses that use air freight. These specialized firms collect shipments and deliver them to the air terminal.

When air freight is handled by a major airline such as United, Delta, or Air Canada, it is often carried as cargo in the luggage space of passenger flights. This allows passenger airlines to use excess capacity that would otherwise be lost. When air freight is carried by specialized air freight companies, it is usually carried in the body of the plane.

The Federal Aviation Administration (FAA) regulates air transportation. It does not regulate charges for air freight. Airlines and air transport companies set their own rates. Air freight carriers offer such things as wide-bodied jets that can ship more goods and specialized packaging designed to help prevent

REAL WORLD MARKETING

Changing Channels

What happens when manufacturers suggest to customers where to buy their goods? Baume & Mercier, the luxury Swiss watchmaker, took out a full-page ad in the Wall Street Journal warning consumers not to buy their goods through the discount retailer Ashford.com. This cut-throat competition isn't exactly fashionable. The e-tailing sector has a term for the trouble that Ashford.com is stirring up—channel conflict. It happens when a manufacturer threatens its existing retailers by selling products through a more efficient channel like the Web. Is this really bad news for Baume & Mercier? On the day the ad ran, Ashford's sales of the $1,000-plus Swiss watches doubled!

Thinking Critically
What are the pros and cons of Baume & Mercier not doing business with certain retailers?

damage. Specialized freight planes now under development will soon allow air carriers to reach and serve even more markets.

ADVANTAGES AND DISADVANTAGES OF AIR TRANSPORTATION The greatest advantage to air transportation is its speed. Many companies, such as Airborne, DHL, Federal Express, United Parcel Service, and the U.S. Postal Service advertise overnight delivery. This fast delivery time allows businesses to satisfy customers who need something quickly. It also reduces inventory expenses and storage costs for warehousing products.

The greatest disadvantage of air transportation is its cost. It is the most expensive form of distribution. Air shipment rates are usually twice as costly as truck rates. For some shippers, however, the advantage of greater speed of delivery may outweigh the extra costs. Other disadvantages of air transportation include mechanical breakdowns and delays in delivery caused by bad weather.

Transportation Service Companies

Transportation service companies handle small- and medium-size packages. Some examples of these companies are the *U.S. Postal Service, express carriers, bus package carriers,* and *freight forwarders.*

■ U.S. Postal Service

The U.S. Postal Service ships small packages by parcel post or fourth-class mail. This includes packages weighing more than 16 ounces, as well as newspapers and magazines and printed matter that weighs less than 16 ounces (but not postcards and letters). Parcel post is used most often for shipping large and oversized packages weighing less than 70 pounds and not more than 130 inches in combined length and girth (distance around). Parcel post can be insured against loss or damage or sent COD (cash on delivery). Parcel post can also be express-mailed at higher rates to guarantee next-day delivery.

In recent years the U.S. Postal Service has seen tremendous growth with its *Priority Mail* product. *Priority Mail* is marketed as a quick, convenient, reliable, and cost-effective way to deliver important correspondence within a two–three day period or for an extra charge, overnight delivery.

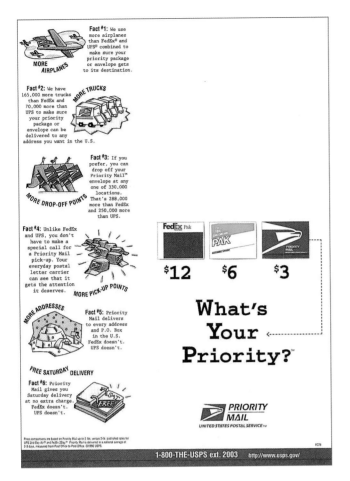

■ **Through Rain, Hail, Sleet, or Snow** The U.S. Postal Service competes with other transportation service companies. *After looking at the advantages in the ad, why do shippers use other express companies?*

BRIGHT IDEAS
Postal Partners

When there is a task at hand that someone else can handle better, it is best to delegate. LeShop, the first online store of its kind in Europe, heeds this lesson well! LeShop sells packaged food and personal products, such as soaps, diapers, and toothpaste, to Swiss customers. Next morning delivery is guaranteed for orders received by 4:30 p.m. LeShop knew that meeting this guarantee would be a challenge and found an outside business partner in a most ingenious place—the Swiss Post Office. The Post Office controls the logistics for the entire distribution. Validated orders are electronically transmitted to postal employees who fill LeShop's boxes with the requested inventory. Boxes are then placed into the traditional mail postal circuit. Customers are charged an additional 10 Swiss francs (about $7.00), but demand keeps rising. Convenience is worth the price in a country where things are expected to run like fine Swiss clockwork.

Thinking Creatively

What other products could LeShop offer with its timely delivery to attract customers?

Case Study

From Your Computer to Your Home

Federal Express—a company known for its business-to-business next-day air express service—is looking at a new market. The company is starting a new division called FedEx Home Delivery, which will handle delivery of products ordered online.

E-tailing is changing physical distribution systems. More customers are beginning to order products online and have them delivered directly to their homes or apartments. A study by Ernst & Young states that approximately 50 percent of online shoppers state convenience as their motivation to shop on the Web. FedEx Home Delivery hopes to make this process even easier for customers. FedEx Home Delivery faces keen competition from United Parcel Service (UPS) and the U.S. Postal Service. UPS handled about 55 percent and the U.S. Postal Service about 30 percent of the holiday 1999 deliveries ordered over the Web. Only 10 percent was handled by the existing Federal Express ground-based system.

Experts feel that UPS is currently more focused on the business-to-consumer market than Federal Express is. The U.S. Postal Service already delivers mail to every household in the country.

Federal Express is interested in securing a bigger piece of the action. In 1999, $20 billion in goods was ordered and shipped over the Internet. Internet sales are expected to rise to $180 billion by 2004. Although delivering to homes is more costly than business-to-business deliveries, it still adds to profits. Schedules can be maximized because air express work can be done in the morning, business-to-business deliveries in the afternoon, and residential deliveries in the evening.

FedEx Home Delivery will use smaller trucks to deliver packages in the evening and on Saturdays when most people are home. Federal Express is also offering customers the option of scheduling an appointment at a time that is convenient for the customer. Federal Express plans to provide a Web site that will allow both shippers and customers to track their orders. This service aids not only consumers but also telecommuters who work from home. As an increasing number of employees work from home, there is a greater need for guaranteed and timely home delivery.

Case Study Review

1. Why does Federal Express want to enter the home delivery market?
2. Why are home deliveries more expensive?

A Matter of Ethics

3. Is it ethical for a government agency to compete with private companies for business? Why or why not?

■ Express Carriers

Express carriers specialize in delivering small, lightweight packages and high-priority mail usually weighing less than 150 pounds. Express parcel carriers, such as Federal Express, DHL, and United Parcel Service, offer door-to-door pickup, delivery, and COD service. Express shipments may be made nationally or internationally by airplane, truck, bus, or train. Rates are based on speed, weight, distance to be sent, size of package, and type of service used. Regular service usually takes from two to three days; more expensive, next-day service is also available.

Over the last 30 years, express carriers have become a more important part of physical distribution. Federal Express, which began operations in 1973, now transports more than 3.3 million packages daily. It has a worldwide fleet of more than 650 aircraft, 150,000 employees, and 1200 service centers serving 210 countries.

DHL, another popular express carrier, started in 1969 shipping from San Francisco to Honolulu. They were the first to introduce express international shipping via airplane to the Eastern Bloc in 1983 and to China in 1986. Today, DHL Worldwide Express is the largest company that specializes in international express shipping. They can send packages to approximately 635,000 destinations in over 233 countries and territories.

■ Bus Package Carriers

Bus package carriers provide transportation services for packages weighing less than 100 pounds. Bus package carriers, such as Greyhound, can provide same-day or next-day service to cities and towns along their scheduled routes. As with other forms of shipping, the cost of bus package transportation depends on the weight of the package and the distance it will travel.

Greyhound may run numerous buses daily to major cities, such as New York, Boston, Chicago, or San Francisco. This is attractive to shippers as they have many options to deliver their products quickly, while at a reasonable rate.

■ Freight Forwarders

Freight forwarders are private companies that combine *less-than carload* or *less-than truckload* shipments from several different businesses and deliver them to their destinations. They accumulate small shipments into larger lots and then hire a carrier to move them, usually at reduced rates. By combining shipments, freight forwarders can often obtain truckload or carload rates and lower transportation costs for shippers. Freight forwarders also provide logistical services that help businesses select the best transportation methods and routes.

22.1 ASSESSMENT

Reviewing Key Terms and Concepts

1. What is physical distribution?
2. What function does transportation play in marketing a product?
3. Identify five transportation systems for the distribution of products.
4. What is the difference between a common and a contract carrier?
5. List four different examples of transportation service companies.

Thinking Critically

6. Many retail distribution and transportation executives support federal legislation that would reduce state trucking regulations. What do you see as potential benefits and disadvantages of this effort?

Integrating Academic Skills

7. **COMMUNICATION** Research and write a 100-word paper about the advantages and disadvantages of federal deregulation of the trucking industry.

Inventory Storage

The Storage of Goods

Storage is the marketing function of holding goods until they are sold. The amount of goods stored is called an inventory. We will talk more about inventories in Chapter 24.

Storing goods is an essential activity for most businesses. Each business member in a channel of distribution needs to store its products until orders are received from customers.

Products might also need to be stored because production has outpaced consumption or demand decreases. Sometimes, certain agricultural commodities such as corn, wheat, and soybeans may be available only during certain times. Commodity storage helps to stabilize prices for the product. Some purchasers buy in quantity to get discounts on their purchases and then store the items until they are needed. Finally, products are stored at convenient locations to provide faster delivery to customers.

Storing goods adds time and place utility to products. Products should be available for customers when and where they want them. The costs involved in storing products include space, equipment, and personnel. Storage also involves the cost of tying up money (or capital) in inventory rather than investing it in an activity that could provide a larger return. Businesses must balance the costs of holding merchandise in inventory against the possibility of not having merchandise available for customers when they want to purchase it.

Determining where to store goods is an important decision. Products are stored in a number of ways. Cars and trucks are frequently stored in outdoor lots, petroleum products in specialized storage tanks, and grain in grain elevators. Efficient, adequate storage reduces the storage costs for a business and helps assure good customer service. Most products are stored in warehouses—facilities in which goods are received, identified, sorted, stored, and dispatched for shipment. Let's take a closer look at the type of warehouses businesses use.

■ Private Warehouses

A private warehouse is a facility designed to meet the specific needs of its owner. Any producer, wholesaler, or retailer has the option of owning its own private warehouse. A private warehouse is valuable for companies that move a large volume of products. Specialized conditions, such as a temperature-controlled environment, may be built into the facility. Private warehouses often house other parts of the business operation, such as offices.

• What You'll Learn

- The concept and function of inventory storage
- The types of warehouses
- How distribution planning works for international markets

• Why It's Important

Most products must be kept for a time in a safe location until they are needed or ready to be sold. In this section, you will be introduced to the concept of inventory storage and learn about the places where products are kept until they are distributed to customers.

Key Terms

- storage
- private warehouse
- public warehouse
- distribution center
- bonded warehouses

■ Ensuring a Rapid Turnaround Distribution centers are designed to speed delivery of products while minimizing the time that they are stored. *Why is moving the product quickly so important?*

Private warehouses are costly to build and maintain. In a recent survey, large retailers reported spending 51 percent of their total physical distribution costs on warehouse expenses; transportation costs accounted for the remaining 49 percent. Larger retailers, such as Sears, Radio Shack, and Kmart link their private warehouses to the purchasing and distribution activities of their retail outlets. Private warehouses should be considered only when a significant amount of merchandise needs to be stored, and the total operating costs are lower than those of public warehouses.

■ Public Warehouses

A public warehouse offers storage and handling facilities to individuals or companies. It is a facility available to any company that will pay for its use. Public warehouses not only rent space but also provide services to businesses. These services include shipment consolidation, receiving, unloading, inspecting, reshipping, order filling, and truck terminal operation services. Public warehouses are helpful to businesses that have low volume storage needs or seasonal production.

There are five types of public warehouses:

- *Commodity warehouses* are used primarily for agricultural products, such as tobacco, cotton, or grain.

- *Bulk storage warehouses* keep products only in bulk form, such as chemicals and oil.
- *Cold storage warehouses* store perishables such as fruits, vegetables, and frozen products.
- *Household goods warehouses* handle personal property storage, household articles, and furniture.
- *General merchandise warehouses* store any item that does not require specialized handling.

■ Distribution Centers

A variation of the private and public warehouse is the distribution center—a warehouse designed to speed delivery of goods and to minimize storage costs. The main focus in a distribution center is on moving products, not on storing them. Distribution centers are planned around markets rather than transportation requirements. They can cut costs by reducing the number of warehouses and cutting excessive inventory. Because companies are in business to sell goods, not to store or ship them, warehousing and delivery times must be cut to a minimum. Distribution centers help in this regard. Since warehousing adds 5 to 7 percent to the cost of merchandise, there is no value added in keeping merchandise stored for very long. Goods in storage do not make money for a business.

Some distribution centers also assist in physically changing the final customer product by changing its appearance, mixing ingredients, labeling, and repackaging it. Sherwin-Williams and Benjamin Moore are paint companies that use their distribution centers in this way.

Distribution centers consolidate large orders from many sources and redistribute them as separate orders for individual accounts or stores within a chain. Merchandise normally stays only a short time in a distribution center.

■ Bonded Warehouses

Bonded warehouses, either public or private, store products that require the payment of a federal tax. Imported or domestic products cannot be removed from a bonded warehouse until the required federal tax is paid. Businesses save on taxes by taking goods out of storage only when they are needed.

■ Challenges of International Distribution
Distribution planning for an international marketplace has several unique challenges.
What are some of the challenges?

© 2000 FedEx. See FedEx Service Guide for terms of carriage.

ORDERING CHINESE?

FedEx provides direct service from the U.S. to the most Asian cities, including Hong Kong, Beijing, Shanghai and Shenzhen. From Taipei to Tokyo, from Seoul to Singapore, FedEx is your gateway to the Far East. And now FedEx introduces the International Resource Center, the one stop for all your international trade needs. Let our International Document Assistance program guide you through the customary red tape of international shipping. Find out more about the International Resource Center and our full menu of FedEx services at **fedex.com** or call 1-800-Go-FedEx. **Be absolutely sure.**

FedEx Express

■ Distribution Planning for International Markets

Distribution is of critical importance in global marketing. Exports now support one-sixth of the manufacturing and agricultural output of the United States. International trade will continue to expand along with the need for worldwide physical distribution systems. This is because of the growing importance of electronic commerce, the increasing popularity of free-market economics, the sweeping away of global trade barriers, and the establishment of regional trading blocs such as the European Union, the Association of South East Asian Nations, and the North American Free Trade Agreement (NAFTA).

Selling to customers in the international marketplace requires even more planning than for selling within domestic markets. Businesses that sell internationally must follow U.S. export laws as well as the import laws of the countries to which they are selling. Some countries also have legal restrictions about how products may be transported. Businesses frequently have to deal with bureaucratic regulations, language barriers, and tedious negotiations.

The need for extensive planning becomes even more obvious when you consider that parts for many products are made in different countries. Car manufacturers often use parts made in several countries. The parts are shipped to assembly plants in other countries where the final product is put together and ultimately shipped to still other destinations. Planning for the best method of transporting parts from each country for each step of the process is the key to keeping the assembly lines running and the final products getting to buyers like you.

To deliver their goods successfully, businesses must understand other countries' physical transportation systems. Once a product reaches a foreign nation, that country's distribution channels take over. The sophistication of a country's distribution channels increases as its economic infrastructure develops. In some less developed nations, the postal system may not be reliable enough to assure delivery of small packages by mail. Other countries may not have well-developed roads and highway systems to support dependable motor carrier deliveries. In China, for example, much of the distribution of goods is done through human labor. Most goods are carried by hand, in handcarts or via bicycle.

Another consideration is how retail institutions in other countries differ from American retail institutions. In most of the world, retailers have little or no capacity for refrigeration. For example, when Coke and Pepsi entered China, both had to create direct-distribution channels, investing in trucks and refrigerator units for small retailers. American-style supermarkets are rare in developing countries. In Japan, the term supermarket refers to a type of retail outfit that is very different from an American supermarket. They are often multi-story buildings that sell food as well as clothing, furniture, and appliances.

As global trade becomes more important to the success or failure of firms of all types and sizes, a well-planned global logistics strategy becomes increasingly important. Uncertainty regarding international distribution channels is the number one reason companies stay out of international markets.

Electronic Frontiers

Digital Distribution

Who would have thought that physical distribution would become a "dinosaur" in the music industry? As technology adjusts how basic things are done, there are new ways to listen to and receive music. Digital technology now allows music to be sent and received over the Internet. Anyone with a powerful computer, speakers, and an Internet connection can hear music electronically. Streaming audio allows for radio-like Web casts or songs to be played online. Advances in technology such as satellite or cable modems and MP3 players have made for quicker and broader distribution of music. Unfortunately, digital distribution also allows for the "piracy" or trading of music without payment. This loophole has the recording industry fuming.

Thinking Critically

With the evolution of technology, what other products could evolve from physical to digital distribution?

22.2 ASSESSMENT

Reviewing Key Terms and Concepts

1. What is the function of storage?

2. Give four reasons why merchandise is stored.

3. What is a warehouse? List the four types of warehouses.

4. How does a distribution center differ from a warehouse?

5. Describe at least three reasons why planning is important for distribution in international markets.

Thinking Critically

6. Most of the inland waterways were developed with federal funds, while the oil companies built pipelines themselves. Why do you think the federal government supports one mode of transportation and not the other?

Integrating Academic Skills

7. **MATH** The George A. Stinson is the second largest freighter on the Great Lakes. Normally, it carries 57,000 tons of taconite ore each voyage between Superior, Wisconsin, and Detroit, Michigan. Due to lower lake levels, it can only carry 50,000 tons per trip. At $5 per ton, how much revenue is lost per trip?

Careers in Marketing

SERVICE MARKETING

Eddie Habbaz
Logistics Manager, International Warehouse Logistics Association

What does your job entail?

"My job is to ensure the availability of the specified product, in the correct quantity, at the right place and time. It is necessary to get the product to the customer in good condition and at the best cost. Logistics managers work with managers who are responsible for the operation of the company. The job requires evaluating company systems that handle the acquisition, transportation, storage, and distribution of supplies, materials, and finished products. By analyzing the systems controlling the flow of materials and products, they propose improvements to increase profitability and customer satisfaction."

What skills are most important?

"Logistics managers must use observational and analytical skills to assess the efficiency of existing distribution systems. Logistics managers gather information from staff and customers and communicate their findings with those in charge of management systems. Logistic managers work with many different people; this requires good people skills."

What kind of training do you recommend for students?

"Students should take business courses in high school and seek an internship. It is recommended to go on to college for business administration or industrial engineering. Experience with a company working in such areas as project management, planning, inventory control, purchasing, or customer relations is valuable."

What is your key to success?

"My key to success lies in the understanding that each customer must be made to feel that his or her business is the single most important business in the universe. If customers do not feel valued, they may take their business somewhere else."

Thinking Critically
What other professionals do you think logistics managers work with frequently?

Career Facts

Education and Training: Logistics managers generally have a minimum of a bachelor's degree in business administration or industrial engineering. Five to six years of experience in areas such as project management, planning, inventory, purchasing, or customer relations provide valuable background experience for logistics managers. Coursework in statistics, economics, and quantitative mathematics is recommended.

Aptitude, Abilities, and Skills: Strong observational and analytical skills, in addition to mathematical skills, are required. Good communication skills, ability to delegate, effective management, and computer familiarity are vital.

Career Outlook: The outlook for logistics managers is excellent, with the demand exceeding the supply.

Career Path: Because logistics managers are exposed to many operations within an organization, they can advance to supervisory and management positions.

Chapter 22 ASSESSMENT

VOCABULARY REVIEW

Write the term that best matches each definition given below.

1. Minimum number of pounds of freight to fill a boxcar

2. Process of transporting, storing, and handling goods

3. Provide transportation services to any business for a fee

4. Owned and operated by an individual business to provide transportation services

5. Marketing function of moving goods from sellers to buyers

6. Free from direct regulation with respect to rates and operating procedures

7. The movement of one ton of freight one mile

8. Marketing function of holding goods

FACT AND IDEA REVIEW

1. What is the transportation function and why is it important to physical distribution? (22.1)

2. Explain the differences among the four types of motor carriers. (22.1)

3. Identify the advantages and disadvantages of motor carriers. (22.1)

4. What are two advantages and one disadvantage of railroads? (22.1)

5. What types of products are typically shipped by water? (22.1)

6. Why are most pipelines classified as private carriers? (22.1)

7. What is an advantage of air transportation? (22.1)

8. What is the difference between private and public warehouses? (22.2)

9. How might international distribution differ from distribution in the United States? (22.2)

THINKING CRITICALLY

1. Identify six examples of merchandise that would be shipped by motor carrier, rail carrier, air carrier, and water carrier. Tell whether this mode of transportation would be the only one used and support your answer.

2. Identify the primary mode of physical transportation for each of these items:

    a. flowers transported from Holland to Detroit

    b. iron ore shipped from Duluth, Minnesota to New Jersey

    c. gasoline to be delivered to a local retailer

3. Why would a business use a public warehouse rather than a private warehouse?

4. Give five examples of businesses that do not require product storage.

5. Why is distribution planning for international markets increasingly important?

BUILDING WORKPLACE SKILLS

1. **Human Relations** You are a clerk in a warehouse. A carton of snack items has been damaged during a shipment. As you are filling out a report for the damaged merchandise, a coworker suggests you have some of the snacks because the warehouse will never miss them. What would you say to your coworker? How do you believe management would view your coworker's suggestion?

2. **Technology** Use trade professional journals such as *Air Cargo World, Air Transport,* and *American Shipper,* or information from the *American Trucking Association, Association of American Railroads,* or the *National Transportation Library* to research the latest technologies used by shipping companies to track merchandise from place of origin to final delivery.

APPLYING MARKETING CONCEPTS

1. **Analyzing Transportation Methods** Talk to a local businessperson about why the company uses a particular type of transportation for physical distribution. Use a word processing program to prepare a 150-word report and share it with your class.

2. **Comparing Transportation Methods** Your company is shipping out samples of a new product to potential buyers around the United States. Research the least expensive and most effective way to distribute these goods if delivery time is not an issue. Create a table using a spreadsheet program comparing the different options that you have, including rail, bus, truck, or air.

3. **Visiting a Warehouse** Visit a warehouse and observe its receiving, storing, and shipping processes. Use a presentation software program to develop at least five visuals about your observations during the field trip.

4. **Finding a Warehouse** Research a warehouse business in your area using the Internet. Develop a word-processed outline identifying the Internet address, where the business is physically located, services offered, number of employees, and the type of merchandise stored there.

5. **Investigating Small Package Express Carriers** Investigate a small package express carrier (i.e. FedEx, RPS, UPS) or the U.S. Postal Service using the Internet. Prepare a report on online services and technologies available to shippers.

LINKING SCHOOL TO WORK

Systems Skills Research the transportation systems used at cooperative education training stations or places of employment. Prepare a written report on your findings, including a description of the method(s) used most frequently and the rationale for using it.

THE **DECA** CONNECTION

Role Play: Traffic Manager

Situation You are to assume the role of assistant traffic manager for a large company that grows oranges. Your plant superintendent (judge) has asked you to assist in the training of new employees.

Activity You must give a 15-minute talk on various types of distribution methods approved for shipping oranges. You are to explain the advantages of each method, including the methods most appropriate and most inappropriate for shipping oranges.

Evaluation You will be evaluated on how well you meet the following performance indicators:

- Explain the nature and scope of distribution
- Describe the use of technology in the distribution function
- Explain shipping procedures
- Explain storage considerations
- Explain the relationship between customer service and distribution

inter NET CONNECTION

Fly Like an Eagle

The U.S. Postal Service maintains a Web site for business and household use.

Connect

- Locate the U.S. Postal Service Web site.
- Find the business "Domestic Rate Calculator" page on the Web site.
- Calculate the cost to send a large package (length plus girth more than 84″ and less than or equal to 108″) from your city to Chicago, Illinois.

Chapter 23

Purchasing

Marketing: What It Takes

Online Purchasing

You have been asked to conduct research on online purchasing for a manufacturer of mountain climbing gear. You need to prepare a written analysis of how purchasing is presently being conducted and your recommendation on how the Internet may be used to reduce costs.

WHAT WILL YOU DO?

What factors will you consider when conducting your analysis and making your recommendation?

The Role of the Buyer

Planning Purchases

Who does the shopping in your household? How does that person know what to buy, how much to buy, and when and where to shop? Those questions are not very different for the people who do the purchasing for businesses. What is different is what they buy and the quantity purchased.

Organizational buyers buy goods for business purposes, usually in much greater quantities than the average consumer. Much of what they buy requires technical knowledge and knowledge of the operations of the firm, especially in manufacturing and service operations. Having a handle on the business trends that affect their industry is also important, especially when buying for resale purposes. Let's look at industrial and reseller markets to see how each plans its purchases.

■ Industrial Markets

In manufacturing and service businesses, the people responsible for purchasing may be called purchasing managers, industrial buyers, or procurement managers. Although the job titles may differ, the key function is to buy goods and services for use in the business.

To plan purchases in manufacturing businesses, industrial buyers are often directly involved with production planning. To get an idea of the responsibilities this entails, consider the case of a purchasing manager for an outerwear apparel manufacturer.

The company's master production schedule would provide the purchasing manager with details of production needed to meet sales requirements. Let's say that the marketing department predicts the company will sell 500 Style No. 1900 jackets in the coming season. The purchasing manager must know how much fabric, insulation, and thread and how many zippers it takes to produce one Style No. 1900 jacket. This is called a *bill of materials*. The total of all the materials necessary to make one jacket can be multiplied by 500 to determine exactly what needs to be purchased to meet the sales goal.

To determine *when* to buy those items, the purchasing manager would be responsible for materials requirement planning (MRP). MRP includes an analysis of when to make the purchases so they are available when needed according to the production schedule. The purchasing manager must therefore know the capacity of the manufacturing facility. He or she must be sure the company has room for the supplies, raw materials, and inventory of finished goods.

Time lines and delivery of all supplies must be followed and checked on a regular basis to maintain the master production schedule. This ensures that everything is as it should be for manufacturing to progress at an appropriate rate.

● What You'll Learn

- The terms used to describe organizational buyers
- How planning purchases differs between an industrial market and a reseller's market
- The six-month merchandise plan and its calculations
- The concept of chain store buying

● Why It's Important

The purchasing function in any business is important because the costs associated with running a business are often a direct result of the competence of the person responsible for buying the goods and services required to run the business.

Key Terms

- organizational buyers
- wholesale and retail buyers
- six-month merchandise plan
- open-to-buy
- centralized buying
- decentralized buying

■ **Industrial Buyers** Industrial buyers in manufacturing businesses buy the materials required to make products the company sells. *What does an industrial buyer have to know in order to purchase the correct quantity at the right time?*

■ Resellers

The resellers' market is found in wholesaling and retailing operations, where the person responsible for purchasing is simply called a buyer. Wholesale and retail buyers purchase goods for resale—they forecast customers' needs and buy the necessary products. Buyers must plan far in advance of the selling season to know how much of each item to purchase.

SIX-MONTH MERCHANDISE PLAN Buyers plan their purchases by preparing a six-month merchandise plan—or the budget that estimates planned purchases for a six-month period. Let's look at how the figures on a six-month merchandise plan are calculated and what factors are taken into consideration to arrive at those figures.

The first figure calculated on a merchandise plan is the *planned sales* figure. In most cases, this is determined by using the previous year's monthly sales figures and adjusting them to reflect the firm's current-year sales goal.

Suppose sales for a particular month last year were $100,000 and this year's goal is to increase sales by 10 percent. This year's planned sales for the month would be calculated as follows:

Desired increase: $100,000 × .10 = $10,000

Planned sales: $100,000 + $10,000 = $110,000

You could also reach the same result in a single step: $100,000 × 1.10 = $110,000

A firm's goal for the current year is derived from a study of last year's sales, current market and economic conditions, and an analysis of the competition. Projection of accurate planned sales figures is important because all other figures on the merchandise plan are computed on the basis of this figure.

Buyers must ensure that there is enough stock to accommodate the sales volume planned; this is also known as *beginning-of-the-month (BOM) inventory*. To project this figure, a buyer checks the previous year's records for how much stock was needed in relation to monthly sales. Sales were $40,000 in a given month and the BOM stock for that month was

■ **Planning Ahead** Employee pilferage and customer shoplifting must be considered when planning purchases in a six-month merchandise plan. *If your business upgraded its security system, how would you adjust your planned reductions figure for the coming season?*

$120,000; therefore, the stock-to-sales ratio is 3 to 1. The buyer can apply that same ratio to the planned figure for another month if economic and market conditions are similar.

Here is how the BOM figure on the merchandise plan would be calculated. Suppose the stock-to-sales ratio is 2:1 (usually reported as 2). This means that to accommodate a given sales volume it is necessary to keep twice that amount of stock on hand. BOM inventory should be twice the amount of anticipated sales—if sales are $5,000, then the BOM would be $10,000.

There is also an EOM (end-of-the-month) stock figure, which is closely related to the BOM stock figure. The BOM stock figure for any given month is the EOM stock figure for the previous month.

Planned retail reductions take into account reductions in the selling price and shortages of merchandise caused by clerical mistakes, employee pilferage, or customer shoplifting. Such reductions in earnings and merchandise shortages ultimately affect the amount of money that must be planned for purchases.

Planned retail reductions can be calculated in two different ways. One is to calculate reductions as a percentage of planned sales. Suppose planned reductions have historically been 10 percent of planned sales; if planned sales for the month are $25,000, planned reductions for that month would be calculated as follows:

$25,000 × .10 = $2,500

Some firms set goals of reducing planned reductions from the previous year. Assume a firm's goal is to reduce this year's planned reductions by 5 percent from last year's figure. Last year's reductions were $700; therefore this year's planned reductions would be figured this way:

Desired decrease: $700 × .05 = $35

Planned reductions: $700 − $35 = $665

This result could also be reached in a single step: $700 × .95 = $655

The planned purchase entry shows the retail-dollar purchase figures a firm needs in order to achieve its sales and inventory projections for each month. All of the figures discussed above—planned sales, BOM stock, and reductions—are needed to determine planned purchases (P). That includes planned sales (PS), planned EOM/BOM stock, and planned reductions (R). The formula for planned purchases is

(PS + EOM stock + R) − BOM stock = P

Assume that planned sales are $10,000, planned EOM stock $25,000, planned reductions $500, and BOM stock $20,000. Using the formula, planned purchases would be arrived at this way:

($10,000 + $25,000 + $500) − $20,000 = $35,500 − $20,000 = $15,500

Figure 23-1 on page 414 shows a nearly completed merchandise plan. Study it carefully, then duplicate the buyer's computations based on what you have learned in this section.

OPEN-TO-BUY During the buying season, a buyer may want to know the open-to-buy (OTB). This is the amount of money left for buying goods after all purchases received and on-order have been considered. It is calculated:

P − (goods received + goods ordered) = OTB

Assume that merchandise received against the planned purchase figure computed above is $6,500 thus far and merchandise on order against it is $2,000. The present OTB would be as follows:

$15,500 − ($6,500 + $2,000) = OTB

$15,500 − $8,500 = $7,000

This $7,000 figure represents the retail value of the goods that the buyer may purchase at the time. However, the problem is not solved here. If a buyer did not continue to work this problem, he or she would have an incorrect estimation of potential funds available to spend.

There is a way to determine the actual money the buyer has to spend. You must calculate the markup percentage used by the buyer and deduct that figure from the retail value. Assuming that the markup percentage is 45 percent based on the retail value of the merchandise, the buyer would actually be able to spend $3,850. The formula for determining the OTB at cost is shown below:

100% − markup % = % attributed to cost of the item

% attributed to cost × retail value = OTB at cost

100% − 45% markup = 55% (cost)

55% (cost) × $7,000 (retail) = $3,850 OTB at cost

Therefore in the end, the buyer has $3,850 to spend with all other costs considered. You can see how this extra step makes a big difference in the final amount.

FIGURE 23-1

Six-Month Merchandise Plan

Spring Season 20___   Department _____Toys_____

No. _____6124_____

		February	March	April	May	June	July	Total
Sales	Last year	82,000	96,000	90,000	100,000	94,000	80,000	
	Plan	90,200	105,600	99,000	110,000	103,400	88,000	
	Actual							
Retail Stock BOM	Last year	328,000	336,000	297,000	360,000	291,400	224,000	
	Plan	360,800	369,600	326,700	396,000	320,540	246,400	
	Actual							
Retail Reductions	Last year	12,300	14,400	13,500	15,000	14,100	12,000	
	Plan	11,685	13,680	12,825	14,250	13,395	11,400	
	Actual							
Retail Purchases	Last year	N/A	N/A	N/A	N/A	N/A	N/A	
	Plan	110,685	76,380	181,125				
	Actual							

■ **Making Merchandise Plans** This nearly completed model merchandise plan is based on the following assumptions: sales are expected to increase by 10 percent over last year; last year's stock-to-sales ratios should be used to compute this year's BOM stock figures; this year's planned reductions should be 5 percent lower than last year's; and the planned BOM for August is $264,000. *What are the planned purchase figures for May through July?*

PLANNING PURCHASES FOR A CHAIN STORE OPERATION Buying for all branches in a chain store operation is usually done in a central location (company headquarters) and is called **centralized buying**. Buyers involved in centralized buying generally buy all the items for a department or part of a department. There may be three buyers for women's shoes—one in charge of casual shoes, another of traditional shoes, and still another of better shoes. To coordinate the efforts of those three buyers, there would be a merchandise or division manager. This person would oversee all shoe buyers, which may include those for men's, children's, and women's shoes.

Chain stores use centralized buying in order to create a unified image for the chain. Customers can expect to find the same goods in every branch. How can centralized retail buyers for national chains adjust for slight variations in customer preferences? Computers allow buyers to study sales daily. They can determine where goods are selling quickly and slowly. A certain style of shoe may be selling well in one branch store but poorly in another.

Do It Yourself Furniture

Where can you buy a futon, a rice paper lamp, and a dresser, all for approximately $750? Ikea, of course. What's the catch? The reasonable prices come with a catch—self-assembly. Since 1985, Ikea has kept customers coming back for more with their minimalist attitude and do-it-yourself style. Stressing safe construction, simple design, and good prices, Ikea has held customers' attention since 1985. Consumers can browse the catalog or check out simulated rooms in stores, copying down the item numbers to pick up in the self-serve warehouse. The unassembled products are stored easily, and Ikea can stock large quantities of items packaged in flat boxes.

Thinking Critically
What are the benefits to Ikea of stocking do-it-yourself furniture kits?

PRACTICE

On a separate sheet of paper, do the following merchandise plan calculations for Granny's Gift Shoppe:

1. Last March the shop had sales of $4,200. The owner's goal is to increase sales by 7 percent. What would be the planned sales for this March?

2. Last year's stock-to-sales ratio for March was 1.5:1. What should be the BOM stock figure for this March?

3. The owner would like to cut planned reductions by 5 percent this year. Last year's reductions for the month were $500, therefore what would be this year's target figure?

4. Using the figures already given or calculated and an EOM stock figure of $5,000 for March, determine planned purchases for the gift shop.

5. Assuming merchandise received and ordered amounted to $1,200, what would be the open-to-buy position at retail?

6. The customary markup percentage for an item is 60 percent. What is OTB at cost?

Note: The answers to this practice set are on page 416.

The buyer can have the shoes transferred from the store with poor sales to the other store. Another benefit of centralized buying is the quantity discounts that chain stores can negotiate with vendors because of the large volume of goods that they purchase at one time.

There are a few instances, however, when chain stores want to have special goods in their stores that are not available elsewhere in the chain. In these cases, local store managers or their designated buyers are authorized to make special purchases for their individual stores. This would be considered **decentralized buying**. Decentralization is when authority for retail decisions is made at low levels in the organization.

Each approach for coordinating buying has limitations. Retailers constantly make trade-offs between the efficiency gained through centralized buying and the greater sales potential obtained through decentralized buying decisions that tailor merchandise to local markets.

Government Markets

In the same way that there are special markets such as industrial or reseller, there are also buyers for government markets. *Government Units* are the federal, state, or local agencies that are responsible for purchasing goods and services for their specific markets. There are approximately 85,000 government units in the United States. These would include the Federal Aviation Administration (FAA), the Department of Sanitation, the Public Library, or the local school board.

Government markets make up one of the largest single markets for retail goods and services in the world. In the United States, the federal government is a huge consumer of goods, ranging from food for school lunches to equipment for the military and the U.S. Postal Service. A large portion of the federal government's buying is centralized. However, there is not one federal agency that is entirely responsible for all government buying.

Government markets are not unique to the United States. As we see a global marketplace expanding trading networks, we see many international government agencies doing business with U.S. organizations. For example, the world's second-largest aircraft manufacturer—Europe's Airbus Industries—purchases mechanical goods from the U.S. company Pratt & Whitney.

PRACTICE (ANSWERS)

1. $4,494

2. $6,741

3. $475

4. $3,228

5. $2,028

6. $811.20

Institutions

There is one final segment of the market that cannot be overlooked when discussing buying power. This market includes institutions and non-profit organizations that do not compete in the business world in the same way that retailers and wholesalers do. These institutions include hospitals, schools, colleges, churches, civic clubs, and foundations that do not work solely for profit. Institutions and nonprofit organizations may have unique buying requirements. They often provide specialized marketing needs.

23.1 ASSESSMENT

Reviewing Key Terms and Concepts

1. What are the differences between organizational buyers and consumers?

2. What products might an industrial buyer purchase?

3. What do wholesale and retail buyers purchase?

4. In a retail buying situation, what does a buyer prepare in advance of the selling situation?

5. Why do chain stores use centralized buying?

Thinking Critically

6. What would happen if a buyer computed a planned sales figure for the next planning period that was 20 percent too high?

Integrating Academic Skills

7. **COMMUNICATION** As an employee of a chain store operation, you have been told to call other branch stores if a customer requests something that is not in stock. Your customer wants a particular dress you carry, but prefers a different color. Role play your telephone conversation with a branch store that has the dress in the color the customer requested. Include all necessary information such as model number, size, color, and make arrangements for getting the dress to your customer.

The Purchasing Function

The Buying Process

Planning purchases is the preliminary step in the buying process. Now it is time to look at how that function is actually performed. Let's review the types of purchase situations, the way suppliers are selected, how terms are negotiated, and how the Internet is changing the entire process.

■ Types of Purchase Situations

How difficult is the task of a purchasing manager or a buyer? The answer depends on which type of purchase situation is considered. Let's review the three types of purchase situations: new-task purchase, modified rebuy, and straight rebuy.

NEW-TASK PURCHASE In a new-task purchase situation, a purchase is made for the first time, possibly triggered by a formerly unrecognized need. This can be the most complicated buying situation, as it involves a first time purchase. In a retail or wholesale operation, salespeople prepare want slips, like the one shown in Figure 23-2 on page 418. These are customer requests for items that are not carried in the store.

Another reason for a new-task purchase may be a desire to change an existing operation in a firm. Let's say a manufacturer may be considering a new way to make its product, such as using robots instead of people to handle one phase of the manufacturing process. In this new-task purchase, many people in the organization may be responsible for determining the characteristics of the equipment needed. In both the industrial market and the reseller market, it is quite common to see buying committees. Some of the people who may be asked to serve on the committee might be people who will use the equipment, as well as top executives in the manufacturing division. Other influential people, such as the president of the company, may get involved too, because they may be the ones who make the final buying decision. The purchasing manager will generally be part of the team and will most likely be responsible for doing research into possible supply sources.

MODIFIED REBUY In a modified-rebuy situation, the buyer has had experience buying the good or service, but some aspect of the purchase changes. Perhaps the buyer is purchasing from a new vendor because the previous vendor went out of business or increased prices significantly. Other reasons for investigating new vendors may come from an analysis of the competition (through comparison shopping) or from current trade information (found in trade journals or trade shows).

• What You'll Learn

- The three types of purchase situations
- The criteria for selecting suppliers
- The factors involved in negotiating terms of a sale
- The various Internet purchasing methods

• Why It's Important

Knowing the details of the purchasing function will give you a better idea of what is involved in the overall job description. It is especially important to recognize the impact of the Internet on the purchasing function. You can expect changes in job descriptions for buyers in the near future due to the significant increase in online purchasing.

Key Terms

- want slips
- resident buying offices
- consignment buying
- memorandum buying
- reverse auction

FIGURE 23-2

Want Slip

Item requested _____ Brand name _____

Size _____ Style _____ Quantity _____

Item description _____

_____

Your name _____

Address _____
      (Street)   (City)   (State)   (Zip code)

Telephone ( ) _____

EMPLOYEE: PLEASE FORWARD IMMEDIATELY TO YOUR
SUPERVISOR.

Employee Signature _____

Store No. _____ Dept. No. _____ Date _____

■ **Want Slip** Salespeople often prepare want slips and give them to the buyer for their department. *Why are want slips so valuable to a buyer?*

Comparison shopping involves researching competing businesses in order to see what goods and services they offer. Buyers in retail operations will note and compare brands carried, prices, and quantities of items. In a modified-rebuy situation, the buyer usually gets proposals from several vendors before making a buying decision.

To stay abreast of industry trends, reading trade journals and general business publications is a must. A trade journal is a business publication that covers a specific business. *Women's Wear Daily* covers the women's apparel industry. Other good sources of business information are general business publications, such as *Forbes, Business Week,* and *Investor's Business Daily.* Attending trade shows to see what is current is another means of learning about new products and vendors. At trade shows, suppliers for a given industry present their goods for buyers to see. Many trade shows publish a directory of all participating vendors to make it easy for buyers to contact them at a later date.

Finally, retail buyers may hire the services of a resident buying office. Resident buying offices are retailers' representatives in a central market. A central market is a geographic area where many suppliers of a given product are located. New York

■ **Factory Issues** Sweatshops are often in the news and create poor publicity for a company. *Why do you think social issues are part of the vendor evaluation process for clothing and toy manufacturers?*

City's garment district, for example, is a central market for apparel. Resident buying offices send information to retail buyers on a regular basis. They inform buyers about new merchandise offerings, closeouts, fashion trends, special buys in the market, and market conditions.

STRAIGHT REBUY In a straight-rebuy situation, the buyer routinely orders the goods and services purchased from the same vendor(s) as in the past. Staple goods such as office supplies fall into the straight-rebuy category for wholesale and retail buyers. The purchase of certain manufacturing supplies may be considered a straight rebuy for most purchasing managers.

Some manufacturing companies purchase all materials and parts in a straight-rebuy situation. This is because of an inventory control system called just-in-time (JIT), which you will learn more about in Chapter 24. JIT links a company via computer to its supplier so the supplier knows exactly what, how much, and when to deliver to meet production needs. Suppliers deliver parts and raw materials just before they are needed for production. Computerized orders are placed when parts and supplies run low. The company is essentially in a partnership with suppliers to guarantee frequent shipments of goods that keep pace with production needs.

■ Selecting Suppliers

The criteria for selecting suppliers fall into a few key categories. They include production capabilities, past experience, product and buying arrangements, and special services.

PRODUCTION CAPABILITIES When dealing with a source for the first time, buyers may request specific information about the source's production capabilities. They may even visit a facility in person to see it in operation. Buyers may solicit business references to determine the source's reputation in the industry. These factors would be extremely important when selecting suppliers and transportation firms as partners in a just-in-time production arrangement.

Production capabilities for some companies go beyond the actual physical plant into social issues, such as review of facilities to ensure that they are not sweatshops. *Sweatshops* are factories characterized by poor working conditions and negligent treatment of employees. Production costs are reduced because factory owners underpay staff workers. Companies may require suppliers to sign a contract stating that they will follow a fair code of conduct. Factory audits performed by human-rights groups may be conducted to ensure that these rules are being followed.

Companies, such as Reebok and Liz Claiborne, often hire the services of manufacturing facilities outside the United States to produce their goods. To show social responsibility and to avoid abuse of workers, these companies require foreign manufacturers to adhere to specific labor standards.

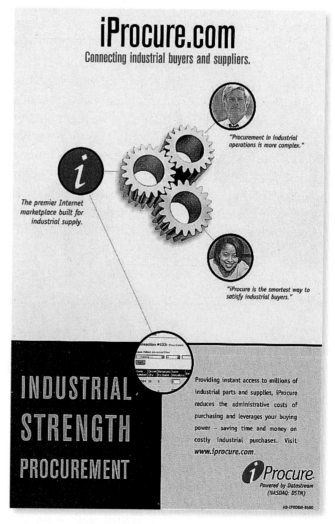

■ **Going Electronic** This dot-com company is an example of an electronic exchange in a specific industry. *How might this e-business change the role of an industrial buyer?*

PAST EXPERIENCES Many buyers maintain resource files that document past experiences with vendors. All basic information, such as products carried, prices, delivery and dating terms, and the names of sales representatives, is recorded. Also noted are evaluations of products, delivery performance, and customer service. A major factor in selecting a supplier is the quality of goods it offers. Retail buyers keep accurate records of customer returns and the reasons for them. Returns relating to the quality of the goods may cause a vendor to be dropped as a supplier.

SPECIAL BUYING ARRANGEMENTS Suppliers may have special policies regarding merchandise returns and sales arrangements. Two special types of sales and return policies are called consignment buying and memorandum buying.

In **consignment buying**, goods are paid for only after they are purchased by the final customer. This special arrangement is applicable to wholesale and retail buying situations. The supplier owns the goods until the wholesaler or retailer sells them. Many suppliers offer consignment buying as an incentive when introducing a new line of goods. No money is tied up in inventory because the buyer pays for goods after they are sold. This is virtually a no-risk situation. The problem with consignment buying occurs when merchandise is stolen or damaged,

which raises the question of who is responsible and who must pay.

Memorandum buying occurs when the supplier agrees to take back any unsold goods by a certain preestablished date. The buyer pays for all of the goods purchased but is later reimbursed for all of the goods returned in accordance with the agreement. This buying arrangement allows for returns. Each agreement may be a little different from other similar agreements with regard to the time lines for accepting returns.

SPECIAL SERVICES Businesses today demand more services from their suppliers than just the basic return policy. Suppliers must keep up with these services to stay competitive.

One special service that many retailers are requesting or demanding is the placement by manufacturers of Universal Product Codes (UPCs) on goods. Having the codes on all products saves the retailer time because individual items do not have to be marked with a price. It also helps retailers keep track of what they have in stock.

Even the large boxes that hold products now have bar codes on them to identify the contents. Machines that read those codes can use them to route the products to various departments within a business or, in the case of a chain store, to branch stores within a chain.

BRIGHT IDEAS
Smart Cart

Silicon Valley inventor George Cokely has a modern solution to one of the supermarket industry's oldest problems—stolen shopping carts. His invention, Stop Z-Cart, consists of a small computer chip inside one of the cart's wheels. The system is activated when the cart rolls over a special mat. Once the cart is a certain distance away from the store, the wheels lock. After the store retrieves the stolen cart they can easily release the locked wheels with a Stop Z-Cart magic wand. Why are supermarkets interested in Stop Z-Cart? Supermarkets lose up to 25 percent of their shopping carts every year to theft. This leaves supermarkets with major additional purchasing costs. Carts can cost up to $200 each, which adds up pretty quickly to $80 million annually industry wide. Stop Z-Cart is worth the extra cost, since it virtually eliminates shopping cart theft.

Thinking Creatively
Retail stores lose millions of dollars in theft. What are other creative ways that stores can prevent stealing?

Case Study

FreeMarkets.com

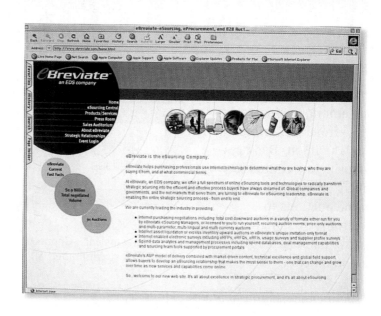

FreeMarkets.com was one of the first Internet companies to link industrial buyers and sellers through computerized auctions. In addition to overseeing online trading, it also helps buyers find and qualify new suppliers.

Online bartering is becoming so popular that there are many more companies that are carving a niche in this expanding market. To compete against FreeMarkets.com, eBreviate.com offers flat rates rather than the industry standard cut of one percent to six percent from each sale.

At one time, FreeMarkets.com only catered to large companies, while other auction companies targeted mid-sized and smaller firms. To counter that competition, FreeMarkets.com began offering software to let buyers and sellers set up their own online transactions. This action makes one wonder how soon companies may reject third-party auction service providers and simply do it themselves.

Case Study Review

1. In the business-to-business e-marketplace, how are new companies competing with FreeMarkets.com?
2. Why would companies prefer to register with a B2B e-marketplace provider instead of conducting an online auction by themselves?

A MATTER OF ETHICS

3. Is it ethical for a company that was registered with an online auction company to set up its own company-run online auction?

■ Negotiating Terms

To evaluate suppliers, buyers must negotiate their prices, dating terms, delivery arrangements, and discounts. You have already learned about dating terms and delivery arrangements in Chapter 16. Discounts are any reductions from the quoted price. Such reductions are generally granted for the buyer's performance of certain functions. These will be discussed in Chapter 26.

Dating terms involve when a bill must be paid and the discount permitted for paying early. You learned about ordinary dating (2/10, net 30) in Chapter 16, but you should also know that there are several variations for specific situations. A company may

allow the dating terms to take effect later than the invoice date. This type of dating, which is known as advance dating, is sometimes offered to businesses as an incentive to buy before the buying season. An invoice may be dated January 15 and include the following advance dating terms: 2/10, net 30—as of March 1.

In other situations, additional days may be granted for the discount (called extra dating). This special dating may be used to encourage a buyer to purchase new merchandise. In still another situation, the terms begin when the buyer's firm receives the goods, which is called "ROG dating" (receipt of goods).

FIGURE 23-3

HOW B2B E-COMMERCE WORKS

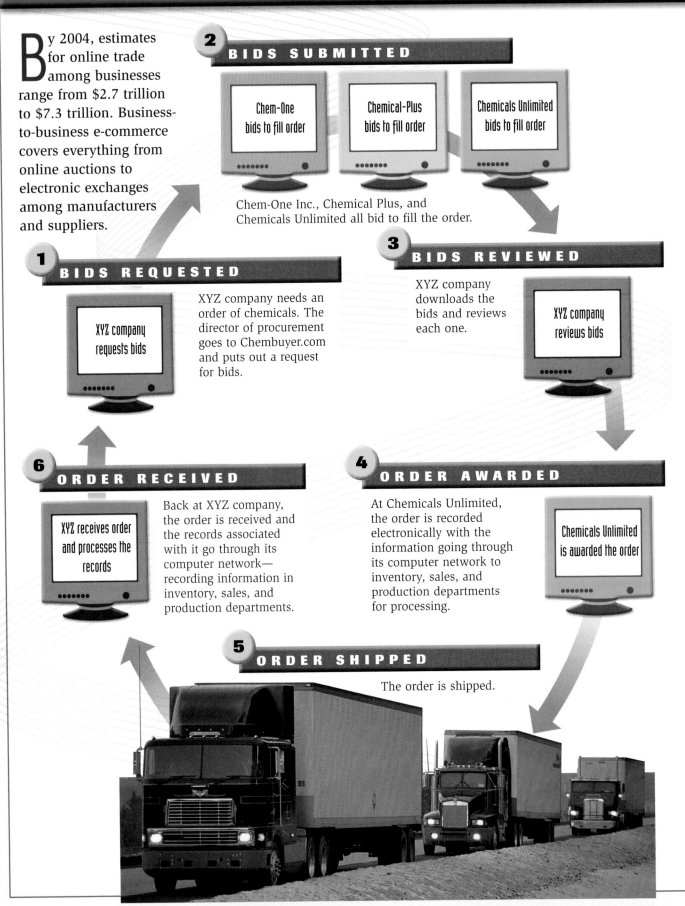

By 2004, estimates for online trade among businesses range from $2.7 trillion to $7.3 trillion. Business-to-business e-commerce covers everything from online auctions to electronic exchanges among manufacturers and suppliers.

2 BIDS SUBMITTED

Chem-One bids to fill order

Chemical-Plus bids to fill order

Chemicals Unlimited bids to fill order

Chem-One Inc., Chemical Plus, and Chemicals Unlimited all bid to fill the order.

1 BIDS REQUESTED

XYZ company requests bids

XYZ company needs an order of chemicals. The director of procurement goes to Chembuyer.com and puts out a request for bids.

3 BIDS REVIEWED

XYZ company downloads the bids and reviews each one.

XYZ company reviews bids

6 ORDER RECEIVED

XYZ receives order and processes the records

Back at XYZ company, the order is received and the records associated with it go through its computer network—recording information in inventory, sales, and production departments.

4 ORDER AWARDED

At Chemicals Unlimited, the order is recorded electronically with the information going through its computer network to inventory, sales, and production departments for processing.

Chemicals Unlimited is awarded the order

5 ORDER SHIPPED

The order is shipped.

■ Internet Purchasing

Business-to-business, or B2B, electronic commerce has revolutionized the purchasing function for businesses in the industrial and reseller markets. Figure 23-3 on page 422 illustrates how B2B e-commerce works. Estimates for online trade among businesses range from $2.7 trillion to $7.3 trillion by 2004, according to *Investor's Business Daily*. Organizational buyers account for 80 percent of the total dollar value of all online transactions.

The popularity of online buying is expected to continue to grow into the twenty-first century. This is partly because organizational buyers have come to depend heavily on timely supplier information, and such information can be easily and quickly conveyed via the Internet. Another reason is that businesses have found that online purchasing dramatically reduces marketing costs for many types of products and services.

Life In The Diverse

MARKETPLACE

Don't Whistle While You Work

As the soccer team scores the winning goal, the stadium erupts in shouts, cheers, and...whistles? Maybe in the United States, but in other countries this would be offensive. While whistling is a sign of appreciation or approval at U.S. sporting events or concerts, it is a symbol of disrespect in other countries. In Europe, it is the equivalent of being booed, whether the setting is a stadium, opera house, or political gathering. In the Middle East, whistling at a woman is not only rude, but it breaks political and social rules!

Thinking Critically
Are there times when whistling is considered inappropriate in the United States?

■ **Grainger.com** Business-to-business electronic commerce has changed the way buyers conduct business. Some vendors have established their own Web sites, like Grainger.com. *Why might a buyer buy supplies like those noted in this ad?*

The bulk of B2B e-commerce transactions are routine purchases made more efficient by the Internet. For example, the sale of standardized products, such as office supplies, and commodities such as stock steel, require little or no buyer-seller interaction. An increasing number of businesses are using the Internet to facilitate the buying of such standardized goods.

Some companies have their own Web sites from which other companies may make purchases directly. The company W. W. Grainger sells over $40 million worth of maintenance, repair, and operating supplies annually through its Web site to other businesses.

Growing in popularity are electronic exchanges where registered users can buy and sell their goods online. Most of these electronic exchanges are in specific industries, such as NECX Global Electronics Exchange (necx.com), which is an electronic exchange for electronic components, computer products, and networking equipment. According to its Web site, NECX has over ten billion items available and access to $30 billion in inventory. Medibuy.com connects buyers and sellers of medical equipment, while Chemdex Corporation maintains an electronic exchange for the biotech and drug industries.

Another Internet purchasing trend involves online auction companies, which register those parties interested in selling an item or service. An auction usually involves having a seller set an asking price and buyers try to outbid each other. This type of auction is found in online exchanges in farming and other industries. In other cases, a reverse auction takes place. In a **reverse auction**, companies post what they want to buy and suppliers bid for the contract.

There are advantages and disadvantages of purchasing online through third parties. The biggest advantage is lower prices; however, as with most businesses on the Internet, privacy is a problem. Some companies fear that competitors will know how much was paid for materials and supplies. To combat that problem, some big companies, like Intel and General Electric, have decided to run their own reverse auctions. GE only spent $15,000 to write its own reverse auction software. This has inspired other companies to follow.

GE's Trading Process Network (TPN) enables GE buyers to post requests for quotes, negotiate, and place orders with global suppliers. The TPN has lowered GE's purchasing costs by over 20 percent.

Another problem with the online purchasing process, especially in a reverse auction, is that unknown companies could artificially deflate prices by bidding low prices. Such a practice would benefit buyers, but cause bad relationships with suppliers.

Electronic Frontiers

To Order...Don't Dial Now

We've seen cellular phones develop from a communication tool used merely to make phone calls to a tool that displays e-mail and stock quotes as well as messages. Cell phone technology is going further as unique bar codes are developed that make ordering by telephone even easier. These codes will be embedded on products, in ads, or even shown on television. Next time you see an infomercial for that must-have product or CD, you may just be a click away from being its proud owner. When a consumer clicks on the code with his or her phone, the product is ordered instantly at the advertised price. Using the personal data stored on the device, the selection, purchase, and shipment will take place via the Internet—completely invisible to the user. This technology is expected to be available in hand-held computing devices as well as traditional television remote controls.

Thinking Critically

Would you like to have a cellular phone with this capability? Why or why not?

23.2 ASSESSMENT

Reviewing Key Terms and Concepts

1. List the three types of purchase situations.
2. What four things can buyers do to stay abreast of industry trends?
3. Name four criteria buyers use in selecting supply sources.
4. What is the difference between consignment and memorandum buying?
5. What are electronic exchanges and in what types of industries are they found?

Thinking Critically

6. How do you see the job description of a buyer or procurement manager changing with the advent of Internet purchasing?

Integrating Academic Skills

5. **MATH** Assuming all discounts are taken, determine which vendor is granting a better deal based on the following facts. Vendor A offers to sell you 1,500 stuffed animals at a unit cost of $3.45 and will pay for shipping. Dating terms are 2/10, net 30. Vendor B's offer is $3.35 per stuffed animal, shipping charges of $65, and payment must be made COD for all 1,500 stuffed animals.

Careers in Marketing

RETAIL MANAGEMENT

Bob Ricketts
Buyer
Barney Greengrass

What skills are most important to you?

"A buyer needs to be knowledgeable about trends and products. My job is to select and purchase merchandise from a number of different sources. I need to be at the nexus of everything, and so communication skills are very important. I must be able to relate to sellers and know the difference between the hype and the reality. This is an extremely stressful job at times, and you need to handle your customers and coworkers well. My job requires a good deal of creativity!"

What kind of training did you have?

"I have been in food service all of my life. My family had a restaurant business in Chicago. I did not go to college for restaurant management; instead I worked my way up the ladder, developing my sales skills along the way. I took some short-term classes in culinary school. The growing importance of computers in my line of business has encouraged me to broaden my horizons."

Why did you focus on a career in retail buying?

"This job allows me to combine my retail knowledge with my personal communication skills. Knowledge is useless without application and I have been able to apply all of my knowledge in my work. The sky is the limit as long as you apply the knowledge that you have gained."

What is your key to success?

"My key to my success is to know my product. I need to recognize quality and turn down inferior products that are not up to our standards."

Thinking Critically
How does a job as a retail buyer differ from that of a retail salesperson?

Career Facts

Education and Training: High school courses in marketing, accounting, business, and consumer education help to develop skills needed to become a retail purchaser. Two-year as well as four-year college programs in business administration, marketing, or finance provide good preparation for becoming a buyer. Some companies offer in-store training.

Aptitudes, Abilities, and Skills: Ability to organize and coordinate goods, attention to detail, computer skills, and accuracy are necessary. Buyers must be able to discern quality, recognize trends, work well with people, negotiate terms, manage budgets, and make decisions.

Career Outlook: Slower than average growth is projected through the year 2006.

Career Path: A typical career path begins as a sales clerk or trainee and proceeds through assistant to head buyer. Some individuals may advance to business executive and manager positions.

VOCABULARY REVIEW

Write one sentence per each group of vocabulary terms.

- Organizational, retail, and wholesale buyers
- Six-month merchandise plan and OTB
- Centralized vs. decentralized buying
- Consignment and memorandum buying
- Electronic exchange and reverse auctions

FACT AND IDEA REVIEW

1. In manufacturing and service businesses, what are three job titles that people responsible for purchasing might have? (23.1)

2. How do industrial buyers use materials requirement planning (MRP) in their purchasing function, and how is it related to the master production schedule? (23.1)

3. What is the main role of wholesale and retail buyers? (23.1)

4. Why are projected accurate planned sales figures important in a merchandise plan? (23.1)

5. Explain three buying situations in which all buyers may find themselves. Provide an example of each. (23.2)

6. What is the significance of want slips to retail buyers? (23.2)

7. What is a resident buying office, and how might it help a local retail buyer? (23.2)

8. Explain the importance of one special service that retailers may demand from suppliers. (23.2)

9. What are customer advantages and disadvantages of online purchasing through third parties? (23.2)

THINKING CRITICALLY

1. Why wouldn't you prepare a new merchandise plan every month? What is a planning method that is more effective?

2. Why is it a good idea to keep a stock-to-sales ratio low?

3. Your high school is purchasing a new copier. Who in the school system might influence the purchasing decision?

4. In recent years, there has been an increased effort to put an end to employing individuals in sweatshops. Why do you think this is so?

5. As a result of online purchasing, are face-to-face negotiations between suppliers and industrial and retail buyers a thing of the past? Why or why not?

BUILDING WORKPLACE SKILLS

1. **Writing** You work in a men's clothing store. A customer approaches you and asks for a sweater that the store does not carry. Design and prepare a want slip for this request.

2. **Human Relations** Top level management has instructed you to speak with a buyer who has been with the company for twenty years. The purpose of the meeting is to let the buyer (who is not computer literate) know that management wants him to purchase online.

1. **Preparing a Six-Month Plan** Use a spreadsheet program to prepare a six-month merchandise plan (from January to June) based on the following information. Last year's sales figures are: January $100,000; February $120,000; March $150,000; April $155,000; May $160,000; and June $145,000. July's sales were $130,000 (needed to calculate planned EOM figure). Sales are expected to increase 10 percent this year. The stock-to-sales ratio for each month is the same as last year at 3:1. Reductions are done at 15 percent of planned sales.

2. **Selecting a Vendor** You have been asked to select a vendor for the purchase of 150 pairs of jeans. Using a word-processing program, prepare a memo that includes your analysis of the two potential vendors and your recommendation for one of them. Provide calculations used in determining the final price for one pair of jeans for each vendor (taking into consideration all available discounts and shipping charges), as well as a rationale for your recommendation.
   - Vendor A has a reputation for late deliveries. The price per pair of jeans is $20, and there is a one percent quantity discount on all purchases over 100. Vendor A has dating terms of 2/10, net 30 and delivery charges of $79 (FOB shipping point).
   - Vendor B has an excellent reputation for delivering on time. The price per pair of jeans is $22 with dating terms of 2/10, net 60 and free delivery (FOB store).

LINKING SCHOOL TO WORK

Personal and Information Skills Interview someone who is responsible for purchasing supplies or merchandise for resale. Ask about his or her job responsibilities and the skills required. Share your findings with your classmates.

THE DECA CONNECTION

Role Play: Buying Intern

Situation You are an intern for the buyer of bicycles for a chain store operation. The buyer has asked that you show a new intern how to do the calculations for a merchandise plan.

Activity You will need to explain the basis for planned sales percentage increases. The standard stock-to-sales ratio for your store is 4, and retail reductions are generally 10 percent of sales.

Evaluation You will be evaluated on how well you meet the following performance indicators:
- Compute the figures found on a merchandise plan
- Use current economic information to project the rate of increase, if any, in planned sales
- Communicate knowledge and use of a merchandise plan

*inter*NET CONNECTION

Paper, Pens, and Pencils
Since your business purchases office supplies on a regular basis, you decide to check out e-commerce as a means for purchasing them.

Connect
- Find five different Internet sources for purchasing office supplies.
- Evaluate the prices for one item found on all five sites.
- Present your findings in a memo along with your recommendation.

Stock Handling and Inventory Control

Marketing: What It Takes

Planning and Controlling Your Inventory

You work for a manufacturer that ships products for the domestic as well as international markets. You have been asked by management to identify the criteria to be used when selecting a freight carrier to move your products to market quickly and help your company better manage its inventory.

WHAT WILL YOU DO?
What selection criteria will you identify for the freight carrier?

The Stock Handling Process

Stock Handling

Manufacturers and suppliers all receive many different parts or raw materials for use in making finished products. These items are received in stock and must be tracked just as retailers track the merchandise they receive.

Whether a business receives raw materials, parts, or merchandise, a process is needed for handling items received. The steps in the stock handling process include receiving goods, checking them, marking the goods with information, and delivering them to their selling location.

■ Receiving Merchandise

Merchandise ordered by a store is received, checked, and marked with a selling price before it is transferred to the sales area. In larger businesses, several people do this job. In smaller businesses, a salesperson, manager, or even the owner may perform this function.

Where merchandise is received depends on the type and size of the business. Smaller businesses may have a back room or may even use store aisles for receiving merchandise. Most stores, however, have enough space to devote a part of the basement, upstairs, or first floor to receiving.

Large businesses and chain stores usually have separate warehouses or distribution centers to receive and store merchandise before it is routed within the company. The specific area where deliveries are made by carriers is called a *dock*. Docks usually have covered or enclosed platforms to protect the merchandise from weather damage. They are large enough to accommodate the type and size of shipment the business normally receives.

RECEIVING RECORDS Every business records the goods it receives in a receiving record or log. A receiving record is a form that is used to describe the goods received by a business. The items on a receiving record depend on the needs of the business. They can include the following:

- Person who received the shipment
- Shipper of the merchandise
- Place from which the goods were shipped
- Name of the carrier
- Number of the carrier
- Number of items delivered
- Weight of items delivered
- Shipping charges
- Department or store that ordered the merchandise
- Date the shipment was received

● What You'll Learn

- The need for a stock handling process
- How merchandise is received and checked
- The methods and procedures used to mark merchandise
- The procedures used for transferring merchandise

● Why It's Important

To be successful, businesses must have systems in place to handle and organize their stock. This helps control costs and ensure that operations can continue without interruption.

● Key Terms

- receiving record
- blind check method
- direct check method
- spot check method
- quality check method
- source marking
- preretailing marking method

Some businesses use a short type of receiving record called an *apron*. An apron is a form attached to the invoice before the merchandise moves through checking and marking. The apron system helps prevent the payment of duplicate invoices because the apron is made out only when the shipment is received.

The receiving number may be called an apron number for businesses using this system. In retail business, the apron is prepared by a store's buyers. Apron forms stay with the merchandise until it reaches the sales floor. They list the steps the merchandise takes to reach the selling floor. The information found on the apron includes the receiving number, the department number, the purchase order number, any terms on the purchase order and on the invoice, routing information, and the date the shipment was checked.

■ **Receiving Stock—An Important First Step** Newly arrived merchandise is inspected and recorded. This activity represents the first step in the stock handling process. *Who is responsible for this activity in a business?*

Electronic Elimination

Excess and obsolete equipment is a big problem for big businesses. U.S. industries generate about $18 billion in excess inventory a year that they cannot sell, which is nearly ten percent of all finished goods produced. Manufacturers attempting to get to the bottom of this big problem and sort out their extra-large trash are looking to a new source— the Internet. New commercial Internet software will allow companies to run their own auctions and generate revenue by selling excess and outdated merchandise. This software saves companies the time and effort of creating such marketplaces themselves. Now a clothing company can sell surplus fabric on an online auction to an interested retail company, or a car manufacturer can find a home for unused parts. This saves companies money and saves the environment some space!

Thinking Critically
What types of companies could benefit from online auction software?

■ Checking Merchandise

Checking is the process of going through the goods upon receipt to make sure they arrived undamaged and that the merchandise ordered was the merchandise received. Merchandise must be checked to verify quantity and condition once it is received. All cartons are checked for damage, and the merchandise is sorted and counted. Some businesses use specially trained employees called *receivers* to inspect and record newly arrived merchandise. In larger businesses, checking is usually done in the receiving area. In small retail stores, it may be done in the aisles.

In the past, checking merchandise was a time- and labor-intensive process. Today, however, many distribution systems use electronic data interchange systems that considerably minimize the time required for this process. The distribution center can pre-notify the retailer regarding what should be in each box. UPC coded shipping box labels can be electronically scanned, identifying the carton's contents, and the information is automatically transferred to an inventory management computer system.

There are other merchandise checking methods, as well. Invoices and shipping tickets should always be verified against physical counts. The physical count is also verified against the purchase order. There are four methods that are frequently used to check merchandise. These methods include the blind check, direct check, spot check, and the quality check.

The blind check method requires the receiver to write the description of the merchandise, count the quantities received, and list them on a blank form or dummy invoice. The list or dummy invoice is then compared to the actual invoice after the blind check is made. The blind check method is considered the most accurate checking method, but it can be time-consuming. The blind check method is used when the merchandise needs to be moved quickly to the sales floor and the actual invoice has not yet been received from the seller. Invoices often follow the shipment of goods by two or more days.

With the direct check method, the merchandise is checked directly against the actual invoice or purchase order. This procedure is faster than the blind check method, but errors may not be found if the invoice itself is incorrect. Some receivers do not completely check the total number of items once they see the amount listed on the invoice—if the amount looks correct, they may not bother to take an actual count.

The spot check method is a random check of one carton in a shipment (such as one out of every twenty). The carton is checked for quantity, and then one product in the carton is inspected for quality. When the contents are as stated on the invoice, the remaining cartons are assumed to be the same. Spot checking is often used for products such as canned goods, paper products, and pharmaceuticals.

The quality check method is done to inspect the workmanship and general characteristics of the received merchandise. Although a receiver can do a quality check, a buyer often performs this check. The merchandise is checked to determine whether the quality of the goods received matches the quality of the products which were ordered. If the goods are damaged, a damage report is prepared. Damaged goods should not be discarded without the authorization of the supplier.

REAL WORLD MARKETING

Tracking Time

Do you send documents to a new client for next-day delivery? Do you keep track of the shipper's guarantees for timely delivery? For a monthly fee of $9.95, a Web service will track the status of a regular customer's FedEx and United Parcel Service shipments. The program alerts the sender whenever a package arrives later than the time guaranteed by the delivery company. Once alerted, the shipper can use that information to ask FedEx or UPS to fulfill its on-time guarantee by paying a full refund for the cost of shipping the package, usually between $10 and $20.

Thinking Critically
Why might this service be of value to a business?

RETURNING MERCHANDISE Careful checking practices can save a business large amounts of money. All incorrect items, damaged merchandise, and items ordered but not received are identified and reported according to the policies of the business. When this is done, the business can get proper credit or adjustments from the carrier or the seller.

Apart from damage, there are many other reasons a business might return merchandise. Perhaps it received something it did not order or decided to cancel an order after it was shipped. Sometimes orders get mixed up and delivered to the wrong clients. It is also possible that the seller sent too many items or that the merchandise arrived late.

Upon return of the merchandise, the seller issues a *credit memorandum*. A credit memorandum is notification that the buyer's account has been credited for the value of the returned merchandise.

■ **Marking Merchandise**
Different methods are used for marking merchandise depending on the product. *Why are UPCs often used for source marking?*

■ Marking Merchandise

After it has been received and checked, merchandise must be marked with the selling price and other information. Different methods may be used for various kinds of merchandise. The most common method of marking price is with a UPC, however a hand-operated pricing machine or pricing tickets can be used as well.

Universal Product Codes (UPCs) are widely used in business today for tracking merchandise. Many businesses receive goods that are preticketed with prices and UPCs. As you learned in Chapter 16, UPCs are made up of parallel vertical bars and a row of numbers printed on a package or a label. These codes describe the merchandise and price information. The UPC codes are scanned into a computer for use in tracking sales and inventory levels.

UPCs are often used for source marking. With this method, the seller or manufacturer marks the price before delivering the merchandise to the retailer. Merchandise can be moved directly from the receiving area to the sales floor. The UPCs are scanned at the checkout area, and the price stored in the computer for that code is entered for the sale.

Some businesses use a *preretailing marking method* of marking merchandise. With the preretailing marking method, pricing information is marked in advance on the purchase order. This information is entered in the buyer's computer system, and prices are available for marking merchandise as soon as it is received. Preretailing marking is normally used for staple items that are

unlikely to have price changes between the time of the order and receipt of the merchandise. It saves time because merchandise can be price marked immediately.

Merchandise can also be marked at the store with an electric or hand-operated pricing machine. Few stores use this method today because of the wide use of bar code scanners.

Finally, merchandise can be marked with the familiar price tickets. In large stores, price tickets are prepared by hand or by machine in a marking room or in a stock room. Gum labels are used on merchandise with a flat, hard surface such as books. Pin tickets are used on merchandise that will not be damaged by the pinholes, such as socks or scarves. String or plastic tags are used for larger articles, such as dresses, shirts, and suits. The pricing ticket also helps when a customer needs to return an item to a store as it is difficult to return an item that has no tags.

PRICE TICKET INFORMATION Price marking on the price ticket identifies the price of the merchandise. Other important information may also be included on the price ticket. Many businesses include information such as store numbers, model or style numbers, color, sizes, fabrics, manufacturer's number, and lot numbers. This information is useful for tracking merchandise. It helps a business determine which items, sizes, and colors are popular with customers. This information may also simplify the shopping process for consumers as necessary information is contained in one place.

◾ Transferring Merchandise

Once merchandise is received, checked, and marked, it is ready to be moved to the sales area. From there it is often transferred to different departments within the business.

Stock is generally transferred from a department or store to a warehouse at the beginning of each season. Old merchandise must be removed from the department sales area to make room for new merchandise. The old merchandise is put on sale for a short time, and the merchandise that does not sell is transferred to a warehouse or distribution center.

Transferred merchandise is accompanied by a form describing the items, style numbers, colors, sizes, cost, and retail prices. Duplicate copies of the transfer forms are retained as a record of merchandise on hand.

Stock transfers between departments can occur when merchandise is carried by more than one department or when the demand for merchandise in one department creates a need for additional merchandise. Stock transfers can also occur when the merchandise is used for sales promotions, such as displays, advertising illustrations, or fashion shows or when the merchandise is used for installation or repairs in various departments.

Stock transfers between stores can occur to meet unexpected demand or to fill requests by customers. A customer may find the perfect pair of pants, but find that the branch of the store is sold out. Some stores will call another local store to have it send

Life In The Diverse MARKETPLACE

Swimwear in Winter

Managing inventory is difficult enough for most businesses. When selling to international customers, this job becomes even harder. This is especially true if the clients are in Chili or the far south of South America. Geographic differences find those areas entering the heat of summer while we enter winter—seasons are reversed. While shoppers are snatching up warm coats and snow shovels in the United States, their South American counterparts are trying on bathing suits and new suntan lotions.

Thinking Critically

How can a business maintain storage room if stocking for both summer and winter simultaneously?

over the right size. Finally, stock transfers from store to distribution outlet can occur when off-season and nonsaleable merchandise is moved to surplus or discount stores. A store may choose to transfer all of its bathing suits to an outlet store if the stock doesn't clear out during after-season sales.

24.1 ASSESSMENT

Reviewing Key Terms and Concepts

1. Describe the stock handling process.
2. What is the purpose of a receiving record?
3. What are the four methods used for checking merchandise?
4. Explain two methods used for marking merchandise.
5. What are some reasons for transferring merchandise between various store departments?

Thinking Critically

6. Retailers often code their actual cost of merchandise on price tickets. Do you think this information should be kept from customers? Why or why not?

Integrating Academic Skills

7. **COMMUNICATION** Use word processing software to write a two-page report detailing how an effective receiving process can benefit a business's sales, goods, expenses, and image.

Inventory Control

Why It's Important

The inventory a business owns represents money tied up in products until the inventory is sold. Since inventory is a large part of the total investment of a business, well-managed and controlled inventories increase the profits of a business.

Inventory Management

Inventory is one of the most costly parts of business operations for many businesses. Inventory refers to an amount of goods stored, including raw materials, purchased components, manufactured subassemblies, works in process, packaging materials, and finished goods. Finished goods are often subdivided to reflect the stock at a manufacturing plant and the stock in distribution centers and warehouses. Retail inventory includes all goods for resale. It is important to maintain a certain level of inventory to meet supply and demand needs.

Inventory management is the process of buying and storing products for sale while controlling costs for ordering, shipping, handling, and storage. This is usually the responsibility of the supply chain manager. Unnecessarily high inventories can create many problems for a business. In addition to using up valuable storage space, they increase personnel costs for security, production, and warehouse staff, cause higher inventory insurance premiums, and may lead to increased interest expenses for a business. Businesses lose money and reduce profits when they manage their inventories poorly. They may have the wrong merchandise in stock, holding too many slow-selling items or too few fast-selling ones.

Inventory management has been greatly affected by the just-in time (JIT) inventory management system. This system originated in the 1980s in the auto manufacturing industry and has since been adopted by the other manufacturers. A just-in-time (JIT) inventory system is an arrangement in which suppliers deliver parts and raw materials just before they are needed for production. Orders are placed when parts and supplies run low. Plants keep only small stocks on hand to avoid tying up money and inventory space.

Computer link-ups tell suppliers and transportation companies which items are needed and when to deliver them to meet production needs. Parts are delivered on a schedule—just in time for use in the production process. A late shipment can bring an entire manufacturing operation to a standstill.

In this system, parts go straight to production, where they are assembled immediately. No parts are stored. Finished goods are shipped to customers as soon as they are assembled. Inventories of completed or partially completed products are kept to a minimum.

In essence, the manufacturer enters into a partnership with suppliers to guarantee frequent shipments of goods that keep pace with production needs. JIT inventory management reduces inventory investment and improves cash flow for a business. This type of inventory management system is particularly useful when there is reliable forecasting for goods that will be used quickly.

■ Manual Systems With manual inventory control systems, employees gather paper records of sales information to track inventory. *What are some examples of paper records that can be used to track inventory?*

Inventory management is complex because a business has to correctly anticipate demand for its products while trying to keep overall inventory investment as low as possible. Retail businesses are expected to:

- Maintain the right quantities of merchandise without running out of stock
- Keep a wide product assortment (with low inventory investment) without compromising on customer needs and wants
- Purchase merchandise at large volumes to gain the lowest prices while not buying more than it will sell
- Keep a current inventory on hand

Good inventory management balances the costs of inventory with the benefits of maintaining a large inventory. The costs of inventory include not only the cost of the items in stock, but also storage, insurance, and taxes. Inventory ties up a business's working capital—money that could be used for other purposes. It is not effective for a company to maintain large inventory holdings if that money could be spent more effectively somewhere else or invested. Effective inventory management helps increase working capital and allows a business to use its savings to pay for other business expenses.

BRIGHT IDEAS

Bar Codes: Bionic Fingerprints

Bar codes are everywhere today, on product packages and goods. They are so common you probably don't even think twice about them. Where did they come from? In 1948, a local food chain store owner asked the Drexel Institute of Technology in Pennsylvania to research a method of automatically reading product information during checkout. Graduate students Bernard Silver and Norman Joseph Woodland were assigned to work on a solution. Woodland first used ultraviolet light sensitive ink, which was unsuccessful. Their second attempt, however, proved more fruitful! The duo filed for a patent, and in 1966, the bar code was first used commercially. The first scanner was installed at March's supermarket in Troy, Ohio, in 1974. What was the revolutionary product to carry the first bar code? Wrigley's gum!

Thinking Creatively
Why are bar codes so important today?

Inventory Systems

All merchandise bought and sold must be tracked to gain the information needed for effective inventory management (see Figure 24-1 on page 437). Two methods of tracking inventory are the perpetual inventory system and the physical inventory system.

■ Perpetual Inventory System

A perpetual inventory system tracks the number of items in inventory on a constant basis. The system tracks all new items purchased and returned, as well as sales of current stock. An up-to-date count of inventory is maintained for purchases and returns of merchandise, sales and sales returns, sales allowances, and transfers to other stores and departments. With a perpetual inventory system, a business keeps track of sales as they occur.

MANUAL SYSTEMS Employees gather paper records of sales and enter that information into the inventory system in a manual system. These records can include receiving department records, sales checks, price tickets, cash register receipts, stock transfer requests, and other documents used for coding and tabulation.

Merchandise tags are used to record information about the vendor, date of receipt, department, product classification, color, sizes, and style. The merchandise tags from items sold are sent in batches to a company-owned tabulating facility or to an independent computer service organization where the coded information is analyzed through the use of computer software.

COMPUTER BASED SYSTEMS Computer based systems to control inventory are increasingly popular even among smaller businesses. They are also faster and more accurate than manual systems. As you learned in Chapter 16, a *point-of-sale terminal* uses hand-held laser guns, stationary lasers, light pens, or slot scanners to feed sales transaction data directly from Universal Product Codes (UPCs), sales checks, or merchandise tags into a computer. Businesses then use computer-generated information printouts at different times for review and action.

Offline point-of-sale terminals can also relay sales information directly to a supplier. The supplier then uses the sales transaction data to ship additional items automatically to the business.

■ Physical Inventory System

Under a physical inventory system, stock is visually inspected or actually counted to determine the quantity on hand. A physical inventory can be conducted periodically or on a regular annual basis.

Even if a perpetual inventory system is used, businesses normally complete a physical inventory at least once a year. A physical inventory allows a business to calculate its income tax, determine the correct value of its ending inventory, identify any stock shortages, and plan future purchases. There are several methods used for physical inventory control.

VISUAL CONTROL Visual control is used to monitor physical inventory levels. Hardware stores often place stock cards on pegboards with stock numbers and descriptions for each item displayed. The stock cards specify the number of each item to be kept in stock. It can also be somewhat inaccurate because it does not account for misplaced merchandise. The amount to reorder is the difference between the number on hand and the specified number to be stocked.

Although a visual control system is easy for stock clerks and ordering personnel to use, it does not tell the rate of sales for each item. It can also be somewhat inaccurate because it does not account for misplaced merchandise. The number to stock may be an estimate of sales for a typical period of time.

TICKLER CONTROL Another method of physical control is called tickler control. In the tickler control method, a small portion of the inventory is physically counted each day so that the entire inventory is accounted for on a regular basis. The entire inventory is never counted at one time. Manufacturers' representatives do a variation of the tickler control method. The representative visits a business on a regular basis, takes the stock count, and writes the order. Unwanted merchandise is removed from stock and returned to the manufacturer through a predetermined, authorized procedure.

ANNUAL INVENTORY COUNT Most businesses physically count inventory at least once a year. In many cases, the business will close so employees can count the inventory. Employees usually work in pairs—one counts merchandise while the other records the count. After the counting is finished, the total value of the inventory is determined. This value is reported on the business's financial statements.

FIGURE 24-1

TIPS FOR BETTER INVENTORY MANAGEMENT

All merchandise that is bought and sold must be tracked to gain the information needed for effective inventory management.

1 AT TIME OF DELIVERY

At the time of delivery, it is important to verify counts and carefully inspect for damage. If damage is visible, note it on the delivery receipt and have the driver sign the business's copy.

2 WHEN DAMAGE IS DISCOVERED

When damage is discovered, retain the items in the receiving area and contact the carrier to report the damage and request an inspection.

3 DOCUMENT DAMAGES

Retain the damaged goods in the receiving area until the carrier prepares a damage report, which is checked for accuracy before signing.

4 AFTER INSPECTION

After inspection, the damaged items should not be disposed of without carrier permission and should not be returned without written authorization from the supplier.

■ Using Both Systems

A business does not have to choose between a physical inventory system and a perpetual inventory system. Many businesses find it most effective to use both systems. The perpetual system gives an up-to-date inventory record throughout the year. The physical system gives an accurate count that can be compared to the perpetual records to identify any errors or problems. The two systems actually compliment each other.

The perpetual inventory records are used to help the business track sales and manage its merchandise. After a physical inventory is taken, the ending inventory amount becomes the beginning inventory for the year that follows. Purchases during the year are added to this amount, while sales are subtracted. Ending inventory is calculated in the example that follows.

Number of Items for 1/1/00 to 6/30/00	
Beginning inventory, 1/1/2000	1,000
Net purchases (purchases less purchases and allowances returned)	+ 300
Merchandise available for sale	1,300
Less net sales (sales less returns and allowances)	− 1,050
Ending inventory 6/30/19	250

Sometimes the ending inventory shown in the perpetual inventory system does not match the physical count of inventory. When the physical count shows less merchandise than is supposed to be in inventory, a *stock shortage* or *shrinkage* has occurred. Theft, incorrect counting, and errors at the cash register or point-of-sale terminal can cause stock shortages for a business.

Using the previous example, all records for purchases and sales are ongoing in a business; therefore the data represents a perpetual inventory system. The ending inventory figure of 250 items is the perpetual inventory. However, as you know, it is possible that this is not the most accurate count. If the physical inventory system showed ending inventory of 225, a stock shortage of 25 would have occurred (250 − 225 = 25). It isn't until the physical inventory is taken that the company really knows if its ending inventory records are correct. It is still helpful, however, to use the perpetual inventory as a good estimation.

■ Stock Control

Stock control involves monitoring stock levels and investments in stock so that a business is run efficiently. Planning those stock levels and monitoring them requires the use of several different systems. They include dollar vs. unit control methods, stock turnover calculations, and three stock lists (model, basic, and never-out).

DOLLAR VS. UNIT CONTROL Inventory management involves both dollar control and unit control of merchandise held in inventory. Dollar control represents the planning and monitoring of the total inventory investment that a business makes during a stated period of time. A business's dollar control of inventory involves information about the amount of purchases, sales, dollar value of beginning and ending inventory, and stock shortages. This information helps a business determine the cost of goods sold and the amount of gross profit or loss during a given period of time. By subtracting operating expenses from the gross profit, the business can determine its net profit or loss. Additional information about developing profit and loss statements is found in Chapter 36.

Unit control refers to the quantities of merchandise that a business handles during a stated period of time. Unit control allows the business to keep stock adjusted to sales and lets the business determine how to spend money available under a planned budget. In a unit control inventory system, each item or a group of related items is referred to as a stockkeeping unit (sku). A unit control inventory system tracks merchandise by the merchandise's sku. Tracking the skus gives valuable sales information on those items that are successful and those that are not selling. A business can use this information to make better merchandising decisions. Sales promotions can be run to sell slow-moving items or to spotlight popular ones.

Unit control records also allow purchasing personnel to see what brands, sizes, colors, and price lines are popular. By keeping track of this information, buyers can understand customer preferences and order accordingly. Finally, unit control records specify when items need to be ordered. When a minimum stock amount is reached, an order is placed for more stock. This system ensures that adequate assortments are available and helps avoid out-of-stock situations.

STOCK TURNOVER The most effective way to measure how well inventory is being managed is to look at stock turnover. Stock turnover is the number of times the average inventory has been sold and replaced in a given period of time. The higher the stock turnover rate, the more times the goods were sold and replaced. In retailing and wholesaling operations, the key is moving inventory so there is cash available to buy more fast-selling merchandise. High turnover rates mean that merchandise is selling quickly. That means higher profit for the business because its money is not tied up in inventory. Stock turnover is also a good measure of success for businesses to use in evaluating vendors and products from year to year.

Businesses use *stock turnover rates* to compare a particular store's entire operation with the operations of similar stores. The stock turnover rate for a supermarket can be compared with rates of other supermarkets, but not with those of a furniture store.

Stock turnover rates for selected retailers are available from trade associations and commercial publishers. One such publisher is Dun & Bradstreet, which publishes *Industrial Norms* and *Key Business Ratios*.

Stores that keep records of the retail value of stock compute their stock turnover rates as follows:

$$\frac{\text{Net sales (in retail dollars)}}{\text{Average inventory on hand (in retail dollars)}}$$

When net sales during a period are $49,500 and average inventory is $8,250, the stock turnover is 6:

$$\frac{\$49,500}{\$8,250} = 6$$

To determine the average inventory, use inventory amounts for each of the months included in the time period being considered. Total these, as shown in the second column below, and then calculate the average.

Month	Average Inventory	Net Sales
January	$ 50,000	$ 10,000
February	55,000	15,000
March	68,000	20,000
April	64,000	19,000
May	63,000	21,000
June	60,000	20,000
Totals	$360,000	$105,000

To get the average inventory for the six-month period, divide by the number of months.

$$\frac{\$360,000}{6} = \$60,000$$

Finally, to calculate stock turnover, divide total net sales (see the third column above) by average inventory).

$$\frac{\$105,000}{\$60,000} = 1.75$$

This figure means that the average inventory was sold and replaced 1.75 times during the six-month period.

When only cost information about stock is available, stock turnover can be calculated with this formula:

$$\frac{\text{Cost of goods sold}}{\text{Average inventory on hand (at cost)}}$$

When a store wants to look at the number of items carried in relation to the number of items sold, it calculates its stock turnover rates in units with this formula:

$$\frac{\text{Number of units sold}}{\text{Average inventory on hand in units}}$$

STOCK LISTS There are three plans used to monitor different types of goods—staple items, fashionable items, and very popular items. They are the basic stock list, model stock list, and never-out list.

A basic stock list (see Figure 24-2 on page 440) is used for those staple items that should always be in stock. This list specifies products that a store should always carry based upon the type of business. A basic stock list in a men's clothing store would include items such as tee shirts, underwear, and dress socks. The basic stock list at a card store would include birthday cards, blank cards, thank you cards, and cards for general occasions, such as weddings and anniversaries. Based on expected sales for a given period, a basic stock list specifies the minimum amount of merchandise that should be on hand for particular products. It shows the quantity of items that should be reordered, as well as the colors, styles, and sizes that should be carried. Retailers assign each product a code for ease in recording those products when they are purchased and sold. That code is commonly referred to as its sku (*stock-keeping unit*). An sku is the smallest available unit for keeping inventory control.

FIGURE 24-2

Basic Stock List

Stock	Description	Size	Packing Units	Cost	Retail	Min. Stock	October Sales		November Sales		December Sales	
							This Year	Last Year	This Year	Last Year	This Year	Last Year
1381	Skippy Peanut Butter	32 oz.	24			4						
1382	Skippy Peanut Butter	18 oz.	24			8						
1383	Skippy Peanut Butter	12 oz.	24			8						
1384	Jif Peanut Butter	32 oz.	24			4						
1385	Jif Peanut Butter	18 oz.	24			8						
1386	Jif Peanut Butter	12 oz.	24			8						

■ **Basic Stock List** Buyers use basic stock lists to plan purchases and keep track of items that should always be in stock. *Where on this list is the SKU?*

FIGURE 24-3

Model Stock List

PRODUCT CLASS Misses Sportswear   SEASON Spring

General Style	Specific Style	Price Range	Color	Total Units	Size 6	Size 8	Size 10	Size 12	Size 14
Blouse	Sleeveless Tailored	$25	White	12	1	3	3	3	2
			Black	12	1	3	3	3	2
			Blue	12	1	3	3	3	2
Blouse	Short-sleeve Oversize	$35	Pink	24	2	6	6	6	4
			Orange	24	2	6	6	6	4

■ **Model Stock Lists** Buyers use model stock lists for fashion merchandise. *How and why does this type of list differ from a basic stock list in form and content?*

A model stock list (see Figure 24-3) is used for fashionable merchandise. Fashion items change relatively rapidly; therefore, these lists are less specific than basic stock lists. The information contained in model stock lists identifies goods by general classes (blouses, skirts, dresses, slacks) and style categories (short sleeve, long sleeve), sizes, materials, colors, and price lines. Style numbers are not included because each manufacturer's style numbers change each year. Although model stock lists identify how many of each type of item should be purchased, the buyer must actually select specific models at the market.

A never-out list is used for best-selling products that make up a large percentage of sales volume. Items are added to or taken off the list as their popularity increases or declines. A video rental store will keep a popular movie on the never-out list and keep a large quantity of the videocassettes in the store. After the movie declines in popularity, only regular quantities of it will be maintained. It will be taken off the never-out list and more popular titles will replace it. When a popular new toy is first introduced, a toy store may keep a large amount of the toy in stock. As it decreases in popularity, a smaller inventory will be held.

Case Study

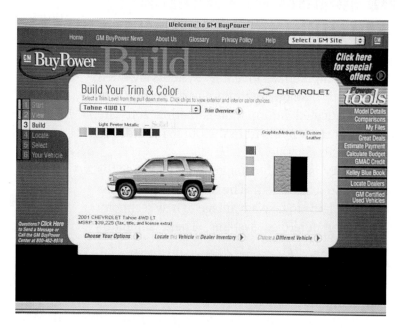

From New Car Order to Delivery—All Within Eight Days

Something revolutionary is happening with the General Motors (GM) Corporation, the world's largest industrial company. Faced with using new information technologies or losing market share to competitors, GM executives are changing their way of doing business. GM executives are recognizing what an important tool the Internet has become for car shoppers. Potential buyers can do their browsing and price comparing online. Now GM wants to take that a step further on their company Web site with e-GM.

The company is creating a new business model, e-GM. Company officials hope to integrate electronic car and supplier orders into its manufacturing operations and existing GM dealer network. A company Web site receives over 4.5 million hits a day from customers and dealers. GM has joined with partners such as AOL and NetZero to help lead Web users to their Web site where they can find out more information about GM products and buying their cars online.

GM also plans to implement a Web-based system that will facilitate the delivery of a customized vehicle to car owners within eight days of an electronic order for a car. E-commerce technologies should save $3,700 on the cost of a new car by reducing inventories, cutting paperwork, and improving communication with suppliers.

The company also plans to save money by ordering parts electronically from its suppliers. This will improve the purchasing process and lead to material cost reductions for the company. Reduced inventories and less paperwork will shorten delivery times to transport the vehicle to dealers and ultimately to the customer.

Reductions in inventory will save GM billions of dollars. The savings will be passed along as increased earnings to shareholders and reduced car prices to customers.

Case Study Review

1. Why did GM feel that it needed to change its way of doing business?
2. How will GM be able to enter other business fields by using this new approach?

A MATTER OF ETHICS

3. Would it be ethical for General Motors to sell its cars directly to customers without involving GM dealers? What are the advantages and disadvantages of this approach?

The Impact of Technology on Inventory Management

Electronic data processing using UPC product codes and computerized inventory systems are often used today to manage and improve inventory control. Sophisticated information-gathering software systems can track items from the purchase order to the final customer sale.

Technology is quickly changing the way stock is handled and controlled. The retail industry has created standards to take advantage of new technologies and computerized systems. These standards include:

- UPCs with standard product identifier bar code symbols to capture sku-level information at the point of sale
- Standard electronic data interchange (EDI) transactions to communicate electronically from business to business
- Standardized shipping container marking (SCM) as a way to identify case and case contents

EDI can shorten order cycles by as much as five days. Savings of two days are possible for manual orders. This time-saving between reorders allows businesses to carry one week less of inventory at their stores. SCM also enables distribution centers to reduce processing time by about two days.

Manufacturers and retailers are teaming up to implement Quick Response Delivery programs. Some *Quick Response Delivery* programs utilize a consolidation facility as a hub to receive, sort, and consolidate materials prior to delivery. This improves inventory control in the retail store, shortens the order cycle, and reduces excess inventory carried in stores.

Even small stores can get low-cost, computer-generated reports containing sales and inventory figures by product classifications. This information improves stock turnover and increases profits by pinpointing inventory that is too high or too low.

The Future of Inventory Management

In the early days of e-commerce, most e-tailers did not check stock until after an order was received. Because most customers who buy online expect their orders to be filled immediately, the ability to process and ship orders without delay has become essential to the success of e-businesses. This has brought about real time inventory systems. Real time inventory management capability lets a company constantly track every product it sells from when it's manufactured, or when it arrives in its warehouse, to when the customer orders it online, and to when it arrives at the buyer's door.

The theory behind real-time inventory management is that by integrating a Web site with such a system, a company will never disappoint an online customer, because its Web site will list only products actually in the warehouse, ready to be shipped, and would reserve those products right when the customer places the order. In the ultra-competitive world of e-commerce, real-time inventory management will make the difference between e-tailers who succeed and those who fail.

24.2 ASSESSMENT

Reviewing Key Terms and Concepts

1. What is inventory management and why is it important?
2. Explain the concept of just-in-time inventory.
3. Name the two different types of inventory systems used for inventory management.
4. What is the difference between dollar control and unit control as they relate to inventory management?
5. What is stock turnover?

Thinking Critically

6. Do you think a just-in-time inventory control system could be used in a retail or wholesale operation? Why or why not?

Integrating Academic Skills

7. **MATH** What is the amount of the ending inventory if beginning inventory was $280,000, net purchases were $756,000, and net sales were $872,000?

Careers in Marketing

Alisha Eads
Manager of Customer Service
E-Toys.com

Career Facts

How does your workload vary?

"You will never be bored in customer service and you will always be provided with challenges. Your work will never be complete and you will never stop striving to 'do better' for the customer. There are always improvements that can be made in customer service so you are always thinking of new and creative ways to motivate staff to achieve your goals."

What skills do you find most important?

"Strong interpersonal skills and relationship building skills are vital. It is important to have relationships in all areas of the company. You must work hard to build the respect and confidence of your peers and coworkers."

Why do you like managing a customer service team?

"I like the challenge of working with many different personality types. You learn to become a better leader by working with such a variety of individuals. You also learn to adjust your personality style to get the best out of each person you work with. Achievements are team achievements, not just individual achievements."

What is your key to success?

"Recognizing the potential of every staff member is my key to success. A rule to live by in this job is that you will only be as successful as your staff. Once you assess what people are capable of, your job will become much easier. Recognizing and utilizing that 'special something' in each person who reports to you will make you successful. Every person has something that they do well and every person can add value to your organization. It is your job as a manager to ensure that you know what those areas are in each of your employees."

Education and Training: A college degree with course work in business administration, operations management, public relations, marketing, or communications provides valuable background. Experience supervising personnel and handling sensitive customer problems is required.

Abilities, Aptitudes, and Skills: Strong leadership skills and the ability to motivate employees are necessary. Strong goal orientation, skill and productivity promoting efficiency, and the ability to maintain excellent service standards are needed.

Career Outlook: Job availability is projected to increase rapidly, but competition for the best jobs is expected to be keen.

Career Path: Work as an entry-level customer service employee may lead to customer service training jobs or assistant supervisor positions, and then to customer service management. Customer service managers may advance to public relations work.

Thinking Critically
What is meant by the statement "You will only be as successful as your staff"?

Chapter 24 ASSESSMENT

VOCABULARY REVIEW

Pair up with another student and quiz each other on the following vocabulary words.

- receiving record
- blind check method
- direct check method
- spot check method
- quality check method
- source marking
- preretailing marking method
- inventory management
- just-in-time (JIT) inventory system
- perpetual inventory system
- physical inventory system
- dollar control
- unit control
- stockkeeping unit (sku)
- stock turnover
- basic stock list
- model stock list
- never-out list

FACT AND IDEA REVIEW

1. What is a receiving record? Why is it an important document? (24.1)

2. Why must merchandise be checked after it has been received? (24.1)

3. Why do buyers perform quality checks? (24.1)

4. Identify three reasons for transferring merchandise between departments. (24.1)

5. How can inventory be tracked in a perpetual inventory system? (24.2)

6. What is a point-of-sale terminal? What are some of its advantages? (24.2)

7. What advantage does unit control provide? (24.2)

8. Name three recent developments in the retail industry that take advantage of computerized systems and new technologies. (24.2)

THINKING CRITICALLY

1. Explain why source marking is important for a small business.

2. Why do stock turnover rates vary by the type of business? Give examples of businesses with high and low turnover rates.

3. What problems might occur if a business used only a perpetual inventory system and never made an actual count of its inventory? How can this be avoided?

4. How does computer technology assist in inventory management?

5. What expectations should be placed on a business that oversees inventory management?

BUILDING WORKPLACE SKILLS

1. **Human Relations** You work in a receiving room of a large department store. You know that a coworker has been damaging incoming merchandise through deliberate and careless behavior. Unfortunately, your manager suspects that you are at fault and has approached you regarding this. Explain how you would handle this situation.

2. **Technology** Find an article about just-in-time inventory management at the library or on the Internet. Use a word processing program to prepare a summary focussing on the article's main points. Identify the name of the article, the author, source, and date of publication.

APPLYING MARKETING CONCEPTS

1. **Understanding Stock Turnover Rates**
Research why stock turnover rates vary by type of retail institution. Use a word processing program to list five different types of retail institutions and their stock turnover rates.

2. **Analyzing Sales Patterns** Use a design software program to make a sales chart for your school store for each hour of the business day or for each day in a month. Analyze the slow and peak sales times.

3. **Making Inventory Purchases** Research catalogs of merchandise to be sold in a school store. Use a spreadsheet program to list ten items and make a description of each by type, brand, style, cost, and retail price. Decide the quantities to stock for each item chosen.

4. **Improving Inventory Management** Research business magazines to find an example of a company that has improved its inventory management system. Use presentation software to create an oral presentation describing the situation and how the solution increased profit.

5. **Researching Inventory Management Systems** Research computer-based inventory management systems on the Internet. Develop a list of five to ten questions you would ask a company representative if you were converting from a physical inventory system to a computer-based system.

LINKING SCHOOL TO WORK

Systems Skills Investigate the receiving process used at a place of employment or at your cooperative education training station. List the job tasks that a receiver would perform from the time the stock is delivered until it is placed on the sales floor.

THE DECA CONNECTION

Role Play: Store Manager

Situation You are to assume the role of store manager of a large discount store. A problem has come up with inventory shortages. Your department manager (judge) has asked you to prepare a presentation about inventory control for an upcoming associates' meeting.

Activity You must make a presentation about the possible causes of inventory shortages as well as specific inventory control procedures that could be used to reduce inventory shortages.

Evaluation You will be evaluated on how well you meet the following performance indicators:
- Explain the possible causes for inventory shortages
- Identify unit inventory control systems that are appropriate for your company
- Develop a plan identifying specific procedures to reduce inventory shortages
- Make oral presentations

inter NET CONNECTION

Inventory Management
There are currently many companies that sell software programs for computer-based inventory management systems.

Connect
- Research the Internet to identify a software company specializing in inventory management programs.
- Use a word processing program to write a report detailing the company's Web site address, name, and physical location, as well as at least five advantages that the company advertises about its inventory management software applications.

The Zazz Lab

A Sports and Entertainment Marketing Simulation

WELCOME

Welcome to Zazz Sports and Entertainment Marketing Company. Zazz is devoted to serving the needs of its clients who include college, university, and professional sports teams, professional athletes, sporting events, and sports arenas plus major consumer product corporations, as well as television networks and movie studios. As an intern, you will have the opportunity to work on different clients' projects. All of your work will be assigned and reviewed by your department supervisor.

ESTABLISH DISTRIBUTION FOR A TEEN SPORTS MAGAZINE

SITUATION

A new Zazz client is *MW* Sports Magazine, a monthly magazine geared to teenage sports enthusiasts. *MW* covers football, baseball, volleyball, soccer, ice hockey, track and field, golf, tennis, and extreme sports, including special amateur events. Zazz has been hired to come up with a new name for the magazine and to establish an effective distribution system. The client is also interested in establishing a Web site.

ASSIGNMENT

Your supervisor wants you to consider the purchasing habits of buyers for magazines of *MW's* target market. Review all possible channels of distribution for the new magazine. Decide on the desired intensity of distribution (intensive, selective, exclusive) and provide your rationale. Provide a sales plan to include the type of sales personnel that should be used to sell to resellers and individual subscribers. Suggest methods of physical distribution, and explain inventory control methods that will be used to keep all customers supplied on a monthly basis. Design the subscription order form that will be inserted in the magazine. Finally, build a Web site for the magazine and make recommendations for online publishing.

Tools and Resources

To complete this assignment you will need to conduct research at a library or on the Internet. You will also need a word processing program, a spreadsheet program, and presentation software. Helpful trade publications include *BrandWeek, Advertising Age, Sports Business Journal,* and *Sports Business Daily.*

Research

Research sports magazines that target teens to determine the market share of competitors. Research all possible outlets for distribution of the magazine to determine what intermediaries may be needed to get this new magazine into the hands of the final customer. Investigate physical distribution methods used to transport these magazines to intermediaries and individual subscribers. Research magazines on the Internet to determine how they are sold and find about about the required links for resellers and individual subscribers.

Report

Prepare a written report and a computer presentation for the client. Use a word processing program to prepare a double-spaced report. Use a spreadsheet program to create a pie chart illustrating the current market share enjoyed by the major competitors in the teen sports magazine market. Arrange your written report around the following headings:

- The teen sports magazine market
- Possible outlets for distribution
- Physical distribution methods
- New name for magazine
- Suggested channel(s) of distribution
- Channel(s) for resellers and individual subscribers
- Intensity of distribution
- Use of the Internet
- Physical distribution (for intermediaries and individual subscribers)
- Sales methods
- Sales staff vs. agents
- Sample subscription order form
- Web site design
- Inventory control

Using computer presentation software, prepare a presentation of your ideas for the client that includes:

- Key topics covered in your written report
- Graphic illustrations that relate to each slide's topic
- Very little text
- Minimum of 10 slides

Presentation and Evaluation

Present your ideas in a written report and an oral presentation. The presentation will later be shown to the client. You will be evaluated on your oral presentation skills, including:

- Knowledge of distribution, sales, and inventory control used in publishing
- Knowledge of e-commerce and online publishing
- Continuity of presentation
- Voice quality
- Eye contact

Portfolio

Print a copy of your completed report and presentation for your Portfolio.

THE DECA CONNECTION

DECA Business Services Marketing Series
Consulting is an occupational area in this event, so the concept of suggesting a channel of distribution for a new sports magazine is a possible role play.

DECA Marketing Management Series
Deciding on the channels of distribution, physical distribution, sales methods, and inventory control are all areas of marketing management.

DECA Hospitality and Recreation Research Event
Researching current distribution methods used for sports magazines and then developing a Web site and the channels of distribution for it could be a topic for this event.

DECA Sports and Entertainment Marketing Management Team Decision-Making Event
Working on this project with a partner would make the experience similar to what is expected in a DECA Team Decision-Making Event.

Portfolio

Develop a New Product

To demonstrate your understanding of pricing concepts, you will research a specific product category, such as chocolate chip cookies, children's cereal, cologne, compact automobiles, or CD players. Assume you have developed a new product in that category and must determine a price for it. Using all the pricing concepts, strategies, and computations in this unit, prepare a written report and an oral presentation (using computer presentation software), on how you would price that new product. In making your decision, assume current economic and market conditions.

Pricing

Unit Overview

As you recall from Chapter 2, the four Ps of the marketing mix are product, place, price, and promotion. Unit 8 addresses the marketing mix decision regarding price. Throughout the unit you will see how essential price is to a company's marketing plan and its ultimate success or failure.

Chapter 25 explores the importance of price and all the factors that affect the pricing decision. In Chapter 26 various pricing policies and strategies provide a wide range of ideas on how one goes about deciding on a price for products. Pricing computations, including how to calculate markups, markdowns, and discounts are explained in Chapter 27. You will learn the relationship between pricing and a company's profitability based on pricing calculations. Chapter 27 ties the profit and loss statement to the concept of pricing.

In this Unit:

Foundations of Marketing

⬤ Economics

⬤ Business, Management, Entrepreneurship

Functions of Marketing

◢ Pricing

Chapter 25

Price Planning

Marketing: What It Takes

Arts and Crafts

You have designed a line of stuffed animals that your friends think you should sell at arts and crafts shows. The problem is that you don't know how to go about pricing your creations.

WHAT WILL YOU DO?
How will your pricing goals affect the price you charge customers? What other considerations are important in pricing your unique stuffed animals?

The Steps of Price Planning

What Is Price?

Price is the value of money (or its equivalent) placed on a good or service. It is usually expressed in monetary terms, such as $5.50 for a pen. It may also be expressed in nonmonetary terms, such as free goods or services in exchange for the purchase of a product. The oldest form of pricing is the barter system. *Bartering* involves the exchange of a product or service for another product or service, without the use of money. For example, a business might exchange some of its products for advertising space in a magazine or newspaper. Some companies also will exchange advertising spots on their Web pages as a form of bartering, or an equal trade.

■ Relationship of Product Value

The key to pricing is understanding the value that buyers place on a product. The value that a customer places on an item makes the difference in his or her spending $100 on a new bicycle or $500. If the buyer is an avid cyclist, it is likely that he or she will pay a high price for the desired quality. If the buyer is merely looking into purchasing a bike as a new hobby or to get around on the weekends, he or she may not place as high of a value on the item. Value is a matter of anticipated satisfaction—if consumers believe they will gain a great deal of satisfaction from a product, they will place a high value on it. They will also be willing to pay a high price.

A seller must be able to gauge where a product will rank in the customer's estimation—whether it will be valued much, valued little, or valued somewhere in between. This information can then be considered in the pricing decision. The seller's objective is to set a price high enough for the firm to make a profit and yet not so high that it exceeds the value potential customers place on the product.

■ Various Forms of Price

Price is involved in every marketing exchange. The fee you pay a dentist to clean your teeth, the amount you pay for a new pair of shoes, and minor charges such as bridge tolls and bus fares are all prices. Rent is the monthly price of an apartment. Interest is the price of a loan. Dues are the price of membership. Tuition is the price you pay for an education. Wages, salaries, commissions, and bonuses are the various prices that businesses pay workers for their labor. Price comes in many forms and goes by many names.

● What You'll Learn

- The different forms of price
- The importance of price
- The goals of pricing
- The difference between market share and market position

● Why It's Important

Price—one of the four Ps of the marketing mix—is an essential element in marketing a product to the correct target market. The goals of company and government regulations are two issues that must be considered in that process. Understanding the steps involved in determining the price of a product is essential for business success.

Key Terms

- price
- market share
- market position
- return on investment

Importance of Price

Price is an important factor in the success or failure of a business. It helps establish and maintain a firm's image, competitive edge, and profits.

Many customers use price to make judgments about products and the companies that make them. A higher price means better quality from an upscale store or company to some customers; to other customers, a lower price means more for their money. Price is a vital component of a business's image.

Price is sometimes the main thrust of a firm's advertising strategy. Some retailers stress that they offer the lowest prices in town or promise that they will beat any other store's prices. In such cases, price plays an important role in establishing the edge a firm enjoys over its competition.

Finally, price helps determine profits. Marketers know that sales revenue is equal to price times the quantity sold. Sales revenue can be increased either by selling more items or by increasing the price per item, in theory. The number of items sold may not increase or even remain stable if prices are raised. Figure 25-1 shows what may happen.

It is also important to remember that an increase in price can increase profits only if costs and expenses can be maintained. You will explore this limitation later in the chapter.

Goals of Pricing

While marketers are concerned primarily with earning a profit, they do have other pricing goals. They include gaining market share, achieving a certain return on investment, and meeting the competition.

Gaining Market Share

A business may forgo immediate profits for long-term gains in some other area. One goal, for example, might be to take business away from competitors. The business is trying to increase its market share in this case. Market share is a firm's percentage of the total sales volume generated by all competitors

FIGURE 25-1

Projected Effects of Different Prices on Sales

Price per Item ×	Quantity Sold =	Sales Revenue
$50	200	$10,000
$45	250	$11,250
$40	280	$11,200
$35	325	$11,375
$30	400	$12,000
$25	500	$12,500

■ **Increased Price or Increased Sales?** An increase in the price of an item may not produce an increase in sales revenue. *Why is this true?*

in a given market. Businesses constantly study their market share to see how well they are doing with a given product in relation to their competitors.

Visualize the total market as a pie. Figure 25-2 on page 453 depicts the total market for digital cameras. Each slice of the pie represents each competitor's share of that market. The biggest slice of the pie represents the firm that has the largest percentage of the total sales volume. In addition to market share, marketers are interested in their relative standing in relation to their competitors, or their market position. To monitor market position, a firm must keep track of the changing size of the market and the growth of its competitors. According to market position, the number one cookie brand in the United States is Oreo (see Figure 25-3 on page 453).

Pricing may play a role in establishing and maintaining a firm's market share and market position. Businesses must watch their competitors to maintain or improve their market share and position. A company that wants to increase its market share will engage in price competition in order to take business away from its competitors. This may be accomplished by increasing advertising or using new advertising media and messages.

Return on Investment

Return on investment is a calculation that is used to determine the relative profitability of a product. The formula for calculating return on investment is as follows:

Profit/Investment

Profit is another word for return, which explains the expression return on investment.

Assume your company sells trash cans for $8 each. Your cost to make and market the trash cans is $6.50 per unit. Remember that profit is money earned by a business minus costs and expenses, so that your calculation on investment is:

$8 − $6.50 = $1.50/$6.50 = .23

This means that your rate of return on investment is 23 percent.

A company may price its products to achieve a certain return on investment. Let's say that your trash can company wants to achieve a return on investment of at least 15 percent on a new model. To determine the price at which the new trash can would have to sell, you would work backward. Start with a target price, the price at which you want to sell the new trash cans. Then, determine how your company can get costs down so that that price will generate your target return. You will learn more about target pricing in Chapter 26.

FIGURE 25-2

Digital Camera Market Share

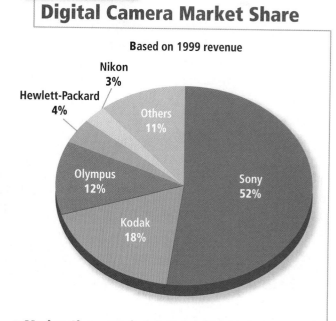

■ **Market Share** Market share is a firm's percentage of the total sales volume generated by all competitors in a given market. *Which brand has the largest share of the digital camera market? If total sales for this market are $3 billion, what is the sales revenue for the market leader?*

FIGURE 25-3

Cookies—The U.S. Market

$510 million

$396 million

$172 million

$143 million

■ **Market Position** Market position is the relative standing a competitor has in a given market in comparison to its competitors. *Which brand is the market leader in the U.S. cookie market? Given total sales of $1,221 (in millions) for the U.S. cookie market, what is the leader's market share?*

■ **At What Price?** The concept of price comes in a variety of ways. *Besides paying money for products or services, what other means is there to exchange products and services?*

■ Meeting the Competition

Some companies simply aim to meet the prices of their competition. They either follow the industry leader or calculate the average price and then position their product close to that figure. Two products priced in this manner are automobiles and soft drinks. Competing products in both these categories tend to be very similar and are therefore priced closely to one another. Prices may vary slightly, but the figures are in the same ballpark. It is unlikely that you would find a can of soda priced over $1.00 if the rest of the soft drinks in that category match that price. Manufacturers want to ensure that they match their competition in price and quality.

How does one compete when there is no price competition? You compete on the basis of other factors in the marketing mix. These might include quality or uniqueness of product, convenience of business location or hours, and level of service. A television manufacturer might offer a longer term or more comprehensive warranty than its competitors. A bookstore might engage a local drama group to do weekly readings from popular titles. A local restaurant may offer luncheon specials for certain businesses within a certain zip code. Businesses would try to meet competition based on a marketing strategy that takes more than price into consideration in these situations.

25.1 ASSESSMENT

Reviewing Key Terms and Concepts

1. What is bartering?
2. Why is price an important factor in the success or failure of a business?
3. Name three goals of pricing in addition to making a profit.
4. Distinguish between market share and market position.
5. Define and show the formula for return on investment.

Thinking Critically

6. Setting prices higher than the competition will put your business on a fast track to failure. Is this statement true or false? Explain the reasons for your answer.

Integrating Academic Skills

7. **COMMUNICATION** Deliver a two-minute talk explaining why knowledge of the consumer is so important in pricing decisions.

Factors Involved in Price Planning

Market Factors Affecting Prices

How do businesses make price decisions? The answer is not an easy one, as you have probably already realized.

Most price planning begins with an analysis of costs and expenses, many of which are related to current market conditions. The cost of raw materials may increase a manufacturer's costs to make an item. Passing that increase on to customers may seem an easy remedy for the situation; however, it is not that simple. An organization's goals must be considered. When a firm's goal is to increase market share, pricing decisions must be in line with that goal. The manufacturer must fully consider the effect the higher price will have in the marketplace.

■ Costs and Expenses

In today's competitive economic environment, businesses constantly monitor, analyze, and project prices and sales in the light of costs and expenses. They do this because sales, costs, and expenses together determine a firm's profit.

RESPONSES TO DECLINING PROFIT MARGINS What do marketers do when costs or expenses increase or when sales decline? Some pass the costs to their customers. When oil prices go up, you will often see an increase in rates charged by airlines, shipping companies, and at the gas stations. How else could businesses maintain their profit margins? Let's look at other options available to improve a firm's profit picture.

Some businesses have found that price is so important in the marketing strategy of a product that they will hesitate to make any price changes. They will reduce the size of an item before they will change its price. A candy manufacturer might reduce a candy bar from 4 to 3.5 ounces rather than increase its price. This would reduce the cost of making the candy bar, so the manufacturer could still make a profit at the established price.

Manufacturers drop features their customers don't value. Some airlines have stopped serving meals and offer only beverages. Eliminating a small portion of its service helps the company to compete more effectively based on price.

Some manufacturers respond to higher costs and expenses by improving their products. They add more features or upgrade the materials in order to justify a higher price. The increase caused by higher costs or expenses is merged with the increase resulting from improvements in the product. For example, the Ford Motor Company designed more comfortable supercabs on some of their trucks and charged more for those models.

• What You'll Learn

- The four market factors that affect price planning
- What demand elasticity is in relation to supply and demand theory
- The government regulations that affect price planning

• Why It's Important

Pricing a product may seem like an easy task, until you take all the factors affecting that decision into consideration. Skipping even one aspect of this process could cost a business millions of dollars in lost sales, or even in fines or lawsuits from not following the laws governing pricing.

Key Terms

- break-even point
- elastic demand
- law of diminishing marginal utility
- inelastic demand
- price fixing
- price discrimination
- loss leader
- unit pricing

Electronic Frontiers

Virtual Yard Sale!

Aiming to mimic the pricing deals available at yard sales, where prices tend to decline as the day wears on, an e-commerce site called WebSwap.com has introduced an online service in which prices decline over time. Sellers set starting prices and minimum prices for items they want to sell. WebSwap automatically decreases the starting price by a set amount each hour. The price continues to decline over the course of a week, until it hits the minimum price the seller is willing to accept. Buyers must decide whether to risk losing the item and wait for a lower price or pay a slightly higher price and get their item for sure.

Thinking Critically

How would a seller determine the starting and minimum prices for a virtual yard sale?

RESPONSES TO LOWER COSTS/EXPENSES Prices may occasionally drop because of decreased costs and expenses. Aggressive firms are constantly looking for ways to increase efficiency and decrease costs. Improved technology and less expensive materials may help create better-quality products at lower costs. Personal computers have fallen in price because of the improved technology.

BREAK-EVEN POINT Manufacturers are always concerned with making a profit. They are especially concerned, however, in two situations—when marketing a new product and when trying to establish a new price. In these circumstances manufacturers carefully analyze their costs and expenses in relation to unit and dollar sales. To do this they calculate their break-even point.

The break-even point is the point at which sales revenue equals the costs and expenses of making and distributing a product. After this point is reached, businesses begin to make a profit on the product.

Suppose a toy manufacturer plans to make 100,000 dolls that will be sold at $6 each to retailers and wholesalers. The cost of making and marketing the dolls is $4.50 per unit, or $450,000 for the 100,000 dolls. How many dolls must the toy manufacturer sell to cover its costs and expenses? To calculate the break-even point, the manufacturer divides the total amount of costs and expenses by the selling price:

$$\$450,000 \div 6 = 75,000$$

To break even, the firm must sell 75,000 dolls. After 75,000 are sold, the firm will begin to make a profit.

■ Supply and Demand

In Chapter 3, you learned about supply and demand theory. You might recall that demand tends to go up when price goes down and down when price goes up. This statement is accurate as a general rule. However, demand for some products does not respond readily to changes in price. The degree to which demand for a product is affected by its price is called *demand elasticity*. Products are said to have either elastic demand or inelastic demand.

Elastic demand refers to situations in which a change in price creates a change in demand. Changes in the price of steak can serve as an example. If the price of steak were $8 per pound, few people would buy steak; if the price were to drop to $5, $3, and finally $2 per pound, however, demand would increase at each price level.

These increases would not continue indefinitely, however. At some point, they would be limited by another economic law—the law of diminishing marginal utility, which states that consumers will buy only so much of a given product, even though the price is low. Let's say that detergent went on sale, and you bought two cases of it. Three weeks later a new sale is announced for the same detergent, but you already have enough to last for months; therefore, you don't take advantage of the new sale.

Inelastic demand refers to situations in which a change in price has very little effect on demand for a product. Certain food products, such as milk and bread, fall into this category. Most people would not buy less milk or bread if prices were to increase sharply. The same holds true if the prices were to decrease sharply—there would be only so much bread and milk that we could use.

What determines whether demand for a product is likely to be elastic or inelastic? Figure 25-4 suggests some answers.

FIGURE 25-4

DEMAND ELASTICITY

D emand elasticity varies with five factors. Most depend on the consumer's personal situation or attitudes about the purchase.

AVAILABILITY OF SUBSTITUTES

When substitutes are readily available, demand becomes more elastic. In the case of detergents, there are many competing brands, most of which will clean your clothes equally well. Demand for detergents would therefore be elastic.

BRAND LOYALTY

Some customers will not accept a substitute product, even though there are many competing brands. In such situations, demand becomes inelastic.

LUXURY VS. NECESSITY

When a product is a necessity (such as medicine for a sick person), demand tends to be inelastic. When a product is a luxury, just the opposite is true. Note that here again the classification is relative. What is perceived as a luxury by one person may be perceived as a necessity by another.

PRICE RELATIVE TO INCOME

Changes in price are relative to the income of the customer. If a price increase is slight and does not have a major impact on the customer's budget, he or she will probably buy the product. If the increase is large and far more than the customer's budget allows, he or she will probably not buy it. Thus, if the increase is significant relative to one's income, demand is likely to be elastic.

URGENCY OF PURCHASE

If you are running out of gasoline and the next gas station charges $.15 more per gallon than you usually pay, you will probably still stop and buy gas. If a purchase must be made immediately, demand tends to be inelastic.

■ Consumer Perceptions

Consumer perceptions about the relationship between price and quality or other values also play a role in price planning. Some consumers equate quality with price. They believe a high price reflects high quality. A high price may also suggest status, prestige, and exclusiveness.

Some businesses create the perception that a particular product is worth more than others by limiting the supply of the item in the market. They do this by coming out with a limited edition of a certain model and charging a higher price. Why? The reasoning is that the value of the item will increase as a result of its exclusiveness.

Personalized service can add to the consumer's perceptions about price. Many consumers are willing to pay more for items purchased from certain businesses because of the service those businesses might offer. Marketers can charge slightly higher prices because consumers are willing to pay for the added service.

A marketer must be concerned with subjective price—that is, the price consumers see as the value they are getting for what they are buying. The perception of the price is what counts.

Extravagant. Excessive. Exorbitant. But enough about the engine.

The new Bentley Arnage Red Label. An overwhelming 400 hp. An overpowering 590 lb-ft of torque. What else could overshadow 550 sq-ft of hand-sewn leather? Call 1-877-300-8803 or visit bentleymotors.com

BENTLEY MOTOR CARS

■ **Presenting Quality** Some businesses want to establish a quality image for their company and products. *What does a high price for this car suggest?*

BRIGHT IDEAS

The Pet Rock—Selling Nothing for Something

You're planning a big vacation. Only problem—you can't find someone to feed your parakeets. A California advertising man had this in mind when he created the infamous fad—the pet rock. Gary Dahl argued to his friends one evening that pets misbehaved, cost too much money, and made a mess. His idea of a great pet was a rock—something with a nice personality and low maintenance. Dahl spent the next two weeks writing the "Pet Rock Training Manual," which included instructions on the essentials of house-training and teaching your new pet to play dead. Dahl packaged the manual in a cardboard case resembling a small pet carrier along with an individual stone, purchased for one penny. In one month's time, a million rocks sold for $3.95 each, making Dahl an overnight star (and millionaire)!

Thinking Creatively

For what inexpensive items could you recreate other uses?

Special Editions Special editions of a product are limited in quantity to create an exclusivity for the item. *How do most businesses price special editions?*

Competition

Price must be evaluated in relation to the target market and is one of the four Ps of the marketing mix. A company can use a lower price to appeal to that market when its target market is price conscious. When its target market is not price conscious, a company can resort to various forms of *nonprice competition*.

Nonprice competition minimizes price as a reason for purchase; instead, it creates a distinctive product through such means as product availability and customer service. The more unusual a product is perceived to be by consumers, the greater the marketer's freedom to set prices above those of competitors.

Marketers change prices to reflect consumer demand, cost, or competition. When products are very similar, price often becomes the sole basis on which customers make their purchase decisions. Shoppers are more likely to buy the less expensive brand if they see no difference between Maxwell House coffee and Hills Brothers coffee.

Because of this, competitors must watch each other closely. When one company changes its prices, others usually react. When the manufacturer of Tide detergent reduces its price, its competitors are likely to do the same. The benefit of this kind of competition is lower prices for consumers.

When competitors engage in a fierce battle to attract customers by lowering prices, a price war is the result. The problem with price wars is that firms reduce their profits while trying to undercut their competitors' prices and attract new customers. This may result in excessive financial losses and, in some cases, actual business failure. According to *PC World*, it took two years for the home scanner market to stabilize after a two-year price war. The battle put many vendors out of business.

Government Regulations Affecting Prices

Federal and state governments have enacted laws controlling prices. Marketers must be aware of their rights and responsibilities regarding price fixing, price discrimination, resale price maintenance, minimum pricing, unit pricing, and price advertising.

Same Price for All . . . Sometimes

Imagine that you are a Russian citizen living and working in Germany. While looking for a flight home, you are quoted $2,500 on an airline's Web site. That same flight is available to you for $1,000 if you go through a "gray market." This technique, known as ethnic pricing, offers reduced rates and discounts to nationals living abroad. Gray markets—usually in the form of discount specialized travel agencies—offer cheaper flights. While not legal in the United States and most of Europe, ethnic pricing has been a common practice in countries such as China, India, and Russia.

Thinking Critically

Why do you think that ethnic pricing is illegal in most countries?

MARKETING

REAL WORLD

Too Cool For Cola

On a chilly day could you be persuaded to buy a cold soda at 20 cents off? Would you be willing to pay 20 cents more for the same soda on a sweltering summer day? Coca-Cola Co. found out the hard way that the answer is no. The beverage company experimented with the idea of "smart" vending machines that priced sodas according to inventory levels. After conducting research however, Coke found that customers felt that they were being taken advantage of. Marketing specialists determined that Coke would damage its brand image by focusing on price.

Thinking Critically?

Why didn't Coke's fluctuating pricing scheme work?

Price Fixing

Price fixing occurs when competitors agree on certain price ranges within which they set their own prices. Price fixing can be proved only when there is evidence of collusion. This means that there was communication among the competing firms to establish a price range. Price fixing is illegal because it eliminates competition—the cornerstone of the free enterprise system.

The federal law against price fixing is the Sherman Antitrust Act of 1890, which outlawed monopolies. In 1999, Hoffman-LaRoche and BASF (Badische-Anillin & Soda-Fabrik) were found guilty of price fixing in the human and animal vitamin industry and they paid a $725 million fine.

Price Discrimination

Price discrimination occurs when a firm charges different prices to similar customers in similar situations. The Clayton Antitrust Act of 1914 defines price discrimination as creating unfair competition. The Robinson-Patman Act was passed in 1936 to strengthen the provisions of the Clayton Act. The

Robinson-Patman Act prohibits sellers from offering one customer one price and another customer a different price if both customers are buying the same product in similar situations.

The Robinson-Patman Act was intended to help smaller retailers compete with the large chain stores. It was presumed that bigger stores would be in a position to demand lower prices because of the volume of goods they could purchase. Smaller retailers who could not buy large quantities of product to sell would be at a competitive disadvantage.

The Robinson-Patman Act created restrictions on pricing and other price-related options, such as rebates, credit terms, warehousing, premiums, coupons, guarantees, discounts, and delivery. There are a few exceptions, however. Price discrimination within a channel of distribution is permissible if:

- Products purchased are physically different
- Non-competing buyers are involved
- Prices do not hurt competition
- Costs justify the differences in prices
- Production costs go up
- Prices are changed to meet another supplier's bid

Discounts are permitted if the sellers can demonstrate that they are available to all channel members on a proportional basis, graduated to allow small and large buyers to benefit and qualify, or justified by savings incurred. Price discrimination is obviously a complicated matter that must be studied carefully to be sure pricing is in line with the provisions of the Robinson-Patman Act.

Resale Price Maintenance

Manufacturers' resale price maintenance policies have come under scrutiny by legal authorities. Historically, manufacturers would set a retail price for an item and force retailers to sell it at that price. The manufacturer would punish retailers that sold the item for a lower price by withholding deliveries or refusing promised discounts or allowances. This practice of punishing retailers was outlawed in 1975 in the Consumer Goods Pricing Act.

Nine West Group Inc., one of the largest suppliers of women's shoes, was found guilty of such practices in 2000. Nine West divisions made agreements with retailers that create a fixed retail price for their shoes. They also limited the time when retailers could run promotional sales at discount prices.

Case Study

The Price of Gas

In June 2000, gasoline prices escalated to over $2.00 per gallon, especially in the Midwest. Everyone wanted to know why.

One reason is that oil refiners use a "just-in-time" inventory system so they do not maintain a lot of reserves. Unprepared for increased demand, refiners had to pay higher prices for crude oil.

A second reason involved increased expenses that refiners incurred due to new environmental requirements. The mandate for cleaner air has prompted state legislatures to require different formulas for gasoline to meet requirements in their respective states. That meant a refiner had to create several different versions of reformulated gasoline for each state it served, costing refiners more money. The concept of special formulas for gasoline is not new. In 1996, California auto drivers experienced a 30-percent increase in gasoline prices when that state mandated its own special formula.

The higher prices led to a federal government investigation and new exploration to increase supplies by oil companies. Until supply meets demand, however, you can expect higher gasoline prices.

Case Study Review

1. How are gasoline prices related to the supply and demand theory and to the theory of demand elasticity?
2. Besides a shortage of inventory, what other factor caused higher gasoline prices for consumers?

A MATTER OF ETHICS

3. Is it ethical for oil refineries to pass the higher cost of fuel on to the consumer, when they were the ones who did not anticipate the increased demand?

Those retailers who did not follow these rules were penalized by Nine West. The State Attorney General called for Nine West Group to pay a fine of $34 million. They also may not threaten a stop in shoe supply if retailers don't comply with their rules.

A manufacturer may suggest resale prices in its advertising, price tags, and price lists. There can even be an agreement to fix the maximum retail price as long as the price agreement is not an "unreasonable restraint of trade" or considered "anti-competitive." A business cannot coerce current customers into adhering to such prices. It can tell customers in advance that they will not be permitted to sell its products if they break the established pricing policy. The difference between "coercing customers" and "telling them in advance" is the fine line manufacturers with such policies must walk.

■ Minimum Price Laws

Very closely related to resale price maintenance laws is the practice of selling goods at a very low price. Many states have enacted minimum price laws (also known as unfair sales laws). The laws were enacted to prevent retailers from selling goods below cost plus a percentage for expenses and profit. Some states have passed such laws that cover all products, while others have included only specific products.

In states where minimum price laws are not in effect, an item priced at cost to draw customers into a store is called a loss leader. This means the business takes a loss on the item to lead customers into the store. Retailers select highly popular, well-advertised products to use as loss leaders, such as disposable diapers.

■ Unit Pricing

A number of states have passed laws to make it easier for consumers to compare similar goods that are packaged in different sizes or come in different forms (such as frozen and canned foods). Unit pricing allows consumers to compare prices in relation to a standard unit or measure, such as an ounce or a pound. Food stores have been most affected by these laws and have responded with shelf labels and computer records of unit prices.

■ Price Advertising

The Federal Trade Commission (FTC) has developed guidelines for advertising prices. The FTC's price advertising guidelines forbid a company from advertising a price reduction unless the original price was offered to the public on a regular basis for a reasonable and recent period of time. Another rule says that a company may not say that its prices are lower than its competitors' without proof of such comparison based on a large number of items. Also,

■ Compare and Contrast A number of states have passed laws to make it easier for consumers to compare similar goods that are packaged in different sizes or come in different forms. *How would a customer determine which is a better buy?*

a premarked or list price cannot be used as the reference point for a new sale price unless the item has actually been sold at that price.

Bait-and-switch advertising, in which a firm advertises a low price for an item it has no intention of selling, is illegal. When a customer comes in and asks for the advertised item, salespeople switch the customer to a higher-priced item by saying that the advertised product is out of stock or of poor quality.

25.2 ASSESSMENT

Reviewing Key Terms and Concepts

1. Name four market factors that affect price planning.

2. In response to increased costs and expenses, what three pricing options might a business consider to maintain its profit margins?

3. What is demand elasticity, and how does it alter the theories of supply and demand?

4. What is the difference between price fixing and price discrimination? What laws govern each?

Thinking Critically

5. Many people with diabetes depend on insulin. If the price of insulin went up $10, would the demand for insulin go down as is suggested by the theory of supply and demand? Explain your answer in terms of demand elasticity.

Integrating Academic Skills

6. **MATH** Calculate the break-even point for a notebook that costs a business $1 to make and market and that will be sold for $1.50. The total quantity that will be sold at that price is 60,000.

Careers in Marketing

PROFESSIONAL SALES

Dennis Spiegel
Manufacturer's Agent
Spiegel & Spiegel Sales Associates LLC

What does your job entail?

"My job involves the direct selling of furniture to various corporations. Manufacturers' agents are also known as marketing or wholesale sales representatives. They are the contact between the manufacturers of products and the customers. I travel to customers' business locations and demonstrate new products, write orders, and solve any problems between the customers and the manufacturers. I also communicate special requests from customers to manufacturers. Sales agents help customers to display a manufacturers' merchandise or to write advertising copy to increase retail sales of the merchandise they represent. In addition to traveling to the customers' locations, they conduct sales by phone and at special manufacturers' showrooms."

What skills are most important to you?

"I believe that it is extremely important to offer the customer extraordinary service. To do this you must have excellent product knowledge, as well as the ability to persuade the customer. Sometimes, you might need to overcome objections before you can close the deal. All of this requires very strong communication skills."

What kind of training do you recommend?

"High school students interested in sales should take courses in business, marketing, economics, consumer education, accounting, and English. This will give you a good background for the specialized training programs that are available on the job."

What is your key to success?

"I enjoy the interaction with my customers. I am persistent in meeting my personal goals and corporate goals. In this business, it is necessary to stay flexible and maintain a broad perspective. Enthusiasm and a positive attitude are what will help you stay on top!"

Thinking Critically

Why is on-the-job training vital in this career?

Career Facts

Education and Training: Most employers require a two to four-year college degree involving some technical training related to the product.

Aptitudes, Abilities, and Skills: Self-motivation, high energy, ability to work with little direct supervision, good people skills, excellent sales skills, and a pleasant personality are vital, in addition to average clerical, arithmetic, and computer skills.

Career Outlook: Average growth is projected for manufacturers' agents through the year 2006. New Internet marketing techniques may reduce the need for agents as fewer agents are able to cover sales territories with less traveling.

Career Path: Many manufacturers' sales agents have previous sales experience. Successful sales agents may advance to sales supervisor positions or to account executives.

VOCABULARY REVIEW

Explain the difference between each pair of words listed below.

- price—unit price
- market share—market position
- return on investment—break-even point
- elastic demand—inelastic demand
- price fixing—price discrimination
- loss leader—bait and switch

FACT AND IDEA REVIEW

1. How does the role of product value play a part in price planning? (25.1)

2. Provide one example each of market share and market position. (25.1)

3. How is return on investment calculated? (25.1)

4. Once businesses meet each other's prices, how else can they compete? (25.1)

5. Name one business situation in which prices dropped because of decreased costs and expenses. (25.2)

6. Name five factors that indicate if a product is likely to have elastic or inelastic demand. (25.2)

7. How do consumers' perceptions play a role in price planning? (25.2)

8. What is the role of competition in price planning? (25.2)

9. What are unfair sales laws? (25.2)

10. What is unit pricing? Why have some states passed laws requiring businesses to post the unit prices of items? (25.2)

THINKING CRITICALLY

1. A firm is selling 10,000 shower curtains at $10 each. The cost of manufacturing and marketing the shower curtains is $7.50 each. Calculate the break-even point for the shower curtains. How is this significant to the manufacturer?

2. Determine the return on investment for the following two video games:

	Morris Mania	Berto's Revenge
Manufacturing costs	$10.00	$ 8.75
Selling/marketing expenses	$ 4.00	$ 3.25
Selling price	$17.00	$14.75

Based on return on investment, which video game is more profitable for the company?

BUILDING WORKPLACE SKILLS

1. **Human Relations** A regular customer approaches you at the snack shop where you work to ask about a new package of chewing gum. The ten-stick package for $.50 replaces the six-stack pack for $.25. The customer is not happy with this change. What do you say to maintain her good faith?

2. **Technology** Use a spreadsheet program to prepare a pie chart depicting market shares for the $800 million sports drink market. Use these fictional figures to represent each brand's sales.

Brand	Sales (× 1,000)
Thirstade	$570,000
Drinkade	93,000
Nautilus	55,000
Everlast	33,500
Energade	24,500
Hy-5	15,000
Other	9,000

1. **Identifying Price** You must determine the customer price (wholesalers and retailers) for your new shampoo called Hair Joy. Visit two local beauty supply stores and compare the retail prices and unit prices (per ounce) of four comparable shampoos. Assume that your cost of manufacturing and distributing Hair Joy to wholesalers and retailers will be $1.85 per ten-ounce bottle. Assume that retailers double the price they pay for shampoo from the manufacturer. What would you suggest as the price retailers should be charged? You expect to make 200,000 bottles of shampoo at the chosen price. What will be your break-even point? Use a word processing program to prepare a written report.

2. **Researching Pricing Violations** Use the Internet to research recent legal cases of companies accused of breaking federal or state laws that govern pricing practices. Use a word processing program to write a 200-word report of your findings.

3. **Reviewing Influences on Price** Use presentation software to prepare an oral report on market factors affecting price. Be sure to include examples and appropriate graphics.

4. **Understanding Price Advertising** Research the Federal Trade Commission's guidelines for advertising prices. Using presentation software, prepare a summary of the rules and their effects on manufacturers.

LINKING SCHOOL TO WORK

Basic and Information Skills Investigate the pricing goals of your firm. Ask your supervisor to identify the goals according to the importance for your business. Prepare a written report.

THE DECA CONNECTION

Role Play: Management Trainee

Situation You are to assume the role of management trainee for a unisex clothing store that specializes in jeans and trendy clothing. The store's buyer (judge) wants your opinion about whether or not to carry a new brand of jeans that would sell for $10 more than your most expensive brand. Even at the $80 retail price, you think they will sell.

Activity In ten minutes, you will be meeting with the store buyer to share your thoughts and opinions. What will you say?

Evaluation You will be evaluated on how well you meet the following performance indicators:
- Explain the nature and scope of the pricing function
- Explain factors affecting pricing decisions
- Identify strategies for pricing new products
- Explain the nature of sales forecasts
- Persuade others

*inter*NET CONNECTION

A Fair Price?
Supply and demand theory is alive on the World Wide Web with Web sites such as Priceline.com, where customers name their prices for air fares and other products.

Connect
- Determine the positive and negative features of a Web site that allows customers to buy goods and services online through a bidding system.
- Determine if such a system constitutes price discrimination.

Pricing Strategies

Marketing: What It Takes

At What Price?

You have just been hired as a product manager for a candy company. Your first assignment is to review the pricing structure used for all current products and to develop a price for a new box of candy called "Delectable Delights"— chocolate covered dried fruits, nuts, and crackers, packaged in a fancy tin.

WHAT WILL YOU DO?

What pricing concepts and strategies will you use to arrive at a price for the new box of candy?

Pricing Concepts

Basic Pricing Concepts

A major factor in determining the profitability of any product is price. You need to find the right price for your target market. Only then will you have a chance of being successful.

There are three basic concepts that you will want to consider in determining the price for any given product. They are cost-oriented pricing, demand-oriented pricing, and competition-oriented pricing.

■ Cost-Oriented Pricing

In cost-oriented pricing, marketers first calculate the costs of acquiring or making a product and their expenses of doing business; then they add their projected profit margin to these figures to arrive at a price. Markup pricing and cost-plus pricing are two of the most common methods of cost-oriented pricing.

MARKUP PRICING Markup pricing is used primarily by wholesalers and retailers who are involved in acquiring goods for resale. A markup is the difference between the price of an item and its cost that is generally expressed as a percentage. The markup on products must be high enough to cover the expenses of running the business and must include the intended profit. Details and calculations related to markup pricing are given in Chapter 27.

COST-PLUS PRICING In cost-plus pricing, all costs and expenses are calculated, and then the desired profit is added to arrive at a price. Very similar to markup pricing, cost-plus pricing is used primarily by manufacturers and service companies. The method is more sophisticated than markup pricing because all fixed and variable expenses are calculated separately for different goods and services. When a manufacturer is running at full capacity, the fixed expenses become a smaller percentage of total sales. This permits the manufacturer to charge a lower unit price for goods. Figure 26-1 on page 468 illustrates how cost-plus pricing can be used to calculate price.

■ Demand-Oriented Pricing

Marketers who use demand-oriented pricing attempt to determine what consumers are willing to pay for given goods and services. The key to this method of pricing is the consumer's perceived value of the item. The price set must be in line with this perception or the item will be priced too high or too low for the target market. Inappropriate pricing could cause the product to fail.

Another aspect of demand-oriented pricing involves demand differentials. Demand-oriented pricing is effective when there are few substitutes for an item and there is demand inelasticity. Consumers

● What You'll Learn

- The three basic pricing concepts involving cost, demand, and competition
- The concepts of pricing forward vs. pricing backward
- The idea of one-price policy vs. a flexible-price policy
- The two polar pricing policies for introducing a new product

● Why It's Important

After deciding on pricing goals, marketers must establish pricing strategies that are compatible with the rest of the marketing mix. Understanding the various options helps businesses effectively execute the difficult task of pricing products.

Key Terms

- markup pricing
- cost-plus pricing
- one-price policy
- flexible-price policy
- skimming pricing
- penetration pricing

FIGURE 26-1

Cost-Plus Pricing

Suburban Research Consultants	
Questionnaire Design and Printing	$3,500
Postage	400
Labor (40 hours at $30)	1,200
Refreshments	100
Expenses	350
Profit	950
Final Price to customer	**$6,500**

■ **Cost-plus Pricing** Cost-plus pricing breaks a price down into its component parts. *How might you relabel these entries to show the similarity between markup pricing and cost-plus pricing?*

are generally willing to pay higher prices because they believe an item is different from that offered by competitors. Companies try to achieve this status by developing brand loyalty.

Sometimes prices do not reflect major differences in the good or service, but reflect only the demand for the good or service. Theaters often charge different prices for tickets on the basis of the location of the seats. Front row seats may be significantly more expensive than those located high in a balcony. Everyone who buys a ticket will see the same performance but from a different vantage point. Telephone companies may charge higher rates for long-distance calls made during peak times. The cost of providing that service may not change, but the demand for the service increases.

Manufacturers may also create prices for different styles on the basis of a demand differential that is not a reflection of the cost of making the item but of the demand for a given style. White refrigerators may be priced at $360, but the same refrigerator in yellow or beige might sell for $450. A similar refrigerator with a stylish stainless steel exterior, while functionally identical to the other refrigerators, could command over $1,000. The difference in price is not based on an increase in the cost of producing refrigerators; rather, it is based on consumer demand for fashionable colors.

■ Competition-Oriented Pricing

Marketers who study their competitors to determine the prices of their products are using competition-oriented pricing. These marketers may elect to take one of three actions after learning their competitors' prices: price above the competition, price below the competition, or price in line with the competition (going-rate pricing). There is no relationship between cost and price or between demand and price in this pricing method—marketers simply set prices based on what their competitors charge.

Competitive-bid pricing, one type of competition-oriented pricing strategy, determines the price for a product based on bids submitted by competitors to a company or government agency. Laws require most government agencies to request bids based on certain specifications so they can select the company that offers the lowest prices. In such cases, some companies will elect to enter a very low bid in order to obtain the contract. They will accept a smaller profit in order to keep their employees working.

REAL WORLD MARKETING

The Power of Pricing

$7.2 billion in 1999! How did Ford manage to make more than any other automaker in history? With the help of a new pricing strategy. Even though Ford's U.S. market share fell almost two percent, it concentrated on selling cars that provided the most profit. Ford informed dealers which cars, options, and model packages made the most profit so they would stop pushing low-profit vehicles. The Ford Escort and Aspire, two low-margin vehicles, decreased in sales by 420,000 units, while the high-margin Crown Victorias and Explorers increased in sales by 600,000. Ford cut prices on its most profitable vehicles to spur demand, but not so much that it lost attractive margins.

Thinking Critically

How did Ford realize its best year in sales?

■ Combining Pricing Considerations

Most marketers use all three pricing policies to determine prices. Cost-oriented pricing helps marketers determine the price floor for a product—the lowest price for which it can be offered to still make a profit. Demand-oriented pricing determines a price range for the product that is defined by the price floor and the ceiling price (the highest amount consumers would pay). Competition-oriented pricing may be used to assure that the final price is in line with the company's pricing policies. Combining pricing considerations offers a good range within which a company can establish its selling price. If a company decides to go with the competition-oriented pricing strategy, they still know how much they can lower their prices if necessary based on the cost-oriented pricing figures.

Manufacturers may also consider the prices they will charge wholesalers and retailers for their products. This can be done in one of two ways. You can work backward from the final retail price to find the price for the wholesalers. You can also do this in reverse, working forward from costs and expenses to the final retail price. Figures 26-2 and 26-3 illustrate these two methods.

In Figure 26-2, which describes the steps in working backward, the retail price is set first, on the basis of consumer demand and competition. Next, the markups desired by the wholesalers and retailers are deducted based on the suggested retail price. Finally, the price that the manufacturer will charge the wholesaler is determined. Note that the price to the wholesaler must be high enough to cover the manufacturer's costs, any expenses, and the intended profit. Figure 26-3 illustrates the steps to working forward from the manufacturer's cost. Expenses and intended profit must be considered, and then the wholesalers' and retailers' markups are added to the manufacturer's price to arrive at the final selling price. Competition and consumer demand may be left out of the pricing decision if the price is set at this point. When the marketer does not consider these two factors, the final retail price may be higher than a competitor's and higher than the price consumers are willing to pay. You may have noticed that the methods used in Figures 26-2 and 26-3 produced the same final result. This is not always the case when using these techniques.

FIGURE 26-2

Pricing Backward from Retail Price

Estimated retail price	$50
Retailer's markup (40% of retail)	− $20
Wholesaler's price to retailer	**$30**
Wholesaler's markup (30% of wholesale)	− $9
Manufacturer's price to wholesaler (must cover costs, expenses, and profit)	**$21**

■ **Wholesale Price** To arrive at a wholesale price, a manufacturer can subtract all markups for channel members from the suggested retail price. *What problem would the above manufacturer have if its costs and expenses totaled $22? What might this manufacturer have to do?*

FIGURE 26-3

Pricing Forward from Manufacturer's Cost

Cost of producing item	$16.80
Manufacturer's expenses and profit (25% of cost)	+ $4.20
Manufacturer's price to wholesaler	**$21.00**
Wholesaler's markup (42.9% of cost)	+ $9.00
Wholesaler's price to retailer	$30.00
Retailer's markup (66.67% of cost)	+ $20.00
Retailer's price to consumer	**$50.00**

■ **Markups** Adding markups to cost is another way manufacturers can price their goods. Suppose in the example given here market research had shown that consumers would pay as much as $60 for the item. *What would the manufacturer's options be?*

■ **Name Your Price**
Priceline.com was one of the first Internet companies to conduct auctions for consumer goods and services. *What kind of pricing policy does such an Internet site have?*

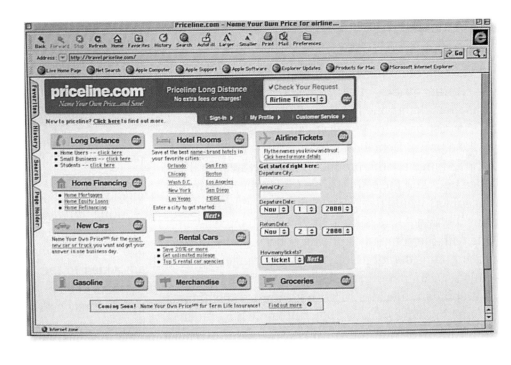

Pricing Policies and Product Life Cycle

A basic pricing decision every business must make is to choose between a one-price policy and a flexible-price policy. A business also needs to consider how a new product will be introduced into the marketplace. That choice will determine the pricing decisions that follow as the product moves through its life cycle.

■ One-Price vs. Flexible-Price Policy

A one-price policy is one in which all customers are charged the same price for the goods and services offered for sale. Prices are quoted to customers by means of signs and price tags and no deviations are permitted. Most of the retail stores that you are familiar with employ this policy.

A flexible-price policy is one in which customers pay different prices for the same type or amount of merchandise. This kind of policy permits customers to bargain for merchandise. The buyer or seller quotes a price and the bargaining begins. Most retail stores avoid using flexible pricing because it can cause legal problems. While many customers do not like the bargaining method, most expect to find a flexible-price strategy in effect with such goods as used cars, antiques, furniture, and selected jewelry.

The concept of flexible pricing is gaining popularity with the rise of e-tailing. Some Internet companies host auctions where buyers state the price they want to pay for an item and wait to see if they find a match. In other situations, sellers note the items they want to sell and let buyers bid on those items. Both situations employ a flexible-pricing policy. There are many advantages and disadvantages to consider when choosing a price policy. A one-price policy offers consistency and reliability. It also allows for retailers to estimate sales and profit because they know the set price. The flexible-price policy, on the other hand, is appealing to customers. It can be used by sellers to generate new customers. It also allows the seller to adjust its prices to meet the competition. On the other hand, a flexible-price policy does not offer consistent profits. It also may turn off some customers who prefer not to haggle to get the best price.

■ Product Life Cycle

Products move through four stages: introduction, growth, maturity, and decline. When products are no longer profitable to a company, they may be dropped from the line. Pricing plays an important role in this sequence of events.

NEW PRODUCT INTRODUCTION A business may elect to price a new product above, in-line, or below its competitors depending on the philosophy of the business and market conditions. When a going-rate strategy is not used to introduce a new product, two polar methods may be used—skimming pricing or penetration pricing.

Skimming pricing is a pricing policy that sets a very high price for a new product. This kind of policy can be used any time demand is greater than supply. Such a policy is designed to capitalize on the high demand for a product during its introductory period. Laptop computers were originally very expensive when they were available from relatively few retailers. When they were first introduced, the target market was technology aficionados and people with high incomes who were willing to pay for the convenience of having a very small computer. At this stage, the high price is geared toward trendsetters, who are generally willing to pay higher prices in order to have or use a new product.

Businesses that use this method recognize that the price will have to be lowered once the market for the product changes to more price-conscious customers. While the product is hot, the business will enjoy a high profit margin. This profit may cover the research and development costs incurred in designing the product and creating a prestigious image. Another advantage of skimming pricing is that the price may be lowered without insulting the target market.

One disadvantage of skimming pricing is that the high initial price generally attracts competition. Once other firms begin to compete successfully, the price will have to be lowered. Another disadvantage becomes apparent if the initial price is far above what consumers (even the trendsetters) are willing to pay. In that case, sales will be lost and profits diminished because the market will not take the item seriously.

Penetration pricing is the opposite of skimming pricing—the initial price for a new product is set

Electronic Frontiers

Price Adjusting Using the Extranet

Need to communicate a price change quickly to clients and manufacturers? Help is on the way in the form of the "extranet." Companies are creating private networks, or extranets, that electronically link them with their suppliers and customers. These systems make it possible to get precise information on inventory, costs, prices, and demand at any given moment. In the past, companies with a large product line were literally "at a loss" when making price adjustments. It could take months for price adjustments to filter down to distributors, retailers, and salespeople. Changing prices resulted in a significant cost known as the "menu cost." Research, market share, and potential lost sales are all factors of menu cost. Streamlined networks, like extranets, reduce menu cost and time to near zero. The best news—it's already benefiting consumers.

Thinking Critically
Why would reducing menu costs be important to consumers?

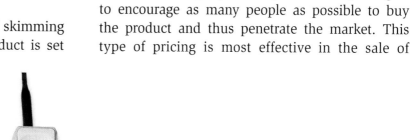

very low. The purpose of penetration pricing is to encourage as many people as possible to buy the product and thus penetrate the market. This type of pricing is most effective in the sale of

■ **The Pricing Cycle** A product's life cycle stage has a bearing on its price. *When these products were first introduced in the marketplace, which type of pricing policy do you think the company used—skimming or penetration pricing? Why? How are the older models priced now?*

price-sensitive products (items with elastic demand). Sony used a penetration pricing strategy when it introduced its first PlayStation game console in 1995. The company's strategy was to saturate the market with low priced PlayStation consoles in an effort to gain market share. Such a strategy deterred competitors and attracted price-conscious customers.

In order to penetrate the market quickly with penetration pricing, mass production, distribution, and promotion must be incorporated into the marketing strategy. The product should take hold in a short period of time. This allows the marketer to save on fixed expenses (through mass production) and to increase the profit margin (through volume sales).

The biggest advantage of penetration pricing is its ability to capture a large number of customers in a relatively short period of time. This blocks competition from other companies. Another advantage is its ability to move into a market in which the leaders are offering higher prices and lure away large numbers of customers.

A major disadvantage of penetration pricing becomes apparent if the product is not in high demand. In that case, the lower price will cause the marketer to suffer a bigger loss than it would have if a higher initial price had been set.

Understanding where a product is in its life cycle is useful in predicting sales. The decision regarding whether to use a penetration pricing strategy during the introductory stage willl influence the product's sales throughout the rest of its life cycle.

OTHER PRODUCT STAGES Pricing during subsequent periods in a product's life cycle is determined by which pricing method was originally used—skimming or penetration. Sales increase rapidly during the penetration stage, and total costs per unit decrease because volume absorbs fixed costs. The main goal of marketers is to keep products in this stage as long as possible.

Sales of products introduced with skimming pricing should be monitored closely. Once sales begin to level off, the price should be lowered to appeal to the price-conscious target market. Prices may lower drastically if the product is considered a fad.

Very little price change will be made in the growth stage for products introduced with penetration pricing. Other promotions will be used to keep sales high.

When demand decreases and sales begin to level off, competition is generally very keen. At this stage, marketers look for new market segments to hold the prices for their products. A baking soda marketer may stress non-cooking uses for baking soda, such as deodorizing or cleaning refrigerators.

The marketer's principal goal during the maturity stage is to stretch the life of a product. Some companies revitalize products in this stage by adding new

BRIGHT IDEAS

Priced to Sell on eBay

How great it would be if one could collect Pez dispensers and interact with other collectors over the Internet? That question, posed by an avid Pez dispenser collector and wife of an early Internet enthusiast, gave birth to eBay. Pierre Omidyar ran with his wife's idea to give people a central location to buy and sell unique items and to meet other users with similar interests. Omidyar lauched eBay in September 1995 and it has since grown to become the world's largest online trading community. It has successfully developed an efficient one-to-one online auction trading system in which buyers determine their own prices. eBay features more than 4,320 categories of merchandise and some 4 million new auctions daily.

Thinking Creatively
Auctions allow users to determine pricing. Why is this pricing strategy effective?

features or improvements. Another option is to seek new markets in other nations in the global marketplace. Products that have been made obsolete in the U.S. by technological advances may be in the introductory or growth stage in other places. Photocopiers and fax machines are examples. Older or superseded models are reconditioned and sold in other countries. By using techniques like these, marketers can significantly extend a product's life cycle. When such efforts are not successful, however, a product moves into its decline.

Sales decrease and profit margins are reduced in the decline stage. Companies are forced to reduce the price to generate sales. To maintain profitability, marketers try to reduce manufacturing costs or cut back on advertising and other promotional activities. Once a product is no longer profitable, it is phased out.

You can see how important pricing is during every stage of a product's life cycle. If all of the stages aren't well considered, a company can lose profits or see a new product experience failure instead of success. On the other hand, if a company implements a well-thought out pricing plan and carries it through, it is much more likely to experience success.

Life In The Diverse

MARKETPLACE

Same Snacks, Different Price

How much would you guess that someone would pay for a snack-size bag of Doritos? $.50? Maybe even $.75? How about $.16? That is the strategy that PepsiCo Inc. took when they took their goods to Mexico. When pricing goods for sales internationally, it is important to keep in mind the income of those consumers and the exchange rate. In most developing nations, income levels and personal spending money is limited compared to the United States. PepsiCo Inc. is just one company that has responded to this with low prices and high availability.

Thinking Critically

Is it fair to U.S. consumers that prices are lower in other countries?

26.1 ASSESSMENT

Reviewing Key Terms and Concepts

1. Name the two most common methods of cost-oriented pricing.

2. Explain how cost-oriented, demand-oriented, and competition-oriented pricing concepts can be combined to determine price.

3. What two methods may manufacturers use when considering the price to charge wholesalers and retailers? How do they differ?

4. What is the difference between a one-price policy and a flexible-price policy?

5. Name and explain two polar pricing methods that may be used when a new product is introduced into the market.

Thinking Critically

6. Would you use skimming pricing or penetration pricing to introduce a new cookie called Coconut Surprise? Why?

Integrating Academic Skills

7. **COMMUNICATION** Prepare a two-minute speech on the pros and cons of a new Internet company using either a one-price policy or a flexible-price policy. Explain why you think the particular policy will be most effective.

Setting Prices

Pricing Techniques

Marketers use specific pricing techniques to determine pricing. These techniques include psychological pricing and discount pricing.

■ Psychological Pricing

Psychological pricing refers to techniques that create an illusion for customers or that make shopping easier for them. In either case, psychological pricing techniques appeal to particular market segments because of their shared perceptions and buying habits. Among common psychological pricing techniques are odd-even pricing, prestige pricing, multiple-unit pricing, bundle pricing, promotional pricing, everyday low prices (EDLP), and price lining.

ODD-EVEN PRICING A technique that involves setting prices that all end in either odd or even numbers is known as odd-even pricing. The psychological principle on which the technique is based is that odd numbers ($.79, $9.95, $699) convey a bargain image. Even numbers ($10, $50, $100) convey a quality image. Whether or not this is true, you will find that many marketers follow the odd-even technique in an effort to project a certain image.

PRESTIGE PRICING Prestige pricing sets higher-than-average prices to suggest status and prestige to the consumer. As noted in Chapter 25, many customers assume that higher prices mean higher quality and are willing to pay more for certain goods and services. Rolls Royce automobiles, Waterford crystal, and Lenox china are all prestige priced.

MULTIPLE-UNIT PRICING Some businesses have found that pricing items in multiples, such as 3 for $.99, is better than selling the same items at $.33 each. Multiple-unit pricing suggests a bargain and helps to increase sales volume.

BUNDLE PRICING Including several complementary products in a package that is sold at a single price is bundle pricing. The one price for all the complementary products and the main item is lower than if a customer purchased each item separately. Computer companies use bundle pricing when they include software and Internet service in the sale of a computer. Travel services use bundling when a single price is offered for a package that includes airfare, hotel accommodations, and meals. Bundling helps businesses sell items (parts of the package) that they may not have sold otherwise, which increases their sales and revenue.

● What You'll Learn

- The various pricing techniques
- The steps in setting prices

● Why It's Important

Now that you have studied pricing concepts and policies, it is time to look at the special pricing techniques that help companies achieve their business goals. Then you will put all of that information into a single process: the steps for determining price.

Key Terms

- psychological pricing
- odd-even pricing
- prestige pricing
- multiple-unit pricing
- bundle pricing
- promotional pricing
- everyday low prices (EDLP)
- price lining
- discount pricing
- trade discounts
- seasonal discounts

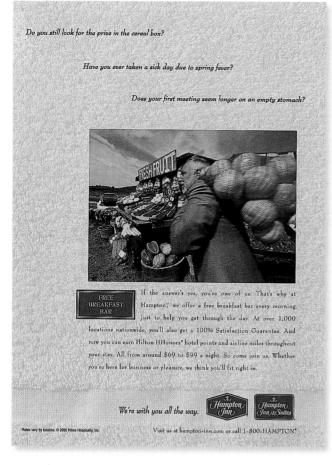

Do you still look for the prize in the cereal box?

Have you ever taken a sick day due to spring fever?

Does your first meeting seem longer on an empty stomach?

FRESH FRUIT

FREE BREAKFAST BAR

If the answer's yes, you're one of us. That's why at Hampton, we offer a free breakfast bar every morning. Just to help you get through the day. At over 1,000 locations nationwide, you'll also get a 100% Satisfaction Guarantee. And now you can earn Hilton HHonors® hotel points and airline miles throughout your stay. All from around $69 to $99 a night. So come join us. Whether you're here for business or pleasure, we think you'll fit right in.

We're with you all the way.

Hampton Inn   Hampton Inn & Suites

Rates vary by location. © 2000 Hilton Hospitality, Inc.   Visit us at hampton-inn.com or call 1-800-HAMPTON®

■ **Even or Odd?** Pricing techniques include psychological pricing in odd numbers. *Why is it referred to as psychological pricing?*

PROMOTIONAL PRICING The psychological technique of promotional pricing is generally used in conjunction with sales promotions when prices are lower than average. Two basic types of promotional pricing are loss-leader pricing (discussed in Chapter 25) and special-event pricing.

As you recall, loss-leader pricing is used to increase store traffic by offering very popular items of merchandise for sale at low prices. In special-event pricing, items are reduced in price for a short period of time, based on a specific happening. Some examples of this technique can be found in back-to-school specials, Presidents' Day sales, dollar days, or anniversary sales. At the end of a season, businesses also run clearance sales to get rid of old merchandise and make room for new merchandise.

Other promotional pricing techniques involving rebates, coupons, and special discounts, will be covered later in this chapter. All types of businesses may offer special promotional discounts to help boost sales at any time. The main characteristic of promotional pricing is that it is temporary—after the promotion ends, prices go back to normal.

EVERYDAY LOW PRICES (EDLP) Everyday low prices (EDLP) are low prices that are set on a consistent basis with no intention of raising them or offering discounts in the future. Everyday low prices are not as deeply discounted as promotional prices might be, which creates sales stability. Other benefits include reduced promotional expenses and reduced losses due to discounting. Wal-Mart is known for its EDLP policy.

PRICE LINING Price lining is a special pricing technique that requires a store to offer all merchandise in a given category at certain prices. A store might price all of its blouses at $25, $35, and $50.

When deciding on price lines, marketers must be careful to make the price differences great enough to represent low, middle, and high prices for the category of goods being offered. Price lines of $25, $26, $27, and $28, for example, would confuse customers because they would have difficulty discerning their basis. (Slight price differences translate into equally slight quality differences.) When price lines are properly drawn, customers can easily compare items.

An advantage of price lining is that the target market is fully aware of the price range of products in a given store. This helps the store maintain its image. In addition, price lining makes merchandising and selling easier for salespeople, who can readily draw comparisons between floor and ceiling prices. The technique also helps salespeople trade up, or offer a higher-priced, better-quality item to a customer to better satisfy the customer's needs.

Manufacturers use a variation of price lining in that they offer three tiers of prices for various models or brands in the same product category. The upper tier is for better quality premium brands, the middle tier for average priced brands, and the lower tier for price-conscious customers.

■ Discount Pricing

Discount pricing involves the seller's offering reductions from the usual price. Such reductions are generally granted for the buyer's performance of certain functions. These discounts include cash, quantity, trade, and seasonal discounts, as well as promotional discounts and allowances.

V 12 ENGINE, LIKE THAT FOUND
IN BMW'S LE MANS WINNER.

PHENOMENAL DRIVING ROAD,
FOUND BY NAVIGATION SYSTEM.

DRIVER'S FAVORITE GEAR, FOUND BY
ADAPTIVE TRANSMISSION CONTROL.

NIRVANA, AS FOUND
BY DRIVER

The New 2000 7 Series. Bristling with a host of ingenious technological features amid sophisticated
elegance, the 7 Series continues to live by the credo that no amount of refinement can ever compensate
for a lack of pure driving zeal. Starting at $62,970. Call 1-800-334-4BMW. Or visit www.bmwusa.com

The Ultimate Driving Machine

■ **Prestige Pricing** The practice of setting higher-than-average prices to suggest status and prestige to the consumer is called prestige pricing. *Do you think prestige pricing is being employed in this ad?*

CASH DISCOUNTS Cash discounts are offered to buyers to encourage them to pay their bills quickly. Terms are generally written on the invoice, for example, 2/10, net 30 means that a 2 percent discount is granted if the bill is paid in 10 days. The buyer who does not take advantage of the discount must pay the full amount within 30 days.

QUANTITY DISCOUNTS Quantity discounts are offered to buyers for placing large orders. Sellers benefit from large orders through the lower selling costs involved in one transaction as opposed to several small transactions. Quantity discounts also offer buyers an incentive to purchase more merchandise than they originally intended to purchase.

There are two types of quantity discounts—noncumulative and cumulative. Noncumulative quantity discounts are offered on one order, while cumulative quantity discounts are offered on all orders over a specified period of time. Cumulative discounts may be granted for purchases made over six months, for example, in which case all purchases for that period are used to determine the quantity discount offered. In other cases, buyers may be required to sign a contract that guarantees a certain level of business. Advertisers who agree to use a specified number of column inches in their newspaper ads might be charged contract rates that reflect usage. Generally, the more you advertise, the less you pay per column inch.

TRADE DISCOUNTS Trade discounts are not really discounts at all but rather the way manufacturers quote prices to wholesalers and retailers. Many manufacturers establish suggested retail prices, or list prices, for their items. They grant members of the channel of distribution discounts from the list price for performing their respective functions. A manufacturer might grant wholesalers a 40 percent discount from the list price and retailers a 30 percent discount.

The manufacturer might also quote the discounts in series, such as 25 and 10 percent for retailers and wholesalers, respectively. Series, or chain, discounts are calculated in sequence, as shown below. The example is based on a list price of $50.

Retailer's discount	$50 \times .25 = \$12.50$
Cost to retailer	$50 - \$12.50 = \$37.50$
Wholesaler's discount	$37.50 \times .10 = \$ 3.75$
Cost to wholesaler	$37.50 - \$3.75 = \$33.75$

Cleaning Up With Promotional Pricing

Dirty laundry makes money—proven by the $4.7 billion laundry detergent market. Procter & Gamble departed from its everyday low price policy to regain market share when it offered off-invoice allowances to retailers for Downy fabric softener and detergent brands Tide, Cheer, Era, and Gain.

This six-month promotional pricing special increased orders, and retailers passed the discounts to their customers through special promotions and more consistent lower prices. Since detergents are often used as loss leaders, the off-invoice discounts allow retailers to run their own promotions without taking a loss on the sale of those items.

In addition to the promotional pricing, Proctor & Gamble also used coupons by dropping FSIs (free standing inserts) during the same period.

Stiff competition from competitor Unilever followed, as it slashed prices on Surf, Wisk, and All brands from 6 percent to 18 percent. Unilever's actions, which made reductions directly to the price, varied greatly from the actions of Procter & Gamble. While Procter & Gamble ran promotions to gain customers, Unilever changed prices permanently. As pricing changes spur more companies into action, it is the consumer who wins—with low prices and fresh-smelling clothes!

Case Study Review

1. What prompted Procter & Gamble to depart from its EDLP pricing policy?
2. What else did Procter & Gamble do to boost sales during that six-month period?

A MATTER OF ETHICS

3. Which pricing policy is more ethical—Proctor & Gamble's special time-limited promotional pricing or Unilever's permanent price reductions?

In series discounts, note that the wholesaler's discount is based on the retailer's discount, not the original list price.

SEASONAL DISCOUNTS Seasonal discounts are offered to buyers willing to buy at a time outside the customary buying season. Manufacturers offer discounts to obtain orders for seasonal merchandise early so that production facilities and labor can be utilized throughout the year.

Other businesses use seasonal discounts to cut anticipated costs. Many retailers, for example, drastically reduce prices on Christmas cards and decorations the day after Christmas. Such retailers prefer to sell this merchandise at a lower markup than pay the costs of warehousing it until the following year. A variation on this device is used by vacation resorts. They offer vacationers lower rates to encourage use of resort facilities during the off-season.

FIGURE 26-4

THE SIX STEPS FOR DETERMINING PRICE

Marketers usually follow six steps in setting the price of a new product. They determine pricing objectives, study costs, estimate consumer demand, study the competition's prices, decide on a pricing strategy, and set the price. Now that you have studied pricing concepts, policies, and techniques, you should be able to establish a price for a given good or service. Imagine that you are the product manager for a candy company and you have been assigned the task of pricing a new box of candy called "Delectable Delights." Evaluate the relevant factors and set an initial price for a box of Delectable Delights.

1 **DETERMINE PRICING OBJECTIVES**

What is your purpose in setting a price for your product? Do you want to increase sales volume or sales revenue? Establish a prestigious image for your product and your company? Increase your market share and market position? Answering these questions will help you keep your prices in line with other marketing decisions.

2 **STUDY COSTS**

Since the main reason for being in business is to make a profit, give careful consideration to the costs involved in making or acquiring the goods or services you will offer for sale. Determine whether and how you can reduce costs without affecting the quality or image of your product.

3 **ESTIMATE DEMAND**

Employ market research techniques to estimate consumer demand. The key to pricing goods and services is to set prices at the level consumers expect to pay. In many cases, those prices are directly related to demand.

4 STUDY COMPETITION

Investigate your competitors to see what prices they are charging for similar goods and services. Study the market leader. What is the range of prices from the ceiling price to the price floor? Will you price your goods lower than, equal to, or higher than your competitors'?

5 DECIDE ON A PRICING STRATEGY

You may decide to price your product higher than the competition's because you believe your product is superior. You may decide to set a lower price with the understanding that you will raise it once the product is accepted in the marketplace.

6 SET PRICE

After you have evaluated all the foregoing factors, apply the pricing techniques that match your strategy and set an initial price. Be prepared to monitor that price and evaluate its effectiveness as conditions in the market change.

PROMOTIONAL DISCOUNTS AND ALLOWANCES

Promotional discounts are offered to wholesalers and retailers willing to advertise or promote a manufacturer's products. The discount may take the form of a percentage reduction in price or free merchandise. Another alternative, discussed in Chapter 19, is cooperative advertising in which the manufacturer and the retailer share the costs of advertising, with the manufacturer paying the lion's share.

Some kinds of promotional discounts are offered directly to the consumer. As you learned in Chapter 17, a rebate is a partial refund on the cost of a particular item from the manufacturer. To receive the rebate, a customer buys the product and then sends in a rebate form along with the product proof of purchase and a store receipt. Manufacturers offer rebates to wholesalers, and retailers too, for purchasing certain quantities of goods during special promotions.

Trade-in allowances also go directly to the buyer. Customers are offered a price reduction if they sell back an old model of the product they are purchasing. Consumers are generally offered trade-in allowances when purchasing new cars or major appliances. Companies are usually granted such allowances when purchasing machinery or equipment.

■ **Promotional Pricing** Often pricing is tied to special promotional events, such as the 4th of July. *What is the main characteristic of promotional pricing?*

26.2 ASSESSMENT

Reviewing Key Terms and Concepts

1. How are odd-even, prestige, multiple-unit, and bundle pricing related? Different?

2. What is the main difference between promotional pricing and everyday low prices?

3. What is the key factor in deciding on price lines?

4. Name five types of discount pricing techniques.

5. List the six steps in setting prices.

Thinking Critically

6. Johnson & Johnson promoted its baby shampoo to adult male athletes by touting the product's gentleness, even when used every day. At what stage in the shampoo's life cycle do you think this promotion took place? What do you think Johnson & Johnson was trying to accomplish by promoting its baby shampoo to adult males?

Integrating Academic Skills

7. **MATH** Determine the price a wholesaler would pay for an item with a list price of $100 if the series trade discounts were 40 percent and 10 percent for retailers and wholesalers, respectively.

Careers in Marketing

Mike McKenzie
Store Manager
Alternate World Comics

Career Facts

What does your job entail?

"I manage a small business, so I am responsible for all phases of that business. I control inventory, manage employees, create shipping schedules, and most importantly, keep the customers happy. As companies grow, they tend to become less efficient; my job is to impart a 'shared vision' to the employees, so that we are all on the right track. Enthusiasm is an important quality in this job. "

What training would you recommend for students?

"When you are the best at something, for example chemistry, you might keep getting promoted until you are the head chemist. The best chemist in the world, however, doesn't necessarily make the best manager. Managers need training, and anyone who wants to go into business needs to know that."

What do you like most about your job?

"I enjoy the daily interaction with the customers. It is really interesting, especially at this time in the comic book industry. The excitement is contagious and it is hard to not be a part of it. It is a great feeling to be able to impart 'industry buzz' to fans. Assuring that people are getting what they want and helping them pursue their hobby is the truly exciting part of selling. People visit stores for more than just a product—and with comics, you can actually talk about the product in the store and develop some really interesting conversations and friendships."

What is your key to success?

"If I knew what that was, I would put it in a bottle and sell it! I would have to say luck and preparation have been my greatest assets. As a manager, you also have to pay attention to every detail of a business. As companies grow, they tend to forget the basics, which are always important!"

Education and Training: A store manager should have a minimum of a high school diploma and good sales experience. Courses in marketing, business administration, consumer education, accounting, psychology, and data processing are recommended. Many companies provide on-the-job training and instruction.

Aptitudes, Abilities, and Skills: Above average communication skills, a good understanding of advertising and display concepts, and average clerical and numerical skills are necessary. Many store managers are required to work weekends and evenings, often working more than 40 hours per week.

Career Outlook: Faster than average growth is expected for store management positions in the next five years.

Career Path: Experience at related jobs such as sales or buying may lead to management positions within a store. It may be necessary to move from a small store to a larger store to advance. Some store managers become divisional or regional managers.

Thinking Critically

Your boss tells you that to become a successful store manager you must be a "Jack of all trades." What does she mean?

Chapter 26 ASSESSMENT

VOCABULARY REVIEW

Write a one-page paper about a fictitious company's pricing practices using ten terms from the list below.

- markup pricing
- cost-plus pricing
- one-price policy
- flexible-price policy
- skimming pricing
- penetration pricing
- psychological pricing
- odd-even pricing
- prestige pricing
- multiple-unit pricing
- bundle pricing
- promotional pricing
- everyday low prices (EDLP)
- price lining
- discount pricing
- trade discounts
- seasonal discounts

FACT AND IDEA REVIEW

1. Name two common methods of cost-oriented pricing. (26.1)

2. How does competition-oriented pricing differ from demand-oriented pricing? (26.1)

3. Once sales level off after product introduction with skimming pricing, what happens to price? (26.1)

4. During the maturity stage of a product's life cycle, what do marketers do to hold the price? (26.1)

5. What psychological principle is associated with odd-even pricing? (26.2)

6. What are the advantages of price lining to customers and to salespeople? (26.2)

7. Why are cash discounts offered to buyers? (26.2)

8. Are trade discounts really discounts? Explain. (26.2)

9. What are seasonal discounts? Why are they offered by manufacturers? By retailers? (26.2)

THINKING CRITICALLY

1. What ill effects could a flexible pricing policy have on customer relations?

2. Select a product and decide what product life cycle stage it is in at the present time. Provide rationale based on its price history and the industry.

3. Why does bundling discourage comparison shopping?

4. If you were a small business with little storage space, which type of quantity discount would be better for you—cumulative or noncumulative? Why?

BUILDING WORKPLACE SKILLS

1. **Human Relations** You work for a retail jeweler who has a flexible-price policy for selected customers. You are alone in the store and ring up the sale of a steady customer. The customer tells you that you did not deduct the customary 20 percent discount. What would you do?

2. **Technology** Set up a spreadsheet that will automatically calculate 20 percent, 30 percent, and 50 percent discounts during special promotions. Assume this will be input into the sales terminal so salespeople will not have to do the calculations in their heads.

1. **Determining Suggested Retail Price** You are product manager for Delectable Delights candy company. The cost to make and market a one-pound tin of Delectable Delights is $4, and the manufacturer hopes to make at least 25 percent profit on the product. Wholesalers and retailers both use a 40 percent markup but are happy when it is higher. Competitors have suggested retail prices between $8.99 and $12.99 per pound. You need to establish the suggested retail price for the product. Use a word processing program to write a memo to your boss exploring your decision. Tell if you are using skimming or penetration pricing, and odd or even pricing. Include the math calculations and prices for the wholesalers.

2. **Understanding Pricing Strategies** The student council purchased 300 tee shirts at $2.50 each as a fund raiser. There are 100 shirts each in three different styles (popular, average, not popular). You need to decide the suggested price for the tee shirts that will generate at least $700. Decide what psychological pricing techniques would be most appropriate. Anticipate how your plan would change if you knew 50 shirts would not sell at all. Use a spreadsheet program to generate possible prices and profits. Use a word processing program to prepare a report with your final pricing plan and rationale.

LINKING SCHOOL TO WORK

Basic Thinking and Information Skills Review the psychological and discount pricing techniques in this chapter in relation to the practices you have observed on your, or a friend's, job. Cite examples of every concept used by the firm. Prepare written and oral reports on your findings.

THE DECA CONNECTION

Role Play: Product Manager

Situation You are to assume the role of product manager. The toy department buyer (judge) has asked for your opinion of a new dinosaur electronic game. There are three models, with the cost (what the retail store pays) ranging from $15.75 to $20.25.

Activity At what retail price(s) should the new items sell? Support your position with known pricing strategies.

Evaluation You will be evaluated on how well you meet the following performance indicators:

- Set prices
- Explain factors affecting pricing decisions
- Explain the nature and scope of the pricing function
- Select promotional pricing strategies used to adjust base prices
- Persuade others

inter NET CONNECTION

What Price to Charge?
You want competitive prices at the electronics store you own. Competition has been keen with brick and mortar retailers, mass merchandisers, and online shopping Web sites. You need to review your prices in relation to competition.

Connect
- Research your competition in your local market and on the Internet.
- Identify the price for three specific products sold by all of your competitors.
- Determine the pricing strategies used by two of your competitors.

Pricing Math

Marketing: What It Takes

Pricing for Profitability

As the new assistant manager of a bookstore, you have been assigned the task of checking retail prices, handling markdowns for sales events, and approving employee discounts. You realize that in this position, you are now responsible for the profitability of the store.

WHAT WILL YOU DO?

How will you calculate the new sale prices and the amount employees will pay for purchases? How will you communicate the relationship between the store's profitability and retail prices?

Calculating Prices

Profit vs. Markup

A businessperson says "We made a profit of $50—buying the radio for $100 and selling it for $150." The businessperson is only partially correct. The difference between the retail price of $150 (which is equal to 100 percent) and the $100 cost ($66\frac{2}{3}$ percent) is the markup of $50 ($33\frac{1}{3}$ percent), not the profit. Profit is the amount left from revenue after the costs of the merchandise and expenses have been paid. The markup on an item, however, is similar to gross profit. Gross profit is the difference between sales revenue and the cost of goods sold. Expenses must still be deducted in order to get net (actual) profit. Therefore, a business must have a markup high enough to cover expenses and provide the profit sought to be successful.

Let's compare a profit and loss statement to retail markup by using the above figures and sales of 300 items. On a profit and loss statement, sales revenue would be $45,000 (100 percent), less cost of goods sold of $30,000 ($66\frac{2}{3}$ percent), which would equal gross profit of $15,000 ($33\frac{1}{3}$ percent). If expenses were $9,000, the gross profit ($33\frac{1}{3}$ percent) would be enough to cover expenses (20 percent) and earn a net profit of $6,000 or $13\frac{1}{3}$ percent ($6,000 divided by $45,000 or $33\frac{1}{3}$ percent − 20 percent = $13\frac{1}{3}$ percent).

■ Basic Markup Calculations

Retailers and wholesalers use the same formulas to calculate markup. We will use only retail prices here to make these formulas easier to understand. Note, however, that wholesale prices can be substituted in any of the formulas.

The most basic pricing formula is the one for calculating retail price. It states in mathematical terms a relationship that has been discussed in the last two chapters—retail price is a combination of cost and markup. Knowing these two figures will enable you to calculate retail price. Here's how.

$$\text{Cost (C)} + \text{markup (MU)} = \text{retail price (RP)}$$
$$\$14 \quad + \quad \$6 \quad = \quad \$20$$

Two other formulas can be derived from this basic formula—cost and markup, respectively.

$$\text{Retail price (RP)} - \text{markup (MU)} = \text{cost (C)}$$
$$\$20 \quad - \quad \$6 \quad = \quad \$14$$

$$\text{Retail price (RP)} - \text{cost (C)} = \text{markup (MU)}$$
$$\$20 \quad - \quad \$14 \quad = \quad \$6$$

You will rely on these three formulas throughout this chapter. The formulas and their terms will be cited in abbreviated form (as C + MU = RP) from this point on.

● What You'll Learn

- **How a firm's net profit or loss is related to pricing**

- **How to calculate dollar and percentage markup based on cost or retail**

- **How to calculate markdown in dollars and how to determine sale price and maintained markup**

● Why It's Important

Now that you understand the principles of pricing, it is time to learn how to perform the mathematical calculations needed to determine prices. You learned earlier that pricing is related to a company's profitability; now you will learn how they are related.

Key Terms

- **gross profit**
- **maintained markup**

PRACTICE 1

Use the retail price formula and its variations to do the following problems.

1. A calculator costs AB Products $15, and the markup is $10. What is its retail price?

2. A tennis racket retails for $175, and its markup is $85. What is its cost?

Note: Answers to all practice sets in this chapter are on page 496.

■ Percentage Markup

In the examples shown, markup was expressed as a dollar amount. In most business situations, however, the markup figure is generally expressed as a percentage. We will distinguish between these two forms of markup (dollar and percentage) throughout the rest of the chapter. In calculations, dollar markup will be represented with the abbreviation MU($) and percentage markup with the abbreviation MU(%).

Expressing markup in either dollar or percentage form is not the only choice that wholesalers and retailers have in making markup calculations. They may also elect to compute their markup on either cost or retail price if they choose to use the percentage form.

Most choose to base the markup on retail price for three reasons. First, the markup on the retail price sounds like a smaller amount. This sounds better to customers and may encourage customers to buy because the price seems reasonable. Second, future markdowns and discounts are calculated on a retail basis. Third, profits are generally calculated on sales revenue. It makes sense to use markup on retail prices when comparing and analyzing data that play a role in a firm's profits.

Here are the steps that are used to calculate the percentage markup on retail. They will be easier to follow if we have an example to work with. Assume that you want to calculate the percentage markup on a pair of bookends that Wright's Department Store stocks for $49.50 (cost) and sells for $82.50 (retail price).

STEP 1 Determine the dollar markup.
RP − C = MU($)
$82.50 − $49.50 = $33.00

STEP 2 To change the dollar markup to the percentage markup, divide it by the retail price. The result will be a decimal.
MU($)/RP = MU(%) on retail
$33.00 divided by $82.50 = .4

STEP 3 Change the decimal to a percentage. This figure is the percentage markup on retail.
.40 = 40%
Shift decimal point two places right.

Retailers may find the percentage markup on cost to be helpful. The calculation is the same, except for Step 2. Using the same facts from above, you calculate the percentage markup on cost as follows:

STEP 1 Determine the dollar markup.
RP − C = MU($)
$82.50 − $49.50 = $33.00

STEP 2 To change the dollar markup to the percentage markup, divide by cost.
MU($)/C = MU(%) on cost
$33.00 divided by $49.50 = .6667

STEP 3 Change the decimal to a percentage. This figure is the percentage markup on cost.
.6667 = 66.67%
Shift decimal point two places right.

PRACTICE 2

Calculate the percentage markup in each of these situations.

1. The retail price of a coffee mug is $10.99 and the cost is $6.50. What is the percentage markup based on cost price? Based on retail price?

2. An electric sander costs $69.74, and its markup is $23.25. Find its percentage markup on cost price. Calculate the retail price, and then calculate its percentage markup on retail price.

3. A gallery sells a framed print for $100, and its markup is $50. What is its percentage markup on cost price? On retail price?

FIGURE 27-1

Markup Equivalents

Markup on Retail	Markup on Cost	Markup on Retail	Markup on Cost
4.8%	5.0%	25.0%	33.3%
5.0	5.3	26.0	35.0
6.0	6.4	27.0	37.0
7.0	7.5	27.3	37.5
8.0	8.7	28.0	39.0
9.0	10.0	28.5	40.0
10.0	11.1	29.0	40.9
10.7	12.0	30.0	42.9
11.0	12.4	31.0	45.0
11.1	12.5	32.0	47.1
12.0	13.6	33.3	50.0
12.5	14.3	34.0	51.5
13.0	15.0	35.0	53.9
14.0	16.3	35.5	55.0
15.0	17.7	36.0	56.3
16.0	19.1	37.0	58.8
16.7	20.0	37.5	60.0
17.0	20.5	38.0	61.3
17.5	21.2	39.0	64.0
18.0	22.0	39.5	65.5
18.5	22.7	40.0	66.7
19.0	23.5	41.0	70.0
20.0	25.0	42.0	72.4
21.0	26.6	42.8	75.0
22.0	28.2	44.4	80.0
22.5	29.0	46.1	85.0
23.0	29.9	47.5	90.0
23.1	30.0	48.7	95.0
24.0	31.6	50.0	100.0

■ **Markup Equivalents Table** A markup equivalents table, one page of which is shown here, allows users to quickly convert markups on retail to markups on cost and vice versa. *A 37.5% markup on retail is equal to what markup percentage on cost?*

■ Markup Equivalents Table

You would notice a correlation between the two figures if you calculated enough problems using the formulas for computing percentage markup based on cost and retail. This correlation led marketers to develop a calculation aid called a markup equivalents table, a portion of which is shown in Figure 27-1. The table lists markup percentages based on retail and the equivalent percentages based on cost. To use the table, you locate the percentage markup on retail and read its cost equivalent in the adjacent column or vice versa.

> **PRACTICE 3**
>
> Use the markup equivalents table to answer the following questions.
>
> 1. When the markup on retail is 28.5 percent, what is its equivalent markup on cost?
>
> 2. The markup on cost is 60 percent; what is its equivalent markup on retail?

■ Cost Method of Pricing

Sometimes marketers know only the cost of an item and its markup on cost. In such a situation, they use the cost method of pricing.

Consider a board game that a toy store buys for $8.50 and sells for cost plus a 40-percent markup on cost. To arrive at the retail price, follow these steps:

STEP 1 Determine the dollar markup on cost. Multiply the cost by the percentage markup on cost in decimal form.

$$C \times MU(\%) = MU(\$)$$
$$\$8.50 \times .40 = \$3.40$$

STEP 2 Add the dollar markup to the cost to get the retail price.

$$C + MU(\$) = RP$$
$$\$8.50 + \$3.40 = \$11.90$$

Often, the situation isn't that simple. Suppose you have the cost, but the only markup figure you know is the markup on retail. What will you do? You cannot use the markup percentage on retail to calculate the markup in dollar unless you know the retail price. This is the perfect time to use the Markup Equivalents Table (see Figure 27-1). You can

FIGURE 27-2

Typical Markup Percentages

Product Category	Typical Markup Percentage Based on Cost
Small Appliances (microwave, coffee maker)	30%
Large Appliances (refrigerator, dryer)	15%–20%
Automobiles	5%–10%* (*note dealers make money on factory incentives and sale of accessories)
Automobile Accessories (sunroof, CD player)	15%–25%
Clothing	100%

■ **Markup Percentages** Markup percentages vary with the type of product and business. *How would you determine how much a microwave whose retail price was $159.99 cost when all you know is the markup percentage based on cost noted in the above table? What would be its cost in dollars?*

convert the markup on retail to the markup on cost and apply it to the cost of the item to arrive at the markup in dollars. (See Figure 27-2.)

Here's an example: A marketer knows that the customary markup for a particular cosmetics firm is 33.3 percent on retail and that the cost of its most popular lipstick is $8.00. To project the lipstick's retail price, follow these steps:

STEP 1 Use the markup equivalents table to get all the information in the same (cost) form. Find the cost equivalent of a 33.3 percent markup on retail.

Markup on Retail	Markup on Cost
32.0	47.1
33.3	50.0
34.0	51.5

STEP 2 Apply the cost method to determine the retail price. First calculate the dollar markup on cost.

$$C \times MU(\%) = MU(\$)$$
$$\$8.00 \times .50 = \$4.00$$

STEP 3 Then calculate the retail price.

$$C + MU(\$) = RP$$
$$\$8.00 + \$4.00 = \$12.00$$

The Drive-In Inventor

Richard M. Hollingshead, Jr. had two interests—cars and movies. It is no irony that he invented the first drive-in movie theater. Hollingshead combined his hobbies to develop a movie theater where movie-goers could watch from their own cars. He experimented in his driveway in New Jersey, projecting movies from a 1928 Kodak projector on to a screen nailed to trees in his backyard. The original Drive-In Theater opened on June 6, 1933, in Camden, New Jersey, charging 25 cents per car and per person.

Thinking Creatively

Drive-ins were once the rage. Today, their popularity has declined. What are some marketing tactics you might employ to bring back the popularity of the drive-in?

FIGURE 27-3

Retail Box

	$	%		$	%
Retail Price	M	J 100	Retail Price	M 11.25	J 100
Markup	N	K	Markup	N 4.50	K 40
Cost	O	L	Cost	O 6.75	L 60

Computation: $L = J - K$ $L = 100 - 40 = 60\%$
                  $M = O \div L$ $M = \$6.75 \div .60 = \$11.25$
                  $N = M - O$ $N = \$11.25 - \$6.75 = \$4.50$

Check: $M \times K = N$ $11.25 \times .40 = \$4.50$

■ **The Retail Method** To compute the retail price using the retail method, fill in the boxes following the letter sequence (J-O). Note that the box labeled "J" (RP%) is always 100%. The amounts that go in the boxes labeled K (MU%) and O (C$) are usually known. *Why is this retail box an example of the retail method for calculating markup?*

■ Retail Method of Pricing

Another way to compute the retail price when all you know are cost and the markup on retail is to use the retail method. This method is based on changing the information that you already have into retail figures.

Let's consider an example: The owner of a sporting goods store wants to know what the markup and retail price should be for a sun visor that costs $6.75. His customary markup on retail is 40 percent. Thus, in algebraic terms 40 percent of "X" equals the retail price. The steps that he follows in his calculation are as follows:

STEP 1 Determine what percentage of the retail price is equal to cost. This is a matter of subtracting the known retail markup figure from 100 percent, which represents the retail price.

$RP(\%) - MU(\%) = C(\%)$
$100\% - 40\% = 60\%$

STEP 2 To determine the retail price, divide the cost by the decimal equivalent of the percentage calculated in Step 1.

$6.75 divided by .60 = $11.25

STEP 3 Calculate the dollar markup.

$RP - C = MU(\$)$
$\$11.25 - \$6.75 = \$4.50$

STEP 4 Check your work by multiplying the retail price you calculated in Step 2 by the percentage markup on retail given originally. The answer will match the dollar markup you calculated in Step 3, if your retail price is correct.

$RP \times MU(\%) = MU(\$)$
$\$11.25 \times .40 = \$4.50$

You can use a visual device called the retail box (Figure 27-3) to help you remember this sequence of calculations. This retail box organizes your information and makes it simple to check your work.

PRACTICE 4

Calculate retail price and markup in these two problems by using the retail method.

1. Find the retail price and dollar markup for a hand-made sweater that costs the Woolens Closet $90 and has a 40-percent markup on retail.

2. A machine-made sweater costs the Woolens Closet $30 and has a 60 percent markup on retail. Calculate this sweater's retail price and dollar markup.

Calculations for Lowering Prices

When a business lowers its prices, a new sale price must be calculated, as well as a new markup. Let's look at the steps used in calculating markdowns (lowered prices), maintained markups (new markup), and the actual sales prices derived from these calculations.

■ Markdowns

To reduce the quantity of goods in stock, a business will sometimes mark down merchandise by a certain percentage [MD(%)]. This reduction is based on the retail price. Consider as an example a record store that wants to mark down by 25 percent compact disks that originally sold for $16. The steps for calculating the sale price (SP) are as follows:

STEP 1 Determine the dollar markdown. Multiply the retail price by the percentage markdown.

RP × MD(%) = MD($)
$16 × .25 = $4

STEP 2 To determine the sale price, subtract the markdown from the retail price.

RP − MD($) = SP
$16 − $4 = $12

Another way to arrive at the same answer is to consider what percentage of the original price will equal the sale price. The procedure is still two steps long, but the percentage calculation is so easy that you can probably do it in your head and save some time. Here are the steps involved.

STEP 1 Determine what percentage of the original price will equal the sale price. This is simply a matter of subtracting the markdown percentage from 100 percent.

RP(%) − MD(%) = SP(%)
100% − 25% = 75%

STEP 2 To find the sale price, multiply the retail price by the decimal equivalent of the percentage calculated in Step 1.

RP × SP(%) = SP
$16 × .75 = $12

PRACTICE 5

Calculate the sale price.

A suit that sells for $225 is to be marked down 40 percent. What is its new price?

■ Maintained Markup

When a marketer marks down goods, the markup and markup percentage change. The difference between an item's final sale price and its cost is called the maintained markup.

Businesses must plan for markdowns, as they are part of being profitable and competitive in the marketplace. Reductions in the original retail price include employee discounts, damaged goods allowances, and special sales events. For businesses to enjoy the profit margin they need to be successful, these factors must be considered. Thus, the concept of maintained markup becomes extremely important in planning the original price of the item and all future markdowns.

Life In The Diverse MARKETPLACE

Driving Others Crazy

When traveling, you expect changes in language, customs, and food. But how about driving? You may be a confident and skilled driver in the United States, but that may change abroad. Other countries often have road standards different from those in the United States. In England, motorists drive on the left side of the road, instead of on the right as in the United States. Speed limits in Canada are based on the metric system, listed in kilometers per hour, not miles per hour. Common rules of the road are nearly disregarded in Brazil, where driving can be a very risky endeavor to an unfamiliar visitor!

Thinking Critically
How can you find out about the driving rules before traveling to another country?

Let's consider an example. Assume that a cassette recorder that cost Zap Electronics $25 and originally sold for $50 is marked down 20 percent. The maintained markup (expressed in both dollars and as a percentage) is calculated as follows:

STEP 1 Calculate the new sale price.

$$100\% - 20\% = 80\%$$
$$\$50 \times .80 = \$40$$

STEP 2 To determine the maintained markup in dollars (MM$), subtract the cost from the sale price.

$$SP - C = MM(\$)$$
$$\$40 - \$25 = \$15$$

STEP 3 To determine the maintained markup percentage, divide the maintained markup in dollars by the sale price.

$$MM(\$) \text{ divided by } SP = MM(\%)$$
$$\$15 \div \$40 = .375$$
$$.375 = 37.5\%$$

PRACTICE 6

Now try the same type of computation on your own.

A hand-held computer that costs Compco Industries $126 to stock sells for $350 (retail price). The firm wants to mark down the computer 20 percent. Determine the sale price and maintained markup in dollars, and then calculate the maintained markup percentage.

Hot Bot

You are purchasing a new camera, but don't know the best value available on the market. You can read consumer magazines, hit the mall, take your best guess, or let someone else do the work for you. Now with the help of a "bot" you can type a request into a Web site and wait for a reply. Most consumers don't have time to comparison shop on the Internet. That's why shopping services with helpers—or "bots"— are popping up all over the Web. These bots comb Web sites for prices. Once a request is made, the agents hunt down product information and prices. Excite.com's shopping service tracks products from over 500 merchants. While these programs offer plenty of bargains for consumers, they also cause many headaches for merchants. Product margins are being pushed down and prices must stay competitive, because shoppers can be directed to another company.

Thinking Critically

How might you use bots for price comparisons?

27.1 ASSESSMENT

Reviewing Key Terms and Concepts

1. Explain how a firm's net profit or loss is related to pricing.

2. How are the dollar and percentage markups calculated based on cost and based on retail? Illustrate the formulas for a book that costs $13.99 and has a retail price of $19.99.

3. Assume that an item that cost $125 and currently retails for $279.99 (RP) is going to be marked down 40 percent for a special sale. Calculate the new sale price, as well as the maintained markup in dollars and as a percent.

Thinking Critically

4. If a buyer wanted to buy goods that cost $100 and the customary markup on retail was 40 percent, what two methods could the buyer use to calculate the retail price? Explain.

Integrating Academic Skills

5. **COMMUNICATION** Your supervisor has requested that you train your coworkers on markdowns that are not automatically deducted at the sales terminal. How should they manually calculate the net price a customer pays in those cases?

Calculating Discounts

• What You'll Learn

- The general procedure for figuring discounts
- How to calculate various kinds of discounts

• Why It's Important

Discounts affect the final price a customer will pay. Therefore, it is essential that you learn how to calculate discounts and the net price payable.

Key Terms

- employee discounts

Discounts

Recall that a discount is a reduction in the price of goods and services sold to customers. Retailers may offer discounts to their employees as a job benefit or to encourage their employees to purchase their goods. Manufacturers and distributors offer discounts to their customers to encourage prompt payment and stimulate business.

The general procedure for calculating discounts involves two steps:

STEP 1 Multiply the price (P) by the discount percentage [D(%)] to get the dollar amount of the discount [D($)].

$$P \times D(\%) = D(\$)$$

STEP 2 Subtract the discount from the price to get the net price (NP), or the amount that the customer will actually pay.

$$P - D(\$) = NP$$

Here is an example. A business is offering a 35 percent discount on an item that sells for $150.

$150 \times .35 = $52.50 D($)
$150 - 52.50 = $97.50 NP

You can simply subtract the discount percent from 100 percent to determine net price's equivalent percentage to determine the net price. Then multiply the original price by that percentage to get the net price. Using the above example, those calculations would be as follows:

100% - 35% = 65%
$150 \times .65 = $97.50 NP

■ Employee Discounts

Businesses offer employee discounts to encourage workers to buy the products they sell or manufacture. Employees who buy and use their company's products project confidence in and enthusiasm about the products. Employee discounts can range from 10 percent to 30 percent for entry-level employees and as high as 50 percent or more for top-level executives.

■ Discounts from Manufacturers and Distributors

Some common types of discounts offered by manufacturers and distributors are cash, trade, quantity, seasonal, and promotional discounts, all of which were already explained in Chapter 26. This section is devoted to explaining how each of these types of discounts is calculated.

CASH DISCOUNTS Recall from Chapter 26 that a cash discount is a discount offered to buyers to encourage them to pay their bills quickly. Consider the invoice terms 3/15, net 60. Recall that the first number (3) represents the percentage of the discount applicable to the invoice total. When that total is $1,000 and the customer takes advantage of the discount, the calculations are as follows:

STEP 1 Determine the dollar discount.

$$P \times D(\%) = D(\$)$$
$$\$1,000 \times .03 = \$30$$

STEP 2 Determine the net price.

$$P - D(\$) = NP$$
$$\$1,000 - \$30 = \$970$$

Cash discounts can also be calculated on a unit basis. The net unit price for 100 items at $10 each listed on the invoice is determined as follows:

STEP 1 Determine the dollar discount.

$$P \times D(\%) = D(\$)$$
$$\$10.00 \times .03 = \$.30$$

STEP 2 Determine the net price.

$$P - D(\$) = NP$$
$$\$10.00 - \$.30 = \$9.70$$

The net amount payable by the customer would still be the same, of course—$970 ($9.70 × 100).

TRADE DISCOUNTS You may recall from Chapter 26 that trade discounts are based on manufacturers' list prices. They are really not discounts at all, but rather the way manufacturers quote prices to wholesalers and retailers. Trade discounts are called trade discounts because different prices are offered to different lines of trade (i.e., wholesalers vs. retailers). They are calculated in the same way as cash discounts. To figure a 40-percent trade discount for an invoice totaling $5,789, you would do the following:

STEP 1 Determine the dollar discount.

$$P \times D(\%) = D(\$)$$
$$\$5,789.00 \times .40 = \$2,315.60$$

STEP 2 Determine the net price.

$$P - D(\$) = NP$$
$$\$5,789.00 - \$2,315.60 = \$3,473.40$$

Invoices containing several items have a trade discount that is applied to each item separately to determine its net unit price to the business.

PRACTICE 7

Determine the amounts payable by the following customers.

1. Southbend Trucking receives an invoice in the amount of $225,000 showing the terms 2/10, net 30. The invoice lists five trucks at $45,000 each. If Southbend takes advantage of the discount, what will be the net amount due on the invoice? The net price per truck?

2. A manufacturer gives retailers a 55-percent trade discount. The invoice received by Wright's Department Store totals $180,775; what is the amount of the store's discount? What is the amount payable to the manufacturer?

QUANTITY DISCOUNTS You may recall from Chapter 26 that quantity discounts are offered to buyers for placing large orders. Sellers benefit from large orders from the lower selling costs involved in one transaction as opposed to several small transactions. They are meant to encourage buyers to buy in bulk and purchase more merchandise than they originally intended to purchase. Quantity discounts may be quoted as either a percentage of price or as part of a quantity price list like this:

No. of items	1–24	25–48	49–72
Unit price	$.95	$.90	$.85

Using the above table, if you purchased 50 items, you would pay $.85 each. Your total bill would be $42.50 ($.85 × 50).

Sometimes businesses offer cumulative quantity discounts, whereby a certain minimum purchase must be made during a specified period of time for the discount to be activated. A firm may offer a 2-percent cumulative quantity discount to any company that purchases $3,000 worth of products in a six-month period. In the case that a firm's purchases total $2,500 during that period, no discount is permitted; if they total $4,000, however, the discount is allowed. It would be calculated in the following manner:

STEP 1 Determine the dollar discount.

$$P \times D(\%) = D(\$)$$
$$\$4,000 \times .02 = \$80$$

STEP 2 Determine the net price.

$$P - D(\$) = NP$$
$$\$4,000 - \$80 = \$3,920$$

Case Study

Costco's Business Plan

Costco Corporation is a unique enterprise that offers low prices in a warehouse setting to businesses and individual consumers. To be eligible to shop at Costco, you must become a member. Originally this membership was only available to small businesses; however, this service has been extended to individuals. Once nonbusiness members began to seek membership at Costco, the first warehouse store opened in Seattle in 1983. Its success is based on several factors, one of which is its low markup on products (about 10 percent above cost), compared with full-service retailers whose markups are 25 percent or more.

Costco keeps expenses low with barebones warehouse facilities, few salespeople, tight control on inventory, and a limited selection of brands and sizes (i.e., two brands of mustard in two sizes) in a product category. To offset its low markup on goods, Costco charges membership fees ranging from $35 to $100. There are different membership categories that require different membership fees—Executive, Business, and Gold Star.

Another part of Costco's success is the variety of goods offered at low prices. You will find high-end items like Waterford crystal and common consumer items like bottles of ketchup. Costco also offers one-hour photo labs, optical centers, pharmacies, and food courts. They also carry business supplies, household products, clothing, electronic equipment, and fresh grocery items. Executive members may also establish health care for small businesses as well as lease business equipment and establish payroll services. Members can even shop online at Costco.com and have deliveries sent to their home or office.

Costco's rivals include Wal-Mart, a subsidiary Sam's Club, and BJ's Wholesale Club, Inc. Even though all three follow the same basic business plan, Costco's average store generates more sales ($94 million) than its competitors ($55 million for Sam's and $44 million for BJ's).

Case Study Review

1. Why is Costco able to mark up its goods only around 10 percent above cost, while other full-service retailers must mark up their products 25 percent or more to be profitable?
2. Who are Costco's rivals, and how does each compare to Costco in average sales revenue generated?

A MATTER OF ETHICS

3. Do you think it is ethical for Costco to charge different customers different membership fees?

PROMOTIONAL DISCOUNTS Promotional discounts are given to businesses that agree to advertise or in some other way promote a manufacturer's products. When the promotional discount is quoted as a percentage, it is calculated the same way as a cumulative discount.

Sometimes, marketers are granted a dollar amount as a promotional discount. In such cases, they may want to determine the net purchase price or the percentage of the promotional discount for themselves. Consider an example. The Cycle Shop buys Speedo bicycles for $10,000 and is granted a $250 promotional discount for displaying the bikes in its store window during the month of March. To determine the percentage discount, follow these steps:

STEP 1 Divide the dollar discount by the original price. The answer will be a decimal.

D($) divided by P = D(%)
$250 ÷ $10,000 = .025

STEP 2 Change the decimal to a percentage. This figure is the percentage discount.

.025 = 2.5%
Shift decimal point two places right.

SEASONAL DISCOUNTS Sellers offer seasonal discounts to encourage buyers to purchase goods long before the actual consumer buying season. Purchasing Halloween costumes before July 27 or ski apparel before May 1 might qualify retailers for seasonal discounts.

Seasonal discounts are calculated in the same way as other discounts. Here is an example. Lobo Inc. offers an 8-percent seasonal discount to all buyers who purchase Christmas decorations before August 1. An order placed on July 20 for $1,500 worth of decorations has a net purchase price that is calculated as follows:

STEP 1 Determine the dollar discount.

P × D(%) = D(S)
$1,500 × .08 = $120

STEP 2 Determine the net price.

P − D($) = NP
$1,500 − $120 = $1,380

REAL WORLD MARKETING

Priced to Fly

Think only first-class passengers can fly in style? Think again! Richard Branson, founder of Virgin Atlantic, is changing this with his price-sensitive service with style. Virgin Atlantic airline soared by selling discount air travel with plush amenities like shower facilities at airport lounges, massages and manicures in flight, and goodie packs with Virgin socks and toothbrushes. But he's no longer flying solo. JetBlue, marketed by ex-Virgin Atlantic employees, offers cheap fares out of New York City's JFK airport. Its hook—economy class with leather seats and personal satellite television. You certainly do get what you pay for!

Thinking Critically
Why do these airlines use price-sensitive services?

PRACTICE 8

Now try these problems involving quantity, promotional, and seasonal discounts.

1. Suppose a firm is required to buy $10,000 worth of goods by September 15 in order to qualify for a 10-percent cumulative quantity discount. Would a firm that purchased $5,000 worth of goods on September 1 get the discount? What about one that purchased $10,500 worth on September 20?

2. A manufacturer offers a retailer $750 as a promotional discount for advertising a certain product. What is the percentage discount if the total invoice was $37,500?

3. Regal Shoe Company offers retailers a 5-percent discount for placing orders by May 1. A retailer takes advantage of the offer and purchases $78,290 worth of shoes by the cutoff date. What is the net amount payable on the invoice?

Answers to Practice Set Problems

PRACTICE 1 (PAGE 486)

1. $25 ($15 + 10 = $25)

2. $90 ($175 − 85 = $90)

PRACTICE 2 (PAGE 486)

1. 69.0% cost ($10.99 − 6.50 = $4.49; $4.49 divided by 6.50 = .690); 40.9% retail ($10.99 − 6.50 = $4.49; $4.49 divided by $10.99 = .4085)

2. 33.3% cost ($23.25 divided by $69.74 = .333); $92.99 RP ($69.74 + 23.25 = $92.99 RP); 25% retail ($23.25 divided by $92.99 = .25)

3. 100% cost ($50 divided by 50 = 1); 50% retail ($50 divided by $100 = .5)

PRACTICE 3 (PAGE 487)

1. 40%

2. 37.5%

PRACTICE 4 (PAGE 489)

1. $150 ($90 divided by .60 = $150)

2. $75 ($30 divided by .40 = $75); $45 ($75 − $30 = $45)

PRACTICE 5 (PAGE 490)

$135 (100% − 40% = 60%; $225 × .60 = $135)

PRACTICE 6 (PAGE 491)

$280 sale price ($350 × .80 = $280); $154 MM$ ($280 − 126 = $154); 55% MM% ($154 divided by $280 = .55)

PRACTICE 7 (PAGE 493)

1. Net amount on invoice $220,500 ($45,000 × 5 = 225,000 × .98) Net amount per truck $44,100 ($45,000 × .98)

2. $99,426.25 discount ($180,775 × .55); $81,348.75 amount payable ($180,775 − $99,426.25)

PRACTICE 8 (PAGE 495)

1. No, because the minimum quantity is $10,000. No, because the deadline date was September 15.

2. 2 percent ($750 ÷ $37,500 = .02)

3. $74,375.50 ($78,290 × .95)

27.2 ASSESSMENT

Reviewing Key Terms and Concepts

1. What procedures are used to calculate the dollar amount of a discount and the final selling price?

2. Carlo's Ice Cream Specialties gives all of its employees a 15-percent discount on ice cream cakes. What would an employee pay for a chocolate ice cream cake that is $13.75?

3. Why do sellers offer seasonal discounts to customers?

Thinking Critically

4. Assume you are given a trade discount of 30 percent and a seasonal discount of 10 percent. You also take advantage of a cash discount of 2 percent. Would you be entitled to a 42-percent discount? Explain.

Integrating Academic Skills

5. **MATH** The dating terms on a $3,000 invoice are 3/10, net 30. If the buyer takes advantage of the cash discount, what will be the net amount due?

Careers in Marketing

CUSTOMER SERVICE

Mary Shipman
Creative Management, Inc.
Customer Service Representative

Career Facts

What does your job entail?

"My job is to find solutions for customer concerns and problems with our software, in addition to training customers on software use. Customers will call with questions regarding how to run their software or general computer troubleshooting. Sometimes customers will call in with complaints about the software. I generally deal with customers on the phone for our software hotline, and I make decisions based on company policy and the facts of each situation. Sometimes it is necessary to send company representatives to the client's company or home to amend the problem, but sometimes it can be handled over the phone."

What skills are important to you?

"Good communication skills are vital. It is impossible to register customer complaints or explain the software's functions without strong verbal communication and problem solving skills. I must listen to concerns and act as a liaison between customers and the company in order to develop changes in a product to meet a customer's specific need. All customer service representatives must have the ability to understand both the customers' need and corporate policies."

What do you like most about your job?

"My job involves a great deal of social interaction, which is rare in computer-based positions. My duties vary daily, ranging from customer training to calming down an unhappy customer. I find it gratifying when I am able to solve someone's problems."

What is your key to success?

"My key to success lies in my ability to remain patient even in stressful situations. There are times when I will be dealing with back-to-back phone calls involving lengthy explanations and sometimes customers become frustrated if there is not a simple answer. It is necessary to always keep a professional attitude—I represent my entire company."

Thinking Critically

What kind of on-the-job training do you think is necessary for a customer sales representative?

Education and Training: High school courses in marketing, accounting, business, office procedures, English, and communications are good preparation for customer service work. Clerical experience and training provide preparation for customer service clerks. Most employers have on-the-job training programs for customer service clerks and professional customer service representatives.

Aptitudes, Abilities, and Skills: Good communication skills, ability to work efficiently under pressure, and good problem-solving skills are necessary. Customer service representatives must be able to gather information accurately in order to arrive at appropriate decisions.

Career Outlook: Faster than average growth is expected through the year 2006.

Career Path: Many customer service representatives gain experience in some area of clerical work, then complete an on-the-job training program in customer service. Experience in customer service is a good preparation for promotion to management.

Chapter 27 ASSESSMENT

VOCABULARY REVIEW

Explain the meanings of the following terms by giving an example of each.

- gross profit
- maintained markup
- employee discounts

FACT AND IDEA REVIEW

1. What is the most basic formula you need in order to calculate retail price? (27.1)

2. List three reasons why most wholesalers and retailers elect to compute their markup on the selling price. (27.1)

3. What is the formula for calculating the percentage markup on retail price? On cost? (27.1)

4. What steps are used to calculate prices according to the cost method? (27.1)

5. What steps do marketers follow when using the retail method to determine the retail price and dollar markup? (27.1)

6. What steps do you follow to calculate maintained dollar markup and maintained percentage markup? (27.1)

7. What is the two-step procedure for calculating a discount? (27.2)

8. Calculate the price for a $40 item with a 2-percent cash discount. (27.2)

9. Company A offers a cumulative discount of 5 percent on orders of $10,000 in a six-month period. Company B purchases $8,000 in one order and $4,000 in another. What would be the dollar discount to Company B? (27.2)

10. What is the formula for determining the percent of a promotional discount? (27.2)

THINKING CRITICALLY

1. Why is a firm's net profit or loss related to pricing?

2. Is the initial markup calculated for an item sometimes the same as the maintained markup? Explain.

BUILDING WORKPLACE SKILLS

1. **Math: Determining Retail Price** A dress costs a business $72, and the markup is $45. What is the retail price?

2. **Math: Calculating Markup** A pair of slacks retails for $110, and the cost is $50. What is the markup?

3. **Math: Calculating Cost** A hammer sells for $16.95, and its markup is $6.75. What is the cost?

4. **Math: Calculating Percentage Markup** A wallet costs a business $27 and sells for $45. What is the percentage markup on cost? The percentage markup on retail?

5. **Math: Calculating Percentage Markup** A stationery store buys greeting cards for $1.90 and puts a $1.60 markup on each of them. What is the percentage markup on cost? The percentage markup on retail?

6. **Math: Calculating Equivalent Markup** What is the equivalent markup on cost for the following percentage markups on retail?
   a. 25.0%   d. 50.0%
   b. 23.1%   e. 40.0%
   c. 33.3%   f. 28.5%

7. **Math: Determining Retail Price** A pencil sharpener that costs a business $12.50 has a markup of 62 percent on retail price. Use a retail box to calculate the sharpener's retail price and check your answer.

APPLYING MARKETING CONCEPTS

1. **Preparing a Quantity Price List** Use a spreadsheet program to prepare a quantity price list for cookies you sell in your school store in order to increase sales volume. Assume your cost to make and market one cookie is $.25. At present, you sell one cookie for $.50. Be sure your quantity prices still generate a profit for the store. Provide a written rationale for your list.

2. **Understanding Markdowns** Research the different ways businesses present markdowns to consumers. Some run sales and advertise those sales in newspapers and direct mail pieces. Others use coupons and rebates. Compare the methods, language, and calculations used to demonstrate the savings a consumer is getting with these markdowns. Contrast those consumer markdown methods with the types of discounts manufacturers and distributors offer retailers (cash discount, trade discount, quantity discount, promotional discount, and seasonal discount). Report your findings in an oral presentation to the class, using presentation software.

LINKING SCHOOL TO WORK

Basic, Information, and Thinking Skills Interview the owner/manager of a business about the use of computers to calculate prices. Ask if the firm uses special software to determine the price for an item or a job for a manufacturing or service concern. Ask what information must be input for the system to work. In a retail concern, ask if markups and markdowns are incorporated into the firm's computer system. Ask who is responsible for inputting the information and checking it for accuracy. Report your findings in both a written and oral report.

THE DECA CONNECTION

Role Play: Sales Associate

Situation You are to assume the role of sales associate in the men's department. Your department manager (judge) asks you to input the prices of newly arrived slacks into the computer inventory system. You notice that the price of $26 appears to be incorrect. According to the invoice, the slacks cost the store $18, not including shipping and handling. You know the customary markup in your store is 50 percent of the retail price.

Activity What will you do and what will you say to your department manager?

Evaluation You will be evaluated on how well you meet the following performance indicators:
* Select approach for setting a base price
* Determine discounts and allowances that can be used to adjust base prices
* Explain factors affecting pricing decisions
* Persuade others
* Foster positive working relationships

*inter*NET CONNECTION

Comparison Shopping
To establish competitive prices for your athletic shoe department, you need to see what rival companies are charging.

Connect
* Locate the Web sites of two manufacturers of athletic shoes and select two different shoes from each one.
* Find three online sporting goods stores that sell those models.
* Create a table depicting the price comparison for the four pairs of shoes. Include the prices manufacturers charge if they sell their shoes online.

The Zazz Lab...

A Sports and Entertainment Marketing Simulation

WELCOME

Welcome to Zazz Sports and Entertainment Marketing Company. Zazz is devoted to serving the needs of its clients who include college, university, and professional sports teams, professional athletes, sporting events, and sports arenas plus major consumer product corporations, as well as television networks and movie studios. As an intern, you will have the opportunity to work on different clients' projects. All of your work will be assigned and reviewed by your department supervisor.

MARKET A GOLF RESORT

SITUATION

A new golf resort in Florida would like Zazz to help market its facility and determine its pricing structure. The resort features two 72 par, 18-hole championship golf courses with rolling hills. Additional amenities include a comprehensive practice facility with a driving range and areas to practice putting, chipping, and sand bunker shots. A pro shop is stocked with golf apparel, equipment, and accessories and a gift shop offers apparel, collectibles, resort logo items, and personal sundries. There are three restaurants in the resort: formal, casual, and a snack bar. The hotel has 250 rooms and suites, as well as 12 conference rooms. There are two swimming pools, ten tennis courts, and a health spa offering fitness equipment, classes, trainers, as well as other personal services such as facials and massages.

ASSIGNMENT

Your supervisor wants you to determine the rates for hotel accommodations, golf greens fees, golf carts, eateries, health spa services, and shop merchandise. Separate seasonal rates for each aspect of the complex need to be established. Design comprehensive golf packages that include breakfast, greens fees, admission to the spa, and any other special features. The pricing structure for the gift and pro shop merchandise should include merchandise examples and reflect the desired markup on items. All restaurant operations will require a name, sample menu, and prices.

Tools and Resources

To complete this assignment, you will need to conduct research at a library or on the Internet. You will also need a word processing program, a spreadsheet program, and presentation software. Trade publications that may be helpful include *Golf Market Today, Golf Digest, Golf Magazine, Restaurant News, Fitness Management, Food Service and Hospitality, Hospitality News,* and *Hotel Management.*

Research

Research competing golf resorts located in Florida, around the United States, and abroad. Compare our client's facilities with its competitors. Analyze the pricing strategies used by comparable competitors. Analyze seasonal supply and demand. Research economic factors, weather, and psychographic trends, such as the type and length of vacations generally taken by various age groups or sports enthusiasts. Research common markup practices for specialty and sports-related merchandise in resorts. Obtain various restaurant menus and research the methods used to determine prices for food service and personal spa services.

Report

Prepare a written report and a computer presentation for the client. Use a word processing program to prepare a double-spaced report. Prepare a spreadsheet to illustrate the formulas and calculations used to arrive at the suggested prices. Arrange your written report around the following headings:

- General background on golf resorts and recreation
  - Economic and psychographic trends
- Pricing principles
  - Suggested pricing objectives for client
  - Researched costs for gift and pro shop and food service operations
  - Estimated demand
  - Competition
    - Major competitors
    - Pricing plan to meet competition
  - Appropriate pricing strategies and techniques
    - Client's image
    - Skimming vs. penetration pricing
    - Use of psychological pricing techniques
- Suggested price structure and rationale
  - Rates for hotel accommodations (fall, winter, and spring; single and double occupancy)
  - Rates for golf
    - Greens fees and cart fees
  - Rates for spa facilities
    - Use of facility
    - Services
  - Packages for sports enthusiasts
  - Gift and pro shop
    - Suggested markup policy (show calculations and provide product examples)
    - Suggested markdown policy (show calculations and provide product examples)
  - Restaurants
    - Names, sample menu items and prices, and calculations and rationale for prices

Using computer presentation software, prepare a presentation of your ideas for the client that includes:
- Key topics covered in your written report
- Graphic illustrations that are relevant to each slide's topic
- Very little text
- Minimum of 10 slides

Presentation and Evaluation

Present your ideas in a written report and an oral presentation. The oral presentation will be shown to the client. You will be evaluated on your oral presentation skills, including:
- Knowledge of pricing principles and practices
- Continuity of presentation
- Voice quality
- Eye contact

Portfolio

Print a copy of your completed report and presentation for your Portfolio.

THE DECA CONNECTION

DECA Business Services Marketing Series
Analyzing research on competitors' pricing and making recommendations for a client could be the basis for a role play in this event.

DECA Marketing Management Series
Pricing is a major function of marketing management and as such could be a topic for a role play in this event.

DECA Hospitality and Recreation Research Event
Researching and developing a pricing structure for a hotel and golf resort could be the basis for a research project in this event.

DECA Sports and Entertainment Marketing Management Team Decision-Making Event
Working on this project with a partner would make the experience similar to what is expected in a DECA Team Decision-Making Event.

Portfolio

Performing Market Research

To demonstrate mastery of the content in this unit, you will conduct a marketing research study on a topic of your choice or for a business of your choice. One idea might be to develop a customer profile for a business based on a survey of its current customers. Prepare a written report that includes a discussion of the secondary research conducted (background information), target population, steps taken to create the survey, steps taken to administer the study, findings, and conclusions. Be sure to include a copy of the survey instrument in your report.

Marketing Information Management

Unit Overview

Marketing information management is an organized attempt by a business to gather information to make better decisions about marketing issues, strategies, and problems. This unit explains how marketing information systems can assist in finding solutions to problems businesses face today.

Chapter 28 introduces marketing research—the process of getting the marketing information needed to make sound business decisions. You will learn the importance of marketing research and the function of a marketing information system. Chapter 29 identifies the five steps in the marketing research process. The chapter also explains how to construct, format, and administer survey questionnaires and explores the effect of computer technologies on marketing research activities.

In this Unit:

Foundations of Marketing

⬤ Business, Management, Entrepreneurship

Functions of Marketing

🔹 Marketing Information Management

Marketing Research

Marketing: What It Takes

Designing a Customer Service Survey

You are working as an assistant to the marketing manager of a recently opened shopping mall. Your manager has asked you to devise a survey to measure whether shoppers have had a pleasant shopping experience and are satisfied with the level of services at the new mall.

WHAT WILL YOU DO?

What important customer service elements would you include in your survey of shopping mall customers?

Marketing Information Systems

Defining Marketing Research

According to the American Marketing Association, marketing research involves the marketing function that links the consumer, customer, and public to the marketer through information. Marketing information is used to identify marketing opportunities, solve marketing problems, implement marketing plans, and monitor marketing performance. Marketing research involves the methods used to gather information, analyze it, and report findings related to marketing goods and services. Marketing research can apply to any aspect of marketing. Kellogg's, a cereal manufacturer, might research the potential sales and market for a new product line of breakfast snacks. Marriott Hotels, Resorts, and Suites might conduct customer satisfaction research on the quality of its guest services.

The primary emphasis of marketing research is to obtain information about the preferences, opinions, habits, trends, and plans of current and potential customers. This information helps marketers in many ways. Before developing a product, marketers can conduct research to determine the type of product customers want. The research can minimize potential losses when introducing the new product. Consumers accept only one out of every ten new products introduced into the marketplace; therefore, gaining information about consumer likes and dislikes is significant.

Why Is Marketing Research Important?

Given the high failure rate of new products on the market, marketing research can make or break a business. The major goal of any business is to increase sales and profits. Businesses that do not pay attention to what consumers are buying are likely to make costly marketing mistakes.

The information obtained from research helps businesses plan their future operations to increase sales and profits. Research answers questions such as what products should be produced, where the products should be sold, how the products will be promoted, and at what price the products will sell.

Research also helps businesses solve marketing problems or anticipate future marketing potential. It took Stouffer's almost 13 years of marketing research and development to start its Lean Cuisine product line. Stouffer's studied consumers' interest in health and dieting. It

• What You'll Learn

- The importance of marketing research
- The function of a marketing information system

• Why It's Important

Successful companies must be able to understand the needs and wants of their customers. Marketing research can provide the necessary information to help a business while planning, solving problems, and making decisions regarding its products and services.

Key Terms

- marketing research
- marketing information system
- database

6.5 million voices free flowing.

You need accurate market research and there's not a moment to lose. Fortunately, the world's largest online database is just a click away. With so many people waiting to be heard, you could ask all the questions in the world

and we'd still be hungry for more.

HarrisInteractive
Harris Heritage. Interactive Power.
www.harrisinteractive.com/cm31
Tel 877-919-4765
Event Code CM31

■ **Marketing Research Information Is Critical** Marketing research is essential for all companies regardless of size. *How can smaller companies obtain necessary marketing information?*

conducted consumer panels to find out what dieters liked and disliked about diet meals. Using the information, the company developed its product, tested its package design, and piloted sales of the product in several large cites before national distribution. The product was a tremendous success, with over $125 million in sales after the first year of national distribution.

Research also helps a company keep track of what is happening with its current markets. Through research, a company can determine its major competitors, what its competitors are offering, and which products consumers prefer.

Who Uses Marketing Research?

Marketing research is valuable for organizations of any size. The size of the business, though, may affect how it conducts the research. Small businesses that do less than $5 million in annual sales usually do not have separate research departments. Here, marketing research is done informally by the owners, managers, or employees. Marketing research is conducted by a variety of business groups and the government (see Figure 28-1).

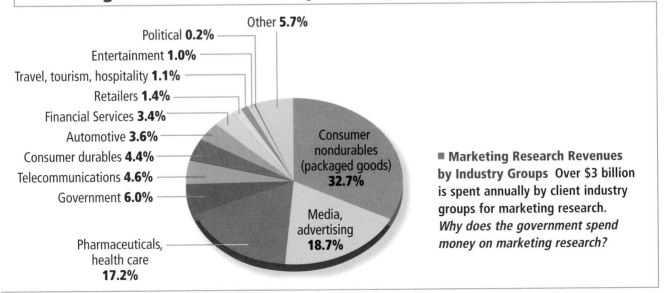

FIGURE 28-1

Marketing Research Revenues by Industry Groups

Other **5.7%**
Political **0.2%**
Entertainment **1.0%**
Travel, tourism, hospitality **1.1%**
Retailers **1.4%**
Financial Services **3.4%**
Automotive **3.6%**
Consumer durables **4.4%**
Telecommunications **4.6%**
Government **6.0%**
Pharmaceuticals, health care **17.2%**

Consumer nondurables (packaged goods) **32.7%**

Media, advertising **18.7%**

■ **Marketing Research Revenues by Industry Groups** Over $3 billion is spent annually by client industry groups for marketing research. *Why does the government spend money on marketing research?*

FIGURE 28-2

Consumer Product Survey of America

INSTRUCTIONS:

Dear Fellow Shopper:

This quick survey is easy and will only take a few minutes. Here's all you have to do:

1) Let me know the products that you or other people living in your home may have used by marking a **dark** "X" in the appropriate boxes.

2) Please take into account products used by you and all other people living in your home.

3) If you get to a category that is not used in your home, just "X" the "DO NOT USE" box and skip it.

4) For each category, "X" as many boxes as apply.

EXAMPLE: in my family, we usually eat Campbell's or Lipton Soup, but we also used Progresso in the past 12 months. I would "X" boxes as follows:

SOUP

☒ WE DO NOT USE (Skip to next category)	Our Usual Brand(s)	Also Used in Past 12 Months
Campbell's	✖	☒
Healthy Choice	☒	☒
Lipton	✖	☒
Progresso	☒	✖
Other	☒	☒

URGENT: Please take a few moments right now to complete this survey. It's important. I appreciate your help.

Sincerely,

Laura

Laura David

P.S. **Please note:** It is extremely important that the information you provide be accurate.

SOUP

☒ WE DO NOT USE (Skip to next category)	Our Usual Brand(s)	Also Used in Past 12 Months
Campbell's	☒	☒
Healthy Choice	☒	☒
Lipton	☒	☒
Progresso	☒	☒
Other	☒	☒

PAPER TOWELS

☒ WE DO NOT USE (Skip to next category)	Our Usual Brand(s)	Also Used in Past 12 Months
Bounty	☒	☒
Brawny	☒	☒
Handi Wipes	☒	☒
Job Squad	☒	☒
Mardi Gras	☒	☒
Sparkle	☒	☒
Viva	☒	☒
Other paper towels	☒	☒

How many days does it usually take to use an entire roll of paper towels in your home?

1 to 6 days	☒
7 to 14	☒
More than 14 days	☒

HAND & BODY LOTION

☒ WE DO NOT USE (Skip to next category)	Our Usual Brand(s)	Also Used in Past 12 Months
Curel	☒	☒
Eucerin	☒	☒
Keri Lotion	☒	☒
Lubriderm	☒	☒
Neutrogena	☒	☒
Nivea lotion	☒	☒
Ponds Ultra Silk	☒	☒
Vaseline Intensive Care	☒	☒
Other	☒	☒

LAUNDRY DETERGENT

☒ WE DO NOT USE (Skip to next category)	Our Usual Brand(s)	Also Used in Past 12 Months
all - regular	☒	☒
- Free & Clear	☒	☒
Cheer - powder	☒	☒
- liquid	☒	☒
Era	☒	☒
Gain	☒	☒
Tide - powder	☒	☒
- liquid	☒	☒
Wisk - powder	☒	☒
- liquid	☒	☒
Other	☒	☒

How many loads of laundry are washed in your household in an average week?

8 or more	☒
5 to 7	☒
4 or fewer	☒

BAR SOAPS

☒ WE DO NOT USE (Skip to next category)	Our Usual Brand(s)	Also Used in Past 12 Months
Caress	☒	☒
Coast	☒	☒
Dial	☒	☒
Dove	☒	☒
Irish Spring	☒	☒
Ivory - original bar	☒	☒
- Moisture Care	☒	☒
Lever 2000	☒	☒
Oil of Olay	☒	☒
Safeguard	☒	☒
Shield	☒	☒
Zest	☒	☒
Specialty brands (eg: Clinique, Bath & Body Works, etc.)	☒	☒
Other beauty bars	☒	☒
Other deodorant bars	☒	☒

1) Does the female adult in your household purchase soap or other products made for sensitive skin?

Yes ☒ No ☒

2) How many bars of soap are used in your household in an average month?

4 or more bars	☒
3 bars	☒
2 bars	☒
1 or fewer	☒

EU-IL9

GENERAL INFORMATION

In order for manufacturers to truly understand what consumers want, it is important for them to know more than simply how much of a product is sold. They need to have a clear picture of who is buying and why they are buying. This survey can help.

The following questions are being asked as a means to place you and your family into sub-groups. This makes it easier for us to understand your preferences and attitudes.

If you are uncomfortable for any reason with answering any of the following questions, please feel free to leave them blank. I would much rather have your survey returned to me without these facts, than not receive your survey at all.

1) How many people, including yourself, are there in your household?

One ☒ Four ☒
Two ☒ Five ☒
Three ☒ Six or more ☒

2) What are the ages of your household members? ("X" all that apply)

INFANTS — Male / Female

0 - 2 months	☒	☒
3 - 6 months	☒	☒
7 - 12 months	☒	☒
13 - 24 months	☒	☒

CHILDREN

2 - 4 years	☒	☒
5 - 8 years	☒	☒
9 - 12 years	☒	☒
13 - 15 years	☒	☒
16 - 17 years	☒	☒

ADULTS — Male / Female

18 - 20 years	☒	☒
21 - 24 years	☒	☒
25 - 34 years	☒	☒
35 - 44 years	☒	☒
45 - 49 years	☒	☒
50 - 54 years	☒	☒
55 - 59 years	☒	☒
60 - 64 years	☒	☒
65 - 69 years	☒	☒
70 years or over	☒	☒

3) If you have grandchildren age 12 or under, how old are they?

Male / Female
0 - 4 years ☒ ☒
5 - 12 years ☒ ☒

4) What is your marital status?

Married ☒
Single or equivalent ☒
Other ☒

5) Do you have a cat(s) or dog(s)?

Cat(s) ☒ Dog(s) ☒

6) Does anyone in your household operate a business from your home?

Yes ☒ No ☒

7) What was the combined income for all members of your household in 1998 (before tax)?

Prefer not to answer ☒
Less than $25,000 ☒
$25,000 to $35,000 ☒
$35,000 to $50,000 ☒
$50,000 to $75,000 ☒
Over $75,000 ☒

8) I would like to receive further mailings and offers that would be of interest to me.

Yes ☒ No ☒

Thank you for taking the time to complete this questionnaire. I hope you found it interesting.

One last thing — please PRINT your name and mailing address below. Contest and coupon deadline is April 30, 1999.

Please allow 12 weeks for delivery of the coupons. If you are moving in the next 12 weeks, write in your NEW mailing address only.

Best Regards

Mr ☒ Mrs ☒ Miss ☒ Ms ☒ *Laura*

PLEASE PRINT

NAME: _____
FIRST NAME   LAST NAME

MAILING ADDRESS: _____

CITY / TOWN   STATE

ZIP CODE: ☐☐☐☐☐ — ☐☐☐☐
(OPTIONAL)

■ **Consumer Product Research**
The largest category of marketing research is for nondurable consumer products. *What information is provided to businesses from the general information section of the survey pictured?*

Larger companies have formal research departments and specialists to plan and conduct marketing research. Some larger companies contract with marketing research companies to investigate special marketing related problems.

In 1997 $3.3 billion was spent on research in the United States in connection with public opinion polls, marketing, and advertising campaigns. The largest percentage of marketing research dollars was spent on consumer nondurables (packaged products).

Individual businesses are not the only organizations that find marketing research valuable. Several departments in state and federal governments, plus trade associations representing various manufacturers, wholesalers, and retailers, conduct marketing research. Industry trade associations, such as the National Retail Merchants Association, collect industry data to help their members understand the markets for their products.

The Consumer Product Safety Commission, a U.S. government agency, tests products to make certain they are safe for consumer use and to give consumers product information. An example of a customer service survey is shown in Figure 28-2. The U.S. Postal Service conducts annual surveys designed to gain input about needed improvements and services (see Figure 28-3 on page 508).

FIGURE 28-3

The U.S. Postal Survey

UNITED STATES POSTAL SERVICE.

GREATER MICHIGAN DISTRICT

Dear Postal Customer:

Once each year your local post office offers an opportunity for customers like yourself to rate the quality of service we provide. The goal of these annual surveys is to solicit your ideas about how we can better serve your needs and provide us with an honest indication of where we need to improve our performance.

In our office and other offices around the country, we've made changes and implemented strategies based on these survey results. Your answers will help us to compare our improvements from year to year. We encourage you to participate in this year's survey, and thank you in advance for taking the time to help us make a difference.

After completing, tear along dotted line and simply drop in your mail box. No postage is necessary.

POSTMASTER

MARKING INSTRUCTIONS
Please use a number 2 pencil or a blue or black ink pen and darken in the ovals completely.

CORRECT MARK ● INCORRECT MARKS ✓ ✗ ● ⊙

We would like your opinion of how this office performed **during the past year** in the following areas. Your answers will give us important information about where we need to make improvements.

TEAR HERE

Based on your own experiences, please rate the U.S. Postal Service on...

	POOR	FAIR	GOOD	VERY GOOD	EXCELLENT	DON'T KNOW
1. Its overall performance	P	F	G	VG	E	D
2. Delivery of your mail at about the same time each day	P	F	G	VG	E	D
3. The convenience of obtaining postage stamps	P	F	G	VG	E	D
4. Delivery of mail to your correct address	P	F	G	VG	E	D
5. Convenience of window service hours at your post office	P	F	G	VG	E	D
6. Telephone courtesy (including speed of answering/helpfulness)	P	F	G	VG	E	D
7. Complaint resolution (including speed of response/easy to complain)	P	F	G	VG	E	D
8. Courtesy/helpfulness of your local letter carrier	P	F	G	VG	E	D
9. Courtesy/helpfulness of your local window clerk(s)	P	F	G	VG	E	D
10. The length of time it takes your mail to get from the sender to the receiver	P	F	G	VG	E	D

11. What would you consider an acceptable overnight delivery area for first class mail?
   ◯ **25 miles or less**   ◯ **26–50 miles**   ◯ **51–75 miles**   ◯ **76–100 miles**   ◯ Other_____
12. Approximately what time is your mail delivered?
   ◯ **10am–12pm**   ◯ **12pm–2pm**   ◯ **2pm–4pm**   ◯ **Other**_____
13. Are you satisfied with the time your mail is delivered?   ◯ **Yes**   ◯ **No**
14. Are your responses based on representing a business?   ◯ **Yes**   ◯ **No**
15. Where do you receive mail?   ◯ **P.O. Box**   ◯ **Street Address**   ◯ **Both**
What can our office do to increase your **overall satisfaction** with the service we provide you? _____

Would you like someone from our office to contact you about this or any other issue?
◯ **Yes** (Please complete the information below.)   ◯ **No** (If no, completion of information below is optional and will be used for internal purposes only.)

Full Name:_____   Phone: (___)_____
Address:_____   City/State/ZIP Code:_____

06404957

■ **Providing Better Postal Services**
Government agencies seek ideas to improve customer services. *What information will the U.S. Postal Service gain from an annual survey?*

Marketing Information Systems

The data collected in marketing research must be sorted and stored so that the results can be put to good use. Many businesses have implemented sophisticated marketing information systems to organize, collect, and store marketing research data for future decisions. A marketing information system is a set of procedures and methods that regularly generates, stores, analyzes, and distributes marketing information for use in making marketing decisions. Most marketing information systems rely heavily on internal data, such as sales reports and inventory figures. However, they also often include information from outside sources such as trade reports and marketing research studies. Both managers and salespeople can use marketing information systems.

Data that should be a part of a marketing information system include:

- Company records, such as sales results, expenses, supplier data, and production schedules

- Competitors' records, such as their prices, products, location, and market share

- Customer profile data, such as the results of previous marketing studies regarding buying behavior, shopping patterns, customer demographics, and lifestyles research

- Government data, such as price trends, new regulations and laws, and future projections for the economy

- Marketing research reports that are produced and sold by research firms

Case Study

Keep Away From My Cookies!

Large companies, like Procter & Gamble, are concerned about Internet advertising services companies using their data, or their "cookies." Cookies are tiny data files that a marketer can download onto the hard drive of a user's computer after the user connects to a Web site. Many Web sites require that a visitor accept a cookie as a condition of access. Cookies hold a log of the user's activities, and this information can be read by the owner of an individual Web site and by the advertising services company used by that site.

Ad service companies help individual advertisers by storing individual company ads on their central computer. This process saves large individual advertisers the trouble of placing their own Internet advertisements, which are often placed into hundreds of different Web pages. However, this arrangement also gives the ad service companies access to the data files. Cookies are extremely helpful to an advertiser because they measure what works and what does not work based on visitors' activity on the Web site.

Procter & Gamble is one company that has banned its advertising service providers from using any data obtained from its popular "Pampers Parenting Institute." On the Parenting Institute Web site, Procter & Gamble has visitors register with their names, address, and children's ages to receive a free newsletter on parenting, information about products, and free coupons. All of this information is logged in cookies.

Case Study Review

1. Why do you think Procter & Gamble has banned its ad service company from using its Web site user's data?
2. What benefits can a company obtain by using cookies collected from a company Web site?

A MATTER OF ETHICS

3. Is it ethical for Procter & Gamble to provide visitors with free information regarding parenting skills in exchange for personal information on its Web site? Why or why not?

■ Marketing Databases

Information technologies have made the collection and analysis of data for marketing decision-making much easier. Bar code scanners at point-of-sale terminals provide information on the merchandise that sells and on inventory levels. Many supermarkets have even gone further in data collection by furnishing "valued customer cards," which add the customer's identity to the purchase. Customers complete an application for this card, which entitles them to special discounts. The store in turn collects data on household demographics, lifestyles, and purchase behavior.

Information about consumers and their buying habits are stored in computer databases. A database is a collection (or file) of related information about a specific topic. L. L. Bean, a sportswear and outdoor products retailer, has a database of the people to whom it sends its catalogs. American Express maintains a database of its card members and their addresses, plus what they buy, where they buy it, where they eat out, and how much money they spend. The company uses the information to send its card members special offers on hotels, restaurants, and travel.

Many companies that collect information about their customers sell that information to others. Banks that provide mortgage loans often sell the names and addresses of the borrowers to insurance companies that then send information on buying mortgage insurance to the borrower. This exchange of information among businesses has led to complaints of invasion of privacy. Consumers don't know what information about them is contained in various databases. This information can be passed on or sold to other companies without the consumers knowledge or permission. The government has stepped in to create laws regarding protecting the privacy of consumers. Marketers defend the need to have information about their customers and their buying habits to better serve them.

■ Difficulties of Marketing Information Systems

Setting up a marketing information system requires a significant investment of time and money. Trained personnel are needed to maintain and analyze the data collected in the system. Vast amounts of data can be readily obtained with computerized systems; therefore, businesses sometimes have to prioritize the kind of information that is most useful to them.

Even smaller businesses that cannot afford to establish their own management information department recognize the need for marketing information. *Sales and Management,* a monthly magazine, publishes a directory of 200 companies that specialize in sales and marketing software to help businesses obtain marketing information.

Honesty Is the Best Policy...

Researching a new product with a focus group is a great idea, right? Sure it is, as long as everyone is telling the truth. That is the catch in marketing research—there is no "Pinocchio's growing nose" or litmus test to detect lying. Media Direct Partners became acutely aware of this problem when hosting a focus group on advertising for a surgical hair replacement company. The participants of the focus group—all bald men—insisted that they were not bothered by their hair loss. Yet most of them were wearing hats in the middle of August! When you can't trust the responses of your research participants, your research is no good—especially not in the billion-dollar advertising business. To solve this problem, new research methods are being developed with tools that track brain waves and measure the skin's reaction to questions.

Thinking Critically

Why would focus group participants lie in a research setting?

28.1 ASSESSMENT

Reviewing Key Terms and Concepts

1. What is marketing research?
2. How does marketing research help businesses?
3. Who uses marketing research?
4. What is a marketing information system?
5. What is a database?

Thinking Critically

6. Supermarkets often require the use of a "valued customer" card to obtain special discounts on the store's products. Do you think that supermarkets should give special bargains in exchange for personal shopping information?

Integrating Academic Skills

7. **COMMUNICATION** Write a business letter to your local chamber of commerce or a state trade association to ask how the organization assists its members in conducting marketing research.

Types, Trends, and Limitations of Marketing Research

Types of Marketing Research

The type of research businesses conduct depends on the problem that they are trying to solve. Some of the most significant areas of research are attitude research, market research, media research, and product research.

■ Attitude Research

Attitude research, also known as opinion research, is research designed to obtain information on how people feel about certain products, ideas, or companies. The Gallup Organization conducts opinion research polls on politics, elections, business and the economy, social issues, and public policy. Through interviewing techniques using random samples of the population, opinion poll results can be generalized to the entire population. A business considering a major expansion might be interested in the attitude of the general population toward the economy. For example, knowing the attitude of Americans who currently wear glasses but would consider laser surgery is important information for companies considering a marketing strategy for corrective laser surgery.

■ Market Research

Market research involves the systematic gathering, recording, analyzing, and presentation of information related to marketing goods and services. Market research is concerned with the size, location, and makeup of the market for a particular product or service. It uses market analysis to obtain the necessary data.

Market research is needed before a product is introduced to the market and on a regular basis throughout a product's life. Research, however, is not limited only to products; it is also conducted to answer questions about market segments, stores, brands, advertising strategies, prices, and every other aspect of marketing.

Market analysis is the study of particular consumer and industrial markets. The goal of market analysis is to investigate the potential markets for a product and to define characteristics of the target market.

Existing and projected sales data are used in performing market research. Sales data helps businesses project the potential sales for a product and anticipate problems related to future sales. Sales trends for various products may also be compared to determine whether a product's sales are increasing or declining.

● What You'll Learn

- The four important areas of marketing research
- The important trends affecting marketing research
- The limitations of marketing research

● Why It's Important

Sometimes more than one type of research is needed to solve a particular problem. In addition, data collected from one research study can often be used to solve other business problems relating to marketing. This section will introduce you to the major types of marketing research, the latest trends in this field, and the limitations of marketing research.

Key Terms

- attitude research
- market research
- media research
- product research
- test marketing

SALES FORECASTING *Sales forecasting* is an effort to estimate the future sales of a product. A total estimate of a market is calculated, and then an individual share is predicted for a business.

The share that is assigned to a business is called its *market share* or *sales penetration* of the market. Based on its research findings, the business can then try to increase its market share through changes in the product, pricing, promotion, or distribution strategies.

ECONOMIC FORECASTING *Economic forecasting* is an attempt to predict the future economic conditions of a city, a region, the country, or another part of the world. This research requires extensive knowledge of economic statistics and trend indicators.

Several federal agencies collect information on key economic indicators, such as new building construction, inflation rates, money supply, and consumer and producer price indexes. Most businesses rely on government data to predict economic conditions and to adjust their business activities depending on the economic outlook.

Businesses use research on general economic conditions to help plan for long-range expansion. This research helps to determine whether to cut costs when unfavorable economic conditions, such as higher interest rates or raw materials costs, are predicted.

Private companies, such as Woods and Poole Economics, Inc., also specialize in long-term economic and demographic projections. The Woods and Poole database for every county, state, and metropolitan statistical area (MSA) in the United States contains projections through 2020 for more than 550 variables. This information helps marketing researchers to analyze the makeup of the economy, population changes, households, and retail sales potential (see Figure 28-4 on page 513).

■ Media Research

Media research focuses on issues of media selection and frequency. It measures the effectiveness of the advertising message and media placement. Media research is done on various forms of media such as print, broadcast, and online.

Businesses often conduct research to determine which media or mix of media are most effective for getting an advertising message to a particular market. To conduct that research, businesses may request information from the print, broadcast, and online media of interest to them. In most cases information received would include a rate card, which lists the advertising costs, as well as its circulation or viewership figures, deadline dates, and other requirements for submission of an advertisement. Other information might be about the readers, subscribers, or viewers with regard to age, income, interests, hobbies, occupations, and attitudes. Another means of conducting research on the various media available would be to subscribe to a publication called *Standard Rate and Data Services* (SRDS), which publishes rates and data for the advertising industry.

BRIGHT IDEAS

Bubbles with Attitude

Bubbles are always in style—and popular everywhere from children's parties to fancy weddings. Looking to re-market a time-tested product, Germany's Swetland family used research and development to find success in the bubble market. They hoped to create bubbles that glowed in the dark, but found that the idea was already taken. Instead they developed Tekno Bubbles. These bubbles look like regular bubbles in the light, but under ultra violet or black lights they take on a special quality—they glow! Tekno bubbles, which are available in a variety of colors and scents, are sold at novelty stores.

Thinking Creatively

Choose an already existing product and determine product enhancements that would improve and extend the life of that product.

FIGURE 28-4

Economic and Demographic Projections

DATA TABLES FOR EVERY COUNTY, STATE, AND MSA IN THE U.S.

SAMPLE COUNTY DATA TABLE

2000 CEDDS 707

Data Table for every County, State, & MSA in the U.S.

Historical Data From 1970

Projected Data to 2025

Population by Race

Employment by Industry

Household Data

Wealth Index

Households by Income

Retail Sales by Kind of Business

ALAMEDA COUNTY, CALIFORNIA

		1970	1980	1990	1997	2000	2001	2002	2005	2010	2015	2020	2025
1	TOTAL POPULATION (in THOUSANDS)	1,073.96	1,108.79	1,307.05	1,374.80	1,423.83	1,434.83	1,445.75	1,478.42	1,535.19	1,595.48	1,656.79	1,716.84
2	UNDER 5 YEARS	[illegible]	73.27	104.35	100.83	96.30	95.98	96.27	96.80	100.06	104.35	[illegible]	109.71
3	5 to 9 YEARS	[illegible]	70.49	91.08	103.57	103.01	100.61	98.12	94.53	95.37	98.84	[illegible]	106.40
4	10 to 14 YEARS	[illegible]	79.26	80.56	89.66	96.41	99.80	102.43	102.98	94.87	96.27	100.13	[illegible]
5	15 to 19 YEARS	94.23	95.65	84.13	88.64	94.06	94.53	95.60	103.33	111.11	102.20	103.70	[illegible]
6	20 to 24 YEARS	112.04	110.83	107.74	91.10	100.28	104.43	107.35	111.88	122.75	131.10	120.61	[illegible]
7	25 to 29 YEARS	86.26	110.08	125.32	107.91	102.09	99.03	98.29	104.22	115.60	125.89	133.98	[illegible]
8	30 to 34 YEARS	65.83	104.72	128.79	122.55	116.76	115.63	113.96	105.89	107.75	118.65	128.60	[illegible]
9	35 to 39 YEARS	58.06	77.64	116.68	129.72	130.34	127.63	124.36	116.55	105.81	107.51	118.12	127.78
10	40 to 44 YEARS	62.13	59.61	104.23	121.93	130.95	132.55	133.30	131.67	117.86	107.09	108.89	119.24
11	45 to 49 YEARS	66.47	53.15	75.10	97.94	107.27	110.13	113.20	119.55	120.58	108.75	99.43	101.39
12	50 to 54 YEARS	58.79	55.94	56.93	73.67	85.54	90.07	90.67	97.93	109.66	111.49	101.71	93.74
13	55 to 59 YEARS	50.65	56.99	47.89	53.36	60.77	62.00	67.23	77.23	89.11	100.40	102.91	94.81
14	60 to 64 YEARS	41.56	46.52	46.49	44.16	47.65	48.75	50.12	56.03	71.44	83.06	94.14	97.26
15	65 to 69 YEARS	32.47	39.01	45.44	42.57	41.73	41.93	42.56	45.40	53.17	67.72	78.77	89.25
16	70 to 74 YEARS	25.60	28.95	35.02	38.10	37.23	37.09	36.51	36.15	39.38	46.14	58.82	68.43
17	75 to 79 YEARS	19.05	21.08	26.82	31.44	33.02	32.90	32.78	32.17	31.51	34.57	40.72	52.16
18	80 to 84 YEARS	12.82	13.72	16.61	19.93	21.14	21.93	22.70	24.10	23.72	23.40	25.95	30.85
19	85 YEARS and OVER	8.61	11.88	13.85	17.54	19.29	19.81	20.32	22.01	25.43	28.03	29.68	32.26
20	WHITE POPULATION	857.40	802.02	844.20	839.94	850.62	849.51	848.28	844.70	841.41	841.73	844.16	847.80
21	BLACK POPULATION	162.19	205.77	248.07	262.30	272.73	275.68	278.58	286.92	299.46	311.41	323.08	333.56
22	OTHER POPULATION	54.37	101.00	214.78	272.57	300.49	309.64	318.89	346.80	394.31	442.34	489.55	535.49
23	HISPANIC POPULATION, ANY RACE	135.02	126.50	192.64	244.49	262.51	265.47	268.49	277.48	294.07	314.06	338.05	365.02
24	POPULATION 0 to 19 YEARS (in THOUSANDS)	373.42	318.66	360.12	382.90	389.78	390.93	392.41	397.64	401.42	401.67	414.48	428.56
25	POPULATION AGE 20 to 64 YEARS	601.80	675.48	809.18	842.34	881.65	890.23	898.47	920.95	960.56	993.95	1,008.39	1,015.33
26	POPULATION AGE 65 YEARS and OVER	98.75	114.65	137.75	149.56	152.40	153.67	154.86	159.83	173.21	199.87	233.93	272.96
27	MALE POPULATION (THOUSANDS)	526.16	539.18	646.49	676.64	701.74	707.39	712.92	729.47	758.76	789.43	820.30	851.30
28	FEMALE POPULATION	547.80	569.61	660.55	698.16	722.10	727.44	732.83	748.95	776.43	806.05	836.49	865.54
29	POPULATION AGE 16 YRS AND OVER	776.05	868.38	1,015.73	1,063.00	1,110.38	1,120.43	1,130.63	1,163.24	1,225.21	1,277.00	1,326.61	1,375.57
30	MEDIAN AGE OF POPULATION (in YEARS)	27.81	30.67	32.32	34.36	35.12	35.30	35.46	35.83	35.97	35.86	36.28	36.82
31	TOTAL EMPLOYMENT (in THOUSANDS of JOBS)	499.79	600.76	758.09	823.54	878.43	891.66	903.59	934.63	985.30	1,035.97	1,086.42	1,136.61
32	FARM EMPLOYMENT	3.76	2.14	1.46	1.24	1.20	1.18	1.16	1.09	1.01	0.94	0.89	0.85
33	AGRICULTURAL SERVICES, OTHER	1.85	3.92	5.11e	7.31	8.21	8.36	8.46	8.70	9.14	9.63	10.15	10.69
34	MINING	1.24	0.96	0.84e	0.67	0.62	0.61	0.60	0.58	0.56	0.56	0.56	0.58
35	CONSTRUCTION	21.87	29.17	38.40	40.78	46.82	47.80	48.60	50.36	52.72	54.92	57.10	59.25
36	MANUFACTURING	85.90	87.23	84.93	99.64	99.87	99.91	99.92	99.97	100.20	100.46	100.75	101.14
37	TRANSPORTATION, COMM. & PUBLIC UTILITIES	33.16	34.21	44.48	48.07	50.99	51.82	52.48	53.89	55.45	56.62	57.63	58.53
38	WHOLESALE TRADE	24.39	31.18	43.19	52.08	57.12	58.58	59.93	63.31	68.87	74.66	80.75	87.13
39	RETAIL TRADE	73.02	97.43	121.89	128.26	133.76	135.47	137.08	141.63	148.69	155.15	161.13	166.74
40	FINANCE, INSURANCE & REAL ESTATE	34.44	45.69	50.73	51.22	54.04	54.50	54.87	55.87	57.50	58.94	60.15	61.12
41	SERVICES	92.44	144.43	222.45	272.28	301.25	308.27	314.82	332.28	362.09	392.85	423.91	454.98
42	FEDERAL CIVILIAN GOVERNMENT	27.84	21.75	23.07	13.40	12.53	12.31	12.10	11.49	10.56	9.72	8.97	8.31
43	FEDERAL MILITARY GOVERNMENT	24.91	12.12	19.23	4.95	4.83	4.83	4.83	4.82	4.82	4.81	4.81	4.81
44	STATE AND LOCAL GOVERNMENT	74.94	90.52	102.32	103.64	107.20	108.03	108.76	110.62	113.70	116.70	119.61	122.48
45	TOTAL EARNINGS (in MILLIONS of 1992 $)	$14,345.02	$17,391.08	$23,047.30	$26,710.84	$30,893.04	$31,632.75	$32,333.51	$34,295.07	$37,634.92	$41,119.25	$44,735.72	$48,472.17
46	FARM EARNINGS	73.78	53.93	26.28	13.24	17.74	17.83	17.89	17.99	18.31	18.79	19.43	20.27
47	AGRICULTURAL SERVICES, OTHER	38.37	57.53	100.33e	123.02	135.47	139.29	142.15	150.06	164.38	180.19	197.23	215.43
48	MINING	61.47	92.65	29.79e	25.48	26.50	26.08	25.73	24.96	24.33	24.26	24.68	25.58
49	CONSTRUCTION	943.30	1,238.42	1,680.02	1,573.68	1,848.71	1,898.21	1,940.84	2,044.78	2,195.21	2,338.94	2,480.29	2,618.92
50	MANUFACTURING	3,076.22	3,526.52	3,360.95	4,539.27	5,133.62	5,188.42	5,241.66	5,399.86	5,662.65	5,915.39	6,155.53	6,384.47
51	TRANSPORTATION, COMM. & PUBLIC UTILITIES	1,181.26	1,459.04	1,864.85	1,959.49	2,162.57	2,215.86	2,262.55	2,379.69	2,541.78	2,687.71	2,825.93	2,957.76
52	WHOLESALE TRADE	865.38	1,163.20	1,636.43	2,136.35	2,519.32	2,597.09	2,670.08	2,861.74	3,183.45	3,523.14	3,883.13	4,262.41
53	RETAIL TRADE	1,649.80	2,042.61	2,434.28	2,507.27	2,691.69	2,740.06	2,786.69	2,921.67	3,138.72	3,345.48	3,543.14	3,732.79
54	FINANCE, INSURANCE & REAL ESTATE	627.31	890.84	1,090.06	1,306.00	1,643.84	1,683.09	1,719.57	1,825.52	2,004.08	2,179.19	2,346.95	2,504.26
55	SERVICES	2,083.58	3,301.28	6,099.98	7,940.33	9,863.36	10,221.04	10,568.41	11,563.85	13,345.99	15,293.04	17,384.20	19,606.70
56	FEDERAL CIVILIAN GOVERNMENT	968.88	788.48	839.20	607.20	601.68	595.53	589.80	573.05	545.88	520.48	497.15	476.14
57	FEDERAL MILITARY GOVERNMENT	490.49	225.93	418.00	88.50	100.48	101.17	101.87	103.95	107.47	111.04	114.64	118.29
58	STATE AND LOCAL GOVERNMENT	2,285.20	2,550.64	3,467.13	3,891.01	4,148.06	4,209.07	4,266.28	4,427.94	4,702.67	4,981.60	5,263.40	5,549.15
59	PERSONAL INCOME (in MILLIONS of 1992 $)	$17,668.72	$22,709.82	$31,242.59	$36,497.59	$41,405.81	$42,363.62	$43,285.51	$45,934.00	$50,504.60	$55,330.87	$60,410.25	$65,741.88
60	WAGES AND SALARIES	12,417.92	14,446.12	18,791.19	21,978.03	25,570.54	26,204.16	26,797.52	28,463.80	31,306.72	34,281.02	37,377.88	40,587.75
61	OTHER LABOR INCOME	671.84	1,395.14	2,049.46	2,172.63	2,469.20	2,522.89	2,572.34	2,708.02	2,934.54	3,166.06	3,401.39	3,639.29
62	PROPRIETORS INCOME	1,255.26	1,549.82	2,206.64	2,560.18	2,853.30	2,905.71	2,963.65	3,123.25	3,393.66	3,672.17	3,956.45	4,245.13
63	DIVIDENDS, INTEREST & RENT	2,456.77	3,626.37	5,309.63	5,910.73	6,485.77	6,626.43	6,768.90	7,206.83	7,971.32	8,777.18	9,621.58	10,500.90
64	TRANSFER PAYMENTS TO PERSONS	2,057.57	3,223.64	4,170.13	5,136.12	5,498.52	5,626.35	5,757.92	6,176.51	6,961.77	7,873.58	8,935.22	10,174.73
65	LESS SOCIAL INSURANCE CONTRIBUTIONS	681.58	903.88	1,530.13	1,798.49	2,086.39	2,149.01	2,213.12	2,413.33	2,784.88	3,216.13	3,717.93	4,303.59
66	RESIDENCE ADJUSTMENT	(509.07)	(627.39)	245.67	538.39	614.86	627.10	638.30	668.92	721.47	776.99	835.66	897.68
67	INCOME PER CAPITA (in 1992 $)	$16,452	$20,482	$23,903	$26,547	$29,080	$29,525	$29,940	$31,070	$32,898	$34,680	$36,462	$38,292
68	INCOME PER CAPITA (in CURRENT $)	$4,852	$11,980	$22,208	$29,683	$34,203	$35,528	$36,896	$41,372	$50,843	$63,028	$77,948	$96,289
69	WOODS & POOLE WEALTH INDEX (U.S. = 100)	113.98	115.15	112.55	114.96	117.26	117.30	117.33	117.21	116.78	116.22	115.54	114.78
70	NUMBER OF HOUSEHOLDS (in THOUSANDS)	366.81	428.82	481.23	507.92	529.32	534.68	540.05	556.04	582.12	606.32	626.17	641.89
71	PERSONS PER HOUSEHOLD (in PEOPLE)	2.82	2.52	2.64	2.63	2.62	2.61	2.61	2.59	2.56	2.56	2.57	2.59
72	RETAIL SALES PER HOUSEHOLD (in 1992 $)	$19,415	$20,079	$21,096	$22,178	$23,436	$23,658	$23,853	$24,384	$25,341	$26,434	$27,755	$29,286
73	MEAN HOUSEHOLD INCOME (in 1992 $)	$46,703	$51,881	$63,525	$70,330	$76,617	$77,587	$78,473	$80,833	$84,836	$89,195	$94,236	$99,909
74	MEAN HOUSEHOLD INCOME (in CURRENT $)	$13,773	$30,345	$59,021	$78,636	$90,112	$93,361	$96,705	$107,637	$131,113	$162,107	$201,456	$251,227
75	HOUSEHOLDS with MONEY INCOME (in thousands)	366.81	428.82	481.23	507.92	529.32	534.68	540.05	556.04	582.12	606.32	626.17	641.89
76	LESS than $10,000 (in 1990 $)	n.a.	n.a.	56.18	50.14	46.74	45.99	45.21	42.49	38.16	34.42	30.54	26.19
77	$10,000 to 19,999	n.a.	n.a.	64.02	57.13	53.26	52.41	51.51	48.42	43.48	39.22	34.81	29.85
78	$20,000 to $29,999	n.a.	n.a.	68.85	61.44	57.28	56.36	55.40	52.07	46.76	42.18	37.43	32.10
79	$30,000 to $39,999	n.a.	n.a.	64.83	58.28	54.34	53.46	52.55	49.39	44.36	40.01	35.51	30.45
80	$40,000 to $49,999	n.a.	n.a.	56.85	66.68	67.18	66.47	65.34	61.41	55.15	49.75	44.15	37.86
81	$50,000 to $59,999	n.a.	n.a.	46.36	58.20	68.12	70.70	73.42	79.87	81.47	74.02	65.70	56.34
82	$60,000 to $74,999	n.a.	n.a.	49.56	62.21	72.81	75.57	78.49	88.78	108.88	128.80	139.04	134.29
83	$75,000 to $99,999	n.a.	n.a.	42.26	53.05	62.09	64.44	66.92	75.71	92.84	112.15	135.41	167.05
84	$100,000 to $124,999	n.a.	n.a.	16.55	20.77	24.31	25.23	26.20	29.64	36.35	43.91	53.02	65.40
85	$125,000 to $149,999	n.a.	n.a.	6.45	8.10	9.48	9.83	10.21	11.55	14.17	17.11	20.66	25.49
86	$150,000 or MORE	n.a.	n.a.	9.33	11.71	13.71	14.22	14.77	16.71	20.50	24.76	29.89	36.88
87	TOTAL RETAIL SALES (in MILLIONS of 1992 $)	$7,121.68	$8,610.34	$10,152.01	$11,264.93	$12,405.05	$12649.72	$12881.87	$13,558.72	$14,751.77	$16,027.75	$17,379.45	$18,798.56
88	BUILDING MATERIALS, HARDWARE	215.61	341.17	466.02	594.95	682.25	694.58	706.30	740.87	803.51	874.90	948.92	1,022.93
89	GENERAL MERCHANDISE	[illegible]	[illegible]	[illegible]	1,271.48	1,452.24	1,496.35	1,537.43	1,647.67	1,806.30	1,932.16	2,037.98	2,124.22
90	FOOD STORES	[illegible]	[illegible]	[illegible]	2,014.57	2,126.13	2,145.73	2,163.74	2,216.29	2,312.64	2,405.75	2,494.49	2,575.57
91	AUTOMOBILE DEALERS	[illegible]	[illegible]	[illegible]	2,397.05	2,647.91	2,697.07	2,743.89	2,882.02	3,137.39	3,438.03	3,743.21	4,041.76
92	GASOLINE SERVICE STATIONS	[illegible]	[illegible]	[illegible]	643.19	640.28	653.23	664.94	696.93	750.91	807.91	[illegible]	950.79
93	APPAREL AND ACCESSORIES	[illegible]	[illegible]	[illegible]	532.08	585.13	595.70	605.67	635.01	688.53	746.92	[illegible]	[illegible]
94	FURNITURE, HOME FURNISHINGS	332.58	430.33	661.12	897.22	1,015.69	1,035.77	1,054.98	1,111.92	1,213.13	1,331.99	1,455.73	[illegible]
95	EATING AND DRINKING PLACES	627.78	885.59	1,143.58	1,239.29	1,393.05	1,432.31	1,469.79	1,580.39	1,777.71	1,989.80	2,230.33	[illegible]
96	DRUG STORES	367.54	381.34	508.68	577.27	664.69	684.08	702.35	752.86	829.50	894.63	953.81	1,007.76
97	MISCELLANEOUS RETAIL STORES	702.92	1,093.40	999.56	1,097.83	1,197.69	1,214.89	1,232.78	1,294.76	1,432.15	1,605.66	1,826.14	2,099.91

Note: Historical employment, earnings, and income data, 1969-1997, and population data, 1969-1998, is from U.S. Dept. of Commerce (USDoC); retail sales data is historical for 1972, 1977, 1982, 1987, and 1992 from USDoC; household data is historical for 1970, 1980, 1985 and 1990 from USDoC; Hispanic data is historical for 1970, 1980, and 1990-1998 from USDoC; all other years of data, 1969-1997, for retail sales, households, and Hispanic population are estimated by Woods & Poole (W&P); "e" indicates withheld employment and earnings data estimated by W&P; all data, 1998-2025 (1999-2025 for population), is projected by W&P; residential population as of July 1; Hispanic population is persons of Spanish origin regardless of race - White, Black, and Other sum to total population; Other is the sum of Asian Americans, Native Americans, and Pacific Islanders; employment in number of jobs includes proprietors and part-time jobs; earnings by industry are earnings of workers - the sum of wages & salaries, proprietors income, and other labor income; historical data on households by money income bracket is for 1990 only (from U.S. Dept. of Commerce) and is not consistent with mean household total personal income data; the projections, 1991-2025, of households by money income bracket (in 1990 $) are based on 1990 data only; please read "Technical Description of the 2000 Regional Projections and Database" (Chapter 2 of this report) for an explanation of data sources, data definitions, and projection methods. HISTORICAL DATA IS SUBJECT TO REVISION; PROJECTIONS ARE UNCERTAIN AND FUTURE DATA MAY DIFFER SUBSTANTIALLY FROM THESE PROJECTIONS. WOODS & POOLE DOES NOT GUARANTEE THE ACCURACY OF THE PROJECTIONS OR HISTORICAL DATA CONTAINED IN THIS TABLE. THIS DATA IS PROVIDED SUBJECT TO ALL TERMS AND CONDITIONS OF THE WOODS & POOLE ECONOMICS, INC. END USER LICENSE AGREEMENT AND IS NOT AUTHORIZED FOR USE IN LEGAL OR FINANCIAL TRANSACTIONS.

COPYRIGHT 2000 WOODS & POOLE ECONOMICS, INC. ALL RIGHTS RESERVED. REPRODUCTION BY ANY METHOD IS PROHIBITED.

© 2000 WOODS & POOLE ECONOMICS, INC. • 1794 COLUMBIA ROAD, N.W. SUITE 4 • WASHINGTON, DC 20009-2808

■ **Obtaining Market Research Data** **Public and private organizations provide valuable information for exploring the market potential for products and services.** ***Why is data such as that found in the chart above important for market research?***

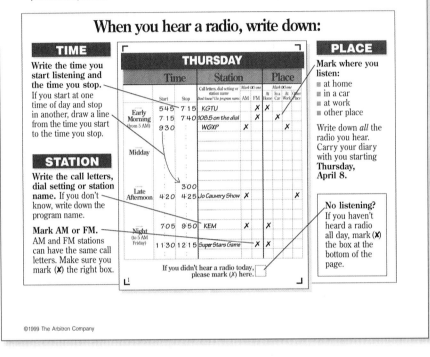

You count in the radio ratings!

No matter how much or how little you listen, you're important!
You're one of the few people picked in your area to have the chance to tell radio stations what you listen to.

This is *your* ratings diary. Please make sure you fill it out yourself.

Here's what we mean by "listening":
"Listening" is any time you can hear a radio – whether you choose the station or not.

When you hear a radio between Thursday, April 8, and Wednesday, April 14, write it down – whether you're at home, in a car, at work or someplace else.

When you hear a radio, write down:

TIME
Write the time you start listening and the time you stop.
If you start at one time of day and stop in another, draw a line from the time you start to the time you stop.

STATION
Write the call letters, dial setting or station name. If you don't know, write down the program name.

Mark AM or FM. AM and FM stations can have the same call letters. Make sure you mark (✗) the right box.

PLACE
Mark where you listen:
■ at home
■ in a car
■ at work
■ other place

Write down *all* the radio you hear. Carry your diary with you starting **Thursday, April 8.**

No listening? If you haven't heard a radio all day, mark (✗) the box at the bottom of the page.

©1999 The Arbitron Company

■ **Researching Radio Advertising** Businesses need to research the effectiveness of their radio advertisements. *What information can be provided through radio diaries?*

RESEARCHING PRINT ADVERTISEMENTS The effectiveness of a printed advertising message can be tested on its recall, communication, and persuasive abilities. Marketing researchers can use different techniques to get people's reactions to an advertisement. In one technique, readers are shown ads from not-yet-released general distribution magazines such as *People, Newsweek,* and *Better Homes and Gardens.* They are queried regarding the ad's effectiveness as to the extent it was noticed, remembered, and associated with the advertised brand. The ad is also measured on its ability to change the consumer's beliefs, attitudes, or intended behavior.

Another technique to measure print advertising effectiveness is through the use of consumer panels. Consumer panels, also called focus groups, are groups of people who are questioned periodically to provide information on research issues. A consumer panel can be comprised of a cross section of people or of people who share common characteristics—senior citizens, single parents, college-educated adults, or teenagers, for example. Oral, written, or observed behavioral responses are recorded to indicate panel members' reactions to an advertisement.

RESEARCHING BROADCAST MEDIA Businesses also want to find out information about various types of broadcast media. The Arbitron Ratings Company, a subsidiary of the Ceridian Corporation, assembles important data on radio advertising. Arbitron produces radio audience measurements and sells software that analyzes advertising expenditure data. Continuous audience measurement in 267 local markets serving 2,300 radio stations makes it the largest radio audience service in the world. Arbitron radio contacts more than 2 million consumers a year and collects more than 1 million diaries to compile its radio station rating reports. *Diaries* are records on which people report such viewer data as who is watching or listening to a station and what programs are tuned in.

Nielsen Media Research, Inc. provides audience measurement information for the television industry. Unlike a magazine or newspaper, where the number of subscribers is known, there is no simple way to know exactly how many people are watching a television program. Nielsen estimates the audience by drawing a sample. It counts the number of viewers in the sample to get a particular television program's rating. The ratings information is generated from a National People Meter Sample of 5,000 homes measuring the viewing habits of 13,000 people.

In meter-equipped households, devices attached to television sets automatically monitor program viewing. Broadcast and cable network providers, program developers, distributors and advertisers use this information to decide on which television programs to advertise (see Figure 28-5).

RESEARCHING ONLINE ADVERTISING As online advertising increases in popularity, researchers have developed marketing research techniques for online copy testing. One technique uses a mock environment similar to traditional copy testing and live testing in an interactive environment. Another aspect to online marketing research is tracking of ad recall and copy effectiveness, as well as evaluation of Web site elements that attract users.

■ Product Research

Product research centers on evaluating product design, package design, product usage, and consumer acceptance of new and existing products. Many new products and their packages are designed, tested, changed, and introduced each year. Product research is also conducted to collect information about competitive products.

NEW PRODUCT ACCEPTANCE Product tests are a way of measuring new product acceptance. One product test has consumers try a product and give their opinions. Product testers are asked questions about specific aspects of the product. A tester of body lotion may be asked about the lotion's texture, scent, consistency, oiliness, and absorption into the skin. Sometimes, two different products are given to test and compare. The products are packaged generically and identified by letter or number. Consumer panels (focus groups) are also used extensively to give feedback on new products.

Have you or your family ever received a small sample box of cereal in the mail? Companies often send samples, usually accompanied by a coupon, to consumers to determine whether they like a product well enough to buy it. You have probably been part of a test market and did not even realize it. Test marketing occurs when a new product is placed in one or more selected geographic areas. Test

FIGURE 28-5

TV Ratings

RATINGS FOR WEEK OF 10/2/00 – 10/8/00

RANK	PROGRAM	NETWORK	RATING	DAY
1	The West Wing	NBC	16.3	Wed
2	Everybody Loves Raymond	CBS	14.6	Mon
3	Who Wants to Be a Millionaire	ABC	14.1	Tue
4	Who Wants to Be a Millionaire	ABC	13.7	Thu
5	Who Wants to Be a Millionaire	ABC	13.4	Wed
6	Who Wants to Be a Millionaire	ABC	13.1	Sun
7	60 Minutes	CBS	12.8	Sun
8	CSI: Crime Scene Investigation	CBS	11.8	Fri
9	Monday Night Football	ABC	11.4	Mon
10	Dark Angel	FOX	11.2	Tue

SOURCE: NIELSEN

■ **Measuring TV Ratings** Advertisers who prepare television advertisements are interested in TV ratings. *What information can TV ratings provide for a television advertiser?*

Peace of mind

FOCUS Suites
We focus on you.

The pressure is on. Your clients are waiting; the group participants are checking in. The last thing you want is an unpleasant surprise. The first thing you need is a responsive staff that supports you.

Focus Suites staff has the experience to anticipate your needs and be flexible when they change. You need to be at your best. From recruitment to project management, Focus Suites does our best to put you there.

visit our website www.focussuites.com

■ **Getting into Focus** Consumer panels are used extensively to give feedback on new products. *What is another term for consumer panel?*

marketing allows marketers to gauge customers' response and to observe a product's sales performance. In the new product development stage, products are test marketed in limited areas. The company monitors the product's sales performance in retail stores that are located in the test market. The results of the test marketing help the manufacturer determine whether the product needs changes before it is introduced to the entire country.

A concern about test marketing is that it offers competitors a chance to see new products before they are ready for national introduction. Competitors can also try to influence the test results by running special advertising and promotions on their own products. Technology has offered one solution to that problem. A company called MarketWare Simulation Services has introduced a program called Visionary Shopper. A computer program allows individuals in a research group to see many different products on screen, including existing products and the new test product. Viewers make choices about which products to put in their on-screen shopping carts. The program tallies the group's responses to different products and gives its clients test market results via computer.

Another marketing research technique to test new products is a product rating board. The Consumer Report magazine for young people, *Zillions,* established a *"Z-Team"* nationwide rating board. This 100-member board of 8- to 14-year-olds was asked to serve for a year and to evaluate various products such as pizza and 35mm cameras.

EXISTING PRODUCT RESEARCH Satisfaction questionnaires and interviews gather information about existing products and services for both the industrial and consumer markets. *Industrial satisfaction surveys* focus upon products and services utilized by business and manufacturing firms. *Customer satisfaction surveys* provide a rich data source for businesses interested in retail customer attitudes toward existing products and services (see Figure 28-6).

FIGURE 28-6

J.C. Penney Customer Survey

America's National Department Store

JCPenney

JCPenney Customer Survey

Marking Instructions
Please use a pencil or a blue or black ink pen only.

Correct ☒ Incorrect ◪

1. Thinking of the JCPenney Store at which you *most* frequently shop, please rate your satisfaction on . . .

	Very Dissatisfied		Somewhat Dissatisfied		Neither Satisfied/ Dissatisfied		Somewhat Satisfied		Very Satisfied	
A. Having the merchandise that you want in stock (e.g., right items, styles, sizes, colors).	1	2	3	4	5	6	7	8	9	10
B. Having good value merchandise for the price paid.	1	2	3	4	5	6	7	8	9	10
C. Having the merchandise that is advertised.	1	2	3	4	5	6	7	8	9	10
D. Having convenient and well-maintained fitting rooms. . .	1	2	3	4	5	6	7	8	9	10
E. Allowing you to make a purchase in a timely manner. . .	1	2	3	4	5	6	7	8	9	10
F. Allowing you to return merchandise without a hassle. . .	1	2	3	4	5	6	7	8	9	10

2. Thinking of the sales service in this JCPenney Store, how satisfied are you on having salespeople who . . .

	Very Dissatisfied		Somewhat Dissatisfied		Neither Satisfied/ Dissatisfied		Somewhat Satisfied		Very Satisfied	
A. Promptly acknowledge you upon entering their department (i.e., within 30 seconds).	1	2	3	4	5	6	7	8	9	10
B. Are available to help you when you have a question and/or need assistance.	1	2	3	4	5	6	7	8	9	10
C. Serve you with a smile and are genuinely friendly and helpful.	1	2	3	4	5	6	7	8	9	10
D. Provide you with useful fashion/product knowledge about the merchandise they sell.	1	2	3	4	5	6	7	8	9	10
E. Are appropriately dressed/have good personal appearance for the merchandise they sell.	1	2	3	4	5	6	7	8	9	10
F. Handle register transactions accurately and efficiently. .	1	2	3	4	5	6	7	8	9	10
G. Thank you by name for shopping JCPenney, whenever possible.	1	2	3	4	5	6	7	8	9	10

3. Thinking of customer service conveniences in this JCPenney Store, how would you rate it on . . .

	Very Dissatisfied		Somewhat Dissatisfied		Neither Satisfied/ Dissatisfied		Somewhat Satisfied		Very Satisfied	
A. Serving you quickly and efficiently at the catalog/credit desk.	1	2	3	4	5	6	7	8	9	10
B. Having clean and well-maintained restrooms.	1	2	3	4	5	6	7	8	9	10
C. Having an overall clean and well-maintained store. .	1	2	3	4	5	6	7	8	9	10

4. In comparison to other department stores you frequently shop, how would you rate this JCPenney Store on. . .

JCPenney is . . .

	Definitely Worse		Somewhat Worse		About Even		Somewhat Better		Definitely Better	
A. Having the merchandise you want in stock (e.g., right items, styles, sizes, colors).	1	2	3	4	5	6	7	8	9	10
B. Having sales associates who are available, friendly, and knowledgeable.	1	2	3	4	5	6	7	8	9	10
C. Making you feel appreciated as a customer.	1	2	3	4	5	6	7	8	9	10

	Definitely No		Probably No		Not Sure		Probably Yes		Definitely Yes	
5. Overall, would you recommend this JCPenney Store to a friend?	1	2	3	4	5	6	7	8	9	10

Thank You!

Please insert survey into reply envelope and mail today.

■ **Providing Information on Existing Products and Service** **Businesses frequently survey their customers about products and services.** ***How is this information useful to a business?***

Trends in Marketing Research

The nature and scope of marketing research are rapidly changing to keep pace with a changing marketplace. The United States is a huge market with many goods and services for almost any consumer need or want. The trend toward a global marketplace means increased international competition for U.S. companies, which must improve or change products frequently to hold on to their customers. In this environment, product quality and customer satisfaction are the keys to business success. Research that measures these qualities has become the fastest growing form of marketing research. It is becoming increasingly important for companies to consider the needs of international consumers.

The basic measure of business success in the future will be customer relationship management, which is measured in continued sales. To maintain a high level of customer satisfaction, companies will need a thorough understanding of their customers' needs and information that tells them how well they are meeting those needs. This can be achieved through effective use of marketing research.

Life In The Diverse MARKETPLACE

Next Door...to the North

Canada may be right next door, but there are many differences to consider when marketing to Canadian citizens. Don't be fooled by the common border and the strong trade history—the cultural makeup is quite different than in the United States. Approximately 25 percent of Canadians call French their first language, 80 percent in the province of Quebec. These French-speaking Canadians are not the only nationals with a foreign influence. Canada was settled by a variety of people from around the world, including France, Britain, Ireland, Germany, Scandinavia, Asia, the Netherlands, Ukraine, Italy, and Poland. How's that for diversity?

Thinking Critically
How can marketers use this information when directing product promotion in Canada?

Another important trend is the use of both internal and external information in managing a business. *Total Quality Management* programs, or *TQM*, place a premium on gathering marketing and other information for use in improving business operations.

As the need and technology for marketing research increases, marketers are faced with a new set of ethical concerns. Some of these concerns include privacy in data collection, privacy in data use, excessive intrusiveness, and deceptive research practices. Such concerns have spurred efforts by the American Marketing Association to discourage unethical research practices among its members.

■ **Research Trends** Advances in technology have resulted in the increased use of marketing research technologies, such as point-of-sale data collection, Internet research, fax broadcasting of surveys to a select group of fax numbers, automated dialing, prerecorded digital surveys, and computerized database management programs. *What effect will the trend toward a global marketplace have on marketing research?*

Limitations of Marketing Research

Each of the major types of marketing research information is used to help businesses make sound business decisions. Few companies, however, can conduct as much marketing research as they would like. The amount of information that can be gathered is limited by the amount of money a company can afford to spend on the equipment and personnel needed to do the research. Often, there is too little time to do the research because decisions must be made before all possible data can be obtained.

Marketing research information also has its limitations. Customers in a test market situation may say they want a particular product, but there is no guarantee they will actually buy the product when it is sold. In addition, fast-changing markets may not allow time for research. There is a time lag between identifying the need for a product, collecting the marketing research, and presenting the findings so the business can decide whether to produce the product. Business conditions, customer buying habits, and customer preferences can change.

Despite these limitations, marketing research provides valuable information. Businesses will continue to rely on marketing research to obtain the best possible information about customers and the marketplace.

REAL WORLD MARKETING

What's in a Name?

Sometimes a change of names can be all it takes to help a product sell. This was the case in 2000 when the California Prune Board (CPB) requested that the Food and Drug Administration (FDA) grant it permission to use the name "dried plums" as an alternative to "prunes." The name change was determined necessary after market research showed that "dried plums" offers a more positive mental image than "prune." The CPB hopes the name change will help to attract its target audience—women age 35 to 44. California prunes aren't the only fruit to change names—the popular kiwifruit was previously called a Chinese gooseberry!

Thinking Critically

Can you think of any products that might benefit from a name change?

28.2 ASSESSMENT

Reviewing Key Terms and Concepts

1. What are the four major areas of marketing research?
2. What is the difference between sales and economic forecasting?
3. What is test marketing?
4. List at least four trends facing marketing researchers today.
5. What are two limitations of marketing research?

Thinking Critically

6. Should every type of business engage in marketing research? Why or why not?

Integrating Academic Skills

7. **MATH** Assume that your company plans to send a marketing questionnaire to 30 percent of the names on a mailing list of 5,000 people. The mailing list was purchased from another company for $0.30 per name. Each questionnaire costs $0.10 to print; mailing costs are $0.36 (including the envelope and return envelope) each; and the cost of writing the questionnaire, analyzing the information, and preparing the report is $15,000. What is the total cost?

Careers in Marketing

MARKETING RESEARCH

Martin Saperstein
Research Analyst
Saperstein Associates, Inc.

Career Facts

What does your job entail?

"Research analysts use statistical data to study potential markets for new products and services. I gather data on customer buying habits, prices, and other market factors. I organize focus groups to help companies make decisions. These focus groups provide information to reduce the possibility of a business making a mistake. We use inferential data, but our sampling error by no means eliminates the chance of being wrong. This information is used to prepare recommendations to management personnel."

What skills are most important?

"Being a good listener is a very important skill. A good analyst can listen and discover what is needed—we find out what the questions are and choose a format for the best answers for a company's research project. We have to be able to collect the data, process it, and share the results with clients. We do not make their decisions, but we offer them recommendations based on the data."

What kind of training did you have?

"I received my undergraduate degree from George Washington University and I have a doctorate in political science from Ohio State University. The rest of the training came from working on the job."

What is the key to your success?

"There are four elements to my success. The first is education, which is the price of admission to this kind of career. The second element is hard work. A strong focus on anticipated goals is the third important element. Many people start businesses and change the direction on a whim, or do too many things at once with no plan. The fourth essential element is my understanding spouse. I cannot overestimate the importance of having a partner who is equally committed, as well as a nonwork environment where I can unwind and be myself. Removing any one of these four aspects would diminish my ability to be successful."

Education and Training: College preparatory classes in advanced math, economics, marketing, merchandising, computer science, English, and psychology are helpful. A bachelor's degree is usually required, and knowledge of current research techniques and online research is helpful.

Aptitudes, Abilities, and Skills: Above-average ability in mathematics, interest in problem solving, ability to plan and develop strategies for gathering and interpreting information, good decision-making skills, strong communication skills, and developed interpersonal skills are necessary.

Career Outlook: Employment opportunities are expected to grow at an average rate through the year 2006. A strong economy and online marketing may increase demand.

Career Path: Senior research analysts begin their careers as interviewers, research assistants, or junior analysts. Some work part-time on these jobs while still in school.

Thinking Critically

Why do you think that being a good listener is important when analyzing research data?

Chapter 28 | ASSESSMENT

VOCABULARY REVIEW

Write the following vocabulary terms and their definitions on index cards. Review the terms and definitions by quizzing a classmate.

- marketing research
- marketing information system
- database
- attitude research
- market research
- media research
- product research
- test marketing

FACT AND IDEA REVIEW

1. What is involved in marketing research? (28.1)

2. What is the major emphasis of marketing research? (28.1)

3. What is the primary function of a marketing information system? (28.1)

4. What is a marketing database? Give an example. (28.1)

5. What is attitude research? (28.2)

6. What is market research? Give an example. (28.2)

7. What is media research? How does research on print media differ from research on broadcast media? (28.2)

8. What is product research? Give an example. (28.2)

9. What are two techniques for researching new product acceptance? (28.2)

10. How has the global economy affected marketing research? (28.2)

THINKING CRITICALLY

1. Surveys indicate that only 34 percent of consumers surveyed trust marketers with regard to their use of consumer marketing information. What can be done to counteract consumer fears about invasion of privacy?

2. Is legislation necessary to make a distinction between legitimate research and telemarketing sales? Explain.

3. Explain what kind of marketing research should be done by a coin-operated car wash.

4. Why are marketing researchers concerned about consumer attitudes and lifestyles?

5. What do you think marketing research would reveal about the differences between the lifestyles of dual-income families with children and the lifestyles of dual-income families without children?

BUILDING WORKPLACE SKILLS

1. **Human Relations** You have a part-time job in the marketing research department of a large corporation. You and three coworkers are gathering information through telephone surveys. Your supervisor wants each of you to complete at least 30 surveys a day, which can be difficult. One coworker makes rude comments to people who do not participate and has told others that the survey is government-sponsored and mandatory. What should you do?

2. **Technology** Investigate database management computer software programs used for marketing research by reviewing advertisements in business publications. Write a letter requesting additional information.

1. **Summarizing Key Concepts** Summarize an article that demonstrates any of the key concepts in this chapter. In the summary, identify the specific concepts in parentheses. Use business publications such as *BrandWeek, Adweek, BusinessWeek, Fortune, Forbes,* and *Marketing News* to find an applicable article.

2. **Identifying Market Factors** Use the Internet to research your city or state's population, income, education, trading area, and purchasing power. Consult city or state offices for additional market information. Create an oral report using presentation software highlighting these marketing factors.

3. **Evaluating Research Agencies** Investigate companies that provide customer research, online database searching, and information-brokering services on the Internet. Identify four questions that you would ask of a large research agency before you would use its services for media research.

4. **Meeting Consumer Needs** Search the Internet for an existing consumer product that you think needs to be changed to raise consumer appeal. Research the product and propose changes. Present your proposal and rationale in an oral report.

5. **Analyzing Marketing Trends** Use presentation software to present an oral report on the trends affecting marketing research within a particular industry, such as electronics.

LINKING SCHOOL TO WORK

Basic Skills Interview your training sponsor or current supervisor to find out how research is conducted at your place of employment. Report your findings orally to the class.

THE DECA CONNECTION

Role Play: Research Consultant

Situation You are to assume the role of employee at a sporting goods store. You have been asked by your store manager (judge) to present your ideas for conducting research on the feasibility of adding a new line of in-line skates and related accessories.

Activity You must make an oral presentation to your store manager (judge) explaining the types of research that will need to be conducted to determine whether the new product line and accessories should be added.

Evaluation You will be evaluated on how well you meet the following performance indicators:
- Explain the nature of marketing research in a marketing information management system
- Assess marketing information needs
- Interpret descriptive statistics for marketing decision making
- Explain the nature of sales forecasts
- Describe the need for marketing information

inter NET CONNECTION

Researching Market Researchers
Visit the Web site for the American Marketing Association and select one of the top 50 U.S. research organizations to investigate.

Connect
- Write a summary of the company in 150–200 words, describing the company's history, number of employees, and the marketing research that it conducts.

Chapter 29

Conducting Marketing Research

Marketing: What It Takes

Surveying Citizens
Imagine that you are surveying people in the community to obtain feedback about government services and ideas for improvements.

WHAT WILL YOU DO?
How will you determine the best way to gain data? How will you ensure a high response rate?

Marketing Research

The Marketing Research Process

The five steps that a business follows when conducting marketing research are *defining the problem, obtaining data, analyzing the data, recommending solutions,* and *applying the results.* Each step is performed sequentially to arrive at solutions to a problem or research issue. Figure 29-1 on page 524 provides more details on each of these steps in the research process.

Step 1: Defining the Problem

The most difficult step in the marketing research process is defining the problem. Problem definition occurs when a business clearly identifies a problem or research issue and the information that is necessary to solve it. An example of a problem may be declining sales. The business needs to decide what it can do to improve sales. It will want to know who is buying its products, who are its present competitors, and why past customers stopped buying. The business will also need to know where, when, and why the product sells or does not sell.

Research issues can focus on any aspect of the marketing process. To study the problem of declining sales, marketers might pose questions such as:
- Are customers satisfied with the present product?
- Are prices competitive?
- Are the products distributed efficiently in the marketplace?
- Are promotion activities effective?

Because money and time are limited, each business has to determine which problems and issues are the most important to address at a given time.

Step 2: Obtaining Data

The second step in the marketing research process is to obtain data. During this second step, data are collected and examined in terms of the problem or problems being studied.

The word *data* means facts. There are two types of data used in marketing research: *primary* and *secondary.* Primary data are data obtained for the first time and used specifically for the particular problem or issue under study. Secondary data have already been collected for some purpose other than the current study. Secondary data are less expensive to collect than primary data. It is most effective for a company to decide what secondary data it will use before collecting any primary data.

What You'll Learn
- The steps in conducting marketing research
- The difference between primary and secondary data
- The various methods used to collect primary and secondary data

Why It's Important

Businesses that want to increase their customer base must have information about the attitudes and behaviors of current and prospective customers. Marketing research can provide information for strategies that will increase sales and profits.

Key Terms
- problem definition
- primary data
- secondary data
- survey method
- sample
- observation method
- point-of-sale research
- experimental method
- data analysis

FIGURE 29-1

THE MARKETING RESEARCH PROCESS

There are five steps in the problem solving process. They start with defining the problem and involve collecting and analyzing data until a potential solution can be found and applied. Following each step in the proper order helps businesses reach effective business decisions.

1 DEFINING THE PROBLEM

The problem or research issue is identified and goals are set to solve the problem.

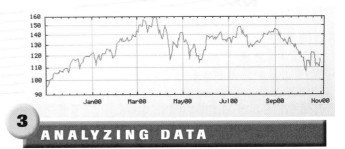

3 ANALYZING DATA

Researchers compile, analyze, and interpret the data.

2 OBTAINING DATA

Researchers obtain data from primary and secondary sources.

4 RECOMMENDING SOLUTIONS

Researchers come up with potential solutions to the problem and present them in a report.

5 APPLYING THE RESULTS

The research results are put into action.

How Secondary Data Are Obtained

Secondary data are obtained from both internal sources (sources within the company) and external sources (sources outside the company). An excellent source of internal secondary data is the marketing information system of a business. As explained in Chapter 28, a marketing information system is an internal method of getting data used to measure monthly sales, determine the geographic distribution of customers, track customer buying patterns, and identify popular items on the market.

INTERNET SOURCES The Internet has increased the availability of secondary data from a variety of sources. *Digital dossiers,* which provide company profiles on public corporations, income statements, and balance sheets, are available online. These reports can be purchased for a fee from online databases such as *Hoover, Fortune 500,* and *Inc. 500.*

Online business clearinghouses such as *Starting Point* and the *Competitive Intelligence Guide* offer commercial directories and company resources.

■ **Obtaining Secondary Data** Government data are an excellent source of secondary data for businesses. *Why should a business review government data sources before launching into a marketing research project?*

U.S. GOVERNMENT SOURCES Federal government studies can provide useful information and statistics about markets, people, and business activities. Data collected by U.S. government agencies regarding population demographics, specific markets, industries, products, economic news, export information, and legislative trends can be accessed on the Internet for free or for a nominal cost. *FedWorld* and *The Federal Web Locator* are two Web directories with links to most government Web sites that provide such data.

The Small Business Administration, U.S. Department of Commerce, U.S. Census Bureau, U.S. Security and Exchange Commission, and the Bureau of Labor Statistics can also be excellent sources for secondary data. Publications such as the *Census of the Population* and the *Statistical Abstract of the United States* contain hundreds of tables, graphs, and charts that can be useful when analyzing various business situations.

CONSUMER AND BUSINESS INFORMATION COMPANIES An active and growing number of specialized research companies or *syndicated services* also offer secondary data for business needs. Specialized companies sell demographic data, five-year forecasts, consumer purchase information, business data, census information, and consumer classification reports to businesses. An example is Audit & Surveys Worldwide (ASW), which provides continuous monthly national measures of retail sales by brand. ASW also provides an annual update of the universe for all U.S. retail and service outlets from the National Retail Census, which is the largest in-person distribution measurement program conducted in the United States, as well as many other types of market research services. Syndicated service companies make data available in print and electronic formats.

BUSINESS AND TRADE PUBLICATIONS Secondary data can also be obtained in publications such as *Forbes, Business Week, The Wall Street Journal,* and *Sales and Marketing Management.* Trade association publications often publish secondary data through articles, reports, and books. Examples of trade associations for marketing research include the American Association for Public Opinion Research, Council of American Survey Research Organizations, and the Marketing Research Association.

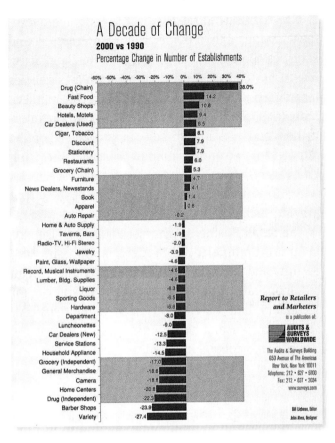

A Decade of Change
2000 vs 1990
Percentage Change in Number of Establishments

Category	Change
Drug (Chain)	38.0%
Fast Food	14.2
Beauty Shops	10.8
Hotels, Motels	9.4
Car Dealers (Used)	8.5
Cigar, Tobacco	8.1
Discount	7.9
Stationery	7.9
Restaurants	6.0
Grocery (Chain)	5.3
Furniture	4.7
News Dealers, Newsstands	4.1
Book	1.4
Apparel	0.8
Auto Repair	-0.2
Home & Auto Supply	-1.9
Taverns, Bars	-1.9
Radio-TV, Hi-Fi Stereo	-2.0
Jewelry	-3.9
Paint, Glass, Wallpaper	-4.6
Record, Musical Instruments	-4.6
Lumber, Bldg. Supplies	-4.6
Liquor	-6.3
Sporting Goods	-6.5
Hardware	-6.6
Department	-8.0
Luncheonettes	-9.0
Car Dealers (New)	-12.5
Service Stations	-13.3
Household Appliance	-14.5
Grocery (Independent)	-17.0
General Merchandise	-18.6
Camera	-18.8
Home Centers	-20.8
Drug (Independent)	-22.3
Barber Shops	-23.9
Variety	-27.4

Report to Retailers and Marketers is a publication of:

AUDITS & SURVEYS WORLDWIDE
The Audits & Surveys Building
650 Avenue of The Americas
New York, New York 10011
Telephone: 212 • 627 • 9700
Fax: 212 • 627 • 2034
www.surveys.com

Bill Liebman, Editor
John Alves, Designer

■ **Call the Specialists** Syndicated service companies provide specialized data to other businesses. *Why would a company want to receive information about their competitors?*

ADVANTAGES OF SECONDARY DATA The greatest advantage of secondary data is that it can be obtained easily because the data are either on the Internet, in corporate, public, and college libraries, or for purchase from syndicated services. In addition, some types of secondary data, such as nationwide population figures, are available through the U.S. Bureau of the Census. Any firm trying to collect similar population data would have to spend a great deal of time and money.

DISADVANTAGES OF SECONDARY DATA There are two major disadvantages associated with secondary data. First, the existing data may not be suitable or available for the problem under study. This situation is most common for new and innovative products. In 1999, secondary data available from *PC Data* showed that Sony's original PlayStation platform had 29 percent of the video game market in the United States. When Sony developed the PlayStation2 video game console, however, no secondary data on this new category of "networked digital entertainment" was available.

The other disadvantage is that secondary data may sometimes be inaccurate. Federal census data are collected every ten years. As a result, projections based on the census most recently completed may not be correct for the current year.

Despite these limitations, a business should first try to find free or low-cost secondary data to avoid the cost and time of collecting primary data.

■ How Primary Data Are Obtained

When marketing researchers cannot find the information they need from secondary data, they collect primary data. Primary research data can be obtained through company research projects or commercial research organizations. Large companies frequently have their own marketing research staff to conduct primary research for the company. Smaller companies that don't have a research staff rely on commercial research organizations. National research organizations often provide attitude and opinion, market, media, and product research services under contract for other businesses and organizations. AC Nielsen, Arbitron, Market Facts, IMS Health, and Westat are some of the leading research organizations in the U.S. In addition, many advertising agencies have research departments that will conduct research for clients.

Primary data may be collected using three methods. These include the survey method, the observation method, and the experimental method.

THE SURVEY METHOD The survey method is a research technique in which information is gathered from people through the use of surveys or questionnaires. It is the most frequently used method of collecting primary data.

When designing a survey, marketers must determine the number of people to include in their survey. Researchers can survey the entire population if the target population is small. This is called a census. Usually, though, the target population is too large, and time and money are too limited to allow researchers to survey the entire population. In this case, researchers would use a sample of the entire target population to get survey results. A sample is a part of the target population that is assumed to represent the entire population. The size of the sample depends upon the amount of money the company has to spend and the degree of accuracy that is needed. Generally speaking, the larger the sample, the greater the accuracy of the results.

After determining the size of the population to survey, you must decide what type of survey to conduct and create the data collection instrument. Surveys can be conducted in person, by phone, (personal and prerecorded), by mail (regular and e-mail), or by using Internet technologies. The decision on how to conduct the survey must be made before the questionnaire is created so that the questions can be written according to the specific needs of each survey type. You will learn more about how to create a survey questionnaire in Section 29.2.

The *personal interview* involves questioning people face-to-face. Since door-to-door interviews are expensive, researchers often conduct interviews in central locations, such as shopping malls and airports. Because this type of interview began in shopping malls, it is called a *mall intercept* interview.

A form of personal interview is the focus group interview. A *focus group interview* involves eight to twelve people who are brought together to evaluate advertising, a particular product, package design, or a specific marketing strategy under the direction of a skilled moderator.

The moderator must direct the discussion to accomplish the objectives of the study. He or she is also responsible for stimulating the group's thinking about the idea or concept. Focus group facilities usually include conference rooms, observation rooms, and audiotape and videotape equipment.

A major advantage of personal interviews is that it is often easier to get people to respond to personal interviews than to mail, phone, or Internet surveys. Interviewers are able to obtain more complete answers to the survey questions. A disadvantage, however, is the cost associated with personal interviews. Personal interviews are generally more expensive than mail, telephone, or Internet surveys because they require hiring experienced interviewers who are skilled at asking nonbiased questions and interpreting the answers correctly. Personal surveys are easy to administer, but it takes time to get survey responses tabulated for data analysis.

The telephone interview is quick, efficient, and relatively inexpensive. A disadvantage of telephone interviews, however, is that some people are unwilling to respond to questions over the telephone. People sometimes resist this approach to data collection because they do not know the caller, dislike responding to a prerecorded digital survey, resent the intrusion on their personal time, or question how their answers will be used.

■ **Mall Intercept Interviews** Mall intercept interviews involve questioning people face to face. *What are some advantages of personal interviews?*

A mail survey is a relatively inexpensive way to reach a potentially large audience. With a direct mail survey a business can use visual presentation techniques. Respondents are generally honest with their responses and find mail surveys to be less of a personal intrusion.

Unfortunately, the average return rate for mail surveys is only 10 percent. Techniques aimed at improving response rates include pre- and post-survey reminders encouraging people to respond to the survey. Average response rates can be improved for questionnaires by offering some type of incentive to complete them. In recent years, some researchers have found that including incentives with the questionnaire, such as discounts on future purchases or pre-paid minutes on a telephone card gets better results. Offering a copy of the results might encourage participation, especially if the survey is of professionals in a given area.

Research information can also be obtained through Internet technologies. *Internet survey* methods include wide-open polls, anybody-can-answer polls, invitation-only surveys, password protected research sites, and Internet-based panels. While

■ **Taking the Mystery Out of Customer Service** Mystery shopping is an observation technique that can improve customer service. *How can the results of a mystery shopping experience improve customer service?*

online research will never completely replace traditional survey methods, the Council of America Survey Research Organizations estimates that by 2005 online research will represent 30–50 percent of the research volume.

Computer-administered surveys are quick and eliminate data entry because the responses are automatically tabulated when the survey is completed. Internet-based research allows for real-time data collection, multiple-choice, and open-ended text-based answers. A drawback is that the use of Internet surveys is limited to individuals who have access to the Web.

THE OBSERVATION METHOD The observation method is a research technique in which the actions of people are watched and recorded either by cameras or observers. Properly performed and recorded observations supply better results than those from survey techniques.

Another use of observation called *mystery shopping* is used to view the interaction between customers and employees. A *mystery shopper* is a researcher who poses as a customer and goes into retail stores to observe employees. A manufacturer, for example, may want to know whether retail employees who sell its products are demonstrating

FIGURE 29-2

Rating Quality of Service

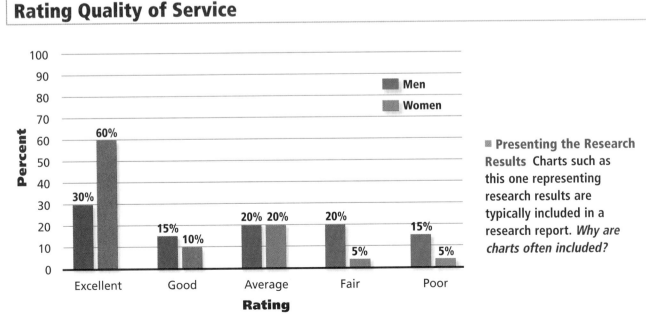

■ **Presenting the Research Results** Charts such as this one representing research results are typically included in a research report. *Why are charts often included?*

them properly and answering customers' questions correctly. The salespeople are observed on approach, sales presentation, product knowledge, and suggestion selling.

One disadvantage of the observation method is that it cannot measure attitudes or motivation. Observation provides information on what the person does, but not why the person does it. Since there is no direct interview of the individuals being observed, a researcher can only speculate on the motives behind the behavior. When knowledge of motivation is important to the business research, another research method may be more useful.

The observation technique may use either *contrived* or *natural* situations. The researcher sets up contrived observations. To decide which toys to market, a toy manufacturer may bring in a group of children to play with the toys. Observers note which toys the children choose and how long they play with them. This is often done using a one-way mirror through which observers can see the children, but the children cannot see the observers. The popular toys are the ones that get marketed. Contrived observations allow researchers to control a testing situation, but respondents may not make the same choices as they would in a real buying situation. Children faced with an entire store of toys might not choose the same toys as they would in the contrived observation.

In natural observation customers or employees are viewed as they would normally act in a given situation. An example of natural observation is when people or hidden cameras observe customers as they enter, shop, or leave a store. Another form of natural observation is the *traffic count*—a count of people or cars as they pass by a store. A traffic count might tabulate the number of people who pass without looking, look and then pass, or stop, look, and enter.

Observation research is faster than personal interviews because participants do not have to be screened by telephone or scheduled for a particular time. Usually people are unaware that they are being observed, which suggests that they are acting how they normally would in a given situation. This type of research can be cost-effective because businesses do not pay for postage or telephone costs, participant fees, or special interviewing facilities.

REAL WORLD MARKETING

Making Tweens Feel At Home

They say that home is where the heart is and furniture designers are stressing that the bedroom is where the heart is for tweens. Tweens—8-to-14 year olds—are one of the hottest consumer groups, and the latest trend is home furnishings. Traditionally adult furniture stores—such as IKEA, Ethan Allen, and Pottery Barn—have expanded their lines to include designer beds, rugs, and dressers that are guaranteed to provide sweet dreams. As more people have children later in life, there is more disposable income; this equals more money to spend on a place where kids like to hang—their rooms. Look out Martha Stewart!

Thinking Critically

How might research firms track the number of tweens in the U.S.?

Point-of-sale research is a powerful form of research that combines natural observation with personal interviews to get people to explain buying behavior. Point-of-sale researchers observe shoppers to decide which ones to choose as research subjects. Researchers may look for shoppers buying a specific type of product, product brand, or who inspect a product but do not buy it.

After observation, researchers approach the selected shoppers and ask them questions. Point-of-sale research combines observation with personal interviews, which offers many benefits to researchers. All participants in the research study are "qualified" respondents because they have been selected by observation. Participants can be chosen based on variables such as shopping time (morning, afternoon, or evening), product price, or any other variable that can be observed. Researchers can also get input from other family members or shopping companions. Participants can easily remember the reason why they purchased a product because the purchase has just been made.

THE EXPERIMENTAL METHOD The experimental method is a research technique in which a researcher observes the results of changing one or more marketing variables while keeping certain other variables constant under controlled conditions. The experimental approach is often used to test new package designs, media usage, and new promotions.

A candy company, for example, may want to compare the effectiveness of two different package color designs for its new candy bar. The company researcher will select two similar groups of consumers. The first group is shown a proposed package for the candy bar. The other group is shown an identical package containing the same product information, except the colors of the package have been changed. Each group's response is measured and the results are determined. The researcher had control over the test environment and only the color of the packaging changed, therefore if one package gets a better response, the company can attribute it to the color.

The experimental method is infrequently used for marketing research. One reason for this is the cost of setting up the research situation. In addition, people respond differently under controlled conditions in contrast to actual buying situations. This difference can make the research data collected less valuable. In situations where different approaches or ideas need to be compared, the experimental method offers an excellent source of information.

Step 3: Analyzing the Data

The third step in the marketing research process is data analysis. Data analysis is the process of compiling, analyzing, and interpreting the results of primary and secondary data collection.

Rupert's Autos surveyed customers about the quality of the dealership's repair service. The number of customers returning the survey was 120. Answers to questions were organized so that the percentage of men and women responding to each question could be shown clearly. Data were cross-tabulated to determine such things as how men and women differ in their perceptions of the service. The answers to a question about the quality of service might be presented as follows. The number of respondents is given in parentheses after the question to tell the reader how many people responded.

Changing Focus

Focus groups—informal discussion sessions of current or potential customers—help companies receive feedback on products and see how they stack up against competition. Now, they are even more effective with the help of technology. In the past, focus groups took place in specially designed boardrooms, with marketers gathered behind a one-way mirror to observe the progress. Today, these rooms are wired with video cameras and satellite networks that allow close-ups or full-group views of focus groups live to interested companies across the country. Online focus groups are becoming more popular, using e-mail to screen and qualify possible focus group candidates. The focus group then operates in an environment similar to an online chat, with all participants seeing all questions and responses. The companies have simplified their research procedures and participants still receive the customary $30–$50 payment sometimes without ever leaving their home!

Thinking Critically

What are some benefits of online chats for market researchers?

Question: *How would you rate the quality of service provided by Rupert's Autos? (N = 120)*

Rating	Men	Women
Excellent	30%	60%
Good	15%	10%
Average	20%	20%
Fair	20%	5%
Poor	15%	5%

As you can see in Figure 29-2 on page 528, female customers of Rupert's Autos generally have a more favorable impression of the quality of service than the male customers do. This information shows that the dealership's image among its male customers needs to be improved.

Case Study

It's a Hit!

All professional baseball teams have Web sites for ticket information, merchandise, and statistics. The new baseball stadiums in Detroit, Houston, and San Francisco have taken technology a step further.

Each new stadium is equipped with advanced fiber optic networks that handle data from voice and data links, concession stands, scoreboards, security cameras, sound systems, interactive kiosks, and video production centers. The data measures attendance, improves services, supports modern sound systems, monitors interactive services, and provides video displays on stadium scoreboards.

In return, owners gather information on fans through fan loyalty programs that provide incentives and rewards for attending games and buying food and merchandise. A condition for receiving fan loyalty cards is that fans must fill out a questionnaire.

Fans receive a card with a magnetic strip that stores personal information. This card is swiped each time the fan attends a game or purchases an item. Points are accumulated which can then be used for free or discounted tickets or team merchandise. Loyalty cards allow owners to capture information such as arrival times, gate access, and purchase habits of each fan. Even the turnstiles use bar code readers, which store information on attendance counts and traffic patterns for stadium entrances. The computer also can invalidate lost or stolen tickets and issue new tickets.

Case Study Review

1. **Why is computerized data collection becoming a part of baseball?**
2. **How can baseball owners use bar coded ticket information to improve customer service?**

A MATTER OF ETHICS

3. **Is it ethical to ask for background information before issuing a fan loyalty card? Why or why not?**

Step 4: Recommending Solutions to the Problem

Successful research results in information that helps businesses make decisions on how to solve a problem. The conclusions drawn from the research are usually presented in an organized and well-written report. Recommendations must be clear and well supported by the research data.

Let's use the example of the auto dealership. Looking at the table of percentages, the researcher would conclude that 55 percent of the male customers thought service was average or worse. The 55 percent is calculated by adding the percentages for average, fair, and poor. The percentage of women who answered that service was average or below was 30 percent. The conclusion to be drawn from these percentages is that service needs to be improved. A recommendation might be to provide additional training for repair staff or to develop a program to communicate better with customers about their repairs.

A typical research report includes the following:

- Title page
- Acknowledgments to people who assisted in the research effort
- Table of contents
- Tables, figures, charts, and graphs
- Introduction (includes the problem under study, its importance, definitions, limitations of the study, and basic assumptions)
- Review of the research information (including the results of any secondary data reviewed for the research effort)
- Procedures used (research technique or techniques used to obtain primary data)
- Findings
- Recommendations
- Summary and conclusions
- Appendices
- Bibliography

Step 5: Applying the Results

Managers use the research report to make decisions about marketing strategies in relation to the researched problem or issue. In evaluating the research, managers may find that the research was inconclusive, additional research may be needed, or the research suggests specific courses of action.

The results are inconclusive if the data gathered by research does not help to solve the problem. Inconclusive results generally require more research. Sometimes the research also points out new areas of a problem that had not been anticipated. That situation may also call for additional research.

After the research has been completed and recommendations acted upon, a business should carefully monitor the results. A business needs to know whether the specific actions taken are successful. The research effort has been a success if decisions made as a result lead to increased profits through better sales, increased efficiency, or reduced expenses.

Marketing research is an ongoing process of problem solving. The results obtained through marketing research should become a part of the total information available to a business for making future decisions.

It is possible that management may choose to not use the findings of a research study. There might have been problems that made the results inconclusive. It may turn out the problem was misdefined from the beginning or it may have disappeared during the research. Sometimes the results and solutions are identified too late to be of any help. The follow-up process helps to determine when and how these problems occurred. It also identifies how research can be better planned in the future.

29.1 ASSESSMENT

Reviewing Key Terms and Concepts

1. What are the five steps in designing and conducting a research study?
2. Explain the difference between primary and secondary data.
3. Name the methods used most frequently to collect secondary data.
4. Name the methods used most frequently to collect primary data.
5. What is meant by the term data analysis?

Thinking Critically

6. Many retail stores ask customers to give their phone number or ZIP code after each sale. Do you support this type of data collection? Why or why not?

Integrating Academic Skills

7. **COMMUNICATION** Write a 100-word memo to your instructor explaining what method of marketing research should be conducted prior to the introduction of new merchandise for your school store. Provide the rationale for your method.

The Marketing Survey

Constructing the Questionnaire

Questionnaires should provide data with validity. Validity exists when the questions asked measure what was intended to be measured. A researcher designs a questionnaire to measure a restaurant's customer service. Questionnaires that feature poorly written questions or do not address customer service will not have validity.

Research questionnaires should also have reliability. Reliability exists when a research technique produces nearly identical results in repeated trials. Reliability requires that the questions ask the same type of information from all the respondents. Questions should be clear and easily understood so that all participants understand the question in the same way. Questions that are unclear and poorly written will not gain reliable responses. Asking a respondent in a restaurant survey, "Was your food hot?" would not yield a reliable answer. "Hot" could be interpreted as either the level of spiciness or food temperature.

To be valid and reliable, a questionnaire must be properly written, formatted, and administered. There are guidelines that can be followed to ensure that a questionnaire is effective.

■ Writing Questions

Survey questions can be either open ended or forced choice. Open-ended questions ask respondents to construct their own response to a question. "How can we serve you better?" is an example of an open-ended question. Some surveys have a space for "general comments" or "suggestions" on the survey instrument. This is also a type of open-ended question. Open-ended questions generate a wide variety of responses that are sometimes difficult to categorize and tabulate. As a result, most researchers prefer forced-choice questions.

Forced-choice questions ask respondents to choose answers from possibilities given on a questionnaire. Forced-choice questions are the simplest questions to write and the easiest to tabulate. They can be two-choice questions, multiple choice questions, rating or ranking scales, and level of agreement scales.

YES/NO QUESTIONS Two-choice questions give the respondent only two options, usually yes or no. Yes/No questions should be used only when asking for a response on one issue. You could use a Yes/No question to ask "Was our facility clean?" but not to ask "Was our facility clean and well-maintained?" The customer may have conflicting answers for the two issues that the question addresses. This would decrease validity and reliability.

● What You'll Learn

- How to construct a survey
- The ways that technology is used in marketing research

● Why It's Important

Businesses need valid and reliable data to make good decisions. Marketing researchers need to know how to construct survey instruments that provide the necessary information to assist in the decision-making process.

Key Terms

- validity
- reliability
- open-ended questions
- forced-choice questions

The following is an example of a Yes/No questionnaire that a bakery and restaurant might administer to customers.

Please answer Yes or No to the following questions:

Did you receive a pleasant greeting upon entering?	Yes	No
Was our facility clean?	Yes	No
Was your server courteous?	Yes	No
Was your menu selection prepared to your liking?	Yes	No
Other comments or suggestions _____		

Yes/No questions are most often used as filter questions. Filter questions help to guide respondents to answer only those questions that apply. Question #5 on the Ford Automobile Ownership Survey in Figure 29-3 serves as a filtering question.

Have you for any reason taken your vehicle to have it serviced (maintenance or repair) during the last year?

Yes   No—Go to question 15

Respondents who answer *No* may skip to other survey questions. While respondents who answer *Yes* are asked a series of questions following

Question #5 related to the quality of repair services that they did receive at the car dealership. In cases where there is a range of choices and yes/no questions are not appropriate, you would use multiple choice questions, rating scale questions, or level of agreement questions.

MULTIPLE CHOICE QUESTIONS Multiple choice questions give the respondent several choices. When constructing multiple choice questions, it is important that the options are made comprehensive enough to include every possible response. Multiple choice options must be mutually exclusive and all encompassing. In order to be sure that all options are covered, many surveys have a space for the option "other."

An outdoor clothing manufacturer might ask its customers the following question.

What is your primary intended use of this product? (check only one)
☐ **A.** Backpacking/Mountaineering
☐ **B.** Camping/Hiking
☐ **C.** Fishing
☐ **D.** Hunting
☐ **E.** Other_____

FIGURE 29-3

Ford Automobile Ownership Survey

Please tell us about your most recent service visit.

ABOUT YOUR SERVICE EXPERIENCE

5 **Have you for any reason taken your vehicle to have it serviced (maintenance or repair) during the past year?**
☐ Yes   ☐ No → *Go to 15*

a. **For the most recent service, what kind of work was done? Mark all that apply.**
☐ Routine maintenance (e.g., oil change, lube, tune–up)   ☐ Recall work
☐ Body work (e.g., collision repairs, paint)   ☐ Other repairs
☐ Engine, transmission or axle repairs

b. **Where did you go for your most recent service visit? Mark one box.**
☐ Grand Ledge Ford, Inc. → *Go to 6*
☐ Another Ford/Lincoln–Mercury Dealer
☐ Independent garage/mechanic   ☐ Some other place (e.g., Goodyear, Sears, Midas, Jiffy Lube)

c. **If you did not return to your selling dealer for this most recent service visit, please tell us why. Mark all that apply.**
☐ Dealer location   ☐ Quality of prior service   ☐ Other_____
☐ Convenience   ☐ Price   _____
☐ Treatment by service personnel   ☐ Parts not available   _____

0017780   *(Please Go To Next Page)*

■ **Importance of Yes/No Questions** Yes/No questions are known as forced-choice questions because there are only two choices. *How can Yes/No questions be used as filtering questions?*

Offering the choice of "other" increases reliability. Respondents who purchased the product for another reason may choose not to answer at all or may choose to pick an inaccurate answer from the list just to give an answer if "other" was not provided. This would cause misleading results.

RATING SCALE QUESTIONS Other forced-choice questions may ask respondents to rate a product based on a scale (see Figure 29-4). A variety of scales may be used, such as a rating scale from *very satisfied* to *very dissatisfied*, or from *excellent* to *poor*. The following is an example of a rating question that might be used by a hotel.

FIGURE 29-4

Holiday Inn Customer Service Survey

Please Tell Us What You Think! *Holiday Inn*

Did you recently stay at the Holiday Inn SAULT STE. MARIE, ON?

If so, please let us know how well we served you.

020833193689120041

■ **Rating Scales** Some forced-choice questions have respondents reply with a rating scale. *Why do businesses often use rating scales to measure customer satisfaction?*

Please rate the following:

Reservations	Excellent	Good	Average	Fair	Poor
Concierge Services	Excellent	Good	Average	Fair	Poor
Check-In Process	Excellent	Good	Average	Fair	Poor
Message Service	Excellent	Good	Average	Fair	Poor
Parking	Excellent	Good	Average	Fair	Poor

LEVEL OF AGREEMENT QUESTIONS When assessing attitudes or opinions, it is often a good idea to write statements that reflect those attitudes or opinions. Then you can ask respondents for their level of agreement with the statements. Commonly used options include *strongly agree* (SA), *agree* (A), *neutral* (N), *disagree* (D), and *strongly disagree* (SD). The following are examples of statements that might be used in a health-related questionnaire.

Indicate your level of agreement with the following statements based on your personal preference:

"I am extremely health conscious."

SA   A   N   D   SD

"I do not like vegetables."

SA   A   N   D   SD

"Eating low cholesterol foods is important to me."

SA   A   N   D   SD

"The cafeteria should serve heart-healthy foods."

SA   A   N   D   SD

As you can see, if someone had to answer Yes or No to these questions, the researcher may not get an accurate picture. That is why it is often easier to use statements for research on attitudes and opinions.

■ Basic Guidelines for Writing Questions

When writing the specific questions you should follow some basic guidelines. Each question should be written clearly and as briefly as possible. Use the same ranking or rating scales for all similar questions. It is important not to ask leading questions, which suggest a correct answer. An example of a leading question is: "Do you prefer X or the more reasonably priced Z?" The phrase "more reasonably priced" could cause respondents to answer Z.

FIGURE 29-5

Century 21 Quality Service Survey

Century 21 **Quality Service Survey**

Dear CENTURY 21® Customer:
Thank you for choosing a CENTURY 21 office to assist you with your recent real estate purchase. We appreciate your confidence in us, and hope you have been very satisfied with our service. Your feedback is very important to us because it lets us evaluate our service and helps us recognize and reward offices and salespeople who provide superior service. We hope that you will take a few moments to answer our survey. -- ***Robert Moles**, President, Century 21 Real Estate Corporation*

Your Overall Experience

1. Overall, how satisfied have you been with your salesperson, his or her office, and their service during your purchase?

Very Satisfied	Satisfied	Dissatisfied	Very Dissatisfied
☐	☐	☐	☐

	Yes	No
2. Would you recommend CENTURY 21 to a friend who is going to buy or sell real estate?..................................	☐	☐

3. How high were your expectations when you chose CENTURY 21?
   Very high..... ☐ High..... ☐ Average..... ☐

4. Overall, how did your experience with CENTURY 21 compare with your expectations?
   Better than expected..... ☐ About the same as expected..... ☐ Worse than expected..... ☐

Who was the principal salesperson you worked with during your purchase? ____________________ *(Please print)*

5. How satisfied have you been with your salesperson's service?

Our CENTURY 21 salesperson:	Very Satisfied	Satisfied	Dissatisfied	Very Dissatisfied
Kept his or her promises..	☐	☐	☐	☐
Understood our specific needs..	☐	☐	☐	☐
Was knowledgeable, well informed..	☐	☐	☐	☐
Went out of his or her way to help us,..	☐	☐	☐	☐
Was available, easy to reach..	☐	☐	☐	☐
Kept in touch with us..	☐	☐	☐	☐
***Overall satisfaction with CENTURY 21 salesperson**..........................*	☐	☐	☐	☐

6. The CENTURY 21 system has awards for outstanding service. Do you want to nominate your salesperson to receive one of these awards? If you do, please check this box: ☐ **YES -- Nominate my salesperson for an award.**

	Yes	No
7. Has your salesperson, or anyone else from your salesperson's office, been in touch with you to follow up since your purchase closed?..	☐	☐

Over→

During Your Purchase

8. Please think back to the first time you called or went to the CENTURY 21® office which helped you with your purchase. What were the main reasons you decided to contact them?

☐ Had worked with them before
☐ Knew the agent
☐ Knew someone else at that office
☐ Another real estate office referred us to them
☐ Someone recommended them to us
☐ Their reputation
☐ Found them on the Internet
☐ Their advertising
☐ Their yardsigns
☐ A home they were selling
☐ Other

	Yes	No
9. While you were looking for your property, did your salesperson give you the BUYER SERVICE PLEDGE,® a form that described what your broker and salesperson would do to help you purchase your property?................	☐	☐
10. Did you receive the office owner's or manager's name and phone number?..	☐	☐

11. How satisfied have you been with the CENTURY 21 office which helped you purchase your property?

a. The office staff:	Very Satisfied	Satisfied	Dissatisfied	Very Dissatisfied
Handled our calls and messages promptly and politely...........................	☐	☐	☐	☐
Were friendly and helpful when we had questions...........................	☐	☐	☐	☐
b. The CENTURY 21 office *(Please skip these two items if you never visited the office)*:				
Looked clean and well maintained...........................	☐	☐	☐	☐
Looked attractive and professional...........................	☐	☐	☐	☐

Other Information (for statistical purposes)

12. Are you...? ☐ Male ☐ Female

13. Are you...? ☐ Married ☐ Single, widowed, divorced, or separated

14. What is your age? ☐ Under 30 ☐ 30-39 ☐ 40-49 ☐ 50-64 ☐ 65 or older

15. What is your family's approximate annual income *(OPTIONAL)*
    ☐ Less than \$30,000 ☐ \$30,000 to \$49,999 ☐ \$50,000 to \$74,999 ☐ \$75,000 to \$99,999 ☐ \$100,000 or more

	Yes	No
16. Did you ever own real estate before this purchase?..	☐	☐
17. Do you know anyone else who is interested in buying or selling real estate?..	☐	☐
18. Are you interested in information about investing in real estate?..	☐	☐
19. Are you interested in information about a career in real estate?..	☐	☐

Again, thank you for your time.
Your opinions are important to us, and we look forward to having the opportunity to serve you again.
Please return this questionnaire in the enclosed, postage-paid envelope, or mail to Quality Research Group
27271 Las Ramblas, Mission Viejo, CA 92691

Century 21
Each Office is Independently Owned and Operated

©1991, 1994, 1995, 1996, 1997, 1998, 1999 Century 21 Real Estate Corporation
® & TM Trademarks of Century 21 Real Estate Corporation

QRG
QUALITY RESEARCH GROUP

101-6-00 Recycled Paper

Identifying the Purpose of a Survey **The purpose of a survey should be identified on the survey itself or in a cover letter mailed with the survey.** ***Why is this information important?***

You should avoid any *bias*, which is a systematic error introduced by encouraging one outcome or answer over the others. It is also important to avoid questions that might cause a respondent to guess at the meaning of your question. The following is an example of a question that might cause a respondent to guess:

"How many students in your high school drink coffee on a daily basis?"

☐ Less than 10
☐ 10–49
☐ 50–99
☐ 100–149
☐ 150–199
☐ over 200

Without asking every student, the respondent can't answer the question without guessing.

When a survey questionnaire is finished, it is a good idea to pretest the wording of the questions. This pretest allows for correction of any misleading questions, directions, or problems on the questionnaire.

Formatting

Questionnaires must have excellent visual appearance and design to appeal to respondents. You should use dark ink (usually black) on light paper and type that is easy to read. Shading sections for contrast and using arrows to lead the reader through the questionnaire are other ways to improve the visual look of the questionnaire.

Section headings or numbers should be placed on all individual survey sections. In addition, numbers should be placed on all individual questions. Respondents are more likely to respond to all sections and questions if they are identified and numbered. Numbered questions are also easier to tabulate. When your questionnaire requires more than one page, place a message at the bottom of each page to continue to the next page.

Directions for completing the questionnaire must be clear for each section or group of questions. Do not assume that respondents will know how you want them to complete the questionnaire.

General demographic questions about gender, age, ethnic background, education are typically grouped together at the end of a questionnaire. This is because respondents are more likely to answer personal questions after completing the other questions. Some people may take offense to personal questions when they are placed at the beginning of the questionnaire. They may choose not to take part in the survey. The only time such information is placed at the beginning of a questionnaire is to qualify a respondent. Here is an example: "Are you between the ages of 20 and 30?" If yes, the interviewer would administer the survey. If no, then the person would not be included in the study.

To increase the response rate the survey should have a variety of question types. It may have a mix of 25 percent yes and no questions, 25 percent agree/disagree items, and 50 percent scaled-response questions.

■ Administering the Questionnaire

All surveys should have deadlines for completion. A mailed questionnaire should be sent first-class with a hand-signed cover letter (attached or part of the survey) and personalized if the potential respondent is known. Figure 29-5 is an example of a survey with a clearly identified purpose. The cover letter should explain the purpose of the survey and give the deadline for returning the questionnaire. A postage-paid return envelope should be included with the questionnaire for the respondent's convenience.

Questionnaires that are not mailed should have a brief explanation of the survey's purpose placed on the questionnaire itself. When conducting personal interviews, the actual selection of the participants for the study is an important issue. It is important that the selection process is unbiased, so a plan should be established for selecting participants. The plan could be as simple as interviewing every third person to exit a store, regardless of age, gender, or appearance. Personal interviews provide a degree of flexibility in collecting data. In a personal interview, probing questions can be asked and reactions to visual materials such as ads or actual product samples can be collected.

To conduct an interview, dress in a businesslike manner and carry a clipboard to hold your questionnaires. Be sure to approach people politely and don't take offense if some individuals don't wish to participate. You may want to hire a marketing research firm, which will have trained professional interviewers on staff.

BRIGHT IDEAS

From Junk Mail to Direct Mail Success

Junk mail received its name aptly—most people throw it out immediately after taking it out of their mailboxes. With the help of mathematician Yuri Galperin this may become a thing of the past for direct-mail marketing companies! This Russian mathematician has used his math skills to create software that tells direct-mail marketers the best avenue to take when marketing new products. His company—MarketSwitch—uses a company's market research on buying patterns and demographics to determine how to best target direct mail campaigns. Why can't these mathematical problems be solved with pen and paper? A large customer database can create ten million different variables to be accounted for. Galperin, with the help of his math expertise, has scaled this down to create manageable equations that produce fast results.

Thinking Creatively

Galperin has merged his math skills to apply to marketing. What other academic areas are useful in marketing? Why?

The Impact of Computer Technologies on Marketing Research

Computer technologies have had a tremendous impact on marketing research. Software programs allow researchers to analyze huge amounts of information. They also allow researchers to find secondary data in computer databases, prepare surveys, and generate lists of potential questionnaire respondents.

Information can be stored, sorted, and used to improve processes in the future. Computerized databases are a source of *data collection* for researchers. Computer programs are available that analyze the information collected, such as competitive, demographic, site, and location data. Finally, specialized software programs can assist with *forecasting*. These programs analyze current market data and use this information to predict future sales.

Survey research can now be conducted through online surveys and focus group chat sessions on the Internet. *Fax broadcasting* allows businesses to send questionnaires to a select group of fax numbers. *Automated dialers* increase the number of telephone survey responses by placing multiple calls and automatically rejecting those with busy signals and answering machines. *Digital surveys* allow a prerecorded voice to qualify a respondent and then ask

a series of survey questions. *Interactive voice response* is similar to voicemail as callers are greeted by a recorded voice that leads them through a series of questions. Responses can be given using the telephone keypad.

Life In The Diverse MARKETPLACE

Vacation Time

While working with companies abroad, you may be pleasantly surprised to see how seriously most other nations take vacation. Vacation time is often referred to as a benefit in the United States and the average allotted time is two weeks. In most European countries, six weeks is the average! In Germany, even those who are unemployed have the right to three weeks of paid vacation. And this is a right that can't be taken away—or replaced with payment—as it falls under labor laws.

Thinking Critically

Why would labor laws require up to six weeks of vacation for employees?

29.2 ASSESSMENT

Reviewing Key Terms and Concepts

1. Why should questionnaires provide data that have validity?

2. Why should research questionnaires have reliability?

3. What are three steps that must be taken to construct a valid and reliable questionnaire?

4. What are some methods of administering a questionnaire?

5. Name six research activities that computers can help researchers perform.

Thinking Critically

6. Can business risks be eliminated by marketing research? Why or why not?

Integrating Academic Skills

7. **MATH** Research indicates that 80 percent of the customers for a pizza store live within one mile of the store, another 15 percent live within two miles of the store, and the remaining five percent live within five miles of the store. Compute the number of customers who live within the various trading areas if the population of the area is 12,540.

Careers in Marketing

MARKETING RESEARCH

Robert W. Cuzner
Research Director
Digital Research, Inc.

What does your job entail?

"Digital Research, Inc. (DRI) is a full-service research firm. As research director, I am responsible for assuring that all clients are satisfied with our services. This involves direct client contact through every stage of the research process. My job includes defining research objectives, recommending the appropriate methodology (telephone, mail, in-person, online), designing the questionnaire, analyzing data, and reporting results. On other projects, I may supervise, train, and mentor the project managers. DRI's areas of specialization are e-commerce, publishing, and tourism."

Why do you like working as a Research Director?

"I enjoy working as a research director because every day offers new and interesting challenges. The process of designing questionnaires and interpreting the results is creative and fulfilling. There are a variety of problems that occur that need to be solved, such as finding eligible survey respondents. One of DRI's major studies is the annual 'Toy of the Year' program for *FamilyFun* magazine. Children test new toys which helps DRI know in advance what each year's hot sellers will be."

How did you get into marketing research?

"I was intrigued by a marketing research course that I took in college. Upon graduation, I sought an entry-level position in research and began doing store location research for a supermarket chain, later moving into consumer research. I then worked for a publishing company where I created a research department and conducted studies for media. After 17 years in that position, I went into consulting."

What is your key to success?

"The key to success is the ability to communicate effectively, not only with the client, but also with the internal staff assigned to work on the project. This includes defining research objectives, reporting survey results clearly, and providing insightful conclusions based on the research."

Thinking Critically

What aspect of this career do you find most appealing?

Career Facts

Education and Training: A college degree in business, marketing, or communications is required, and a master's degree in one of these fields is highly recommended. A minimum of eight years of marketing experience with an emphasis in research and research design is necessary.

Aptitudes, Abilities, and Skills: Excellent communication skills and outstanding analytical and decision-making skills are necessary in this career.

Career Outlook: Employment opportunities are expected to grow through the year 2008.

Career Path: Many directors of research begin their careers as interviewers, research assistants, or junior analysts. They may move up to senior analysts before attaining the position of director.

VOCABULARY REVIEW

Write three paragraphs on conducting marketing research using these vocabulary terms.

- problem definition
- primary data
- secondary data
- survey method
- sample
- observation method
- point-of-sale research
- experimental method
- data analysis
- open-ended questions
- forced-choice questions

FACT AND IDEA REVIEW

1. Why should secondary data be used first when trying to solve marketing research problems? (29.1)

2. What are two advantages and disadvantages of using secondary data? (29.1)

3. What is the survey method of research? Describe four ways to conduct surveys. (29.1)

4. What is the difference between a natural and contrived observation? (29.1)

5. How does survey research differ from observation research? (29.1)

6. Identify the elements in a final marketing research report. (29.1)

7. What is validity? (29.2)

8. What is the difference between an open-ended question and a forced-choice question? (29.2)

9. Why is the answer choice "other" important in multiple choice questions? (29.2)

THINKING CRITICALLY

1. What sources of information would you use to identify the market for a new automated car wash in your community?

2. Under natural observation, customers or employees do not know they are being observed. Do you think that this research technique is an invasion of privacy? Why or why not?

3. Compared to mail surveys, why have telephone surveys become so popular?

4. Why is Internet survey research increasingly important?

5. A small business owner wants to conduct a focus group interview, but is unwilling to pay several thousand dollars to an outside company to conduct one. What could the owner do to reduce costs, but still conduct the focus group?

BUILDING WORKPLACE SKILLS

1. **Human Relations** You work for the manager of a marketing research department. You and five other employees conduct a number of surveys by telephone. Getting people to respond to questions over the telephone is increasingly difficult. The manager has asked each of you to provide suggestions for how the response rates to telephone surveys could be improved. What suggestions would you make?

2. **Social Studies** Review your local newspaper or a weekly magazine for an article dealing with an opinion poll on a local, state, or national issue or election campaign. Write a 100-word summary of when and how the poll was conducted, and what the results indicated.

1. **Finding a Marketing Research Firm** Locate the Web page of *Quirk's Marketing Researcher Sourcebook*. Search for a marketing research firm in your state. Search by research specialty area and identify one firm in your state that performs the specialty research. Make a print-out of the company's home page to share with your class.

2. **Researching Market Information** Choose a business to research. Use a word processing program to prepare a report on at least two secondary data sources for each of the following items: size of the business's market, characteristics of its customers, income of its customers, present sales volume of its competitors, and information about trends in its industry.

3. **Analyzing Census Data** Locate the U.S. Census Bureau's Web site. Find the following information about your community: population, number of restaurants, retail stores, and gas stations; and the total sales for each number of households, average family size, average income, estimated average age of the population, and average education level. Use the research information you found to prepare a 200-word report on what new type of business might be successful in your community, including how the research supports your recommendation.

Basic and Information Skills Research a company in your community or where you are currently employed to find out how it collects demographic information about its customers. Write a 250-word report on how customer information (name, address, phone, occupation, age, etc.) is collected and used.

Role Play: Marketing Research Consultant

Situation You are to assume the role of a marketing research consultant. The owner (judge) of a small floral shop has asked you to identify whether the shop should add a large assortment of greeting cards. The owner knows very little about marketing research.

Activity You must explain the steps used in marketing research and recommend a research method to determine the feasibility of adding greeting cards.

Evaluation You will be evaluated on how well you meet the following performance indicators:

- Identify information monitored for marketing decision making
- Describe sources of secondary data
- Describe the need for marketing information
- Explain the nature of marketing research in a marketing-information management system
- Collect marketing information from others

inter **NET**
CONNECTION

Secondary Data Online
Locate the U. S. Census Bureau's Web site to obtain secondary data about business activity in your county.

Connect
- Locate the *County Business Patterns Economic Profile* for your county.
- Identify the total number of employees in your county and the annual payroll (in $1,000) in your county.
- Find the total estimated employment by size of business and locate the industry area in your county that employs the most people.

The Zazz Lab

A Sports and Entertainment Marketing Simulation

WELCOME

Welcome to Zazz Sports and Entertainment Marketing Company. Zazz is devoted to serving the needs of its clients who include college, university, and professional sports teams, professional athletes, sporting events, and sports arenas plus major consumer product corporations, as well as television networks and movie studios. As an intern, you will have the opportunity to work on different clients' projects. All of your work will be assigned and reviewed by your department supervisor.

CONDUCT MARKETING RESEARCH FOR A NEW MINOR LEAGUE BASEBALL FRANCHISE

SITUATION

A current Zazz client would like to build a Minor League Baseball team and stadium in your community. Our client wants to assess community support, potential target market(s) needs and wants, and how to promote this new source of entertainment.

ASSIGNMENT

Your supervisor wants you to design and administer a marketing research study regarding the creation of a Minor League Baseball team and stadium. You need to address the 4 *P*s of the marketing mix for the new team by conducting primary and secondary research. *Product* decisions may include the name of the new team, stadium design and facilities, and amenities for families and corporate audiences. *Promotional* strategies may include special events, special corporate promotions, advertising media, trade character, and Web site. *Place* decisions would include how tickets are sold. *Price* strategies for tickets, food, and merchandise would also be important. Establish the methodology for the primary research and indicate how the survey should be conducted. Explain how you will ensure a valid and reliable study. Create a questionnaire that includes one open-ended question and a variety of forced-choice questions. Prepare a table to show that your questionnaire items correlate with the objectives of the study. Develop a customer profile of who is likely to use the facility.

Tools and Resources

To complete this assignment, you will need to conduct research at a library or on the Internet. You will also need a word processing program, a spreadsheet program, and computer presentation software. Other resources include local newspapers, real estate agencies, and your local Chamber of Commerce.

Research

Study the demographics and psychographics of the community to determine potential attendance. Demographic information should include population, average household income, household size, number of families with children under 21 years old, level of education, and types of occupations. Research the marketing mix of Minor League Baseball franchises to determine what has made them successful.

Report

Prepare a written report and a computer presentation. Use a word processing program to prepare a double-spaced report. Use a spreadsheet program to create tables illustrating your research findings. Arrange your written report around the following headings:

- Background information
  - Target population demographics and psychographics
  - Minor League Baseball franchises
  - Significant trends
- Primary research design
  - Selected method and rationale
  - Questionnaire design
    - Correlation with objectives of the study
    - Measures taken to prevent instrumental bias
    - Sample questionnaire
  - Administration of the questionnaire
    - Sample vs. census
    - Measures taken to prevent sample bias
- Study's findings and conclusions
  - Customer profile
  - Product
    - Stadium design and amenities
    - Baseball franchise
  - Price
  - Place
  - Promotion
- Recommendations and plan for implementation

Using computer presentation software and other visual aids (sample promotional materials, team name and logo, etc.), prepare a presentation of your ideas for the client that includes:

- Key topics covered in your written report
- Graphic illustrations that are relevant to each slide's topic
- Very little text
- Minimum of 10 slides

Presentation and Evaluation

Present your ideas in a written report and an oral presentation. The oral presentation will later be shown to the client. You will be evaluated on your oral presentation skills, including:

- Secondary research conducted
- Primary research design and administration
- Research findings, conclusions, and recommendations
- Continuity of presentation
- Enthusiasm
- Voice quality
- Eye contact

Portfolio

Print a copy of your completed report and presentation for your Portfolio.

THE DECA CONNECTION

DECA Business Services Marketing Series
Conducting marketing research for a client is part of this occupational area, because it is a business service.

DECA Marketing Management Series
Designing and administering a marketing research study is a possible role play situation in this event.

DECA Hospitality and Recreation Research Event
Since a Minor League Baseball franchise is a form of entertainment and recreation, conducting a marketing research study for such a business is a possible topic for this event.

DECA Sports and Entertainment Marketing Management Team Decision-Making Event
Working on this project with a partner would make the experience similar to what is expected in a DECA Team Decision-Making Event.

Portfolio

Product Research

Once you have completed this unit, you will research the history and development of a consumer product of your choice. Investigate the branding, packaging, and labeling for the product over the years. Detail the warranties available for your product. Then, create a poster showing the product, its features, and where you believe the product would be in its product life cycle.

BUYERS GU

IMPORTANT: Spoken promises are difficult to enforce. Ask deal. Keep this form.

VEHICLE MAKE   MODEL   YEAR   VIN

DEALER STOCK NUMBER (optional)

WARRANT

COSTS FOR ANY REPAI   WARR
y oral statements about this vehic   sumes no resp

WARRANT

☐ LIMITED WARRANTY. The dealer will pay
d systems that fail during the war
rranty   cuments for a full explanation of v
pair obligations. Under state law, "implied w

Product and Service Management

Unit Overview

Product and service management involves all of the decisions a business makes in the production and sale of its products.

Through your study of Chapter 30, you will see how businesses plan, position, and manage the products and services they will produce and sell. This chapter also discusses the concept of product mix, product mix strategies, and new product development. Chapter 31 explores how branding, packaging, and labeling are incorporated into product planning strategy to create perceived product differences. Chapter 32 discusses extended product features with an emphasis on the use of warranties and the use of credit in product planning as well as consumer rights and responsibilities affecting product usage and credit protection.

In this Unit:

Foundations of Marketing

● Business, Management, Entrepreneurship

Functions of Marketing

Product/Service Management

Financing

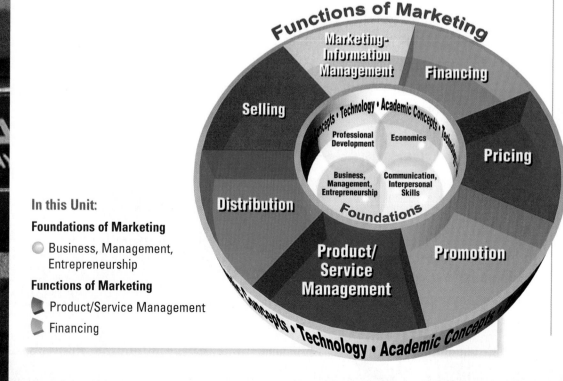

Product Planning

Marketing: What It Takes

Great Products Boost the Bottom Line

As part of the summer internship program at XYZ company, you are required to prepare a written report on the company's product mix. Your analysis must demonstrate your understanding of product planning and product strategies used by companies to achieve success.

WHAT WILL YOU DO?
What major topics will you evaluate in your analysis of the company's product mix?

Product Planning, Mix, and Development

Product Planning

A product is anything a person receives in an exchange. A product can be a tangible item (car), a service (haircut), an idea (a good education), or a combination of all of these concepts. A product, therefore, includes its physical features, the seller's reputation, the seller's services, warranties, and the way the product is viewed by people. Product planning involves making decisions about those features that are needed to sell a business's products, services, or ideas. These decisions relate to product features, such as packaging, labeling, and branding, as well as the services, such as product warranties, necessary to support the product. Product planning allows a business to coordinate existing products and features offered to customers, add new products, and delete products that no longer appeal to customers. Product planning requires creativity as well as the ability to interpret current customer needs and forecast new trends.

Product Mix

Product mix includes all the different products that a company makes or sells. A large manufacturer, such as Kraft Foods, the second-largest packaged-foods company in the world, may have hundreds of different products. Some of Kraft's key brands include Kraft, Maxwell House, Oscar Mayer, and Post products.

A retailer has a product mix that is made up of all of the different products the store sells. Retail stores must plan their product mix carefully because they cannot offer all of the products that customers may want. Stores need to offer a good selection of merchandise. Adding more products, though, may not result in increased sales if those products are not popular. In fact, sometimes adding too many new products can take away from existing sales.

The type and number of products to be carried must be based on the objectives of the business, the image the business wants to project, and the market it is trying to reach. This makes product mixes unique to each business. Even similar types of businesses can offer different product mixes. Gap and Brooks Brothers are both apparel stores, yet they have different product mixes. While Brooks Brothers carries a product mix of classic clothing and accessories for business-people, the Gap carries a product mix of trendsetting, fashion-conscious clothing for the youth market. Each store serves a different market and projects a different image.

What You'll Learn

- The nature and scope of product planning
- The concept of product mix
- The different product mix strategies
- The steps in new product development

Why It's Important

Product planning allows a business to make or sell products that are wanted by customers. Product planning also is used to design appropriate marketing programs that help create increased sales and profit opportunities.

Key Terms

- product planning
- product mix
- product line
- product item
- product width
- product depth
- product modification

■ Product Items and Lines

A product line is a group of closely related products manufactured and/or sold by a business. Examples include all the car models produced by the Saturn division of General Motors, all the cereals produced by Kellogg's, and all the computers produced by IBM.

Retailers frequently sell more than one product line. A motorcycle dealer, for example, might carry both Honda and Kawasaki product lines. A supermarket might stock both the Libby and Del Monte canned fruit lines. A camera and electronics store might sell the JVC, Panasonic, Sharp, and Sony digital camcorder product lines.

A product item is a specific model, brand, or size of a product within a product line. Typically, retailers carry several product items for each product line they sell. A computer dealer handling hand-held organizers might carry several Palm Computer models. These models might include the Palm3, Palm3C, Palm 3X, and Palm 3Xe.

■ **A Look at Product Mix** A company like Frito Lay is able to succeed while carrying a large product mix. *Is it a good idea for all companies to expand their product lines?*

■ **What Is My Target Market?** Similar businesses often have different images and serve different markets. Because of this, they also offer different product mixes. *What is the primary target market for this store?*

FIGURE 30-1

The Concept of Product Mix

Width of the Gillette Product Mix			
Blades and Razors	**Toiletries**	**Writing Instruments**	**Lighters**
MACH 3	Series	Paper Mate	Cricket
Sensor	Adorn	Flair	S.T. Dupont
Trac II	Toni		
Atra	Right Guard		
Swivel	Silkience		
Double-Edge	Soft and Dri		
Lady Gillette	Foamy		
Super Speed	Dry Look		
Twin Injector	Dry Idea		
Techmatic	Brush Plus		

Product ▶

Depth of the Product Lines ▶

■ **Product Mix** The width and depth of product lines define product mix. *What does product depth tell you about the importance of a given product line?*

■ Product Width and Product Depth

The width and depth of its product offerings define a product mix. Product width refers to the number of different product lines a business manufactures or sells. Product depth refers to the number of product items offered within each product line.

As you can see in Figure 30-1, Gillette has a product width of four different product lines including blades and razors, toiletries, writing instruments, and lighters. Product depth for the Gillette product mix is ten product items under blades and razors, ten items under toiletries, and two each under writing instruments and lighters.

A retailer that sells several brands of jeans, such as Levi's, Lee, and Guess? is demonstrating product width. The product depth is the number of sizes, price ranges, colors, and styles for each brand.

Product mix strategies vary with the type of business. Red Lobster restaurants, which specialize in seafood dinners, have product depth within a narrow product line (seafood-related entrees). Other restaurants offer broader menus that include steak, chicken, pork, and pasta dinners, as well as seafood. Their product mix shows greater width but less depth than Red Lobster's.

Both manufacturers and retailers must decide on the width and depth of their product mix. To determine its product mix, a business needs to identify its target market, its competitors, and the image the business wants to project. After a target market and an image are determined, a business must determine its product lines and items to manufacture or sell. Periodically a business also must review whether its existing product lines need to be expanded, modified, contracted, or deleted.

Product Mix Strategies

A product mix strategy is the plan for how the business determines which products it will make or stock. Businesses can use different product mix strategies depending upon their resources and their objectives. Some businesses develop completely new products to add to their existing product lines. Others expand or modify their current product lines. Sometimes businesses drop existing products to allow for new product offerings.

To make these decisions, a business must take an objective look at sales as well as other factors such as current trends. A product that has experienced success in the past may not continue to thrive if consumers' wants and needs are changing.

■ Developing New Products

New products can add substantially to a company's overall sales and boost its market share. Often a slight variation of the original or existing product can lead to increased sales.

Packaged-goods giant Procter & Gamble, with such venerable brands as Tide, Crest, and Pampers in its lineup, devotes roughly 15 percent of its research and development budget to developing new products. Innovative products that have created consumer-goods categories include P&G's Febreze odor remover for fabrics, the Swiffer dry-mop system, and the Dryel home dry-cleaning kit. Other P&G brands introduced in 2000 include Mr. Clean Antibacterial Wipes, Fit Fruit and Vegetable Wash, Thermacare heat wraps, and Impress food wrap.

According to one study, new products (those less than five years old) account for about 35 percent of total sales for major consumer and industrial goods companies. New products also can help a company's image by providing it with a reputation as an innovator and leader with its customers.

New products also increase markups and profits to sellers. This happens when new products are successful because they tend to be priced 10–15 percent higher than older, comparable products.

New products often become a major part of a company's product line. The Sensor for Women Razor, first introduced in July 1992, has become an ongoing product for Gillette. More than 100 million razors and one billion refills have been sold since its introduction.

New product development generally involves seven key steps:
1. Generating ideas
2. Screening ideas
3. Developing a business proposal
4. Developing the product
5. Testing the product
6. Introducing the product (commercialization)
7. Evaluating customer acceptance

Let's take a closer look at these steps (see Figure 30-2 on page 551).

GENERATING IDEAS New product ideas come from a variety of sources, including customers, competitors, channel members, and company employees. Larger companies establish research and development departments that work with marketing staff, marketing research staff, and outside research companies to develop and test new products.

■ **Dirty Work** Procter and Gamble developed "Fit Fruit and Vegetable Wash" after the company's market research found that although nine out of ten consumers wash their fruits and vegetables, 61 percent feel they're not getting them clean enough. *How can new products help a company's image?*

Creativity is essential for new product development. Some companies sponsor idea sessions, which are designed to generate new ideas and new product concepts in as many product categories as possible.

SCREENING IDEAS During the screening process, ideas for products are evaluated. They are matched against the company's overall objectives to see if they fit. Consider the example of a company that comes up with a new idea to develop a home blood-pressure machine. The company's objective, however, is to disband the consumer products division of the company in the next three years. There would be no reason to continue evaluating that new product idea. During the screening process, the new idea would be evaluated on its potential conflict with existing products. What would a manufacturer of digital thermometers do if a new way of taking body temperature was invented? Let's

FIGURE 30-2

THE STEPS IN NEW PRODUCT DEVELOPMENT

Developing new products involves several key steps.

1 GENERATING IDEAS

This involves tracking cultural trends and observing customer behaviors to generate ideas.

2 SCREENING IDEAS

Ideas for new products are screened and evaluated. Some ideas are eliminated while the best ideas are put through further evaluation. Finally, one or two ideas are selected for development and a business proposal is written.

3 DEVELOPING THE PRODUCT

During the development stage, a prototype is made. The prototype is tested, and adjustments are made to improve the final product.

4 TESTING THE PRODUCT

Newly developed products are test marketed to obtain customers' responses.

6 EVALUATING CUSTOMER ACCEPTANCE

After the product has been introduced, marketers track customer acceptance.

5 INTRODUCING THE PRODUCT

If customer response is favorable, the product is introduced into the marketplace.

The mark PT Cruiser® is a registered trademark of DaimlerChrysler Corporation and the PT Cruiser reprints are used with permission from the DaimlerChrysler Corporation.

say a disposable plastic strip that turned different colors based on body heat could be used instead of the standard thermometer. Would that new product be in conflict with the standard thermometer?

Take this idea a step further and screening might involve concept testing with consumers to see if they would actually use a thermometer that provided colored readings instead of digital numbers. Focus groups could be conducted at this stage to see how consumers felt about the new concept of taking one's temperature in this manner. A description of the product would be presented in writing. Consumers would be asked to identify attributes they liked and disliked about the new concept, and their willingness to buy such a product. The purpose of this stage is to find the products that deserve further study. A large number of products are rejected in the screening stage, making it an important preliminary step.

DEVELOPING A BUSINESS PROPOSAL A product idea that makes it through the screening process would then be evaluated in terms of its profit potential. A business proposal would be developed to evaluate the new product in terms of the size of the

market, potential sales, costs, profit potential, technological trends, overall competitive environment, and level of risk. During this stage, production requirements must be considered. How long will it take to produce and introduce the new product? Can it be produced efficiently and at a competitive price? A program to develop the product is planned and someone is assigned the responsibility of studying the feasibility of making and marketing the new product.

DEVELOPING THE PRODUCT During product development, the new product idea takes a physical shape, and marketers develop a marketing strategy. Plans relating to production, packaging, labeling, branding, promotion, and distribution are made.

During this product planning stage, technical evaluations are made to see if the company can produce the new product and if it is practical to do so. Ben & Jerry's ice cream company had difficulties when it first developed Cherry Garcia ice cream. The original idea was to use whole chocolate-coated cherries. The whole cherries were too large to go through the production machinery, which caused the chocolate to break off the cherries. After numerous tests, the company finally separated the cherries and the chocolate; the rest is history.

In addition to detecting difficulties with product production, tests are conducted on products to see how they will hold up during normal and not-so-normal use by the consumer. A new product may be tested for durability in the lab by machines that will reproduce the actions or motions that the product will endure during use. It is at this stage that technical problems should be detected so that they can be corrected before full-scale production begins.

Sometimes millions of dollars can be spent at this stage of development for testing, prototypes, and research. A *prototype* is a model of the product. Usually, only a few models are made at first, as the business tests the idea and makes changes to improve the final product. Companies can experience long delays during this stage of product planning. The government requires extensive testing in various stages for some products, such as prescription drugs and genetically engineered food products. These tests end with testing on human beings to determine side effects and problems with the product's safety. Getting final approval from the government for use by the general public can take years.

REAL WORLD MARKETING

Marketing to Kids: Icing on the …Chocolate Bar?

Kids can now design their own candy bars! Hershey Food Corporation is letting kids do the "dirty work" of filling and decorating their own chocolate treats. Hershey's Candy Bar Factory contains a cleverly designed chocolate bar with four ready-to-fill sections. Kids can use the kit to fill or decorate the bar with Reese's peanut butter filling, colored sprinkles, chocolate cookie bits, and white frosting. Although each candy bar costs nearly $2 per package, people buy them as a special treat. The kits provide kids with creative entertainment and "incr-edible" results!

Thinking Critically
Why do you think personalizing a product leads consumers to believe the value is higher?

TESTING THE PRODUCT After the product is tested in the lab, consumer acceptance of the product is the next step. As you learned in Chapter 28, new products frequently are test marketed in certain geographic areas to see whether consumers will accept them. PepsiCo developed a new soft drink for the European market to try to increase its market share. The new soft drink is called Pepsi Max, a one-calorie cola, and it was made specifically for non-American tastes. International consumers typically do not like diet beverages, so the company spent more than two years testing different flavor combinations on the European market. Finally, one version met the company's goal of having at least 40 percent of the consumers in a taste test choose the new product over Coke.

Not every new product is test marketed in geographic areas. Frequently a focus group evaluation during development can provide additional input into final product design and uncover potential problems before production.

In some cases, the costs of test marketing, focus group evaluations, or direct marketing tests to sample households may be too high. In others, marketers may forgo testing because they would need to ask people to evaluate something that for them does not even exist. Sometimes companies fear that a time delay will allow competitors to enter the market before their product is ready.

INTRODUCING THE PRODUCT When a new product has been researched successfully, it is ready for full market introduction. This stage also is called commercialization. The costs of introducing a new product often are quite high. The product must be advertised to introduce its benefits to consumers. A new or revised distribution network may be needed. The company may need to develop training programs for its sales force. To pay for these costs, the company needs to get its new products into the market as quickly as possible.

The earlier a product can be brought to market, the greater the chance that revenues and profits will be high. The first company to introduce a new product has an advantage in acquiring customers and in building brand loyalty.

EVALUATING CUSTOMER ACCEPTANCE After products have been introduced, marketers track new product performance. This step is done to evaluate customer acceptance of the product and the marketing strategies used to introduce the product.

One way to obtain customer responses is to study sales information. Scanning equipment and computer systems can be used to compile large amounts of sales and market data on existing and new products. From this information, customized reports can be prepared. These reports help answer key questions such as:

- *Who are the best customers for our new product?*
- *What new products are customers buying?*
- *How often do customers buy the new product?*
- *When did customers last buy the new product?*

■ Developing Existing Products

Companies constantly review their product mix to see if they can further expand their product lines or modify existing products. They do this in order to build on an already established image, to appeal to new markets, and to increase sales and profits. Companies that have successful product lines often add products to those lines to take advantage of customers' positive attitude toward the brand name. Sony built on its image as a producer of high-quality

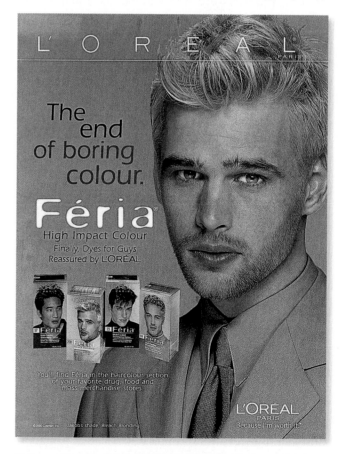

■ **Appealing to New Markets** A business must always look at new markets for its products. *How can new ideas for products or product expansions help a business?*

electronics products when it added the original PlayStation video game to its product line. Sony was able to capitalize on its image and brand awareness when it introduced PlayStation2, a technically more advanced version of the game, in 2000. To appeal to new markets, a hair color line for men was introduced by L'Oréal, which up until that time only sold hair color for women. In these examples, the companies utilized their knowledge of existing products to expand their businesses.

One disadvantage of adding new products to a company's product mix is the cost factor. Adding products or product lines increases inventory, promotion, storage, and distribution costs. New products also may take sales away from existing products and may require additional training for sales representatives who sell the products to suppliers. Finally, when a brand or corporate name is placed on a new product and the product proves harmful or defective, all products with the corporate name suffer.

Even though these disadvantages exist, they are often not significant enough to keep a company from developing its products. Two ways of developing existing products are line extensions and product modifications. Let's look at both options.

LINE EXTENSIONS Companies can expand product offerings by adding new product lines, items, or services, which may or may not be related to current products. To illustrate this strategy, think of all the varieties of Tylenol, such as Tylenol Flu, Tylenol Cold, and Tylenol Allergy/Sinus. Also think about the different forms they come in, such as tablets, caplets, and gelcaps. Each of these products is a line extension of the original Tylenol product.

A line extension is designed to be a different product that appeals to somewhat different needs of consumers. In essence, the company wants to provide a wider range of choices to increase product depth within a line. Line extensions are easy to market because customers are already familiar with the original product on which the extension is based.

In some cases, the line extension may be a product that is not directly related to the original product, but the brand name is used nonetheless. You see Bic pens and Bic disposable lighters. In this case, the company is building a new product line based on an existing brand name that is familiar to consumers.

PRODUCT MODIFICATIONS A product modification is an alteration in a company's existing product. Modified products may be offered in new

Introducing the first step to fast healing: an instant scab

New **BAND-AID** ADVANCED HEALING
BRAND ADHESIVE BANDAGES
is a revolutionary approach to wound treatment. It actually encourages fast healing by taking the place of a scab, instantly creating a protected, nurturing environment. So wounds heal fast. What's more, new BAND-AID® Brand Advanced Healing adhesive bandages are designed to stay in place for days, so they not only seal in the body's healing fluids, they seal out water, dirt and germs.

The Next Generation of Healing

■ **Ouch! Product modifications are a relatively easy and inexpensive way to add new products to a company's product line.** *How did BAND-AID modify its traditional bandages to create a new product?*

and different varieties, formulations, colors, styles, features, or sizes. Product modifications are a relatively quick and easy way to add new products to a company's product line.

When modifying a product, the old product often is phased out. Packaging may be modified to appeal to consumers and attract them to the product. One of the best examples of a product modification is the classic story of Coca Cola.

A few years ago Coke decided to make its cola slightly sweeter to compete for the market that prefers sweeter colas. While the sweeter coke drew new customers, Coke's traditional drinkers responded to the sweeter product with protest. They preferred their old, original Coke. The company soon decided to market two products instead of one. Coke Classic used the old formula, and Coke became the new, sweeter version. The company was able to increase its sales by holding on to its traditional market while gaining new customers for the new product. In this case a product modification actually became a line extension because both products were kept in the product mix.

Nike Gear

Hoping to build on the success of its digital Triax Sports Watch launched in 1998, Nike is developing a new line of electronic products for sports. Its goal is to create technologically advanced products that can enhance athletes' workouts. The oversized digital Triax Sports Watch, which is easy to read while running or jogging, has sold 2.5 million units worldwide.

Nike has formed a new division called Tech Lab, which is introducing a line of sports-focused products including a digital audio player, a high tech walkie-talkie, and portable heart monitors. These new products will be marketed globally.

The new products will bear the trademark swoosh symbol. The portable audio player will be the first product released. It will play MP3 files and Microsoft's Windows Media audio files. These lightweight players will have the software needed to let users mix their own music. An added attraction is that the player will not skip when jogged. To avoid potential problems with digital copyrights and royalties, Nike will get permission from artists and record companies for any songs downloaded from the company's Web site.

Other new products include a heart-rate and speed-distance monitor, a digital compass, and hand-held walkie talkies. The company will also sell related accessories, such as holsters and fanny packs to carry the new gadgets.

Nike will sell the new electronic line and accessories at NikeTown stores, Nike's Web site, sporting goods chains, and retail stores, such as Circuit City. The company will face tough competition in this $2 billion market from Sony, which already has a Sports Walkman unit.

Case Study Review

1. Why does Nike want to enter a new market for its products?
2. Discuss the psychographic trends that have created demand for Nike's new electronic sports accessories.

A MATTER OF ETHICS

3. What steps has Nike taken to avoid copyright infringements by the users of its product?

■ Deleting a Product or Product Line

Sometimes companies decide that they will no longer produce or sell a particular product or perhaps even a whole product line. Let's take a look at other reasons to drop a product or a product line.

OBSOLESCENCE Changing interests and technology have caused many products to be dropped. For example, older models of desktop computers have been dropped because newer models are faster and less expensive to produce. Early computer games have been replaced by games that have life-like graphics.

LOSS OF APPEAL As consumer tastes change, companies drop products that no longer appeal to the old tastes. Products popular with older generations, such as Brylcreem hair cream and Ovaltine hot chocolate, have lost much of their original customer appeal. These products may have some lasting loyalties that generate revenue, so the manufacturers must decide whether to keep them in their product mixes.

CONFLICT WITH CURRENT COMPANY OBJECTIVES Sometimes a product does not match a company's current objectives. Sears sold one subsidiary, Caldwell Banker real estate company, for this reason. Over the past several years, Sears stores had lost market share to other retailers. The company sold some unrelated businesses to focus on its retail objectives.

REPLACEMENT WITH NEW PRODUCTS Supermarkets, drugstores, department stores, and other retail outlets may change product mix frequently. Shelf space is limited, so retailers must make shelf or display space for new products. Products may be dropped because the store decides that it can make more money selling a different brand. One manufacturer might offer better buying terms because the store can buy in volume.

LACK OF PROFIT Seeking to increase profits, retailers will handle only fast-moving and profitable items. Often retailers will carry only those products whose stock turnover exceeds a certain number of turns per month.

Product developers may drop products when sales reach such a low level that the return on sales does not meet company objectives. Examples of products that have been dropped because they were no longer profitable are items such as Beeman's Black Jack gum, bite-size Oreos, Pepsi Crystal soda, and Powerhouse candy bars.

CONFLICT WITH OTHER PRODUCTS IN THE LINE Sometimes products take business away from other products in the same product line. Increased sales of one product can cause decreased sales of another product. In the 1990s, Procter & Gamble dropped many of its "unproductive" products, such as White Cloud tissue and Gleem toothpaste. The company was willing to give up market share to improve its return on similar products.

30.1 ASSESSMENT

Reviewing Key Terms and Concepts

1. What is product planning?
2. What is product mix?
3. Name four product mix strategies.
4. Identify the steps for new product development.
5. Name one advantage and one disadvantage to expanding a product line.

Thinking Critically

6. Suppose a company is developing a new product when a competitor introduces a new product that is similar. What are some things the company should consider in deciding whether to proceed with the development of its new product?

Integrating Academic Skills

7. **COMMUNICATION** Develop a 200-word written product plan for a truck manufacturer that is planning to diversify into the building and selling of buses. Identify possible target markets and product features.

Sustaining Product Sales

The Product Life Cycle

A product life cycle represents the stages that a product goes through during its life. There are four stages of the life cycle: introduction, growth, maturity, and decline (see Figure 30-3 on page 558). As each stage in the product life cycle is reached, marketers must adjust their product mix and their marketing strategies to ensure continued sales.

▪ Managing During the Introduction Stage

When the product is introduced to the market, the focus of the company's efforts is on promotion and production. The major goal is to draw the customer's attention to the new product. The company works to build its sales by increasing product awareness. Special promotions may get the customer to try the new product. As you know, the costs of introducing a product are high. Therefore, this is usually the least profitable stage of the life cycle.

▪ Managing During the Growth Stage

During the growth phase of the product life cycle, the product is enjoying success as shown by increasing sales and profits. Much of the target market knows about and buys the product. Advertising may now focus on consumer satisfaction, rather than on the new product benefits. By this time, the competition is aware of the success of the product and is likely to offer new products in order to compete. To keep its product sales growing, the company may have to introduce new models or modify the existing product to offer more than the competition.

Consider the example of the market for video game consoles. Sales of improved video game players now amount to several million units a year and several companies offer competing products.

▪ Managing During the Maturity Stage

A product reaches the maturity stage when its sales level off or slow down. The product may have more competition now, or most of the target market may already own the product. When a large proportion of potential buyers have the improved video game platforms, sales will slow and the product will enter the maturity stage.

During this stage, a company spends more of its marketing dollars fighting off the competition. Advertising expenses may climb, and the company may have to decide whether it can continue to improve the product to gain additional sales.

What You'll Learn

- The product life cycle
- The concept of product positioning
- The purpose of category management

Why It's Important

After products are introduced in the marketplace, they go through different stages of growth and decline. It is important to understand the different marketing strategies used to sustain product sales over time.

Key Terms

- product life cycle
- product positioning
- category management
- planogram

FIGURE 30-3

The Product Life Cycle

Introduction   Growth   Maturity   Decline

Dollars

Sales

Profits

Time

■ **Understanding the Product Life Cycle** The life cycle of a product can be divided into four stages: introduction, growth, maturity, and decline. *Why are sales not at their highest during the introduction stage?*

A Virtual Test with Real Results

As you walk down the supermarket aisle, you see a box of cereal that looks interesting. You take the box off the shelf and realize that it's one of your favorites—but with a new box design. You turn the box around and read its sides. When you decide to buy the cereal, you click on the shopping cart and lean back in your chair. You are a test shopper in a virtual supermarket! Many marketers use simulation software to see how their products will fare in the real world. Using this technology, marketers can test packaging changes or discount-price promotions. Before spending the money to create prototypes, product engineers can see how consumers like their efforts. Simulation software "virtually" changes the way products are tested.

Thinking Critically

A simulated test can cost up to five times more than conventional testing. Why would a company pay more for a software-simulated test?

■ Managing During the Decline Stage

During the decline stage, sales fall. Profits may reach the point where they are smaller than the costs. Management will need to decide how long it will continue to support the product.

Besides dropping the product, the company can use other product mix strategies to try to gain further sales from a declining or failing product. These strategies include selling or licensing the product, recommitting to the product line, discounting the product, regionalizing the product, and modernizing or altering the product.

SELL OR LICENSE THE PRODUCT Many companies sell or license their poorly performing products to risk-taking companies. Risk-taking companies try to rejuvenate the product by changing the product's image or introducing it to a new market.

RECOMMIT TO THE PRODUCT LINE Some companies decide that a declining product has other uses that can help improve sales. Knox gelatin lost sales as people spent less time cooking and stopped making fancy gelatin desserts. The company found a new use for the product that appeals to a different market. Adding Knox gelatin to Jell-O mixes allows people to make gelatin desserts that can be held in the hand. The new desserts are especially popular with children. Creating this new use helped Knox to improve sales.

Even with recommitment and advertising of new product uses, there is no guarantee that a product will continue to have enough sales. Eventually it may need to be discontinued.

DISCOUNT THE PRODUCT Many declining product lines can be saved from deletion by discounting them to compete with cheaper store or private brands. Lever Brothers discounted Pepsodent toothpaste and Lifebuoy soap and advertised the products with phrases such as "compare and save."

REGIONALIZE THE PRODUCT Sometimes companies decide to sell declining products only in the geographical areas where there is strong customer loyalty. The Nabisco Food Group only markets its My-T-Fine soups in northeastern states because it still has a significant customer base there. By marketing its product only in that area, the company saves the money of national advertising and distribution costs.

MODERNIZE OR ALTER THE PRODUCT OFFERING Some products can be altered or modernized to avoid deletion. Products can be completely redesigned, packaged differently, or reformulated. Tide laundry detergent—available in powder form in a box—was redesigned as New Tide. The product was also introduced in liquid form and repackaged in a plastic bottle. The new product now has a different appeal to existing consumers and a completely different look to new consumers who never used the original Tide.

Companies spend large amounts of money to develop and promote consumer and industrial products. As a result, they are reluctant to delete products without trying one of the above strategies. When products must be dropped, a company needs to plan the move carefully to avoid disappointing customers and damaging the company's overall image.

Product Positioning

The *focus* of product positioning is the image a product projects. The *goal* of product positioning is to set the product apart from the competition. Al Ries and Jack Trout, authors of *Positioning: The Battle for Your Mind,* explain positioning as the way you get into your customer's mind. Product positioning refers to the efforts a business makes to identify, place, and sell its products in the marketplace. It is an attempt to create an image of a product that appeals to customers. Changing the image or repositioning unsuccessful products is costly. To position their products, businesses identify customers' needs and determine how their product compares to the competition. A number of strategies are used to position products in the marketplace. Let's take a closer look at each of these strategies.

BRIGHT IDEAS
FUN, Inc.

Who might like lip gloss with a mirror on the bottom, or makeup and a fortune in a miniature Chinese-food container? How about a line of temporary tattoos that come off with soap and water? Kristin Penta knows what's hot. She dreamed up these and other new products to create and market to teenage girls. How did Penta get started? She teamed with a pencil manufacturer, Pentech International, who helped transform Penta's lip and eye pencils into a line of makeup for teens. Penta's ideas for low-cost—and fun—cosmetics led her to find investors for her start-up company, FUN Cosmetics, Inc. FUN is now expanding its product line and marketing to women in their twenties. Penta's new products and promotions keep her company one step ahead of the competition. For Penta, work truly is fun!

Thinking Creatively
How might Penta plan which products will be future trends?

■ **A Facial A Day** Olay used research to determine how to best place its new product. *How is Olay focusing on product placement?*

■ Positioning by Price and Quality

Companies frequently position their products in a product line based upon price and quality. A company may offer an economy line, a mid-priced line, and a luxury line. Positioning by price and quality stresses high price as a symbol of quality or low price as an indication of value.

The Ford Motor Company deliberately positions its Focus as an economical compact car while still emphasizing quality. It positions its Taurus as a full-size passenger car. Promotional efforts are aimed at creating a price and quality image for each of these Ford products. This strategy enables Ford to give each of its products a unique position in the marketplace.

■ Positioning by Features and Benefits

Companies frequently position products by stressing their features and benefits to the buyer. Products are often associated with a feature, attribute, or customer benefit. For example, Rockport shoes are positioned as comfortable shoes, whether dress or casual.

Olay Daily Facials were introduced in 2000 to appeal to younger women. Research had indicated that consumers would use the product to get rid of damp washcloths next to bathroom sinks. The thin disposable cleaning cloths are designed to remove makeup, wash, and moisturize. They also offer convenience and portability. Olay promoted the new product by emphasizing its benefits using the theme, "a little bit of a facial every day."

Companies frequently position products to highlight the products' unique characteristics. When Palm Computing introduced the Palm Pilot, it tried to position the product as a user-friendly tool for people to access, manage, and communicate information. The Palm Computer was unique from the other personal digital assistants on the market because it could easily fit in a pocket or purse. By 2000, Palm had 72 percent of the world market for hand-held computers.

■ Positioning in Relation to the Competition

Some businesses position their products to compete directly with the products of other companies. Positioning in relation to the competition is a common strategy that is often used when a firm is trying to solidify an advantage over another firm.

When the Warner-Lambert Company introduced Cool Mint Listerine, it did so by positioning its product against the competition. Traditionally, customers of mouthwashes chose between the "therapeutic" benefits of strong tasting, original

Listerine or the "cosmetic" benefits of other brands like Scope. With its "cool mint" flavor, Listerine hoped to compete directly with other cosmetic brands. The company also hoped to retain those customers who believed that Listerine could fight germs, plaque, and gum infection better than other products.

It is not always a good idea to compete head-to-head with the industry leader. It might be better to compete by showing that you are the underdog. Southwest Airlines does a good job of that by telling potential customers that they are the low-fare alternative to full-service airlines.

■ Positioning in Relation to Other Products in a Line

Individual products may be positioned in relation to other products in the same line. Binney & Smith introduced washable crayons and positioned them as a specialty item in the company's Crayola crayon line.

MARKETPLACE

The Customer's Choice

When Coca-Cola first moved into the Indonesian soft-drink market, it was sadly surprised to find low customer interest levels. Carbonated beverages were not popular or well-known to Indonesians, who preferred tea and fruit juices. The solution? Coke started again, keeping customers' preferences in mind. To slowly introduce carbonated beverages, Coke developed strawberry-, pineapple-, and banana-flavored soft drinks. It hoped that once customers developed a taste for these products, they may be more apt to try other Coke products. Building the market share will help build recognition of the Coke name and brand!

Thinking Critically
What are possible disadvantages of the technique that Coke used?

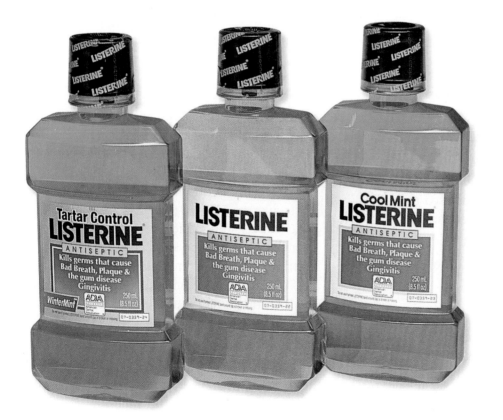

■ **The Scope of Listerine** Products can be positioned to compete directly with other brands. *How did Warner-Lambert position the new, mintier Listerine?*

Category Management

Many manufacturers and retailers are adopting a new process for marketing and selling their products known as category management. Category management is a process that involves managing product categories as individual business units. A category may include a group of product lines that have the same target market and distribution channels. The process is designed to put manufacturers and retailers in closer touch with customer needs.

The position of *category manager* is one that is relatively new. This person is responsible for all of the profits or losses for one specific product line. The position of category manager evolved out of the position of brand manager. The difference between the two job titles is that a category manager is responsible for only one category and has more interaction with the sales force, whereas a brand manager manages an entire brand and has little direct interaction with the sales force.

The manufacturer can customize this category's product mix, merchandising, and promotions according to customer preference on a store-by-store basis. Using scanned data on product sales and other market data, manufacturers assist retailers with their product mix. In examining product mix, a manufacturer determines which of its products a particular retailer does not carry. It also identifies products that would have strong sales potential for both the retailer and the manufacturer. This analysis helps the manufacturer to recommend an optimum product mix by projecting sales volume and profits for a retailer. Suggestions are then made to add or delete certain items to its product mix. If the category manager feels as if one product is taking away from other products in the same category, this product will be discontinued.

Another way manufacturers can help retailers is through planograms. A planogram is a computer-developed diagram that shows retailers how and where products within a category should be displayed on a shelf at individual stores. This is important to maximize a product's potential. Placement can also be used to highlight other products that can be used in conjunction with a product. Manufacturers can even customize planograms for specific types of stores. Each store then can stock more of the products that appeal to people in its trading area and fewer products that do not appeal to its customers.

30.2 ASSESSMENT

Reviewing Key Terms and Concepts

1. What is a product life cycle? Name the four stages in the product life cycle.

2. Explain the concept of product positioning. Why is it important?

3. List and describe four strategies used to position products in the marketplace.

4. What is category management?

5. How can manufacturers use category management to assist a retailer?

Thinking Critically

6. Identify a possible product modification or product extension for an electric shaver, a toothbrush, and animal crackers.

Integrating Academic Skills

7. **MATH** The Griffin Company has two declining products and is considering deleting one of them from its product line. Product A costs $68 per unit to produce and sells for $105. The storage, distribution, and promotion costs average $5.40 a unit. Last year, 18,000 units were sold. Product B costs $46 to produce and sells for $67. Its storage, distribution, and promotion costs average $8.50 a unit. Last year, 80,000 units were sold. Of the two products, which is the less profitable and should be deleted?

Careers in Marketing

PRODUCT MANAGEMENT

Frederick Hacket
Product Planner
London Fog

What does your job entail?

"My job requires me to set the blueprint for the designers. You have to have an understanding of the market on a creative and sales level. You need to know a little bit of everything. I try to travel to the major fashion shows in Paris. I need to have an eye for colors, directions, and trends in Europe, so that when I visit our retail stores I can determine their needs. I love my job because every day offers new opportunities! Every day leads to new learning and new challenges."

What training did you have?

"I have spent my entire working career in retail, which helps me understand the needs of retailers. I also spent two years merchandising for a product group called Façonnable. I was responsible for an entire product line from conception to creation. I have worked my way up through the industry."

Why did you focus on a career in product planning?

"Product planning is the only thing I have ever really wanted to do. In high school geometry, when the teacher asked us to draw different geometric shapes, I drew Argyle socks. I have always dressed pretty normally, but with a small twist here and there. While I don't consider myself a fashion maven, I love doing what I do."

What is your key to success?

"I think the key to success in this business is understanding what customers want and need. I also have the ability to interpret trends and apply them to the product and the personality of brand."

Thinking Critically

What challenges might a product planner face when dealing with a retailer?

Career Facts

Education and Training: A minimum of a BS in engineering along with several years of product marketing experience is necessary. An MBA is highly desirable.

Aptitudes, Abilities, and Skills: Product planners must have exceptional analytical skills to present their assessments to many different groups including management, engineers, and customers. Strong leadership, the ability to promote teamwork, good communication skills, and the ability to work with little supervision are all necessary.

Career Outlook: Opportunities are linked to the growth in the consumer market and vary as the demand for new products increases or decreases.

Career Path: Experience in marketing or engineering design may lead to a career as a product planner, who can move into executive management levels.

Chapter 30 ASSESSMENT

VOCABULARY REVIEW

Using all of the vocabulary terms below, write a 150-word paper on product planning.

- product planning
- product mix
- product line
- product item
- product width
- product depth
- product modification
- product life cycle
- product positioning
- category management
- planogram

FACT AND IDEA REVIEW

1. Explain the difference between a product item and a product line. (30.1)

2. Explain the difference between product depth and product width. (30.1)

3. Summarize the types of criteria that marketers use to screen new product ideas. (30.1)

4. How do marketers evaluate customer acceptance of a new product? (30.1)

5. Identify four reasons for expanding a product line. (30.1)

6. What is a product modification? (30.1)

7. What strategies might a business use during a product's introduction and growth stages? (30.2)

8. What strategies might a business use during a product's growth stage? (30.2)

9. What strategies might a business use during a product's maturity and decline stages? (30.2)

10. List the strategies that a company can use during a product's decline stage. (30.2)

THINKING CRITICALLY

1. Hometown Favorites is a company that will ship over 400 old-time favorite food items, which are largely unavailable on a regular basis at local supermarkets. Why do certain brands of cereal, candy, and staple products have such appeal that consumers will order them specially?

2. You own a small retail store that sells party supplies. What are ten items you should have in your product mix?

3. In response to the "green movement," manufacturers are designing products that are safe for the environment. Choose a type of company, and suggest ways it could modify one of its products to be environmentally friendly.

4. Explain the strategies you would use to manage a computer product, video game, or cosmetic product during each stage of its life cycle.

BUILDING WORKPLACE SKILLS

1. **Technology** Select a favorite sport in which you are either an active spectator or a participant. Investigate how technological improvements have impacted at least one product used in the sport. Using a word-processor, prepare a written report between 150–200 words about the technology and its effect on the sport.

2. **Human Relations** You are a buyer of clothing for a large department store. You are confronted by an exasperated customer who is ready to walk out of the store because of the cluttered merchandise. She complains that too many sizes, colors, and styles are jammed together on too many racks. What might you say or do to pacify the customer and cause her to stay in the store to buy merchandise?

1. **Identifying Product Mix** Explore a Web site for a car manufacturer, such as Chevrolet, Pontiac, Saturn, or another one of your choice. Identify the product mix offered by the car manufacturer. Write an outline detailing each product in the product line and the primary market for each product.

2. **Finding Product Line Extensions** Find a consumer product manufacturer's Web site (Kellogg's, Quaker Oats, Nabisco, Procter & Gamble, Kraft, etc.) to obtain five examples of product line extensions. Use presentation software to give an oral report on the name of the original product and the line extensions for the product.

3. **Investigating Width and Depth of a Product Line** Investigate a consumer product, such as cameras, computers, a line of clothing, or sporting equipment. Evaluate the width and depth of each product line. Use a word processor to prepare a 150-word report on how the selection increases or decreases the potential sales of those products.

4. **Representing a Product Line** Use a spreadsheet program to represent visually a product line carried in a store of your choice. Identify the product line, each item in the product line, its price, and product features.

LINKING SCHOOL TO WORK

Basic Information and Thinking Skills Analyze the product mix of a place of employment. Determine the target market and write a 250-word report on how the product mix appeals to the target market.

THE DECA CONNECTION

Role Play: Ad Agency Employee

Situation You are to assume the role of an employee at an advertising agency. A representative of Consolidated Union Foods (judge) has approached you regarding its High Brow brand of decaffeinated coffee. High Brow's coffee sales are flat, while the industry's sales figures are going up. A possible reason is that High Brow only carries regular and decaffeinated coffee in traditional tin cans.

Activity You have been asked to review High Brow's product mix and make suggestions to position the product in order to increase sales.

Evaluation You will be evaluated on how well you meet the following performance indicators:

- Explain the concept of product mix
- Plan product mix
- Develop strategies to position product/businesses
- Describe factors used by marketers to position products/businesses
- Make oral presentations

inter NET CONNECTION

Product Life Cycles for Services

Locate one of the following Web sites: United States Postal Service, Federal Express, or United Parcel Service.

Connect

- Write a report on the delivery service features offered by the business that you visited.
- Develop a product life cycle for one service that you investigated.
- Indicate in what stage the particular service would fall on your product life cycle.

Marketing: What It Takes

Brand Building on the Internet

You are employed in a leading advertising and media agency that offers a variety of branding services. You have been assigned to develop a brand building campaign for a new dot-com company.

WHAT WILL YOU DO?

What recommendations would you give to your new dot-com company to help with its brand building efforts?

Branding Elements and Strategies

Branding

A brand is a name, term, design, or symbol (or combination of them) that identifies a business or organization and its products. Brands are divided into two categories—corporate brands and product brands.

Corporate brands, such as Coca-Cola, McDonald's, and Citibank, are used not only to identify the business but also to reflect quality, value, and reliability. Corporate brands build relationships with customers and support the product brands offered by the company.

Effective brands have tremendous value and are well known worldwide. A 1999 brand valuation study by Interbrand, a leading international branding company, identified 60 global brands worth more than $1 billion. The Coca-Cola brand was valued at $83.8 billion, Microsoft at $56 billion, and IBM at $43 billion. U.S. companies dominated the ranking, accounting for the top ten brands and two-thirds of the 60 brands analyzed. Figure 31-1 on page 568 identifies some of the best-known worldwide brands.

Product brands, such as Pepsi, Coke, Barbie, Whopper, and Big Mac, also are used to connote quality and reliability. Almost every product has a brand. Product brands are among a company's most important assets and are powerful in the selling process.

Brands can include a number of elements. Some examples of these are brand name, brand mark, trade name, trade character, and trademark.

A brand name is the word, group of words, letters, or numbers representing a brand that can be spoken. Some brand names for products include PT Cruiser, Mountain Dew, SnackWells, and K2. Brand-name products usually cost more than similar unbranded merchandise because of higher advertising costs. A brand mark is the part of the brand that is a symbol or design. It may include distinctive coloring or lettering. A brand mark is the element of the brand that usually is not spoken. Some examples of brand marks are the U.S. Postal Service's eagle, Apple Computer's apple, and Greyhound Bus Company's greyhound.

A trade name identifies the company or a division of a particular corporation. This is the legal name that a company uses when it does business. Dell, Kellogg's, and Xerox are all examples of trade names. A trade character is a brand mark with human form or characteristics. Some examples include Birds Eye's Jolly Green Giant, Kellogg's Tony the Tiger, the Pillsbury Doughboy, and the Keebler Elves. A trademark is a brand name, brand mark, trade name, trade character, or a combination of these that is given legal protection by the federal government.

What You'll Learn

- The nature, scope, and importance of branding in product planning
- The various branding elements
- The different types of brands
- How to classify branding strategies

Why It's Important

The right name is an important part of every successful business. The name of a business or a product projects the personality of the company, product, or service.

Key Terms

- brand
- brand name
- brand mark
- trade name
- trade character
- trademark
- manufacturer brands
- private distributor brands
- generic brands
- brand extension
- brand licensing
- mixed-brand strategy
- co-branding strategy

FIGURE 31-1

Top Ten Brands

Rank	Brand	Company	1999 Advertising (in millions of dollars)
1	Chevrolet vehicles	General Motors Corp.	762.4
2	AT&T telephone services	AT&T Corp.	711.4
3	Dodge vehicles	Daimler-Chrysler	651.7
4	Ford vehicles	Ford Motor Co.	629.5
5	McDonald's restaurants	McDonald's Corp.	627.2
6	Toyota vehicles	Toyota Motor Corp.	569.4
7	Sears department stores	Sears, Roebuck & Co.	556.1
8	Sprint telephone services	Sprint Corp.	470.1
9	Chrysler vehicles	Daimler Chrysler	426.5
10	Nissan vehicles	Nissan Motor Co.	416.9

■ **The World's Most Valuable Brands** Brands are often a company's most valuable asset. *What is the total 1999 advertising spending for these top ten brands?*

■ **Branding** Brands include brand name, brand mark, and trademark. *Can you find these elements on this bottle of Gatorade?*

Trademark branding of products and services has been expanding to include additional elements of sound, color, and smell. Harley-Davidson has applied for a sound trademark consisting of the exhaust sound from its V-Twin motorcycle engine. Every motorcycle that Harley-Davidson sells is in effect a sound billboard for its products. Boston Duck Tours, a sightseeing tour company, received a sound trademark for the sound of a human voice making duck-like quacking noises.

Trademarks are followed by a registered trademark symbol (®). Examples include Frito-Lay's *Doritos®*, Kellogg's *Rice Krispies Treats®* cereal, and *VISA®*. When brand names, brand marks, trade characters, and other elements of branding are registered, they cannot be used or misused by other companies.

Brand names, brand marks, trade names, trade characters, and trademarks are often combined to form a firm's *corporate symbol* or name.

■ Importance of Brands in Product Planning

The use of brands is important in product planning for several reasons.

Branding helps build customer loyalty. Satisfied customers can easily recognize a company's products when they want to make repeat purchases. Nine out of ten people will pay 25 percent more to buy GE Soft White light bulbs. The GE Soft White brand is perceived by customers to be better than competitors.

Branding assures customers that products carrying the same brand are of a consistent quality. Branding identifies the firm that manufactures the product, and reduces the risk of customer dissatisfaction.

Branding is vital as it addresses new target markets. By simply extending the brands, different markets can be reached. Branding also helps when introducing new product lines and categories. Customers are more willing to try new products that carry a familiar brand name. When Burger King announced its Big Kids Meals, aimed at kids 7 to 12, they capitalized on customer familiarity with kids' meals.

Finally, branding establishes an image for a product or company. The company's brand becomes a reflection of its target customers. The Volkswagen Company reinvented its VW image in 2000 by focusing on youth and vitality. They decided to place less emphasis on the traditional engineering approach. The new image has proven very successful with the younger market.

Generating Brands

According to an Interbrand survey for the first six months of 1998, 93 publicly-traded companies registered corporate name changes. It is estimated that 75 percent of all companies introduce a new product name on an annual basis. Some companies find it increasingly difficult to secure the right corporate or product names because so many names are already taken. This fact is not surprising when in 1999 over 79,000 trademarks were registered by the U.S. Patent and Trademark Office.

Some companies with global brands such as Mars, Inc. and Kellogg's Company are doing the opposite. They are reviewing whether they should rename their similar products that have different names. The *3 Musketeers* candy bar is called the *Mars Bar* in England, which may cause confusion. The Coca-Cola Company has already adopted this worldwide approach. Procter & Gamble has reduced the number of brand names from 600 to 400 to take advantage of increased worldwide exposure caused largely by the Internet.

Brand names are often generated internally by employees. There are computer software programs that specialize in generating brand names. Some programs will check to see if a name is already owned and trademarked by another company. Companies hire branding agencies, naming consultants, or public relations firms to generate brand names. Branding is so important to product planning that 50 percent of all marketing firms do research to test new brand names before they are released.

Despite the high costs involved, marketers sometimes must change brand names. Names may change when a business adds new product lines, seeks new markets, or modifies its image. Approximately 50 percent of all corporate name changes occur because of company mergers and acquisitions. Brand names also are changed as a result of lawsuits and court decisions.

Types of Brands

Manufacturers, wholesalers, and retailers often brand their own products. These products are classified by who owns them. Three classifications of brands are manufacturer brands, private distributor brands, and generic brands.

REAL WORLD MARKETING

The Booming Itsy Bitsy Market

Kenn Viselman's company, Itsy Bitsy Entertainment, is growing larger and larger. The company sells merchandise targeted at preschoolers. Viselman takes characters from television programs and well-known children's books and licenses their images to manufacturers of everything from dolls to underwear to shampoo. Some of the characters that Viselman licenses are Thomas the Tank Engine, the Teletubbies, and Eloise. The big money is in licensing, according to Viselman. While a successful movie might bring in $100 million, "a successful licensing program can make $1 billion in its first year."

Thinking Critically
What propels classic books such as *Eloise* into the mainstream years after their first introductions?

MANUFACTURER BRANDS Manufacturer brands, also called *producer brands*, are owned and initiated by manufacturers. Examples of manufacturer brands include General Electric, Heinz, and Motorola.

Manufacturer brands generate the majority of sales for most product categories. Approximately 70 percent of all food products, 65 percent of all appliances, 80 percent of all gasoline, and 100 percent of all automobiles are sold under manufacturer or producer brands.

Manufacturer brands not only identify a given product but also indicate a standard quality and price. They appeal to customers who want consistent quality, dependable product performance, and status.

PRIVATE DISTRIBUTOR BRANDS Private distributor brands—also called *private brands, store brands,* or *dealer brands*—are owned and initiated by wholesalers and retailers. The manufacturer's name does not appear on the product. Some examples of private distributor brands are Radio Shack and Kmart.

■ **Same Store, Different Brands** You will find different types of brands in many retail stores. *Why might a supermarket carry all of these types of macaroni and cheese dinners?*

What's in a Domain Name?

Looking for a name for your new business? Before the "Technology Revolution," finding a name for a business was commonplace. You could file a name with a local county government as a "DBA" (doing business as) and forge into your business activities. Now, with the increase of Internet businesses, people must register for domain names. Over 10,000,000 entrepreneurs have registered dot-com domain names. This means that many memorable domain names already are taken! Some entrepreneurs register names in order to sell them in the future — and make a great profit. One entrepreneur registered the name Business.com and sold the domain name for $7.5 million! Although new top-level domain name extensions, such as dot shop and dot banc are in the works, the original dot com is expected to be most valuable.

Thinking Critically

What problems might occur with the introduction of new top-level domain name extensions?

Private distributor brands appeal to customers who want the quality and performance of manufacturer brands at a lower price. Many large supermarket and retail chains have private distributor brands. At some major department stores, private brands amount to more than 40 percent of all merchandise carried.

Private brands are popular with retailers because they usually carry higher gross margins (and are thus more profitable for the seller) than manufacturer brands. They are better controlled by retailers because they cannot be sold by competitors and thus can lead to retailer, rather than to manufacturer, loyalty. Some private distributor brands, such as the Sears' Kenmore line of appliances and Craftsman tools, have become so popular and respected that they rival manufacturer brands in sales and customer recognition.

GENERIC BRANDS Generic brands represent a general product category and do not carry a company or brand name. The packaging for generic products carries only a description of the product, such as "pancake mix" or "paper towels." They are generally sold in supermarkets and discount stores. Unbranded products are often priced 30 to 50 percent lower than manufacturer brands and 10 to 15 percent lower than the private distributor brands. Generic brands come with a lower price because they are not heavily advertised or promoted.

The Jewel supermarkets in Chicago were the first to introduce generic products in the 1970s. Generic products have expanded to include more than 300 product categories, including vitamins, auto parts, food staples, and pharmaceuticals. Generic products are now offered in more than 250 retail chains throughout the United States, and more than 75 percent of all U.S. supermarkets carry generic items.

■ Branding Strategies

Branding strategies are the ways companies use brands to meet sales and company objectives. Some of these strategies include brand extensions, brand licensing, mixed branding, and co-branding. Effective use of different brand strategies can increase sales of branded products and maximize company profits.

BRAND EXTENSION Brand extension is a branding strategy that uses an existing brand name for an improved or new product in the product line. For example, Ocean Spray Cranberry juice extended its product line by adding Cran®Apple, Cran®Raspberry, Cran®America, and various other fruit blends. Other examples of brand extension include Ann Taylor personal-care products and Starbucks ice cream. As you learned in Chapter 30, launching new products is costly, and the failure rate for new products is high. Companies can reduce the risk of failure by using an already established brand name.

A potential problem with brand extensions is that over-extending a product line may cause *brand dilution*. Brand dilution occurs when the original brand loses its strength in brand identity because it has been stretched to include too many products. The original brand may lose its appeal with customers. Some marketing specialists believe that the Arm & Hammer brand was diluted when the brand was extended to laundry detergent, antiperspirant, toothpaste, and cat litter.

BRAND LICENSING Brand licensing is the legal authorization by a trademarked brand owner to allow another company (the licensee) to use its brand, brand mark, or trade character for a fee. The licensee pays the brand owner a royalty for the use of the product name.

Companies license their brands to enhance their company image and to sell more of their core products. Caterpillar Corporation of Peoria, Illinois has licensed its name to more than 700 products, from marine apparel to scaled replicas of the company's tractors and other machinery.

McDonald's paid a $75 million licensing fee to associate its *Happy Meals* with Disney's 2000 movie, *Dinosaurs*. Licensed products must always support the core product's marketing strategy.

MIXED BRANDS Some manufacturers and retailers use a mixed-brand strategy to sell products. A mixed-brand strategy involves simultaneously offering a combination of manufacturer, private distributor, and generic brands. In mixed branding, a firm markets products under its own name and that of a reseller because the market segment attracted to the reseller is different from their own market. Michelin manufactures tires for Sears and with the Sears brand name as well as under its own brand name. Union Carbide produces and sells generic and national brands of garbage bags. It advertises Glad bags, its national brand, as "superior to the thin, bargain bags." Union Carbide can maximize its profits by selling a generic product without damaging the reputation and the sales of its brand product. A mixed-brand strategy allows a business to reach several target markets, maintain brand loyalty, and increase its overall product mix.

■ **Brand Extension Helps Sell Products** Developing brand extensions is an effective branding strategy. *What are some advantages of using brand extensions?*

Case Study

Building Brand Loyalty on the Internet

PepsiCo has started to experiment with the Internet as a tool for building brand loyalty by promoting its brand on the Web. As the interest for Internet use continues to grow, especially among teens, it seems that cyber-space is the place to build brand awareness.

In August 2000, PepsiCo began jointly co-branding and co-promoting its drink products with the Web site Yahoo! Pepsi will feature Yahoo! on 1.5 billion soft drink labels, while Yahoo! will promote Pepsi products on a co-branded site called PepsiStuff.com. In order to take advantage of the services of this Web site, you need to first register with Yahoo! The desired result is that newly registered users will take advantage of other Yahoo! services.

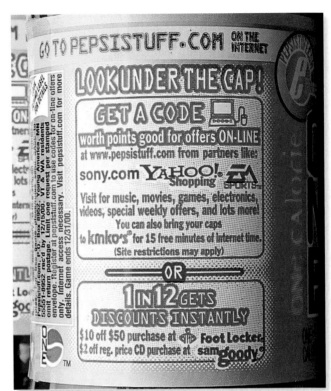

A joint promotional campaign will involve coded bottle caps of Pepsi's products that can be redeemed online for merchandise discounts and prizes. Companies such as The Sports Authority and Sony Pictures offer merchandise that can be "purchased" using PepsiStuff points.

The expenditures of online advertising are smaller than non-Internet advertising. However, consumer product manufacturers prefer to advertise on television and do not feel that Internet banner ads will build brand loyalty. They believe that Internet advertising is limited in what it can convey through sound and video. In 1999, consumer products companies spent only 2 percent of their advertising budgets on Internet advertising.

Promoting and advertising branded products on the Internet does have some potential advantages for manufacturers. Direct feedback can be obtained through e-mail, by tracking respondent behavior. Experimenting with sponsorships and contests can bring fast results. Good results with these types of activities might convince other manufacturers to use the Internet to promote brand loyalty.

Case Study Review

1. How do Pepsi and Yahoo! expect to build brand loyalty through the Internet?
2. Why do consumer product manufacturers prefer television advertising to online advertising?

A MATTER OF ETHICS

3. Is it ethical for consumer product manufacturers to alter promotional campaigns to address changing lifestyles? Why or why not?

CO-BRANDING Have you ever noticed that Kellogg's Pop-Tarts are made using only Smucker's fruit filling? Sometimes companies use a co-branding strategy to sell their products. A co-branding strategy combines one or more brands to increase customer loyalty and sales for each individual brand. For example, the Ford Motor Company wanted to find a marketing tool that would strengthen customer loyalty among Harley-Davidson riders and create a distinctive vehicle for potential owners of Ford trucks. Therefore, they created the Limited Edition 2000 Harley-Davidson F-150 pickup truck. This strategy draws on the customer base for both separate products.

Co-branding can also work when two or more retailers share a location. Starbucks Coffee Co. has an agreement with Barnes & Noble bookstores to open coffee shops inside the store. Book shoppers know that they can buy Starbucks coffee in the bookstore. This helps to draw customers into Barnes & Noble and away from other bookstores that don't offer brand name coffee bar services. The Barnes & Noble/Starbucks partnership is advertised throughout the bookstore's promotional materials to increase customer awareness.

Co-branding strategies primarily build brand recognition for each business. Co-branding works well if both companies' brands complement each other and each brand receives equal billing in

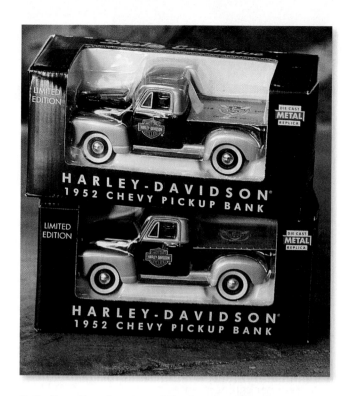

■ **Co-Branding Creates a Winning Combination**
Co-branding techniques work well with well-respected products. *How does co-branding help each business partner?*

advertisements, direct mail, and other promotions. Customer benefits will assure that the arrangement will succeed.

31.1 ASSESSMENT

Reviewing Key Terms and Concepts

1. What is the difference between a brand name and a brand mark?
2. Why is branding important to product planning?
3. Name three types of brands.
4. List four different branding strategies.

Thinking Critically

5. Internet service providers are teaming with airlines, financial institutions, media outlets, celebrities, and non-profit groups to offer private-label Web access. Do you think that individuals want to receive their Internet access from the New York Yankees, David Bowie, Pepsi, or their local bank? Why or why not?

Integrating Academic Skills

6. **COMMUNICATION** Kellogg's sells a cereal called Frosted Flakes in the United States, Frosties in most European countries, and Zucaritas in Italy. Write a 150-word paper explaining why the company uses different product names in various countries.

Packaging and Labeling

What You'll Learn

- The principal functions of product packaging
- The main functions of labels

Why It's Important

While branding gives a specific brand personality, packaging puts a face on a product. Effective packaging creates a good impression, helps to sell the product, and communicates benefits to customers.

Key Terms

- package
- label

Packaging

A **package** is the physical container or wrapping for a product. A package represents the size, shape, and final appearance of a product at the time of sale which makes it important to product planning. It is estimated that 10 percent of a product's retail price is spent on the actual package as well as package development and design.

■ Functions of Packaging

A package does much more than hold a product—it is a selling tool. Companies take great care in designing or redesigning the packages for their products. When Coca-Cola created a new embossed 8-ounce "Georgia green" glass bottle in 2000, the company did a lot of research and promotion. Sampling stations were set up in malls, movie theatres, concerts, skating rinks, and ski areas in more than 75 cities across the country. The green glass contour bottle was also made the focus of new packaging graphics, featuring a visual of the cap popping off of the top of the bottle.

The functions of packaging include promoting and selling the product, defining product identity, providing information, meeting customer needs, ensuring safe use, and protecting the product (see Figure 31-2 on page 575).

PROMOTING AND SELLING THE PRODUCT Customer reaction to a product's package and brand name is an important factor in determining marketplace success or failure. This function is especially important as more stores focus on a self-service layout. Attractive, colorful, and artistic packages have promotional value. The brand name on a package reminds the customer of the product's manufacturer.

A better container can even create new sales or minimize the sales lost to competitors for the same products. Pump soap containers were designed to be neater, cleaner, easier to use, and more germ-free than bar soaps. The new containers have not replaced bar soaps; instead, they provide a choice for customers. Pump type dispensers create new sales and encourage competitors to offer similar new products.

DEFINING PRODUCT IDENTITY Packages are often used to invoke prestige, convenience, status, or another positive product attribute. An example of convenience packaging is Breakaway Foods "Push N' Eat" IncrEdibles. This line of food products including macaroni and cheese and scrambled eggs with cheese and sausage comes in a microwavable cylinder similar to a push-up ice cream bar. The company's slogan is "No forks, no spoons, no plates, no mess!" This food product's packaging was specially designed to allow the food to be frozen and then microwaved.

FIGURE 31-2

THE FUNCTIONS OF PACKAGING

Packaging actually serves many purposes, ranging from product protection to attracting customer's attention. It is a selling tool that should promote and sell the product by catching customers' attention, defining the product's identity, providing information, ensuring safe use, and protecting the product.

PROMOTING AND SELLING THE PRODUCT

A well-designed package is a powerful point-of-purchase selling device because it can make a product stand out from its competition.

DEFINING PRODUCT IDENTITY

Packaging can be a crucial part of an overall marketing strategy for a product—particularly its advertising component.

PROVIDING INFORMATION

Some packages contain preprinted prices and UPC symbols to assist with inventory control.

ENSURING SAFE USE

Proper packaging helps to eliminate potential injuries or misuse of a product. Protective packaging prevents the contamination of products and also makes it difficult for a child to have access to potentially harmful substances.

PROTECTING THE PRODUCT

Packaging can protect a product from damage or spoilage.

■ **Finger Foods Become Popular** New packages are created to address customer needs. *Why are hand-held foods becoming more popular?*

PROVIDING INFORMATION
The package provides information for the customer. Many packages give directions for using the product and information about its contents, product guarantees, nutritional value (where applicable), and potential hazards.

MEETING CUSTOMER NEEDS
Product packages often come in various sizes to meet the needs of different market segments. Family packs are designed to meet the needs of larger families, while smaller packages are made for individuals. Specific examples include multipacks of beverages such as soda and juice, bulk sizes of paper packages, single-serving cans of soup, and family meals at fast-food outlets.

Packages and package design must also keep up with changing lifestyles. Lunch kits with sliced meats and snack kits with cookies did not exist fifteen years ago. Now, this product category is a $1 billion business. Such products are especially popular with time-strapped consumers who purchase these products for their children. Tostitos Snack Kits are another example of product packaging that seeks to meet a consumer need. These snack kits contain a single serving of chips and salsa that can be conveniently eaten on the run.

ENSURING SAFE USE
A package can improve product safety for the customer. Many products formerly packaged in glass now come in plastic containers. To avoid misuse or product tampering, many nonprescription drugs, cosmetics, and food items are now sold in tamper-resistant packages. These include jars and plastic containers with sealed lids and blisterpacks. *Blisterpacks* are packages with preformed plastic molds surrounding individual items arranged on a cardboard backing.

Countless other products are packaged in child-proof containers. These have lids that make them more difficult to open to reduce the chances of accidental spills and poisonings.

PROTECTING THE PRODUCT
A package must protect a product during shipping, storage, and display. The package design should prevent tampering with the product while on display. The package design also might help prevent shoplifting of the product. It must protect the product from breakage and, in the case of food items, from spoilage.

Product planners must consider many factors when designing packaging. A poorly designed package that does not protect the product will cause a business to lose money. Additionally, a damaged or spoiled product creates a bad image and leads to a reduction in sales.

■ **Safety Directions Included** Packaging also encourages the safe use of individual products. *Why are safety directions often placed on a product package?*

Basic protective materials for packages include cardboard, foam, and plastic. Many food items are packaged in airtight containers with resealable foil or plastic covers to prevent spoilage. This is especially important with perishable food products such as cheese, yogurt, or lunchmeat.

■ Contemporary Packaging Issues

Product packaging offers companies unique opportunities to address lifestyle changes and social and political concerns. Companies must consider using environmentally friendly types of packaging as well as packaging that makes social and political statements.

ENVIRONMENTAL PACKAGING The condition of the environment is an important issue facing product planners today. Recent public opinion surveys show that most Americans support less wasteful packaging. They are even willing to pay more for products that reduce waste. In response to consumer concern, companies are making more packages that are reusable, recyclable, less wasteful, and safer for the environment.

Celestial Seasonings, a specialty tea company, uses recycled paperboard for its boxes. Most of Procter & Gamble's plastic laundry detergent containers are made with at least 25 percent recycled plastic. *Budget Gourmet* frozen dinners are packaged in molded paper containers. The molded package eliminates the need for plastic trays,

■ **Sealed for Protection** Some packages have special protective material surrounding the product. *Why are blisterpacks often used in product packaging?*

aluminum tops, and cardboard boxes that would otherwise be used to package frozen dinners.

Many compact disc manufacturers have switched from plastic jewel cases to recycled cardboard packaging to hold CDs. On the same note, many companies that manufacture spray products such as hair products, air freshener, and paint have switched from using aerosol cans to pump dispensers, which do not release ozone-destroying cholorflurocarbons, or CFCs, into the atmosphere.

BRIGHT IDEAS
Cool Placement

Have you ever enjoyed a nice big brownie and a tall glass of . . . soymilk? To make its products more appealing to consumers, White Wave, the Boulder, Colorado, maker of soymilk and soy-based foods, changed its product packaging. Its sealed boxes of soymilk that were tucked away in health-food shelves just weren't "making waves." White Wave changed the look of its product by packaging it in traditional-looking milk cartons in the dairy cases of grocery stores. The company distributed coupons and free samples to shoppers during in-store giveaways in an effort to bring back its followers and find new ones. The result: White Wave obtained 30 percent of the soymilk product market and 78 percent of the refrigerated soy milk category, a $300 million market.

Thinking Creatively
Why did White Wave change its product packaging?

CAUSE PACKAGING As you learned earlier, packages perform a variety of functions to promote products. Packages also can be used to promote non-product issues. Some companies are using their packages to promote social and political causes. This practice is known as *cause packaging*. The issues on the packages may be totally unrelated to the product you buy. Ben & Jerry's Homemade ice cream cartons promote saving the rain forests and oppose the use of bovine growth hormone to stimulate milk production in cows. Body Shop products feature packaging that promotes social justice and environmental responsibility issues.

Stonyfield Farm yogurt company prints "call-to-action" messages on the lids of its yogurt containers. The messages include pleas to protect the rain forests, stop child labor, preserve the environment, end hunger, promote wildlife research, and defend human rights. The company, whose slogan is "Stonyfield Farms. Yogurt on a Mission," hopes to promote commendable causes and link such causes to the company's desire to change the world and make a profit.

Printing messages on packages, bags, and bills encourages consumers to participate in politics. Some marketers believe that companies using cause-packaging take an enormous risk promoting causes that not every consumer may agree with. Others feel that their views on social and political causes may actually help sell the product.

Labeling

A label is an information tag, wrapper, seal, or imprinted message that is attached to a product or its package. Labeling plays a major role in product planning strategy. The information on labels helps customers decide if the product is right for them.

The main function of a label is to inform customers about a product's contents and give directions for use. Labels also protect businesses from legal liability for mishaps involving their products. Fear of litigation, consumer pressure, government regulation, and concern for consumer safety are all factors that have led manufacturers to place more detailed information on labels.

There are three kinds of labels. These are the brand label, descriptive label, and grade label.

The brand label gives the brand name, trademark, or logo. Some bananas are stamped with the Chiquita brand label. Although this is an acceptable form of labeling, it doesn't supply sufficient information alone.

A descriptive label gives information about the product's use, construction, care, performance, and other features. A descriptive label usually includes statements describing the precise type of product. Descriptive labels do not necessarily always contain all of the information wanted by a customer in making a buying decision.

A grade label states the quality of the product. Eggs are grade-labeled, AA, A, and B; corn and wheat are grade-labeled 1 and 2; canned fruit is often grade labeled A, B, or C.

Labels often contain a brand name, logo, ingredients, directions, and special promotional messages. Food labels include product illustrations, weight statements, dating and storage information, a universal product code, product guarantees, and the manufacturer's name and address.

Product illustrations must represent what is in the package. Weight statements give the "net weight" of the entire product minus the package or liquid in which it is packed.

(6g sugars), and 4g protein.
**Percent Daily Values are based on a 2,000 calorie diet. Your daily values may be higher or lower depending on your calorie needs:

	Calories:	2,000	2,500
Total Fat	Less than	65g	80g
Sat Fat	Less than	20g	25g
Cholest	Less than	300mg	300mg
Sodium	Less than	2,400mg	2,400mg
Potassium		3,500mg	3,500mg
Total Carb		300g	375g
Fiber		25g	30g

INGREDIENTS: WHEAT FLOUR, MALTED BARLEY FLOUR, SALT, YEAST. **VITAMINS AND MINERALS:** REDUCED IRON, NIACINAMIDE, ZINC OXIDE (SOURCE OF ZINC), VITAMIN B6, VITAMIN A PALMITATE, RIBOFLAVIN (VITAMIN B2), THIAMIN MONONITRATE (VITAMIN B1), FOLIC ACID, VITAMIN B12, VITAMIN D.

© KRAFT FOODS, INC., BOX GN-64, TARRYTOWN, NY 10591, USA

KRAFT *Good Food & Good Food Ideas!*™

EXCHANGE: 3 Starch/Bread. Exchange calculations based on *Exchange Lists for Meal Planning.* ©1995, American Diabetes Association, Inc. and The American Dietetic Association.

■ **Food Labels Contain Nutritional Information** Food products are required to have ingredients displayed on the label. *What agency regulates the labeling of food products?*

Date and storage information is necessary for food items. Date information includes the packed on date (date food was packed), the sell by date (last date product should be used), the best if used by date (last date for use for top quality), and the expiration date (date after which the product should not be used). Storage information tells how the product should be stored to have the least waste and best quality.

Nonfood labels usually provide consumers with instructions for the proper use and care of products. They also give manufacturers a convenient place to communicate warranty information and product-use warnings. Notices of electrical hazard, flammability, and poisonous ingredients are required on the labels of certain categories of products. Due to increased international business, labels might contain symbols in addition to words. These symbols give graphic instructions on how to wash, cook, or care for the product.

The manufacturer's name and address are provided so consumers can write for more information or to register a complaint. Many packages include the company's Web address, where consumers can find more product information if desired. Some labels include a customer service phone number that can be called regarding any questions or problems with a product.

■ Labeling Laws

In the past, the public has criticized product labeling for failing to offer complete and truthful information. Public complaints about the lack of uniformity in labeling on packages encouraged the government to establish labeling laws. Many package labels must now meet local, state, and federal standards. Federal mandates require the name and address of the manufacturer, packer, or distributor, and the quantity of contents. These standards prevent manufacturers from misleading consumers with deceptive or incomplete packaging labels.

The Fair Packaging and Labeling Act (FPLA) of 1966 requires mandatory labeling requirements and provides the authority to the U.S. Food and Drug Administration (FDA) and the Federal Trade Commission (FTC) to establish packaging regulations. A 1992 amendment to the FPLA requires

Life In The Diverse MARKETPLACE

If The Name Fits . . .

How many different ways are there to say "beans" in Spanish? More than you would think, as realized by Goya Foods, Inc. Goya makes over 800 food products that are popular in the Hispanic food market. The nuances of the Spanish language in different cultures causes obstacles when labeling. Beans are called *frijoles* in Cuba and *habichuelas* in Puerto Rico. Goya already makes bilingual labels for those customers who do not speak Spanish. It also relies on a clear product photo to ensure that different groups know exactly what they are buying—despite any language barriers.

Thinking Critically

What are the benefits of creating bilingual labels for a company?

that the packaging of selected products include metric measurements. The amendment, which went into effect in 1994, mandates that product weight is listed not only in traditional American weights and measures, but also in metric weights and measures.

Careful consideration must also be taken when planning package labeling for foreign markets. Care must be taken to meet all local labeling laws. Some countries require that labeling is bilingual. Other countries require that every ingredient in a product is listed on the label. In the late 1990s, this became a problem for Coca-Cola. An Italian judge ordered all Coca-Cola pulled from store shelves because Coca-Cola keeps part of its recipe a secret.

Labeling is becoming a highly regulated and complex part of product planning. Marketers face the challenge of planning product packaging and labeling that conforms to regulations.

THE FEDERAL FOOD AND DRUG ADMINISTRA-TION The Federal Nutrition Labeling and Education Act passed in 1990 and enacted in 1994 protects consumers from deceptive labeling. This act, which is administered by the FDA, requires that labels give nutritional information on how a food fits into an overall daily diet. Labels must clearly state the amount of calories, fat, carbohydrates, sodium, cholesterol, and protein in each serving, as well as the percentage of a daily intake of 2000 calories. The act also regulates health claims and defines descriptive terms to make them consistent on all products. These terms include *light* and *lite; free* (as in fat free, salt free, cholesterol free); *low; reduced;* and *good source.*

The FDA also requires the manufacturers of certain products to place health warnings on their packages. Beginning in 1989, all alcoholic beverage labels had to carry the following statement: "According to the Surgeon General, women should not drink alcoholic beverages during pregnancy because of the risk of birth defects. Consumption of alcoholic beverages impairs the ability to drive a car or operate machinery and may cause health problems." Similar warnings of health risks are required on cigarette package labels.

The FDA also has proposed new regulations on genetically modified foods. The FDA is developing guidelines for voluntary labeling as to whether food products contain genetically modified organisms.

THE FEDERAL TRADE COMMISSION Another federal agency involved with product labeling is the Federal Trade Commission (FTC). The FTC is also responsible for monitoring for deceptive advertising that is false or misleading.

The Care Labeling Rule, first passed by the Federal Trade Commission in 1972, requires that care labels be placed in textile clothing. The care labeling rules ensure that specific detailed information about the care of garments related to washing, drying, and ironing are placed on labels.

The FTC released guidelines in 1992 for companies to use when making environmental claims on product labels. Many environmental terms previously had loose definitions and could be used freely on labels and in advertisements. When using the term *recycled content,* the FTC requires that proof be given about the amount of material in a product or package that has been kept from a landfill or retrieved as manufacturing scraps. The term *recyclable* can be used only if the product or package can be reused as raw material for a new product or package. The terms *ozone safe* and *ozone friendly* can be used only if the products do not contain any ozone-depleting chemicals. The terms *degradable, biodegradable,* and *photodegradable* can be used only if the product will decompose into elements found in nature within a reasonably short period of time after disposal.

31.2 ASSESSMENT

Reviewing Key Terms and Concepts

1. What is a package?
2. List the principal functions of product packaging.
3. What is a product label?
4. What are the main functions of labels?

Thinking Critically

5. Many popular products have symbols on their packages telling consumers how to cook, clean, and wash. Why have symbols and graphic directions been placed on many packaged products?

Integrating Academic Skills

6. **MATH** Robinson & Perry Advertising Agency billed Sky High Air Cargo Service $3,500 for the development of Sky High's corporate symbol. Robinson & Perry's designer was paid $1,500 for her creative work on this project. Her salary was what percentage of the entire amount?

Careers in Marketing

SPORTS MARKETING

Liam Mooney
Athletic Horizons
Talent Manager

What does your job entail?

"I am a sports agent for international European football (or soccer in the United States) players. I represent individual athletes in the international football market. It is my responsibility to negotiate contracts and fees, and schedule public appearances both in the United States and around Europe and Latin America. I have to look out not only for my clients' income, but also their public image. My clients look to me for advice on business matters."

What do you like most about your job?

"I have been a huge football fan since I was a child and grew up watching the matches. It is an exciting field to be in—I'm doing what I love. Not only do I get to attend games all over the world, but I'm also on the cutting edge of new talent in soccer."

What skills are important to you?

"A thorough understanding of the media and how to use them to the best advantage is essential for my success. I need to know how to troubleshoot when there is bad press, but also be ready for good opportunities to promote my clients and their successes. I have also worked hard to develop my ability to oversee, supervise, and manage people and budgets."

What is your key to success?

"My key to success is keeping my client's best interests at heart. It is important for me to set standards, but in the end I have to remember that behind each athlete is an individual who needs personal attention and consideration."

Thinking Critically
Is it necessary to have a love of sports to work in this field?

Career Facts

Education and Training: High school students interested in becoming talent managers should take college preparatory classes. Courses in English, journalism, communication and marketing, psychology, media, computer science, and graphic art classes are good choices. Many employers now require applicants to have a college degree or related work experience, especially in public relations, journalism, or communications.

Aptitudes, Abilities, and Skills: Talent managers must have excellent communication skills, both verbal and written. They must be able to "size up" a situation quickly and offer advice based on experience. A talent manager must understand each client's strengths and weaknesses and have the ability to present each client in a good light.

Career Outlook: Job growth is expected to be greater than average through the year 2006. Opportunities increase as the numbers of star athletes increase.

Career Path: Talent managers come from varied educational and professional backgrounds. Many have played on college athletic teams, and often have worked in some area of public relations, business, or sales.

Chapter 31 ASSESSMENT

VOCABULARY REVIEW

Select two products that your family uses regularly. Write one paragraph on each product describing the product characteristics by incorporating these vocabulary terms.

- brand
- brand name
- brand mark
- trade name
- trade character
- trademark
- manufacturer brand
- private distributor brand
- generic brands
- brand extension
- brand licensing
- mixed-brand strategy
- co-branding strategy
- package
- label

FACT AND IDEA REVIEW

1. Describe how brands are generated. (31.1)

2. What is the difference between a manufacturer brand and a private distributor brand? (31.1)

3. How does brand extension differ from brand licensing? (31.1)

4. When does a co-branding strategy work well for companies? (31.1)

5. What is a mixed-brand strategy? Why is it used? (31.1)

6. What is the difference between a package and a label? (31.2)

7. Name two contemporary packaging issues. (31.2)

8. Identify three kinds of information commonly found on product labels. (31.2)

9. Summarize the FTC label guidelines concerning environmental claims. (31.2)

THINKING CRITICALLY

1. Burger King is testing see-through bags for its stores. Do you think that this is a good idea? Why or why not?

2. Some childproof packages tend to be adult proof, too. Do some product planning for an over-the-counter drug (such as a pain reliever) that is packaged to be childproof. Address the problems that older people have opening these packages and suggest some ways that product manufacturers can help.

3. McDonald's has designed a salad package that will fit into car cup holders. Explain the rationale behind this product packaging concept.

4. Time-Warner Inc. introduced a new Internet business magazine in 2000 called *E-Company Now*. The company added the word "now" at the last minute. Why do you think they added the word?

5. Why are consumer advocates promoting the labeling of food products that have been genetically altered?

BUILDING WORKPLACE SKILLS

1. **Science** Investigate genetically engineered plants for human consumption. Prepare a two-page research report on a word processor identifying the advantages and disadvantages of gene-altered plants and their impact on food labeling.

2. **Technology** Research the process used to recycle paper, cardboard, glass, plastic, wood, or other packaging materials. Create a chart that illustrates and describes the type of recycling process for the material selected.

1. **Summarizing Key Concepts** Summarize an article that demonstrates any of the key concepts discussed in this chapter. In the summary, identify the specific concepts in parentheses. Use business publications, such as *BrandWeek, Adweek, BusinessWeek, Fortune, Forbes, Marketing News,* and *Nation's Business,* to find an applicable article.

2. **Understanding the Whole Package** Locate the Web site of a consumer products company of your choice, such as Johnson & Johnson, Gillette, Heinz, or Procter & Gamble. Review the Web site and determine the company image, as well as the branding elements and strategies that are used on products. Use presentation software to create a report based on your research.

3. **Identifying Brand Extensions** Locate the Web site for one of the companies in the "billion dollar league" (refer to Figure 31-1 on page 568). Use a spreadsheet program to identify and display the brand extensions that exist for three product lines.

4. **Researching Packaging Trends** Research new packaging trends that respond to changing lifestyles, changing demographics, legislation, or environmental concerns. Identify one product and use word processing software to prepare a report explaining how the product's packaging addresses at least one or more of these concerns.

LINKING SCHOOL TO WORK

Information Skills Select one line of product sold by a business. Identify the various brands sold in that product line. Use product brochures to create a posterboard presentation of the product features of the various brands sold in the product line.

THE DECA CONNECTION

Role Play: Brand Manager

Situation You are to assume the role of a brand manager for a large company. Your supervisor (judge) has asked you to develop a brand name, brand mark, trade character, and corporate symbol for a new type of hand-held food product: a frozen, chocolate-covered banana on a stick. You have also been asked to develop a package and label for your product.

Activity You must present all of the elements of your new brand in a meeting.

Evaluation You will be evaluated on how well you meet the following performance indicators:

- Explain the nature of branding
- Describe factors used by marketers to position products/businesses
- Develop strategies to position product/business
- Develop appropriate branding, package, and label elements for your product
- Make oral presentations

inter NET CONNECTION

Brand Games

Locate the Nabiscoworld Web site and play one of the several games sponsored by a Nabisco product.

Connect

- Write a one-page report using a word processing program about the game, how it could be improved, and why Nabisco might sponsor a Web site for games.

Extended Product Features

Marketing: What It Takes

Understanding Warranties

You have been hired to work in the service department of an automobile dealership. Your dealership offers warranties with its car sales. To assess your knowledge of product and service planning, your supervisor has asked you to explain the importance of warranties in product planning.

WHAT WILL YOU DO?

What sources will you use to research and verify your report on service warranties?

Warranties

Warranties

A **warranty** is a promise, or guarantee, given to a customer that a product will meet certain standards. Typically, these standards apply to materials, workmanship, and/or performance.

A *guarantee* is another term for warranty. The major difference in the use of the two terms is in the promotion of goods and services. The term guarantee (or guaranteed) is usually used for promotional phrases, such as "money-back guarantee," "results guaranteed," "guaranteed for 1,000 average hours," or "satisfaction guaranteed."

Warranty text is usually framed as a series of specific promises. An example is "D & A Auto Body will repair any defects in workmanship billed on the repair invoice unless caused by or damaged from unreasonable use, maintenance, or care of the vehicle, excluding paint work if the vehicle's original finish is defective."

Most warranties set time or use limits for coverage and limits the seller's liability. The most familiar language is usually found in auto warranties—"Warranty ends at 36 months or 36,000 miles, whichever occurs first." The typical warranty limits the seller's liability to some degree.

Businesses are not required by law to issue warranties, though most do to convince their customers of their quality products and services. Some companies, notably automobile manufacturers, make warranties a key component of their product advertising.

Warranties come in two different forms—*express* and *implied*. These forms, in turn, can be divided into specific types.

■ Express Warranties

An **express warranty** is one that is explicitly stated, in writing or spoken words, to induce a customer to buy. A written warranty can appear in a number of places—on the product packaging, in the product literature, in an advertisement, or as part of a point-of-purchase display. All that is required is that the location of the warranty is easily accessible to customers before purchase. The warranty must always be clearly worded so that customers can easily understand its terms. Spoken warranties, however, even if clearly worded, may not be enforceable unless they are in writing.

Here is an example of how an express warranty works. A print ad states that a portable stereo headset will operate while the user jogs. You purchase a headset and discover almost immediately that it shorts out when you jog. You are entitled to whatever relief the warranty specifies. Now imagine that the headset package features a runner using the product in the rain. You find that the product shorts out in the rain. Once again, you are entitled to warranty relief because

● What You'll Learn

- The different types of warranties
- The importance of warranties to product planning
- Additional extended product features
- The major provisions of product safety legislation
- Consumer responsibilities and rights related to product performance

● Why It's Important

Warranties are used by sellers to encourage customers—whether a wholesaler, retailer, or final consumer—to purchase a product or service. Depending on how warranties are used and the quality of the product or service, they can either boost sales or become a major problem for a business.

Key Terms

- warranty
- express warranty
- full warranty
- limited warranty
- implied warranty
- warranty of merchantability
- warranty of fitness for a particular purpose
- disclaimer

We care, and it shows
in a lush, green, worry-free
lawn your family will enjoy!
RESULTS GUARANTEED!

CHEMLAWN®
We care, and it shows.

■ **A Guarantee or Warranty?** A guarantee is another term for warranty. *What is the major difference between the two terms?*

the illustration constitutes a promise of performance, even though the promise is not a written one.

There are two types of written warranties—a *full warranty* and a *limited warranty.* A full warranty guarantees that if a product is found to be defective within the warranty period, it will be repaired or replaced at no cost to the purchaser. A manufacturer that offers a full warranty agrees to repair a defective product "within a reasonable time and without charge." A defective product must be replaced or a full refund offered if the product does not work after a reasonable number of repair attempts. Full warranties are rarely offered on consumer goods as they incur high costs for the manufacturer.

A limited warranty may exclude certain parts of the product from coverage or require the customer to bear some of the expense for repairs resulting from defects. It is not uncommon, for example, for a limited warranty to specify that the manufacturer will pay for replacement parts but charge the customer for labor or shipping. See Figure 32-1 for an example of a limited warranty.

FIGURE 32-1

Limited Warranty

ANDERSEN WINDOWS, INC.
Windows and Patio Doors Limited Warranty

Glass
Twenty (20) Year Transferable Limited Warranty
   The glass in Andersen factory glazed sash and patio door panels glass *(including annealed double pane, High-Performance™ glazing, High-Performance Sun™ glazing, FineLight™ grilles, full divided light grilles, High-Performance tempered glazing, and High-Performance Sun tempered glazing)* is warranted to be free from defects in manufacturing, materials, and workmanship for twenty (20) years from the date of purchase from the retailer/dealer. It is also warranted not to develop, under normal conditions, any material obstruction of vision resulting from manufacturing defects or as a result of premature failure of the glass or organic seal for twenty (20) years from the date of purchase from the retailer/dealer. This limited warranty on glass does not apply to special glazings, Andersen® art glass and glass that is not factory installed by Andersen.
   In the event a glass failure occurs as a result of a defect in manufacturing, materials, or workmanship within the limited warranty period, Andersen, at its option, will: (1) provide the appropriate replacement glass product to the Andersen retailer/dealer you specify—installation labor is not included; or (2) provide a factory authorized repair to the existing glass at no cost to you; or (3) refund the purchase price or the retailer's/dealer's price at the time of the original purchase, whichever is less. Such replacement or repair is warranted for the remainder of the original warranty period.

Components Other Than Glass
Ten (10) Year Transferable Limited Warranty
   Non-glass portions of Andersen windows and patio doors *(including non-electric operators, locks, lifts, balance systems, hinges, handles, insect screens, weather-stripping, sash and frame members)* are warranted to be free from defects in manufacturing, materials and workmanship for a period of ten (10) years from the date of purchase from the retailer/dealer. This limited warranty does not apply to Andersen electric window operators, retractable insect screens and solid bright brass patio door hardware.
   In the event a component other than glass fails as a result of a defect in manufacturing, materials, or workmanship within the limited warranty period, Andersen, at its option, will: (1) provide replacement parts to the Andersen retailer/dealer you specify—installation labor is not included; or (2) provide a factory authorized repair to the existing component at no cost to you; or (3) refund the original purchase price or retailer's/dealer's price at the time of the original purchase, whichever is less. Such replacement parts and repairs are warranted for the remainder of the original warranty period.

■ **Stating the Specifics** A limited warranty states the time period and specific ways products are warranted. *What does this long-term warranty tell you about the company and its products?*

Implied Warranties

Most major purchases that customers make are covered by written warranties provided by manufacturers. Where there is no written warranty, implied warranty laws apply.

An implied warranty is one that exists automatically by state law whenever a purchase takes place. There are two types of implied warranties— a warranty of merchantability and a warranty of fitness for a particular purpose.

A warranty of merchantability is a promise from the seller that the product sold is fit for its intended purpose. Some examples are that an automatic coffee maker will make coffee or a washing machine will clean clothing.

A warranty of fitness for a particular purpose arises when the seller advises a customer that a product is suitable for a particular use and the customer acts on that advice. A customer, for example, might buy a small truck based on a salesperson's recommendation that it will pull a trailer of a certain weight. The dealership must take back the truck and refund the buyer's money if it turns out that the truck cannot tow the anticipated load.

Warranty Disclaimers

Warranties often have disclaimers to protect the businesses issuing them. A disclaimer is a statement that contains exceptions to and exclusions from a warranty. Disclaimers are used to limit damages that can be recovered by a customer. A common form of disclaimer limits recovery to a refund of the purchase price. It can specifically exclude any other costs that may have been incurred by the owner as a result of product failure. Another common disclaimer waives customers' rights under implied-warranty laws.

Role of Warranties in Product Planning

Warranties are an important element of product planning. Customers may make their decisions to purchase based on the extended product feature. Warranties are significant to a business because they:

- Force a company to focus on customer needs
- Set clear standards of performance
- Generate customer feedback
- Encourage quality control
- Boost promotional efforts

FIGURE 32-2

Extended Warranty

■ **Increasing Sales Revenue** Extended warranties and service contracts provide repair and maintenance service beyond the life of the original product warranty. *How does a business benefit from extended warranties?*

Extended warranties or *service contracts* provide repairs or preventative maintenance for a specified length of time beyond a product's normal warranty period (see Figure 32-2). Customers pay extra for such a contract at the time of purchase. Costs range from a few dollars on a low-cost item to hundreds of dollars on a higher-priced item, such as a car. There is often a deductible amount, which the customer pays before work is performed.

FIGURE 32-3

THE IMPORTANCE OF WARRANTIES TO PRODUCT PLANNING

L'eggs Satisfaction Guarantee:
We are very proud of all our products. And, we want you to feel the same way. That's why we guarantee your satisfaction by promising that every pair of L'eggs® hosiery will be free of manufacturing defects and provide a great fit. The L'eggs Satisfaction Guarantee does not cover snags, runs, or other damage caused by normal wear. Just send L'eggs® hosiery along with an explanation of the defect or problem to:

L'eggs Satisfaction Guarantee
P.O. Box 450
Winston-Salem, NC 27102.

We'll gladly send you your choice of a refund or a replacement. Health considerations require that hosiery must be washed before returning. Satisfaction Guarantee limited to U.S.A.

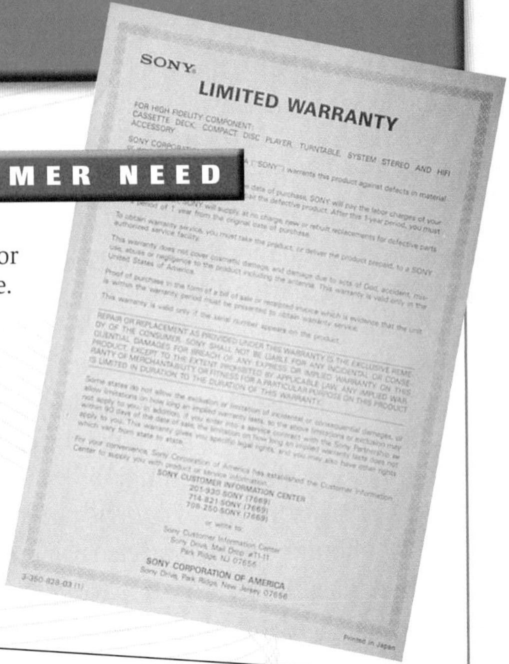

FOCUS ON CUSTOMER NEED

Warranties help to guide expectations for product performance.

SET CLEAR STANDARDS OF PERFORMANCE

Warranties tell the customer how the product is manufactured or how it will perform.

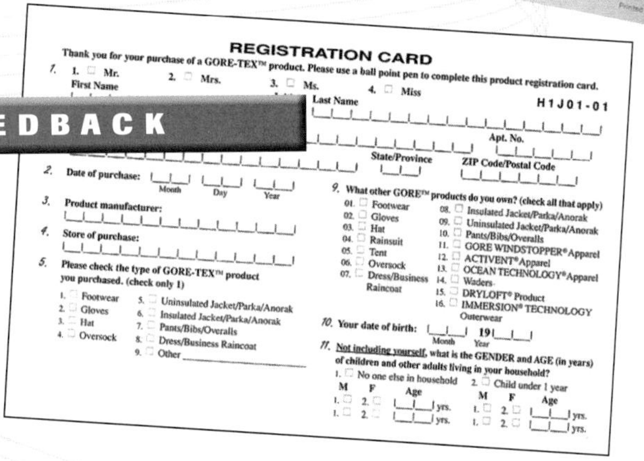

GENERATE CUSTOMER FEEDBACK

Product or warranty registrations help provide customer feedback about the product.

ENCOURAGE QUALITY CONTROL

Quality manufacturing is necessary, since products that are defective or cannot be repaired must be replaced under a warranty program.

BOOST PROMOTIONAL EFFORTS

Long-term warranties speak for the reputation of the company and the confidence it has in its products.

WITH AMERICA'S BEST **WARRANTY** WE SEE A VERY **LONG LIFE** IN YOUR FUTURE.

The Hyundai Sonata. With the freedom of America's Best Warranty, the Hyundai Advantage: 10 year/100,000 mile powertrain protection, 5 year/60,000 mile bumper-to-bumper coverage and 5 year/unlimited mileage roadside assistance. Hey, don't you deserve a fortune this good? 800-826-CARS www.hyundaiUSA.com

HYUNDAI DRIVING IS BELIEVING

Extended warranties, or service contracts, are beneficial to both businesses and customers. Businesses benefit by receiving additional money (and more profit, if the product performs as expected) on the original sale of a product. Customers benefit from the assurance of long-term satisfaction with their purchase.

There are also disadvantages to service contracts. *Consumer Reports* magazine estimates that only 12 to 20 percent of people who buy extra repair or service protection ever use it. This happens because some service contracts overlap existing warranty coverage—the consumer is paying for something that is already available. It is also common for customers to forget that they have the service contract. Figure 32-3 on page 588 shows how important warranties are in product planning.

■ Other Extended Product Features

Product planners provide additional extended product features, in addition to warranties, to help create customer satisfaction. These features include delivery, installation, billing, service after the sale, directions for use, technical assistance, and training.

Product planners must constantly evaluate a product's extended features from a customer's viewpoint. They should be able to answer yes to questions such as these:

- *Was the product delivered on time?*
- *If installation was necessary, was it done properly?*
- *Was the bill for the good or service accurate and timely?*
- *If needed, was the service provided promptly, courteously, and correctly?*
- *If needed, were technical assistance and training provided?*
- *Were directions clearly written?*

Consumer Laws and Agencies

A working knowledge of relevant federal, state, and local laws is essential for businesspeople. Manufacturers must be sure that their products meet all the requirements of the law. They must be safe, adequately labeled, and accurately advertised; if they are not, the manufacturer could face fines or product recalls.

A DVD That's Book Smart

Graduate students at some dental schools across the country are lightening the load—of their backpacks, that is. Their coursework remains the same, but they'll be spared lugging heavy textbooks around campus. They don't even need any of the usual 400 pounds of books and manuals that previous classes used. Each incoming student purchases a DVD containing the four-year curriculum—including all textbooks, manuals, and lecture slides. Each DVD will replace more than two million pages of printed matter and costs roughly the same as the four-year total for books, roughly $3,000 to $6,000 paid over time. In order for financial aid programs to cover the costs, the dental schools are making the DVD and a laptop with a DVD player requirements for all students.

Thinking Critically

What are the benefits and disadvantages of changing the product features of a traditional print textbook to a DVD format?

Larger companies often employ consumer affairs or legislative specialists to advise management on requirements. Smaller companies often join trade associations to stay informed on existing and pending laws that affect their products.

■ Federal Statutes

Many of the warranty features discussed in this chapter have their origins in a federal statute called the *Magnuson-Moss Consumer Product Warranty Act* of 1975. This statute governs written warranties for all consumer products costing $15 or more. It sets minimum standards for such warranties, rules for making them available before a product is sold, and provisions for lawsuits against manufacturers if a warranty is not fulfilled.

Other federal statutes protect consumers by forcing companies to manufacture and sell safe products. The *Consumer Product Safety Act* of 1972, for example, established the Consumer Product Safety Commission (CPSC). This agency monitors the safety of more than 11,000 nonfood items, such as toys, televisions, and appliances. The agency is empowered to issue standards for the construction, testing, packaging, and performance of these products.

When the CPSC finds any product that it believes to be defective or dangerous, it can:

- Require that warning labels be attached to the product
- Recall the product and order repairs
- Prohibit the product's sale

The CPSC recalled about seven million infant swings manufactured by Graco in April 2000. The swings were made from 1970 until 1998. During its investigation, the CPSC found that the swings were often sold second-hand without a strap necessary for protection. The absence of this strap caused injury and even death of many infants. Under the Graco recall, swing owners received a new safety attachment that ensured that the strap is used.

To ensure consumer awareness of product recalls, notices for unsafe children's products, appliances, toys, and other items are placed in all 33,000 U.S. Post offices since April 2000. The CPSC had found that less than 5 percent of recalled toys were being returned for repairs or replacement, 60 percent for child safety seats, and 90 percent for major appliances.

The *Food, Drug, and Cosmetic Act* of 1938 is another federal statute designated to assure consumers that the products they buy will be safe. "Safe" in this case means pure, wholesome, and effective, as well as informatively labeled and truthfully advertised. The Food and Drug Administration, which certifies new drugs and inspects drug and food processing plants, enforces the act. The agency also regulates the advertising and sale of imported and exported foods, drugs, cosmetics, medical devices, animal drugs, animal feed, and products that emit radiation.

Some products are regulated by more than one agency. Cars and trucks, for example, have their emission standards set by the Environmental Protection Agency (EPA), their price stickers regulated by the Federal Trade Commission, and any potentially dangerous design flaws investigated by the National Highway Traffic Safety Administration. Making sure products meet this multiplicity of standards is an important function of product planning.

■ State Statutes

Many states have passed their own consumer protection laws. Most are aimed at poorly made or poorly serviced products. Nearly all states have passed lemon laws to protect customers.

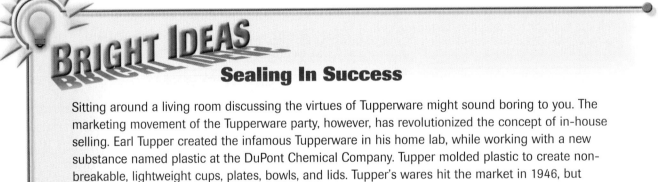

BRIGHT IDEAS

Sealing In Success

Sitting around a living room discussing the virtues of Tupperware might sound boring to you. The marketing movement of the Tupperware party, however, has revolutionized the concept of in-house selling. Earl Tupper created the infamous Tupperware in his home lab, while working with a new substance named plastic at the DuPont Chemical Company. Tupper molded plastic to create non-breakable, lightweight cups, plates, bowls, and lids. Tupper's wares hit the market in 1946, but hardware and department stores were not successful sales places. With no demonstrations, consumers were confused by the lids and uninterested in the potential. Tupper ingeniously pulled all merchandise from store shelves in 1951, and developed the sale of his products through in-home demonstrations known as Tupperware Parties. Today, a Tupperware demonstration begins approximately every two seconds with yearly sales exceeding $1.2 billion.

Thinking Creatively

What other product sales might benefit from in-home demonstrations? What product features of this product would you highlight?

Lemon laws are statutes designed to protect consumers from poorly built cars. Under most lemon laws, a car is a "lemon" if it is out of service at least 30 days during the first year of ownership or if four attempts have been made to fix the same problem. Lemon owners are entitled to a refund or a comparable replacement car.

Many states have incorporated *arbitration programs* into their lemon laws. In arbitration, an impartial third party, such as a representative of the Better Business Bureau, decides the crucial issues—for example, whether a vehicle is a lemon and how much the refund should be. In most cases, the arbitrator's ruling is not binding on the parties. The owner can sue the carmaker in a court of law if he or she is not satisfied with the outcome. The principal benefit of arbitration is that it saves all parties long delays and excessive costs often associated with a lawsuit.

The most common form of state regulation mainly affects service businesses. Most states require certain individuals—for example auto mechanics, realtors, building contractors, barbers, and police officers—to meet training requirements. It is necessary to hold a license or state certification before legally practicing in their professions. The process frequently involves testing and the payment of a substantial fee.

Consumer Rights and Responsibilities

Consumers have a right to expect quality products at fair prices. What happens when the extended features that a business has placed on a product or service fail? What happens when, for example, buyers do not feel that the warranty has protected them adequately?

Consumers can take several steps when they have not been adequately protected by a warranty.

- The consumer should contact the business that sold the product or the product manufacturer.
- If the problem is still unresolved, the consumer should contact the local, state, or federal offices that can assist with consumer complaints. These numbers can be found on the World Wide Web or in a telephone directory.
- Finally, if the problem is still not resolved, consumers can take legal action.

REAL WORLD MARKETING

Yesterday

The classic retro Volkswagen Beetle is back, and some might say, better than ever. Modern conveniences such as four air-bags and power outlets for cell phones appeal to a new generation of "bug" drivers. Its familiar bubble shape symbolizes carefree youth for most consumers, even those who weren't around for the original. By developing an advertising strategy using symbols of the 1960s, Volkswagen has hit a home run and other companies are following suit. Maxwell House has rolled their old ads into their new TV spots, while Charlie Tuna has once again returned from the sea. Consumers can't seem to get enough of the good old days and nostalgia marketing!

Thinking Critically
What other products have reinvented themselves with a hint of the past?

Because part of being a consumer is getting the best value for your money, you must be compensated for products that are defective.

Consumers can sue manufacturers or retailers on at least three grounds—breach of federal law (written warranty), breach of state law (implied warranty), and negligence. When a company does not hold up its end of a warranty or when it shows carelessness, consumers have the right to take a case to court. *Negligence* means failure to take proper or reasonable care. Courts have held manufacturers and retailers liable for defects in products, or when injury is caused by use of the product. Individuals can also bring food suppliers to court if sickness is caused by unhealthy practices or bad food. Class action suits—filed by more than one party—can be filed by consumers, cities, and states against manufacturers for making unsafe products. Some states brought a class-action suit against tobacco companies for health-related costs caused by smoking. This led to a $206 billion settlement in November 1998.

Businesses can take steps to minimize liability suits during product planning. Manufacturers should examine product design and consider what might go wrong. Products should be tested thoroughly. Items such as cars are repeatedly tested before they are put on the market. Besides federally mandated tests, there are extensive-use tests that manufacturers can do to make suggestions for recommended product use. It is more effective to spend money on precaution measures ahead of time instead of risking lawsuits and a ruined reputation. Manufacturers should give special attention to package design and provide warnings on the package and labels about any potential hazards involved in using the product. When a manufacturer suspects a problem with a product, it is often more cost efficient to recall that product than to risk liability.

Private distributors can limit their liability by questioning manufacturers before accepting a product for sale. They should obtain the manufacturer's test data and determine the company's ability to stand behind the product before it is put on store shelves.

As a final line of defense against product liability, businesses should encourage their customers to be responsible consumers. They should take every

■ **Protecting the Consumer** Product warnings are often printed on packages to make the consumer aware of potential health concerns and to protect the consumer from unsafe product use. *What are some other benefits for businesses of putting warnings on products?*

opportunity to remind customers of their duty to be informed. Customers are responsible for reading and following the safety directions provided with products. This is especially important with items for children, such as car seats, cribs, and even toys.

32.1 ASSESSMENT

Reviewing Key Terms and Concepts

1. What are two types of warranties?

2. Why are warranties important for product planning?

3. Identify three additional extended product features that are frequently part of product planning.

4. What are the basic provisions that product safety legislation requires of manufacturers?

5. What can consumers do when they do not feel that a product's warranty has protected them adequately?

Thinking Critically

6. Many unsafe and potentially dangerous toys enter the country from other countries. What should the federal government do to prevent this from happening?

Integrating Academic Skills

7. **COMMUNICATION** While warranties are supposed to be written in clear, simple language, many consumers still find them hard to understand. Find an example of a detailed warranty for a household appliance, electronic equipment, or a motor vehicle. Rewrite the warranty in your own words.

Credit

Credit and Its Importance

Credit allows businesses or individuals to obtain products or money in exchange for a promise to pay later. The use of credit is essential to our economy. In 2000 there were over 500 million credit cards in circulation. Visa USA—the nation's largest credit card system—had over $724 billion in transactions in 1999. There are over 6,000 individual credit card issuers and the average household receives about two dozen credit card solicitations every year.

Credit allows most people to buy major purchases such as homes, autos, appliances, furniture, and recreational vehicles. Credit is also used by individuals for less costly purchases, such as meals, clothing, groceries, and movies. Credit cards can be used to purchase just about any good or service. Even the Internal Revenue Service now accepts credit cards for payment of taxes.

Credit is used by businesses to purchase goods and services. Credit is also used between manufacturers, wholesalers, and retailers to buy materials, equipment, supplies, and services for use either within their business or to sell to other businesses.

Millions of people and thousands of businesses would not be able to buy necessary goods and services without credit. This is because income (business or personal) often does not match buying needs when they occur. When buying a new car, you will probably need to use some of your savings; however, it is often difficult to save enough to buy a car. Credit allows you to purchase a car on regular monthly payments—you can buy a car and pay for it over a period of time. Extending credit to customers gives consumers an incentive to purchase, which increases businesses' sales and profits.

Credit helps build long-term relationships with customers. J.C. Penney has incorporated special programs for customers who use a store credit card. The company sends mail-order catalogs and notices of special sales to these customers.

▪ Consumer Credit

Companies who offer credit to consumers, such as banks, department stores, and oil companies, typically issue credit cards. Customers fill out credit applications that ask about customers' sources of income and credit history. If they meet the company criteria, they are issued a credit card and agree to a credit contract, which establishes the rules governing the use of the credit card.

Credit cards are issued with a *credit limit* based upon customers' ability to pay and their payment history. A credit limit is a preapproved dollar amount, which customers can use to purchase items on credit.

● What You'll Learn

- The importance of credit
- The five sources of consumer credit
- The four types of credit accounts extended to consumers
- How businesses use trade credit
- The most important credit legislation

● Why It's Important

Extending credit to customers or accepting credit cards for purchases is an important part of product planning. The wise use of credit can be a great benefit to a business and its customers.

● Key Terms

- credit
- regular, or 30-day, charge accounts
- installment accounts
- revolving accounts
- budget accounts

Credit limits can range from several thousand dollars per card to as little as $250 for first time cardholders.

Purchases made by credit cards go through a computerized preapproval process prior to the purchase. This assures a customer has not exceeded the credit limit. A point-of-sale terminal typically scans the approved card and prints sales receipts for the customer and business.

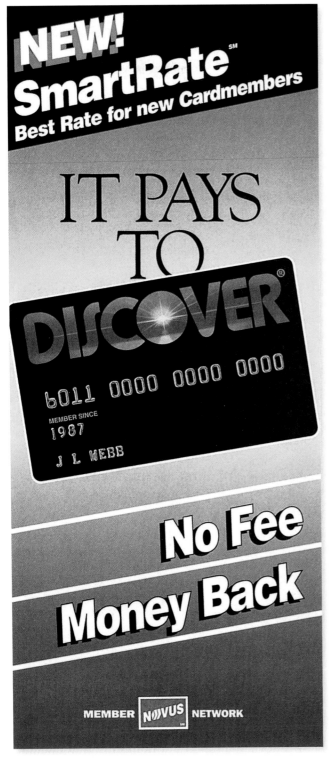

BANK CREDIT CARDS Bank credit cards are issued by banks and their subsidiaries. VISA, MasterCard, and Discover sponsor bank credit cards but do not issue them directly. Banks that issue credit cards, such as Bank One, Citibank, or First USA, set their own interest rates and fees. An *annual fee* is a flat yearly charge similar to a membership fee. Some credit card interest rates are tied to other rates such as the prime rate or the treasury bill rate and are called *variable rate* plans. Others are not explicitly tied to changes in other rates and are called *fixed rate* plans. Banks frequently issue *gold* or *platinum* cards for people earning higher incomes. Depending on the type of card, different credit limits and services are available. Originally, special bank cards carried a certain amount of prestige with owning them, but today they are used as a promotional tool. First USA bank recently issued a *titanium* card. *Standard* or *classic* bank cards, issued for people with lesser incomes, may carry a higher annual percentage rate (APR) and higher fees.

Retailers who belong to a bank credit card system either electronically process credit card sales or mail the credit card forms to the bank for payment. The bank charges a service fee to process the amount of the purchase and sends the balance to the retailer. Often the service fees can be lowered for a business by letting a third party, such as a trade association, process the credit card sales.

After the credit card sales are processed, the bank bills the customer for credit card purchases. Banks that issue bank cards receive their income from finance charges, annual membership fees, and servicing fees.

STORE AND GASOLINE CREDIT CARDS Some businesses are large enough to offer their own credit cards, known as proprietary cards. Some store and gasoline credit cards include those issued by J.C. Penney, Sears, Target, Sunoco, and Shell. Usually proprietary cards do not have an annual fee, but instead have very high interest rates. The individual company handles the processing and billing of all customer purchases.

■ **Do You Qualify for a Credit Card?** Credit applications are completed to determine credit worthiness and to establish a credit limit for customers. *What general types of information are normally collected on a credit application?*

Charge your Gas - Save your Cash!

3 Credit Cards...

THE GASOLINE CARD
Primarily for gas. $250 credit line.
No revolving charges. No annual fee.

THE SUNOCO CARD
Higher credit limits for gas and other
products or auto repairs and services.
No annual fee.

THE PRESTIGE CARD
All the advantages of The Sunoco Card PLUS
towing and roadside insurance. Low annual fee.

4 ways to apply!

PHONE
1-800 2 SUNOCO
(1-800-278-6626)
FAX
1-918-586-6066
ONLINE
www.SunocoCreditCard.com
MAIL
Postage paid

The Choice is Yours

5901 2345678 0001
G. WILLIAMS

■ **A Card for Every Customer** Retail stores and gasoline companies often issue different types of credit cards. *Why do businesses issue different credit cards?*

Businesses that issue credit cards receive their income from finance charges. Finance charges on unpaid credit card balances are very expensive. In most states, the legal annual percentage rates can not exceed 18 percent, but in some states they can be as high as 21.6 percent.

TRAVEL AND ENTERTAINMENT CARDS Travel and entertainment companies include American Express, Discover, and Diners Club. Travel and entertainment credit card companies require that payments be made in full each month, in addition to an annual fee or service charge.

These types of cards are often accepted for non-travel and entertainment-related goods and services. American Express's main business is travel, which makes up more than two-thirds of its sales.

Travel and entertainment credit card companies also charge retailers a service fee when retailers submit customers' charge slips to the credit card companies. This fee is payment for the service provided by the travel and entertainment card company. Because some businesses are unwilling to pay the service fee, these cards are not accepted everywhere.

REBATE CARDS Rebate cards offer some type of reward or incentive to use their credit. Rebate cards are frequently co-branded and offer rewards in cash, airline miles, long distance service, or special merchandise offers. Individuals who carry a balance on a credit card should look for the card with the lowest interest rate. Those who use a credit card for convenience, however, and pay the balance every month may find the best deal in a rebate card.

Rebate cards have higher interest rates because they are subsidizing the membership costs by offering special incentives on future purchases. The General Motors Mastercard, for example, allows you to transfer 5 percent of your purchases toward the purchase or lease of a new GM vehicle. You can accumulate up to $500 a year toward the rebate.

AFFINITY CARDS Affinity Cards are credit cards issued by issuing banks to show your loyalties to a particular sports team, university, charity, or other organization. The issuer gives a small percentage (usually less than 1%) of the interest toward the organization that is supported by the customer.

DEBIT CARDS A variation of the credit card is a *debit card*. These cards look like credit cards and allow the funds to be withdrawn directly from a checking account and applied to the place of purchase. The customer receives a receipt showing the transfer and the transfer appears on your bank statement as a withdrawal. The ATM machine automatically deducts a customer's purchase from his or her bank checking or savings account.

SPECIAL CUSTOMER CARDS While not really a credit card, many stores are using plastic *special customer cards* as part of product planning. Special customer cards are offered to frequent shoppers.

They allow customers to receive reduced prices on items purchased or reward certificates for cash discounts on future purchases. These cards provide customers with an incentive to shop at the store, and for the business, they provide marketing research information about customers and their purchase patterns.

Chapter 32 ■ *Extended Product Features* **595**

Benefits...

ThankQ Annual Reward
When you shop any Quality Stores Inc. store, present your ThankQ card or key tag and you'll earn from 1% to 3% on your purchases. These rewards will be mailed to you in the form of certificates good toward purchases at any Quality Store, Inc. store listed below.* Total reward is based on annual spending levels.**
1% on first $500**,
1.5% on $501-$1,000,
2% on $1,001-$1,500,
2.5% on $1,501-$2,000,
3% on purchases greater than $2,000.

Members' Specials
Watch for special promotions and premium offers all year long. We'll be mailing members notices and reminders on selected merchandise at low, members-only prices so you can make the most of shopping with us.

Members-Only Shopping Events
We've got a lot in store for you! Our festive members' shopping events are fun for the whole family. ThankQ members will be invited to come in and meet other members for conversation, refreshments and great savings!

ThankQ Newsletter
Our newsletter will bring you helpful information on our products and services. You'll find articles and offers on lawn and garden equipment, animal care, home improvements, and much more.

Personal Purchase Record
To help keep you organized, we'll automatically keep track of your purchases. ThankQ members will receive a convenient personal purchase summary yearly.**

Itemized Statement
If you provide us with your tax I.D. number, we will send you an itemized year-end purchase statement. We're sure you'll find this handy at tax time.

Lost Key Service
Attaching the ThankQ tags to your key chain is a safe move. In the event that your keys are misplaced, the protection of our Lost Key Service will ensure that your keys are returned to you promptly.

Heartland™ Home Delivery Pharmacy Program
This mail service drug program is ideal for members who take prescription medications on an ongoing basis. You'll enjoy savings of up to 50% on prescription and non-prescription items and delivery right to your mail box.

The Program That Rewards You For Shopping!

ThankQ Advantage card is good at the following locations: Quality Farm & Country, CT Farm & Country, Quality Farm & Fleet, Country General and County Post. *$1,000 minimum (pretax) annual purchase required.

■ **Rewarding Special Customers** Special plastic customer cards are given to loyal shoppers and the sales are recorded for each purchase. *What are the benefits of these special cards for customers and the business?*

SECURED AND UNSECURED LOANS Loans are also a form of credit. Consumers and businesses can obtain *secured loans* and *unsecured loans* for the purchase of goods and services. In secured loans, something of value, such as property, motor vehicles, machinery, or merchandise is pledged as collateral, or security. The collateral helps to ensure that a loan will be repaid; if the loan is not repaid, the lender can keep the secured items to repay the debt.

Consumers and businesses can also obtain unsecured loans, which represent a written promise to repay a loan. Unsecured loans do not require any security. They rely on the excellent credit reputation of the borrower who pledges to repay the loan.

In either case, a credit contract is signed, which provides the details for payment and penalties for not meeting payment deadlines.

■ Types of Accounts

There are four major consumer credit plans in use today. They are regular, or 30-day accounts installment accounts, revolving accounts, and budget accounts. The dollar amount a customer pays to use credit is called the finance charge. A *finance charge* may include interest costs and other charges associated with transactions. Let's take a closer look at each type.

REGULAR Regular charge accounts or 30-day accounts allow customers to charge purchases during a month and pay the balance in full within 30 days after they are billed. There is no finance charge for this type of credit plan as long as the bill is paid on time.

INSTALLMENT ACCOUNTS Installment accounts, or time payment plans, allow for payment over a period of time. Installment accounts are normally used for large purchases, such as a college education, travel, automobiles, appliances, and furniture. Installment accounts offer a certain interest rate over a set period of time. Installment accounts sometimes require a down payment and a separate contract for each purchase.

REVOLVING ACCOUNTS The retailer determines the credit limit and when payments are due with a revolving account. The minimum payment is usually a certain percentage on the balance owed or a minimum dollar amount, such as $15. The customer can choose to pay more than the minimum payment to reduce the balance owed. An interest charge is added to the unpaid balance for the billing period.

Customers can make purchases up to the credit limit when using a revolving account. Under most credit card arrangements, regular accounts become revolving accounts if the full amount is not paid for the billing period. Most billing cycles are 25-day periods.

BUDGET ACCOUNTS Budget accounts allow for the payment of a purchased item over a certain time period without a finance charge. The most typical interest-free time period is 90 days, but some businesses have extended the time period to as much as one year. Some retailers who handle expensive products, such as furniture and appliances, offer budget accounts. Budget accounts do not require the customer to pay an interest charge if the amount owed is paid within the interest-free time period. Finance charges are applied if not paid within the specified time period. Offering budget accounts is one way that a company can stay competitive. Customers are attracted to this because they don't have to pay large amounts up front and can budget their money accordingly.

Case Study

A New Kind of Bank

Commerce Bancorp, based in New Jersey, is a different kind of bank. Unlike many banks, Commerce Bancorp provides a variety of extended product features to its banking customers. As more retail banks consolidate, creating impersonal service and higher fees, consumers are looking for better banking features.

Commerce Bancorp gives free checking for the first year and requires only a $100 minimum balance for free checking after the first year. Other banks frequently have several different fees for a variety of checking accounts. Commerce also offers free money orders, keeps extended hours and has branches open on Saturdays, Sundays, and holidays.

Commerce Bancorp has adopted many of the same branding and service concepts used in quick-serve restaurants. All of the bank's 150 branches have a big red "C" on the front of the bank, open glass architecture, and red and gray design.

Commerce Bancorp spends about $100,000 on marketing each new branch opening. Grand openings for the new branches are special. Magicians, disk jockeys, sports celebrities, raffles, and free food and gifts are all part of the event.

Case Study Review

1. **How can Commerce Bancorp provide free checking services when other banks have different fees for different checking accounts?**
2. **Why does Commerce Bancorp make all of the branches look the same?**

A MATTER OF ETHICS

3. **Do you think that so much money should be spent on marketing new branches? Why or why not?**

■ Business Credit

Business credit, or trade credit, is similar to consumer credit in that money is lent for goods and services. Suppliers provide raw materials, equipment, and inventory to businesses under an arrangement to pay later. Businesses often use credit for the same reasons that individual consumers do.

Unlike consumer credit, trade credit does not involve the use of credit cards. Credit memorandums, letters of credit, and credit drafts are used in trade credit arrangements. Money is lent with an agreement to pay later. As you learned in Chapter 16, cash discounts are frequently offered to businesses that promptly pay their bills.

Legislation Affecting Credit

There are many government regulations that protect consumers and their credit standing while providing information on the proper use of credit. The following are some of the principal credit laws:

The *Truth in Lending Act* of 1968 requires that lenders disclose information about annual percentage rates, the name of the company extending credit, and the amount financed. It also requires lenders to provide the total purchase price minus any down payments and taxes, the actual finance charge in dollars, a payment schedule, and late payment penalties.

The *Fair Credit Reporting Act* of 1971 requires that a lender report the name and address of the credit bureau that was used by the lender when a consumer is denied credit. The Act gives consumers the opportunity to check their credit histories for errors that prevent them from obtaining credit.

The *Equal Credit Opportunity Acts* of 1975 and 1977 set guidelines for the review of applications for credit. These acts also prohibit discrimination based upon age, gender, race, religion, or marital status.

The *Fair Debt Collection Act* of 1980 prevents businesses from harassing or abusing bad-debt customers in order to collect from them.

The *Credit and Charge Card Disclosure Act* of 1988 helps consumers by requiring credit card issuers to provide information about card costs.

Life In The Diverse MARKETPLACE

Kids Today!

"I walked eight miles to school" will soon be replaced with "When I was a kid, we rode bikes and played outside!" This strange concept of outdoor play and free time to children in the future could be true globally if trends continue in the pattern that market researchers are finding. Studies of children ages 6 to 11 from several countries, including Brazil, Germany, and the United States, find that kids today just don't play. From London to Singapore, the rise in technology, accessibility to computers, popularity of video games, and the push to get into the right college find more kids clicking a mouse than tossing a football.

Thinking Critically
Why is this trend apparent in many different cultures?

32.2 ASSESSMENT

Reviewing Key Terms and Concepts

1. Why is credit important to our economy?
2. List the types of consumer credit.
3. Identify the four major credit plans extended to consumers.
4. How do businesses use trade credit?
5. Why do federal and state governments pass legislation regulating credit?

Thinking Critically

6. More and more banks are issuing credit cards that offer low interest six-month "teaser" rates. What are some possible disadvantages of accepting these offers?

Integrating Academic Skills

7. **MATH** The average American charges $2,800 per year on a card. How many years would it take to earn 25,000 miles for a free airline trip, if the rebate was 1 mile earned per $1 spent?

Careers in Marketing

RESTAURANT MANAGEMENT

Joe O'Brien
Executive Chef
H2O Inc.

What does your job entail?

"I'm responsible for managing the business to success in both profitability and recognition. The chef's reputation and specialties are very important marketing tools for a dining establishment. I develop menus, set prices, design the presentation of the food, oversee the preparation of the food, hire and train kitchen staff, and educate the service staff about menu offerings. Other tasks include ordering food and accounting for and controlling food costs."

What kind of training did you have?

"I started out in this business at the age of 14, working in a restaurant as a dishwasher. I later got a position as a cook, and after I got my speed and coordination, I became a line cook in a full-service restaurant. My life changed when I got an apprenticeship with a master French chef. Over the course of three years, I got a solid European-style education in true cooking. Then I was able to get a position at Lutèce, a first-rate French restaurant in New York City. Three years later, I opened my own restaurant. I designed the kitchen, staffed it, and ran it for two years. After that, I accepted my first 'multi-unit' executive chef position, supervising several operations at a private resort in Florida. I went on to work as chef of the Blue Door restaurant at the Delano Hotel in Miami, and I later moved to Las Vegas to open, staff, and design the menus for four new restaurants. Now I'm the director of operations for an eight-unit restaurant operation in Las Vegas."

What skills are most important?

"You truly have to train your palate to develop a strong sense of taste and a sense of smell. It is also important to have an eye for presentation and design. You have to be able to use both hands at once."

What is your key to success?

"The most important key to my success is hard work. After hard work, the key to advancement is asking questions and listening. Not just hearing, but truly listening, to the answer and to the person."

Thinking Critically

Why would a solid background in business education be important for an Executive Chef?

Career Facts

Education and Training: Valuable college courses include health and nutrition, botany, consumer education, marketing, and business math. French is also recommended. Most chefs receive formal training in culinary schools, while some train through apprenticeships. Some four-year colleges offer culinary programs.

Aptitudes, Abilities, and Skills: The ability to work under stress is important. Good communication, interpersonal, and listening skills are needed. Organizational skills are very important. Chefs must be able to prioritize many tasks, and move from one to another quickly. It is also important to know how to give directions effectively.

Career Outlook: Average growth is projected in this field. Competition for the best jobs is likely to be high.

Career Path: Many chefs begin their careers as apprentices to experienced chefs. They often advance to supervisory or management positions. Some become entrepreneurs by opening their own restaurants.

VOCABULARY REVIEW

Create four-member teams. Use the vocabulary terms below to create hangman puzzles. Each team takes turns guessing the missing letters until the term is identified. The team that correctly identifies and defines the term gets a point.

- warranty
- express warranty
- full warranty
- limited warranty
- implied warranty
- warranty of merchantability
- warranty of fitness for a particular purpose
- disclaimer
- credit
- regular, or 30-day, charge accounts
- installment accounts
- revolving accounts
- budget accounts

FACT AND IDEA REVIEW

1. What is a warranty? (32.1)
2. How does an express warranty differ from an implied warranty? (32.1)
3. Is a full warranty different from a limited warranty? (32.1)
4. What are consumer advantages and disadvantages regarding extended warranties or service contracts? (32.1)
5. What steps should consumers take to remedy a problem they have with a product? (32.1)
6. Explain the difference between credit and credit limits. (32.2)
7. Summarize how bank, store, and gasoline credit card issuers receive income. (32.2)
8. How do travel and entertainment charge cards differ from bank credit cards? (32.2)
9. Compare consumer and business credit. (32.2)
10. What does the Truth in Lending Act of 1968 require of lenders? (32.2)

THINKING CRITICALLY

1. In your opinion, what criteria should be part of a good guarantee?
2. Why does a company sell extended warranties to its customers if its advertising stresses product quality? Doesn't this imply that the company's products are subject to failure?
3. Federal legislation has been proposed to place a product liability limit of $250,000 on small businesses for selling a defective product. What are the pros and cons of this proposal?
4. Many credit card issuers provide new college students free tee shirts, Frisbees, and other gifts to apply for credit cards. Do you think college students should be targeted for credit card offerings? Why or why not?

BUILDING WORKPLACE SKILLS

1. **Communication** Write a business letter to the Federal Reserve Board requesting informational material regarding how to choose a credit card. In your letter, ask if it has information on how to maintain good credit. Find the address on the World Wide Web, or use a telephone directory.

2. **Science** Investigate the recent recall of three consumer products by the Consumer Products Safety Commision (www.cpsc.gov) or the National Highway Traffic Safety Commission (www.nhtsa.dot.gov). Prepare a chart of the reasons that the products were recalled.

1. **Obtaining Warranty Quotes** Use the Internet to find a direct marketer of extended warranties. Obtain a quote for an automobile, recreational vehicle, motorcycle, or boat.

2. **Researching Credit Advice** Use the library or the Internet to investigate how to use credit wisely. Prepare a one-page report using a word processing program.

3. **Finding the Better Business Bureau** Find a Better Business Bureau located in your state. Use presentation software to create an oral report that summarizes the various services it provides and where it is located.

4. **Protecting Your Credit** Use the Internet to search for "credit repair services." Investigate how to prevent identity theft. Write a one-page report using a word processing program.

5. **Comparing Credit Cards** Locate the Federal Reserve Board Web site and find information about comparison shopping for bank credit cards. The Board's site provides information on interest rates, grace periods, annual fees, and telephone numbers for the 150 largest banking institutions offering credit cards. Prepare a spreadsheet using computer software that compares the advantages and disadvantages of three credit cards. Compare annual fees, annual percentage rates, and other pertinent information.

LINKING SCHOOL TO WORK

Interpersonal and Basic Skills Develop a one-page written report on the process used at your or another's place of employment to honor product or service guarantees.

THE DECA CONNECTION

Role Play: Service Manager

Situation You are to assume the role of service manager in an auto dealership. An angry customer (judge) is complaining about rattles and noises, which are occurring in his/her car. The customer's (judge's) new car warranty has recently expired. The customer (judge) is complaining that prior to expiration, he/she requested the necessary repairs, but they were not completed correctly.

Activity Your task is to represent the warranty conditions to the customer (judge) and to resolve the situation to the satisfaction of the customer (judge).

Evaluation You will be evaluated on how well you meet the following performance indicators:
- Explain warranties and guarantees
- Handle customer/client complaints
- Demonstrate problem-solving skills
- Interpret business policies to customers/clients
- Show empathy for others

interNET CONNECTION

Finding Great Rates
Locate the *Consumers Digest* Web site for the best credit card rates.

Connect
- Use a spreadsheet program to create a table showing the bank and the best annual percentage rates for each type of credit card.

The Zazz Lab

A Sports and Entertainment Marketing Simulation

WELCOME

Welcome to Zazz Sports and Entertainment Marketing Company. Zazz is devoted to serving the needs of its clients who include college, university, and professional sports teams, professional athletes, sporting events, and sports arenas plus major consumer product corporations, as well as television networks and movie studios. As an intern, you will have the opportunity to work on different clients' projects. All of your work will be assigned and reviewed by your department supervisor.

CREATE A SPORTS PRODUCT

SITUATION

Zazz's client, Good Sports, would like to develop a new piece of sports equipment and/or apparel for teens. The client's research and development department has not come up with any satisfactory ideas. Zazz has volunteered to take on the challenge. Think of how surfing was the impetus for snowboarding and skateboarding. Consider how in-line skating transformed regular roller skating into a new dimension. This is the kind of creative new idea that Good Sports is looking for.

ASSIGNMENT

Your supervisor wants you to develop your ideas using the steps for new product planning. You may want to create an entire product line or just one item. Create a prototype of your product if possible, or draw your design. If it's not a new concept, decide what will differentiate your product from others like it. Identify the product positioning, brand name, and packaging, including any warnings that should be part of the package design. Develop a warranty for the product and note any other extended product features. Design a brand mark or trade character to attract attention.

Tools and Resources

To complete this assignment, you will need to conduct research at a library or on the Internet. You will also need a word processing program, spreadsheet program, and presentation software. Trade publications that may be helpful include *Brandweek, Sports Business Journal, Sports Business Daily, Women's Wear Daily,* and *Sporting Goods Dealer*.

Research

Research traditional and current trends in sports, such as extreme sports, to identify an unfulfilled equipment or apparel need. Once you have a solid product design, conduct a small-scale marketing research study among your peers to test your concept. Use your findings to make adjustments to your original plan. Research the target market for this product, identifying characteristics and numbers in the population who may buy such an item. Research any laws that may pertain to the use of your product, as well as labeling laws. Research other similar products or product lines to determine how best to position your new product idea. Finally, research your competition to find out how you can differentiate your product.

Report

Prepare a written report and a computer presentation for the client. Use a word processing program to prepare a double-spaced report. Arrange your written report around the following headings:

- Product idea
  - Concept and design
  - Target market
  - Features and benefits
  - Brand name, brand mark, and/or trade character
- Market and business analysis
  - Sporting goods trends
  - Market demand (number of potential customers in target market)
  - Competition (market share enjoyed by each competitor)
  - Product's potential profitability (selling price, estimated cost, estimated sales)
  - Product development program
- Packaging, labeling, and extended product features
  - Package design
  - Pertinent labeling laws
  - Label design
  - Warranty
- Product positioning
  - Relation to competition
  - Differentiation
  - Positioning methods
- Distribution
  - Identified retail markets
  - Rationale for distribution method

Using computer presentation software, prepare a presentation of your ideas for the client that includes:

- Key topics covered in your written report
- Graphic illustrations that are relevant to each slide's topic
- Very little text
- Minimum of 10 slides

Presentation and Evaluation

Present your ideas in a written report and an oral presentation. The oral presentation will be shown to the client. You will be evaluated on your oral presentation skills, including:

- Knowledge of market and business analysis for the proposed product
- Product design
- Creativity
- Ability to meet the customer's needs
- Program to develop the product (packaging, labeling, positioning, distribution)
- Continuity of presentation
- Enthusiasm
- Voice quality
- Eye contact

Portfolio

Print a copy of your completed report and presentation for your Portfolio.

Apparel and Accessories, Management Level
Designing a new piece of apparel and determining how to position it in the marketplace could be a topic for this event.

DECA Business Services Marketing Series
Designing a new product, package design, extended features, and positioning for a client is a possible role play topic for this event.

DECA Hospitality and Recreation Research Event
Since the product involved in this unit lab is a sporting goods product, the research involved in developing a new product and its design is a potential topic for this research event.

DECA Sports and Entertainment Marketing Management Team Decision-Making Event
Working on this project with a partner would make the experience similar to what is expected in a DECA Team Decision-Making Event.

Portfolio

Preparing a Business Plan

Once you have completed this unit, you will prepare a business plan for a business of your choice. A good business plan describes every part of a proposed business to potential investors and lenders. It also helps you develop your ideas and provides a way for you to evaluate your results. To ensure that all required elements are present, follow the outline detailed in Chapter 35.

Entrepreneurship and Finance

Unit Overview

Entrepreneurship is highly stressed in marketing education because it is so important to the U.S. economy. Chapter 33 introduces you to the process of starting and managing a business. Chapter 34 discusses the economic, natural, and human risks inherent in business ownership and the steps business owners take to reduce and manage risk by careful planning. Chapter 35 explains how potential business owners create a business plan to give an overall picture of a proposed business to potential investors and lenders. Chapter 36 shows how to identify capital needs for a business and develop a financial plan that will meet those needs.

In this Unit:

Foundations of Marketing

- Professional Development
- Economics
- Business, Management, Entrepreneurship

Functions of Marketing

- Financing

Entrepreneurial Concepts

Marketing: What It Takes

Entrepreneurship 101

Look seven years into the future. You've graduated from college and worked in computer software sales for three years. You've dreamed of having your own business. You're ready to pursue your dream, but you have many questions.

WHAT WILL YOU DO?

How will you know where to find the answers you need as you prepare to start up a business?

Entrepreneurship

What Is Entrepreneurship?

Entrepreneurship is the process of starting and managing your own business. Everyone in the United States is free to start, own, and operate a business. Entrepreneurs are people who organize, manage, and take the risk of owning and operating a business. You are an entrepreneur if you have provided baby-sitting services or cut someone's lawn.

Entrepreneurs have made major contributions to our economy. Henry Ford introduced the mass production of automobiles, thus making them affordable to the average person. Ray Kroc made McDonald's the largest fast-food restaurant chain in the world. Bette Graham, a secretary, developed Liquid Paper to cover errors in typed, printed, or photocopied documents; the product is now sold worldwide. Steven Jobs and Steven Wozniak began Apple Computer, Inc., working mostly from their homes, and soon turned it into an international business.

These entrepreneurs became famous and wealthy; however, there are many entrepreneurs who do not dream of fame and riches. They are people who want to be their own bosses and to make their own business decisions. They are willing to put in the effort and dedication it takes to be successful at running their own businesses.

■ The Risk of Entrepreneurship

Starting a new business is a risk because it requires a major commitment of time, money, and effort. New business owners must be risk takers. It is often necessary to quit a job, work long hours, invest savings, and borrow money—all with no guarantee that the new business will succeed.

Approximately 60 percent of those who start a business are between the ages of 25 and 40. People between these ages usually have the work experience, the personal drive, the financial resources, and the willingness to take business risks. People over the age of 40 are usually established in life. They may have the money and experience it takes to start a business, but they may be reluctant to do so because of family commitments or the fear of losing what they have achieved.

The threat of losing money or of not making enough money with a new business venture is very real. Most new businesses that survive employ only a few people and provide a living only for the business owner and his or her family. More than 3,000 new businesses are started each week in the United States. Studies show that two out of three new firms close their doors within four years.

● What You'll Learn

- The meaning of entrepreneurship
- How to identify the risks involved in entrepreneurship
- The advantages and disadvantages of entrepreneurship
- How to identify the personal characteristics and skills necessary for entrepreneurs
- The scope of small business in the American economy

● Why It's Important

In this section, you will learn some important advantages and disadvantages of business ownership.

Key Terms

- entrepreneurship
- entrepreneurs

■ Small to Big Business McDonald's started out as a single drive-in restaurant in California. *What other big businesses began as small entrepreneurial ventures?*

■ Advantages of Entrepreneurship

You can see that owning and operating your own business can be risky. There are no guarantees of success. Nevertheless, being an entrepreneur has its advantages.

There are many reasons why people choose to start their own businesses despite the risks. If you become your own boss, you can enjoy great benefits. Some of these advantages include personal freedom, personal satisfaction, increased income, and increased self-esteem.

Entrepreneurs are not controlled by any other managers in their organizations. They set their own work schedules and control their own fate. They make their own decisions, try out their own new ideas, and direct their energies into business activities as they see fit.

Personal freedom leads to the satisfaction of doing what you enjoy each day. By being in control of their businesses and their work settings, entrepreneurs are much more in control of their lives.

Personal satisfaction usually leads people to work hard at what they enjoy. Working hard generally results in making more money. The incentive to make money—coupled with the personal satisfaction that comes from doing so—is always present.

Freedom, satisfaction, and increased income add up to a greater feeling of self-esteem. People who work hard and are well rewarded for it, both personally and financially, are truly successful people.

■ Disadvantages of Entrepreneurship

The advantages of being an entrepreneur are definitely exciting and motivating. There are also some disadvantages. These include the potential loss of income, long and irregular hours, and the necessity for strong self-discipline.

New businesses usually have a restricted cash flow because of start-up costs. This may mean that an entrepreneur's first year or more of operation does not meet his or her personal financial needs. Entrepreneurs enjoy improved earnings only if the business is successful. If they do not have the necessary personal or technical skills, their businesses will probably fail. The failure of a business may cause the loss of employment, status, and invested money.

Entrepreneurs are not 40-hour-a-week people. It is quite possible that a new business will demand 12 to 16 hours a day in addition to weekends and holidays. New business owners often do not take vacations until the business proves successful.

Running a business requires doing many tedious, time-consuming tasks. The business owner may do general cleaning and maintenance because there is not enough money to hire someone else to do it. There is usually a lot of paperwork. Accounts payable, accounts receivable, payroll, and forms to fill out for all levels of government regulations require precise record keeping.

■ **Satisfaction Guaranteed** The satisfaction of working for yourself is a great advantage for entrepreneurs. *What other advantages are there to owning and managing your own business?*

REAL WORLD MARKETING

From Germany to eBay...And Back

Based on the quick success of eBay, it was only a matter of time before the trend went international. Brothers Oliver, Marc, and Alexander Samwer saw their opportunity as eBay interns and ran with it—back to their native Germany. They returned to Berlin to model their own auction site—Alondo.de—on eBay's. In three months, the twenty-somethings sold Alondo.de to eBay for $43 million. The young entrepreneurs have become German celebrities. Alondo.de, now called eBay Germany, has set off a wave of young start-up companies throughout their country.

Thinking Critically
What are some advantages of an unpaid internship for people who want to start their own businesses?

It takes a great deal of self-discipline to keep up with all these things on a daily, weekly, and monthly basis. They are just as important as selling the product or service.

Despite these disadvantages, the lure of being one's own boss attracts countless people each year. Those who are successful at it have certain personal characteristics that enable them to succeed where others fail. What are these personal qualities? Are you a budding entrepreneur?

To be a successful entrepreneur, you must have strong organizational skills, tremendous drive, and very good leadership ability. You must have the special skills and knowledge necessary to operate the business you have chosen. You must also be in good physical and mental condition to work the necessary hours.

It helps to have parents or relatives who are already in business for themselves. Studies have shown that the family is a major influence on who becomes an entrepreneur. Being around people who are successful entrepreneurs influences children to

feel that they can be successful entrepreneurs, too.

People who become entrepreneurs usually feel that they are in control of their career and daily work activities. They think that their hard work and determination—not luck or fate—will make their business successful. They also have a spirit of adventure. They get a great deal of satisfaction from taking risks and achieving goals.

■ Do You Have What It Takes?

Being an entrepreneur is a huge responsibility. You are responsible not only for your own welfare but also for the welfare of your company and employees. An entrepreneur is responsible for owning the business and for managing the basic functions as well. Without the proper skills or training, entrepreneurs can quickly go out of business and lose all of the money that they invested. Being a smart entrepreneur requires not only strong business skills but also tremendous dedication to the vision of the company. Entrepreneurs have many personal skills and characteristics that their job demands of them.

Before you think about owning your own business, you have to ask yourself if you have what it takes to go into business for yourself. This may seem like an obvious question to ask, but committing to owning your own business requires serious thought.

You can answer this question by doing a self-evaluation—an assessment of your personal qualities, abilities, interests, and skills. The self-evaluation in Figure 33-1 was developed by the Small Business Administration. Take a few minutes to answer each question and write your answers on a piece of paper. Think before you answer—and be honest with yourself.

As you can see from answering the questions in Figure 33-1, starting a business requires careful self-evaluation. Answering "yes" to most or all of these questions should be an indication that you may have the right characteristics for success. You should also consider the experiences of family, friends, and other businesspeople who are in the same or a similar business. Find out about their experiences. Do research on the type of business you want to start. All this information taken together should give you a good indication of whether you are ready and able to join the millions of small business owners in the United States.

FIGURE 33-1

Self-Evaluation

The first seven questions relates to your personality characteristics.	YES	NO
1. Do you like to make your own decisions?	——	——
2. Do you enjoy competition?	——	——
3. Do you have willpower and self-determination?	——	——
4. Do you plan ahead?	——	——
5. Do you like to get things done on time?	——	——
6. Can you take advice from others?	——	——
7. Can you adapt to changing conditions?	——	——

The next series of questions relates to your physical, emotional, and financial well-being.

	YES	NO
8. Do you understand that owning your own business may entail working 12 to 16 hours a day, probably six days a week and maybe on holidays?	——	——
9. Do you have the physical stamina to handle a business?	——	——
10. Do you have the emotional strength to withstand the strain?	——	——
11. Are you prepared to lower your living standard for several months or years?	——	——
12. Are you prepared to lose your savings?	——	——
13. Do you know which skills and areas of expertise are critical to the success of your business?	——	——
14. Do you have these skills?	——	——
15. Does your idea for a business use these skills?	——	——
16. Can you find the people who have the expertise you lack?	——	——
17. Do you know why you are considering this business?	——	——
18. Will your business meet your career aspirations?	——	——

■ **Self-Evaluation** Be honest as you answer each of these self-evaluation questions. Being clear about where you stand is the only way to learn what improvements you need to make. *What do your answers say about you?*

The Importance of Entrepreneurship in Our Economy

Small businesses are those with less than 500 employees in manufacturing and less than 100 in retailing. As you learned in Chapter 4, small businesses make up the majority of U.S. businesses. In addition, they provide jobs for about 55 percent of the labor force. Eighty percent of the new jobs created annually come from businesses that are less than five years old.

Small businesses produce 50 percent of the Gross Domestic Product (GDP). As you may recall from Chapter 4, the GDP is a measure of the goods and services produced using labor and property in this country.

Small businesses benefit the economy and society in other ways, too. They offer consumers more choices of goods and services. They help improve products and processes. They challenge existing businesses to become more efficient and provide better goods and services. They also offer on-the-job training to many students who then use this valuable experience to open small businesses of their own. In addition to providing goods and services people need, small businesses generate jobs and create income for the community.

Life In The Diverse MARKETPLACE

What Time Was That Meeting?

From lunchtime to siesta time, there are many rules that govern when to call a business meeting around the world. Don't schedule a breakfast meeting when in France or Germany—anything before 10:00 A.M. is absurd! Most of the real business gets taken care of in a social setting in China, so don't be shocked if your deals are made during dinner or drinks. Finally, it's best not to schedule more than two appointments in one day in Latin America, as the clock does not hold the same almighty power that it might elsewhere.

Thinking Critically

Why is it important to schedule a meeting at the best time for all participants?

33.1 ASSESSMENT

Reviewing Key Terms and Concepts

1. What is entrepreneurship?
2. Why is starting a new business such a risk?
3. What are four advantages and three disadvantages of being an entrepreneur?
4. What are three characteristics of a successful entrepreneur?
5. What are three reasons small businesses are important to the economy?

Thinking Critically

6. Do you think money and material gain are the most important reasons for becoming an entrepreneur? Explain. If your answer is no, what do you consider the most important reasons for becoming an entrepreneur?

Integrating Academic Skills

7. **COMMUNICATION** Using this book and other sources, write a 250-word paper on why the entrepreneur is so important to the U.S. economy.

Logistics of Business Ownership

What You'll Learn

- How to discuss business ownership opportunities
- How to identify forms of business ownership
- The legal steps to take in establishing a business

Why It's Important

Considering whether and how to become an entrepreneur requires knowledge of the several forms of business organization, along with the legal steps for establishing a business.

Key Terms

- franchise
- sole proprietorship
- unlimited liability
- partnership
- general partnership
- limited partnership
- corporation
- stockholders
- foreign corporation
- Subchapter S corporation
- DBA
- Articles of Incorporation

Business Ownership Opportunities

According to Dun & Bradstreet, some 150,000 businesses are started each year. There are four ways to enter business: 1) develop a new business, 2) purchase a franchise business, an agreement to operate a business in the name of a recognized company, 3) purchase an existing nonfranchise business, or 4) take over the family business (See Figure 33-2 on page 613).

Forms of Business Organization

Just as you can choose which good or service to provide, you can also choose the legal organization or structure your business will take. The legal form of business organization you select may make the difference between success and failure. It determines how fast you implement your business decisions, how well you compete in the marketplace, and how quickly you can raise money for expansion.

As an entrepreneur, your choices of business organization are sole proprietorship, partnership, or corporation. The one you select depends on circumstances such as your financial condition, the type of business you want to start, the number of employees you will hire, the business risk involved, and your tax situation.

You can change your initial decision about the type of business organization you choose. As your business grows and prospers, your financial and tax situations may require you to change organization.

■ Sole Proprietorship

A sole proprietorship is a business owned and operated by one person. This is the most common form of business ownership. Approximately 70 percent of all U.S. businesses fall into this category. People usually become sole proprietors when they have a special skill by which they can earn a living. Plumbers, auto mechanics, and writers are often sole proprietors.

The sole proprietor must provide the money and management skill to run the business. In return for all this responsibility, the sole proprietor is entitled to all the profits.

There are several other advantages to a sole proprietorship. It is relatively easy to start, and all business decisions are made on your own. It is generally taxed less than other forms of business, and there is more freedom from government regulation.

Choosing this form of ownership offers you complete control over

FIGURE 33-2

WAYS TO ENTER BUSINESS

The manner by which you choose to enter business will depend on your experience, needs, and financial resources.

PURCHASING AN EXISTING BUSINESS

When you buy an existing nonfranchise business, you usually receive little or no help from the previous owner. You must investigate why the business is being sold. You must carefully examine the business records and the condition of the property and inventory. You must also determine the reputation of the business in the community.

TAKING OVER THE FAMILY BUSINESS

Some of the same considerations for purchasing an existing business also apply for a family business. You must review business records and the overall condition of the property and inventory. You must determine the reputation of the business in the community. In addition, you need to explore potential conflicts and concerns with family members.

STARTING YOUR OWN BUSINESS

Starting your own business allows you to start the business of your choice. You can decide where to locate your business and how you will set it up. You do not have to take on old debts, a bad reputation, or a poor location that you may inherit when you buy an existing business. However, you must establish every aspect of your business from ground up. In addition, you must create and build a reputation with your customers.

PURCHASING A FRANCHISE BUSINESS

A franchise is a legal agreement to operate a business in the name of a recognized company. The *franchisee* (the person purchasing the franchise) buys an existing business operation. All business planning is done by the *franchisor*, the owner of the recognized company. Planning generally includes management training and assistance with advertising, merchandising, and day-to-day operations. The biggest disadvantages of franchising are the large amount of capital needed to purchase most franchises and the high initial fees charged to begin operations. Also, the franchisor may limit the franchisee's choices as to how the business is run.

the business. However, you are also responsible for all business debts or legal judgments against the business.

In the event that the debts of your business exceed its assets (that is, all of its resources), your creditors can claim all of your own personal assets, such as your car, home, and savings. This is called unlimited liability, which means that your financial liability is not limited to your investment in the business, but extends to your total ability to make payments.

Problems can develop in a sole proprietorship when it becomes necessary to expand business operations but the only money available is the owner's personal assets. This is why making all the decisions yourself, without the input and advice of others, can be difficult.

■ The Partnership

A partnership is a legal agreement between two or more people to be jointly responsible for the success or failure of a business. The least common form of U.S. business, partnerships represent just 10 percent of U.S. businesses. A partnership agreement, usually prepared by an attorney, specifies the responsibilities of each partner. Profits in a partnership are usually divided in a proportion equal to the amount of time and money invested. Partners share the profits if the business is a success and share the losses if it fails. Common partnerships in your community may include real estate agencies, law offices, and medical offices.

Like a sole proprietorship, a partnership is subject to relatively little regulation and is fairly easy to establish. Partnerships are more complicated than sole proprietorships because more than one person is involved.

There are two types of partnerships: general and limited. In a general partnership, each partner shares in the profits and losses. As in the sole proprietorship, each partner has unlimited liability for the company's debts. Also, each partner's share of the profits is taxed as personal income.

Based on the unlimited liability that you face as a member of a general partnership, you might want to establish a limited partnership. In a limited partnership, each limited partner is liable for any debts only up to the amount of his or her investment in the company.

Every limited partnership, however, must have at least one general partner who has unlimited liability. In exchange for their limited liability, limited partners have no voice in the management of the partnership. The withdrawal of a limited partner does not dissolve the partnership if you and your partners decide to continue doing business.

When establishing a limited partnership, you

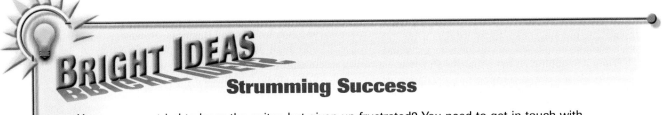

BRIGHT IDEAS
Strumming Success

Have you ever tried to learn the guitar, but given up frustrated? You need to get in touch with Nicholas Ravagni from Seattle. At only eleven years old, he created and marketed a device that helps people learn how to play the guitar. Nicholas began playing the guitar when he was five years old. He came up with his invention one year later, while watching another child struggle while practicing musical scales. His device, a self-adhesive strip of plastic that fits under the strings, allows a player to see exactly where to place his or her fingers. It uses a color-coded and letter system to teach where the notes are. Nicholas has marketed his device up and down the West Coast and on the Internet.

Thinking Creatively
Nicholas's invention was the result of trying to simplify a process. Brainstorm some ideas that might simplify some of your everyday chores.

■ **Inc.** Most small businesses are not incorporated because of complicated legal requirements. *What are some advantages of corporate ownership?*

must give public notice stating that one or more partners have limited liability. Otherwise, it is assumed that a general partnership exists, and all partners have unlimited liability. You can get additional information regarding limited partnerships by contacting your state department of commerce.

There are several advantages to a partnership. It combines the skills of the owners. Partnerships may offer more money, which allows easier operation and expansion. It allows each partner a voice in the management of the business. A partnership is taxed and regulated less heavily than a corporation.

Despite these advantages, there are some disadvantages to partnerships. The owners may not always agree on business decisions, yet the actions of one partner are legally binding on the other partners. This means that all partners must assume their share of the business debt. They must also be responsible for the shares of the other partners if they cannot pay. Finally, the business is dissolved if one partner dies. It can be reorganized as a new partnership, but the process is time consuming and costly.

■ The Corporation

A corporation is a business that is chartered by a state and legally operates apart from the owner or owners. It is the most complicated form of business organization we've looked at in this chapter.

Although a corporation can be any size, larger firms are usually organized as corporations. Those who work for a corporation are not necessarily the people who own it. Corporations form governing bodies called *boards*, who hire directors and officers to manage the affairs of the business and the interests of the stockholders.

The value of a corporation is divided into equal units called shares of stock. These shares of stock are sold through the *stock market* to individual investors called stockholders. The stockholders are the people who actually own the corporation with limited liability. The liablity for the losses of the corporation belong to the stockholder only to the extent of his or her individual investment. Stockholders are not responsible for debts incurred by the corporation.

A corporation can own assets, borrow money, and perform business functions without directly involving the shareholders. Therefore, it is subject to more government regulation than a sole proprietorship or a partnership.

Corporations can be *incorporated* (established) in the state where they will do business or in another state. It is best for most small businesses to incorporate in the state where they are going to do business. Otherwise, they may have to do business as a foreign corporation. A foreign corporation is incorporated under the laws of a different state from the one in which it does business. Foreign corporations must seek approval from and register with each state in which they intend to do business.

Some new businesses can also be established as Subchapter S corporations. A Subchapter S corporation is a small business that is taxed like a partnership or proprietorship.

There are strict provisions for Subchapter S cor-

Finding Your Niche

Seeing a need that's not being met and turning it into a business—that's an entrepreneur's dream. That is exactly what the Yee sisters of Columbus, Ohio did and now they are enjoying their success.

The Yees are Chinese-American women who never tired of looking for make-up tints that flattered their complexions. When the eldest, Susan, came out of a cosmetic counter makeover looking "awful," the five sisters decided to pool their savings and start a company to serve the Asian-American market.

The big cosmetic companies have developed lines for African-American skin tones, but none had addressed the Asian-American market. The Yees realized their frustration trying to find cosmetics was shared by millions of other Asian-American women.

They found a chemist to develop make-up formulas, designed their catalog themselves, and modeled for the photographs. Susan's husband developed and sent out press kits. Zhen Cosmetics was born. An employee at a local Asian-language newspaper saw their ad and told a contact at Nordstrom's who was immediately interested. Nordstrom was Zhen's first retail customer.

The operation, which began in 1994 in Susan's home has grown to include 24 employees, a suite of offices, a warehouse, cosmetics counters in 47 J.C. Penney's locations, and a Web site for sales online. They expanded their product line from make-up products to include facial cleansers and other skin care products. They have even developed a line of personal care products for men, including after shave and moisturizer. Their Web site includes beauty tips as well as a forum where product users can interact with each other.

Zhen cosmetics holds an estimated 2 percent of the ethnic cosmetics market, with about $8 million in revenues in 2000. The next move? Asia, of course!

Case Study Review

1. What characteristics of entrepreneurs do the Yee sisters have?
2. Does it make sense to invest your life savings in a new business? Why or why not?

A MATTER OF ETHICS

3. Do large cosmetics companies have an ethical responsibility to create makeup for all skin colors? Defend your position.

porations. The business, for example, can have no more than 35 shareholders. It must be incorporated in the United States. It can have no more than 20 percent of its gross revenues from investment income and no more than 80 percent of its gross revenues from foreign sources. You can learn more information about Subchapter S corporations by consulting Internal Revenue Service (IRS) publication number 589 or by calling your IRS office.

Whether or not you choose to file as a Subchapter S corporation, you must show your internal corporate organization when forming a corporation. This requirement includes the development of corporate bylaws, the selection of a board of directors, and the election of officers who will actually run the corporate operations. In small corporations, the members of the board of directors frequently are elected as the officers of the corporation. There are four key advantages to this form of business organization.

- Each owner has limited liability.
- It is easier for a corporation to raise money for expansion than it is for other forms of business.
- People can easily enter or leave the business simply by buying or selling their shares of stock.
- Each operation area of the business can be professionally managed by an expert in that area.

As you can see, there are many advantages of forming a corporation. There are times when this is not the best option, however. Among the disadvantages to the corporation are:

- The complexity of forming it
- Increased government regulation
- Higher taxes on the profits of the corporation and on each stockholder
- Intricate accounting and record keeping

It is important to be flexible in approaching the legal form of ownership when establishing a new business. A business may start out as a sole proprietorship, grow into a partnership, and ultimately end up as a corporation. The entrepreneurs you read about at the beginning of the chapter—Henry Ford, Ray Kroc, Bette Graham, Steven Jobs, and Steven Wozniak—watched their businesses grow from sole proprietorships or partnerships to major corporations.

Legal Steps in Establishing Your Business

Before you can officially open the doors of your business, you will need to take specific legal steps to establish your business. These will vary if you form a sole proprietorship, partnership, or corporation.

When you establish a sole proprietorship or partnership, you must file for a DBA (Doing Business As) at your local county clerk's office. A DBA is a registration process by which your county government officially recognizes that your business exists. This legitimizes your business.

There is usually a filing fee for registration, but the process protects the name of your business for a certain number of years. This name protection applies only to the county where your business is registered.

You must check with the county clerks in your trading area and with your state department of commerce to see if any other business is using your chosen business name. This reduces the chances that someone will sue later if you are using his or her same business name.

When forming a corporation, you must file Articles of Incorporation with the corporation and securities bureau in your state department of commerce. Articles of Incorporation identify the name and address of your business, its purpose, the names of the initial directors, and the amount of stock that will be issued to each director.

There is a filing fee, but your business becomes protected and no other business may register under your business name. The necessary forms, applications, and information on filing fees can be obtained from your state department of commerce.

The type of business organization that you choose is important to the overall success of your business. The decision is somewhat complicated, so you must get the best advice possible before starting operations. Discuss the advantages and disadvantages of each business form with an accountant, an attorney, or another business advisor. Do your research and investigate all of the options. When forming a corporation, the laws of your state may require you to hire an attorney. Check your state laws for specific requirements regarding incorporating a business. These may vary from state to state.

Depending on what business you enter and where you locate, you may have to obtain one or more licenses. Individual states license many businesses and occupations, such as doctors, accountants, cosmetologists, barbers, marriage counselors, and pharmacists. Licensing is done to protect the public from unqualified people practicing in a business and to maintain the health and welfare of the citizens. Licenses establish minimum standards of education and training for people who practice in a particular profession. They also regulate where businesses can locate, and protect neighborhoods and the environment.

In addition to state licenses, your community may require special local licenses or permits to comply with zoning ordinances, building codes, and safety standards. Local governments use licensing as a way to regulate people who plan to enter certain types of businesses. Most communities require you to obtain a license before you open a hotel, restaurant, or movie theater. Check with your local government and your state department of licensing and regulation prior to starting your business.

As an entrepreneur, it is important to protect yourself and your ideas—other legalities may include safeguarding your intellectual property. Patents, trademarks, or copyrights can protect these products and ideas.

Send the Work Out

While small- to mid-size companies have many advantages over larger companies, available resources is not one of them. MSPs, or management service providers, are a new type of business that assists these businesses with a level of help that only large corporations have had in the past. Limited financial or human resources can sometimes undermine a small entrepreneurial company's ability to implement successful information technology management programs. MSPs evaluate technology management to find out where companies need the most help. MSPs are able to monitor clients' computer networks and perform network maintenance, upgrades, and fixes off-site. This allows in-house labor to focus on more pressing work.

Thinking Critically
Before hiring an MSP, what qualifications might a company check for?

33.2 ASSESSMENT

Reviewing Key Terms and Concepts

1. What are four ways to enter into a business?
2. What are the three basic forms of business ownership?
3. What legal steps must you take to establish a sole proprietorship or partnership?
4. What legal steps must you take to establish a corporation?
5. What is a Subchapter S corporation?

Thinking Critically

6. Which of the four ways to enter a business would you use to start your own business? Explain your decision.

Integrating Academic Skills

7. **MATH** An entrepreneur works 11 hours a day, five days a week, 52 weeks a year. How many hours is the person working annually?

Careers in Marketing

ENTREPRENEUR

Ron Wilson
Chief Executive Officer
Big Bang Products

What does your job entail?

"I started Big Bang Products with my partner Brian Le Gette when we were MBA students at the Wharton School of Business (University of Pennsylvania) in 1993. While in school, Brian and I developed a product called Arctic 180s—earwarmers that wrap around the back of the head. We handled every aspect of the business in the beginning, including product design, finding contract manufacturers, standing on street corners selling the product, collecting market research, making cold calls to retailers, designing packaging, creating logos, raising money, and even assembling the product on occasion. As CEO, my role is now focused on shaping our vision and market strategy to clearly define and maintain focus on our customers."

What do you like most about your work?

"I still remember the first person I saw on the streets of Philadelphia wearing our earwarmers. The realization that a stranger was wearing something that I worked hard to create, was amazing."

How does your workload vary?

"The first few years my workload was extremely heavy with an average of 80+ hours a week. The workload is still heavy, but it's now about 60 hours a week. This seems like a lot, but when you love what you do you don't notice. Every day I get up and can't wait to get to work. If you like marketing, the entrepreneurial environment can provide a demanding, yet satisfying career."

What is your key to success?

"Most successful entrepreneurs I know have two common traits: tenacity and love of their job. My other key to success has been education. After earning a bachelor's degree in Industrial Engineering, I went on to business school. The results paid off! In 1996, we launched the product on QVC, selling over 5000 units in four minutes, and we are now a $10 million dollar company."

Thinking Critically

What are some things that you can do to make work more manageable when starting on an entrepreneurial venture?

Career Facts

Education and Training: Business courses and experience are helpful, especially in the small business field.

Aptitudes, Abilities, and Skills: Creativity, willingness to take risks, resilience, good people skills, strong leadership skills, and a good understanding of economics and government policies are necessary.

Career Outlook: The number of small businesses is growing and is expected to continue to grow.

Career Path: Many entrepreneurs have some experience working in a line of business similar to the type they plan to enter as an owner.

Chapter 33 ASSESSMENT

VOCABULARY REVIEW

Divide the class into teams for a Marketing Quiz Bowl. Your teacher will call out the terms below. Teams should raise their hands when they feel they know the correct definition for the term. The team that raises a hand first has ten seconds to respond; if they incorrectly define the term, the other team then has ten seconds to respond. The team that correctly defines the term first gets a point.

- entrepreneurship
- entrepreneurs
- franchise
- sole proprietorship
- unlimited liability
- partnership
- general partnership
- limited partnership
- corporation
- stockholders
- foreign corporation
- Subchapter S corporation
- DBA
- Articles of Incorporation

FACT AND IDEA REVIEW

1. Why should you do self-evaluation if you want to become an entrepreneur? (33.1)

2. How does franchising work? (33.2)

3. List three advantages and three disadvantages of the sole proprietorship. (33.2)

4. How does unlimited liability affect the type of business organization selected by an entrepreneur? (33.2)

5. Explain the difference between the two kinds of partnerships. (33.2)

6. List three advantages and three disadvantages of a partnership. (33.2)

7. List three advantages and three disadvantages of a corporation. (33.2)

8. What three groups of people are involved with the corporate form of ownership? (33.2)

9. What is a foreign corporation? (33.2)

10. What are five reasons for licensing certain occupations and businesses? (Sec. 33.2)

THINKING CRITICALLY

1. What are the disadvantages of working for others as opposed to being your own boss? Are the disadvantages enough to make you consider starting your own business? Why?

2. A franchisee has a new product idea. Who should get credit for it—the franchisee or the franchisor?

3. Imagine you are starting a restaurant. Which type of business organization would you choose? Explain the reasons for your decision.

BUILDING WORKPLACE SKILLS

1. **Human Relations** A very good friend of yours has an idea to start a small video rental business. You have heard, however, that small video stores are being replaced by video rental superstores. You have also heard that the cost of opening a store has risen from $50,000 a few years ago to between $150,000 and $200,000 today. What would you tell your friend to do before she invests in this kind of business?

2. **Technology** You have always wanted to own a small sporting goods store. You have a friend who is interested in joining you in a partnership. Use the library or the Internet to research how much competition you would have in your geographical area.

1. **Opening Your Own Business** Using a word processing program, write a description of a business you might want to open in preparation for DECA's Entrepreneurship Written or Participating Event.

2. **Understanding Risk** Work with a partner to prepare a debate on the advantages and disadvantages of entrepreneurship. Stage the debate for your class.

3. **Investigating Small Business** Interview a small business owner in your community to find out why that person started his or her own business. Present an oral report about the job duties and tasks typically performed by the business owner on a daily, weekly, and/or monthly basis.

4. **Buying a Franchise** Use the Internet to research and identify factors you need to know when you buy a franchise. Use presentation software to create a report on what you have learned.

5. **Identifying New Market Possibilities** Entrepreneurs often look into the future to see new market possibilities. Use a word processing program to explain the kinds of businesses that you think will boom in the next 25 years. Explain how you would go about getting the knowledge or training to enter one of them.

LINKING SCHOOL TO WORK

Resources and System Skills Research whether a local business was originally organized as a proprietorship, partnership, or a corporation. Write a 300-word report on how the business got started and whether it has changed its type of ownership over the years.

THE DECA CONNECTION

Role Play: Bookstore Manager

Situation You are to assume the role of manager of a local bookstore that is operated as a sole proprietorship. The owner (judge) is interested in changing the ownership to either a partnership or a corporation.

Activity You have been appointed to research the benefits of each. You must report to the store owner (judge) about your findings.

Evaluation You will be evaluated on how well you meet the following performance indicators:

- Explain the types of business ownership
- Describe legal issues affecting businesses
- Explain the nature of tax regulations on businesses
- Describe the nature of legally binding contracts
- Explain types of business risk

inter NET CONNECTION

Entrepreneurs Online
Knowing that many new companies start up every day, you want to discover what makes a successful startup.

Connect
- Locate information online about successful entrepreneurs.
- E-mail entrepreneurs and ask if they are willing to share what factors they think led to their success.
- Hold an "Entrepreneurship Week" at your school and invite entrepreneurs to come and talk to your marketing class.

Chapter 34

Risk Management

Marketing: What It Takes

Stopping "Drive-offs"
You work as an assistant manager for a 24-hour a day self-service gas station and convenience store. Because of rising gasoline prices, you are experiencing an increasing amount of "drive-offs." More individuals are filling their tanks and driving away without paying. Your manager has asked for your input in designing a plan to reduce external theft at your gas station.

WHAT WILL YOU DO?

How will you find a solution that doesn't offend your regular customers, but will help lower gasoline theft for your store.

Risk Management

What Is Risk Management?

As a business owner, one of your primary goals will be to make a profit. Unfortunately, there is no guarantee that this will happen. Your business may realize a lower return on investment than you expected or may experience a loss after you have paid all your expenses. The possibility of financial loss is called risk.

A business cannot eliminate all risks, but marketers can reduce and manage risks. According to the American Risk and Insurance Association, risk management is the systematic process of managing an organization's risk exposure to achieve objectives in a manner consistent with public interest, human safety, environmental factors, and the law. Risks are managed by using the best available marketing information, analyzing opportunities, and making wise decisions.

Kinds of Risks

Business risks are the possibility of business loss or failure. There are three kinds of business risks—*economic, natural,* and *human.* Let's take a closer look at each of these types of risks.

▪ Economic Risks

Economic risks occur from changes in overall business conditions. These changes can include the amount or type of competition, changing consumer lifestyles, population changes, limited usefulness or style of some products, product obsolescence, government regulation, inflation, or recession.

Businesses that fail to change their products when competitors offer more features and benefits lose sales and experience economic risk. Foreign competition is also an economic risk for many U.S. companies, because foreign products can often be produced and sold for less than similar domestic products. The positive aspect of foreign competition is that it forces U.S. companies to improve productivity and efficiency to compete successfully in the marketplace.

Consumer lifestyles and population changes are other economic risks facing modern businesses. More single-parent households, dual-income families, the aging of the Baby Boom generation, and the increasing number of single individuals delaying marriage all present potential risks for businesses that fail to adapt products to meet changing needs.

The limited usefulness or style of some products is another potential economic risk. Prices have to be reduced on unsold products at the end of the season to sell them. This obviously reduces profits.

• What You'll Learn

- The nature and scope of risk management
- The various types of business risks

• Why It's Important

Businesses must manage risks in ways that accommodate public interest, human safety, the environment, and state and federal laws. Risk management is necessary for effective financial, marketing, production, and human resource management decisions. Risk management reduces the adverse effects of risk on business resources, cash flow, and profits.

Key Terms

- risk
- risk management
- business risks
- economic risks
- natural risks
- human risks

■ **Keeping Up with the Times** Products that were once successful often become outdated and obsolete in time. *Why do some products experience product obsolescence?*

Some products inevitably become obsolete or outdated. Known as *product obsolescence*, this represents another type of economic risk for businesses that depend on fashion and the latest trends to market goods and services. This is because new products are constantly being developed. When a new product is faster, more efficient, or more convenient than its predecessor, the predecessor becomes obsolete.

Changes in the general business environment caused by inflation or recession can present economic risks. All businesses in an area experiencing high unemployment will suffer through reduced product sales.

Government laws and regulations can also result in economic risks. Laws requiring businesses to pay for such things as street and sewer improvements, or parking and general maintenance, reduce profits.

Product recalls, or even the threat of recalls, by government agencies can affect sales and profits. Companies that have to recall products often face high legal costs and expensive repairs and replacements. DaimlerChrysler AG recalled 380,000 Dodge Ram 1998–2000 model year pickup trucks in 2000 to reinforce trailer hitches that had shown signs of cracking. The company incurred costly expenditures because it had to notify all owners by mail, provide free inspections, and then make the needed repairs on the vehicles.

BRIGHT IDEAS

If the Shoe Fits...

How would you feel if you made a product and everyone walked all over it? If you were Mark Thatcher—inventor of the Teva sports sandal—you would be feeling good! For Thatcher, the saying "You don't know a man until you've walked in his shoes," has truth! Thatcher spent some time living as a nomad in the deserts of Israel. On his return, he became an engineering student in Arizona, but found his zest for life was working the summers as a river guide, or "boatman," on the Colorado River in the Grand Canyon. Thatcher decided to return to his love for river rafting with a business concept. He knew there was no adequate footwear for boatmen who traveled by river. Tennis shoes never dried out, and flip-flops seemed to always slip off. Thatcher came up with Teva (the Hebrew word for nature) as the first modern sport sandal. Thatcher's sandals are available in 140 styles and have generated $106 million in sales.

Thinking Creatively

Think of other types of sports that could benefit from new equipment. What new type of product would suit that sport?

FIGURE 34-1

The Top Catastrophes of 1999

1. Winter Storm Lothar	Western Europe	$4.5 billion
2. Typhoon Bart	Southern Japan	$2.98 billion
3. Hurricane Floyd	Eastern United States	$2.36 billion
4. Winter Storm Martin	Southwest France	$2.2 billion
5. Earthquake	Izmit, Turkey	$2 billion
6. Tornadoes	Midwest United States	$1.49 billion
7. Earthquake	Nantou, Taiwan	$1 billion
8. Hailstorm	Sydney, Australia	$982 million
9. Snowstorm	Midwest United States	$755 million
10. Explosion	Ford Motor Company plant, Dearborn, Michigan	$650 million

■ **The Top Catastrophes of 1999** Businesses face natural risks from floods, hurricanes, fires, and other natural causes. *How many times greater were the damages caused by Hurricane Floyd compared to the Ford Motor Company plant explosion and fire?*

■ Natural Risks

Natural risks are risks resulting from natural causes such as floods, tornadoes, hurricanes, fires, lightning, droughts, earthquakes, and even unexpected changes in normal weather conditions.

Businesses can insure against unexpected losses from some natural risks, but not all. Some businesses and products depend on predictable weather conditions for success. Unexpected weather conditions can often spell financial ruin or reduced profits for a business. Ski resorts depend on a season of normal to above-normal snowfall levels so they can operate ski lifts, sell ski packages, and fill restaurants. A mild or below-normal winter represents lost revenues and a natural risk to the business (see Figure 34-1).

Conversely, a hot summer will have a positive effect on sales of certain products like air conditioners, cooling fans, boats, and swimming pools. Protecting your business against the natural risk of fire is simpler. Smoke detectors and fire sprinklers will protect your staff and your property. Cash and important documents should be stored in a fireproof safe.

■ Human Risks

Human risks are caused by human mistakes, as well as the unpredictability of customers, employees, or the work environment. They range from the negative effects of thefts to the issues involved with injury on the job.

Customer dishonesty, such as theft, fraudulent payment, or nonpayment, is a human risk. Additional examples of customer dishonesty include the nonpayment of accounts or paying for goods and services with fraudulent checks or credit cards.

Employees represent another human risk for business. Employee error, negligence, incompetence, and theft also pose a human risk. Another employee risk can be seen when employees take advantage of employee discounts by extending his benefit to non-employees.

In a restaurant, failing to properly cook or handle food can lead to customers becoming ill or hospitalized. To lessen risks of this type, many companies have instituted food safety programs that stress the importance of proper food handling. Employees must be *competent.* They must possess the skills and direction to do their jobs well.

The business environment or work setting itself often becomes a risk. Customer or employee accidents are potential human risks. Airlines train crews to prepare for emergencies caused by mechanical problems, but to consider human factors as well. A customer might fall on the premises, break an arm, and sue the store. Businesses must be especially careful during inclement weather when rain or ice may cause injuries in the building or on the property. An employee might be injured in a work-related accident caused by faulty machinery or improperly built structures. Another risk is employee illness caused by toxic fumes or other hazards at the workplace. Asbestos in old buildings is an ongoing issue that companies must deal with.

Over the past decade, computer crime has emerged as a significant new human risk that businesses must protect against. Employees may pass along confidential information through an e-mail, either intentionally or unintentionally. Computer criminals penetrate the security of computer systems for mischievous or criminal purposes. This type of crime can be committed by a disgruntled employee or by an outsider. The simplest and least expensive way to protect your business from computer crime is to secure the computer network using passwords, encoding programs, and virus detectors. It is also necessary to train employees on the proper handling of computers and the proper use of software.

Life In The Diverse MARKETPLACE

If the Gift Fits

In some countries, gift giving in business can be a sensitive event. Even the most well-intentioned gifts can be offensive. Never give a clock as a present in Hong Kong, as it connotes death. In Ecuador, bring flowers when invited to someone's home—but avoid lilies and marigolds, which are used in funerals. The only article of clothing that is appropriate to give in Germany is a scarf—items such as perfume, soap, and other clothing are considered too personal.

Thinking Critically

What might you bring as a gift when invited for dinner to a client's home in Ecuador?

34.1 ASSESSMENT

Reviewing Key Terms and Concepts

1. What is a business risk?
2. What is risk management?
3. What are the three kinds of business risks?
4. Why does product obsolescence represent an economic risk?
5. Give three examples of human risks.

Thinking Critically

6. A business faces risks daily. Why are business owners willing to assume risks when it would be much easier to work for someone else?

Integrating Academic Skills

7. **COMMUNICATION** Write a 100-word paper on parents' responsibilities to instill honesty and respect for personal property in their children so they do not shoplift.

Handling Business Risks

Ways of Handling Business Risks

There are four basic ways that businesses can handle risks: risk prevention and control, risk transfer, risk retention, and risk avoidance (see Figure 34-2 on page 628). Let's take a closer look at each of these.

■ Risk Prevention and Control

Business risks can be handled through prevention and control. Risks can be prevented and controlled by screening and training employees, providing safe conditions and safety instruction, preventing external theft, and deterring employee theft.

SCREENING AND TRAINING EMPLOYEES The best way to prevent the human risk of employee carelessness and incompetence is through effective employee screening, orientation, and training. Many businesses have human resource development departments to screen, test, and train new and existing employees to minimize the risk caused by improperly trained personnel.

Most larger companies and some smaller ones now require prospective employees to undergo drug testing before being hired. Drug abuse can lead to increased human risk by making employees careless and more likely to forget safety rules.

When employees begin a new job, some form of orientation, training, and instruction is normally provided. The training may be brief verbal instruction or extensive training that lasts several weeks or months.

Effective orientation and training programs are essential in minimizing business risk. Properly trained personnel are better able to meet customer needs and wants and to prevent the risk of lost sales through human error.

Chapter 11 outlines the basic necessities of an effective orientation. In addition to these, workers should be trained in rules and regulations relating to safety. Many companies support continuing education for all of their employees through individual company training activities or support for college training and education related to the field.

PROVIDING SAFE CONDITIONS AND SAFETY INSTRUCTION According to the National Safety Council, each year U.S. businesses lose over $42 billion to work-related illness and injuries. The financial impact of workplace accidents is staggering. Based on these numbers, it seems clear that safety and health information needs to improved.

What You'll Learn

- The ways businesses handle risks

Why It's Important

Businesses use certain strategies to help prevent, avoid, and protect against accidents, injuries, fires, thefts, defective products, and environmental disasters.

Key Terms

- insurance policy
- extended coverage
- fidelity bonds
- performance bonds

FIGURE 34-2

HANDLING BUSINESS RISKS

There are four basic ways that businesses can handle risks: risk prevention and control, risk transfer, risk retention, and risk avoidance.

RISK PREVENTION AND CONTROL

Risk prevention and control are important ways to handle business risks. Effective employee screening and orientation can help a business.

RISK TRANSFER

Risk transfer attempts to place some or all of the risk on other parties. Product warranties transfer the risk to the manufacturer.

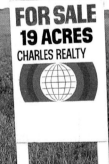

RISK RETENTION

Risk retention frequently occurs when a company is unaware of the risks, under-estimates the risk, or anticipates a profit by taking a risk. A risk is often held by a business in hopes of a future profit.

RISK AVOIDANCE

Risk avoidance attempts to minimize risk through good information and research. Marketing research on a new product is carried out to reduce risk exposure.

When employees receive safety instruction and are provided with safe work conditions, the potential for on-the-job accidents is greatly reduced. In marketing jobs, for example, common accidents include falls that occur while moving merchandise, or injuries due to improper lifting techniques.

To prevent such risks, businesses can design stock and selling areas for efficient foot traffic and merchandise storage. They can also provide training on proper ways to lift and store merchandise.

Many companies address workplace safety by developing accident management programs which include:

- Creating a safety committee to check for hazards
- Correcting hazards before accidents occur
- Developing procedures to comply with all state and federal health and safety regulations
- Investigating and recording all workplace accidents
- Providing employees with protective clothing and equipment
- Placing first aid kits near work stations
- Posting the address and phone number of the nearest hospital and clinic
- Offering employee classes in first aid and cardiopulmonary resuscitation (CPR)
- Keeping track of how many work days were missed due to accidents or injuries
- Scheduling regular safety meetings
- Preparing written safety plans and circulating them to all employees
- Offering incentives for improved safety records, such as prizes or bonuses for accident-free months

PREVENTING EXTERNAL THEFT One of the largest and most costly forms of human risk is internal and external theft from stores. It has been estimated that total theft from retail stores costs the American public between $20–30 billion every year.

Shoplifting is a form of external theft that involves stealing merchandise from a business. Shoplifting is one of the fastest-growing crimes against property in the country. According to the Federal Bureau of Investigation (FBI), about 15 percent of all thefts committed in the United States involve shoplifting.

While shoplifting losses vary by store type, it is estimated that one-third of the total inventory shrinkage is caused by shoplifting. According to an annual Price Waterhouse *Shrinkage Survey,* 1.5 to 1.9 percent of mass merchandisers retailers' net sales and 2.4 percent of apparel specialty retailers' net sales are lost to shoplifting. This means that if a specialty retailer's net sales are $100 million, approximately $2.4 million are lost to shoplifters!

There are many ways to deter shoplifting. Businesses can educate store employees about shoplifting prevention guidelines. Effective store layouts, with adequate lighting, orderly displays, and expensive items stored in locked display cases or tagged with electronic devices can cut down on shoplifting. In clothing stores, employees typically monitor how many items are brought in and returned. Many stores use security personnel and security devices such as two-way mirrors, closed circuit television, and wall and ceiling mirrors to cut down on the risk of theft.

Many states have passed strict legislation regarding shoplifting. Still, apprehending shoplifters is not without its own risks. Aside from any necessary physical contact, merchants can be sued for allegations of false arrest, false imprisonment, malicious prosecution, excessive use of force, or assault. To limit their liability, retailers must know acceptable shoplifter detention policies, and be sure that employees are trained in this.

Robbery is the stealing of money or merchandise by violence or threat. No matter where a business is located, it has a chance of being robbed. Many local police departments provide instruction on how to prevent and handle robberies. Sometimes businesses band together to form business watch programs that are similar to neighborhood watch programs.

Businesses can lower their risk from robberies by:
- Limiting the amount of money kept on hand and handling bank deposits discreetly
- Installing video cameras to help identify robbers
- Hiring extra employees so that no one is alone in a business at any time
- Hiring security guards
- Installing bulletproof glass in cashier cubicles
- Opening back doors only for freight or trash
- Installing switches near cash registers that allow employees to lock outside doors
- Increasing lighting inside and outside of the establishment
- Making sure doors are locked and alarms are set at night

■ **Helping to Deter Shoplifting** Businesses often use a variety of techniques to reduce the threat of shoplifting. *How do electronic article surveillance systems deter shoplifters?*

CONTROLLING EMPLOYEE THEFT Employee theft—stealing merchandise, funds, or other company property—is another problem businesses face. Most employee theft occurs at the point-of-sale (POS) terminal, or cash register. To protect themselves from employee theft, many businesses have installed closed-circuit television systems and POS terminals that generate computerized reports.

POS computerized reports monitor void transfers, cash discrepancies, sales reports, refunds by employees, employees' discounts, and cash register transactions. By carefully analyzing these data, businesses improve the chances of apprehending dishonest employees.

Closed-circuit television systems used in conjunction with POS terminals lower the risk of employee theft. Closed-circuit systems include cameras concealed in mannequins, ceilings, or walls. Usually operated by security personnel in a control room, they are backed up with a video recorder.

It is important to set internal business standards regarding dishonest behavior and incorporate polices to prosecute dishonest employees. Open discussion about employee honesty and company policies keeps all employees aware of expectations. Another prevention techniques is preemployment testing to detect attitudes about honesty. Some states, however, have banned the use of lie detectors for preemployment screening.

■ Risk Transfer

Some business risks can be handled by transferring the risk to another business or to another party. Three common risk transfers are insurance, product and service warranties, and the transference of risks through business ownership.

PURCHASING INSURANCE Businesses can insure property and people against potential loss by purchasing insurance policies. An insurance policy is a contract between a business and an insurance company to cover a certain business risk. A business can buy an insurance package that includes several types of insurance policies.

Insurance companies estimate the probability of loss due to such natural risks, such as fire, lightning, and wind damage, and human risks, such as theft and vandalism. The insurance company then looks at the business's location, past experience, and type of business, and determines an insurance rate depending on the degree of risk.

A business located in a neighborhood with a high risk of robbery will be charged higher rates for adequate coverage against theft. This business has a higher likelihood of being robbed and therefore of making a claim against the insurance company for coverage of its losses.

One of the most common forms of business insurance is property insurance. *Property insurance* covers the loss of, or damage to, buildings, equipment, machinery, merchandise, furniture, and fixtures. Coverage can be purchased for the full replacement value of the building, merchandise, and other items, or for a portion of the replacement value in the case of fire.

In addition, property insurance often covers off-premise accidents, outdoor property, loss of valuable papers and records, fire department service charges, and the personal property losses of others. Some policies provide added coverage for theft of personal property. Property insurance typically includes the following features:

■ **Transferring Risks Through Insurance** Businesses often purchase insurance to transfer some of the risks of doing business. *What does an insurance policy represent?*

REAL WORLD MARKETING

Abracadabra. The E-mail Is Gone!

Presto Chango! Imagine, E-mail that vanishes before your very eyes! E-mail can be risky to a business with trade secrets. An employee forwards sensitive information by e-mail, and it circles the world almost instantaneously. San Francisco's Disappearing, Inc. thinks it has found a solution. Its e-mail service automatically destroys messages after a set time, be it one or 90 days. Each time a message is read, it must first access an encrypted key—a bit of software—on a server provided by Disappearing. When a message expires, the key and the message are both destroyed. Poof!

Thinking Critically
Who might benefit from disappearing e-mail?

- *Replacement Cost Coverage* This covers the replacement cost of buildings and other personal property. A *coinsurance policy* has the insured business and the insurance company both sharing the risk if there is a loss. A business may be insured for 80 percent of the replacement value. This means that in case of a loss, the insurance company pays 80 percent of the covered items and the business pays 20 percent.
- *Automatic Increase Protection* This policy feature automatically adjusts the coverage to compensate for inflation on both the building and the personal property.
- *Loss of Income* This feature compensates a business for loss of income during the time that repairs are being done to a building or property after a natural disaster. Loss of income coverage also covers certain expenses that continue during the repair period, such as interest on loans, taxes, rent, advertising, telephone, and salaries.

Property insurance policies can be purchased with extended coverage, which represents optional coverage on a basic property coverage policy. Extended coverage can be purchased to cover items that may not be covered on the basic property insurance policy, such as employee dishonesty, exterior glass, outdoor signs, rented cars, and valuable paper and records.

Business liability insurance protects a business against damages for which it may be held legally liable, such as an injury to other persons or damage to others' property. Business liability insurance is usually provided with limits up to $1 million. This type of insurance includes features such as premises and operations coverage, medical expense, personal injury coverage, employee and advertising liability.

Personal liability insurance covers damage claims made by customers and employees. The damages must have occurred near or in the business establishment.

Product liability insurance protects against business loss resulting from personal injury from

Case Study

Fighting the Cyberpirates

While major companies seek to expand and increase their commitments to e-commerce and the Internet, they are faced with new business risks. Companies now have to fight cyberpirates. Cyberpirates make their Web site's domain name similar to an established company's Web domain name. The similarity can cause customers to be directed to the cyberpirate's Web site.

DaimlerChrysler AG recently won a trademark infringement case against a Web site that used a domain site similar to their foradodge.com. Ford Motor Company has also been aggressively fighting the cyberpirates. In February 2000, Ford won an injunction against a Cleveland man who tried to sell 52 domain names, including ford-quality.com on eBay's auction Web site.

The pirating of established brand names has become such a big problem that the federal government passed the *Anticybersquatting Consumer Protection Act* in November 1999. Pirates may be other companies or individuals who want to make a fast buck by trading on the brand name of an established company.

Other risks force companies to protect themselves from rumors, product disparagement, and false accusations against top executives. Stock swindlers have used the Internet to spread rumors about a company that affect the price of its stock. The Internet has proven to be a tremendous marketing tool for companies, but it also creates new and different types of business risks.

Case Study Review
1. Why are companies concerned about Web site cyberpirates?
2. What can companies do about rumors and false accusations that occur on the Internet?

A MATTER OF ETHICS
3. Is it ethical for companies and individuals to develop Web sites that sound similar to established companies and brands? Why or why not?

---

products manufactured or sold by a business. Many businesses purchase product liability insurance to guarantee against losses even after products have been tested extensively by private companies and government agencies.

Fidelity bonds protect a business from employee dishonesty. Businesses usually require employees who handle money, such as bank tellers and cashiers, to be bonded. If a bonded employee steals money, the bonding company pays the loss. Individuals who are bonded undergo personal character reviews and background checks before they are bonded.

Performance bonds (also called surety bonds) insure against losses that might occur when work or a contract is not finished on time or as agreed. A building contractor might be required to purchase a performance bond to guarantee completion of the job on time and according to specifications. The company that issues the performance bond is responsible for damages if the contract is not completed.

Life insurance is often purchased to protect the owners or managers of a business. A sole proprietor (sole business owner) is usually required to have life insurance in order to borrow money. The policy will guarantee that there will be money to pay off the sole proprietor's debts and obligations if he or she dies. Life insurance on a deceased partner can provide the money needed for other partners to continue the business if the partners are named as *beneficiaries* —those who will receive the money from the policy.

Credit insurance protects a business from losses on credit extended to customers. *Credit life insurance* pays the balance of any loans granted by banks, credit unions, and other financial agencies in the event the borrower dies.

Workers' compensation insurance is a type of insurance paid by employers to cover employees that suffer job-related injuries and illness and to protect employers from being sued by an employee who is injured on the job. Most states require all public employers, and those private employers who regularly employ a predetermined minimum number of employees for prescribed time periods, to have workers' compensation insurance coverage.

PRODUCT AND SERVICE WARRANTIES *Warranties* are promises made by the seller or manufacturer with respect to the performance and quality of a product and protection against loss. Product and service warranties were discussed in depth in Chapter 32.

TRANSFERRING RISKS THROUGH BUSINESS OWNERSHIP As you learned in Chapter 33, the amount of risk a business must handle depends in part on the type of business ownership. In a sole proprietorship, the individual owner assumes all risks. Partnerships enable the partners to share in the business risks. Corporations allow the stockholders, as owners, to share the business risks. The corporate form of ownership offers the most protection from losses.

■ **Protecting the Business** Businesses can purchase insurance to protect themselves against many forms of risk. *What type of insurance would help protect a bank from employee theft?*

■ Risk Retention

In some cases, it is impossible for businesses to prevent or transfer risks so they *retain* or assume responsibility for them. This is called *risk retention*. A business has to assume the loss—or retain the risk—if customer trends change and merchandise remains unsold. Most retail shops assure they will assume the loss of a certain percentage of goods to damage or theft.

Businesses and businesspeople may retain certain business risks because they are unaware of the risk. It is also possible to underestimate the risk, such as when merchandise is purchased in anticipation of high sales, but weather, trends, and customers' habits change. A business could anticipate a profit by taking a risk, such as purchasing land for development and future sale for a subdivision.

■ Risk Avoidance

Certain risks can be avoided by anticipating them in advance. Market research can lead businesses to conclude that investment in a product is not worth the risk. All business decisions should be made with the consideration of both potential benefits and potential risks. Risk avoidance should be a key consideration in any marketing decision.

As you can see, businesses have several ways of handling risks. Owning and operating a business, however, always involves a degree of risk. The way a business manages its risks determines its success or failure.

Electronic Frontiers

When Computers Get Sick!

"An apple a day keeps the doctor away," or so the adage goes. It means, "Prevention is the best medicine." Companies are always seeking ways to immunize themselves against computer viruses. Disabling executable files that can carry viruses into corporate e-mail networks is a major focus. Hackers have used e-mail messages with subject lines such as "I Love You" or "Jokes," which seemed to be harmless. However, many people opened the messages to realize they were part of a virus that shut down some of the largest e-mail systems around the world. A virus attacks by installing itself in a computer system and can spread by mailing itself to all of the addresses registered in a computer's electronic address book. This can reduce system performance and clog mail servers. The best way to avoid viruses is to check with the sender and not open any unknown file attachments.

Thinking Critically

What kind of corporate e-mail policy might a shipping company develop to help reduce the risk of spreading computer viruses?

34.2 ASSESSMENT

Reviewing Key Terms and Concepts

1. Identify the four ways businesses handle risk.
2. Name four ways that companies prevent and control risks.
3. How can businesses reduce the human risk of on-the-job injuries?
4. What are the three principal ways to transfer risk?
5. What is the difference between risk retention and risk avoidance?

Thinking Critically

6. What important factors should a business consider when selecting an insurance company?

Integrating Academic Skills

7. **MATH** Calculate the amount of net sales lost to shoplifting in a discount store with sales of $400 million and a shoplifting rate of 1.5 percent.

Careers in Marketing

SERVICE MARKETING

Heather Lowry
Insurance Agent
GEICO

What does your job entail?

"I spend most of the day on the phone. My job is to keep customers happy and to make sure that they have the coverage they need and want. I also prepare reports, maintain records, and assist clients in making insurance claims. Insurance agents need to be able to analyze data and make recommendations. I must be familiar with insurance policies and be able to communicate the details of these policies clearly. It's important that I do my job well and always treat the customer with respect."

What kind of training did you have?

"The GEICO training process took approximately six months. The first six weeks are spent learning all of the commands on the computer. After that, I learned about the phone system and I studied for a state government mandated certification course. My calls were monitored to ensure that I was providing the right information to customers. GEICO offers training seminars and continuing education."

What skills are most important?

"Communication is the most important skill; I must be able to articulate the details of policies to my customers, and I have to listen carefully to their concerns. It is important to be equally comfortable working alone and as part of a team."

What is your key to success?

"Persistence—you have to keep learning every day. Problem solving is also very important; you need to know how to adapt to any given situation."

Thinking Critically
Why is it important to know the insurance laws and policies for different states?

Career Facts

Education and Training: Most insurance companies require a college degree. High school and college courses in accounting, economics, marketing, business law, investments, psychology, and communication are recommended.

Abilities, Aptitudes, and Skills: The ability to analyze data, make recommendations, understand different policies, and communicate clearly are helpful. Successful agents are self-motivated, self-disciplined, and self-confident.

Career Outlook: Because of the increasing popularity of online insurance agencies, the number of positions is expected to grow more slowly than average.

Career Path: Some apprenticeship opportunities exist that prepare employees for state insurance agent exams. Insurance agents may advance to sales managers of local offices, to district or regional executive positions, or to establish their own businesses.

Personal Insurance Policy

Chapter 34 ASSESSMENT

VOCABULARY REVIEW

Use the following vocabulary terms to write a song on how businesses can manage risks.

- risk
- risk management
- business risks
- economic risks
- natural risks
- human risks
- insurance policy
- extended coverage
- fidelity bonds
- performance bonds

FACT AND IDEA REVIEW

1. Why is risk management an important marketing function? (34.1)

2. Why do companies fear product recalls? (34.1)

3. How can businesses reduce the human risk of carelessness and incompetence? (34.2)

4. Why can drug abuse lead to increased human risk? (34.2)

5. What is an insurance policy? (34.2)

6. Compare property coverage and business liability coverage. (34.2)

7. Identify some features and types of coverage found in property coverage policies. (34.2)

8. Explain the difference between personal and product liability insurance. (34.2)

9. What is workers' compensation insurance? What are its two basic purposes? (34.2)

10. How can the type of business ownership affect the risks of the business owners? (34.2)

THINKING CRITICALLY

1. Some people think that shoplifting only affects retailers. Explain the consequences of shoplifting to individuals and society.

2. Identify some factors that may affect the insurance rates a retailer pays for fire protection.

3. How does a business decide what kinds of insurance it needs? Do you think it's possible for a business to carry too much insurance? Explain your answer.

4. Insurance rates are partially based on past experience. Do you think it is appropriate to deny auto insurance to companies that have employees with poor driving records or robbery insurance to businesses that are located in high crime areas? Analyze the two situations and defend your answer.

5. How can warranties and guarantees transfer business risks to other parties?

BUILDING WORKPLACE SKILLS

1. **Human Relations** You are planning to start a small arts and crafts shop with a friend. You believe that the business should be free from risk through the purchase of insurance coverage on the building, vehicles, merchandise, staff, etc. Identify the types of insurance you will need.

2. **Social Science** Jury judgments on personal and product liability cases have led to huge cash settlements for injured parties. How do these claims affect businesses? How do they affect you? Should there be limits on the cash amounts given for injury or death? How would you determine the settlement amounts?

APPLYING MARKETING CONCEPTS

1. **Understanding Workplace Safety** Locate the address of the National Safety Council (NSC) at the library or the Internet. Write a letter requesting business safety information for your class. Prepare an oral report using presentation software based on the materials.

2. **Researching Shoplifting** Locate the Web site of your local chamber of commerce, Retail Merchants Association, police department, or state retail trade association. E-mail a request for information about your state's legislation on shoplifting. Report your findings orally.

3. **Comparing Life Insurance** Research life insurance on the Internet or at the library. Use a word processing program to write a two-page report. Explain the various forms of life insurance and how rates are established. Present your oral report to your class.

4. **Evaluating Insurance Policies** Locate the Web site of a local insurance agency. E-mail a request to obtain sales brochures on business operations protection policies. Bring any brochures you receive to class, and display them on posterboard for your classmates.

5. **Understanding Product Recall Reasoning** Locate the Web site of the Federal Consumer Information Center. Search for product recall information and identify three recent recalls. Create a spreadsheet using computer software outlining the reasons for recall.

LINKING SCHOOL TO WORK

Writing Systems Skills Write a report on an employer's company policies when observing a shoplifting incident. Explain the procedures and actions taken at your place of business when dealing with a shoplifter.

THE DECA CONNECTION

Role Play: Assistant Manager

Situation You are to assume the role of assistant manager for a large department store. Your store manager (judge) has assigned you a special assignment to develop a risk management plan for your store.

Activity You are to describe the risks your business faces and develop a checklist of ways to handle these risks.

Evaluation You will be evaluated on how well you meet the following performance indicators:
- Explain the types of business risk
- Explain the nature of risk management
- Explain routine security precautions
- Describe the concept of insurance
- Follow safety precautions

interNET CONNECTION

Business and the Environment
There are often environmental risks involved with conducting a business. The U.S. Environmental Protection Agency plays a significant role in preventing and correcting environmental damages caused by businesses.

Connect
- Perform a search of the EPA Web site for information about a recent case involving a business.
- Identify the actions taken by the EPA and the impact on public interest.

Developing a Business Plan

Marketing: What It Takes

Realizing Your Dream

You have worked part-time at a small market during your high school years and have really enjoyed the job. You have an idea for a unique type of fish market you could successfully operate. This market would be different from the other franchise operations. You will need financing to lease a building and the necessary equipment.

WHAT WILL YOU DO?

How will you determine what kind of capital you will need? How will you learn where to find the right kind of financing?

The Business Plan

Developing the Business Plan

Once you have determined that you want to establish your own business, you need to develop a business plan. A business plan is a proposal that describes a new business to potential investors and lenders. Although business plan formats vary somewhat, the outline in Figure 35-1 on page 640 is an excellent model.

It is expensive to open a business, and you will probably need financial assistance. A business plan maps out the course of your business and helps you to obtain financing, guide the opening of a business, and plan the successful management of the business.

Your business plan should convince investors and lenders that your business idea is profitable; identify procedures necessary to legally establish the business; and, work as a management tool to identify the month-to-month steps necessary to operate a profitable business.

A business plan must be well organized and easy to read. It should contain three main sections:
- Description and analysis of the proposed business situation
- Organizational and marketing plan
- Financial plan

Description and Analysis of the Proposed Business

The description and analysis section introduces the proposed business concept. This section should clearly identify the products and services the business will sell. It includes your personal business philosophy, as well as a self-analysis that describes your business experience, education, and training. This section of your business plan also includes a trading area analysis, a market segment analysis, and an analysis of potential locations.

■ Type of Business, Business Philosophy, and Type of Products

Begin your business plan with a description of the type of business you plan to open. In this section you will present marketing research data or significant trends that will influence the success of your business. Explain how a current or changing situation has created an unfulfilled consumer want that your business will address.

Next, give your business philosophy, which tells how you think the business should be run and shows your understanding of your business's role in the marketplace. It reveals your attitude toward your customers, employees, and competitors.

● What You'll Learn

- The purpose and importance of a business plan
- The major sections of a business plan
- How to describe and analyze a proposed business situation

● Why It's Important

It takes financing to start a new business. To obtain financing you must have a well-developed business plan. A business plan is an invaluable tool that helps an entrepreneur plan business goals, determine necessary resources, and clearly identify how the new business will operate and be managed.

Key Terms

- business plan
- business philosophy
- trading area
- buying behavior

FIGURE 35-1

OUTLINE FOR A BUSINESS PLAN

A business plan details every part of a proposed business to potential investors and lenders.

1

Section 1 describes the general concept of the proposed business, outlines the entrepreneur's special skills, and analyzes the potential market.

2

Section II discusses how the business will be organized, describes the product or service to be offered, and details the marketing plan.

3

Section III identifies the sources of capital and projects income and expenses.

I. **Description and analysis of the proposed business situation**
   A. Type of business
   B. Business philosophy
   C. Description of good or service
   D. Self-analysis
      1. Education and training
      2. Strengths and weaknesses
      3. Plan for personal development
   E. Trading area analysis
      1. Geographic, demographic, and economic data
      2. Competition
   F. Market segment analysis
      1. Target market
      2. Customer buying behavior
   G. Analysis of potential location

II. **Organization and marketing plan**
   A. Proposed organization
      1. Type of ownership
      2. Steps in establishing business
      3. Personnel needs
   B. Proposed good/service
      1. Manufacturing plans and inventory policies
      2. Suppliers
   C. Proposed marketing plan
      1. Pricing policies
      2. Promotional activities

III. **Financial plan**
   A. Sources of capital
      1. Personal sources
      2. External sources
   B. Projected income and expenses
      1. Personal financial statement
      2. Projected start-up costs
      3. Projected personal needs
      4. Projected business income
      5. Projected business expenses
      6. Projected income statement(s)
      7. Projected balance sheet
      8. Projected cash flow

■ **Having the Required Skills** **Some types of businesses require special training and education.** *Why does the government require special licensing for certain occupations?*

Your business philosophy will help you attract new customers and maintain existing customers once you start a business. Wal-Mart's business philosophy states that the company will match the advertised sale prices of any competitor. The principal pricing policy is that Wal-Mart will not be undersold and the return policy is that customers can always return merchandise if they are dissatisfied with it. This business philosophy has earned Wal-Mart a loyal following of customers.

After identifying your business philosophy, describe the product or service you will offer. Explain the potential consumer benefits and why your product or service will be successful. Include as many facts as you can—speculation and statements of belief do not convince investors and lenders to lend you money. For regional and national business information, consult recent issues of *Business Week, Entrepreneur, Fortune, Inc., Money, The Wall Street Journal,* and other business publications.

■ Self-Analysis

The next part of your business plan includes a self-analysis. A *self-analysis* is a description of your personal education, training, strengths, weaknesses, and a plan for personal development in the field of marketing.

Imagine that you are interested in apparel and accessories marketing and want to start a related business. You must be able to accurately predict current fashion trends. You also must be able to buy, display, price, and advertise your merchandise correctly. In this part of the business plan, highlight your strengths and skills in this area. Describe how you will acquire the skills you need through training or hiring a professional.

Indicate the education and training you have had so far to prepare you for operating your new business. In addition to mentioning your marketing education program, you should discuss other courses that you have taken and related job experience that will benefit you in your endeavor. Your education and work experience shows potential lenders that you can understand and interpret your business's financial statements.

Discuss any future educational plans, such as attending a community college, technical institute, or university. Plans for continuing education show that you intend to improve on your existing skills for operating your business.

Some businesses require applying for a special license. In this section, you should explain if you already have this license or are in the application process. Some businesses that require licensing are adult and childcare facilities; automotive, electrical, and mechanical repair businesses; construction companies; and, styling salons and barbershops.

Finally, include the special personal traits and work habits you possess that will help you to operate the proposed business. Examples of past leadership activities, personal initiatives, and willingness to work hard, all add strength to your business plan.

■ Trading Area Analysis

Following an explanation of your personal strengths and skills, you should begin to define your trading area. A trading area is the geographical area from which a business draws its customers. Before going into business, you must analyze the trading area with respect to geographic, demographic, and economic data, as well as competition.

REAL WORLD MARKETING

Legal Grounds

Would you like an "Equal Rights Espresso"? Sounds silly, but that is what you might hear David Musslewhite say when you enter his Legal Grounds Café. Knowing that meeting with an attorney can be stressful, Musslewhite opened the Legal Grounds Café, where customers can sip on capuccino while seeking legal counsel. They can order lunch and have their will or trusts prepared. After years of drinking bad coffee and conducting legal practice at a large Texas law firm, Musslewhite finds the overstuffed chairs at the café a perfect setting for consultations. You can find him on the café floor providing advice, cappuccino, and a smile.

Thinking Critically
What types of businesses could profit from an environment similar to that of Legal Grounds?

Information about the population in your trading area is available from your local chamber of commerce or state department of commerce. You can also consult the most recent local census data in your local library or on the Internet.

GEOGRAPHIC, DEMOGRAPHIC, AND ECONOMIC DATA *Geographic* data includes population distribution, or how many people live in a certain area. *Demographics* are identifiable and measurable population statistics such as age, gender, marital status, and race/ethnicity. Knowing the demographics of your trading area will help you identify market trends that may have a direct impact on your business. Your plans to open a travel agency might be adjusted if you learned that your trading area has an older population with high incomes.

Prevailing economic conditions are among the major factors affecting a business. *Economic factors* include economic growth projections, trends in employment, interest rates, business mergers, and governmental regulations. Tax increases or decreases levied by the local, state, or federal government will affect consumer buying power.

It is important to include how much *disposable income* the potential consumers in your trading area are likely to have. This is the personal income remaining from wages after all taxes are taken out. Disposable income is also referred to as *buying income.*

A special measurement called a *buying power index* has been developed to help new business owners determine the buying power for a given area. The index factors disposable income, population size, and retail sales figures to determine an overall indicator of an area's sales potential. These factors are then expressed as a percentage of total sales. You can find more information on buying power indexes in the *Survey of Buying Power,* which is published annually by *Sales and Marketing Management* magazine.

National and international economic conditions can have an effect locally, too. International trade agreements, like NAFTA, may affect your business by increasing or decreasing the demand for your product or service.

Will your business be affected by seasonal fluctuations? Could technological advancements that may occur now or in the future affect the demand or need for your product or service? You should know how to find the information you need to help you answer these questions.

A good source of information on local economic conditions is your local bank. Bank officials often have business projections for major geographical areas and for most types of businesses located in their immediate area. In addition, the U.S. Small Business Administration (SBA) has funded over 900 small business development centers (SBDCs) to provide management and technical assistance to small businesses and new entrepreneurs. Other good sources of information are related business publications available at schools, public libraries, colleges, universities, or on the Internet.

COMPETITION As a new business owner, you must analyze your competition. List all the competitors in your trading area, along with their types of products, prices, locations, general quality of products, and their strengths and weaknesses. Try to estimate your competitors' sales volume and identify how they promote and sell their products. You should be able to use these factors to demonstrate how your business will be superior to the competition.

■ **Knowing Your Customer**
New businesses need to identify a target market for their products and services. *Why must businesses carefully identify a target market?*

Some good sources of information about your competitors can be found through annual reports, the local chamber of commerce, trade associations, the Yellow Pages, the Internet, business publications, and reports such as those published by as *Dun & Bradstreet*.

■ Market Segment Analysis

The next part of your business plan should contain a market segment analysis. A market segment analysis is a description of your target market and the buying behavior of your potential customers.

TARGET MARKET As you know, your target market represents the specific group of people you want to reach. You can identify your target market by common geographic characteristics such as region, county size, size of city, density of population, and climate of the area. You can also categorize it by demographic characteristics such as age, gender, marital status, family size, income, occupation, education, religion, and culture or ethnic background.

You must carefully identify your target market because the needs and wants of different markets must be addressed differently in the marketing of goods and services. Families can live in the same city and have similar education levels, occupations, and incomes, but have varying needs for entertainment, furniture, food, clothing, or personal services depending on their religious or ethnic background.

Your task as an entrepreneur is to decide which market to target and how to do it. The best way to make this decision is to be guided by the way the members of the target market perceive themselves and their own needs.

CUSTOMERS' BUYING BEHAVIOR After you have identified your target market, you will need to explain how the chosen market's *buying behavior* will be good for your business. Buying behavior is the process individuals use to decide what they will buy, from where they will buy it, and who they will buy it from. Imagine that you are planning to open a children's toy store. You have used demographic information to determine how many families with children are in your target market. You also know the approximate average family income. From your earlier analysis of the competition (other toy stores serving the same target market), you have an idea of how much disposable income these families have spent on children's toys and which toys they bought. You also know which stores in which locations did the most business. This is your target market's buying behavior.

Electronic Frontiers

A Road Map to Success

Imagine that you wanted to drive from Gotham, New Jersey, to Metropolis, Illinois. Would you just start driving? Or, would you carefully map out your route? Now, imagine that you wanted to start a business. Would you just start your company or would you carefully map out your route? Business plans are the roadmap to success for businesses! A business plan is a good way to take a look at a business from a critical viewpoint. A company can use a business plan to target strengths and weaknesses, as well as address finances and marketing plans. Writing a business plan is usually a tremendous amount of work; however, individuals can get a head start on writing a business plan by using online resources, such as downloadable templates or programs. One such program, BizPlanBuilder, includes templates for every aspect of a successful business plan.

Thinking Critically

How might a template of a business plan assist in gaining financing?

You can then put this information together to make decisions about how your store might best serve these same customers. Do you want to try to take business away from other toy stores, or do you want to try to sell items not offered in the other stores? Do you want to entice your customers to buy a lot of low-priced items or a few high-priced ones?

■ Analysis of Potential Locations

You can select your location after you have analyzed your trading area and your market segment, including your target market and your competition. Location has a direct effect on your sales, making this a vital decision.

BUY, LEASE, OR BUILD Your analysis should include whether you want to buy, lease, or build your facility. The advantages of leasing outweigh the other options for most new businesses. When leasing, a large initial outlay of cash is avoided, risk is reduced because of a shorter commitment, and lease expenses are tax deductible. The process of buying or building is more complex and almost always requires applying for financing.

Regardless of whether you buy, lease, or build, you need to compare certain terms of each potential property. Those terms include monthly rent or payments and length of commitment. You will also need to find out who is responsible for insurance.

You should have an attorney review any lease or contract before you sign it. This will help you fully understand your obligations and negotiate the best possible terms before completing the deal.

■ **Location, Location, Location!**
A location is very important to a business. *What are the advantages and disadvantages of locating along a heavily used thoroughfare?*

COMPETING AND COMPLEMENTARY BUSINESSES A major consideration in a business location should be the nearness to your competition. Consider the number and size of potential competitors in the area—if your business is similar in size and merchandise to its competitors, you may want to locate near them. This can encourage comparison shopping. That's why it's not uncommon to see an entire block of furniture stores or auto dealers. On the contrary, a larger business that offers more variety than the competition should be able to generate its own customers and therefore can be located away from the competition.

A complementary business is one that would help generate store traffic. A shoe or accessories store located next to a clothing store is one example of a complementary business.

HOURS OF OPERATION Whether you locate your business in a mall, neighborhood shopping center, freestanding location, or your own home depends upon the nature of your business. Your location will determine your hours of operation and the number of customers who will see and patronize your business.

A business located in a shopping mall will probably have regular hours that are set by the mall management. In such a situation, you can also usually depend on fairly constant customer traffic generated by the other businesses in the same location.

If you run your own small business, you can set your own hours based on when you have the most customers or clients. For example, if you own a nail salon and know that other nail salons in the area are closed on Sunday, you may consider having hours that day. If you run a coffee shop located in an office park or business complex, you may open very early and close in the early evening. Establishing your hours in this manner may give you an edge over your competition.

VISIBILITY Businesses that rely on high visibility, such as restaurants, may spend the extra money to locate in a highly visible location. A highly visible site may not be a priority for all businesses, but the money you save on the building can be used for advertising or promoting your business.

SAFETY Neighborhood safety should be a consideration when choosing a business location. Research the community's crime rate. You don't want to open your operation in an area where customers feel uncomfortable or are unlikely to visit in the evening or during off-peak hours.

Closeness to fire hydrants and the fire department is also important. Find out what type of fire department the community has, volunteer or municipal.

BRIGHT IDEAS
LEGO Maniac

The LEGO Empire was created brick by brick, literally! In 1932, Ole Kirk Christiansen established a carpentry firm in Denmark, which manufactured stepladders, ironing boards, and wooden toys. Formed from the Danish words "LegGOdt" ("play well"), the company adopted the name LEGO. The stepladders and ironing boards sold slowly, but the toy sales took off—mainly because of the beautiful varnish and attention to detail. In 1947, LEGO became the first company in Denmark to buy a plastic injection molding machine for making toys. Over the next decade, the LEGO company phased out production of their wooden toys and started to manufacture plastic building blocks, called LEGO Bricks. To make the product more interesting, Christiansen designed play sets modeled from everyday life, including cars, houses, and buildings. To keep models sturdy, LEGO patented the stud-and-tube coupling system, which allowed children's imagination to run wild, as the possible brick combinations are astronomical!

Thinking Creatively

How would you improve on LEGO?

CUSTOMER ACCESSIBILITY Identify the highways, streets, and transportation routes that lead to your business site. Customer accessibility should be a priority—if there is no convenient route to your business, customers can't reach you. Other important considerations include whether traffic congestion will be a problem and whether there is sufficient parking space. Also keep in mind that special considerations must be made to accommodate customers with special needs, including wheelchair accessible entrances and convenient parking spots.

PERSONAL ISSUES There are some personal issues regarding the location of your business. Do you want to be near family and friends? Do you want to locate in a neighborhood or city different from where you currently live? Intangible issues such as atmosphere, character, and personal preference will enter into a final decision.

ZONING AND OTHER REGULATIONS Now that you have answered these questions, you are ready to find a specific site. Your first step should be to learn about any local ordinances or laws that may affect your business. Research any restrictions that exist which might prevent you from locating in a particular commercial or residential area.

Plans to build or renovate will require the necessary building permits. Operating a regulated business, such as a childcare center or a service

Life In The Diverse
MARKETPLACE

Sealed with a Kiss

One of the most common non-verbal signals one can make is the "kiss." While kissing is reserved as a greeting for close friends or family in North America, it is not so in all countries. Don't be surprised if you see acquaintances greeting each other with a kiss. Latins, Europeans, and Russians, both men and women, are no strangers to this form of "hello." It is even more common for the kiss to land on the air next to the face rather than square on—but this "air kiss" symbolizes a proper greeting for some. A word of advice—don't try this with a stranger, as it may be returned with a slap across the face!

Thinking Critically

What are the more common forms of greeting in the United States?

station, will call for the necessary local zoning approvals and state licenses. You may want to meet with your local or county officials to learn about local regulations.

35.1 ASSESSMENT

Reviewing Key Terms and Concepts

1. What is a business plan and why is it important?
2. What are three sections of a business plan?
3. What is a business philosophy? Why is it important?
4. Define buying behavior. Why is it important to understand customer buying behavior in your target market?
5. Identify at least three factors to consider when planning a location for a business.

Thinking Critically

6. What are some of the factors that a new business can control? What are some uncontrollable factors?

Integrating Academic Skills

7. **COMMUNICATION** Under the direction of your instructor, use a word processing program to develop a business letter inviting a local businessperson to speak to your marketing class on the importance of store location to the success of a business.

The Marketing Plan

Organizing the Plan

The second section of the business plan tells how you plan to organize the new business. It contains a description of your current and anticipated staffing needs. It also details how you plan to sell your product and how you intend to reach and satisfy customers with your product. The details of your proposed product are explained along with your potential suppliers, manufacturing or selling methods, and inventory policies.

Finally, it includes your marketing plan. Your marketing plan details your pricing strategies and promotional plans.

■ Proposed Organization

The organization part of your business plan is essentially a blueprint. It lays the foundation for the structure of your proposed business. It must be clearly laid out and solid, as the rest of your business will be built around it.

TYPES OF OWNERSHIP As you learned in Chapter 33, there are three main types of business ownership which include sole proprietorships, partnerships, and corporations. In this part of the business plan, you will need to identify the form of business ownership appropriate for your business and the rationale behind your choice. The rest of your plan will be affected by how you choose to establish ownership.

STEPS IN ESTABLISHING YOUR BUSINESS Once you have detailed what type of business ownership you have chosen, you need to show the steps you will take to establish your business. As you know from Chapter 33, the specific steps you will take will depend on how you organize your business.

PERSONNEL NEEDS Your personnel needs must be detailed in your business plan. Potential investors and lenders need to know that you can identify the jobs essential for your business to run properly. They also will want you to identify, as much as you can, the people who will do those jobs. If you are opening a small coffee shop, you need to consider what staffing needs you have to address. You will need various service staff, depending on your business's size, as well as people to manage the business and marketing for your shop. This information can all be worked out in the business plan.

Figure 35-2 on page 648 shows the typical functions in a business. Notice that some of the functions are repeated under more than one category. By identifying all the necessary functions, you will be able to begin planning an organizational structure for your business.

• What You'll Learn

- How to develop a business's organization plan
- How to provide details related to goods or services to be offered
- How to develop a marketing plan

• Why It's Important

The organization and marketing section of the business plan outlines how you plan to organize the business. It also explains how you will use advertising and promotional activities to help your business grow and prosper in the competitive marketplace.

Key Terms

- job descriptions
- organization chart

FIGURE 35-2

Business Functions

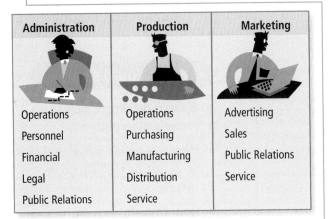

Administration	Production	Marketing
Operations	Operations	Advertising
Personnel	Purchasing	Sales
Financial	Manufacturing	Public Relations
Legal	Distribution	Service
Public Relations	Service	

■ **Business Functions** This table shows the typical functions performed in most businesses in three general categories: administration (running the business), production (making the product), and marketing (selling the product). *What are two positions you would find in any one of the above functions?*

Many new businesses begin as one-person operations in which that person does most or all of the business functions. It is not unusual for an entrepreneur to handle everything from the management duties to the financial oversight functions to the advertising and promotional activities. As a business grows, these responsibilities need to be divided among additional partners or employees. Entrepreneurs must identify how everyone fits into the organizational structure.

You need to prepare job descriptions for your partners, employees, and yourself. **Job descriptions** are written statements listing the requirements of a particular job. Each job description includes the purpose of the job, qualifications needed, duties to be performed, equipment to be used, and expected working conditions.

Job descriptions set a standard against which all applicants for a job or employees in the same position can be rated. A sample of a solid job description is illustrated in Figure 35-3. Notice how it contains a long list of job functions, from the most basic to more specific. This leaves little room for confusion about what is expected on the job.

After job descriptions have been prepared, you are ready to develop an organization chart. An organization chart is a diagram of the various jobs and functions that are found in a company. It should be

FIGURE 35-3

Job Description

Position Purpose

Performs general warehouse duties including shipping/receiving, picking and packing orders, processing orders in the system, stocking and reshelving merchandise, and other warehouse related job tasks as assigned.

Essential Functions

- Conducts inventory audits on a regular basis to detect discrepancies.
- Marks materials with identifying information.
- Opens bales, crates, and other containers.
- Record amounts of materials or items received or distributed.
- Weighs or counts items for distribution within plant to ensure conformance to company standards.
- Responds in a professional, polite, and helpful manner when dealing with customers.
- Helps load and unload shipments into and out of transporting vehicles.
- Refers non-routine problems to supervisor.
- Learns, understands, and complies with all company and customer policies.
- Move material through facility with the use of material handling equipment (i.e., pallet, handcart) as required.
- Use the computer to dispense and receive information such as product codes, part numbers, quantities, locations, comments, etc.
- Must be able to lift up to 50 pounds, stoop, kneel, crouch, reach, stand, walk, push, pull, and grasp materials.
- Additional duties as assigned to meet department and company objectives.

Required Skills

Level of reading, writing, and math ability as demonstrated by a competent high school student or high school graduate. Personal computer literate. Ability to operate various types of material handling equipment, including a pallet jack, hand truck, and carton dolly.

Physical Requirements

Must be able to lift 50 pounds. Must be able to lift, carry, stoop, reach, pull, push, and bend repeatedly to transport materials from racks and bins for shipment. Must be able to climb stairs and ladders to stock and pull materials from shelves.

Scheduling Requirements

Must be available to work up to the required hours as scheduled in compliance with 1978 Public Act 90 (Youth Employment Standards Act).

■ **Job Description** Written statements of job requirements help employees recognize their responsibilities. *What items are typically found on a job description?*

■ **Knowing Your Competitors** Analyzing your competitors is important for determining your pricing strategy. *How can you determine a competitor's pricing policies?*

drawn with the jobs and major duties identified and lines of authority clearly shown. Ideally, an organization chart outlines who each employee reports to and the chain of command in a company. This answers any questions regarding responsibility and how problems should be handled if they arise. It also makes clear what kind of work each department is responsible for. If you work for a large company in the public relations department and need to work with someone in the design department for a project, an organization chart should tell you to whom you would need to report.

Sometimes outside professional help is needed to keep a business going and growing. Entrepreneurs are often afraid to spend money on such professional services as accounting. This can be a fatal mistake. Trained professionals will help you avoid making serious mistakes that can result in business failure. If you decide to use outside professionals, identify them and their responsibilities on your organization chart. Professionals that can help you include accountants, attorneys, bankers, and insurance agents.

You can also use technical assistance to identify employment practices in your state or locality. New business owners must be familiar with laws regulating nondiscrimination laws, wages and hours regulations, occupational health and safety issues, unemployment compensation, and workers' disability insurance. State agencies—such as state departments of civil rights, commerce, labor, licensing and regulation—publish many inexpensive or free publications and offer technical assistance to help new entrepreneurs understand various employment laws, rules, and regulations.

■ Proposed Good or Service

One part of your business plan should include information on the types of goods and services you will offer, as well as your potential suppliers, manufacturing plans, and inventory policies. Let's say you plan to introduce a new service, such as a pre-school center, to your trading area. Perhaps you are going to sell or produce an existing product in a new and creative way. In both cases, you would prepare a list of possible suppliers and develop a manufacturing plan that details all of the purchasing and manufacturing requirements.

Closely related to your manufacturing plan is your inventory policy. You need to show how you will manage the goods you purchase or manufacture. How much, for example, will you keep on hand? How will you keep track of what to order and what has been sold? Where will you store the goods that you have in stock?

Your inventory system depends on the size and scope of your proposed business. Trade associations and many suppliers can give you suggestions for the best inventory control system for your business.

Planning for a service business requires that you develop a plan that addresses how, when, and who will provide the service to your customers. State the services provided by your competitors, then describe the additional services you will provide, and estimate their costs.

Proposed Marketing Plan

At this point in your business plan, you have selected your business organization, identified your staffing needs, and detailed your goods and services policies. You are now ready to develop your marketing policies—that is, the way you will price and promote your product. These two aspects are vitally important because they can make or break your customer relations. The promotional activities get your business's name out there, and the appropriate price will ensure a profit for your business.

PRICING POLICIES As you learned in Unit 8, pricing is a vitally important aspect of running a successful business. You must be able to set a price high enough to cover your costs and make a profit, but competitive enough to attract customers. Your business plan must show your pricing policies.

The three main factors in reviewing pricing policies are cost, demand, and competition. Review Chapters 25, 26, and 27 about the important factors in pricing.

PROMOTIONAL ACTIVITIES Once pricing policies have been established, you need to describe your promotional activities. You must identify ways to reach the greatest number of potential customers in your target market. This must be done considering the most economical use of your time and money.

The simplest method of promoting your business is by providing top quality products and services to your customers. Satisfied customers generate word-of-mouth advertising when they pass the news on to their friends. This will attract additional customers, as people usually trust the opinions of friends.

As you may recall, a firm's promotional mix may comprise activities involving advertising, public relations, promotions, and personal selling. A business decides on the promotional mix that will be most effective in persuading potential customers (wholesalers, retailers, and consumers) to purchase and support their product.

A convincing business plan provides a rationale for your selection of activities and the costs involved. You need to present a yearlong budget for promotion, listing the types of promotional activities you intend to use and their costs in the budget. Make sure the dollar figures generated from this budget correspond to the promotional expenses noted on your income statement.

35.2 ASSESSMENT

Reviewing Key Terms and Concepts

1. What elements should be included in the proposed organization part of the business plan?
2. Why are job descriptions important?
3. What is the purpose of an organization chart?
4. What information should be included in your proposed good or service part of the business plan?
5. What items should be covered in the marketing plan for a new business?

Thinking Critically

6. How could a poorly written business plan hurt a new business venture?

Integrating Academic Skills

7. **MATH** An employee was paid $7.75 an hour and double time on Sunday. What was the total weekly wage, if the employee worked 4 hours on Sunday, 4 hours on Wednesday, $3\frac{1}{2}$ hours on Thursday, and 6 hours on Saturday?

Financial Plan

Financial Plan

The financial plan section shows lenders and investors what monies are needed to start and operate the business. It includes statements of personal and external sources of capital. It also shows statements of projected income and expenses expected for at least the first year of operation.

Sources of Capital

Capital means the funds needed to finance the operation of a business. The term *capital* also includes all goods used to produce other goods. In business, capital may also include owned property and cash resources. When we refer to capital in this chapter, we are talking about anything that can be converted into money.

Entrepreneurs usually need a substantial amount of capital to open a business. There are several ways to raise the capital for a new business. You can use money from personal savings or borrow money from banks, credit unions, relatives, friends, suppliers, and previous business owners.

The method you choose to raise money depends on the amount that you need. Money needed for operating expenses is usually repaid within a year. A large amount of money borrowed to build a new facility, to purchase equipment, or to start an inventory will be repaid over a longer period of time.

■ Equity Capital

Raising money from within your company or by selling part of the interest in the business is called using equity capital. The advantage of using equity capital is that you do not need to repay the money or pay interest. However, the investor becomes a co-owner in your business. The larger the amount of interest in your business you sell, the greater degree of control you lose to your investors.

Equity capital sources include personal savings, partners, and shareholders. The most common method of financing a business is using personal savings. Even though you might not want to do this, you probably cannot avoid investing all or part of your savings. As you know, starting any new business involves risk. Your prospective investors and lenders will expect you to share in that risk.

As you learned in Chapter 33, having partners is another way to raise money for your business. Partners may bring in their own money and have access to other sources. As with investors, forming

What You'll Learn

- How to describe the elements found in the financial section of a business plan
- How to identify sources of equity capital
- How to identify sources of debt capital

Why It's Important

It takes money to start and operate a business. Most entrepreneurs need to borrow money to begin business operations. Potential investors and lenders want to look at the financial estimates for a new business to ensure that their efforts will be profitable for them.

Key Terms

- equity capital
- debt capital
- collateral
- credit union

■ **Meeting with the Owners** Issuing stock can raise equity capital. *What is the principal disadvantage of selling stock to raise equity?*

a partnership will lessen your degree of ownership, and you may have to share control of the business.

You may sell stock to shareholders as a way of raising capital—this is known as forming a corporation. As you learned in Chapter 33, to operate as a corporation, you'll need to incorporate and obtain a charter. Each shareholder in a corporation has limited liability or responsibility for debt; therefore a corporation can raise large amounts of money from its shareholders. Shareholders influence general corporate policy decisions, but as long as you hold a majority of the shares, you control the corporation's daily activities.

■ Debt Capital

Raising funds by borrowing money that will be repaid later is called using debt capital. Debt capital can work to your advantage because borrowing money and repaying it builds your credit standing. Good credit standing makes it easier for you to borrow money in the future. While you must pay interest when you repay your loan, the interest you pay is a tax-deductible business expense. In addition, if you raise money by borrowing it, no ownership passes to the lender.

There is a major disadvantage to debt capital. If you cannot pay back your debt, you could be forced into bankruptcy. Investors or co-owners may not force bankruptcy; they might instead insist on telling you how to run the business. Some debt capital sources include banks, credit unions, the Small Business Administration, friends, relatives, suppliers, and previous business owners.

BANKS Commercial banks are the most numerous and widespread lending agencies in the United States. They are one of most common sources of business financing. They know their local area and local economy well and offer a number of different loans and services on competitive and government-regulated terms. A 1998 study of small owners and midsize businesses indicated that 45 percent of the businesses surveyed used commercial bank loans to finance their companies.

Banks evaluate potential borrowers on criteria called the six Cs of credit. The six Cs are made up of *capital, collateral, capability* and *character,* and *coverage* and *circumstances.*

How much of your own money, or *capital,* is to be invested in your new business? Banks, like other potential investors, will want to know how much capital you are willing to invest into your new venture.

What assets (things of monetary value) can be used as collateral for a loan? Collateral is something of value that a borrower pledges to a lender to ensure repayment of a loan. Some examples of collateral are jewelry, vehicles, bonds, stocks, machinery, the cash value of insurance policies, and real estate. Some businesses may use accounts receivable, which is the sum of money owed to a business by its customers, as collateral. Lenders will usually require the value of the collateral to be greater than the amount of the loan.

Some banks will require a guarantee of personal assets (in effect, a promise that you have the assets you claim to have) and a pledge that you will repay the loan. Banks want to know that your loan will be repaid, even if your business fails.

A résumé of your previous training and related work experience, including professional and personal references, will answer questions about your *capability* and *character.* Your personal credit history will also be reviewed to see if you regularly pay your bills on time.

Case Study

Seeing Red!

GET THE *Red-i*® OUT OF YOUR FLASH PHOTOS!

Flexpoint® Ultra Fine Nib.

Archival Quality.
Acid Free.
Restores Natural Eye Color Instantly Right On Your Prints.

BEFORE

AFTER

i®FLASHPOINT®

Copyright © 1997 Private Label Products Inc.

How do you get rid of red-eye? Here's a hint: You won't need eye drops! The answer is no riddle to the Private Label Products Company of New Jersey. The company creates unique and creative uses for existing products—pens and markers. Their first products were red-eye retouching pens used to "clean up" photographs. Specialty camera and photography shops originally sold the red-eye pens in stores for $12.95.

After realizing that distributors were making the profit, co-owners Jim Michael and David Naor decided to mass market the pens. The company began to produce and package the pens for the consumer market. The company targeted supermarkets and drugstores first because 60% of photo developing is done there. The company's first big order came from a Walgreen manager for 60,000 pens.

The pens are now available through the CVS and Walgreen chains and retail at about half of the original price. Increased volume allows the company to reduce the product price and make more money.

The company has expanded on the uses for its pens and markers, including surgical markers for marking skin during a surgery; invisible inks for security that are readable under ultraviolet light; fabric pens to permanently mark laundry; and food coloring markers for writing on cookies, pastries, and other edible products. The Private Label Products Company relies on creativity to market existing products for a new and ever-changing marketplace.

Case Study Review

1. Why is creativity an important ingredient for most new businesses?
2. What risks did the company's co-owners take to establish the business?

A MATTER OF ETHICS

3. Was it ethical for specialty photo stores to sell the red-eye pen for $12.95 when chain stores now sell it for approximately half of the original price? Why or why not?

Banks will want to know the amount of insurance *coverage* that you carry and the general *circumstances* of your business. This is outlined in the description and analysis section of your business plan.

CREDIT UNIONS A credit union is a cooperative association formed by labor unions or groups of employees for the benefit of its members. Credit unions often charge lower interest rates on loans than banks do. To borrow money from a credit union, however, you must be a member. Check with your parents, guardians, and relatives to determine your eligibility, since credit unions often accept memberships for relatives. Credit unions also use the six Cs of credit to determine if they will accept your loan application.

FRIENDS AND RELATIVES Many people begin their businesses with funds borrowed from relatives and friends. While this may seem like the most convenient option, you should be cautious about doing this. Remember the saying that two of the quickest ways to lose friends are to lend them money or to borrow money from them.

When borrowing money from family or friends, put all agreements in writing to avoid future problems and misunderstandings. Identify the period of the loan, any interest to be paid, and your payment schedule. It is essential to remember that even if you are borrowing money from a personal friend or family member, it is still a business situation.

SUPPLIERS AND PREVIOUS OWNERS Some suppliers may provide you with a low-interest loan to purchase inventory, furniture, fixtures, and equipment on a delayed payment basis. This method of raising capital can improve your credit rating and stretch available cash. Remember, the interest on loan payments is a tax-deductible business expense.

When purchasing an existing business, consider the previous owner as a potential source of capital. Many sole proprietors want to see their businesses continue after their retirement. They may be willing to provide you with a loan and a favorable repayment plan to get you started. The rates on a loan negotiated in this manner are often lower than those from a bank or credit union.

■ **A Popular Funding Source** Banks are a common source of business financing. *What criteria do banks use to evaluate borrowers?*

Financial Statements

After you have identified your source or sources of capital, the last part of your business plan is to develop your financial statements. Your financial statements display your business's projected income and expenses and help persuade investors to loan you money. These financial statements and the math needed to complete them will be discussed in Chapter 36.

35.3 ASSESSMENT

Reviewing Key Terms and Concepts

1. Name the two major parts in the financial section of a business plan.
2. Identify three main sources of equity capital.
3. How can a corporation raise capital?
4. What are the main sources of debt capital?
5. What are the six Cs of credit?

Thinking Critically

6. What factors would you consider in selecting a lender for a business?

Integrating Academic Skills

7. **TECHNOLOGY** Interview a small business owner about a new technological process or piece of equipment that is used in his or her business today, but was not available when the business was first started. Write a 100-word report on your findings.

Careers in Marketing

FINANCIAL SERVICES

Trudy Brame
Bank Teller
ALL First Bank

What is your key to success?

"The key to success is ensuring that the customers stay happy and feel satisfied with the bank. We try to provide a friendly atmosphere—we want our customers to leave feeling satisfied with the services that we have provided. We must provide courteous, prompt, and efficient customer service."

What kind of training did you have?

"My company provides classroom training for customer service representatives. We aren't just tellers—we are expected to be more than that. The course lasts two weeks and teaches important skills for banking."

What kind of training would you suggest for students?

"On-the-job training in retail and cash handling are very important skills. Classes in marketing, business math, data processing, and accounting are recommended for high school or college course work."

What skills are most important?

"People skills are extremely important—it is very important to establish rapport with every customer. The technical skills of banking are also important—the teller must have not only an aptitude with the computer and math, but also a familiarity with our product. We are a service provider, offering banking products and packages to customers. I need to be able to answer questions about accounts, loan options, funds, investments, bonds, and money markets, as well as questions about overdraft, withdrawals, and deposits. After banking hours, we sort though the activity of the accounts that day."

Thinking Critically
How is technology affecting the banking industry?

Career Facts

Education and Training: A high school diploma, with classes in marketing, business math, data processing, and accounting, is usually required to become a bank teller. Similar course work at a community college provides good preparation. Jobs that require cash handling skills and customer service skills are excellent preparation for bank teller positions.

Aptitudes, Abilities, and Skills: Good arithmetic skills, organizational skills, basic clerical skills, ability to learn and apply the required banking standards, and good communication skills, both written and verbal, are essential.

Career Outlook: Growth is expected to be lower than average through the year 2006. Competition for bank teller positions is generally keen.

Career Path: A bank teller is often an entry-level position, which can lead to top positions in banking. Tellers may advance to supervisory positions such as bank operations officer and loan officer or to management training programs.

VOCABULARY REVIEW

Use each of the following terms in a sentence.

- business plan
- business philosophy
- trading area
- buying behavior
- job descriptions
- organization chart
- equity capital
- debt capital
- collateral
- credit union

FACT AND IDEA REVIEW

1. Why is self-analysis critical in a business plan? (35.1)

2. What is a trading area? Why is an analysis of the trading area important in a business plan? (35.1)

3. What is disposable income? Why is it important to know the disposable income of potential customers? (35.1)

4. How can an entrepreneur research existing competition for a proposed product? (35.1)

5. Why is the identification of your target market essential to your business plan? (35.1)

6. Why is planning for personnel needs important for a new business? (35.2)

7. What is the simplest method to promote a business? (35.2)

8. What is the difference between debt capital and equity capital? (35.3)

9. What is the most common method of financing a business? (35.3)

10. Why is a credit union a good source of debt capital for a new business owner? (35.3)

THINKING CRITICALLY

1. "Employees are the most valued asset to a small business." Do you agree or disagree with this statement? Explain your answer.

2. How can you determine whether there is a need for a product or service?

3. How would you determine which job positions you need to fill in your new business?

4. Why would you have an accountant, attorney, or business advisor assist you in establishing your business?

5. "While debt capital can work to your advantage when establishing a business, there are many disadvantages if you cannot pay back your debt. Bankruptcy is one of these disadvantages, however it may not be the worst one." Explain what this statement means. Decide whether you agree or disagree with this idea.

BUILDING WORKPLACE SKILLS

1. **Political Science** Political and legal considerations affect all types of businesses. Prepare a 250-word paper on the reasons businesses establish and support political action committees (PACs).

2. **Technology** In 2000, over 123 million Americans had Internet access at home. Write a 250-word report on the impact of the Internet on small businesses.

APPLYING MARKETING CONCEPTS

1. **Researching New Business Ventures** Use business magazines to research a successful new business venture. Develop a 150-word report or an article on a word processing program.

2. **Finding SBA Resources** Find the U.S. Small Business Administration (SBA) Web site. Summarize at least five resources that are available through the SBA for new business start-ups in a 150-word report.

3. **Developing a Business Plan** Use word processing software to begin developing a business plan using instructor or DECA guidelines. Describe the type of business, the product/service involved, appealing factors about the business, and the factors you think will make it successful. Describe your aspirations and career objectives, educational experiences, and related work experiences. Finally, make a chart of your competitors' strengths and weaknesses.

4. **Establishing Pricing Strategies** Continue with the business plan that you created in the previous activity. Establish pricing policies and a one-year promotional plan for your business. The plan should contain a budget, selection of media, and a plan to evaluate its effectiveness. List special promotional events that would be conducted for each month of the year for your business.

LINKING SCHOOL TO WORK

Basic Writing and Information Skills Investigate a product line available at your place of employment or a local business. Compare the pricing policies used for selected items in the product line. Use word processing software to create a 100-word report on your findings.

THE DECA CONNECTION

Role Play: Restaurant Employee

Situation You are to assume the role of an employee at a restaurant. A co-worker (judge) plans to establish his own quick-serve restaurant. He believes that he will be successful because there is an available location and he is a good cook. He thinks he will have no trouble obtaining a loan because his proposed business has so much potential. He does not believe that it will be necessary to develop a business plan.

Activity Your task is to explain the importance of a business plan and convince your co-worker to develop one.

Evaluation You will be evaluated on how well you meet the following performance indicators:
- Explain the nature of business plans
- Develop a business plan
- Develop company objectives
- Develop strategies to achieve company goals
- Explain external planning considerations

*inter*NET CONNECTION

Learning From the Pros
The Senior Corps of Retired Executives (SCORE) is a voluntary group of counselors that helps America's small businesses. SCORE provides many resources to help individuals write business plans.

Connect
- Locate the SCORE Web site and find the address of the SCORE office nearest to your school.
- List at least three resources available from SCORE to help you develop a comprehensive business plan.

Chapter 36

Financing the Business

Marketing: What It Takes

Digging Up Some Cash

You and your friends in the manufacturing technology program have designed and built a prototype for a new and improved two-wheeled personal scooter. Your personal scooter is fun to use, and it can also transport an individual easily in crowded urban areas. You have determined that you will form a partnership with your friends and start a business. You currently have a facility to manufacture the units, but you need additional capital to purchase equipment, materials, supplies, and pay for operating expenses.

WHAT WILL YOU DO?
What will it take to convince a lender to provide the required capital for your new business?

658

Preparing Financial Documents

The Financial Part of a Business Plan

A major purpose of the business plan is to put together the financial information relating to your business. This information is presented on financial documents that describe your personal financial situation, as well as the financial needs of your business. Preparing financial statements helps you determine the amount of money you need to operate the business. The process also helps you estimate how much money you may need to borrow.

When you inquire about borrowing money, the lender will want to know that you will be able to repay a loan. A lender will look at your credit history, items you own that can be sold to pay off the loan (collateral), and your prospects for business success. Your financial documents give a potential lender a picture of you and your business.

Five important financial documents are the personal financial statement, the start-up cost estimate, the income statement, the balance sheet, and the cash flow statement. In this section you will look at the first two financial statements.

The Personal Financial Statement

The personal financial statement is a summary of your current personal financial condition. A personal financial statement is like a snapshot of your finances. It is an important part of any loan application for a new business. It measures your financial progress to date and shows how well you have met your personal expenses in the past. It compares your *assets* to your *liabilities* at a particular point in time. An asset is anything of monetary value that you own. A liability is a debt you owe.

To develop a personal financial statement, you first list your assets. You should be realistic about the current value of your assets. For example, if you have a van worth $9,000, do not round it up to $10,000. Be sure to list all your cash assets (checking and savings accounts) and any investments (stocks, bonds, mutual funds, and retirement funds) and personal assets (furniture, cars, clothes, and home). You will need to estimate the present value for each item. A lender will look for assets that you can sell to pay off the business loan if your business does not do as well as expected.

Next, list your debts, including your charge accounts, mortgage balance, and school and automobile loans. Add all your assets and all your debts to find a total for each. Then calculate your personal

What You'll Learn

- The purpose of preparing financial documents
- How to develop a personal financial statement
- How to determine start-up costs for a business

Why It's Important

The most common reason for writing a business plan is to obtain financing for a business. In order to get the money you will need to start your business, you will need to prepare financial statements.

Key Terms

- personal financial statement
- asset
- liability
- start-up costs

net worth by subtracting your debts from your assets. Figure 36-1 shows an example of a personal financial statement.

Your personal financial statement will be one aspect used to determine whether you and your business are a good credit risk. In addition, a lender will require a copy of your personal tax returns. Your tax returns will show how you have earned money in the past. A credit report will also be requested to show how well you have paid off debts in the past. If you plan to continue working at another job, the lender will be interested in whether that income can support your personal expenses until your new business becomes profitable.

PRACTICE 1

1. You have assets of $10,000 (car), $8,000 (savings), $1,000 (cash value of life insurance), $1,500 (cash), and personal property worth $1,500. What are your total assets?

2. You have liabilities of $7,000 (car loan), $2,500 (student loan), and $500 (credit card balances). What are your total liabilities?

3. What is your net worth?

Note: Answers to all practice sets in this chapter are on page 678.

FIGURE 36-1

Personal Financial Statement

August, 20--

Assets

Cash	$	500.00
Savings accounts		1,500.00
Stocks, bonds, other securities		750.00
Life insurance cash value		0.00
Auto (2000 van)		18,000.00
Real estate (residence)		75,000.00
Vested pension plan		25,000.00
Other assets (lakefront property)		15,000.00
TOTAL ASSETS	$	135,750.00

Liabilities

Accounts payable (credit cards)		1,875.00
Contracts payable		0.00
Notes payable (mortgage)		28,500.00
Taxes payable		2,500.00
Real estate loans		0.00
Other liabilities (2000 van)		15,000.00
TOTAL LIABILITIES	$	47,875.00

TOTAL ASSETS	$	135,750.00
TOTAL LIABILITIES	$	47,875.00
NET WORTH	$	87,875.00

■ **Personal Financial Statement** A personal financial statement shows your financial condition to date. *Based upon the figures shown here, what is your total net worth? How is net worth calculated?*

Estimating Start-up Costs

Before starting your business, you need to know how much it will cost you. Start-up costs are a projection of how much money you will need for your first year of operation. You also need an estimate of operating costs after the first year.

Assessing these start-up costs prior to getting involved in a project protects you as you start your business. You will need to spend money on goods and services ranging from furniture to advertising. Some examples of these costs are listed in Figure 36-2. As you can see, these costs vary depending on the type of business.

FIGURE 36-2

Start-Up Costs

Type of Costs	Type of Business			
	 **Manufacturing**	 **Retail**	 **Wholesale**	 **Service**
Deposits (rents, utilities, telephone)	$7,500–$20,300	$3,900–$35,300	$7,400–$17,700	$4,200–$14,000
Furniture and Equipment	$20,100–$42,000	$21,300–$42,300	$22,500–$54,900	$19,700–$54,100
Machinery and Equipment	$10,000–$60,000	$5,000–$32,500	$19,900–$33,900	———
Transportation Equipment	$32,000–$45,000	$32,000–$45,000	$32,000–$45,000	———
Building Improvements	$11,300–$42,000	$11,300–$52,500	$15,000–$30,000	$15,000–$60,000
Professional Fees	$1,500–$4,000	$1,500–$4,000	$1,500–$4,000	$1,500–$4,000
Advertising	$3,000–$10,000	$10,000–$15,000	$3,000–$10,000	$3,000–$10,000
Working Capital	$9,900–$45,000	$3,800–$93,700	$25,200–$75,000	$9,900–$35,100
Inventory	$13,000–$57,500	$35,000–$157,500	$23,000–$122,500	———
Totals	$108,300–$325,800	$123,800–$477,800	$149,500–$393,000	$53,300–$177,200

■ **Start-up Costs** Start-up costs vary depending on the type of business. *Why is less money generally needed to establish a service business than to establish a manufacturing, franchise, retail, or wholesale business?*

Start-up costs vary for each type of business, but are based on factors such as:

- *The nature of your proposed business* Manufacturing, wholesale, or retail businesses all have different needs and requirements.
- *The size of your business* Small businesses usually do not require as much money to start as big businesses.
- *The amount and kind of inventory needed* For example, it is much more costly to purchase inventory for a large supermarket than for a neighborhood convenience store.
- *The estimated time between starting the business and earning income from the first sales*
- *The operating expenses that must be paid before cash is received from sales*

Business start-up costs may be one-time costs or continuing costs. *One-time costs* are expenses that will not be repeated after you begin operating the business. Examples of one-time costs include licenses and permits, deposits for telephone installation, and charges for installation of equipment, fixtures, and machinery.

Continuing costs are operating expenses you will pay throughout the life of the business. Examples of continuing costs include payroll, monthly rent, advertising, supplies, insurance, repairs, maintenance, and taxes. Most businesses are not profitable immediately, so estimate at least three months of continuing costs when deciding the amount of cash you will need for start-up costs.

You can find information to help you plan your financial needs from several sources. The Small Business Administration (SBA) provides information to people who want to start a new business. The SBA offers a wide variety of loan programs. These programs help small businesses borrow money at reasonable interest rates from traditional lenders. The SBA has developed a worksheet for estimating start-up costs and operating expenses for new businesses (see Figure 36-4 on page 663).

You can also get estimates of start-up costs from people who are already in a similar business or from related trade associations. State and local government agencies, such as your state department of commerce and local chamber of commerce, are also valuable sources of cost information. Better Business Bureaus and local, regional, and state business development agencies are also sources of information. Figure 36-3 details sources of financing for a start-up business.

> ### PRACTICE 2
>
> You have one-time costs of $18,000 and average monthly costs of $3,200. What are your total costs for the first quarter of operation? Using the same average monthly costs, what are total costs for the year?

FIGURE 36-3

Financing Sources

Primary Sources		Secondary Sources	
Long-term financing	*Short-term financing*	*Long-term financing*	*Short-term financing*
• Personal financing • Family and friends • Private Investors • Equity financing • Leasing • Credit unions • SBA LowDoc	• Personal financing • Family and friends • Credit cards • Credit unions • Trade credit • Banks • SBA Microloans • SBA LowDoc	• Business alliances • SBA regular 7(a) program • Venture capital • SBICs • State and local public financing • Franchising • Asset-based financing	• SBA CAPlines • Consumer finance companies • Commercial finance companies • State and local public financing

■ **Financing Options** There are several funding sources used to start up a business. *Why are the sources divided into primary and secondary sources?*

FIGURE 36-4

Start-Up Cost Worksheet

ESTIMATED MONTHLY EXPENSES			
Item	Your estimate of monthly espenses based on sales of $_____ per year	Your estimate of how much cash you need to start your business (See column 3)	What to put in column 2. (These figures are typical for one kind of business. You will have to decide how many months to allow for your business.)
	Column 1	Column 2	Column 3
Salary of owner	$	$	2 times column 1
All other salaries and wages			3 times column 1
Rent			3 times column 1
Advertising			3 times column 1
Delivery expense			3 times column 1
Supplies			3 times column 1
Telephone and telegraph			3 times column 1
Other utilities			3 times column 1
Insurance			Payment required by insurance company
Taxes, including Social Security			4 times column 1
Interest			3 times column 1
Maintenance			3 times column 1
Legal and other professional fees			3 times column 1
Miscellaneous			3 times column 1
STARTING COSTS YOU ONLY HAVE TO PAY ONCE			Leave column 2 blank
Fixtures and equipment			Fill in worksheet 3 on page 12 and put the total here
Decorating and remodeling			Talk it over with a contractor
Installation of fixtures and equipment			Talk to suppliers from whom you buy these
Starting inventory			Supplies will probably help you estimate this
Deposits with public utilities			Find out from utility companies
Legal and other professional fees			Lawyer, accountant, and so on
Licenses and permits			Find out from city offices what you have to have
Advertising and promotion			Estimate what you'll use for opening
Accounts receivable			What you need in order to buy more stock until credit customers pay
Cash			For unexpected expenses or losses, special purchases, etc.
Other			Make a separate list and enter total
TOTAL ESTIMATED CASH YOU NEED TO START WITH	$	$	Add up all the numbers in column 2

■ **Start-Up Cost Worksheet** The SBA provides worksheets to assist new business owners in estimating monthly expenses. *Why is a worksheet helpful to beginning businesses?*

Personal Costs

Unless you are starting your new business while still working at another job, you will need money to live on during the start-up phase. Your *personal costs* are those expenses that are necessary for you to live. You will need to project your monthly living expenses and household cash needs for at least the first year of business. When starting a new business, you may be able to meet your personal expenses by working at another job or by relying on a spouse's income.

You may choose not to work outside your business or to have any other source of income, but you must plan to have enough cash on hand to pay your personal expenses. Some experts suggest that you have enough start-up capital available to pay for up to six months of living expenses.

Set aside the money for living expenses in a savings account. Do not use the money for any other purpose. This fund will help you get through the start-up period. The chart in Figure 36-5 on page 665 will help you estimate how much money you should have in this account. Figure 36-5 illustrates a cost-of-living budget for an average month. The table includes regular monthly payments, household operating expenses, food expenses, personal expenses, and tax expenses. Under each category is a breakdown of estimated and actual costs.

REAL WORLD MARKETING

Virtual Banking

New breeds of Internet banking companies such as Wingspan have sprung up to meet the demands of businesses. Wingspan refers to themselves as more than a bank, but more as a "one-stop resource" for personal finance. It offers services such as checking and saving accounts, online bill payment, credit cards, ATM locations, mortgage loans, research resources, and financial tools. Without the traditional cost of increased payroll and rent associated with established brick-and-mortar banks, virtual banks offer greatly reduced rates for loans and higher rates for deposit interest.

Thinking Critically

What might an online bank not offer that a traditional brick-and-mortar bank does?

The bottom right hand corner of the chart shows a summary of each category and ends with a monthly total.

BRIGHT IDEAS
Sack It to Me!

Kicking around beans in a sack? The idea is not new, as team sports using bean sacks can be traced back to ancient times. Countries including China and Thailand have historical documentation showing the existence of recreational games very similar to soccer. In 1972, John Stalberger and Mike Marshall of Oregon City, Oregon, created a new version of an old game. Marshall designed a hand-made beanbag that he enjoyed kicking around. Stalberger, recovering from knee surgery, was looking for a way to exercise his knees. Together, they called the new game "Hackin' the Sack." They marketed the game under their new catchy trademark—Hacky Sack. Stalberger went on to form the National Hacky Sack Association and later sold the rights to Kransco, under the Wham-O label.

Thinking Creatively
You need financing to begin a business. Research typical means of financing today. What are the obstacles? What are some creative means of financing?

FIGURE 36-5

Estimating Personal Living Expenses

Cost-of-Living Budget for an Average Month
Based on an Average Income of $38,000

Regular Monthly Payments		Personal Expenses	
Rent or mortgage (including taxes)	$ 550.00	Clothing, cleaning, laundry	110.00
Cars (including insurance)	350.00	Medications	10.00
Appliances/TV	0.00	Doctors and dentists	50.00
Home improvement loan	200.00	Education	0.00
Personal loan	55.00	Dues	10.00
Health plan	50.00	Gifts and contributions	40.00
Life insurance premiums	15.00	Travel	50.00
Other insurance premiums	20.00	Newspapers, magazines, books	10.00
Miscellaneous (bank account service fees)	10.00	Auto upkeep, gas, and parking	50.00
		Spending money, allowances	20.00
TOTAL	**$ 1,250.00**	**TOTAL**	**$ 350.00**
Household Operating Expenses		Tax Expenses	
Telephone	50.00	Federal and state income taxes	175.00
Gas and electricity	120.00	Personal property taxes	350.00
Water and garbage	30.00	Other taxes	25.00
Other household expenses repairs, maintenance	20.00	**TOTAL**	**$ 550.00**
		BUDGET SUMMARY	
TOTAL	**$ 220.00**	Regulary Monthly Payments	1,250.00
Food Expenses		Household Operating Expenses	220.00
Food—at home	500.00	Food Expenses	560.00
Food—away from home	60.00	Personal Expenses	350.00
		Tax Expenses	550.00
TOTAL	**$ 560.00**	**MONTHLY TOTAL**	**$ _____**

■ **Estimating Personal Living Expenses** This form will help you to estimate how much you need for your living expenses when you start your business. *Based upon the figures shown here, what is your monthly total for cost-of-living expenses?*

36.1 ASSESSMENT

Reviewing Key Terms and Concepts

1. Why is financial information included as part of a business plan?

2. What items should be identified on a personal financial statement?

3. What is the difference between an asset and a liability?

4. What are start-up costs?

5. What is the difference between one-time costs and continuing costs?

Thinking Critically

6. Why are friends and family usually consulted first when looking for loans?

Integrating Academic Skills

7. **COMMUNICATION** Use a word processing program to write a business letter to your department of commerce requesting general information about the steps involved with starting a business in your state.

Financial Aspects of a Business Plan

What You'll Learn

- How to estimate business income and expenses
- How to prepare an income statement
- How to calculate payroll and other expenses itemized on an income statement
- How to prepare a balance sheet
- How to prepare a cash flow statement

Why It's Important

Financial institutions and investors in any new business will want to know why you need their money, how you are going to use it, and how you plan to repay them. The financial section of a business plan provides this information to prospective lenders.

Key Terms

- income statement
- gross sales
- net sales
- net income
- interest
- principal
- balance sheet
- net worth
- cash flow statement

Estimating Business Income and Expenses

After estimating your start-up costs and personal living expenses, the next step is to estimate the money you expect to earn and to spend in operating your business. Many small businesses fail because they do not bring in enough revenue to pay their costs and expenses. Estimating your business income and expenses is a key part of your business plan. Lenders will want to see your estimates before deciding to lend you money.

If you are buying an existing business, you will have previous operating results to use as a guide. You will need to estimate your potential revenue and the costs and expenses of operating the business if you are starting a new business.

The financial document that is used to calculate a business's revenue, costs, and expenses is the income statement. The income statement is a summary of your business's income and expenses during a specific period, such as a month, a quarter, or a year. This statement is often called a *profit and loss statement.*

The income statement for an existing business shows the previous year's income, costs, and expenses. The income statement for a new or planned business estimates earnings and expenses for the first few months (or the first year) of operation. Figure 36-6 on page 667 shows a sample projected quarterly income statement. Refer to this figure as you read about the different parts of the income statement.

Income statements have several major parts: total and net sales, cost of goods sold, gross profit, expenses of operating the business, net income from operations, net profit before income taxes, and net profit after income taxes. Each item on the income statement is added to or subtracted from total sales to find the amount of profit.

Total Sales
2 Returns and Allowances
5 Net Sales
2 Cost of Goods Sold
5 Gross Profit
2 Expenses of Operating the Business
5 Net Income from Operations
2 Income Taxes
5 Net Profit

Let's look at how you calculate the amounts for each part of the income statement.

FIGURE 36-6

Projected Quarterly Income Statement

	Month 1	Month 2	Month 3	TOTAL
Sales	30,900	34,000	36,400	101,300
Less Returns & Allowances	900	1,000	1,400	3,300
NET SALES	30,000	33,000	35,000	98,000
Cost of Goods Sold	19,500	21,000	22,750	63,250
GROSS PROFIT	10,500	12,000	12,250	34,750
Operating Expenses				
Variable Expenses				
Advertising	300	350	350	1,000
Automobile	450	400	525	1,375
Dues and Subscriptions	15	20	18	53
Legal and Accounting	300	400	350	1,050
Miscellaneous Expenses	360	480	420	1,260
Office Supplies	120	160	140	420
Security	300	400	350	1,050
Telephone	90	120	105	315
Utilities	90	120	105	315
Total Variable Expenses	2,025	2,450	2,363	6,838
Fixed Expenses				
Depreciation	180	180	180	540
Insurance	300	300	300	900
Rent	800	800	800	2,400
Salaries and Payroll Taxes	5,600	5,600	5,600	16,800
Total Fixed Expenses	6,880	6,880	6,880	20,640
TOTAL EXPENSES	8,905	9,330	9,243	27,478
NET INCOME FROM OPERATIONS	1,595	2,670	3,007	7,272
Other Income	0	0	0	0
Other Expenses (Interest)	300	300	300	900
NET PROFIT (LOSS) BEFORE TAXES	1,295	2,370	2,707	6,372
Taxes	325	590	680	1,595
NET PROFIT (LOSS) AFTER TAXES	970	1,780	2,027	4,777

Net Sales is determined by subtracting returns and allowances from total sales.

Gross Profit is the difference between net sales and the cost of goods sold.

Operating Expenses are the costs of operating a business. They are divided into variable and fixed expenses.

Total Expenses is determined by adding the total variable expenses to the total fixed expenses.

Net Income From Operations is found by subtracting total expenses from gross profit.

Net Profit Before Taxes is calculated by adding other income to net income from operations, then subtracting interest expense.

Net Profit After Taxes is found by subtracting taxes from net profit before taxes. This amount represents the actual profit after income taxes are paid from operating the business for a certain period of time.

■ **Projected Quarterly Income Statement** An income statement is a summary of your business's income and expenses during a specific period. *Based on the figures shown here, what are your total expenses and your net profit after taxes for the quarter?*

■ Estimating Total Sales

The income generated by a business depends on the yearly volume of sales. Most new businesses grow slowly in the beginning, so you should be conservative in estimating your first-year sales.

Most people who start a new business have some idea about where they will sell their products. You may already have discussed your new product with potential buyers. You may even have a contract to produce a certain number. Suppose you are starting a new tee shirt printing business. You have a contract for 2,000 tee shirts, which you will sell at $6 wholesale. Your estimated total sales will be $12,000. You would estimate your total sales at $120,000 if you think you can produce and sell ten times that amount during your first year.

It is important to calculate a reasonable estimated sales volume. You must verify your estimated sales volume by comparing it with projected industry figures for your size of business and location. Trade associations, bankers, and industry publications can help you make sales and income estimates.

The accuracy of your sales estimates will also depend on the quality of your market analysis. Losses instead of profit are not uncommon during the first year in business. In your business plan, you will need to show how you will support any losses and your ability to invest more capital or reduce your operating expenses.

■ Calculating Net Sales

The total of all sales for any period of time is called gross sales. Your gross sales will simply be the total of all cash sales if your company sells only on a cash basis. When your company accepts credit and charge cards, sells gift certificates, and sells merchandise on account, then all of these different types of sales must be totaled to arrive at gross sales.

Most businesses have some customer returns and allowances (credit granted to customers for damaged or defective goods kept by the customer); therefore, the gross sales figure does not reflect the actual income from sales. The total of all sales returns and allowances is subtracted from gross sales to get net sales. Net sales, then, represents the amount left after gross sales have been adjusted for returns and allowances. Look at Figure 36-6 on page 667 to see the net sales line.

■ Cost of Goods Sold

The total amount spent to produce or to purchase the goods that are sold is called the *cost of goods sold*. To calculate cost of goods sold, add goods purchased during the year to the beginning inventory. Then subtract the amount of the ending inventory.

$$
\begin{array}{l}
\quad \text{Beginning Inventory} \\
+ \ \text{Net Purchases} \\
- \ \text{Ending Inventory} \\
\hline
= \ \text{Cost of Goods Sold}
\end{array}
$$

As you learned in Chapter 24, beginning and ending inventory amounts are determined by figuring how much stock is on hand and calculating its value.

Service businesses do not provide goods to their customers. Therefore, they don't have to determine their cost of goods sold. Their gross profit is the same as net sales. Other businesses that produce or buy products to sell must calculate the cost of goods sold.

■ Determining Gross Profit

Gross profit on sales is the difference between the net sales and the cost of goods sold.

The formula for calculating gross profit is:

$$
\begin{array}{l}
\quad \text{Net Sales} \\
- \ \text{Cost of Goods Sold} \\
\hline
= \ \text{Gross Profit}
\end{array}
$$

Once you know the cost of goods sold, you can calculate your gross profit by subtracting the cost of goods sold from net sales. Suppose you are employed by Seaside Surfboards, a company that sold $96,785 worth of surfboards last year. The company books show a total of $1,470 in sales returns and allowances. When you subtract the sales returns and allowances from total (gross) sales, you get net sales of $95,315. The cost of goods sold for last year totals $53,769; therefore, your gross profit is: $95,315 − $53,769 = $41,546.

■ Projecting Business Expenses

The next major part of the income statement is the operating expenses. *Operating expenses* are the costs of operating the business, which include both variable and fixed expenses.

CALCULATING VARIABLE EXPENSES *Variable expenses* change from one month to the next. Variable costs can fluctuate up or down depending upon the needs of the business. Variable expenses include items such as advertising, office supplies, telephone, and utilities.

Variable expenses are often calculated as a percentage of some baseline amount. Advertising expenses may be planned to be 5 percent of total sales.

CALCULATING FIXED EXPENSES *Fixed expenses* are costs that remain the same for a period of time. Expenses that are fixed for a certain period of time include items such as depreciation, insurance, rent, and office salaries.

Depreciation is a complicated fixed expense. *Depreciation* essentially represents the amount by which the value of a business's assets has fallen in a given period of time. An accountant or financial advisor can assist you in determining the asset depreciation schedule for assets on your income statement.

Projecting other fixed expenses usually is easier because you simply add all your fixed costs, such as rent or insurance. Employee wages may be a significant part of your business expenses. Let's look at how to calculate payroll costs.

CALCULATING PAYROLL EXPENSES To calculate payroll expenses, you must estimate the number of employees you need to operate your business. Then research typical salaries in your area for the work you will have the employees perform. You can get help on salary information by consulting with your state employment security agency (SESA) office and by reviewing the help-wanted ads in the newspaper for similar jobs. You can also use the minimum wage as a starting point and decide how much more to pay for more skilled workers, recognizing that a skilled worker should have a higher salary than an unskilled worker.

When setting up your business, you need to pay particular attention to your payroll records. Payroll records are important to your employees and to your company. They are used to prepare income tax returns, so the federal and state governments are interested in their accuracy, too.

Your payroll records may be part of the cash disbursements journal where you keep records of all cash payments. You may prefer to keep your payroll records in a separate payroll journal. When using a separate journal for payroll records, you will want to use a separate record for each employee. Each record will show one employee's pay period, hours worked, earnings, deductions, and net pay. See Figure 36-7 for a payroll journal that is used to record payroll information for employees.

The amount earned by an employee is that person's *gross pay*. *Net pay* is what the employee receives after deductions for taxes, insurance, and voluntary deductions. Nancy Baker earns $11 an hour and worked 40 hours during the week; therefore, her gross pay is $440 ($11 times 40 hours).

Nancy's deductions total $125.66, so you would calculate her net pay by subtracting the deductions from her gross pay:

$$\$440 - \$125.66 = \$314.34 \text{ (net pay)}$$

Tax tables are available for calculating the amount to be deducted from each employee's pay for local, state, and federal income tax. The percentage of gross pay to be deducted for FICA (Social Security and Medicare taxes) changes almost every year. Get the latest information from your local social security office.

Example: Find the net pay for Carmen Lopez, who worked a total of 44 hours during a week at $12 per hour. Carmen is paid time and a half for overtime (hours worked beyond 40 hours in a week).

FIGURE 36-7

Payroll Journal

Name _Nancy Baker_   Wage rate _$11.00/Hr_

Date of Birth _11-19-64_   Date employed _8-1-86_

Soc. Sec. No. _514-62-5254_   Employee No. _9_

No. of Allowances _1_   Department _B_

Address _317 Sycamore_

Pay Period Ending	S	M	T	W	T	F	S	Total Regular	Over-time	Earnings	Social Security	Medicare	Federal Income tax	State Income tax	Misc.	Net Pay
8-14		8	8	8	8	8		40		440.00	27.28	6.38	53.00	22.00	17.00	314.34
8-21		7	8	8	8	8		39		429.00	26.60	6.22	50.00	21.45	17.00	

■ **Payroll Journal** A payroll journal summarizes each employee's pay period, hours worked, earnings, deductions, and net pay. *What is Nancy Baker's net pay for the period ending August 21?*

STEP 1 Find the gross pay.

$480.00 ($12 × 40 hours)
+ 72.00 ($12 × 4 hours × 1.5)
$552.00

STEP 2 Subtract the total deductions.

$552.00 (gross pay)
+ 98.40 (total deductions)
$453.60 (net pay)

In estimating your total payroll expenses, you will need to use current tax rates for local, state, and federal income taxes. Remember that as the employer, you will also pay FICA and unemployment payroll taxes on your employees' earnings. You will need to include those amounts in your total payroll expense estimate.

CALCULATING TOTAL EXPENSES Once you have calculated all your operating (variable and fixed) expenses, you are ready to total your expenses. To calculate total expenses, add all the variable expenses to the fixed expenses.

Total Variable Expenses
+ Total Fixed Expenses
= Total Expenses

■ Net Income from Operations

After calculating your total expenses, the next step is to calculate net income from operations. Net income is the amount left after the total expenses are subtracted from gross profit.

The formula for calculating net income from operations is:

Gross Profit on Sales
− Total Expenses
= Net Income from Operations

Suppose that you own Worldwide Travel Agency and had gross profit on sales of $145,540 during the year. Your total operating expenses for the year were $79,630, so your net income from operations was:

$145,540 − $79,630 = $65,910

During the first years of operation, a business may have a net loss from operations. A net loss results when total expenses are larger than the gross profit on sales. The financial plan should address how the business intends to pay its debts in the short term, especially if a loss is probable during the first months of operation.

CALCULATING OTHER INCOME In the "Net Income From Operations" section of the income statement, list money earned from sources other than sales. You may earn dividends on stocks or interest on money in the bank. Interest is the money paid for the use of money borrowed or invested.

To estimate your interest earnings, check with local banks and find the current interest rate paid on similar accounts. It is likely that you will use some of this money during the year, so you will need to calculate interest only on the amount actually on deposit. Unless the interest income you expect to earn is significant, you may want to list this amount as zero in your business plan.

CALCULATING OTHER EXPENSES You will pay interest on any money that you borrow to start your business. This is called the principal.

Interest is expressed as a percentage of the principal and is called the *rate* of interest. Imagine that you borrow $100 and the interest rate is 11 percent. The principal is $100 and the rate of interest is 11 percent. To find the amount of interest for one year, multiply the principal (p) times the rate of interest (r) times the length of time (t). This formula is stated as:

$$i = prt$$
($100 × 11% × 1 = $11).

You would pay $11 in interest for the example above.

The units in the rate of interest and time must agree. That is, if the rate of interest is expressed in years, then the time must be expressed in years as well. Both may be expressed in months. Check this before you do your math or your answers will be wrong. If the rate is given without reference to a time period, you can assume that it is for one year.

Suppose you are quoted a yearly rate and need to convert it to a monthly rate. There are 12 months in a year, so you would divide the yearly rate by 12, and you will get the monthly rate. When you are quoted a monthly rate and want to convert it to a yearly rate, multiply the monthly rate by 12.

Once you decide how much money you will need to borrow and how long it will take you to repay the loan, you can calculate your total annual (or monthly) interest. This amount is listed on the financial statement as "Other Expenses."

◼ Net Profit or Loss Before Taxes

Net profit or *net loss before taxes* is calculated by adding other income to net income from operations. Then subtract other expenses from the total.

$$
\begin{aligned}
&\text{Net Income from Operations} \\
+\ &\text{Other Income} \\
-\ &\text{Other Expenses} \\
\hline
=\ &\text{Net profit (or loss) before taxes}
\end{aligned}
$$

◼ Net Profit or Loss After Taxes

Net profit (or loss) after taxes is the amount of money left over after federal, state, and local taxes are subtracted. This amount represents the actual profit from operating the business for a certain period of time.

The projected income statement should be done on a monthly basis for new businesses. After the first year, projected income statements can be prepared on a quarterly basis.

The steps that follow are a summary of how to prepare a monthly projected income statement.

STEP 1 Estimate total sales.

STEP 2 Subtract sales discounts, returns, and allowances from total sales to calculate net sales.

STEP 3 List the estimated cost of goods sold.

STEP 4 Subtract the cost of goods sold from net sales to find gross profit on sales.

STEP 5 List each monthly operating expense, categorizing each as a variable or fixed expense.

STEP 6 Total the monthly operating expenses.

STEP 7 Subtract total operating expenses from gross profit on sales to find net income from operations. Put parentheses around any projected losses; for example, a projected loss of $1,000 would be identified as ($1,000).

STEP 8 Add other income such as interest on bank deposits and subtract other expenses, such as interest expense, from net income from operations. The result is net profit (or loss) before income taxes.

STEP 9 Estimate total taxes on the net income and subtract that amount from net profit. The result is net profit (or loss) after taxes.

PRACTICE 3

Using the income statement shown below, answer the following questions:

1. How much did Mountain Air pay for the bikes it sold?

2. How much was the gross profit for the year?

3. How much were total operating expenses?

4. Which operating expense was the most costly?

5. How much net income was earned during the year?

Mountain Air Bikes
Income Statement for the Year Ended December 31, 20--

Net Sales	$ 212,015
Cost of Goods Sold	109,614
Gross Profit	$?
Operating Expenses:	
Salaries	$ 24,019
Rent	$ 11,211
Utilities	4,514
Advertising	2,422
Total Operating Expenses	$?
Net Income from Operations	$?

Bringing it Together

Cross your knees, but be sure not to show the bottom of your feet. Bow only after being acknowledged at a meeting. There are books filled with tips and hints for businesspeople doing business abroad. How can one person remember all of these facts? The folks at Globesmart, a global training and consulting company in San Francisco, wondered the same thing. Globesmart offers Web-based training for individuals who do business abroad. The program includes 30 different countries, and while it will not help you learn the language, it will fill you in on the most important dos and taboos of the culture.

Thinking Critically

Familiarizing yourself with foreign traditions is important. How is Globesmart helpful in this area?

FIGURE 36-8

Balance Sheet

August, 20--	Year 1	Year 2
Current Assets		
Cash	$ 7,000	$ 10,000
Accounts receivable	10,000	10,000
Inventory	150,000	265,000
Fixed Assets		
Real Estate	$ 100,000	$ 100,000
Fixtures and equipment	50,000	45,000
Vehicles	25,000	24,000
Other Assets		
Licenses	$ 100	$ 100
TOTAL ASSETS	$ 342,100	$ 454,100
Current Liabilities		
Notes payable (due within one year)	$ 125,000	$ 250,000
Accounts payable	10,000	15,000
Accrued expenses	5,000	5,000
Taxes owed	7,000	7,500
Long-Term Liabilities		
Notes payable (due after one year)	$ 75,000	$ 80,000
Other	15,000	20,000
TOTAL LIABILITIES	$ 237,000	$ 377,500
NET WORTH (ASSETS minus LIABILITIES)	$	$
TOTAL LIABILITIES plus NET WORTH should equal ASSETS		

■ **Balance Sheet** A balance sheet is a dollar and cents description of your existing or projected business. *Based on the figures shown here, what is the net worth of your business for year 1 and year 2?*

The Balance Sheet

A balance sheet is a summary of a business' assets, liabilities, and owner's equity. Figure 36-8 shows a typical balance sheet.

Assets are anything of monetary value that you own. They are classified as either current or fixed. *Current assets* are expected to be converted into cash in the upcoming year. Examples of current assets include cash in the bank, accounts receivable (money owed to you by your customers), and inventory. *Fixed assets* are used over a period of years to operate your business. Examples of fixed assets include land, buildings, equipment, furniture, and fixtures. The assets of the business are important because they are needed to operate the business. When borrowing money to start a business, assets are also often used as collateral for the loan.

The next section of the balance sheet reports the liabilities of the business. Liabilities are amounts the business owes, including amounts owed for merchandise bought.

Liabilities are classified as current or long-term. *Current liabilities* are the debts the business expects to pay off during the upcoming business year. An example of current liabilities are accounts payable (money owed to suppliers), notes payable (money owed to a bank), taxes payable, and money owed to employees for salaries. *Long-term liabilities* are debts that are not due in the next 12 months. Some examples of long-term liabilities are mortgages and long-term loans.

The third section of the balance sheet is the equity, or net worth, section. When you start a new business, you will most likely invest some savings in the business. The amount of the savings is your equity, or ownership interest, in the business. The money invested will be used to buy assets and to operate the business. The assets owned by the business and the debts the business owes, then, affect your equity. Net worth is the difference between the assets of a business and its liabilities:

$$\text{Assets} - \text{Liabilities} = \text{Net Worth (Equity)}$$

Analysis of Financial Statements

Lenders use ratio analysis as a way of determining how a business is performing as compared to other businesses in the industry. Ratios tell whether a business has too much debt, is carrying too much inventory, or is not making enough gross profit. Information on the balance sheet and the income statement may be used to calculate these ratios. Lenders use ratio analysis to determine whether your business would be a good investment risk and whether it could repay a loan.

Figures on the balance sheet will show you the amount of your (stockholder's equity) ownership interest and the financial strength of a business on a given date. Figures on the income statement can give you an idea of how well the business is operating over a period of time. Sometimes you will need information from both statements to calculate the ratios. The following are some of the most basic operating ratios and how they may be used to analyze or interpret financial statements.

Liquidity Ratios are used to analyze the ability of a firm to meet its current debts. One Liquidity Ratio is *Current Ratio*. Its formula is current assets divided by current liabilities. In this case, the higher the ratio the better.

The *Acid Test Ratio* is used to see if the company can meet its short-term cash needs. Its formula is cash plus marketable securities plus net receivables divided by current liabilities.

Activity Ratios are used to determine how quickly assets can be turned into cash. One such ratio is *Accounts Receivable Turnover,* which tells you the number of days it takes to collect the money owed by customers. To calculate this ratio, divide net sales by average trade receivables. In this case, the lower the ratio, the better.

The *Stock Turnover Ratio* measures how many days it takes to turn the inventory. Excessive inventory ties up cash that a company can use to grow its business. The basic formula for this ratio is cost of goods sold divided by average inventory.

Profitability Ratios measure how well the company has operated the past year. One ratio is *Profit Margin on Sales*, which shows the rate of profit in percentages. This information is found on the income statement. Its formula is net income divided by net sales. Another Profitability Ratio is the *Rate of Return on Assets,* which shows how well you are doing when compared to other companies. The formula for this ratio is net income divided by average total assets.

A number of sources and directories exist to help you determine the common business ratios for your type of business. These include *Parameters of Small Businesses* published by the Accounting Corporation of America, *Costs of Doing Business* by Dun & Bradstreet, and *Annual Statement Studies* by Robert Morris Associates.

PRACTICE 4

Using the balance sheet shown below, answer the following questions:

1. How much are the total assets for Mountain Air Bikes?

2. How much are the total liabilities?

3. What is Mountain Air's net worth?

Mountain Air Bikes
Balance Sheet December 31, 20--

Current Assets	
Cash	$ 10,000
Accounts Receivable	15,000
Inventory	68,000
Fixed Assets	
Building	120,000
Equipment	80,000
Vehicles	30,000
Total Assets	$?
Current Liabilities	
Notes Payable	$3,000
Accounts Payable	12,000
Salaries Payable	5,000
Taxes Payable	1,000
Long-Term Liabilities	
Notes Payable	90,000
Total Liabilities	$?
Net Worth	$?

Cash Flow Statement

A cash flow statement is a monthly plan that shows when you anticipate cash coming into the business and when you expect to pay out cash. A cash flow statement helps you to see if you will have enough money when you need it to pay your bills.

Businesses need cash to pay bills, their employees, and unexpected expenses. The cash flow statement itemizes how much cash you started with, projected cash expenditures, and how and when you plan to receive cash. It also tells you when you will need to find additional funds and when you will have cash left over. Figure 36-9 on page 675 shows a typical cash flow statement for the first three months of operation. Most lenders will require you to estimate cash flow for the first year of operation.

When operating a retail business, one of your largest payments of cash will be for your merchandise. You will most likely have to pay for part of the merchandise in cash and part in credit. When estimating sales for the income statement, you include both cash and credit sales. In contrast, the cash flow statement shows only the amount you expect to receive in cash (for cash sales and payments for credit sales) during the month. You may receive payment for most of your credit sales 30 days after the sales.

You will also need to calculate your monthly costs for operating the business. Use the following steps to prepare a cash flow statement for your business.

STEP 1 Add the total cash on hand (in bank accounts) and money received from any loans to find your total start-up money.

STEP 2 Subtract the start-up costs to determine the amount of cash left for operation.

STEP 3 Enter the estimated cash you expect to receive from cash sales and credit sales for each month during the first year. Enter the amount of any income from business investments or additional loans.

STEP 4 Add all sources of cash receipts to find the total cash income for the month.

STEP 5 List the cost of goods that you will buy for your inventory. This cost should be separated into purchases for which you will pay cash and purchases on credit, which you will pay for the next month. For example, the cash flow statement shows goods bought on credit in Month 1. This is a payment for items bought on credit prior to the opening of the business. Add the cash and credit purchases to find the total cost of inventory purchases.

STEP 6 List the expenses you expect to pay during the month. These amounts are the same as those listed on the income statement, except for depreciation expense. Depreciation is a means of spreading the cost of an asset over a period of years. The amount of depreciation is not an actual payment made by the business, so it is not listed on the cash flow statement.

STEP 7 Total all expenses for the month.

STEP 8 List amounts that will be paid out for capital expenditures. A capital expenditure is money paid for an asset used to operate the business. The purchase of a delivery truck would be a capital expenditure.

STEP 9 List any other payments that will be made, such as repayment of the principal and interest for the loan.

STEP 10 Add all the cash expenditures (cost of inventory purchased, expenses, capital expenditures, and other payments). Subtract the total cash payments from the total cash received during the month to determine net cash flow. The amount of any cash payments that are higher than cash receipts should be placed in parentheses.

STEP 11 Add the beginning cash balance from the start-up column to the net cash flow for the month. The result is the cash surplus for the month. When the costs of operating the business are higher than income added to the beginning of the cash balance, the business will have a deficit rather than a surplus. In that case, the business will need additional cash for its operations. The amount is listed on the "Cash Needs" line. Figure 36-9 shows cash flow projections with a need for additional cash of $175 by the end of month 2. If you compare month 2 on the income statement, you will see net profit for the month. What the income statement does not take into account is how long it may take a business to collect the cash from sales made on credit.

FIGURE 36-9

Projected Cash Flow Statement

Beginning of Month:	Start-Up	Month 1	Month 2	Month 3
Cash in Bank	$25,000			
Loans	$ 5,000			
	$30,000			
Less Start-up Costs	$20,000			
Total Beginning Cash	$10,000			
Income (during month):				
Cash Sales		$20,000	$20,000	$27,000
*Credit Sales			10,000	13,000
Investment Income		200	200	200
Loans		0	0	0
Other Cash Income		0	0	0
TOTAL CASH INCOME		$20,200	$30,200	$40,200
Inventory Purchases				
Purchases for Cash		$15,000	$16,000	$14,750
*Purchases for Credit		4,500	5,000	8,000
Total Inventory Purchases		$19,500	$21,000	$22,750
Expenses				
Variable Expenses				
Advertising		300	350	350
Automobile		450	400	525
Dues & Subscriptions		15	20	18
Legal & Accounting		300	400	350
Miscellaneous		360	480	420
Office Supplies		120	160	140
Security		300	400	350
Telephone		90	120	105
Utilities		90	120	105
Fixed Expenses				
Insurance		300	300	300
Rent		800	800	800
Salaries/Taxes (including owner's)		5,600	5,600	5,600
Total Expenses		$ 8,725	$ 9,150	$ 9,063
Capital Expenditures				
Purchases of Equipment and Other Assets		1,000		
Other Payments				
Loan Repayment		600	600	600
TOTAL CASH EXPENDITURES		$29,825	$30,750	$32,413
NET CASH FLOW (end of month)	$10,000	($ 9,625)	($ 550)	$ 7,787
CASH SURPLUS (monthly)	$10,000	$ 375	($ 175)	$ 7,612
CASH NEEDS	0	0	$ 175	0

* payment based on previous month

■ **Projected Cash Flow Statement** A cash flow statement is a helpful financial tool for a business. *What is the purpose behind completing a monthly cash flow statement?*

Case Study

Your Own Personal Franchise

Ever dreamed of owning your own fast food restaurant? That's right, as unlikely as it may seem, you can own your own McDonald's, Burger King, or Taco Bell. This is possible thanks to the franchise. A franchise is an agreement between a corporation and an independent individual or group who wishes to operate the business locally.

Quickserve restaurants first began in 1925 with A&W walk-up root beer stands. Baskin-Robbins, Dairy Queen, Kentucky Fried Chicken, McDonald's, and Taco Bell followed. The continued growth of both full and quickserve restaurants since the 1990s has been attributed to a booming economy.

Quickserve restaurants have become an international phenomena. From the original international franchises led by KFC and McDonald's in the 1960s, more and more companies are opening overseas stores. Because of the continuing growth in dining on the go, there will be a continuing need for entrepreneurs to start and investors to finance quickserve restaurants.

Franchisers make up a big part of the teams that lead these quickserve restaurants. Many entrepreneurs look to quickserve restaurants because of the tremendous growth in overall restaurant industry sales. The restaurant industry has nearly $400 billion in annual sales and employs 11 million people or 8 percent of the total number of workers in the United States.

Most quickserve restaurants require $10,000 to $20,000 for an initial franchise fee. The total investment, excluding real estate, usually runs between $100,000 to $250,000, according to the International Franchise Association. As more restaurants are popping up, one can only imagine that quickserve restaurants equal quick cash for investors!

Case Study Review

1. Why is the concept of quickserve restaurants so popular with today's consumers?
2. In your opinion do most quickserve restaurants build their marketing concept around adults, children, or teenagers? Provide your rationale.

A MATTER OF ETHICS

3. Do you think that it is ethical to take the U.S. quickserve restaurants to overseas markets? Why or why not?

■ Loans

What can you do if you project that you will need additional money during the year? You should be able to borrow additional money if your business has potential and your balance sheet shows enough assets to serve as collateral. A loan can help you keep the business going during the start-up period and during slow sales months. When your cash flow projections indicate that you need to borrow money to meet monthly expenses, you will want to include monthly payments on the loan as a part of your cash needs for the rest of the year.

PRACTICE 5

1. You have total cash of $23,000 to start your business and start-up costs of $12,000. What amount of cash is available for operating the business?

2. Suppose cash income for the first three months is $100, $750, and $980. Total expenses for these same months are $4,800, $3,400, and $2,700. What is the cash flow for each month?

3. What is the cumulative amount of cash available at the end of each month?

Electronic Frontiers

Cyber Cash

The classic thwarted dream—an individual brainstorms an innovative and potentially successful business idea for a new business, but does not have the time to pursue it while making a living. This scenario is becoming a scene from the past, because the Internet has brought changes. The Web is becoming a vast source of capital for the entrepreneur who doesn't have the business connections or the time to find money the old-fashioned way. Web sites provide access to experts, free downloadable forms, and opportunities to chat with professionals who may be able to match new entrepreneurs with investors. A businessperson can post a proposal on a Web site where venture capitalists, banks, and others seeking investment opportunities get involved. In order to succeed, the entrepreneur can't show up unprepared. The standard principles of good business apply— a business plan and funding proposal are still necessary for consideration.

Thinking Critically

How would investors verify the legitimacy of an online start-up looking for capital?

36.2 ASSESSMENT

Reviewing Key Terms and Concepts

1. What financial document can you use to calculate a business's earnings and expenses?

2. What are the major categories that are calculated on the income statement?

3. How are payroll expenses calculated?

4. What is the purpose of a balance sheet?

5. What is a cash flow statement? What is its purpose?

Thinking Critically

6. What steps could a business take to improve cash flow?

Integrating Academic Skills

7. **MATH** Total first-quarter sales for the Leon Company were $285,000. Goods returned by customers amounted to $4,100. The cost of goods sold to customers was $112,000. The company's total fixed and variable expenses were $84,500. Interest paid on a loan was $2,400. Taxes were estimated at a rate of 20 percent. Calculate the following amounts: net sales, gross profit, net income from operations, net profit before taxes, and net profit after taxes.

Answers to Practice Problems

PRACTICE 1 (PAGE 660)

1. Total assets are $22,000 ($10,000 + $8,000 + $1,000 + $1,500 + $1,500 = $22,000).

2. Total liabilities are $10,000 ($7,000 + $2,500 + $500 = $10,000).

3. Net worth is $12,000 ($22,000 − $10,000 = $12,000).

PRACTICE 2 (PAGE 662)

Total costs for the first quarter are $27,600 [$18,000 + ($3,200 × 3) = $27,600]; Total costs for the year are $56,400 [$18,000 + ($3,200 × 12) = $56,400].

PRACTICE 3 (PAGE 671)

Mountain-Air Bikes
Income Statement For the Year Ended December 31, 20--

Net Sales	$212,015
Cost of Goods Sold	109,614
Gross Profit	$102,401
Operating Expenses:	
Salaries	$ 24,019
Rent	11,211
Utilities	4,514
Advertising	2,422
Total Operating Expenses	$ 42,166
Net Income from Operations	$ 60,235

1. $109,614

2. $102,401 ($212,015 − $109,614 = $102,401)

3. $42,166 ($24,019 + $11,211 + $4,514 + $2,422 = $42,166)

4. Salaries

5. $60,235 ($102,401 − $42,166 = $60,235)

PRACTICE 4 (PAGE 673)

Mountain Air Bikes
Balance Sheet December 31, 20--

Current Assets	
Cash	$ 10,000
Accounts Receivable	15,000
Inventory	68,000
Fixed Assets	
Building	120,000
Equipment	80,000
Vehicles	30,000
Total Assets	$323,000
Current Liabilities	
Notes Payable	$ 3,000
Accounts Payable	12,000
Salaries Payable	5,000
Taxes Payable	1,000
Long-Term Liabilities	
Notes Payable	90,000
Total Liabilities	$ 111,000
Net Worth	$212,000

1. $323,000 ($10,000 + $15,000 + $68,000 + $120,000 + $80,000 + $30,000 = $323,000)

2. $111,000 ($3,000 + $12,000 + $5,000 + $1,000 + $90,000 = $111,000)

3. $212,000 ($323,000 − $111,000 = $212,000)

PRACTICE 5 (PAGE 677)

1. The amount of cash available for business operations is $11,000 ($23,000 − $12,000 = $11,000).

2. The cash flow is as follows: month 1; ($4,700) [$100 − $4,800 = ($4,700)]; month 2; ($2,650) [$750 − $3,400 = ($2,650)]; month 3; ($1,720) [$980 − $2,700 = ($1,720)].

3. The cumulative cash available at the end of each month is as follows: month 1; $6,300 ($11,000 − $4,700 = $6,300); month 2; $3,650 ($6,300 − $2,650 = $3,650); month 3; $1,930 ($3,650 − $1,720 = $1,930).

Careers in Marketing

FINANCIAL SERVICES

Amanda Patterson
Financial Analyst Controller
UBS Warburg

Career Facts

What does your job entail?

"Financial analysts evaluate the cost and income effects of decisions that a company makes. Another job duty is forecasting the income from various investments and analyzing the costs of capital improvements. Financial analysts prepare and present budgets, income statements, and other financial reports. I am responsible for overseeing the process and accounting for trades that are booked by the Emerging Markets desk. My workload may be more intense during the end of the month when reports are issued. I have a routine of daily procedures that are required every day, and from there, specific projects may be assigned during the month."

What kind of training did you have?

"I have a background in accounting. I worked in public accounting in auditing and then moved away from auditing in this job. My training has included both formal classes and informal working with mentors."

What skills are most important?

"All jobs require you to be able to write effectively and properly. This specific job requires above-average math and computer skills as well. You must be accurate, detail-oriented, and familiar with laws and regulations related to investments and taxation."

What is your key to success?

"In my experience, the key to success is to be open to new opportunities. The hardest thing to accept when I started working was that I didn't know everything. There were times when I felt like I didn't know anything! It is necessary to be self-confident and willing to learn as you go along. The learning experience is challenging, but there are always people willing to help you."

Education and Training: High school students desiring to work in financial services should take college preparatory courses. Additional classes in business law, math, and administration as well as classes in marketing, accounting economics, and computer science are recommended. Most employers require applicants to have an MBA degree. Preparation specific to the industry of employment may also be required.

Aptitudes, Abilities, and Skills: Above-average ability to work with numerical data and to understand financial concepts is required, in addition to good communication and computer skills.

Career Outlook: Average growth for the employment of financial analysts is projected through the year 2006. The growth in interstate and international banking as well as international investing may create greater than average demand for financial analysts.

Career Path: An MBA from a desirable school and a strong background in computer science are increasingly important for candidates seeking jobs as financial analysts. Success as a financial analyst can lead to financial management positions such as treasurer, controller, or portfolio manager.

Thinking Critically
How has technology increased efficiency in a career such as that of a financial analyst controller?

VOCABULARY REVIEW

Review the definitions for each of the following vocabulary terms with a classmate.

- personal financial statement
- asset
- liability
- start-up costs
- income statement
- gross sales
- net sales
- net income
- interest
- principal
- balance sheet
- net worth
- cash flow statement

FACT AND IDEA REVIEW

1. Why are financial documents important in a business plan? (36.1)

2. What factors determine start-up costs for a new business? (36.1)

3. What are personal costs? (36.1)

4. List the steps in projecting income for a new business. (36.2)

5. Compare fixed and variable expenses. (36.2)

6. What does a balance sheet show? (36.2)

7. Explain the difference between current and fixed assets. (36.2)

8. What is net worth? (36.2)

9. What different type of financial information does an income statement, a balance sheet, and a cash flow statement provide? (36.2)

THINKING CRITICALLY

1. Many states and the federal government have economic development programs devoted to the needs of small business. Why do a majority of economic development loans originate from banks rather than from the state or federal agencies?

2. What sources could you use to determine the total amount of cash needed to start a business?

3. What do you think are some of the legal issues that have impact on financial statements?

4. What do you think a lender looks for in considering a loan application for a new business?

5. What are some techniques that a small business owner can use to cultivate a good relationship with a local lending institution?

BUILDING WORKPLACE SKILLS

1. **Human Relations** A friend has decided to open an Internet consulting business. He believes that he will not need extra capital for personal living costs—the business will generate enough revenue when it gets started to cover this. What would you tell your friend about his lack of concern about personal living costs?

2. **Technology** Locate the *Inc.com* Web site on the Internet. Download the *Initial Cash Requirements Worksheet* and use the template and your estimate of expenses to calculate the total amount of cash needed to start a new business.

1. **Finding Franchise Opportunities** Find the International Franchise Association Web site on the Internet. Find an existing franchise opportunity to investigate. Use a word processing program to write a report describing the franchise opportunity, including the type of franchise, primary product or service, potential for growth and other pertinent facts about it.

2. **Calculating Projected Cash Flow** Use a spreadsheet program to calculate projected cash flow for a six-month period. Use the cash flow information to assist you in developing the financial section of a business plan.

3. **Preparing an Income Statement** Locate the American Express Small Business Exchange Web site on the Internet. Under "Financials" on the home page find the template for preparing an income statement. Place your projected income figures into the template to prepare an income statement for the financial section of your business plan.

4. **Developing a Personal Financial Statement** Develop a personal financial statement using a word processing program and a spreadsheet program. Create a one-year report based on the average month, including personal living expenses, projected monthly sales, fixed and variable expenses, estimated profits, and start-up costs. Include the cost of equipment, supplies, and inventory.

LINKING SCHOOL TO WORK

Information and Foundation Skills Interview your supervisor or training station sponsor regarding three business ratios that have proven to be most helpful to running the business. Identify the ratios and the reasons your supervisor has found them to be helpful.

THE DECA CONNECTION

Role Play: Bookkeeper

Situation You are to assume the role of recently hired part-time bookkeeper for a newly opened home repair service. The business owner (judge) has excellent technical skills but little experience with financial statements.

Activity The business owner (judge) has asked you to explain the difference between an income statement, a balance sheet, and a cash flow statement. He has also asked you to explain to him how to develop a cash flow statement for the business.

Evaluation You will be evaluated on how well you meet the following performance indicators:
- Explain the concept of accounting
- Explain the nature of balance sheets
- Describe the nature of cash-flow statements
- Prepare cash-flow statements
- Make oral presentations

inter NET CONNECTION

Investigate Funding Sources
Locate the Quicken Web site and find the *Quick Pick Chart for Financing Sources.* Investigate one primary source for long-term financing of a start-up business.

Connect
- Select one of the primary sources of long-term financing.
- Summarize the information presented in a 2-page report.

The Zazz Lab

A Sports and Entertainment Marketing Simulation

WELCOME

Welcome to Zazz Sports and Entertainment Marketing Company. Zazz is devoted to serving the needs of its clients who include college, university, and professional sports teams, professional athletes, sporting events, and sports arenas plus major consumer product corporations, as well as television networks and movie studios. As an intern, you will have the opportunity to work on different clients' projects. All of your work will be assigned and reviewed by your department supervisor.

PREPARE A BUSINESS PROPOSAL FOR A NEW AMUSEMENT PARK

SITUATION

Zazz wants to tap the amusement and/or water park market. You need to research the amusement and water park industry to test the idea's feasibility.

ASSIGNMENT

Your supervisor wants you to prepare a business proposal for a new amusement and/or water park that Zazz would own and operate. You will need to study the market for this type of venture, as well as costs involved in a project of this magnitude. The organizational structure for operation and a comprehensive marketing plan are required. You have also been asked to design the theme and attractions to be included in this magnificent complex. Location and weather are important factors, as is park management. A "guest friendly" atmosphere needs to be established, from the park design to the training of employees. Practical considerations, such as the location of food services and infrastructure, are vital. Parking, the configuration of lines for rides, and customer hospitality services are also important details. The success of an amusement park is based on customer satisfaction with the experience—return rates and guest recommendations are very important.

Tools and Resources

To complete this assignment, you will need to conduct research at a library or on the Internet. You will also need a word processing program, a spreadsheet program, and presentation software. Trade publications and organizations that may be helpful are *Splash Magazine*, published by the World Waterpark Association, *Amusement Today*, and the Themed Entertainment Association.

Research

Research theme amusement parks and water parks. Identify the demographics and psychographics of typical attendees. Research locations and Web sites. Identify major competitors and their market shares. Identify strategies used by competitors with regard to product (theme and design of park), place (location), price (individual and group rates), and promotion (message and media used). Obtain samples of the competitors' park designs and promotional materials. Research the cost to build and operate a new amusement/water park. Consider the number of employees needed, employee training, and the park's mission statement.

Report

Prepare a written report and a computer presentation for your supervisor. Use a word processing program to create a double-spaced report. Use a spreadsheet program to prepare pie charts to depict market share and other variables where parts of a whole are shown, as well as financial reports. Arrange your written report around the following headings:

- Analysis of the amusement/water park market
  - Market size and trends
  - Competitors
    - Location and market share
  - Customer profile
- Proposed amusement/water park
  - Theme and design
  - Suggested location
    - Weather
    - Trading area analysis
      - Population
      - Economic factors
    - Transportation—highways and roads
    - Other possible locations
  - Market segment analysis
    - Geographics, demographics, and psychographics
- Planned operation of amusement/water park
  - Proposed organization
    - Legal ownership
    - Mission statement
    - Personnel needs/training
  - Proposed products and services offered
    - Attractions
    - Food services
    - Merchandise (gift shops, souvenirs)
  - Proposed marketing plan
    - Pricing (individual/group)
    - Promotional plans
    - Selling
      - Major selling points—feature/benefit chart
      - Training sales office personnel
- Proposed financing
  - Project income statement
  - Projected balance sheet
  - Projected capital needs
  - Project cash flow statement
- Conclusion

Presentation and Evaluation

Present your ideas in a written report and an oral presentation. You will be evaluated on your oral presentation skills, including:

- Knowledge of the amusement/water park market
- Expertise in preparing a business proposal
- Comprehensiveness of business plan
- Creativity
- Continuity of presentation
- Voice quality
- Enthusiasm
- Eye contact

Portfolio

Print a copy of your completed report and presentation for your Portfolio.

THE DECA CONNECTION

DECA Hospitality and Recreation Marketing Research Event
Conducting market research to determine who would attend an amusement/water park near your community and what they would want included in the design and operation of such a park could be a possible topic for this event.

DECA Entrepreneurship Participating Event
Developing and presenting your proposal for a new amusement/water park is a potential topic for this event.

DECA Entrepreneurship Written Event
Writing a comprehensive business proposal for a new amusement/water park, complete with details and financial plans, could be a topic for this event.

DECA Advertising Campaign Event
Creating an advertising campaign for an existing amusement/water park in your community is a potential resource for this event.

DECA Sports and Entertainment Marketing Management Team Decision-Making Event
Working on this project with a partner would make the experience similar to what is expected in a DECA Team Decision-Making Event.

Portfolio

Assessing Your Job Needs

In this unit, you will assess your own needs and attributes. While doing this, keep a record of your assessment in a file or notebook titled "Career Planning Notebook." You might label this information "Self-Assessment File." Summarize your various assessments in paragraph form or, where appropriate, using a rating scale. Label the second part of your career planning notebook "Careers Assessment." In this section, include records of all your research on careers that you investigate. Having written records of all of your self-assessment and careers assessment information in one notebook will help you evaluate your choices and make your career decision.

EMPLOYMENT HISTORY

Career and Professional Development

Unit Overview

The work you do to earn a living will most likely become the central activity around which you plan your daily life. You'll spend close to half your waking hours working, and your career will span about 40 years. The focus of this unit—career planning—is the logical conclusion to *Marketing Essentials*.

Chapter 37 provides a six-step procedure to guide you in assessing your own needs and attributes along with the demands and opportunities of careers. It also shows you how to evaluate career choices, make a career decision, and develop a plan of action. Chapter 38 provides guidance in finding and applying for a job, including how to use the Internet for these purposes.

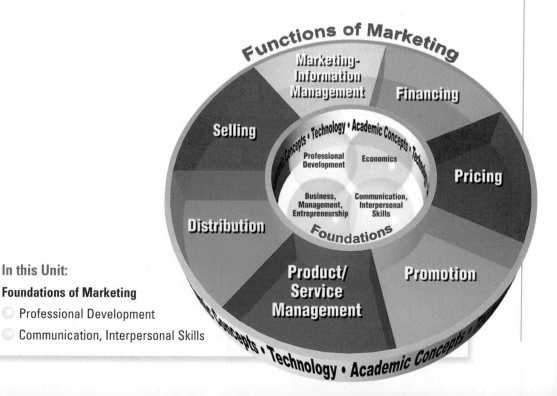

In this Unit:

Foundations of Marketing

○ Professional Development

○ Communication, Interpersonal Skills

Identifying Career Opportunities

Marketing: What It Takes

Marketing Yourself
Two very important elements of marketing any product are knowing your product well and researching the market in which you plan to sell the product. As you join the "race" to make a career choice, *you* are the product—and the world is your potential market.

WHAT WILL YOU DO?
What are some of the things you will want to learn about yourself and your potential market?

Important Career Decisions

Choosing a Career

Like many high school students, you may not have thought about what kind of career you would like to have. A career differs from a job in that it is a series of progressively more responsible jobs in one field or in related fields. Choosing a career requires careful thought and preparation. The following six-step procedure will help guide you in making important career choices:

1. Conduct a self-assessment.
2. Identify possible career choices.
3. Gather information on each choice.
4. Evaluate your choices.
5. Make your decision.
6. Plan how you will reach your goal.

■ Assessing Yourself

The first step in your career search is to conduct a self-assessment. You can begin by assessing your values, interest, and skills and aptitudes. Then you can assess your personality, learning style, lifestyle goals, and work environment and relationship preferences. As you make your assessment, record your findings in a notebook. Label the notebook "Self-Assessment File." Summarize your various assessments in paragraph form or, where appropriate, using a rating scale.

YOUR VALUES Values are beliefs that guide the way people live. Just as people have different abilities and personalities, they also have different values. Defining your system of values is essential in choosing a career. When you understand your values, you know what you want out of life. You can then choose a career that is suited to your values.

You can identify your values by identifying the kinds of actions that are important to you. If you are willing to work very hard to succeed, you value achievement. If you want your work to be acknowledged, you value recognition.

YOUR LIFESTYLE GOALS The word *lifestyle* refers to the way you spend your time, energy, and money. Your lifestyle goals reflect your vision of how you see yourself living in the future. Your career has a great effect on your lifestyle. The happiest, most satisfied people have the greatest control over their lifestyle. Most of these people are well educated, motivated to succeed, and have incomes well above the average.

● What You'll Learn

- **How to assess your values, lifestyle goals, interests, skills and aptitudes**
- **How to appraise your personality**
- **How to visualize your work environment and relationship preferences**

● Why It's Important

Understanding yourself is the first step in finding a career you'll enjoy. It is necessary to know your own attributes well when trying to select the most satisfying career for you. This section will help you begin to assess your attributes so you can match them with the right career.

Key Terms

- values
- lifestyle goals
- aptitude

As a child, your lifestyle was dependent almost entirely upon your family and your relationships with family members. As a student, your life revolves around your school, your studies, and your friends. As an adult, your lifestyle is made up of many things, but the following are major influences:

- where you live (city or rural area)
- the type of housing in which you live
- your choice of foods, clothing, and leisure activities
- your mode of transportation
- your relationships with your family and friends
- the work you do to earn a living

If attaining a certain lifestyle is important to you, then choosing a career that will allow you to reach your lifestyle goal is essential. Your career is the key because your earnings will pay for your lifestyle. The ideal career will be compatible with all of the other elements in life as well.

YOUR INTERESTS It is likely that you will spend 30 to 40 years working—so you will want to choose work that interests you. Your interests are the things you enjoy doing.

When you research careers, you will make judgments about how interesting each career would be. Your judgments will probably be more accurate if you first survey your own interests. To evaluate your interests, write down the things you like to do, including leisure activities, school activities, favorite classes, sports, and social activities. If you feel that your list is too short or unvaried, then you may want to try out some new activities to learn whether you enjoy them.

Another way to find out about your interests is to take a career interest survey. A career interest survey is similar to a test, but there are no right or wrong answers. You are given a long list of activities and you decide how much you would like doing each of them. Then you score your own survey to learn which career areas you would find most interesting. Your school counselor or marketing teacher can probably arrange for you to take one of these surveys.

YOUR SKILLS AND APTITUDES Values and interests are important in self-assessment because they help you picture what you want your life to become. They may even suggest certain careers. It takes

■ **Work or Play?** Your interests or hobbies can be a guide to help you narrow your career search. *What careers might be related to this young man's interest in cars?*

certain skills, and an aptitude for the work, to be successful in any career. An aptitude is an ability, or a potential, for learning a certain skill. Pursuing a career without having an aptitude for the required skills might prove to be a struggle instead of a pleasure—and real success would be harder to achieve. A person who can't describe the benefits of products won't have much success selling. You can see that it is important to identify your aptitudes before you choose a career.

Begin a new page in your self-assessment file, and list all the things you have done well. Do you find it easy to sell cookies, candy bars, or other items that your DECA chapter sells to raise funds? Are you good at organizing committees and getting everyone to do their jobs? Is math easy for you? Have you won any prizes for your creative ability?

The grades you earn in school may indicate some of your aptitudes. If most of your written reports earned A's and B's, you probably have an aptitude for writing. There are several tests that can help identify areas of strength.

Perhaps you have already developed certain skills that will be useful in a career that interests you. List them on a separate sheet of paper in your self-assessment file and update your list as you develop new skills. Your skills list will be very helpful when you apply for a job.

Case Study

Making Your Career Decision: From Doodles to Prime Time

While growing up, Matt Groening spent his time doodling when he was supposed to be working on his spelling. His unconventional personality made people think that he would not go far in life, but he proved them wrong.

After graduating from college, he went to Los Angeles to make a living as a writer. He worked at a sewage treatment plant, and then as a chauffeur. He kept up his doodling, and in 1977 he invented a comic strip that was syndicated to 250 newspapers. He quit his chauffeur job and began to make a living from his doodling.

In 1986, Groening was asked to create a 2½ minute animated feature for a television variety show and "The Simpsons" was born. In 1990, the half-hour "Simpsons" series began—the first animated prime time TV program in 20 years. It immediately became the most popular show on television. Ten years later the show was still among the ten most-watched TV programs in America every week, in addition to airing in many other countries. Simpsons merchandise is sold all over the world.

Matt Groening turned his love of doodling into a very profitable career. His interests and aptitude led him to the work that was right for him.

Case Study Review

1. What interests do you have that could lead to a career? What aptitudes?
2. What sort of personality do you think a television cartoonist needs?

A MATTER OF ETHICS

3. Sometimes the television network tries to control the content of the Simpsons. Do you think it is ethical for the network to overrule the creators of the show?

YOUR PERSONALITY Your personality is the combination of all of the unique qualities that make you who you are. Understanding your personality characteristics will help you to determine what types of work situations will best suit you. There are tests that you can take that will help you identify your personality type. It may not be necessary, however, to take a test to learn how your personality will fit with certain careers. To assess your personality traits, use a new page in your self-assessment file to list words that describe you. As you perform this exercise, remember that there is no right or wrong kind of personality. There are only different kinds of people.

FIGURE 37-1

DATA, PEOPLE, THINGS

All jobs involve working with data, people, or things. Most jobs involve working with combinations of these.

DATA

Accountants work mostly with data. Do you like doing involved math problems? Do the hours seem to pass quickly when you are working on a computer? If you answered yes, then you probably like working with data.

PEOPLE

Salespeople deal mostly with people. Think about your own preferences. Do you prefer working with large groups or with one person at a time? Do you get lonely working alone for hours on a project? A little reflection will probably tell you how much you like working with people.

COMBINATIONS OF DATA, PEOPLE, THINGS

In most marketing careers, you will work with more than one of these three. A hotel registration clerk works mostly with people and data.

THINGS

Carpenters spend most of their time working with things. Do you enjoy woodworking, building, working on your car, or fixing things around the house? If so, then you probably like working with things.

YOUR WORK ENVIRONMENT Your work environment refers to where you work—the place and the working conditions. Working conditions include sights, sounds, and smells.

Many factors affect working conditions, such as geographic location. If you are a carpenter who works outdoors, your working conditions would be quite different in California as opposed to Alaska.

Whether you work during the day or at night also affects your working conditions. If you prefer not to work nights, there are many careers you should rule out. For example, doctors and nurses as well as hotel and restaurant employees often work evening shifts and night shifts. While an event planner may book events during the day, he or she is often required to be on hand to see that things go smoothly during the event, regardless of what time of day or night it is held.

You don't have to know all your preferences about working conditions now, but start thinking about them. When you read about the working conditions of a certain career, you will have a better idea of your criteria for a positive work environment.

YOUR RELATIONSHIP PREFERENCES All jobs require working with data, people, or things—alone or in some combination (See Figure 37-1 on page 690). These categories can form the basis for describing different kinds of careers. Since any career you choose will likely involve an overlapping of these categories, think about which interests you most.

REAL WORLD MARKETING

Buxx for Young Bucks!

In its latest effort to capture a portion of the $153 billion teens spend annually, Visa USA has introduced VISA Buxx. Visa Buxx allows teens to spend money loaded onto cards by their parents. The card looks like a credit card and can be used to spend online or in stores to get cash at automated teller machines. Visa Buxx are not attached to any line of credit or bank accounts, but parents receive statements and can track their teen's spending. One added safety feature—parents must acknowledge they've given their teens a financial literacy test.

Thinking Critically
Why is Visa requiring that kids take financial literacy tests before using VISA Buxx?

37.1 ASSESSMENT

Reviewing Key Terms and Concepts

1. What should you consider when conducting a self-assessment?

2. What are values?

3. What are three influences on the lifestyle of an adult?

4. Why is it important to know what skills and aptitudes you have?

Thinking Critically

5. Why is it important to set goals? What can happen to someone who does not set goals?

Integrating Academic Skills

6. **COMMUNICATION** Select an area vocational school, technical institute, community college, college, or university in which you are interested. Write a letter requesting information about entrance requirements and courses of study. Conclude with a request for an admission application.

Career Planning

• What You'll Learn

- How to complete a career assessment
- Where to look for career research resources

• Why It's Important

The more career information you have, the easier it will be to decide which one is right for you. Research can provide you with a wealth of information on subjects such as salaries, working conditions, and prospects in your field.

Key Terms

- career outlook
- *Dictionary of Occupational Titles (DOT)*
- *Occupational Outlook Handbook (OOH)*
- *Guide for Occupational Exploration (GOE)*
- career consultation
- internship

Career Assessment Planning

Once you identify careers that interest you, it's time to research if those careers are right for you. Even if you have already chosen a career goal, select two or three other careers to research and assess. You will save time by learning about several careers now if your first choice doesn't work out.

Now begin a new section in your career planning notebook and label it "Career Assessment File." Later, you will compare this information with that in your self-assessment section to help make your career decision.

■ Work Values

Certain values are important to success on the job. These include honesty, dependability, diligence, and team spirit. Each job and career field has its own special work values. Most retail marketing careers would place a high value on working long hours, getting along with others, coping with stress, and being willing initially to work for lower pay.

Study the work involved in potential jobs, but also look beyond the duties and responsibilities. Consider the values that are important for success in each field.

■ Lifestyle Fit

Some careers will fit your lifestyle goals better than others will. Try to determine how compatible each career will be with the other elements of your lifestyle goals.

You probably don't want a career that requires a lot of travel if spending time with your family is important to you. Similarly, you probably won't look for a job that requires working weekends if you cherish weekends for religious or leisure activities. Look for a career that enhances the other elements of your lifestyle, not one that conflicts with them.

■ Salaries and Benefits

Consider if each potential career will provide the financial support for your desired lifestyle. You must look at both salary and benefits such as paid vacations, life insurance, health insurance, and a pension (or retirement) plan.

Companies and businesses offer employees different kinds of benefit packages. Paid vacations will be a priority if you like to travel. Life insurance is especially important for families, and you can save money if your employer pays for this or offers lower premiums through an employer-sponsored group plan. The high cost of health care today makes health insurance a necessity. Some employers pay the premiums for all their employees, while others have group plans that save you money. You may not think a retirement plan is important because retirement seems a long way off. Many older workers find themselves working into their seventies because they are not covered by such a plan. Others must rely on social security alone, which barely supports the most basic lifestyle.

Some careers provide more benefits than others do. Some, for example, regularly pay bonuses, give discounts on merchandise, or offer low interest loans on homes and autos. Others make recreational facilities available to their employees.

■ Career Outlook

Suppose you find a career that seems interesting, one in which you could do well and one that will satisfy your lifestyle goals. You now need to research the career outlook, or the availability of jobs in the field. A job with a good career outlook is one in an area that is growing and provides opportunities for advancement.

■ Higher Education Many careers require a college degree even for entry-level jobs. *What kinds of jobs do you know of that require only a high school diploma?*

■ Education and Training

Every job requires a certain level of education and training. Some require only graduation from high school or minimal post-high school education or training. Others will require four or more years of college.

Look at the education and training requirements of various careers. What if the career that fits your values, interests, aptitudes, and lifestyle goals requires more education and training than you are willing to pursue?

■ Duties and Responsibilities

Jobs are primarily distinguished by their duties and responsibilities. Job duties are the things you will be doing on the job. Responsibilities are the things for which you must be accountable. A duty may be to type business reports, while responsibilities include completing the work neatly, correctly, and on time. Learn all you can about the duties and responsibilities of each job you are considering. This offers certainty as you search for a career that you will find interesting and in which you can excel.

■ Skills and Aptitudes Required

You know that it takes more than just an interest in a job or career to succeed. Every job requires different types and levels of skills. First, you need to determine what skills are necessary to handle the required duties and responsibilities; then you can determine what aptitudes would be helpful in learning those skills. Suppose you are considering a career in advertising. When you look at the job description for an advertising copywriter, you learn that the skill used most is writing. In the event that you haven't done much writing, you must ask yourself what you can do to develop your writing skills.

Consider another example: when you look at the job description of an advertising layout artist, you learn that you would need good artistic skills. Perhaps you've done a lot of sketching and are developing your art skills further. You must determine if you have an aptitude for sketching and design work.

■ Helpful Personality Traits

You have probably noticed that people in certain careers have similar personality traits. Does the type of work you do affect your personality? Do people with certain personality traits tend to choose specific careers? Do people with similar personalities choose the same type of career? The answer to these questions is yes.

Your personality is affected by all your life experiences. Your job is likely to become the central activity in your life, therefore it will affect your personality. Your interpersonal relationships with other people at your workplace will also shape your personality.

A popular belief about salespeople is that they must have outgoing personalities. This is not completely true. You learned in the sales unit of this book that many successful salespeople do not have outgoing personalities; in some cases, they simply enjoy helping other people. Someone who is very quiet and uncomfortable with strangers however, will have a difficult time on most sales jobs.

■ Work Environment

Working conditions vary from one job to another. There are big differences in the work environments of an office, a department store, and a factory.

As you study the working conditions of the careers you have selected, try to learn these things about each job:

- Is the work done indoors or outdoors?
- Is the work done sitting down or standing up?
- Is the work environment dusty, smelly, or especially noisy?
- Is the work environment dangerous? What are the risks?
- Is the work physically tiring (does it involve a lot of lifting, stretching, or walking)?
- Is the work done on a 9–5 shift, at night, on weekends, or from home?

■ **Work Environment** Working conditions include the physical environment you will be working in, as well as the people you will be working with. *Which aspects of the working conditions of these three workplaces do you think you would like? Which would you rather avoid?*

■ Work Relationships

As you research careers, note the data/people/ things relationships in the specific jobs you have selected. Most jobs require working with other people to some extent. Some jobs, like those in retail sales, offer constant exposure to people. Other jobs require you to work almost constantly with data or things.

Research Resources

To research careers, you will need to gather information from a variety of sources. You'll find current information at libraries or on the Internet. You can also learn a great deal through career consultations and actual work experiences.

■ Libraries

You can find many good career information resources in your school or public library. Many school libraries have a special section devoted to career information. You will find books, magazines, pamphlets, films, videos, and special references with information about careers.

The U.S. Department of Labor publishes three reference books that are especially helpful in career research. They are the *Dictionary of Occupational Titles,* the *Occupational Outlook Handbook,* and the *Guide for Occupational Exploration.* Most school and public libraries have these reference books.

The *Dictionary of Occupational Titles (DOT)* describes about 20,000 jobs and their relationships with data, people, and things. Several hundred more jobs that have emerged since the publication of the dictionary are defined in the *DOT Supplement.* Following each job title you will find a nine-digit code number. Use this number to locate the job description you want in the front section of the *DOT.* The *DOT* number provides a sophisticated way of classifying jobs into career clusters and worker functions. Recall that every job requires a worker to function to some degree in relation to data, people, and things. The middle three digits of the *DOT* number indicate the nature of this relationship for the given job title. This is explained fully in the *DOT* introduction.

Write down the *DOT* numbers of the jobs you are researching. This will save you some time because other sources also use these numbers to organize their information.

■ **Finding it at the Library** Public libraries often have sections devoted to career research. *What might you find at the library that could help you discover the right career?*

Job Listings...At Your Service

You may be aware of the popularity of Web sites that help you find a job. Some companies have taken it one step further, making the search process even easier for job seekers. Hotjobs.com is one Web site that offers job search agents. Job seekers submit a form listing their job criteria. Every day a search agent checks any new job listings to check for matching criteria; if the agent finds a match, it will send an e-mail informing the job seeker. Hotjobs.com adds hundreds of new jobs to their database every day. This service keeps seekers updated while cutting down on the work!

Thinking Critically

What other helpful services can job search Web sites offer?

The *Occupational Outlook Handbook (OOH)* provides information on more than two hundred occupations and is updated every two years. It is especially helpful and easy to use in locating such information as:

- Education and training requirements
- Usual hours of work
- Working conditions
- Salaries
- Job or career outlook
- Sources of additional information

Information on salaries and job outlook can change quickly. You should always use the latest edition of the *OOH*. Refer to the supplement to *OOH*, the *Occupational Outlook Quarterly*, for the most recent information.

The *Guide for Occupational Exploration (GOE)* is a reference that organizes the world of work into 12 interest areas that are subdivided into work groups and subgroups. The interest area Selling, for example, is divided into the three work groups: *Sales Technology, General Sales,* and *Vending.* Each work group is further divided into the subgroups *Wholesale, Retail, Demonstration, Sales,* and five others. The *GOE* includes the following types of career information:

- Kind of work done
- Skills and abilities needed
- Interests and aptitudes
- Required background or preparation

■ The Internet

The Internet is becoming a primary source for researching any topic. Career information is no exception. Information that was previously most easily accessible in a library is now available on the Internet, enabling you to do your research from home.

The Internet offers a multitude of career planning resources. You can find everything from accepted starting salaries to projected career paths. The Internet is not only a helpful tool while searching for a career, but for staying on top of developments in your career once you have chosen it.

In 1998, the U.S. Labor Department introduced the Occupational Information Network (O*NET). This online career information database was designed to eventually replace the DOT. O*NET online offers an interactive framework for exploring career information. You can enter key words relating to the career you wish to research, or you could search on Web sites that are devoted to career options.

BRIGHT IDEAS
Slippery Business

Does the name Frank Zamboni sound familiar? If you are a hockey fan it might, because he is responsible for the invention that has simplified the process of maintaining the ice. Having been in the refrigeration and ice-block business for some years, Frank and some family members decided to build an open-air skating rink in 1940. It was one of the largest at the time. The intense Southern California sun and hot winds were one challenge that reduced ice quality. The Zamboni family covered the rink with a dome and came up against the next challenge—keeping the ice smooth. At the time, resurfacing meant pulling a scraper behind a trailer, scooping away the shavings, spraying water, using a squeegee to clean it, and finally allowing it to freeze. The process took more than an hour. It wasn't long before Frank began engineering a machine that would do all of that yet reduce time and effort—the Zamboni.

Thinking Creatively
What are some other inventions that could simplify a sports game?

■ Career Consultations

A career consultation is an informational interview with a professional who works in a career that interests you. You can learn about the demands and opportunities of a career from someone with experience. You also get the opportunity to learn about the day-to-day realities on a job. Those who have met the challenges of a career are usually happy to talk about it.

Ask both your teacher and your counselor for suggestions about whom you should interview. They may have lists of people in the community who enjoy talking with young people about their work. Family members and friends of the family can also sometimes give you leads.

When you don't get some good suggestions from others, use the telephone directory to compile your own list of potential interviewees. You can then call each person from the list to find out whom you should interview. Suppose you are interested in becoming a retail buyer. Buyers are not listed under their own category in the Yellow Pages, so you will have to call the store that you are interested in first to get the name of someone you can contact.

It is always best to interview the person where he or she works. That's usually more convenient for the person. It will also give you a chance to see the workplace and form your own opinions. You may even get to see others actively engaged in the work you want to learn about.

You may also consider "shadowing" a person who works in a career field that interests you. This experience lets you follow a professional on the job for the day to see what the work is like—the daily duties, responsibilities, and challenges. Some schools set aside Groundhog Day for this purpose, while at others your guidance counselor can match you with a person in the career of your choice.

Before any career consultation, prepare a list of questions that you want to ask. Here are some suggestions.

- How do you spend most of your time on the job? Which work activities do you like most?
- What skills will I need to do this type of work? What skills will I need to advance?
- What education and training will I need? Can I complete some of the training after I begin working?
- How much time do you spend working with data? With people? With things?
- Will there be an increase in job opportunities in this field over the next several years? What impact will automation and new technology have on job opportunities in the next few years?

■ **Work to Learn** Work experience programs can give you valuable first-hand knowledge of what a job is like. *What can you learn from participating in such a program?*

■ On-the-Job Experience

You can learn a great deal about a career by reading and by interviewing those who work in the field. There are many things, however, that you cannot learn about a job until you try it for yourself.

Many students work part-time after school, on weekends, or during the summer months. If you have an idea of what career you might be interested in pursuing, it is great experience to find an entry-level position in that field. Even if you are not sure exactly what you want to do, a part-time job can teach you valuable working skills. If you choose a job in a career field that interests you, you will benefit in the following ways:

- You can try out some of the work activities in your career field and decide how much you like doing them.

- You can experience the work environment of the career.

- You can develop work habits that will help you succeed in your career.

- You can broaden your understanding of the world of work and smooth the transition from school to work.

- You can make career contacts that can serve as mentors or assist you when you are searching for a job later.

- You can build up your résumé which will grow as you gain more working experience.

Does your school have a work-experience program? You may know it by another name, such as cooperative education, cooperative work-experience, work study, or diversified occupations. Many vocational work-experience programs include the word cooperative in their names because the programs represent a cooperative effort by schools and employers. In these programs, the teacher-coordinator teaches a class related to the job (such as marketing) and also supervises students on the job. This allows you not only to study an occupation but also to gain practical experience.

You may also look into an internship program at a company or organization that interests you. An internship offers a student direct work experience and exposure to various aspects of a career, either with or without pay. If you are considering a career in public relations, you might find an internship in a local public relations firm. While most of your duties will be basic, you will gain good exposure to the field through the professionals you work with.

The value of an internship is in the experience and the contacts that you make; often, students on internships are asked to stay on with a company after they have put in their time. Even if you choose not to stay at the company, your internship supervisor can be a great source of job contacts in addition to being a good reference. Employers seriously consider internship experience when reviewing candidates for new positions. It demonstrates high interest and a willingness to put in time to gain valuable experience.

37.2 ASSESSMENT

Reviewing Key Terms and Concepts

1. What are the major areas you should consider when you investigate possible careers?

2. Name three sources for information about careers.

3. What are the benefits of a career consultation?

Thinking Critically

4. You would love to work for a magazine but do not think that you have the necessary experience or talent as a writer. Is it possible for you to work for a magazine even if you don't have superior writing skills? Explain your answer.

Integrating Academic Skills

5. **MATH** Use the Occupational Outlook Handbook to find the current salaries for two marketing careers that interest you. What is the annual difference in those two salaries? Disregarding pay increases over the years, how much more would you make in the higher paying job over a ten-year period?

Develop a Career Plan

Evaluating Your Choices

In the next step of the career planning process, you will match what you learned about yourself in your self-assessment with the career information you gathered. The best match that you find should be the most logical career choice.

You will be more efficient in evaluating your choices if you organize your task before you begin. Gather all of your self-assessment notes and research on different careers. It may be helpful to begin this matching process on paper. Create a personal career profile, or an evaluation format that allows you to compare your self-assessment side-by-side with a particular career assessment (see Figure 37-2 on page 700).

On the left side of the profile, write the information about yourself. Then make several photocopies of this form—one for each career that you researched and are interested in. Using these copies, fill in the career information on the right by referring to your notes. After you complete each profile, reread all the information carefully. Then ask yourself the following questions:

- Does this career match my personal values? Do the work values important in this career match my personal values?
- Does this career fit my lifestyle goals?
- Will this career provide an adequate income?
- Is the job outlook good for this career?
- Am I willing to continue my education and training as required for this career? Can I afford to do so? Will my employer possibly pay for it if I wait?
- Will the duties and responsibilities of this career interest me? Will I be able to perform them well?
- Will I have the skills required for this career? Do I have the aptitudes to learn the skills needed to advance in this career?
- How will my personality fit this career?
- Will I find the work environment and work relationships in this career satisfactory?

Using a personal career profile has a major advantage—you can refer to it again and again in the months and years ahead. Some people may doubt their decision after they have made their choice. It is not rare for an individual to choose one career path and later realize that it is not the best fit. The profile makes it easy to review your evaluation; then you can remind yourself of your priorities, change your decision based on your review, or change your profile based on what you have learned. It is helpful to constantly update your profiles as you develop new skills and find new possible career interests.

What You'll Learn

- How to match your own needs, wants, and potential qualifications with a realistic and satisfying career
- How to develop a plan to reach your career goals

Why It's Important

Once you have set a career goal, you must figure out the steps you must take to reach your goal. In this section, you will learn how to create a detailed plan of action that will show the steps leading to one of your career choices.

Key Terms

- planning goals
- specific goal
- realistic goal

FIGURE 37-2

Personal Career Profile

Name ___Joan Smith___ Date ___September 4, 20--___

Personal Information	Career Information	Match (1–5, with 5 being the best match)
Your Values: The value scales I took showed that I like to help other people (humanitarianism). I like to be a leader. Doing creative things is fun, too.	**Values:** As a teacher I would have a chance to help others—that's what it's all about. Teachers certainly have plenty of opportunities to be leaders, too. Teachers also need to be creative!	
Your Interests: My hobby interests have always been photography, reading, and theater. My career interest survey showed that I might like a career in leading/influencing, selling, the arts, or maybe a humanitarian career.	**Career Duties and Responsibilities:** As a teacher, I would present information, and direct student discussions and activities in class. I would help each student individually, too. (Maybe I could teach marketing or general business.) A teacher's working conditions would be good in most schools. (Summers off!)	
My Personality: I like people, and I have a good attitude toward learning. I have an open mind. I'm enthusiastic, too. However, I don't have the energy and drive that some people have. I don't know if I could work night after night.	**Type of Personality Needed:** A teacher must like kids, even when they aren't very likeable. I would have to prepare my lessons every day—couldn't just forget about them. Teachers need to be organized, too.	
Data-People-Things Preferences: I think I like working with people most of all. I wouldn't want to be stuck in an office all day with only "data" to talk to. I also wouldn't like working only with things. Some data would be all right, though.	**Data-People-Things Relationships:** Teachers work mostly with people—their students, the principal, parents. They work with data (information), too, though. I don't think they work much with things.	
Skills and Aptitudes: I may have some natural teaching skills—the kids at the YMCA always come to me for help. I helped several kids in Miss Moore's class. Business classes are easy for me.	**Skills and Aptitudes Needed:** Being able to present information so students can understand it is a very important skill. Of course, you must know your subject. An appetite for learning new approaches to teaching is important, too.	
Education/Training Acceptable: I sure never thought I would go to college—I never even liked doing the homework in high school. However, here I am a senior with no real prospects of a good job. Maybe college is the answer.	**Education/Training Required:** Four years of college (it sounds like forever, but I guess it does go fast) are required before you can begin teaching in most states. Some states require course work beyond that.	

■ **Personal Career Profile** A personal career profile helps you compare your self-assessment with a particular career assessment. *Based on this personal career profile, how does Joan Smith's personal information match the career information shown? Rank each category from 1–5.*

Making Your Decision

You are now ready to choose which career you would like to pursue. You may feel that you aren't ready to make such an important decision, or fear making a mistake that could affect you for years.

Your choice of a career is one of the most important decisions you will make. It is not necessary, however, to wait until you are absolutely certain about a career choice before you make your decision. You may wait for years if you do that. Make the best choice you can now, even if you think you may change it later. A flexible goal will give you something to aim for.

Making your first career decision now, even one you may change later, will be a positive influence on your life. It will give you a sense of direction. You can review your career planning process anytime. If you decide that another career is better for you, then it is no disgrace to change your goal. In fact, it's the right thing to do. You may find your career path taking many twists and turns before you establish yourself in the right job for you. Don't be afraid of making the wrong career decision—it is possible to learn from all of your experiences.

Developing a Plan of Action

Have you decided which of the marketing careers you researched is the best match with your self-assessment? If so, begin planning how you will achieve your career goal. A plan doesn't guarantee success, but it will outline the steps that you will need to follow to reach your ultimate goal.

■ Formulating Planning Goals

The small steps you take to get from where you are now to where you want to be are planning goals. They give your life a sense of direction and move you steadily toward your ultimate career goal. Every time you reach a planning goal, you gain confidence to move on boldly toward the next one.

BE SPECIFIC You can make progress toward your ultimate goal by making your planning goals specific. A specific goal is stated in exact terms and includes some details. The goal statement "I want to become

a success," is not specific; however, "I want to complete my class in marketing this semester and earn at least a B," is specific. This is the type of planning goal that moves you toward your ultimate goal. The more specific you are about your career goals, the more likely it is that you will be able to formulate a plan to reach those goals. Each time you achieve a goal—no matter how small—it serves as motivation for you to keep working hard.

BE REALISTIC Planning goals must also be realistic. A realistic goal is one that you have a reasonable chance of achieving. Few people can reasonably expect to become the president of General Motors. If you have limited artistic talent, you can't realistically expect to become a commercial artist. Think about all of the different skills and aptitudes that you possess. They will guide you in both your ultimate career goal and your planning goals.

WORK BACKWARD When you set your planning goals, begin with your ultimate career goal. Then decide what goals you need to reach to achieve your ultimate goal. Work backward, starting with your most distant objective (long-term goals) and moving closer to your present position in time (medium- and short-term goals).

Suppose your career goal is be to become a chef. One short-term goal is to investigate what type of training you will need. Another short-term goal may be to work in a kitchen to gain practical experience. You may subscribe to a cooking magazine or keep up-to-date with new cookbooks. A medium-term goal may be to earn a degree from a culinary institute. Another medium-term goal is to get a job at a well-respected restaurant in your town or city. Finally, a long-term goal may be to study with a world-class chef.

Having a progressive series of goals allows you to test your ultimate career goal and make corrections along the way. While progressing toward your career goal, your experiences may reinforce your career decision or lead to your changing your career goal. You may discover another career that you find more interesting. On the basis of work experience in a kitchen, you may discover that you would rather own a restaurant than be a chef. At any point along the way you can adjust your path and your ultimate goal.

Choosing the Best Education for You

Whatever your career choice, your plan of action to reach your goal will include some education and training. The amount can vary from a few days of on-the-job training to four or more years of college.

Choosing education is much like choosing a career. Follow the complete decision-making process to select the best program and the best school for you. Your school counselor is a good place to start when you want information on vocational schools and centers, technical institutes, community colleges, and colleges and universities. Your school and public libraries are also likely to have useful information. You can also search the Internet and visit the Web sites of those schools that you are interested in.

If you are planning education and training beyond high school, consider the following questions:

- What is my ultimate career goal?
- What course can I take now that will help me to reach that career goal?
- What education and training beyond high school is required to reach my career goal? Is there a specific college degree required?
- How much of this education and training must I complete before I enter this career?
- Where can I get this education and training?
- How much will this education and training cost, and how will I get the money? Are there scholarships or loans available to help me finance this education?
- How much education and training can I get on the job? What part-time jobs will help?

Outlining Your Plan

After you have answered these questions, begin writing your personal plan of action. Write down all of your goals, the date that you plan to begin working toward each one, and the date you expect to reach each goal. This will help keep you on track toward your ultimate career goal—the one that turns your dream lifestyle into reality!

Life In The Diverse MARKETPLACE

The Best Medicine

When traveling in Singapore, you may notice that Singaporeans sometimes smile or laugh during situations that Westerners might deem laughing inappropriate. These behaviors may hide anxiety, shyness, bitterness, or loss of face. It is considered disrespectful and shameful to lose one's temper in public—and laughing is used as a way to hide negative feelings.

Thinking Critically

When might it be appropriate to hide feelings of anger in public?

37.3 ASSESSMENT

Reviewing Key Terms and Concepts

1. How does a career profile help in evaluating careers?
2. After evaluating career choices, what is the next step to take in choosing a career?
3. What steps should be involved in developing a plan of action?

Thinking Critically

4. Why is it important that your plan of action be written down?

Integrating Academic Skills

5. **COMMUNICATION** Your guidance counselor has requested that you write a personal plan of action for the summer. You are applying to colleges in the fall and would like to study fashion design at school. Considering these goals, develop an action plan following the suggestions discussed in this section.

Careers in Marketing

SPORTS MARKETING

E.J. Narcise
The SFX Sports Group
Senior Vice President

What does your job entail?

"I oversee our team, league, and venue services. My function is to develop and manage our goals and objectives. As part of SFX entertainment, the Sports Group merges entertainment and sports to maximize opportunities. Some of our clients are the Cleveland Browns, Denver Broncos, and San Francisco 49ers, as well as the University of Maryland, University of Connecticut, University of Miami, and Towson University. We work to develop incremental revenue streams—usually revolving around a new stadium or new project development. We also market sponsorships such as naming rights, for example the Baltimore Ravens' PSINet, and the Washington Redskins' FedEx Field."

What skills are important to you?

"People skills are most important in this career because you deal with an array of personalities, from owners of professional sports teams to project managers and contractors."

How did you get into sports management?

"I had a good friend who was the marketing director for the Baltimore Orioles. He introduced me to the owner of a minor league baseball team. At the time, I was a marketing manager for General Electric Company. I left GE to take a job running the AA affiliate of the Chicago Cubs. The rest is history . . . I've worked for several teams and went into the sports marketing business four years ago."

What training do you recommend for students?

"It is extremely important that students stay well rounded, especially through a liberal arts education. I think that specialization should be saved for graduate school. Maintaining an open mind and striving to broaden your academic horizons will open up many opportunities."

What is your key to success?

"Tenacity and passion for what I do. One breeds the other. I believe that your passion is your power."

Thinking Critically

Could you work in sports marketing if you were not a sports enthusiast?

Career Facts

Education and Training: Courses in marketing, accounting, communication, and business classes, and a strong interest in sports are necessary.

Aptitudes, Abilities, and Skills: Good communication and negotiation skills, administrative and supervisory ability, and financial aptitudes are necessary.

Career Path: Most sports and entertainment marketing managers come from college or professional sports programs. Many have previously worked in marketing or business prior to becoming a team manager.

Career Outlook: Average growth is projected in this field. Competition for the best positions is expected to be keen.

703

Chapter 37 ASSESSMENT

VOCABULARY REVIEW

Use these vocabulary terms in a paragraph on career research.

- values
- lifestyle
- aptitude
- career outlook
- *Dictionary of Occupational Titles (DOT)*
- *Occupational Outlook Handbook (OOH)*
- *Guide for Occupational Exploration (GOE)*
- career consultation
- internship
- planning goals
- specific goal
- realistic goal

FACT AND IDEA REVIEW

1. List six elements of lifestyle. (37.1)
2. How can making a list of your hobbies help you in the career planning process? (37.1)
3. How does personality type relate to career research? (37.1)
4. Why should you assess your preferences for working with data, people, or things? (37.1)
5. Name three benefits of a job or profession that could affect your career choice. (37.2)
6. List the career resources you might find in a school or public library. (37.2)
7. What are the three final steps in the career planning process outlined in the text? (37.3)
8. Name three specific planning goals. (37.3)
9. What is a short-term goal if you want to be a retail buyer? (37.3)

THINKING CRITICALLY

1. Think of your own hobbies or interests. Brainstorm ways that these could become professions.
2. How do you think your values were formed? What effect do you think your personal values will have on the career you choose?
3. Describe someone you know whose personality is a good match for the job he or she is in. Explain how their personality affects his or her work. Is the person happy in the job?
4. Childcare is a sought after benefit. Why do you think this is so? What are the advantages for the companies who provide childcare?
5. A successful friend tells you that she got to where she is because she is lucky, not because she set career goals. How would you respond to this?

BUILDING WORKPLACE SKILLS

1. **Human Relations** You love plants and flowers and have decided that your long-range goal is to own a retail garden shop. You have an opportunity to work in a local garden shop as soon as you graduate, get on-the-job training, work your way up, and eventually buy into the business. Your parents want you to go to college first. What should you do?
2. **Technology** A career in marketing sounds appealing to you, and you have always enjoyed looking for answers to problems. Some type of research in marketing seems like a possible career choice, but you're also interested in having a comfortable lifestyle. Use the Internet to find the salary ranges of some specific jobs in marketing research.

APPLYING MARKETING CONCEPTS

1. **Researching Careers** Use a spreadsheet program to list the areas to consider when researching careers: work values, lifestyle goals, salary, benefits, career outlook, responsibilities, skills and aptitudes, education and training, personality traits, work environment, and involvement with data/people/things. Rank these items in importance when making a career choice. Compare your list with a classmate's and discuss differences.

2. **Considering Career Choices** Interview two people who work in the field of marketing. Ask them about the important considerations in choosing a career. Ask them if these considerations contribute to their like or dislike of their work. Ask them what was most important to them when they were job hunting. Use a word processing program to summarize your findings.

3. **Conducting a Career Consultation** Conduct a career consultation in one of the career areas you are researching. Use a presentation program to illustrate the importance of different job requirements. Present your findings to the class.

4. **Summarizing Career Concepts** Find a magazine article about someone who has made a mid-life career change. Summarize the article orally or in writing for your classmates. Be sure to explain why the career change was made and whether it turned out to be worthwhile.

LINKING SCHOOL TO WORK

Thinking Skills and Personal Qualities Ask your employer to describe how he or she chose his or her career, and the steps taken to achieve his or her short-, medium-, and long-range goals. Share this information with the class, comparing different paths taken by businesspeople.

THE DECA CONNECTION

Role Play: Interviewer

Situation You are to assume the role of interviewer for a local employment agency. You will be going into schools to talk to students about career planning.

Activity You must demonstrate to the agency manager (judge) that you are ready to begin your assigned task.

Evaluation You will be evaluated on how well you meet the following performance indicators:

- Identify tentative occupational interests
- Identify sources of career information
- Explain possible advancement patterns for jobs
- Describe techniques for obtaining work experience (e.g., volunteer activities, internships)
- Identify desirable personality traits important to business

*inter*NET CONNECTION

Virtual College Visits

You have decided on a career in online marketing, and need to discover where you can get the skills and education you need.

Connect

- Use the Internet to identify colleges or technical schools with good programs in both computer science and business.
- Look at the different schools' Web sites and compare the programs and tuition costs.
- Choose the school that best fits your needs.

Chapter 38

Finding and Applying for a Job

Marketing: What It Takes

The Marketing Plan for Your Career

Every marketing activity has a better chance of success with proper planning. Certainly, this is true when you are ready to market yourself. You will be looking for the best opportunity to enter your chosen career—the career around which your daily life will revolve as an adult. Take some time to reflect on what you've learned in this course, then consider how you will plan the most important marketing process of your life.

WHAT WILL YOU DO?

How will you organize your job finding program?

Finding a Job

Finding Job Openings

When you are ready for a full-time job, you will want one that matches your needs, wants, and qualifications. Your main interest right now, however, is probably to find a job to gain work experience and earn some money. You should search for a job that you can enjoy and at which you can be successful.

How do you go about finding such a job? A productive first step is to contact all of the sources available to you that might produce a job lead. A job lead is information about a job opening. You may hear that a nearby department store is looking for part-time salespeople, but you don't know for which department or to whom you should apply. Sometimes you may have to act like a detective, following up skimpy leads and filling in the rest of the information yourself. Finding the right job requires getting as many leads as possible and following up on them.

▪ Networking

One of your best sources of job leads is often family, friends, and acquaintances. The people that you know—family and friends, former employers, and professional people you know personally—form a network of individuals connected to you. Finding contacts among them is called networking.

Some young people are not comfortable asking people they know for job leads. They want to get a job on their own. There is nothing wrong with getting a job through networking, if you are qualified. While a friend may help you get your foot in the door, it is your hard work that will bring you success. Many jobs are never advertised because acquaintances of present employees fill them; therefore, it is important not to overlook this important source of job leads.

FAMILY AND FRIENDS Family members and friends often hear of job openings where they work. They may not immediately know of the perfect job for you, but they can ask their friends and coworkers about openings.

Do you have any friends who have started new jobs recently? Ask them if they have any leads. Make a list of family and personal friends who might help you find job leads. Do any of them own or manage their own business? They may need someone with your qualifications or have a business contact that is looking for a good worker like you.

List friends who work for companies where you would like to work to your list. Then add the names of school friends and neighbors who are somehow connected with a business that interests you. Perhaps

What You'll Learn

- How to locate job leads from a variety of sources
- The best ways to contact your job leads
- How to expand your list of job leads

Why It's Important

This section will help you understand how to use the best sources of job leads to find the job that will start you on your way to success in your chosen career.

Key Terms

- job lead
- networking
- public employment agencies
- private employment agencies
- résumé
- direct contact

a classmate's mother or father works for a company that has an opening that's just what you are looking for. Most businesses welcome applications from friends of their employees because they trust their opinions. Valued company employees are good people to make referrals and recommendations because they understand the skills, values, and work ethic necessary to work for their company.

SCHOOL COUNSELOR Retail stores and other businesses often call school counselors for qualified students for part-time or temporary jobs. School counselors usually have contacts in the business community, therefore they sometimes hear about full-time jobs, too. Your counselor may know of a job that matches your interests and abilities and might be able to put in a good word for you.

PROFESSIONAL PEOPLE IN YOUR PERSONAL LIFE You probably have periodic contact with professional people in your personal life—doctors, businesspeople, dentists, or lawyers. If you have established a good rapport with these people, they will be happy to help you in your job search. Ask them for names of people that you can contact.

FORMER EMPLOYERS Have you ever held a job? Even if it was a temporary or part-time job, such as babysitting or mowing lawns, your former employers may be good sources of job leads. It is likely that they will want to help you find a job if they were pleased with your work. That is why it is always important to give every job your best effort.

■ Cooperative Education and Work Experience Programs

Many high schools have a cooperative education program in which students work part-time on a job related to one of their classes. You may already be working on a part-time job in marketing if the marketing class you are enrolled in is part of a cooperative education program. Cooperative education teachers have contacts in the business community because they place and supervise students on part-time jobs. Cooperative work experiences sometimes offer students both course credits and minimum wage payments.

Many schools also offer a work experience program that is not limited to just one career area,

■ **Getting Connected** There may be professional people in your life who could be a source of job leads. *Who are some of the adults you know who could help you find a part-time job?*

such as marketing. The work experience coordinator has hundreds of contacts in the business community and may be a good source of job leads.

Schools have a good record of placing students in jobs that fit their interests and abilities. This is because teachers, counselors, and work experience coordinators know their students well. They also have the experience of seeing how former students fit into a particular career. Don't sit back and relax, however, thinking a teacher or someone else in your school will find the right job for you. There are almost always going to be more students looking for jobs than there are jobs to be filled. That means several well-qualified students will probably be referred for every job opening. It is possible to follow up several good leads and still not get a job because of the competition. You can't let this discourage you though—if you keep looking, the right job will eventually come through.

Newspaper Ads

Read the Help Wanted ads in your local newspaper, especially the Sunday edition. Most papers separate jobs by type. The Help Wanted ads are not only a good source of job leads, but they will also teach you about the local job market. You will learn the qualifications required for different types of jobs and the salaries offered.

Promptly follow up every ad that looks like it could lead to the job you want. The job will probably be filled quickly. Be aware, however, that not every ad represents a legitimate job offer. Ads that require you to make a deposit of money or enroll in a course are not usually genuine job offers but disguised attempts to sell you something. People who place ads like these will take your money, but they don't usually have any jobs to offer.

Employment Agencies

The main function of employment agencies is to match workers with jobs. Most larger cities have two types of employment agencies—public and private. Public employment agencies are supported by state or federal taxes and offer free services to both job applicants and employers. Private employment agencies, which are not supported by taxes, must earn a profit to stay in business. They charge a fee for their services, which is paid by either the job applicant or the employer.

Public employment agencies are identified by the names of the states in which they are located. The Texas Employment Commission and the California State Employment Development Department are examples. In some cities, the state employment service is the only one available.

When you fill out an application form at the public employment agency near you, you will be interviewed to determine your qualifications and interests. The agency will call you if they find a job that is a good match. You will be told about the company and the job duties, then referred for an interview if you are interested.

Private employment agencies often have job leads that are not listed with public agencies. Remember, however, that private agencies charge a fee if they place you on a job. Make sure you know who is expected to pay the fee—it might be you. This will be stated in a contract you must sign. The fee for matching workers with higher-level jobs is often paid

■ Getting Acquainted A company's personnel office can be a source of leads for the career you are interested in. *How can you show your interest to a personnel manager?*

by the employer. The employee usually pays the placement fee on entry-level jobs. The fee is usually a percentage of your salary for the first several months or even the first full year of employment.

Company Personnel Offices

Large companies have personnel offices to handle employment matters, including the hiring of new workers. You may check on job openings by telephoning that office or by scheduling a personal visit. Some personnel offices list openings on a public bulletin board. If this is the case, you can stop by at your convenience and see if any new jobs have been posted.

When you know that you would like to work for a certain company, make an effort to get to know the people who work in the human resources department. This way you will have a better chance of being hired.

◾ Searching the Internet

You will certainly want to look into cyberspace for job openings. By searching the Internet using Web sites like Hotjobs.com or Monster.com, you can easily find out which companies have job openings.

Most large companies now list their job openings either on their own Web page or with an online employment service. There are tens of thousands of career-related Web sites, so the challenge will be locating the ones having jobs that interest you. Look for sites with up-to-date listings—nothing more than two months old.

Once you've narrowed your career decision to a specific job title, career, industry, or even location, begin your search with sites that specialize in those areas. Start with a Web directory like Yahoo! to get a listing of career-related Web sites from which to choose. Then, do a keyword search of the site, using words such as salesperson, research assistant, or marketing. You can also search by job location, selecting to view only jobs in the area where you live or want to move to.

Another way to begin your search is to look at the Web sites of companies that spark your interest. The Web site for *Fortune* magazine lists 100 companies that offer noteworthy education benefits, stock options, and childcare.

ELECTRONIC RÉSUMÉS When using the Internet for your job search, you may come across the option to apply for a particular position online. This can be done using an electronic résumé. A résumé is a brief summary of personal information, education, skills, work experience, activities, and interests. Applying for jobs over the Internet is different than submitting a traditional résumé and requires a different résumé writing technique. It is important to learn the different formats as applying for jobs online is increasingly popular. You will learn about traditional résumés later in this chapter.

You can write your electronic résumé using a word processing program. Upon completion, you can submit your résumé as part of an e-mail. It is best to "cut and paste" the résumé into the body of an e-mail rather than including it as an attached file. Attached files can be difficult to read if the file is created in a different word processing program, and some employers may be hesitant to open files because of the risk of computer viruses.

There are three main differences between electronic résumés and traditional résumés. These are format, phraseology, and confidentiality.

The format of your electronic résumé should be text only. Make sure to save your résumé as a text file; this is the easiest way to transmit and read electronic files. Avoid bold type, italics, and underlining, which does not transmit well and makes your résumé difficult to read. Stick to a commonly used traditional font, such as Times New Roman, and keep your font size between 12 and 14 point. Do not use tabs; use the space bar instead.

Many companies that accept résumés electronically will search for job qualifications by looking for key words. It is very likely that your résumé will not be read by a person, but will be scanned by a computer program instead. In the scanning process, key words and phrases are searched for and the résumé is summarized and ranked among other qualified candidates.

It is important to use key words to describe what you can do because of this. Key words consist primarily of nouns and are usually divided into three categories: job title, industry, and personal

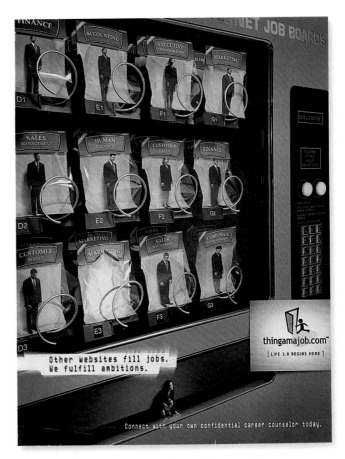

◾ Help Wanted Thingamajob.com is an online career service featuring résumé posting, job alerts, industry news and confidential career counseling. *How would you go about finding job listings, company research, and salary information on the Web?*

traits. It is important to include industry specific jargon, as many employers will search by industry language. Be sure to spell out all acronyms—include your membership in the Distributive Education Clubs of America (DECA), not just DECA. You will not be considered for a job that you are qualified for if key words don't appear on your résumé.

Confidentiality is an issue when posting your résumé on the Internet. Remember that once posted on a career Web site, your résumé is a public document that is out of your control. You have the option of limiting your personal information by only including an e-mail address or post office box so that potential employers can contact you without the use of a phone number or address. Since most employers prefer to contact applicants by telephone, you could hire a voice mail account during your job search. This may become an issue for job seekers who already have a job. The concern is that the current employer will realize its workers are looking to change jobs.

Before e-mailing your résumé to employers, e-mail a copy to yourself so that you can review it. Be sure to include your cover letter in the body of the e-mail as well. Creating your résumé in a standardized, electronic, scannable format keeps you on top of the competition.

Contacting Your Job Leads

The more job leads you have, the better your chances of finding a job that is right for you. There are different ways to approach potential job contacts. You may choose to contact employers directly or to send a letter expressing your interest.

■ Direct Contact

The process of visiting potential employers in person or calling them on the telephone is known as direct contact. Do this when you think you would like to work for certain companies but are unsure whether they have any openings. Be sure to call ahead for an appointment. Showing up unannounced could be inconvenient to the potential employer and may start the relationship on the wrong foot.

You may get more consideration by calling in person than by inquiring about a job on the telephone with direct contact. Direct contact can be time consuming; however, if you contact enough employers you may find a job that interests you. It also shows your high level of interest in a company and your dedication and commitment to finding a job.

BRIGHT IDEAS
The Launch of the MoonPie

In the early 1900s, Earl Mitchell, a salesman for the Chattanooga Bakery, was servicing his territory. He came across a company store for coal miners. While asking coal miners what they might enjoy as a snack, the need was identified for something solid and filling for their lunch pails. The salesman asked, "How big?" About that time the moon was rising, so a miner held out his hands to frame the moon and said, "About that big!" Earlier, the salesman had noticed some workers dipping graham crackers into marshmallow and laying them on the window to harden. He headed back to the bakery with an idea. The salesman asked a baker to experiment by adding another cookie to this graham cracker/marshmallow concoction, and then dip it in chocolate. They sent the product over to the workers to try. The experiment was a success and the MoonPie was launched!

Thinking Creatively

Design your own favorite snack food, determining your market, necessary ingredients, and selling price.

Do You Want to Be a Star?

You've walked through the application process, sailed through the interview, and got your dream job. Are you ready for the next step? What kind of employee will you be?

Robert E. Kelley, a professor at Carnegie Mellon University, wants you to be a star. He has written a popular book called *How To Be a Star at Work: A Breakthrough Strategy You Need to Succeed* that outlines what sets star employees apart from the rest. He has studied successful workers to see what makes them different from their more average coworkers.

Surprisingly, it isn't brainpower or technical skill that is most important. What makes a star isn't what the employee does so much as how he or she does it. An employee can have the most advanced on-the-job skills and a college degree from a top school; however, if his or her people-skills are poor, it is unlikely that he or she will succeed.

Some of the tactics that Kelley focuses on include: initiative, networking, self-management, teamwork, leadership, perspective, and organizational skills. Star employees take the initiative to discover what might need doing that the manager hasn't thought of yet. Most employees make the effort to be on friendly terms with the boss. Kelley says that what sets stars apart is that they also make the effort to know the people who know how things work in the company, whether they are managers or coworkers. It is important to show respect for all people in the workplace—not just your own boss.

Star employees focus on the big picture—they make sure the way they do their job fits into the overall strategy of the company. They don't just go along with "business as usual." Instead, they offer their ideas to management even if they differ from the way the company usually does business. Showing initiative illustrates that you value your role in the company and are not just seeking personal success.

Companies work to keep and promote star employees. Won't you choose to be a star?

Case Study Review

1. How do you think helping others succeed could make you a star?
2. What qualities of a star employee do you already have?

A MATTER OF ETHICS

3. Do you think it is ethical to befriend someone at work because you think the friendship will help you improve your work?

■ Letters of Inquiry

Writing a letter of inquiry is a variation of direct contact. You use the technique under the same circumstances and for the same reason—when you want to know whether a company has openings in the career area of your interest.

You must do some research to learn to whom you should address your correspondence. Call the company and ask for the name of the individual who hires new employees. At that point you will learn whether the company has a human resources department or whether department heads do their own hiring. Confirm the spelling of any names you are given and the position of the person to contact. Verify the company's address, particularly the zip code, postal box, floor, or suite numbers. Now you are ready to write a letter of inquiry. See Chapter 8 to review the elements of a business letter and Figure 38-1 for an example.

Expanding Your List of Job Leads

You should always be looking for new job leads even as you follow up on existing ones. Expand your list by getting referrals from people. Each time you follow up a lead that doesn't result in a job, ask your interviewer to suggest someone else to contact. Having other possibilities will keep you from getting discouraged if you don't get the job you want right away. If you have a long list of leads, you can simply follow up on the next one.

FIGURE 38-1

Letter of Inquiry

327 Hoyt Avenue
Berkeley, California 95212
April 27, 20—

Susan W. Peterson
Appleton Kitchen Products
5134 State Street
Berkeley, CA 95214

Dear Ms. Peterson:

On May 17, I shall graduate from Sam Houston High School with a major emphasis in sales and marketing. While in high school, I have worked in sales part-time, but I am most eager to begin my first full-time job in sales.

As I have always been impressed by the courteous, efficient salespeople in your store, I am very interested in a job at Appleton. If you anticipate a need for any full-time, permanent employees in the next several months, I would like to apply.

May I have an application form, or should I call for an interview at your convenience? My home telephone number is 924-7884.

Sincerely,

Charlene J. Graham

Charlene J. Graham

■ **Inquiry Letters** You will probably need to send letters of inquiry to many companies in order to come up with a few leads. *Why do you think that is true?*

38.1 ASSESSMENT

Reviewing Key Terms and Concepts

1. What are six possible sources of job leads?
2. What is networking?
3. What are two methods that you can use to contact job leads?
4. How can you expand your list of job leads?

Thinking Critically

5. How would you feel about getting a job through a family member or personal friend? Would you rather find a job on your own? Why or why not?

Integrating Academic Skills

6. **COMMUNICATION** Imagine that you would like to work for a local mail-order company that sells electronic gadgets, but you don't know if there are currently job openings. Write a letter of inquiry regarding summer employment.

Applying for a Job

What You'll Learn

- The legal document that you must have before you can begin working
- How to write a letter of application and complete an application form
- How to write a résumé and cover letter

Why It's Important

You've contacted the sources of job leads and found some jobs that interest you; your next step is to apply for them. This is done by completing application forms, writing letters of application, and preparing your own résumé.

Key Terms

- standard English
- references
- cover letter

Getting a Work Permit

Most states require that you have a work permit before you can legally begin working if you are under the age of 18. In some states, such as Michigan, a cooperative education training agreement can serve as a legal work permit.

State and federal labor laws designate certain jobs as too dangerous for young workers. Most of these jobs are performed in hazardous environments or involve the use of power-driven machinery. The laws also limit the number of hours that young people can work in one day or one week. More hours of work are allowed during summer vacations than during the school year.

A work permit establishes that it is legal for a young worker to do the type of work offered. In some states, work permits must specify the exact job duties and hours of work. In these cases, both the employer and the worker fill out sections of an application for the permit. The employer, worker, and the worker's parent must sign the application before a work permit is issued.

Ask your marketing teacher or counselor whether you will need a work permit and, if so, where you can get one. A designated school official usually issues work permits. Check on this now so you can avoid possible delays when you are ready to go to work.

Applying for a Job

Employers look for the most qualified person to fill a job. They will decide whether to hire you based in part on how you present yourself during an interview. More than anything else, they will want to know whether you have the ability to do the work.

Employers have several ways of getting this information. Many ask job seekers to fill out an application form. Some request additional documents—a separate letter of application or a résumé. Finally, some employers administer one or more employment tests to applicants.

How you present your qualifications is likely to be the determining factor in whether you are hired. Following the suggestions on the next few pages should increase your chances of success.

■ Using Standard English

Everything you write and say to a prospective employer should be in standard English. Standard English is the formal style of writing and speaking that you have learned in school. It is standard because it means the same thing to everyone.

Most people do not use standard English for all of their communications. When you write a letter to a close relative, for example, you simply write what is on your mind and don't usually worry about form. When you speak with a friend on the telephone, you may use slang or informal language. These practices make for comfortable and easy personal conversation, but they have no place in business. Most communication in business is formal, and that means standard English.

Standard English employs correct grammar, spelling, pronunciation, and usage. "Marilyn *has* a job interview" is standard English, while "Marilyn *have* a job interview" is not. The repeated use in conversation of the interjections *you know* or *like* is nonstandard English. Nonstandard pronunciations are another common lapse, although an accent, either regional or foreign, does not indicate non-standard English.

Employers will have several opportunities to evaluate your English. When they read your application form, they will notice whether you use and spell words correctly. Your letter of application or résumé will indicate your ability (or inability) to write. Finally, when you are interviewed, the employer will listen to you speak and will evaluate your grammar and pronunciation.

■ Filling Out Application Forms

Most employment application forms are short (from one to four pages) and ask similar questions. Companies usually design their own application forms, so you may find differences between various applications. You can see an example of a completed application form in Figure 38-2 on page 716.

The application form provides information about your qualifications so company personnel can decide whether to interview you. The first rule of filling out an application form is to complete the form neatly. Spell all words correctly and use a dictionary to look up the spellings of any words you aren't sure about. When filling out the form at the place of employment, use words you know how to spell.

Take the application form home and fill it out on a typewriter if possible. Make a photocopy of the form if you are not a good typist, so you can practice first. When asked to complete the form at the place of employment, use a pen with blue or black ink;

REAL WORLD MARKETING

Spinning CDs

How about some listening enjoyment while you read that magazine? Riffage.com, an online music destination, and Spin Magazine, a leading music and youth culture magazine, broke new ground in marketing for the music industry. Five issues of Spin magazine were assembled with a special CD-ROM produced by Riffage.com. The deal marked the first time a music CD-ROM was distributed by a major national magazine to its entire newsstand circulation base of over 500,000 issues. The CD-ROM contained a collection of 150 MP3-formatted songs by artists whose music is available on Riffage.com.

Thinking Critically
Determine another innovative way to distribute CD-ROMs. What type of packaging would you use?

colored inks are considered to be not serious and inappropriate.

Answer every question that applies to you. Write "NA" (meaning "Not Applicable") or draw a short line in the space for those questions that are not applicable. This shows that you did not overlook the item.

Use your full name, not a nickname, on the form. On most applications, your first name, middle initial, and last name are requested. Provide your complete address, including your zip code.

List a specific job title if they ask for job preference; do not write "anything" as an answer. Employers expect you to know what type of work you can and want to do.

Most application forms include a section on education. Write the names of all the schools you have attended and the dates of attendance. There will also be a section on previous work experience. You may not have had much work experience, but

FIGURE 38-2

Job Application

Date April 6, 20 - -

SEARS, ROEBUCK AND CO.
APPLICATION FOR EMPLOYMENT

SEARS IS AN EQUAL OPPORTUNITY EMPLOYER and fully subscribes to the principles of Equal Opportunity unity. Sears has adopted an Affirmative Action Program to ensure that all applicants and employees are considered for hire, promotion and job status, without regard to race, color, religion, sex, national origin, age, handicap, or status as a disabled veteran or veteran of the Vietnam Era.

To protect the interests of all concerned, applicants for certain job assignments must pass a physical examination before they are hired.

PLEASE PRINT INFORMATION REQUESTED IN INK

NOTE: This application will be considered active for 90 days. If you have not been employed within this period and are still interested in employment at Sears, please contact the office where you applied and request that your application be reactivated.

Name Graham (Last) Charlene (First) Joan (Middle) Social Security Number 541-62-6351
(Please present your Social Security Card for review.)

Address 753 (Number) North Fairfield Street (Street) Dallas (City) Texas (State) 75221 (Zip Code)

County Dallas

Current phone or nearest phone (214) 924-7486

Previous Address _____ (Number) (Street) (City) (State) (Zip Code)

Best time of day to contact after 4 p.m.

(Answer only if position for which you are applying requires driving.)

If hired, can you furnish proof of age? Yes ☒ No ☐   Licensed to drive car? YES ☐ NO ☐
If hired, can you furnish proof that you are legally entitled to work in U.S.? Yes ☒ No ☐   Is license valid in this state? YES ☐ NO ☐

Have you ever been employed by Sears or a subsidiary of Sears? YES ☐ NO ☒   If so when and where last employed? _____   Position _____

Former employees of Sears and certain Subsidiaries may be entitled to service credit under the Pension Plan based on prior employment with Sears, Roebuck and Co., Homart Development Co., Sears Investment Management Co., Sears Roebuck Acceptance Corp., Sears, Roebuck de Puerto Rico, Inc., Sears Roebuck Overseas, Inc., Sears Securities Sales, Inc., Terminal Freight Handling Co., Allstate Insurance Company and their Subsidiaries, Lifetime Foam Products, Pacific Installers, and Sears, S.A. (Central America), Dean Witter Reynolds Organization, Inc. and their Subsidiaries, Coldwell Banker and their Subsidiaries and Sears World Trade.

Have you a relative in the employ of Sears in the store or unit to which you are applying? No

A PHYSICAL OR MENTAL DISABILITY WILL NOT CAUSE REJECTION IF IN SEARS MEDICAL OPINION YOU ARE ABLE TO SATISFACTORILY PERFORM IN THE POSITION FOR WHICH YOU ARE BEING CONSIDERED. Alternative placement, if available, of an applicant who does not meet the physical standards of the job for which he/she was originally considered is permitted.

Do you have any physical or mental impairment which may limit your ability to perform the job for which you are applying? No

If yes, what can reasonably be done to accommodate your limitation? _____

	School Attended	No. of Years	Name of School	City/State	Graduate?	Course or College Major	Average Grades
EDUCATION	Grammar	7	Esperanza Elementary	Dallas, TX	Yes		B+
	Jr. High	3	Andrews Junior High	Dallas, TX	Yes		B
	Sr. High	3	Sam Houston High School	Dallas, TX	Yes	Marketing/Bus.	A–
	Other						
	College					Degree	

	BRANCH OF SERVICE	DATE ENTERED SERVICE*	DATE OF DISCHARGE*	HIGHEST RANK	SERVICE-RELATED SKILLS AND EXPERIENCE APPLICABLE TO CIVILIAN EMPLOYMENT
MILITARY SERVICE					

*Do not complete if applying in the state of California.
What experience or training have you had other than your work experience, military service and education? (Community activities, hobbies, etc.)

I am interested in the type of work I have checked: ☒ Sales ☐ Office ☐ Mechanical ☐ Warehouse ☐ Other Specify _____

Or the following specific Job _____

I am seeking (check only one):

☐ Temporary employment (6 days or less)
☐ Seasonal employment (one season, e.g. Christmas)
☒ Regular employment (employment for indefinite period of time)
If temporary, indicate dates available _____

I am available for (check only one):

☐ Part Time
☒ Full-Time

If part-time, indicate maximum hours per week _____ and enter hours available in block to the right.

HOURS AVAILABLE FOR WORK	
Sun.	To
Mon.	8 a.m. To 6 p.m.
Tues.	8 a.m. To 6 p.m.
Wed.	8 a.m. To 6 p.m.
Thurs.	8 a.m. To 6 p.m.
Fri.	8 a.m. To 6 p.m.
Sat.	8 a.m. To 6 p.m.

Have you been convicted during the past seven years of a serious crime involving a person's life or property?
☒ NO ☐ YES If yes explain _____

10534 Rev. 9/83

(SEE REVERSE SIDE)

REFERENCES

LIST BELOW YOUR FOUR MOST RECENT EMPLOYERS, BEGINNING WITH THE CURRENT OR MOST RECENT ONE. IF YOU HAD LESS THAN FOUR EMPLOYERS, USE THE REMAINING SPACES FOR PERSONAL REFERENCES. IF YOU WERE EMPLOYED UNDER A MAIDEN OR OTHER NAME, PLEASE ENTER THAT NAME IN THE RIGHT HAND MARGIN. IF APPLICABLE, ENTER SERVICE IN THE ARMED FORCES ON THE REVERSE SIDE.

NAMES AND ADDRESSES OF FORMER EMPLOYERS BEGINNING WITH THE CURRENT OR MOST RECENT	Nature of Employer's Business	Name of your Supervisor	What kind of work did you do?	Starting Date	Starting Pay	Date of Leaving	Pay at Leaving	Why did you leave? Give details
NOTE–State reason for and length of inactivity between present application date and last employer								
Name Merchandise Mart / Address 2800 Tyler Avenue Tel No 925-9021 / City Dallas, State Texas Zip Code 75221	Depart-ment Store	Mr. Travis	Sales	Month Nov. Year 95	Per Week	Month Year	Per Week	Still employed part-time
NOTE–State reason for and length of inactivity between last employer and second last employer								
Name Chicken Annie's / Address 1700 S. Vernon Avenue Tel No 924-6318 / City Dallas, State Texas Zip Code 75221	Fast Food	Mrs. Riley	Sales	Month Jan. Year 95	$80 Per Week	Month Oct. Year 95	$95 Per Week	To accept a job with more hours
NOTE–State reason for and length of inactivity between second last employer and third last employer								
Name Mr. Paul Crawford (former teacher) / Address 3614 Rayburn Avenue Tel No 925-1163 / City Dallas, State Texas Zip Code 75221				Month Year	Per Week	Month Year	Per Week	
NOTE–State reason for and length of inactivity between third last employer and fourth last employer								
Name Miss Irene Jenkins / Address 1222 Oakwood Street Tel No 925-7611 / City Dallas State Texas Zip Code 75221				Month Year	Per Week	Month Year	Per Week	

I certify that the information contained in this application is correct to the best of my knowledge and understand that any misstatement or omission of information is grounds for dismissal in accordance with Sears, Roebuck and Co. policy. I authorize the references listed above to give you any and all information concerning my previous employment and any pertinent information they may have, personal or otherwise, and release all parties from all liability for any damage that may result from furnishing same to you. In consideration of my employment, I agree to conform to the rules and regulations of Sears, Roebuck and Co., and my employment and compensation can be terminated with or without cause, and with or without notice, at any time, at the option of either the Company or myself. I understand that no unit manager or representative of Sears, Roebuck and Co. other than the President or Vice-President of the Company, has any authority to enter into any agreement for employment for any specified period of time, or to make any agreement contrary to the foregoing, in some states, the law requires that Sears have my written permission before obtaining reports on me, and I hereby authorize Sears to obtain such reports.

Applicant's Signature *Charlene G. Graham*

NOT TO BE FILLED OUT BY APPLICANT

INTERVIEWER'S COMMENTS	Date of Emp.		Tested	(Store will enter dates as required)	Mailed	Completed
	Dept. or Division	Regular ☐ Part-Time ☐	Physical examination scheduled for	References Requests		
	Job Title		Physical examination form completed	Consumer Report		
	Job Title Code	Job Grade		With. Tax (W-4)		
	Compensation Arrangement		Review Card prepared / Minor's Work Permit	State With. Tax		
	Manager Approving		Time card prepared / Proof of Birth			
Prospect for			Training Material Given to Employee			
1. 2.	Employee No.	Rack No.	Unit Name and Number _____			

■ **Best Foot Forward** Filling out a job application carefully using a typewriter or printing in ink very neatly shows an employer that you are serious about the job. It is your introduction to the company, and will be used in deciding whether you will be interviewed. *Where do you list the names of people who the company could contact to learn more about your work habits and character?*

you can include short-term or unpaid jobs. Fill out this section in reverse chronological order—begin with your current or most recent job and end with your first job.

Be prepared to list several references. **References** are people who know your work habits and personal traits well and who will recommend you for the job. Try to use professional references such as your teachers, friends established in business, or former employers. Make sure you ask permission of your references before listing them on an application form. Do not list classmates, relatives, or personal friends.

Sign your name using your first name, middle initial, and last name. Your signature should be written, never typed or printed.

■ Writing Letters of Application

Most employers prefer application forms because they provide just the information employers need to reach a decision on interviews. Some employers, however, request a letter of application.

Writing a letter of application is like writing a sales pitch about yourself. You must convince an employer that you are the best person to fill a specific job opening. Tell why you are interested in the position and what your special qualifications for it are. Don't write a sad story about needing the job. You want your enthusiasm to convince the employer that you are needed by the company.

Write a first draft to get down most of the main points, then revise your letter until you are pleased with the end result. Ask a teacher, parent or guardian, or friend in business to read and critique your letter; then, put the final touches on it and print out a copy.

Describe how you learned about the job opening in the first sentence. You might say, "At the suggestion of Mr. Charles Williams, I am writing about the job as mail-order clerk in your store" if a friend gave you a lead. When responding to a newspaper ad, you might say, "I am responding to your ad in the *Daily News* for an advertising assistant." State that you are applying for the job in the second sentence, for example, "I would like to be considered an applicant for this position."

The second paragraph should contain a description of how your education and experience qualify you for the job. Use a separate paragraph for each

Can You Repeat That in Spanish?

You have morning meetings with representatives from a large department store in Argentina. The only problem? Your translator is late and you don't speak Spanish! Knowledge of a foreign language is important for international business and advertising within the United States where there are large Hispanic and Asian-American populations. Learning Spanish or Japanese can give you an edge when applying for jobs. And now is the best time to start—the Modern Language Association estimates that 600 class hours are needed to establish fluency.

Thinking Critically
How can you illustrate your strong abilities in a foreign language when applying for a job?

if you have a lot to say about both your education and job experience. Don't worry if you don't have much experience—just write about your education in more detail. Mention classes you have taken that are related to the job. You may want to mention any class projects that you have excelled in, for example, developing a new advertising campaign for a local company.

List your references in the next paragraph. Finally, in your last paragraph, ask for an interview at the employer's convenience. State when you will be available and provide your telephone number.

Many businesses receive dozens of application letters every week. Businesses that advertise jobs in the newspaper may receive hundreds of letters. Businesses interview only a small portion of those who write—those people who have effectively presented their qualifications in a neatly written letter. Doing this gives you a big advantage over most applicants. Take the time to develop an effective letter of application that you are really proud of. You can use it as a model for other letters for other jobs, personalizing details of the letters to each job.

FIGURE 38-3

Letter of Application

Guadelupe Gomez-Pomeda
2517 Bath Street
Winfield, Colorado 36145
May 18, 2001

Mr. Harrison E. Frank
Sales Manager
Ferguson Aircraft Inc.
823 Dutton Avenue
Golden, Colorado 36053

Dear Mr. Frank:

Mr. Bernard Hubert, my marketing instructor at Winfield Community College, advised me this morning of the commercial artist position that you have open. I wish to apply for this position.

On May 17, I will graduate from Winfield Community College with a major in marketing and a special emphasis on advertising and commercial art. I have also taken commercial art courses during the past two summers at Colorado College. My overall grade average in college is B+.

For the past three years, I have assisted the advertising manager at Rubbermaid, here in Winfield, by preparing more than 30 ads that have run nationally. One of these ads, which I prepared myself, won an award at a recent advertising convention in Chicago.

My father taught me to fly while I was in high school, so a job in advertising with an aircraft manufacturing company would combine my two greatest interests. It would be a dream come true! May I have an interview at your convenience? You can reach me most weekdays after 3 P.M. at (316) 221-5288.

Yours truly,

Guadelupe Gomez-Pomeda

Guadelupe Gomez-Pomeda

■ **A Letter of Application**
A good letter of application lets the prospective employer know why you have the best qualifications for the job offered. Guadelupe took several classes in fashion design at Colorado College. *Why doesn't she mention those in her letter to Mr. Frank?*

As with any sales pitch, a good first impression counts. Use the spell check function of your word processing program to eliminate any spelling errors. Before you send your letter, make sure you have read it over for accuracy.

The sample letter shown in Figure 38-3 will give you some idea of how your finished letter should look. Notice how this letter is not only neat and clear, but it follows the rules outlined in this section. The applicant focuses on special classes she has taken, as well as previous job experience. The letter conveys a personal interest, and uses standard English. Be sure to include all the elements of a business letter; in particular, duplicate the salutation and complimentary closing as shown.

FIGURE 38-4

RÉSUMÉ

Arésumé tells prospective employers what you are like and what you can do for them. A good résumé shows you at your best in a one or two page outline. It usually includes the following information.

1

Identification Include your name, address, telephone number, and e-mail address.

2

Objective Your objective statement should indicate the type of job you are looking for. Don't forget to change this item if you use the same résumé to apply for a different job.

3

Experience List experience related to the specific job for which you are applying, including volunteer work. It is a good idea to list any other work you have done if you have not worked in a related field.

4

Education List schools attended from high school on, the dates of attendance, and diplomas or degrees earned. It is fine to emphasize the courses that are related to the job you are applying for.

5

Activities and Awards This is the place to list school clubs or sports awards, any recognition you have received in work, school, or extracurricular settings.

6

References Include up to three references on a short résumé. Otherwise, indicate that they are available. Always ask people ahead of time if they are willing to be listed as references for you.

Frank Johnson
1235 East Tenth Avenue
Ventura, CA 93003
(805)964-6264
frankjohnson@yourname.com

Objective:
A marketing analyst position that would complement my academic and experiential skills.

Experience:
9/96-present Assistant Marketing Analyst
Ventura Volvo
6580 Leland Street
Ventura, CA 93003

Used computer to estimate sales by model and make recommendations for inventory. Accessed databases using computer terminal to study inventory in relation to buying estimates. Studied historical applications, including media ads, price and color changes, and impact of season.

9/95-9/96 Marketing Assistant
KVEN Radio
Ventura, CA 93003

Assisted Communications Manager in publishing articles and ads, sales presentations, vendor contracts, and trade shows. Contacted vendors for advertising needs (charts, overheads, banners).

Education:
1992-1996 Ventura College. AA in Marketing. Dean's Honor Roll four semesters.

Courses included:
Marketing I and II
Marketing Information Systems
Advertising
Economics I and II
Computer Science

1989-1992 Ventura High School, Graduated in upper 10 percent of class. Served as Vice President of DECA two years.

Personal:
Hobbies include writing computer programs, tennis, and photography.

References:
Available upon request.

FIGURE 38-5

Cover Letter

1235 East Tenth Avenue
Ventura, CA 93003
April 6, 2001

Ms. Linda Morrison
Metromedia-West Television
3200 Beverly Drive
Beverly Hills, CA 90123

Dear Ms. Morrison:

Your ad for a marketing analyst in Sunday's Los Angeles Times described exactly the position that I am seeking. As you will see from the résumé I have enclosed, my qualifications match up very well with the requirements listed in your ad.

My education, experiences, and DECA participation (for which our school won a national award) have prepared me to fulfill your needs in marketing analysis.

After you have read my résumé, I would appreciate an appointment for an interview. I will call you next week to arrange a time convenient to meet.

Sincerely,

Frank Johnson

Frank Johnson

■ **Cover Letter** A short cover letter accompanies your résumé. *Since your résumé includes the information about you that is relevant to the job, what is the purpose of sending a cover letter along with it?*

■ Preparing Résumés and Cover Letters

A good letter of application may convince an employer to grant you an interview; however, a résumé and cover letter sent together are even more impressive. You can see an example of a traditional print résumé in Figure 38-4 on page 720. A résumé organizes the facts about you related to the job, which saves the employer time before and during an interview.

A cover letter is similar to a letter of application but without the information on education and experience (see Figure 38-5). It simply introduces you and allows you to say why you can do a good job for the company. Your cover letter should reflect your understanding of the company and how you may be able to meet its needs. Emphasize facts that make you especially well qualified for the job.

Your résumé outlines your qualifications for a particular job; therefore, you won't need to accompany it with a complete letter of application. When you send an employer a résumé, include a brief cover letter. The résumé makes filling out job applications a simpler process because you have all of the information organized already. Many people prepare a résumé as the first step in the job application process.

Even if you are not hired, many employers will keep your résumé on file for a certain period of time. If they have an opening for which you qualify in the future, they may call you.

38.2 ASSESSMENT

Reviewing Key Terms and Concepts

1. What are four important components of standard English?

2. Why do most employers prefer application forms?

3. What is the purpose of a letter of application?

4. What are the basic types of information that are contained in a résumé?

5. What is the purpose of a cover letter?

Thinking Critically

6. If you were an employer, what qualities do you think you would look for in a job seeker's application, application letter, or résumé?

Integrating Academic Skills

7. **MATH** Your prospective employer tells you that you can have your choice of being paid two ways. Either you will be paid a straight salary of $400 per week or a base salary of $200 per week, plus commissions of 13 percent of your sales. In your last job, you sold $2,000 a week. Assuming you will continue to sell at least that amount, which salary option should you take? What is the difference between the two?

The Job Interview

• What You'll Learn

- How to prepare for and conduct yourself properly during a job interview
- How to follow up a job interview

• Why It's Important

Almost all decisions to hire are made during or following an interview of an applicant. The goal of your search is to secure a job interview in which you may present yourself as the best applicant for the job.

Interviewing for a Job

Preparing application forms, letters of application, and résumés and cover letters, and using the Internet are all important parts of the job application process. Their purpose is to make an employer want to interview you. It is what happens during the interview that causes most employers to choose one applicant over others.

You, of course, want the interviewer to choose you for the job, so you will need to plan for a successful interview. Your plan should include three steps—preparing for an interview, conducting yourself properly during an interview, and following up an interview.

■ Preparing for an Interview

The employer's first impression of you will greatly affect whether you are offered a job. Remember that you never have a second chance to make a first impression. Appropriate grooming and dress, body language that shows confidence, and use of standard English all combine to make a good first impression. These are all things that you can control with some preparation.

DRESS AND GROOMING Employees in sales and office jobs followed a strict dress code in the past. Men wore suits, white shirts, ties, and leather shoes with dark socks, while women wore business suits or very conservative dresses, medium heeled shoes, and nylons. Today, employees in many stores and offices have adopted a dress code known as corporate casual. This does not mean, however, that you should dress casually for an interview. It is better to make the extra effort to make a good impression.

Your clothes should always be neat, clean, and wrinkle-free for every interview. In some cases, appropriate interview dress depends on the job. In sales, for example, people dress formally to make a good impression on customers. You need to show in the interview that you are aware of that and can dress appropriately. Many employers feel that if you don't care enough to dress up for the interview, then you don't care enough about the job.

Regardless of its style, your hair should be clean and neat. While this may seem unfair, you will have to please your employer if you truly want the job.

Employers will notice whether your hands are clean and your nails are neatly trimmed. Wearing a great deal of jewelry, for both men and women, can be distracting in an interview; too much makeup on women can also distract the interviewer. Also beware of wearing too much perfume or cologne. Strong scents can be overwhelming and distracting.

THINGS TO KNOW Before you schedule an interview, do some research on the company. You will make a better impression if you can talk intelligently about the company's products. It will show that you are interested in the firm. You can read company brochures or catalogs, check out information on a company's Web site, search for related newspaper articles, or talk with family members or teachers.

Once you call for an interview appointment, write down the date and time and ask for the interviewer's name. Check the spelling and make sure you can pronounce it correctly.

Before your interview, carefully review your résumé. Be ready to answer any questions about your education, work experience, or other qualifications.

The following questions are often asked of job applicants during interviews. Practice answering these questions so that you feel more confident. Get a family member or friend to help you by asking the questions and giving you feedback on how you answer.

- Why do you want to work for this company?
- Do you want permanent or temporary work?
- Why do you think you can do this job?
- What jobs have you had? Why did you leave?
- What classes did you like best in school?
- In what school activities did you participate?
- What do you want to be doing five years from now?
- Do you prefer working alone or with others?
- What is your main strength?
- What salary do you expect?
- What grades have you received in school?

- How do you feel about working overtime?
- How many days were you absent from school last year?
- Why should I hire you?
- When can you begin work?

■ Conducting Yourself Properly During an Interview

Always go alone for a job interview. Some young people take a friend along for moral support, but this is a mistake. Employers seldom hire anyone who can't handle an interview alone.

Plan to arrive for your interview five to ten minutes early. Always allow some extra time in case you run into traffic. You will appear careless and make a bad impression if you are even a little late or rush in at the last minute. Don't be too early, though. Waiting outside the interviewer's door for half an hour is not comfortable for you or the employer.

Before you meet the interviewer, you may meet a receptionist, administrative assistant, or other employees. Be courteous and polite to anyone you meet—these people might be your future co-workers. The interviewer may ask these people for their opinion of you after you are gone.

You may be asked to complete an application form before you are interviewed if you have not already done this. Be prepared by having a good pen (or two) with you. Bring along two copies of your résumé to the interview—one to leave with your interviewer if he or she wants it and one to help you fill out an application form.

■ **Dress Code** Although there is a trend to dress more casually in many jobs now, presenting yourself well at an interview includes being well dressed. *What can you tell about the man in this picture?*

■ **Sending Signals** Your body language tells as much about you as your actual words. *What is this young man's body language telling his interviewer about him?*

The receptionist or assistant may introduce you to the interviewer, or you may have to introduce yourself. In the latter case, say something like, "Good afternoon, I'm Mario Spinello, and I'm here about the sales associate position." Speak clearly and audibly and remember to smile. You should never chew gum during an interview. Grasp the interviewer's hand firmly in a handshake.

Remain standing until you are asked to sit down. When you do sit down, lean forward slightly toward the interviewer to show your interest. Relax and focus on your purpose: to make the best possible impression.

Place your purse or briefcase on the floor by your chair. Never put anything on the interviewer's desk, even if there is room. This may appear disrespectful or too casual. Don't let your eyes wander over papers on the interviewer's desk—it may look as though you are trying to read company correspondence.

It is normal to feel a little nervous at the beginning of an interview. You will relax as the interview progresses. Keep your hands in your lap, and try to keep them still. Never place your hands on the interviewer's desk. Look the interviewer in the eye most of the time and listen to him or her carefully. Most importantly, act confident and be yourself. The employer has taken his or her time to interview you because he or she has confidence that you are a qualified candidate.

WHAT TO SAY IN AN INTERVIEW Most interviewers begin by asking specific questions. Answer each question honestly—if you don't know the answer to a particular question, say so. The interviewer will probably realize it if you try to fake knowing the answer. Keep your answers short as no interviewer wants to listen to long stories. It may be necessary to elaborate a little if many of the questions seem to call for a simple yes or no.

Two particular questions often cause problems for young job applicants. These questions are, "What type of work would you like to do?" and "What wage (or salary) do you expect?" You can answer the first question by giving the name of the specific job you want. The question about expected wage or salary is a little more difficult if you don't have a specific wage or salary in mind. The best answer is something like, "What do you usually pay for this type of work?" Try to turn the question back to the interviewer.

You might not be offered the job if you request too large a salary; however, you may find yourself making less than other employees in the same job if your request is too low. You could mention a rate you know others get for the same type of work if it seems acceptable to you. Prepare for this before the interview by finding out what the going rate is for the type of work you want.

Your interviewer may simply say something like, "Tell me about yourself." You will have to do most of the talking in this situation. You should anticipate what the interviewer would like to know and present the information clearly. This type of interview is often difficult for the job applicant. Be sure to cover all your qualifications for the job. You should also say why you would like to work for this particular company, which is where your company research will help you.

Your interviewer may not mention pay at all. In that case, wait until the interview is almost over, then ask how much the job pays. It may appear that you are only interested in the money if you ask too soon. You also may want to ask about benefits if you are applying for a full-time, permanent job. These may include a paid vacation and insurance coverage. Wages and benefits are usually discussed toward the end of an interview.

The interviewer will expect you to ask some questions. It may appear that you aren't interested in the job or the company if you don't ask anything. Your interviewer will probably pause after telling you about the job and asking about your qualifications when it is time for you to ask questions. This is your time to ask a question referring to an article that you read, a new product that you learned about, or new markets that the company might be entering. Specific questions show the interviewer that you have done your research and are interested in learning more. The questions listed below are often asked by young applicants:

- Why is the position vacant?
- What are the hours of work?
- Does the company allow flex time?
- Would I be expected to work on the weekend?
- Is overtime common on this job?
- What are the opportunities for advancement?
- What is the pay?
- When will I be notified if I am hired?
- Will I have regular evaluations or reviews?
- What are some of the issues the person hired will need to address immediately?
- Does the company have plans for national or international expansion?
- How are the departments structured?
- Would I report to you if I am offered this job?
- What is the typical career path of someone starting in this position?
- What kind of benefits do you offer?
- Would I work individually or with a team?
- What is the dress code?
- Does the position require any travel?

You may be asked to a second interview with someone else in the company, such as a department head. This usually means you've made a good impression in your first interview, and your chances of being offered the job are good.

CLOSING THE INTERVIEW At the close of the interview, one of several things can happen. You may be offered the job and accept, you may be offered the job but decline, or you may be told that you will not be hired. More likely, however, you will be told that a decision will be made later. Don't be discouraged if no definite offer is made or a specific salary is not discussed. The interviewer will probably want to communicate with others in the company first or interview more applicants before making a decision immediately. It is also possible that the interviewer may want for you to meet with another person in the company. This is always a good sign.

If you are interested in the position, let the interviewer know. You can ask for the job or ask for the next interview if another interview is required. Be a good salesperson and say something like: "Mr./Ms. Employer, I am very impressed with what I've seen and heard here today and am confident that I could do an excellent job in the position you've described to me. When might you be in a position to make an offer?" Your enthusiasm should make a favorable impression.

If an offer is extended, accept it only if you are ready. If you are sure that you want it, accept it on the spot. If you want some time to think it over, be courteous and tactful in asking for that time. It is not unreasonable to want to think about this decision before making a commitment. Set a definite date when you can provide an answer (usually no more than 24–48 hours).

You will be able to sense when the interview is almost over. The interviewer will say something like, "Well, Mario, thank you for coming in" or "We'll decide by the end of the week." This is your cue to ask any last-minute questions. Then you should stand, smile, and thank your interviewer for his or her time and consideration. If you have expressed why you are you interested in the company and what can you offer, you have done all that you can. Usually, the interviewer will extend a hand for a handshake. Shake hands and go. Be sure to thank the receptionist or administrative assistant on your way out.

■ Following Up an Interview

Evaluate your performance after every interview whether you were offered the job or not. Which questions did you answer best? Which ones did you not answer very well? Were there any total disastrous questions? Did you use standard English? Each interview is a learning experience that will help prepare you for the next one.

It is unlikely you will be offered the job the same day as your interview if the employer is interviewing many people. The employer will want some time to consider all the applicants before making a decision. Many employers will check your references and call the school for a recommendation. This may take several days to a week or more. You can follow up your interview with a telephone call, a short thank-you letter sent a day or two after your interview, or a visit.

A thank-you letter is an appropriate way to follow up many interviews. Your letter should be brief and to the point. Simply thank the employer for the time given you and reaffirm your interest in the job. Include any information that you forgot to mention during the interview that will help qualify you for the position. Your letter may be either handwritten or typed, but it must be neat.

Unless you were told not to call, it is all right to telephone the employer five or six days after the interview. Ask to speak with the person who interviewed you. Then give your name and ask if he or she has made a decision on the job. This will let the employer know that you are still interested.

Over the Counter Interviews

Imagine having your big job interview with a computer. Dozens of big-name retailers, including Target and Macy's, are replacing paper applications and in-person interviews with in-store computer kiosks for screening applicants. The computer programs ask prospective employees about job history and work habits. They even serve up psychological tests that can help match an applicant's job skills and personalities with openings. Employers say that automated applications provide an edge in a tight labor market. They are able to sift through these new types of applications more quickly, weed out duds, identify talent, and attract candidates who might not have otherwise taken the time to apply. Some companies are beginning to offer computer applications over the Internet. Companies even foresee putting prospective employees into virtual video environments to see how they react in a stressful environment.

Thinking Critically

Do you think these applications can replace face-to-face interviews?

38.3 ASSESSMENT

Reviewing Key Terms and Concepts

1. What steps can you take to plan for a successful interview?

2. Why is it important to know something about the company before you interview?

3. How should you dress for a job interview?

4. How would you follow up a job interview?

Thinking Critically

5. What do you think about a situation in which a potential employer denies an applicant a job because he has long hair or a beard?

Integrating Academic Skills

6. **COMMUNICATION** Write a thank-you letter to follow-up an interview. The interview was for a job that you think you would enjoy doing and that you believe you could do very well. Remember to keep your letter brief and to the point.

Careers in Marketing

FASHION MERCHANDISING

Renie Hanna
Fashion Illustrator

Career Facts

Education and Training: A bachelor's or master's degree in graphic arts, or training from specialized art schools is recommended.

Aptitudes, Abilities, and Skills: Ability to visualize finished designs and to make detailed visual comparisons, as well as an accurate color sense, neatness, and precision are required to translate clients' ideas into two-dimensional representations.

Career Outlook: Employment is expected to grow through 2006 with keen competition, while the impact of computer-aided design programs may affect the need for trained artists.

Career Path: Internships, work as a paste-up artist, and freelancing help develop a reputation and clientele. Fashion artists may advance to art or design directors.

What does your job entail?

"As a fashion illustrator, I draw sketches of models, clothing, and fashion accessories for clients. I have to be both a business manager and an illustrator—I handle client billing, set up new contracts, and manage my own marketing through networking or my Web site. I always have new clients coming in which keeps my very busy. I have also been sent by my clients to various fashion shows worldwide to act as a consultant or to review my designs after they have been produced. "

What kind of training did you have?

"I have been a fashion illustrator for 20 years. I am always perfecting and refining my talents. When I was younger, I had a very realistic style, but it has become more stylized—it's my signature style. I attended the Fashion Institute of Technology in New York, The Parsons School of Design, and the John Murray School of Art, and have studied with Antonio Lopez in the Dominican Republic. "

How does your workload vary?

"I have to be my own business manager, and secretary, in addition to being an illustrator. On some days, I work on billing, updating my Web site, or answering e-mail, while other days I focus on my project designs in my studio or meet with clients. While I do get to set my own hours and be my own boss, I also always have to be available for the client at any time."

What is your key to success?

"The key to my success would have to be the level of professionalism I bring to my job. The development of my online portfolio was a great idea and brought many new clients. In the 20 years I have been working, I have NEVER missed a deadline. Every deadline is important—and everyone seems to need everything yesterday. I am prompt, enthusiastic, and professional. This industry is fueled by word of mouth, and I try to never disappoint my clients because that can come back to hurt you professionally."

Thinking Critically

Why is it essential to always meet deadlines?

VOCABULARY REVIEW

Use the following vocabulary terms in a paragraph describing an effective job search.

- job lead
- networking
- employment agencies
- private employment agencies
- direct contact
- standard English
- references
- résumé
- cover letter

FACT AND IDEA REVIEW

1. How old do you need to be to work without obtaining a work permit? (38.2)

2. What is standard English? Why should it be used when communicating with an employer? (38.2)

3. Who are good people to list as references on a job application? (38.2)

4. When listing your previous experience on a job application, what is the usual form? (38.2)

5. How long should your résumé be? (38.2)

6. How should you dress for a job interview? (38.3)

7. Describe how you would introduce yourself to an interviewer. (38.3)

8. What should you say if an interviewer asks what kind of work you would like to do? (38.3)

9. How should you respond if an interviewer asks you what salary you want? (38.3)

10. Why should you study your résumé before a job interview? (38.3)

THINKING CRITICALLY

1. How would you respond if you applied for a job at age 15 and the prospective employer told you it wasn't important for you to have a work permit, even though the law requires one?

2. If you were interested in working for a particular company, would you prefer to visit the personnel office in person, call on the phone, or write a letter of inquiry? Why?

3. What are some benefits to a company in advertising open positions online?

4. After the interview, John feels pretty confident he will get the job at Dal Pozzo Tires. When he doesn't hear anything in a week, John calls back a couple of times, but the manager doesn't return his calls. What further follow-up should John do?

BUILDING WORKPLACE SKILLS

1. **Human Relations** You are scheduled for a job interview. You arrive at the receptionist's desk terribly nervous and suddenly go completely blank. You can't remember the name of the person with whom you have the interview. What do you say to the receptionist? What might you have done to avoid this situation?

2. **Technology** Suppose that you are planning to attend a college in the Pacific Northwest—Washington or Oregon. You've previously spent some time in that area and think you would like to find a job there and make it your home after you graduate. Use the Internet to investigate the job market in that area. Use key words to focus on several specific market jobs in the Pacific Northwest, and list or print out your findings.

APPLYING MARKETING CONCEPTS

1. **Analyzing Body Language** With a classmate, use a word processing program to write a series of skits showing how body language and verbal communication can contribute to or detract from the success of a job interview. Present your skits to the class. Consider including the following characters:

   - the know-it-all applicant

   - the shy, nervous applicant who is unwilling (or unable) to provide information

   - the applicant who does not speak standard English

2. **Finding Jobs in Marketing** For one week, go through your newspaper's classified section and find jobs in the marketing field. Choose one company to research. Prepare for an imaginary interview at this firm by preparing the answers to the list of questions commonly asked by interviewers using a word processing program. Working in groups of four to five with one student acting as the interviewer, interview for the job. Have group members give you suggestions on ways to improve your performance.

3. **Creating a Networking System** Use a database program to create a file of all the professionals, friends, family members, and former employers who might be able to help you find work.

4. **Applying for a Job** Use your word processing program to prepare a letter of application and a résumé for a marketing job of your choice.

LINKING SCHOOL TO WORK

Interpersonal and Information Skills Ask an employer what the most important qualities are that he or she looks for during an interview. Write them down in order of importance. Compare your list with that of your classmates'.

Role Play: Interviewee

Situation You (participant) are going to be interviewed for a job at a financial services company.

Activity You have fifteen minutes to demonstrate to your career counselor (judge) that you are ready for the interview.

Evaluation You will be evaluated on how well you meet the following performance indicators:

- What clothing you should wear to the interview and why

- What 15 questions you are likely to be asked by the interviewer

- The attitude and body language you will use during the interview

- Familiarity with the elements of a typical résumé

*inter*NET CONNECTION

Jobs Online

You want a job in automotive retailing, and you are willing to move just about anywhere for the right position. You decide to make a search for openings nationwide.

Connect

- Find job search Web sites.
- Narrow your search to focus on auto sales.
- Compare job offerings in different parts of the United States.
- Write e-mail job queries in response to three of the most attractive offerings.

the Zazz Lab...

A Sports and Entertainment Marketing Simulation

WELCOME

Welcome to Zazz Sports and Entertainment Marketing Company. Zazz is devoted to serving the needs of its clients who include college, university, and professional sports teams, professional athletes, sporting events, and sports arenas plus major consumer product corporations, as well as television networks and movie studios. As an intern, you will have the opportunity to work on different clients' projects. All of your work will be assigned and reviewed by your department supervisor.

RESEARCH AND APPLY FOR A JOB OR AN INTERNSHIP PROGRAM

SITUATION

Due to its tremendous success this past year, Zazz is expanding its operations. As a result, there are many permanent job opportunities available at Zazz for qualified applicants. Your internship at Zazz is now over and it is time for you to make career decisions and prepare for the job application process.

ASSIGNMENT

Before you can start your career search, conduct a self-assessment. Consider your values, interests, personality; preferences for data, people, or things; skills and aptitudes, and level of education. Analyze three career areas related to sports and/or entertainment marketing that interest you. Prepare a Personal Career Profile that shows the degree to which your personal assessment matches the career area you have researched. Select one area to pursue, and formulate goals (ultimate, short-, medium-, and long-range) and a plan for reaching those goals. Apply for a position that will help you satisfy your first job-related goal outlined in your plan. Prepare a cover letter, application, resume, list of references, and a sample thank-you note you would send to the person who interviewed you. Prepare responses to ten common job interview questions to use in an interview role play.

Tools and Resources

To complete this assignment you will need to conduct research at a library or on the Internet. You will also need a word processing program and possibly a typewriter to complete the job application. Other resources include *Dictionary of Occupational Titles, Occupational Outlook Handbook, Occupational Outlook Quarterly, Guide for Occupational Exploration,* and *General Aptitude Test Battery.*

Research

Research three career areas of your choice related to sports and/or entertainment marketing. Investigate career trends, career outlook, duties, responsibilities, salary range, benefits, necessary education or training, and required skills and aptitudes. Also consider the work environment, work relationships, and what a typical day would be like. Arrange an informational interview with someone in that occupation to get first-hand information about your career choice. Research the company where you are applying to gain insight into its current and future status in that industry.

Report

Prepare a written report of your research findings, as well as written documents required for a job search (cover letter, résumé, and list of references). All written work is to be prepared using a word processing program. Arrange your written report around the following headings:

- Self Analysis
  - Values
  - Skills
  - Aptitudes
  - Interests
  - Preferences
  - Personality
  - Education
  - Other considerations
- Career research
  - Description of career area
    - Job responsibilities
    - Salary range and benefits
    - Education and/or special training
    - Experience required, if any
    - Employment trends and outlook
    - Skills and aptitudes required
    - Work environment
    - Work relationships
    - Interview with someone in the field
  - Personal career profile
  - Research on a prospective employer
  - Ten commonly asked interview questions and responses

- Job-search documents
  - Résumé
  - Sample application
  - Cover letter
  - List of references
  - Sample thank-you note

Presentation and Evaluation

In addition to preparing your written report, your supervisor wants you to conduct a simulated job interview role play. You will be evaluated on the following:

- Knowledge of the career area and job for which you are applying
- Knowledge of the company with which you are seeking employment
- Knowledge of yourself
- Ability to sell yourself
- Personal appearance
- Enthusiasm
- Voice quality
- Eye contact

Portfolio

Print a copy of your completed report and presentation for your Portfolio.

THE DECA CONNECTION

DECA Marketing Management Series
Reviewing job applicants and conducting job interviews with them could be a role play in this event.

DECA Sports and Entertainment Marketing Management Team Decision-Making Event
Establishing criteria for employment of new personnel in sports and entertainment industries, as well as deciding on an applicant's potential could be a topic for this event.

Glossary ✳

A

absolute advantage A country has special natural resources or talents that allow it to produce an item at the lowest cost possible.

ad layout A rough draft that shows the general arrangement and appearance of a finished ad.

adjacent colors Colors located next to each other in the color wheel that contrast only slightly.

advertising Any paid form of nonpersonal presentation and promotion of ideas, goods, or services by an identified sponsor.

advertising agencies Companies that work jointly with business clients to develop advertising campaigns.

advertising campaign The creation and coordination of a series of advertisements (both broadcast and print) around a particular theme to promote a product.

advertising proof Prepared by a newspaper or magazine to show exactly how an ad will appear in print.

agents Intermediaries that bring buyers and sellers together.

agreement A specific commitment that each member makes with a group.

allowance A partial return of the sale price for merchandise that the customer has kept.

aptitude An ability or potential for learning a certain skill.

Articles of Incorporation Filed with the corporation and securities bureau in a state department of commerce; they identify the name and address of your business, its purpose, the names of the initial directors, and the amount of stock to be issued to each director.

assertive Standing up for your rights, beliefs, and ideas.

asset Anything of monetary value that you own.

attitude research Marketing research designed to obtain information on how people feel about certain products, ideas, or companies.

B

Baby Boom Generation The 76 million babies born in the United States between 1946 and 1964.

balance of trade The difference in value between exports and imports of a nation.

balance sheet A summary of a business's assets, liabilities, and owner's equity.

banner ad A wide shallow rectangle at the top or bottom of a Web page that takes the user to the advertiser's Web page when clicked with a mouse.

bar graph A drawing made up of parallel bars whose lengths are proportional to the qualities being measured.

basic stock list Inventory monitoring plan used for staple items that should always be in stock.

benefits Privileges, or monetary payments beyond salary or wages, that go with a job.

blind check method Way of checking inventory that requires the receiver to write the description of the merchandise, count the quantities received, and list them on a blank form or dummy invoice.

blocks Things that interfere with understanding the message, including distractions, emotional blocks, and planning a response.

body language The gestures, posture, mannerisms, and eye contact through which persons communicate their thoughts with others.

bonded warehouse Public or private warehouses that store products requiring the payment of a federal tax.

boomerang method Handling an objection by bringing it back to the customer as a selling point.

brand extension A branding strategy that uses an existing brand name for an improved or new product in the product line.

brand licensing The legal authorization by a trademarked brand owner to allow another company (the licensee) to use its brand, brand mark, or trade character for a fee.

brand mark The part of the brand that is a symbol or design.

brand name The word, group of words, letters, or numbers representing a brand that can be spoken.

brand A name, term, design, or symbol (or combination of them) that identifies a business or organization and its products.

break-even point The point at which sales revenue equals the costs and expenses of making and distributing a product.

brick and mortar retailers Traditional retailers that sell goods to the customer from their own physical stores.

broadcast media Advertising that uses radio and television.

browser The software program that allows you to view Web pages.

budget accounts Charge accounts that allow for the payment of a purchased item over a certain time period without a finance charge.

bundle pricing Psychological pricing technique that includes several complementary products in a package that is sold at a single price.

business cycle Recurring slow-down and growth of an economy.

business philosophy Describes how you think your business should be run and shows your understanding of your business's role in the marketplace.

business plan A proposal that describes a new business to potential investors and lenders.

business risks The possibility of business loss or failure.

business All of the activities involved in producing and marketing goods and services.

business-to-business selling Form of selling that takes place in a manufacturer's or whole-salers' showroom (inside sales) or a customer's place of business (outside sales).

buying behavior The process individuals use to decide what they will buy, from where they will buy it, and who they will buy it from.

buying signals The things customers do or say to indicate a readiness to buy.

C

capital The money needed to start and operate a business.

capitalism An economic system characterized by private owner-ship of businesses and market-place competition.

career consultation An informational interview with a professional who works in a career that interests you.

career outlook The availability of jobs in any field.

carload The minimum number of pounds of freight needed to fill a boxcar.

cash flow statement A monthly plan that shows when you anticipate cash coming into the business and when you expect to pay out cash.

cash on delivery (COD) sale A transaction that occurs when a customer pays for merchandise at the time of delivery.

cash sale A transaction in which the customer pays for the pur-chase with cash or a check.

category management A process that involves managing product categories as individual business units.

CD-ROM A type of optical storage device identical to audio music CDs.

centralized buying Buying for all branches in a central location, such as company headquarters.

channel of distribution The path a product takes from producer or manufacturer to final user.

channels The avenues by which a message is delivered.

circle graph A geometric repre-sentation of the relative sizes of the parts of a whole.

clip art Illustrations that take the form of images, stock drawings, and photographs.

closing the sale Obtaining posi-tive agreement from the customer to buy.

co-branding strategy A brand-ing strategy that combines one or more brands to increase customer loyalty and sales for each indi-vidual brand.

cold canvassing A salesperson tries to locate as many potential customers as possible without checking out leads beforehand.

collateral Something of value that a borrower pledges to a lender to ensure repayment of a loan.

command economy The government is responsible for answering the three basic eco-nomic questions.

common carrier A company that provides transportation services to any business in its operating area for a fee.

communication The process of exchanging information, ideas, and feelings.

communications programs Software applications used to establish communication between your computer and other computers.

communist Countries that have a totalitarian form of government which runs everything.

community relations The activities that a business uses to acquire or maintain the respect of the community.

comparative advantage The value that a nation gains by selling the goods that it produces most efficiently.

competition The struggle between companies for customers.

complementary colors Colors opposite each other on the color wheel that create the greatest contrasts.

consensus A decision that each team member agrees to.

consignment buying Goods are paid for only after they are purchased by the final customer.

consumer Person who uses the product.

consumer affairs specialists People who design programs to reflect customer needs for information.

Consumer Price Index (CPI) Measures the change in price over a time of some 400 specific retail goods and services used by the average urban household.

consumerism The societal effort to protect consumer rights by putting legal, moral, and economic pressure on business.

contract carrier A for-hire carrier that provides equipment and drivers for specific routes, accord-ing to agreements between the carrier and the shipper.

Glossary

controlling The process of comparing what you planned with actual performance that involves setting standards, evaluating performance, and solving problems revealed.

cooperative advertising A cost-sharing arrangement whereby both a supplier and a local advertiser pay for advertising.

copy The selling message in a written advertisement.

corporation A business that is chartered by a state and legally operates apart from the owner or owners.

cost per thousand (CPM) The media cost of exposing 1,000 readers to an ad.

cost-plus pricing Pricing concept in which all costs and expenses are calculated, and then the desired profit is added to arrive at a price.

cover letter Letter that introduces you and allows you to say why you can do a good job for the company.

credit The opportunity to obtain money, goods, or services immediately in exchange for a promise to pay in the future.

credit union A cooperative association formed by labor unions or groups of employees for the benefit of its members.

customer Person who buys the product.

customer advisory boards Panels of consumers who make suggestions about products and businesses.

customer benefits The advantages or personal satisfaction a customer will get from a good or service.

customer profile Information about the target market with regard to the age, income level, ethnic background, occupation, attitudes, lifestyle, or geographic residence of the targeted customer.

customization The product and promotion strategy of creating new products for foreign markets.

customs brokers Specialists licensed by the U.S. Treasury Department.

D

data analysis The process of compiling, analyzing, and interpreting the results of primary and secondary data collection.

database programs Software applications used to collect related data, which can be sorted, searched through, and printed as needed.

database A collection or file of related information about a specific topic.

DBA "Doing Business As" designation for a sole proprietor or partnership.

debit card An ATM card used to make a purchase at a store.

debt capital Raising funds by borrowing money that will be repaid later.

decentralized buying Local store managers or their designated buyers are authorized to make special purchases for their individual stores.

decimal number A fraction or mixed number whose denominator is a multiple of 10.

demand The amount or quantity of goods and services that consumers are willing and able to buy at various prices.

demographics Statistics that describe a population in terms of personal characteristics.

denominator The bottom number in a fraction.

depression A period of prolonged recession.

derived demand The demand for industrial goods based on the demand for consumer goods and services.

desktop publishing programs Software applications used to design and produce professional printed materials.

Dictionary of Occupational Titles (DOT) U.S. Department of Labor publication that describes about 20,000 jobs and their relationships with data, people, and things.

digits The ten basic symbols: 0, 1, 2, 3, 4, 5, 6, 7, 8, 9.

direct check method Way of checking inventory in which the merchandise is checked directly against the actual invoice or purchase.

direct close The method of asking for the sale.

direct contact The process of visiting potential employers in person or calling them on the telephone.

direct distribution Goods or services are sold from the producer directly to the customer.

disclaimer A statement that contains exceptions to and exclusions from a warranty.

discount pricing Pricing technique that involves the seller's offering reductions from the usual price.

discretionary income The money left from a person's gross income after paying for basic living necessities such as food, shelter, and clothing.

disk drive Hardware used to read data from and write data to a disk.

display The visual and artistic aspects of presenting a product to a target group of customers.

disposable income The money left from a person's gross income after taking out taxes.

distractions Blocks to effective listening that include noises, environmental factors, interruptions, and competing thoughts.

distribution center A warehouse designed to speed delivery of goods and to minimize storage costs.

dollar control Method of stock control that represents the planning and monitoring of the total inventory investment that a business makes during a stated period of time.

drop shippers Wholesalers that own the goods they sell but do not physically handle the actual products.

DVD A high-density optical storage device capable of storing a full-length movie on a single disk the size of a CD.

E

e-commerce The buying and selling of goods through the use of electronic networks, usually the Internet.

economic risks Type of business risks that occur from changes in overall business conditions.

economy The way a nation makes economic choices.

elastic demand Situations in which a change in price creates a change in demand.

e-mail A system of exchanging written messages as well as voice and video messages.

e-marketplace An online shopping location.

embargo A total ban on specific goods coming into and out of a country.

emotional blocks Biases against the opinions expressed by the sender that prevent understanding.

emotional motive A feeling experienced by a customer through association with a product.

empathize To understand a person's situation or frame of mind.

employee discounts Discounts to encourage workers to buy the products their employer sells or manufactures.

empowerment Encouraging team members to contribute to and take responsibility for the management process.

endless chain method Salespeople ask previous customers for names of potential customers.

entrepreneurs People who organize, manage, and take the risk of owning and operating a business.

entrepreneurship The process of starting and managing your own business; the skills of people who are willing to risk their time and money to run a business.

equilibrium The point at which the amount of a product supplied equals the amount demanded.

equity capital Raising money from within your company or by selling part of the interest in the business.

e-tailing Retailers selling products over the Internet to the customer.

ethics Guidelines for good behavior.

euro The currency of the European Union.

European Union (EU) Europe's trading bloc.

everyday low prices (EDLP) Low prices are set on a consistent basis with no intention of raising them or offering discounts in the future.

exchange When something is sold in the marketplace; merchandise brought back to be replaced by other merchandise.

exclusive distribution Form of distribution that involves protected territories in a given geographic area.

excuses Insincere reasons for not buying or not seeing a salesperson.

exempt carrier Carrier of agricultural products, free from direct regulation of rates and operating procedures.

experimental method Research technique in which a researcher observes the results of changing one or more marketing variables while keeping certain other variables constant under controlled conditions.

exports Goods and services that are sold to other countries.

express warranty Warranty that is explicitly stated, in writing or spoken words, to encourage a customer to buy.

extended coverage Optional insurance coverage on a basic property coverage policy.

extension The result of multiplying the number of units by the cost per unit.

extensive decision making Used when there has been little or no previous experience with an item.

F

factors of production The technical term economists use for resources.

feature-benefit selling Matching the characteristics of a product to a customer's needs and wants.

feedback The receiver's response to the message.

fidelity bonds Protects a business from employee dishonesty.

finance Money or anything that can be sold very quickly to get money; borrowing money.

fixtures Permanent or movable store furnishings, such as display cases, counters, shelving, racks, and benches.

flexible-price policy Pricing policy that permits customers to bargain for merchandise.

floor limit The maximum amount a salesperson may allow a customer to charge without getting special authorization.

Glossary

forced-choice questions Survey questions that ask respondents to choose answers from possibilities given on a questionnaire.

foreign corporation Corporation incorporated under the laws of a different state from the one in which it does business.

form utility Changing raw materials or putting parts together to make them more useful; dealing with making, or producing, things.

formal balance When a large item is placed on one side of a display, an equally large item should be placed on the other side.

fractions Numbers used to describe a part of some standard amount.

franchise A grant or right to sell a parent company's product or service within a given area or territory.

free enterprise system System in which individuals start and operate their own businesses without government involvement.

freight forwarders Private companies that combine less-than carload or less-than truckload shipments from several different businesses and deliver them to their destinations; in international business, companies licensed by the U.S. Maritime Commission to handle export details.

full warranty A warranty that guarantees that if a product is found to be defective within the warranty period, it will be repaired or replaced at no cost to the purchaser.

G

general partnership Each partner shares in the profits and losses of the business.

Generation X The more than 40 million Americans born between 1965 and 1976.

Generation Y The 77 million Americans born between 1977 and 1997.

generic brands Brands that represent a general product category and do not carry a company or brand name.

geographics Segmentation of the market based on where people live.

globalization The product and promotion strategy of keeping a product and its advertising message the same around the world.

goods The kinds of things you can touch or hold in your hand.

graphics and design programs Software applications used to produce drawings and designs.

green marketing Companies make an effort to produce and promote environmentally safe products.

greeting approach method The salesperson welcomes the customer to the store.

gross domestic product (GDP) A measure of the goods and ser-vices produced using labor and property located in this country.

gross profit The difference between sales revenue and the cost of goods sold.

gross sales The total of all sales for any period of time.

Guide for Occupational Exploration (GOE) Reference that organizes the world of work into 12 interest areas that are sub-divided into work groups and subgroups.

H

hardware The physical components of a computer system.

headline The saying that gets the readers' attention, arouses their interest by providing a benefit, and leads them to read the rest of the ad.

home page Web site page that has links to other pages throughout the site.

horizontal organization Self-managing teams that set their own goals and make their own decisions.

human risks Type of business risks caused by human mistakes, as well as the unpredictability of customers, employees, or the work environment.

hypertext markup language (HTML) Language in which Web pages are written.

hypertext transport protocol (http) links together documents on the World Wide Web.

I

illustration The photograph or drawing used in a print advertisement.

implied warranty A warranty that exists automatically by state law whenever a purchase takes place.

imports Goods and services purchased from other countries.

incentives Higher-priced products earned and given through contests, sweepstakes, and rebates.

income statement A summary of a business's income and expenses during a specific period, such as a month, a quarter, or a year; often called *profit and loss statement.*

indirect distribution Selling the goods or services involves one or more intermediaries between the producer and customer.

industrial market Based on, or derived from, the demand for consumer goods and services.

inelastic demand Situations in which a change in price has very little effect on demand for a product.

inflation A period of rising prices.

informal balance Balancing a large item with several small ones.

information utility Communication with the consumer.

infrastructure The physical development of a country, including its roads, ports, sanitation facilities, and utilities, especially telecommunications.

initiative Doing what needs to be done without being urged.

installment accounts Charge accounts that allow for payment over a period of time.

institutional advertising Advertising attempts to create a favorable impression and goodwill for a business or an organization.

institutional promotion Communication used by a business to create a favorable image for itself.

insurance policy A contract between a business and an insurance company to cover a certain business risk.

integrated distribution Form of exclusive distribution in which manufacturers own and run their own retail operations.

intensive distribution Form of distribution that involves the use of all suitable outlets to sell a product.

interest The money paid for the use of money borrowed or invested.

intermediaries Distribution channel that provides value to producers because they have expertise in areas that producers do not have.

international trade The exchange of goods and services between nations.

Internet The world's biggest computer network.

internship Student's direct work experience and exposure to various aspects of a career, either with or without pay.

inventory management The process of buying and storing products for sale while controlling costs for ordering, shipping, handling, and storage.

inventory An amount of goods stored, including raw materials, purchased components, manufactured subassemblies, works in process, packaging materials, and finished goods.

invoice Customer bill included with delivered merchandise when filling a PO-based order.

J

jargon Technical or specialized vocabulary used by members of a particular profession or industry.

job descriptions Written statements listing the requirements of a particular job.

job lead Information about a job opening.

joint ventures Partnerships that allow companies to participate in another country's economy.

just-in-time (JIT) inventory system An arrangement in which suppliers deliver parts and raw materials just before they are needed for production.

L

label An information tag, wrapper, seal, or imprinted message that is attached to a product or its package.

labor All of the people who work in the economy.

land Everything on the earth that is in its natural state.

laptop A small, portable personal computer.

law of diminishing marginal utility Law that states that consumers will buy only so much of a given product, even through the price is low.

layaway Merchandise removed from stock and kept in a separate storage area until the customer pays for it.

layman's terms Words the average customer can understand.

liability A debt that you owe.

lifestyle goals Reflect your vision of how you see yourself living in the future.

limited decision making Used when a person buys goods and services that he or she has purchased before but not regularly.

limited partnership Each limited partner is liable for any debts only up to the amount of his or her investment in the company.

limited warranty A warranty that may exclude certain parts of the product from coverage or require the customer to bear some of the expense for repairs resulting from defects.

line graph A graph that uses a line joining points representing changes in a variable quantity, usually over a specific period or time.

local radio advertising Advertising done by a local business for its target market.

loss leader An item priced at cost to draw customers into a store.

M

mainframe Large computers, sometimes filling a whole room.

maintained markup The difference between an item's final sale price and its cost.

management The business function used to plan, organize, and control all available resources to reach company goals.

manufacturer brand Brand owned and initiated by manufacturers; also called *producer brands*.

market All potential customers who share common needs and wants, and who have the ability and willingness to buy the product.

market economy Economy in which there is no government involvement in economic decisions.

Glossary

market position Marketers' relative standing in relation to their competitors.

market research The systematic gathering, recording, analyzing, and presentation of information related to marketing goods and services.

market segmentation A way of analyzing a market by specific characteristics in order to create a target market.

market share A firm's percentage of the total sales volume generated by all competitors in a given market.

marketing concept Businesses must satisfy customers' needs and wants in order to make a profit.

marketing information system A set of procedures and methods that regularly generates, stores, analyzes, and distributes marketing information for use in making marketing decisions.

marketing mix Four basic marketing strategies, collectively known as the four Ps—product, place, price, and promotion.

marketing research The marketing function that links the consumer, customer, and public to the market through information.

marketing The process of developing, promoting, and distributing products to satisfy customers' needs and wants.

marketplace Wherever two or more people agree to buy and sell a product.

markup pricing Pricing concept used by wholesalers and retailers involved in acquiring goods for resale; based on the difference between the price of an item and its cost.

marquee An architectural canopy that extends over store's entrance.

media research Marketing research that focuses on issues of media selection and frequency.

media The agencies, means, or instruments used to convey advertising messages to the public.

memorandum buying The supplier agrees to take back any unsold goods by a certain date.

merchandise approach method The salesperson makes a comment or asks questions about a product in which the customer shows interest.

microcomputer Personal computer (PC) used in most medium and smaller businesses.

middle management Implements the decisions of top management.

minicomputer Computers ideal for organizations and companies that cannot afford or do not need a mainframe system.

mini-nationals Midsize and smaller companies that have operations in foreign countries.

mission statement Describes the ultimate goals of a company.

mixed number A whole number and a fraction together.

mixed-brand strategy A branding strategy that involves simultaneously offering a combination of manufacturer, private distributor, and generic brands.

model stock list Inventory monitoring plan used for fashionable merchandise.

monopoly Exclusive control over a product or the means of producing it.

multinationals Large corporations that have operations in several countries.

multiple-unit pricing Setting prices to suggest a bargain and help to increase sales volume.

N

national spot radio advertising Used by national firms to advertise on a local station-by-station basis.

nationalize Government takes ownership of property and the owners get nothing in return.

natural risks Type of business risks that result from natural causes such as floods, tornadoes, hurricanes, fires, lightning, droughts, earthquakes, and unexpected changes in normal weather conditions.

net income The amount left after the total expenses are subtracted from gross profit.

net sales The amount left after gross sales have been adjusted for returns and allowances.

net worth The difference between the assets of a business and its liabilities.

network radio advertising A broadcast from a studio to all affiliated radio stations throughout the country.

networking Finding contacts among people you know, including family and friends, former employers, and professional people you know personally.

never-out list Inventory monitoring plan used for best-selling products that make up a large percentage of sales volume.

news release A prewritten story about a company that is sent to the various media.

nonprice competition Businesses choose to compete on the basis of factors not related to price.

nonprofit organizations Service organizations not operated for the purpose of making a profit.

nonverbal communication Expressing yourself through body language.

North American Free Trade Agreement (NAFTA) An international trade agreement among the United States, Canada, and Mexico.

numerator The top number in a fraction.

O

objection analysis sheet Lists common objections and possible responses to them.

objections Concerns, hesitations, doubts, or other honest reasons a customer has for not making a purchase.

observation method A research technique in which the actions of people are watched and recorded either by cameras or observers.

occupational area A category of jobs that involves similar skills and aptitudes.

Occupational Outlook Handbook (OOH) U.S. Department of Labor publication that provides information on more than two hundred occupations; updated every two years.

odd-even pricing Setting prices that all end in either odd or even numbers.

on-approval sale Customer permitted to take merchandise home for further consideration.

one-price policy Pricing policy in which all customers are charged the same price for goods and services.

online advertising Advertising messages on the Internet.

open-ended questions Questions that require more than a yes or no answer; survey questions that ask respondents to construct their own response.

opening cash fund The coins and currency designated for the register for a given day's business.

open-to-buy The amount of money left for buying goods after all other expenses have been considered.

organization chart A diagram of the various jobs and functions that are found in a company.

organizational buyers People who buy goods for business purposes, usually in much greater quantities than the average consumer.

organizing A coordinated effort to reach a company's planning goals.

P

package The physical container or wrapping for a product.

paraphrase Restating (objections) in a different way.

parcel post A type of standard surface package delivery offered by the U.S. Postal Service.

parliamentary procedure A structure for holding group meetings and making decisions.

partnership A legal agreement between two or more people to be jointly responsible for the success or failure of a business.

PDAs The smallest portable computers.

penetration pricing Pricing policy that sets the initial price for a new product very low.

percent Number expressed in parts per hundred.

performance bonds Insurance against losses that might occur when work or a contract is not finished on time or as agreed; also called *surety bonds.*

perpetual inventory system Tracks the number of items in inventory on a constant basis.

personal financial statement A summary of your current personal financial condition.

personal selling Any form of direct contact occurring between a salesperson and a customer.

physical distribution All the activities that help to ensure that the right amount of product is delivered to the right place at the right time.

physical inventory system Method of physical inventory control in which stock is inspected or actually counted to determine the quantity on hand.

pie chart A circle graph that looks like a pie cut into slices of different sizes.

place utility Having a product where customers can buy it.

planning goals Small steps you take to get from where you are now to where you want to be.

planning The first step in the management process that involves deciding what will be done and how it will be accomplished.

planogram Computer-developed diagrams that show retailers how and where products within a category should be displayed on a shelf at individual stores.

point-of-sale research A powerful form of research that combines natural observation with personal interviews to get people to explain buying behavior.

point-of-sale (POS) system Computers used in retailing that feed information directly from merchandise tags or product labels into a computer.

possession utility The exchange of a product for some monetary value.

preapproach Getting ready for the face-to-face encounter in a selling situation.

premiums Low-cost items given to consumers at a discount or for free.

preretailing marking method Pricing information is marked on merchandise in advance on the purchase order.

presentation software Software applications used to create slide shows or multimedia presentations all in one program.

Glossary

press conference A meeting in which a business or organization invites media members to hear an announcement about a news-worthy event.

press kit A folder containing articles, news releases, feature stories, and photographs about a company, product, or person.

prestige pricing Setting higher-than-average prices to suggest status and prestige to the consumer.

price competition Competition that focuses on the sale price of a product.

price discrimination A firm charges different prices to similar customers in similar situations.

price fixing Competitors agree on certain price ranges within which they set their own prices.

price lining Pricing technique that requires a store to offer all merchandise in a given category at certain prices.

price The value of money (or its equivalent) placed on a good or service.

primary data Data obtained for the first time and used specifically for the particular problem or issue under study.

principal Amount of money that you borrow to start your business.

print media Written advertising that may be included in every-thing from newspapers and magazines to direct mail, signs, and billboards.

private carrier Carrier that trans-ports goods for an individual business.

private distributor brand Brand owned and initiated by whole-salers and retailers; also called *private brands, store brands,* or *dealer brands.*

private employment agencies Employment agencies not sup-ported by taxes, that must earn a profit to stay in business.

private sector Businesses not associated with government agencies.

private warehouse A facility designed to meet the specific needs of its owner.

privatization The process of selling government-owned busi-nesses to private individuals.

problem definition A business clearly identifies a problem or research issue and the informa-tion necessary to solve it.

Producer Price Index (PPI) Measures wholesale price levels in the economy.

product depth The number of product items offered within each product line.

product features Basic, physical, or extended attributes of the product or purchase.

product item A specific model, brand, or size of a product within a product line.

product life cycle The stages that a product goes through during its life, including introduction, growth, maturity, and decline.

product line A group of closely related products that are manu-factured or sold by a business.

product mix All of the different products that a company makes or sells.

product modification An altera-tion in a company's existing product.

product planning Making deci-sions about those features that are needed to sell a business's products, services, or ideas.

product positioning Focused on the image a product projects.

product promotion Commu-nication used by a business to convince potential customers to buy its products instead of buying from a competitor.

product research Marketing research that centers on evaluating product design, package design, product usage, and consumer acceptance of new and existing products.

product width The number of different product lines a business manufactures or sells.

production The process of cre-ating, growing, manufacturing, or improving on goods and services.

productivity Output per worker hour.

products Goods and services, both of which have monetary value and satisfy customers' needs and wants.

profit The money earned from conducting business after all costs and expenses have been paid.

promotion Any form of communi-cation a business or organization uses to inform, persuade, or remind.

promotional advertising Adver-tising designed to increase sales.

promotional mix A combination of the different types of promotion.

promotional pricing The psy-chological pricing technique generally used in conjunction with sales promotions when prices are lower than average.

promotional tie-ins Sales promotional arrangements between one or more retailers or manufacturers.

proportion The relationship between and among objects in a display.

prospect A potential customer; also called a *lead.*

prosperity Point in the business cycle when the economy flour-ishes; also called *expansion.*

psychographics Studies of consumers based on social and psychological characteristics.

psychological pricing Pricing techniques that create an illusion for customers or that make shopping easier for them.

public employment agencies Employment agencies supported by state or federal taxes that offer free services to both job applicants and employers.

public relations Any activity designed to create a favorable image toward a business, its products, or its policies.

public sector Local, state, and federal government agencies and services, such as public schools and public libraries.

public warehouse A facility that offers storage and handling facilities to individuals or companies.

publicity A specific kind of public relations that involves placing positive and newsworthy information about a business, its products, or its policies in the media.

pull policy Promotion policy designed to create consumer interest.

purchase order A legal contract between the buyer and the supplier.

push policy Promotion policy used only with the next partner in the distribution channel.

Q

quality check method Checking inventory to inspect the workmanship and general characteristics of the received merchandise.

quorum A proportion of the membership needed to conduct official business.

quota Limits either the quantity or the monetary value of a product that may be imported.

R

rack jobbers Wholesalers that manage inventory and merchandising for retailers by counting stock, filling it in when needed, and maintaining store displays.

rational motive A conscious, logical reason for a purchase.

realistic goal Goal that you have a reasonable chance of achieving.

real-time inventory system System of inventory that lets a company constantly track every product it sells from when it's manufactured, or when it arrives in its warehouse, to when the customer orders it online, to when it arrives at the buyer's door.

receiving record A form that is used to describe the goods received by a business.

recession A period of economic slowdown that lasts for two quarters, or six months.

recovery The increase in the overall economic activity.

references People who know your work habits and personal traits well and who will recommend you for the job.

referrals The names of other people who might buy a product or use a service.

regular, or 30-day, charge accounts Charge accounts that allow customers to charge purchases during a month and pay the balance in full within 30 days after they are billed.

relationship marketing Strategies businesses use to stay close to their customers.

reliability A research technique that produces nearly identical results in repeated trials.

resident buying offices Retailers' representatives in a central market.

resources All the things used in producing goods and services.

résumé A brief summary of personal information, education, skills, work experience, activities, and interests.

retailers Channel of distribution that buys goods from wholesalers or directly from manufacturers and resells them to the final consumer.

return Merchandise brought back for a cash refund or credit.

return on investment A calculation used to determine the relative profitability of a product.

reverse auction Companies post what they want to buy and suppliers bid for the contract.

revolving accounts Charge accounts for which the retailer determines the credit limit and when payments are due.

risk management The systematic process of managing an organization's risk exposure to achieve objectives in a manner consistent with public interest, human safety, environmental factors, and the law.

risk The possibility of financial loss; the potential for loss or failure in relation to the potential for improved earnings.

routine decision making Used when a person needs little information about a product that he or she is buying.

S

sales incentives Awards given to managers and employees who successfully meet or exceed a sales quota.

sales promotion All marketing activities, other than personal selling, advertising, and public relations, that are used to stimulate consumer purchasing and sales effectiveness.

sales tax A fee placed on the sale of goods and services.

Glossary

sales transaction The process of recording a sale and presenting the customer with proof of payment.

sample A part of the target population that is assumed to represent the entire population.

scanner Hardware that reads documents and transforms images into digital data.

scarcity The difference between wants and needs and available resources.

seasonal discounts Offered to buyers willing to buy at a time outside the customary buying seasons.

secondary data Data that have already been collected for some purpose other than the current study.

selective distribution Form of distribution in which a limited number of outlets in a given geographic area are used to sell the product.

service approach method The salesperson asks the customer if he or she needs assistance.

service close Explains services that overcome obstacles or problems.

services The kinds of things you can't physically touch; tasks performed for a customer.

setting Where communication takes place.

shortages Market situation in which demand exceeds supply.

signature Logotype (logo) symbol used to distinctly identify a business.

six-month merchandise plan The budget that estimates planned purchases for a six-month period.

skimming pricing Pricing policy that sets a very high price for a new product.

slogan A catch phrase or small group of words that are combined in a special way to identify a product or company.

slotting allowance A cash premium paid by the manufacturer to a retail chain for the costs involved in placing a new product on its shelves.

socialist Countries that try to reduce the differences between rich and poor.

software A set of electronic instructions that directs the CPU to carry out a specific task.

sole proprietorship A business owned and operated by one person.

source marking Use of Universal Product Codes (UPCs) in which the seller or manufacturer marks the price before delivering the merchandise to the retailer.

specialty media Relatively inexpensive, useful items with an advertiser's name printed on them.

specific goal Goal stated in exact terms that includes some details.

sponsorship The promotion of a company in association with a property.

spot check method Way of checking inventory in a random check of one carton in a shipment.

spreadsheet programs Software applications used to organize, calculate, and analyze numerical data.

standard English The formal style of writing and speaking that you have learned in school.

standing-room-only close Used when a product is in short supply or when the price will be going up in the near future.

start-up costs A projection of how much money you will need in your first year of operating a business.

stock turnover The number of times the average inventory has been sold and replaced in a given period of time.

stockholders The people who own the corporation with limited liability.

stockkeeping unit (sku) Each item or group of related items in a unit control inventory system.

storage The marketing function of holding goods until they are sold.

store layout The way store floor space is used to facilitate and promote sales and to best serve the customer.

storefront The store's sign, marquee, outdoor lighting, banners, planters, awnings, windows, and the building itself (its design and setting).

Subchapter S corporation A small business that is taxed like a partnership or proprietorship.

suggestion selling Selling additional goods or services to the customer.

supercomputer The largest and most powerful type of computer used for the most sophisticated work.

superior point method Salesperson acknowledges objections as valid yet still offset them with other features and benefits.

supervisory-level management Front-line managers that supervise the activities of employees who carry out the tasks determined by the plans of middle and top management.

supply The amount or quantity of goods and services that producers will provide at various prices.

surpluses Market situation in which supply exceeds demand.

survey method A research technique in which information is gathered from people through the use of surveys or questionnaires.

T

target marketing Focusing all marketing decisions on a very specific group of people who you want to reach.

tariff A tax on imports; also called *duty*.

telemarketing The process of selling over the telephone.

test marketing Type of marketing research that occurs when a new product is placed in one or more selected geographic areas.

third party method Handling objections by using a previous customer or another neutral person who can give a testimonial about the product.

tickler control Method of physical inventory control in which a small portion of the inventory is physically counted each day so that the entire inventory is accounted for on a regular basis.

till The cash drawer of a cash register.

time utility Having a product available at a certain time of year or a convenient time of day.

ton-mile The movement of one ton of freight one mile.

top management Those who make the planning decisions that affect the whole company.

trade character A brand mark with human form or characteristics.

trade discounts The way manufacturers quote prices to wholesalers and retailers.

trade name Identifies the company or a division of a particular corporation.

trademark A brand name, brand mark, trade name, trade character, or a combination of these, that is given legal protection by the federal government.

trading area The geographical area from which a business draws its customers.

transportation The marketing function of moving products from a seller to a buyer.

trial close An initial effort to close a sale.

U

unit control Method of stock control which measures quantities of merchandise that a business handles during a stated period of time.

unit pricing Method of pricing that allows consumers to compare prices in relation to a standard unit or measure, such as an ounce or a pound.

Universal Product Code (UPC) Bar code used for electronic entry.

Universal Vendor Marketing (UVM) Product code that appears as a series of numbers across the top of a price tag.

unlimited liability As a sole proprietor, your financial liability is not limited to the investment in the business, but extends to your total ability to make payments.

Uniform Resource Locator (URL) The code used to identify and locate Web pages on the Internet.

utility The attributes of a product or service that make it capable of satisfying consumers' wants and needs.

V

validity The questions asked in a questionnaire measure what was intended to be measured.

values Beliefs that guide the way people live.

vertical organization Up and down structure of an organization.

visual merchandising The coordination of all the physical elements in a place of business that are used to project the right image to its customers.

W

want slips Customer requests for items that are not carried in the store.

warranty A promise, or guarantee, given to a customer that a product will meet certain standards.

warranty of fitness for a particular purpose The seller advises a customer that a product is suitable for a particular use and the customer acts on that advice.

warranty of merchantability A promise from the seller that the product sold is fit for its intended purpose.

Web page Contains text, photos, graphics, and hyperlinks.

Web page editors Software applications used to create Web pages.

which close Customer is encouraged to make a decision between two items.

wholesale and retail buyers People who purchase goods for resale; they forecast customers' needs and buy the necessary products to meet those needs.

wholesalers Obtain goods from manufacturers and resell them to industrial users, other wholesalers, and retailers.

word processing programs Software applications used to create documents that are primarily text and some graphics

World Trade Organization (WTO) A global coalition of 135 governments that makes the rules governing international trade.

World Wide Web A collection of interlinked documents that resides on the Internet.

Index

Index

Index

Index

Index

Index

Index

Index

Index

Index

Index

Virtual tours, 245
Virtual yard sale, 456
VISA, 281–283, 568, 594, 691
Viselman, Kenn, 569
Visionary Shopper, 516
Visual control of inventory, 436
Visual merchandising, 308
  defined, 319
  interior displays, 322–324
  store interior, 322
  store layout, 321
  storefront, 320–324
Volkswagen Beetle, 591
Volkswagen Company, 568

W

W.W. Grainger, 423
Walgreen, 653
Wall Street Journal, The, 336, 399, 525, 641
Wal-Mart
  business philosophy, 641
  cost and control by, 383
  as Costco rival, 494
  discontinuing products, 46
  one-stop shopping at, 43
Walt Disney World, 328
Want slips, 417–418
Warehouses
  private, 403–404
  public, 404
  self-serve, 415
Warehouse Logistics Association, 407
Warner Brothers, 308
Warner-Lambert Company, 168, 388, 560, 561
Warranties, 585–589
  defined, 585
  disclaimers, 587
  express, 585–586
  extended, 587
  full, 586
  implied, 587
  limited, 586
  product planning and, 587–589
  product and service, 633
Warranty of fitness for a particular purpose, 587
Warranty of merchantability, 587
Water transportation, 397–398
Waterford crystal, 474, 494
Watson, Al, 239

Watson and Associates, 389
Web, 170. *See also* Internet; Web site; Web sites; World Wide Web
Web page editors, 165–166
Web site
  development and maintenance, 355
  e-marketplace vs. private, 387
  e-tailers', 377
  job-hunting, 695
  photo sharing company, 221
  physicians, 148
Web sites
  Amazon.com, 377
  Ashford.com, 399
  Cameraworld.com, 237
  Direct Focus, 384
  Discovery.com, 173
  ebay.com, 245, 472, 609, 632
  eBreviate.com, 421
  e-GM, 441
  Excite.com, 491
  Expedia.com, 285
  FreeMarkets.com, 421
  General Motors, 260
  Grainger.com, 423
  HomeGrocer.com, 341
  IRS, 137
  HomeTownStores.com, 237
  Hotjobs.com, 710
  Medibuy.com, 423
  Monster.com, 710
  necx.com, 423
  Panasonic B2B, 386
  Priceline.com, 285
  Ticketmaster.com, 386
  Travelocity.com, 285
  Wal-Mart, 43
  WebSwap.com, 456
Westat, 526
Weyerhauser Lumber Company, 81
Wham-O, 387, 664
Which close, 259
White, Krista Brennecke, 187
White Pages, 338
White Wave packaging, 577
Whole numbers, writing, 119–120
Wholesale and retail buyers, 412
Wholesalers, 84, 376
Wilkinson, William, 200
Will-call, 284
Wilson, Ron, 619
Window display, 321
Wired hotel rooms, 90

Women
  food for, 180
  in top positions, 202
Women's Wear Daily, 418
Woodland, Norman Joseph, 435
Woods, Tiger, 42
Woods and Poole Economics, Inc., 512
Word processing programs, 162
Work experience program, 708
Workers' compensation insurance, 633
Work to Learn, 697
Workplace trends, 30, 91–92
World Trade Organization (WTO), 102–104
World Wide Web, 84–85, 170, 377. *See also* Internet; Web site; Web sites
Wozniak, Steve, 201, 607, 617
Writing
  basic considerations, 148
  business letters, 150–151
  company publications, 152
  e-mail, 151
  letters, 151
  memos, 151–152
  reports, 151–152
  writing style, 148–149

X

Xenophobia, 112
Xerox, 567
X-Files, 308

Y

Yahoo!
  for job search, 710
  loyalty marketing programs, 309
  origin of, 221
  PepsiCo promotion, 572
Yang, Jerry, 221
Yee sisters, 616
Yellow Pages, 338, 642, 697
Yes/no questions, 533
"You've Got Mail," 308

Z

Zamboni, Frank, 696
Zhen cosmetics, 616
Zillions magazine, 516
Zing, 221
Zoning regulations, 646

Competitive Event Correlation

Role Play

DECA Connections

Technology Connections

※

• Internet Activities

School-to-Work Connections

School-to-Work Connections

School-to-Work Connections

School-to-Work Connections

Photography Credits

Photography Credits: AFP/Corbis 683; Adidas 313; Colin Allen, Vice President of Sales, RefrigiWear Inc and for design: Katherine Hook 219(ml); Allstate 311; Barbara Alper/Stock Boston 380(l); Anderson 586(b); Apple Computer 361; The Arbitron Company 514; Arctic Cat Inc. 301; Bill Aron/PhotoEdit 326, 338, 425, 463; Daniel Arsenault/The Image Bank 539; Audit & Surveys Worldwide 526; Auto-Owners Insurance 631(br); Bruce Ayres/Stone 457(ml); BMW 476; Bachmann/PhotoEdit 145, 694(t); Baking Buyer 217(tr); Band-Aid 554; Jose Luis Banus-March/FPG International LLC 78(t); Barbie 459; Tim Barnwell/Stock Boston 63; Paul Barton/The Stock Market 613(tl); Bentley Motor Cars 458; Big Bang Products 619; Bloomingdale's 43(l); Mark Bolster/International Stock 394(bl); Dan Bosler/Stone 4(r), 604(r); Robert Brenner/PhotoEdit 46, 340(br); Michelle Bridwell/PhotoEdit 410; Tim Brown/Stone 628(tr); Mark C. Burnett/Stock Boston 298; Gary Buss/FPG International LLC 111, 237; Peter Byron/PhotoEdit 16; Campbell Soup Company 108(mr); John Caremolla/Allsport 242; Chris Carroll/Corbis 203; Steve Casimior/Stone 509; Myrleen Ferguson Cate/PhotoEdit 22(ml), 340(tr), 724; Charmin 357; Chemlawn 586(t); Steve Chenn/Corbis 502(t); Chrysler, 551(br), 551(mr); Columbia Sportswear Company 251; Paul Conklin/PhotoEdit 83, 398; Gary A. Conner/PhotoEdit 690(tl); Corbis 317(l), 371(r), 543(l); Cosmair, Inc. 553; Tony Craddock/Stone 389; Bill Crump/Image Bank 282; Jim Cummins/FPG International LLC 708; Cure'l 308; DECA 302; Michael K. Daly/Stock Market 686; Phil Degginger/Stone, 169; Delta Airlines 362; Doug Denginger/Allsport USA 703; Stephen Derr/Image Bank xvi, 606; Disario/The Stock Market 628(mr); Discover Card 594; David Doody/FPG International LLC 231; Mark Douet/Stone 275(tl); E-billboards 339; Sean Ellis/Stone 435; Bob Elsdale/The Image Bank 208(b); Amy C.Etra/PhotoEdit 87, 479(ml), 588(bl), 608, 628(ml), 630; FPG International LLC 118, 638; Federal Express 405; Jon Feingersh/Stock Market 256; Jon Ferrey/Allsport 296(t); Ken Fisher/Stone 153, 457(bl); Focus Suites 515; Food Logistics 217(bm); Ford Motor Company 534; Jim Foster/The Stock Market 394(mr); Owen Franken/Stock Boston 466; David Frazier/Stone 274; Tony Freeman/PhotoEdit 93(tr), 201, 323(br), 613(tr); Tim Fuller Photography 214, 222, 253(2), 265(ml), 265(tr), 269, 300(br), 323(tl), 376, 448(b), 448(t), 572; Geisser/H. Armstrong Roberts 53; General Mills 576(t); General Motors 360; Glencoe Stock 2, 55, 207(r), 295, 447(l), 447(r), 501(b), 501(t), 543(r), 581; Gore-Tex Fabric 588(mr); Grainger 423; Spencer Grant/Photo Edit 9(bl), 9(m), 9(tr), 108(tr), 163, 252, 275(bm), 275(tr), 399, 461, 524(tl), 525, 527, 615; Jeff Greenberg/International Stock 548(b); Jeff Greenberg/Leo de Wys xvii, 709; Jeff Greenberg/PhotoEdit 9(bl), 108(bl), 235, 300(mr), 323(mr), 413, 524(bl); Howard Grey/Stone 192(ml); Charles Gupton/The Stock Market 609; Dennis Hallinan/FPG International LLC 276; Mia Hamm© 1999 America's Dairy Farmers and Milk Processors 25; Harris Interactive 506; Hastings Mutual Insurance Company 631(tr); Tom Hauck/Allsport 531; Hewlett-Packard 160(mr), 160(br), 173; Hilton Hospitality, Inc. 475; Hilton Hotels 309; Walter Hodges/Stone 190, 394(tr); Holiday Inn 535; Katherine Hook, Director of Marketing and Internet Development, RefrigiWear Inc. 219(tr); Hulton Getty Picture Library 69(tl); Billy Hustace/Stone 93(br); Hyundai 588(tr); Index Stock 4(l), 60, 69(mr), 159, 219(br), 230(bl), 244, 291, 323(bl), 329, 394(tl), 454, 566, 684(b), 723, 731; Internal Revenue Service 359; International Stock 58, 395, 517; Invensys PLC 358; Iprocure.com 419; J.C. Penny 516(2); Bob Jacobson/International Stock 133; Janeart/Image Bank 246; David Joel/Stone 192(br); Johnny Stockshooter/International Stock 432; Chris Jones/Stock Market 80; Jonsered 588(bl); Zigy Kalunzy/Stone 5(r); Bonnie Kamin/PhotoEdit 170, 457(tr); Keyphotos Image Photography/The Stock Market 604(b); Bob Krist/Leo de Wys 135; Robert Laberge/Allsport 296(b); Richard Laird/FPG International LLC 69(bl); Richard Laird/Leo de Wys 655; Peter Langone/International Stock 17, 90; L'eggs Products 588(tl); Leo de Wys 694(m); Barbara Leslie/FPG International LLC 622; Llewellyn/Uniphoto 92(tr); Romilly Lockyer/Image Bank 210, 727; Macy's 480; MailStation 349; Mike Malyszko/FPG International LLC 524(br); Gregg Mancusco/Stock Boston 138; Marriott Photo Services 264; Marshall's 43(r); Felicia Martinez/PhotoEdit 92(ml), 331, 479(tr), 599; Mattel 303; Tom & DeeAnn McCarthy/Stock Market 695; McDonald's Corporation 307; Mathew Neal McVay/Stone 412; Meat & Poultry 217(ml); Lawrence Migdale/Stone 641; Jean Miele/The Stock Market 679; Bill Miles/The Stock Market 690(bl); Art Montes De Oca/FPG International LLC 320, 428; Montgomery Ward 587; Scott Morgan/FPG International LLC 116(b); Alese Mortpechter/The Stock Market 321; John Neubauer/PhotoEdit 613(bl); Michael Newman/PhotoEdit xv, 5(l), 40, 88, 93(tl), 160(ml), 263, 265(br), 322, 340(ml), 374, 380(r), 384, 437(br), 437(ml), 437(tl), 437(tr), 443, 471, 478(bl), 522, 524(mr), 551(bl), 551(ml), 560, 712; Dwayne Newton/PhotoEdit 573; Wayne E. Newton/PhotoEdit 628(bl); Steve Niedorf/Image Bank ix, 229; James Nielsen/UPI 42; David Noble/FPG International LLC 100(tr); Patrick Olear/PhotoEdit 82(r), 85, 323(tr); Oscar Mayer Foods, 300(tl), 300(tr); Kunio Owaki/The Stock Market xxviii; White/Packert/Image Bank 236; Tony Page/Stone 250, 684(t); Parker Brothers 108(tl); Richard Pasley/Stock Boston 690(br); Greg Pease/Stone 478(ml); Peggy & Ronald/The Stock Market 38(b); Jose L Pelaez/The Stock Market 478(tr), 504, 551(tr); Pepsico 33; Peter Paul 31; Steven Peters/Stone 149, 524(tr); Pfizer Pharmaceuticals 239; Pictor xi, 156 187, 208(t), 334, 497; Pioneer State Mutual 631(bl); Polaroid 22(bl), 22(mr), 22(tr); David Pollack/The Stock Market 394(br); Andreas Pollok/Stone 199; Peter Poulides/Stone 272; Tom Prettyman/PhotoEdit 401; Clayton J. Price/The Stock Market 624; Private Label Products Company 653; Quality Research Group 536; Quality Stores Inc. 596; Patric Ramsey/International Stock 192(tr), 649; Refrigerated & Fozen Foods 217(tl); RefrigiWear 217(tr); Reuters NewsMedia Inc./Corbis 555; Mark Richards/PhotoEdit 166, 172, 181, 315, 494, 544(b); Jon Riley/Stone xxvii, 38(t), 176, 182, 184, 633, 690(tr); Marc Romanelli/Image Bank 220; Don Romero/International Stock 706; Dave Rosenberg/Stone 120; David Roth/Stone 226; Rothman's 340(mr); Royalty Free/Corbis 78(b) 207(l), 354; S.I.N./Corbis 115; Robin L. Sachs/PhotoEdit 230(tr) 697; Chuck Savage/The Stock Market xiii, 258 575(mr), 484, 658; Bob Schatz/Stone 198; Max Schneider/The Image Bank 73; Shopper's Voice 507; Rhoda Sidney/PhotoEdit 141; Elizabeth Simpson/FPG International 367; Stephen Simpson/FPG International LLC 116(t); Frank Siteman/Stone 694(b); Skechers Sport Footwear 26; Ariel Skelley/The Stock Market 688; Don Smetzer/Stone 69(tr), 232(tl) 528, 613(mr); Steve Smith/FPG International LLC 479(bl); Sony Computer Entertainment ® 44; W.B. Spunbarg/PhotoEdit 260; Barbara Stitzer/PhotoEdit 457(tl); Stock Boston 212, 592; Stone 654; Ted Streshinsky/Corbis 481; Sunoco 595; Superstock vi, 49, 92(bl), 98, 129, 147, 160(tl), 167, 219(mr), 306, 404, 430, 450, 502(b), 519, 603, 693; Jeffrey Sylvester/FPG International 160(tr); Telegraph Colour Library/FPG International LLC vii, 9(tl), 178, 351, 372(t), 584, 643; Texaco 336; thingamajob.com by Glen Wexler 710; Scott Thode/International Stock 652; Bob Torrez/Stone v, 20; Toyota Motor Sales, U.S.A., Inc. 47, 342; Tropicana 27(l), 27(r); Tryfit.com 550; John Terence Turner/FPG International LLC xii, 392, 422, 563; Craig/Tuttle/The Stock Market 95; US Postal Service 400, 508; Univision 29; VCG/FPG International LLC 372(b); Robert Van Der Hilst/Stone 62; Susan Van Etten/PhotoEdit 635; Vignette Corporation 383; Peter Weber/Stone 103; Weinberg & Clark/Image Bank 77; Westerman/International Stock 197; Ed Wheeler/The Stock Market 259; Dana C. White/Dana White Productions 165 185, 462; Lee White Photography 223, 453(4), 457(br), 477, 546, 548, 561, 568, 570, 571, 575(bl), 575(br), 575(ml), 575(mr), 575(tr), 576(b), 577, 578; Woods & Poole Economics, Inc. 513; Worldcom 340(bl); Xerox 365; Michael S. Yamashita/Corbis 418; Ed Young/Corbis 397; David Young-Wolff/PhotoEdit 12, 82(l), 100(bl), 143, 217, 232(tr), 245, 281, 318, 341, 343, 377, 407, 421, 441, 470, 544(t), 597, 632, 644, 676, 689; Jeff Zaruba/Stone 179; Zhen Cosmetics 616